Trade and the Environment

The International Library of Critical Writings in Economics

Series Editor: Mark Blaug

Professor Emeritus, University of London
Professor Emeritus, University of Buckingham
Visiting Professor, University of Exeter

This series is an essential reference source for students, researchers and lecturers in economics. It presents by theme a selection of the most important articles across the entire spectrum of economics. Each volume has been prepared by a leading specialist who has written an authoritative introduction to the literature included.

A full list of published and future titles in this series is printed at the end of this volume.

Wherever possible, the articles in these volumes have been reproduced as originally published using facsimile reproduction, inclusive of footnotes and pagination to facilitate ease of reference.

For a list of all Edward Elgar published titles visit our site on the World Wide Web at http://www.e-elgar.co.uk

Trade and the Environment

Economic, Legal and Policy Perspectives

Edited by

Alan M. Rugman

Thames Water Fellow of Strategic Management
Templeton College, University of Oxford, UK

John J. Kirton

Associate Professor of Political Science
University of Toronto, Canada

with Julie A. Soloway

Doctoral Candidate, Faculty of Law
University of Toronto, Canada

THE INTERNATIONAL LIBRARY OF CRITICAL WRITINGS IN ECONOMICS

An Elgar Reference Collection
Cheltenham, UK • Northampton, MA, USA

Published by
Edward Elgar Publishing Ltd
8 Lansdown Place
Cheltenham
Glos GL50 2HU
UK

Edward Elgar Publishing, Inc.
6 Market Street
Northampton
Massachusetts 01060
USA

A catalogue record for this book
is available from the British Library

Library of Congress Cataloguing in Publication Data

Trade and the environment : economic, legal and policy perspectives /
edited by Alan M. Rugman, John J. Kirton with Julie A. Soloway.
(The international library of critical writings in economics ; 87)
Includes bibliographical references and index.
1. International trade—Environmental aspects. 2. Commercial policy—Environmental aspects. 3. Environmental policy—Economic aspects. I. Rugman, Alan M. II. Kirton, John J. III. Soloway, Julie A. IV. Series.
HF1379.T719 1998
363.7—dc21

97–44700
CIP

Printed and bound in Great Britain by Bookcraft (Bath) Ltd.

ISBN 1 85898 662 1

Contents

Acknowledgements

The editors and publishers wish to thank the authors and the following publishers who have kindly given permission for the use of copyright material.

American Economic Association for articles: Adam B. Jaffe, Steven R. Peterson, Paul R. Portney and Robert N. Stavins (1995), 'Environmental Regulation and the Competitiveness of US Manufacturing: What Does the Evidence Tell Us?', *Journal of Economic Literature*, **XXXIII**, March, 132–63; Michael E. Porter and Claas van der Linde (1995), 'Toward a New Conception of the Environment–Competitiveness Relationship', *Journal of Economic Perspectives*, **9** (4), Fall, 97–118.

Blackwell Publishers Ltd for articles: John Whalley (1991), 'The Interface between Environmental and Trade Policies', *Economic Journal*, **101** (405), March, 180–89; Arvind Subramanian (1992), 'Trade Measures for Environment: A Nearly Empty Box?', *World Economy*, **15** (1), January, 135–52.

British Institute of International and Comparative Law for article: Damien Geradin and Raoul Stewardson (1995), 'Trade and Environment: Some Lessons from *Castlemaine Tooheys* (Australia) and *Danish Bottles* (European Community)', *International and Comparative Law Quarterly*, **44**, Part I, January, 41–71.

Colorado Journal of International Environmental Law and Policy for article: J. Owen Saunders (1994), 'NAFTA and the North American Agreement on Environmental Cooperation: A New Model for International Collaboration on Trade and the Environment', *Colorado Journal of International Environmental Law and Policy*, **5** (2), Summer, 273–304.

Elsevier Science, Inc. for article: Robert Howse and Michael J. Trebilcock (1996), 'The Fair Trade–Free Trade Debate: Trade, Labor, and the Environment', *International Review of Law and Economics*, **16** (1), March, 61–79.

Kluwer Law International for article: Cees van Beers and Jeroen C.J.M. van den Bergh (1996), 'An Overview of Methodological Approaches in the Analysis of Trade and Environment', *Journal of World Trade*, **30** (1), February, 143–67.

Minnesota Journal of Global Trade for article: Robert E. Hudec (1996), 'Differences in National Environmental Standards: The Level-Playing-Field Dimension', *Minnesota Journal of Global Trade*, **5** (1), 1–28.

MIT Press Journals for article: Robert O. Keohane (1982), 'The Demand for International Regimes', *International Organization*, **36** (2), Spring, 325–55.

National Policy Association for article: Don Munton and John Kirton (1994) 'North American Environmental Cooperaion: Bilateral, Trilateral, Multilateral', *North American Outlook*, March, 59–86.

Northwestern University School of Law for article: C. Ford Runge (1990), 'Trade Protectionism and Environmental Regulations: The New Nontariff Barriers', *Northwestern Journal of International Law & Business*, **11** (1), Spring, 47–61.

Sage Publications, Inc. for article: Steve Charnovitz (1996), 'Trade Measures and the Design of International Regimes', *Journal of Environment & Development*, **5** (2), June, 168–96.

Stanford Journal of International Law for article: Robert Housman (1994), 'The North American Free Trade Agreement's Lessons for Reconciling Trade and the Environment', *Stanford Journal of International Law*, **30**, 379–422.

University of California, Hastings College of the Law for article: Robert Housman and Durwood Zaelke (1992), 'Trade, Environment, and Sustainable Development: A Primer', *Hastings International and Comparative Law Review*, **15** (4), 535–612.

University of Chicago and *Journal of Law & Economics* for article: R.H. Coase (1960), 'The Problem of Social Cost', *Journal of Law & Economics*, **III**, October, 1–44.

Washington and Lee Law Review for article: John H. Jackson (1992), 'World Trade Rules and Environmental Policies: Congruence or Conflict?', *Washington and Lee Law Review*, **49** (4), 1227–78.

John Wiley & Sons, Inc. for articles: David Vogel (1993), 'Environmental Protection and the Creation of a Single European Market', *Business & the Contemporary World*, **V** (1), Winter, 48–66; Alan M. Rugman (1995), 'Environmental Regulations and International Competitiveness: Strategies for Canada's Forest Products Industry', *The International Executive*, **37** (5), September/October, 451–65.

Every effort has been made to trace all the copyright holders, but if any have been inadvertently overlooked the publishers will be pleased to make the necessary arrangement at the first opportunity.

In addition the publishers wish to thank the Marshall Library of Economics, Cambridge University for their assistance in obtaining these articles.

Introduction

Alan M. Rugman, John J. Kirton and Julie A. Soloway

Part I Economic Perspectives

1. In order to generate a foundation for economic analysis of the environment, there is no better place to start than with the now classic work of Ronald Coase. His paper on 'The Problem of Social Cost', published in 1960, is one of the two papers which won him the Nobel Prize in Economics in 1991 (the other one dealt with the theory of the firm). In this paper, Coase discusses the nature of externalities, that is, activities where there is a divergence between private and social cost (and price). Throughout the paper, Coase applies his thinking to environmental issues, such as factory smoke pollution, the contamination of a stream, straying cattle and crop damage. The basic problem with an environmental externality, for an economist, is that the underlying neoclassical pricing system cannot provide a ready solution; instead judgement about relative social costs and benefits has to be introduced. This leads to a debate about the assignment of property rights (to the manufacturer or the society) and the responsibilities of the owner for external effects. Coase's article is a provocative introduction to these issues.

Coase challenges the conventional thinking of neoclassical economists, who would argue that in a case of a polluting smokestack, the factory owner should be liable for damage caused by the smoke, or, alternatively, a tax should be placed on the factory owner, varying with the amount of smoke produced. Coase questions the assumption that the person who causes the harm (A) is automatically responsible for repairing the harm that is inflicted on another person (B). Coase digs beneath that assumption by introducing a method of reciprocal analysis. In searching for the optimal solution, the appropriate question should be whether A is allowed to harm B or B is allowed to harm A. In finding such an answer, it is necessary to examine the value of what is obtained as well as the value of what is sacrificed to obtain it. Coase aptly illustrates this point with the example of straying cattle which destroy crops on neighbouring land. If cattle inevitably stray on to neighbouring lands, that would mean that an increase in the suply of meat would be obtained at the expense of a decrease in the supply of crops. The choice would be meat or crops. The answer to this question will depend on the value of the additional meat and the value of the decrease in crops.

Our reading of Coase suggests that, in many ways, it would seem that the simplest method to overcome the problem of an environmental externality is to internalize it. One solution that has been extended into the literature on the theory of the firm (and on multinationals) is a full assignment of all property rights to the producer. It is then in the self-interest of the producer to conserve the resource and otherwise to set the private equal to the social net benefit. Likewise, especially in a closed economy, this can be accomplished by a full assignment of property rights by the state to society. A producer would internalize the cost of pollution by buying from society the ability to pollute a given amount. This is, however, especially difficult for environmental issues of the global commons as a supranational government or trade organization does not exist to regulate such a scheme. We believe that this issue of internalization and ownership lies at the heart of economic analysis of trade and the environment.

2. The next article in the collection, 'An Overview of Methodological Approaches in the Analysis of Trade and Environment', brings together the issue of externalities in both trade and the environment. Two Dutch writers, van Beers and van den Bergh, offer a clear discussion of the methodology for the integration of the two types of externalities. They present a solid introduction to the rich treasury of theoretical work undertaken by economists that is relevant for analysis of trade and environment. Different models which underlie theories of international trade are discussed in the context of how they interact with the environment, with an analysis of the benefits and limitations of such models. One issue arising in environmental economics is that it has mainly dealt with externalities in a closed economy model, whereas trade economists have concerned themselves with market imperfections other than environmental ones. Here the authors review partial (single market) and general (more than one market) equilibrium trade theories of perfect competition and relate them to certain basic environmental externalities. They also do this for situations of imperfect competition; with distributional effects incorporated in the general equilibrium (but not partial) economic analysis.

The authors conclude that any serious approach to environmental policy analysis should take account of the open character and international dependence of most economies. They also conclude that international coordination of environmental policy is a necessity for maintaining free trade. These conclusions highlight the modern interdependence of trade and environment policy: the externality problems between neighbours analysed by Coase can be extrapolated to an international scale.

3. John Whalley brings together two related points. First, he uses a general equilibrium model to assess the impact of a carbon emissions tax (to help offset global warming) on the global economy. This is typical of the empirical work that economists can perform on the efficiency aspects of an environmental tax. Whalley estimates the global economic cost of carbon taxes to be in the range of $280 billion per year, or approximately 2 per cent of world product. How this cost is distributed depends more particularly on the policy instrument chosen, but Whalley effectively makes the point that any carbon limitation initiative will have major implications for the international economy. Second, he predicts the emerging importance of two related issues prominent in the trade and environment debate: the use of trade sanctions as an enforcement mechanism for environmental law and the pressure on trade policies created by national differences in environmental regulation. He canvasses the institutional framework of the General Agreement on Tariffs and Trade (GATT), now the World Trade Organization (WTO), to assess its efficacy in dealing with the emerging interface between trade and environmental problems. He states that the GATT is very poorly equipped to deal with these issues, since they are outside the original scope of this trade-related agency. This is due in part to the fact that the trading rules and institutional framework were developed before the emergent environmental movement. However, some of his concerns have begun to be addressed in the Uruguay Round and the new WTO.

4. Arvind Subramanian, an economist at the GATT/WTO head office in Geneva, provides an articulate summary of the ways in which trade policy measures can be used (actually misused) to address environmental problems in his article, 'Trade Measures for the Environment: A Nearly Empty Box?'. He finds that, in general, trade policy is not an efficient method of correcting domestic environmental externalities; indeed, it usually introduces a protectionist distortion. Unilateral trade sanctions are both inefficient and inequitable in correcting environmental externalities. Such market failures are better corrected at source, by domestic tax and subsidy measures, rather than by introducing a new trade-related distortion. This thinking goes back to work carried out in the 1960s on trade and domestic distortions by Jagdish Bhagwati and Harry G. Johnson, among others.

Subramanian offers a good taxonomy of the interactions between trade policy and environmental problems, and on the basis of that taxonomy he analyses the role that trade measures can play. He classifies different trade measures dealing with both transborder and domestic environmental problems. With transborder environmental problems, trade measures are taken to correct for an environmental externality, such as a ban on fur caught in leghold traps. With domestic environmental problems, measures are taken to compensate for the loss of competitiveness in a trading relationship caused by, for example, lax environmental standards. This latter type of issue finds its theoretical grounding not in Coase's theory of externalities, but rather in David Ricardo's theory of comparative advantage. The question becomes whether environmental regulation is an appropriate basis on which a country may base its comparative advantage. If it is not, as many people argue, then how may a country negate the source of the comparative advantage which could be legitimately based on differences in environmental capabilities and preferences? Measures used to counter such advantages, such as a restriction or tax on their import, Subramanian argues, are flawed as they are protectionist in intent. The basic difficulty here is how to differentiate between a valid environmental regulation and one which is protectionist in nature. The legal and policy papers in the later parts of this book address these issues in further detail.

5. Michael Porter is the most influential scholar on business policy, with his classic works on competitive strategy, competitive advantage and the firm-level sources of international competitive advantage. In his article, 'Toward a New Conception of the Environment–Competitiveness Relationship', written with Claas van der Linde, he challenges another assumption that underlies the trade and environment debate. He contends that the struggle between ecology and the economy is incorrectly derived from a static view of environmental regulation, whereas there is a shift towards a more dynamic and responsive model of technical innovation. Porter argues that competitive advantage does not depend on static efficiency or on optimizing within fixed constraints, but is a function of the capacity of a firm for innovation and improvements which shift those constraints. He also argues that tight domestic environmental regulations can, at times, act as an incentive to domestic firms with a strong home base to create a first mover-type of competitive advantage. In other words, certain industries will improve their (environmentally related) productivity in response to 'properly crafted environmental regulations'.

While there may be some point to this allegation for large, closed trade economies such as the United States (and possibly the European Union (EU), if it ever becomes an integrated single market), it is extremely doubtful that a Porter-type environmental policy will ever help industries in smaller, open economies. Instead, these firms need to benchmark their activities to the markets of their customers (that is, to look into export markets) and understand their customers' environmental regulations rather than those of their home base. While Porter's specific recommendations for a closed economy are of limited general applicability when trade is introduced, it is essential that the corporate policy dimension of international competitiveness be added to the economics of the environment and this well-written article helps to provide this linkage. It is clear, however, that Porter's work cannot be extended to the trade side of trade and the environment for small, open economies without the modification suggested above.

6. Rugman also introduces concepts of corporate strategy into the domain of trade and the environment. Using the Canadian forest products sector as a case study, he demonstrates that environmental regulations (especially in a large triad country such as the United States) can be used as a barrier to entry against the exports of smaller, open economies. This asymmetry in market power calls for imaginative managerial responses by corporations in smaller economies, including the ability to lobby in larger markets or to anticipate the discriminatory use of host-country environmental regulations. An additional factor is that the national treatment provisions of the North American Free Trade Agreement (NAFTA) do not necessarily offer practical entry rights to outside producers when a domestic environmental regulation has trade-restricting effects. Rugman also demonstrates that Porter-type tight environmental regulations would not be a sensible policy for Canadian governments to pursue, since Canadian firms need to set benchmarks in the larger markets of key customers (the United States and the EU) rather than re-engineer to their relatively small Canadian home base. More work needs to be done on the interaction between corporate strategy and environmental/trade policies, and Rugman helps to set the agenda for such future research.

7. The managerial and business component of the trade and environment debate is represented in this economics section by the survey of the empirical literature on competiveness conducted by Adam Jaffe and three co-authors. After an extensive and intensive investigation of the literature on the competitiveness of US manufacturing as affected by environmental regulations, they conclude that there is no evidence to suggest that environmental regulations adversely affect competitiveness. Their survey thus rejects two schools of thought. First, Jaffe et al. cannot find evidence to support an economics/business literature which suggests that environmental regulations impose significant costs on US firms and reduce their productivity and growth. Neither do they find evidence to support the use of 'pollution havens' by firms. Second, Jaffe et al. find no evidence to support the Porter hypothesis that strict domestic environmental regulations can lead to first mover advantages for home-based firms which are forced to develop green capabilities. In other words, the impact of environmental regulations is largely neutral when measured by economists. It is difficult to believe that this finding is divorced from the economic techniques and methodologies used to conduct the empirical research. Indeed, Jaffe and his co-authors conclude that their work is limited by a lack of reliable cross-national data and methodological difficulties in measuring the effectiveness of enforcement of environmental regulations within the context of different regulatory regimes.

Part II Legal Perspectives

As discussed above, Ronald Coase presents a method of economic analysis to deal with divergence between private and social costs. Using the example of the polluting smokestack, Coase presents an economic argument about how best to allocate property rights between the polluting firm and the damaged party. In the face of such conflict, the law must define the rights and obligations of each party to the dispute. The legal rules and the adjudication of those rules will specify who will bear the cost of such a divergence. The law is not always clear about who should bear the cost of an externality (that is, pollution), yet the law has the potential to avoid such disputes through internalization. These issues also arise at the international level when environmental costs and benefits are not internalized in the price of goods.

The theory underlying trade policy posits that free markets are the most efficient means by which to allocate resources. The theory underlying environmental policy is based on non-market grounds and seeks to conserve and protect the Earth's resources. The legal agreements that enshrine these separate goals of efficiency versus environmental protection contain inherent conflicts. The framework of the international trading system was designed half a century ago, before the current range of environmental considerations became important. The recent proliferation of international trade agreements, combined with rising environmental consciousness in wealthy nations, has forced legal scholars to deal with environmental issues. Likewise, environmentalists have sought to further their goals through the reform of trading rules. This has exacerbated the tensions in reconciling goals that often appear to be at odds with each other.

8. Robert Housman and Durwood Zaelke provide a useful starting point from which to examine this tension. As lawyers at the Center for International Environmental Law in Washington, DC, an environmental non-governmental organization, they are well positioned to give a unique insight into this issues area. Their article, 'Trade, Environment, and Sustainable Development: A Primer', offers an overview of the major trade agreements and environmental treaties, in which they argue that 'both trade and the environment must be disciplined to serve the overarching goal of sustainable development'. This would mean, in accordance with Coase's analysis, that trading rules should encourage the internalization of environmental costs.

Housman and Zaelke begin with the GATT, 'the legal framework under which almost all trade among nations occurs'. In reviewing its central provisions and environmental implications, they demonstrate that seemingly benign trade provisions can potentially have profound environmental implications. For example, the GATT's cornerstone provision, Article I, imposes a most-favoured nations obligation on all contracting parties, requiring that parties treat all like products equally. This provision seems to prevent GATT members from using trade restrictions to deal with goods produced in a way that unduly degrades the environment. Thus if Country A imposed a tax on a good produced by Country B, because it was produced in an environmentally harmful manner (and Country A is seeking to internalize the cost of the environmental damage incurred by Country B), then such a tax will be contrary to Article I of the GATT.

Housman and Zaelke present options for reducing or eliminating friction between environmental protection and trade agreements. They begin this analysis by relying on the classic tools of the international lawyer, such as Article 30 of the Vienna Convention on the Law of Treaties which provides general rules governing the relationships between treaties. They identify the limits of such an analysis, for while traditional legal rules can deal with narrow legal questions regarding specific conflicts between treaties, such rules fail to advance the trade–environment discourse in a meaningful way. They then canvass a variety of creative approaches for incorporating environmental considerations into trade agreements.

9. Professor John H. Jackson takes up the challenge of examining the GATT in his detailed article, 'World Trade Rules and Environmental Policies: Congruence or Conflict?'. One of the world's leading trade law scholars, Professor Jackson examines the legal and policy provisions of the GATT in relation to the environment. The institutional issues touched on by Whalley in Chapter 3 are fully developed by Jackson in this article. Jackson further elaborates on the central theme presented by Housman and Zaelke: that trade and environmental policies must evolve to be mutually compatible. Citing the difference in 'policy cultures' between traders and environmentalists, Jackson sees the hostilities between the opposing interest groups as part of a broader trend in international economic relations stemming from the growth in international economic interdependence. Such interdependence leads to efficiency gains which will increase welfare. At the same time, however, government regulation in all areas (consumer protection, competition policy, banking and financial institutions), as well as the environment, designed to promote worthy goals, will increasingly clash with free trade policy. This will force a rethinking of previously held attitudes towards government regulation, especially in the area of the environment.

Jackson makes the point that trade and environment cultures differ in important ways. Trade policy experts come from a culture of international diplomacy: 'secrecy, negotiation, compromise', and a 'behind the scenes catering to a variety of special economic interests'. Environmental policy groups come from a tradition of domestic transparency, public participation and access which has not been realized in international affairs. Institutional provisions within legal agreements thus become extremely important, because the decision-making and dispute resolution process can substantially affect outcomes. Jackson concludes that there is potentially a congruence between the welfare objectives that both trade and environment policies are designed to promote. However, his optimism is tempered by the fact that there will need to be a great deal of accommodation and compromise to achieve this congruence.

10. Owen Saunders presents the North American experience in developing a trade and environment legal framework in 'NAFTA and the North American Agreement on Environmental Cooperation: A New Model for International Collaboration on Trade and the Environment'. Against a backdrop of the political debate in the five years leading up to NAFTA, he outlines the environmental provisions of NAFTA and its environmental side agreement. Owen argues that NAFTA's overwhelming significance lies in the fact that it demonstrates the effectiveness of the environmental community in placing environmental issues on the international trade agenda and implanting environmental concern in a meaningful way into a major trade agreement. Saunders offers an effective analysis of NAFTA's environmental side agreement, the star thus far of the trade and environment world. A review of these legal obligations reveals that many are at best 'soft law', in that the substantive provisions are not particularly onerous. Rather, they reflect an attempt both to give effect to the principle of state sovereignty with respect to domestic environmental law and to

recognize the interests of all states in environmental protection. In contrast, the innovative institutional provisions and dispute resolution regime of the environmental side agreement may prove to be highly effective, depending on how they operate. It is these provisions that will ultimately determine the real value of the agreement. Owen also argues that the NAFTA experience has applicability beyond North America, especially with respect to defining the trade–environment relationship in a north–south context. However, whether the unique combination of factors which led to the formation of NAFTA and its side agreement could be applied in such a way, even in the case of NAFTA accession, remains an open question.

11. The varying rules governing the trade–environment relationship at the regional and national levels are highlighted by Damien Geradin and Raoul Stewardson. In 'Trade and Environment: Some Lessons From *Castlemaine Tooheys* (Australia) and *Danish Bottles* (European Community)', a comparative study of a classic trade and environment issue is presented. By comparing how two different jurisdictions deal with a similar environmental regulation with a trade-hindering effect, they demonstrate the impact of two different legal regimes. In doing so, they focus on the law in practice as it affects individual actors. While the discussion of broad questions of international trading rules and national sovereignty can sometimes obscure the individual, Geradin and Stewardson show how the law is ultimately a tool which allows individuals to live beside their neighbour, as citizen to citizen rather than state to state. Both of the cases reviewed in this article involve a judicial examination of 'the validity of State legislation attempting on its face to establish or promote schemes for the return and recycling of used bottles'. Such schemes, although ostensibly motivated by environmental concerns, are trade restricting in nature. They effectively disadvantage importers against domestic producers as importers must bear additional costs in order to establish a recycling scheme, which may be a long distance from their home base. Importers must thus absorb extra additional transport costs. In addition to their extremely thorough discussion of the relevant legislation in both jurisdictions, Geradin and Stewardson compare the relevance of central legal terms. Must a trade-restrictive measure be *discriminatory* between domestic and imported goods? What does it mean to assert that a trade-restrictive measure is *necessary or proportional* in meeting an environmental goal? They conclude that the Australian High Court and the European Court of Justice have used similar tests in their analysis, although the Australian High Court has placed much more importance on the concept of discrimination. Not surprisingly, they also conclude 'that it is very difficult to design a workable, practicable test that perfectly resolves the conflicting interests involved where local legislation protects the local environment at the expense of interstate trade'.

12. In an integrated global economy, attempts to set higher domestic environmental standards will often be seen as protectionist by 'free traders'. Likewise, 'fair traders' seek to link environmental concepts to trade concepts for non-economic goals, and see 'free traders' as overly committed to the objective of unencumbered global trade. This fairness of trade concept is explored by two international trade law experts, Professors Robert Howse and Michael Trebilcock, in their article, 'The Fair Trade–Free Trade Debate: Trade, Labor, and the Environment'. Motivated by the contention that 'fair trade' claims represent 'the most fundamental challenge to the liberal trading order that has arisen in decades', Howse and Trebilcock examine fairness claims, paying particular attention to the north–south dimension of the debate.

Howse and Trebilcock propose a framework for sifting through and evaluating 'fair trade' claims stemming from labour and environmental standards. This framework distinguishes between, on the one hand, 'claims that trade measures should be used to attain a specific non-trade goal' and, on the other, 'arguments for a level competitive playing field ... or establishing "fair" rules of the game that are internal to the trading system'. They conclude that the former are far more justifiable than the latter. Fair trade claims relating to the environment, they find, often have real merit and are not necessarily threatening to a liberal world trading order. However, they also conclude that the class of fair trade claims which seek to level the competitive playing field are threatening to a liberal world trading order, as they are almost always protectionist in nature.

This framework advances the trade–environment debate in two significant ways. First, it assesses the welfare effects associated with various claims for fairness. The opposing cases of when trade sanctions succeed or fail to succeed in inducing higher environmental standards are examined, with an analysis of the welfare effects in the targeted country, the global welfare effects and the welfare effects in the sanction-imposing country. In a similar way, competitive fairness claims are examined. Second, Howse and Trebilcock clarify the institutional challenge to be one of trade law regime design. To preserve the integrity and credibility of the world trading system, trade law regimes must incorporate the ability to distinguish between those claims which promote a worthy environmental value and others which function largely to serve protectionist interests.

13. Treaty-based approaches stand in sharp contrast to the use of 'aggressive unilateralism' as a means to deal with unfair trade. Such unilateralism has been evident in numerous recent legislative attempts by the United States 'to offset the price advantages of weak environmental regulations elsewhere'. These are catalogued by Professor Robert Hudec, a noted trade lawyer and academic, in his article, 'Differences in National Environmental Standards: The Level-Playing-Field Dimension'. Like Howse and Trebilcock, Hudec evaluates the claim that imports from countries with low environmental standards are unfair, through an exploration of the roots of the fairness concept in US legal and political history and its ongoing importance in the US trade policy debate. He challenges the 'simple-minded' concept that equality of competitive conditions is the predominant determinant of fairness. Naturally occurring competitive advantages between countries, such as factor endowments (natural resources, fertile soil, sunshine), are considered a fair and proper basis for international trade. Environmentally degrading standards are not considered to be a fair and proper basis by which to compete. It is at this point where disagreement arises between the claims of the 'free trade economists' and the 'fair traders'. Hudec provides alternative approaches in the analysis of these legitimate differences.

Hudec concludes that fairness complaints are inherently difficult to correct through policy intervention because the value judgements on which fairness claims are based 'are simply not coherent' in an international trade context. It is impossible to know if the playing field is indeed truly level. Despite that, fairness claims will continue 'as long as those claims exert political leverage'. Their impact will thus depend on the access and weight they are accorded, at the national and international level, within those institutions where trade–environment tradeoffs are ultimately made and productive synergies potentially forged.

Part III Policy Perspectives

A third essential and frequently employed perspective from which to analyse the trade and environment relationship is that of government policy, and in particular the way in which sovereign national governments have constructed international institutions and 'regimes' that shape the way in which the values of trade liberalizers and environmental regulators intersect. Indeed, within the discipline of political science, drawing on the intellectual contributions of both law and economics, regime theory has emerged over the past decade as a key intellectual lens through which international trade and international environmental relationships, and thus the linkage of the two, have been explored.

14. In the initial contribution in this integrative section, Robert Keohane, one of the leading regime theorists, develops the general concept of international regimes that underlies much of the work on the trade–environment interface at the international level and its effect on national policy outcomes. In 'The Demand for International Regimes', Keohane uses the rational choice, supply–demand concepts of microeconomics to explain the demand for such regimes, defined in Stephen Krasner's classic formulation, as 'sets of implicit or explicit principles, norms, rules, and decision making procedures around which actor expectations converge'. Keohane begins with a 'constraint–choice analysis' that views overall trends in the creation, development, decay and dissolution of regimes as a result of changes in both the international system where powerful actors exert exceptional impact, and in the particular international regimes that actors choose. The competitiveness, uncertainty and conflicting interests that pervade world politics lead rational states to demand regimes as 'nests' through which specific agreements can be efficiently arrived at in ways that compensate for Coasian market failures, reduce transactions and information costs, and diminish the fear of being taken advantage of in the future.

Regimes rather than *ad hoc* arrangements are needed to produce specific agreements in situations, such as world politics, where there is no clear legal framework establishing liability for action, where information is costly and where transactions costs are positive. Regimes also arise in situations of complex interdependence, where there are many important issues in a single policy area, and where complex linkages and side-payments, and a low cost vehicle for organizing agreements, are needed. They can also arise where states forgo maximizing short-term interests in the expectation of long-run gains, to reduce uncertainty by providing high quality information equally to all, to reduce moral hazard and to minimize deception and irresponsibility. Such information flows most freely in an ongoing relationship in which open governments, with intense transnational relations among subunits of governments, provide knowledge of otherwise internal evaluations, intentions, the intensity of preferences and willingness to keep commitments in difficult circumstances. Thus regimes with highly regularized procedures and rules, that provide such high quality information, may be relied on long after the hegemonic country that created them has lost its dominance. Such regimes can be aimed not only at controlling the behaviour of their members and non-members, but also at providing insurance to members against specific risks. This analysis implies that trade–environment regimes, while first supplied by predominant actors such as the United States, will be increasingly demanded among the advanced industrialized societies where the ties of trade and ecological interdependence and thus issue density are most intense. It further suggests, however, that the well-developed and effective separate trade regimes and environment regimes, each grounded in open transborder communication among different agencies in national governments, will be difficult to merge into a single trade–environment regime at the international level, despite the rising number of linked issues arising in this sphere.

15. The demand for international regimes carries with it the task of designing such regimes, and in particular embedding in institutions particular principles, norms, rules and procedures that specify which environmental values will be respected and which trade-restricting or -enhancing measures will be permitted in their support. Steve Charnovitz, one of the most prolific writers on the trade–environment issue, focuses on the world's major environmental regimes and the use of trade measures within them. His central argument in 'Trade Measures and the Design of International Regimes' is that trade measures do indeed promote the effectiveness of environmental regimes, as they do when lodged within the trade regimes that stand alongside them. Charnovitz first proposes a conceptual framework for how trade measures are used in environmental and other regimes. Here he identifies seven purposes for which trade measures are employed, and the three types of harm they are designed to prevent, for a resulting matrix with 21 cells. He next applies the framework to 30 case studies in which trade measures were embedded within bilateral, plurilateral and multilateral treaties dating from 1878 to 1995.

Charnovitz's work makes three central contributions. First, in contrast to those who argue that trade measures have limited or no value in environmental regimes, Charnovitz demonstrates that such measures are longstanding, legitimate, widely used in other regimes and effective in accomplishing their environmental purposes. Second, he grounds his findings in an extensive list of case studies, advancing the debate from the self-contained deductive logic and convictions of isolated trade or environment communities to a careful examination of solid historical evidence. Third, he moves the debate from policy prescription and self-justifying argumentation into the realm of analysis, by providing a conceptual framework for purposes of classification and the identification of trends. Although this framework does not extend into the generation of propositions to guide further research, it does allow him to address critical issues – notably inter-regime linkage – highlighted in Keohane's seminal theoretical work.

16. In his article, 'Trade Protectionism and Environmental Regulations: The New Nontariff Barriers', C. Ford Runge shifts the focus to the world's major trade liberalization regimes, the environmental provisions within them and the stress placed on these regimes by the growing, unilateral use of stringent national environmental regulations, which can constitute disguised barriers to trade. Since 1947, the GATT regime, under Article 20(g), has allowed countries to adopt and enforce national measures to conserve exhaustible natural resources, if such measures were accompanied by domestic restrictions, not applied arbitrarily or in a discriminatory fashion, or used as a disguised restriction on trade. Moreover, while the 1979 Standards Code sought to prevent environmental standards from creating unnecessary obstacles to trade, US domestic implementing legislation underscored the US sovereign right to choose nonconformance with international standards to ensure environmental protection at home.

More recently, growing concern about the poisons embedded in traded products, rising and hard-won environmental regulations in the United States, the move of the EU and the 1989 Canada–United States Free Trade Agreement to set regional standards, and the plethora of standards established by subnational governments, have assaulted the free trade bias of the existing regimes. The resulting restrictions on trade, imposed primarily by rich northern countries, have created particular tensions with the poorer south, which argue that they prefer growth-through-exports more than environmental quality, and lack the resources to establish well-developed national systems of environmental regulation. These dynamics are particularly acute in the agrifood sector, where the need to recoup the high research and development costs of pesticides provides incentives for US producers to export pesticides to poorer countries, where they can easily be improperly used to the detriment of agricultural workers and consumers in the south and, potentially, their customers in export markets in the United States. The effort to set common international standards was advanced by the 1989 Canada–US salmon and herring case, which pointed to three criteria: the estimated costs of the regulations; who bears the costs; and whether the regulations would be imposed in the absence of trade effects. Yet because common international standards should reflect differences in national priorities related to levels of economic development and culture, allowance should be made for intermediate standards for poorer countries. The policy task is to strengthen environmental standards both domestically and internationally, by having the United States lead in the relevant multilateral organizations.

17. In his article, 'Environmental Protection and the Creation of a Single European Market', David Vogel deals with the effort to construct such an integrated regime on a regional level, by reconciling free trade with national environmental regulation within the highly integrated market and geographically compact space of the EU. Here divergent national standards and growing environmental activism, but differing environmental consciousness across member countries, presented obstacles to intra-European trade and controversy over how to cope with the ensuing conflicts. In its effort to define a trade–environment regime, the European Community wavered in the emphasis it placed on trade and environment priorities, until the Single European Act of 1987 finally moved the regime from a preference for trade over the environment to a more equal balance between the two. Its passage inaugurated an era of Community-level environmental activism that was strengthened again with the ratification of the Maastricht Treaty in 1993. Throughout this experience, the effort to construct common, strong Community-wide environmental standards has often proved difficult, as in the case of automobile emissions. The eventual construction of strong, harmonized environmental standards reflected the dominance of major European producers, who wished to export their products throughout the Community and to the United States, and who often formed *de facto* coalitions with national environmental movements.

Vogel's analysis provides strong evidence that freer trade produces stronger and more widespread environmental regulation, provided that the free trade area's most powerful members are also its most environmentally conscious ones, and that the common institution's decision rules allow the stronger members' views to prevail. Implicit in this analysis is the proposition that the richest members – Germany, Denmark and the Netherlands – are the greenest because they are rich, in addition to the tight ecological interdependencies they experience. In contrast to the emphasis in Keohane's formulation, Vogel's analysis is at its core a confirmation of realist theory, in that the preferences of the powerful – Germany within the Community and the United States beyond – determine the content of the international regime, by virtue of their sheer market power, the interests that derive directly from them and the leverage that comes from the singular ability of these countries to defect from the regime. But Vogel also points to the way regimes are politically constructed as export-oriented, technologically advanced industries form alliances with environmental non-governmental organizations (ENGOs) and others to impose their will.

18. The importance of the specific values and rules embedded in a particular regime is central to Robert Housman's analysis of the innovative features of the regional trade–environment regime created by NAFTA and its accompanying North American Agreement on Environmental Cooperation. In 'The North American Free Trade Agreement's Lessons for Reconciling Trade and the Environment', Housman argues that there are many environmentally desirable innovative features and valuable lessons contained in the negotiating process and provisions of the NAFTA, and in the rules of its parallel environmental accord. The core NAFTA text provided an overarching commitment to sustainable development, measures to prevent derogations in environmental enforcement to attract transborder investment, preferential respect for major multilateral environmental agreements, the first systematic attempt to develop environmental standards in a trade agreement, and advances in dispute resolution. Moreover, the institutions created along with NAFTA created a beneficial 'carrot and stick' model, with the Commission for Environmental Cooperation (CEC) empowered to impose monetary assessments and trade sanctions for a persistent pattern of non-enforcement of environmental standards, and the bilateral Border Environmental Cooperation Commission and North American Development Bank able to mobilize funds to produce needed environmental infrastructure along the US–Mexico border. In Housman's judgement, from an environmental perspective NAFTA's provisions represent a major advance in devising balanced trade–environment regimes. Their value has already been demonstrated by the infusion into the final Uruguay Round texts of several NAFTA innovations, particularly in the field of standards. Looking ahead, NAFTA will serve as an important laboratory for shaping solutions to many difficult issues in the trade–environment field.

19. Assessing the power and potential of the central environmental institution established by NAFTA – the CEC – is a task taken up by Don Munton and John Kirton in 'North American Environmental Cooperation: Bilateral, Trilateral, Multilateral'. Placing the CEC in the broader context of the longstanding bilateral environmental cooperation between the United States and Canada, the CEC represents a potentially revolutionary development by integrating major environmental concerns directly into a trade agreement, by expanding bilateral cooperation into a trilateral arrangement, and by introducing key features of supranational governance such as organizational and procedural powers and political legitimacy. The CEC could serve as the vehicle to deliver the required trilateral eco-management, performing the tasks of joint fact-finding, policy advice, prior notification, dispute resolution and the provision of a foundation for north–south cooperation in the wider world.

Yet Munton and Kirton's analysis of the CEC's prospects is a contingent as well as an optimistic one. The United States and Canada are two rich, law-based democracies, enjoying the intense interdependence of the world's largest two-way trading relationship and an exceptionally ecologically integrated border. Yet their century-long record of bilateral environmental cooperation has regularly seen bold commitments made and then broken, and once effective institutions fall into irrelevance. These 'realist' conclusions from what should be an 'easy case' for regime theory, suggest that the CEC, even with its majority voting provisions (comparable to those Vogel emphasizes in the EU case), will require additional advantages to succeed. These include the hard political factors of support from ENGOs, business and the public and, above all, direction supportive of sustainable development from political leaders whose responsibility it is to devise a regime that uses modern economic and legal concepts as a basis for cooperative international behaviour.

Part I
Economic Perspectives

[1]

The Journal of

LAW & ECONOMICS

VOLUME III OCTOBER 1960

THE PROBLEM OF SOCIAL COST

R. H. COASE
University of Virginia

I. The Problem To Be Examined[1]

This paper is concerned with those actions of business firms which have harmful effects on others. The standard example is that of a factory the smoke from which has harmful effects on those occupying neighbouring properties. The economic analysis of such a situation has usually proceeded in terms of a divergence between the private and social product of the factory, in which economists have largely followed the treatment of Pigou in *The Economics of Welfare*. The conclusions to which this kind of analysis seems to have led most economists is that it would be desirable to make the owner of the factory liable for the damage caused to those injured by the smoke, or alternatively, to place a tax on the factory owner varying with the amount of smoke produced and equivalent in money terms to the damage it would cause, or finally, to exclude the factory from residential districts (and presumably from other

[1] This article, although concerned with a technical problem of economic analysis, arose out of the study of the Political Economy of Broadcasting which I am now conducting. The argument of the present article was implicit in a previous article dealing with the problem of allocating radio and television frequencies (The Federal Communications Commission, 2 J. Law & Econ. [1959]) but comments which I have received seemed to suggest that it would be desirable to deal with the question in a more explicit way and without reference to the original problem for the solution of which the analysis was developed.

areas in which the emission of smoke would have harmful effects on others). It is my contention that the suggested courses of action are inappropriate, in that they lead to results which are not necessarily, or even usually, desirable.

II. The Reciprocal Nature of the Problem

The traditional approach has tended to obscure the nature of the choice that has to be made. The question is commonly thought of as one in which A inflicts harm on B and what has to be decided is: how should we restrain A? But this is wrong. We are dealing with a problem of a reciprocal nature. To avoid the harm to B would inflict harm on A. The real question that has to be decided is: should A be allowed to harm B or should B be allowed to harm A? The problem is to avoid the more serious harm. I instanced in my previous article[2] the case of a confectioner the noise and vibrations from whose machinery disturbed a doctor in his work. To avoid harming the doctor would inflict harm on the confectioner. The problem posed by this case was essentially whether it was worth while, as a result of restricting the methods of production which could be used by the confectioner, to secure more doctoring at the cost of a reduced supply of confectionery products. Another example is afforded by the problem of straying cattle which destroy crops on neighbouring land. If it is inevitable that some cattle will stray, an increase in the supply of meat can only be obtained at the expense of a decrease in the supply of crops. The nature of the choice is clear: meat or crops. What answer should be given is, of course, not clear unless we know the value of what is obtained as well as the value of what is sacrificed to obtain it. To give another example, Professor George J. Stigler instances the contamination of a stream.[3] If we assume that the harmful effect of the pollution is that it kills the fish, the question to be decided is: is the value of the fish lost greater or less than the value of the product which the contamination of the stream makes possible. It goes almost without saying that this problem has to be looked at in total *and* at the margin.

III. The Pricing System with Liability for Damage

I propose to start my analysis by examining a case in which most economists would presumably agree that the problem would be solved in a completely satisfactory manner: when the damaging business has to pay for all damage caused *and* the pricing system works smoothly (strictly this means that the operation of a pricing system is without cost).

A good example of the problem under discussion is afforded by the case of straying cattle which destroy crops growing on neighbouring land. Let us suppose that a farmer and a cattle-raiser are operating on neighbouring proper-

[2] Coase, The Federal Communications Commission, 2 J. Law & Econ. 26–27 (1959).

[3] G. J. Stigler, The Theory of Price 105 (1952).

ties. Let us further suppose that, without any fencing between the properties, an increase in the size of the cattle-raiser's herd increases the total damage to the farmer's crops. What happens to the marginal damage as the size of the herd increases is another matter. This depends on whether the cattle tend to follow one another or to roam side by side, on whether they tend to be more or less restless as the size of the herd increases and on other similar factors. For my immediate purpose, it is immaterial what assumption is made about marginal damage as the size of the herd increases.

To simplify the argument, I propose to use an arithmetical example. I shall assume that the annual cost of fencing the farmer's property is $9 and that the price of the crop is $1 per ton. Also, I assume that the relation between the number of cattle in the herd and the annual crop loss is as follows:

Number in Herd (Steers)	Annual Crop Loss (Tons)	Crop Loss per Additional Steer (Tons)
1	1	1
2	3	2
3	6	3
4	10	4

Given that the cattle-raiser is liable for the damage caused, the additional annual cost imposed on the cattle-raiser if he increased his herd from, say, 2 to 3 steers is $3 and in deciding on the size of the herd, he will take this into account along with his other costs. That is, he will not increase the size of the herd unless the value of the additional meat produced (assuming that the cattle-raiser slaughters the cattle), is greater than the additional costs that this will entail, including the value of the additional crops destroyed. Of course, if, by the employment of dogs, herdsmen, aeroplanes, mobile radio and other means, the amount of damage can be reduced, these means will be adopted when their cost is less than the value of the crop which they prevent being lost. Given that the annual cost of fencing is $9, the cattle-raiser who wished to have a herd with 4 steers or more would pay for fencing to be erected and maintained, assuming that other means of attaining the same end would not do so more cheaply. When the fence is erected, the marginal cost due to the liability for damage becomes zero, except to the extent that an increase in the size of the herd necessitates a stronger and therefore more expensive fence because more steers are liable to lean against it at the same time. But, of course, it may be cheaper for the cattle-raiser not to fence and to pay for the damaged crops, as in my arithmetical example, with 3 or fewer steers.

It might be thought that the fact that the cattle-raiser would pay for all crops damaged would lead the farmer to increase his planting if a cattle-raiser came to occupy the neighbouring property. But this is not so. If the crop was previously sold in conditions of perfect competition, marginal cost was equal to price for the amount of planting undertaken and any expansion would have reduced the profits of the farmer. In the new situation, the existence of crop damage would mean that the farmer would sell less on the open market but his receipts for a given production would remain the same, since the cattle-raiser would pay the market price for any crop damaged. Of course, if cattle-raising commonly involved the destruction of crops, the coming into existence of a cattle-raising industry might raise the price of the crops involved and farmers would then extend their planting. But I wish to confine my attention to the individual farmer.

I have said that the occupation of a neighbouring property by a cattle-raiser would not cause the amount of production, or perhaps more exactly the amount of planting, by the farmer to increase. In fact, if the cattle-raising has any effect, it will be to decrease the amount of planting. The reason for this is that, for any given tract of land, if the value of the crop damaged is so great that the receipts from the sale of the undamaged crop are less than the total costs of cultivating that tract of land, it will be profitable for the farmer and the cattle-raiser to make a bargain whereby that tract of land is left uncultivated. This can be made clear by means of an arithmetical example. Assume initially that the value of the crop obtained from cultivating a given tract of land is $12 and that the cost incurred in cultivating this tract of land is $10, the net gain from cultivating the land being $2. I assume for purposes of simplicity that the farmer owns the land. Now assume that the cattle-raiser starts operations on the neighbouring property and that the value of the crops damaged is $1. In this case $11 is obtained by the farmer from sale on the market and $1 is obtained from the cattle-raiser for damage suffered and the net gain remains $2. Now suppose that the cattle-raiser finds it profitable to increase the size of his herd, even though the amount of damage rises to $3; which means that the value of the additional meat production is greater than the additional costs, including the additional $2 payment for damage. But the total payment for damage is now $3. The net gain to the farmer from cultivating the land is still $2. The cattle-raiser would be better off if the farmer would agree not to cultivate his land for any payment less than $3. The farmer would be agreeable to not cultivating the land for any payment greater than $2. There is clearly room for a mutually satisfactory bargain which would lead to the abandonment of cultivation.[4] But the same argument applies not only to the whole tract cultivated by the farmer but also to any

[4] The argument in the text has proceeded on the assumption that the alternative to cultivation of the crop is abandonment of cultivation altogether. But this need not be so. There may be crops which are less liable to damage by cattle but which would not be as profitable as the crop grown in the absence of damage. Thus, if the cultivation of a new crop would yield a return to the farmer of $1 instead of $2, and the size of the herd which would cause $3 damage with the old crop would cause $1 damage with the new crop, it would be profitable to the cattle-raiser to pay any sum less than $2 to induce the farmer

subdivision of it. Suppose, for example, that the cattle have a well-defined route, say, to a brook or to a shady area. In these circumstances, the amount of damage to the crop along the route may well be great and if so, it could be that the farmer and the cattle-raiser would find it profitable to make a bargain whereby the farmer would agree not to cultivate this strip of land.

But this raises a further possibility. Suppose that there is such a well-defined route. Suppose further that the value of the crop that would be obtained by cultivating this strip of land is $10 but that the cost of cultivation is $11. In the absence of the cattle-raiser, the land would not be cultivated. However, given the presence of the cattle-raiser, it could well be that if the strip was cultivated, the whole crop would be destroyed by the cattle. In which case, the cattle-raiser would be forced to pay $10 to the farmer. It is true that the farmer would lose $1. But the cattle-raiser would lose $10. Clearly this is a situation which is not likely to last indefinitely since neither party would want this to happen. The aim of the farmer would be to induce the cattle-raiser to make a payment in return for an agreement to leave this land uncultivated. The farmer would not be able to obtain a payment greater than the cost of fencing off this piece of land nor so high as to lead the cattle-raiser to abandon the use of the neighbouring property. What payment would in fact be made would depend on the shrewdness of the farmer and the cattle-raiser as bargainers. But as the payment would not be so high as to cause the cattle-raiser to abandon this location and as it would not vary with the size of the herd, such an agreement would not affect the allocation of resources but would merely alter the distribution of income and wealth as between the cattle-raiser and the farmer.

I think it is clear that if the cattle-raiser is liable for damage caused and the pricing system works smoothly, the reduction in the value of production elsewhere will be taken into account in computing the additional cost involved in increasing the size of the herd. This cost will be weighed against the value of the additional meat production and, given perfect competition in the cattle industry, the allocation of resources in cattle-raising will be optimal. What needs to be emphasized is that the fall in the value of production elsewhere which would be taken into account in the costs of the cattle-raiser may well be less than the damage which the cattle would cause to the crops in the ordinary course of events. This is because it is possible, as a result of market transactions, to discontinue cultivation of the land. This is desirable in all

---

to change his crop (since this would reduce damage liability from $3 to $1) and it would be profitable for the farmer to do so if the amount received was more than $1 (the reduction in his return caused by switching crops). In fact, there would be room for a mutually satisfactory bargain in all cases in which a change of crop would reduce the amount of damage by more than it reduces the value of the crop (excluding damage)—in all cases, that is, in which a change in the crop cultivated would lead to an increase in the value of production.

cases in which the damage that the cattle would cause, and for which the cattle-raiser would be willing to pay, exceeds the amount which the farmer would pay for use of the land. In conditions of perfect competition, the amount which the farmer would pay for the use of the land is equal to the difference between the value of the total production when the factors are employed on this land and the value of the additional product yielded in their next best use (which would be what the farmer would have to pay for the factors). If damage exceeds the amount the farmer would pay for the use of the land, the value of the additional product of the factors employed elsewhere would exceed the value of the total product in this use after damage is taken into account. It follows that it would be desirable to abandon cultivation of the land and to release the factors employed for production elsewhere. A procedure which merely provided for payment for damage to the crop caused by the cattle but which did not allow for the possibility of cultivation being discontinued would result in too small an employment of factors of production in cattle-raising and too large an employment of factors in cultivation of the crop. But given the possibility of market transactions, a situation in which damage to crops exceeded the rent of the land would not endure. Whether the cattle-raiser pays the farmer to leave the land uncultivated or himself rents the land by paying the land-owner an amount slightly greater than the farmer would pay (if the farmer was himself renting the land), the final result would be the same and would maximise the value of production. Even when the farmer is induced to plant crops which it would not be profitable to cultivate for sale on the market, this will be a purely short-term phenomenon and may be expected to lead to an agreement under which the planting will cease. The cattle-raiser will remain in that location and the marginal cost of meat production will be the same as before, thus having no long-run effect on the allocation of resources.

IV. The Pricing System with No Liability for Damage

I now turn to the case in which, although the pricing system is assumed to work smoothly (that is, costlessly), the damaging business is not liable for any of the damage which it causes. This business does not have to make a payment to those damaged by its actions. I propose to show that the allocation of resources will be the same in this case as it was when the damaging business was liable for damage caused. As I showed in the previous case that the allocation of resources was optimal, it will not be necessary to repeat this part of the argument.

I return to the case of the farmer and the cattle-raiser. The farmer would suffer increased damage to his crop as the size of the herd increased. Suppose that the size of the cattle-raiser's herd is 3 steers (and that this is the size of the herd that would be maintained if crop damage was not taken into account). Then the farmer would be willing to pay up to $3 if the cattle-raiser would reduce his herd to 2 steers, up to $5 if the herd were reduced to 1 steer and would pay up to $6 if cattle-raising was abandoned. The cattle-raiser would therefore receive $3 from the farmer if he kept 2 steers instead of 3. This $3 foregone is therefore part of the cost incurred in keeping the third steer. Whether the $3 is a payment which the cattle-raiser has to make if he adds the third steer to his herd (which it would be if the cattle-raiser was liable to the farmer for damage caused to the crop) or whether it is a sum of money which he would have received if he did not keep a third steer (which it would be if the cattle-raiser was not liable to the farmer for damage caused to the crop) does not affect the final result. In both cases $3 is part of the cost of adding a third steer, to be included along with the other costs. If the increase in the value of production in cattle-raising through increasing the size of the herd from 2 to 3 is greater than the additional costs that have to be incurred (including the $3 damage to crops), the size of the herd will be increased. Otherwise, it will not. The size of the herd will be the same whether the cattle-raiser is liable for damage caused to the crop or not.

It may be argued that the assumed starting point—a herd of 3 steers—was arbitrary. And this is true. But the farmer would not wish to pay to avoid crop damage which the cattle-raiser would not be able to cause. For example, the maximum annual payment which the farmer could be induced to pay could not exceed $9, the annual cost of fencing. And the farmer would only be willing to pay this sum if it did not reduce his earnings to a level that would cause him to abandon cultivation of this particular tract of land. Furthermore, the farmer would only be willing to pay this amount if he believed that, in the absence of any payment by him, the size of the herd maintained by the cattle raiser would be 4 or more steers. Let us assume that this is the case. Then the farmer would be willing to pay up to $3 if the cattle raiser would reduce his herd to 3 steers, up to $6 if the herd were reduced to 2 steers, up to $8 if one steer only were kept and up to $9 if cattle-raising were abandoned. It will be noticed that the change in the starting point has not altered the amount which would accrue to the cattle-raiser if he reduced the size of his herd by any given amount. It is still true that the cattle-raiser could receive an additional $3 from the farmer if he agreed to reduce his herd from 3 steers to 2 and that the $3 represents the value of the crop that would be destroyed by adding the third steer to the herd. Although a different belief on the part of the farmer (whether justified or not) about the size of the herd that the cattle-raiser would maintain in the absence of payments from him may affect the total payment he can be induced to pay, it is not true that this different belief would have any effect on the size of the herd that the cattle-raiser will actually keep. This will be the same as it would be if the cattle-raiser had to pay for damage caused by his cattle, since a receipt foregone of a given amount is the equivalent of a payment of the same amount.

It might be thought that it would pay the cattle-raiser to increase his herd above the size that he would wish to maintain once a bargain had been made, in order to induce the farmer to make a larger total payment. And this may be true. It is similar in nature to the action of the farmer (when the cattle-raiser was liable for damage) in cultivating land on which, as a result of an agreement with the cattle-raiser, planting would subsequently be abandoned (including land which would not be cultivated at all in the absence of cattle-raising). But such manoeuvres are preliminaries to an agreement and do not affect the long-run equilibrium position, which is the same whether or not the cattle-raiser is held responsible for the crop damage brought about by his cattle.

It is necessary to know whether the damaging business is liable or not for damage caused since without the establishment of this initial delimitation of rights there can be no market transactions to transfer and recombine them. But the ultimate result (which maximises the value of production) is independent of the legal position if the pricing system is assumed to work without cost.

V. The Problem Illustrated Anew

The harmful effects of the activities of a business can assume a wide variety of forms. An early English case concerned a building which, by obstructing currents of air, hindered the operation of a windmill.[5] A recent case in Florida concerned a building which cast a shadow on the cabana, swimming pool and sunbathing areas of a neighbouring hotel.[6] The problem of straying cattle and the damaging of crops which was the subject of detailed examination in the two preceding sections, although it may have appeared to be rather a special case, is in fact but one example of a problem which arises in many different guises. To clarify the nature of my argument and to demonstrate its general applicability, I propose to illustrate it anew by reference to four actual cases.

Let us first reconsider the case of *Sturges v. Bridgman*[7] which I used as an illustration of the general problem in my article on "The Federal Communications Commission." In this case, a confectioner (in Wigmore Street) used two mortars and pestles in connection with his business (one had been in operation in the same position for more than 60 years and the other for more than 26 years). A doctor then came to occupy neighbouring premises (in Wimpole Street). The confectioner's machinery caused the doctor no harm until, eight years after he had first occupied the premises, he built a consulting room at the end of his garden right against the confectioner's kitchen. It was then found that the noise and vibration caused by the confectioner's machin-

[5] See Gale on Easements 237–39 (13th ed. M. Bowles 1959).

[6] See Fontainebleu Hotel Corp. v. Forty-Five Twenty-Five, Inc., 114 So. 2d 357 (1959).

[7] 11 Ch. D. 852 (1879).

ery made it difficult for the doctor to use his new consulting room. "In particular . . . the noise prevented him from examining his patients by auscultation[8] for diseases of the chest. He also found it impossible to engage with effect in any occupation which required thought and attention." The doctor therefore brought a legal action to force the confectioner to stop using his machinery. The courts had little difficulty in granting the doctor the injunction he sought. "Individual cases of hardship may occur in the strict carrying out of the principle upon which we found our judgment, but the negation of the principle would lead even more to individual hardship, and would at the same time produce a prejudicial effect upon the development of land for residential purposes."

The court's decision established that the doctor had the right to prevent the confectioner from using his machinery. But, of course, it would have been possible to modify the arrangements envisaged in the legal ruling by means of a bargain between the parties. The doctor would have been willing to waive his right and allow the machinery to continue in operation if the confectioner would have paid him a sum of money which was greater than the loss of income which he would suffer from having to move to a more costly or less convenient location or from having to curtail his activities at this location or, as was suggested as a possibility, from having to build a separate wall which would deaden the noise and vibration. The confectioner would have been willing to do this if the amount he would have to pay the doctor was less than the fall in income he would suffer if he had to change his mode of operation at this location, abandon his operation or move his confectionery business to some other location. The solution of the problem depends essentially on whether the continued use of the machinery adds more to the confectioner's income than it subtracts from the doctor's.[9] But now consider the situation if the confectioner had won the case. The confectioner would then have had the right to continue operating his noise and vibration-generating machinery without having to pay anything to the doctor. The boot would have been on the other foot: the doctor would have had to pay the confectioner to induce him to stop using the machinery. If the doctor's income would have fallen more through continuance of the use of this machinery than it added to the income of the confectioner, there would clearly be room for a bargain whereby the doctor paid the confectioner to stop using the machinery. That is to say, the circumstances in which it would not pay the confectioner to continue to use the machinery and to compensate the doctor for the losses that this would bring (if the doctor had the right to prevent the confectioner's using his

[8] Auscultation is the act of listening by ear or stethoscope in order to judge by sound the condition of the body.

[9] Note that what is taken into account is the change in income after allowing for alterations in methods of production, location, character of product, etc.

machinery) would be those in which it would be in the interest of the doctor to make a payment to the confectioner which would induce him to discontinue the use of the machinery (if the confectioner had the right to operate the machinery). The basic conditions are exactly the same in this case as they were in the example of the cattle which destroyed crops. With costless market transactions, the decision of the courts concerning liability for damage would be without effect on the allocation of resources. It was of course the view of the judges that they were affecting the working of the economic system—and in a desirable direction. Any other decision would have had "a prejudicial effect upon the development of land for residential purposes," an argument which was elaborated by examining the example of a forge operating on a barren moor, which was later developed for residual purposes. The judges' view that they were settling how the land was to be used would be true only in the case in which the costs of carrying out the necessary market transactions exceeded the gain which might be achieved by any rearrangement of rights. And it would be desirable to preserve the areas (Wimpole Street or the moor) for residential or professional use (by giving non-industrial users the right to stop the noise, vibration, smoke, etc., by injunction) only if the value of the additional residential facilities obtained was greater than the value of cakes or iron lost. But of this the judges seem to have been unaware.

Another example of the same problem is furnished by the case of *Cooke v. Forbes*.[10] One process in the weaving of cocoa-nut fibre matting was to immerse it in bleaching liquids after which it was hung out to dry. Fumes from a manufacturer of sulphate of ammonia had the effect of turning the matting from a bright to a dull and blackish colour. The reason for this was that the bleaching liquid contained chloride of tin, which, when affected by sulphuretted hydrogen, is turned to a darker colour. An injunction was sought to stop the manufacturer from emitting the fumes. The lawyers for the defendant argued that if the plaintiff "were not to use . . . a particular bleaching liquid, their fibre would not be affected; that their process is unusual, not according to the custom of the trade, and even damaging to their own fabrics." The judge commented: ". . . it appears to me quite plain that a person has a right to carry on upon his own property a manufacturing process in which he uses chloride of tin, or any sort of metallic dye, and that his neighbour is not at liberty to pour in gas which will interfere with his manufacture. If it can be traced to the neighbour, then, I apprehend, clearly he will have a right to come here and ask for relief." But in view of the fact that the damage was accidental and occasional, that careful precautions were taken and that there was no exceptional risk, an injunction was refused, leaving the plaintiff to bring an action for damages if he wished. What the subsequent developments

[10] L. R. 5 Eq. 166 (1867–1868).

were I do not know. But it is clear that the situation is essentially the same as that found in *Sturges v. Bridgman,* except that the cocoa-nut fibre matting manufacturer could not secure an injunction but would have to seek damages from the sulphate of ammonia manufacturer. The economic analysis of the situation is exactly the same as with the cattle which destroyed crops. To avoid the damage, the sulphate of ammonia manufacturer could increase his precautions or move to another location. Either course would presumably increase his costs. Alternatively he could pay for the damage. This he would do if the payments for damage were less than the additional costs that would have to be incurred to avoid the damage. The payments for damage would then become part of the cost of production of sulphate of ammonia. Of course, if, as was suggested in the legal proceedings, the amount of damage could be eliminated by changing the bleaching agent (which would presumably increase the costs of the matting manufacturer) and if the additional cost was less than the damage that would otherwise occur, it should be possible for the two manufacturers to make a mutually satisfactory bargain whereby the new bleaching agent was used. Had the court decided against the matting manufacturer, as a consequence of which he would have had to suffer the damage without compensation, the allocation of resources would not have been affected. It would pay the matting manufacturer to change his bleaching agent if the additional cost involved was less than the reduction in damage. And since the matting manufacturer would be willing to pay the sulphate of ammonia manufacturer an amount up to his loss of income (the increase in costs or the damage suffered) if he would cease his activities, this loss of income would remain a cost of production for the manufacturer of sulphate of ammonia. This case is indeed analytically exactly the same as the cattle example.

Bryant v. Lefever[11] raised the problem of the smoke nuisance in a novel form. The plaintiff and the defendants were occupiers of adjoining houses, which were of about the same height.

> Before 1876 the plaintiff was able to light a fire in any room of his house without the chimneys smoking; the two houses had remained in the same condition some thirty or forty years. In 1876 the defendants took down their house, and began to rebuild it. They carried up a wall by the side of the plaintiff's chimneys much beyond its original height, and stacked timber on the roof of their house, and thereby caused the plaintiff's chimneys to smoke whenever he lighted fires.

The reason, of course, why the chimneys smoked was that the erection of the wall and the stacking of the timber prevented the free circulation of air. In a trial before a jury, the plaintiff was awarded damages of £40. The case then went to the Court of Appeals where the judgment was reversed. Bramwell, L.J., argued:

[11] 4 C.P.D. 172 (1878–1879).

> . . . it is said, and the jury have found, that the defendants have done that which caused a nuisance to the plaintiff's house. We think there is no evidence of this. No doubt there is a nuisance, but it is not of the defendant's causing. They have done nothing in causing the nuisance. Their house and their timber are harmless enough. It is the plaintiff who causes the nuisance by lighting a coal fire in a place the chimney of which is placed so near the defendants' wall, that the smoke does not escape, but comes into the house. Let the plaintiff cease to light his fire, let him move his chimney, let him carry it higher, and there would be no nuisance. Who then, causes it? It would be very clear that the plaintiff did, if he had built his house or chimney after the defendants had put up the timber on theirs, and it is really the same though he did so before the timber was there. But (what is in truth the same answer), if the defendants cause the nuisance, they have a right to do so. If the plaintiff has not the right to the passage of air, except subject to the defendants' right to build or put timber on their house, then his right is subject to their right, and though a nuisance follows from the exercise of their right, they are not liable.

And Cotton, L.J., said:

> Here it is found that the erection of the defendants' wall has sensibly and materially interfered with the comfort of human existence in the plaintiff's house, and it is said this is a nuisance for which the defendants are liable. Ordinarily this is so, but the defendants have done so, not by sending on to the plaintiff's property any smoke or noxious vapour, but by interrupting the egress of smoke from the plaintiff's house in a way to which . . . the plaintiff has no legal right. The plaintiff creates the smoke, which interferes with his comfort. Unless he has . . . a right to get rid of this in a particular way which has been interfered with by the defendants, he cannot sue the defendants, because the smoke made by himself, for which he has not provided any effectual means of escape, causes him annoyance. It is as if a man tried to get rid of liquid filth arising on his own land by a drain into his neighbour's land. Until a right had been acquired by user, the neighbour might stop the drain without incurring liability by so doing. No doubt great inconvenience would be caused to the owner of the property on which the liquid filth arises. But the act of his neighbour would be a lawful act, and he would not be liable for the consequences attributable to the fact that the man had accumulated filth without providing any effectual means of getting rid of it.

I do not propose to show that any subsequent modification of the situation, as a result of bargains between the parties (conditioned by the cost of stacking the timber elsewhere, the cost of extending the chimney higher, etc.), would have exactly the same result whatever decision the courts had come to since this point has already been adequately dealt with in the discussion of the cattle example and the two previous cases. What I shall discuss is the argument of the judges in the Court of Appeals that the smoke nuisance was not caused by the man who erected the wall but by the man who lit the fires. The novelty of the situation is that the smoke nuisance was suffered by the man who lit the fires and not by some third person. The question is not a trivial one since it lies at the heart of the problem under discussion. Who caused the smoke nuisance? The answer seems fairly clear. The smoke nuisance was caused both by the man who built the wall *and* by the man who lit the fires. Given the fires, there would have been no smoke nuisance without the wall: given the wall, there would have been no smoke nuisance without the fires. Eliminate the wall *or* the fires and the smoke nuisance would disappear. On the marginal principle it is clear that *both* were responsible and *both* should be forced to include the loss of amenity due to the smoke as a cost in deciding whether to continue the activity which gives rise to the smoke. And given the possibility of market transactions, this is what would in fact happen. Although the wall-builder was not liable legally for the nuisance, as the man with the smoking chimneys would presumably be willing to pay a sum equal to the monetary worth to him of eliminating the smoke, this sum would therefore become for the wall-builder, a cost of continuing to have the high wall with the timber stacked on the roof.

The judges' contention that it was the man who lit the fires who alone caused the smoke nuisance is true only if we assume that the wall is the given factor. This is what the judges did by deciding that the man who erected the higher wall had a legal right to do so. The case would have been even more interesting if the smoke from the chimneys had injured the timber. Then it would have been the wall-builder who suffered the damage. The case would then have closely paralleled *Sturges v. Bridgman* and there can be little doubt that the man who lit the fires would have been liable for the ensuing damage to the timber, in spite of the fact that no damage had occurred until the high wall was built by the man who owned the timber.

Judges have to decide on legal liability but this should not confuse economists about the nature of the economic problem involved. In the case of the cattle and the crops, it is true that there would be no crop damage without the cattle. It is equally true that there would be no crop damage without the crops. The doctor's work would not have been disturbed if the confectioner had not worked his machinery; but the machinery would have disturbed no one if the doctor had not set up his consulting room in that particular place. The matting was blackened by the fumes from the sulphate of ammonia manufacturer; but no damage would have occurred if the matting manufacturer had not chosen to hang out his matting in a particular place and to use a particular bleaching agent. If we are to discuss the problem in terms of causation, both parties cause the damage. If we are to attain an optimum allocation of resources, it is therefore desirable that both parties should take the harmful effect (the nuisance) into account in deciding on their course of action. It is one of the beauties of a smoothly operating pricing system that, as has already been explained, the fall in the value of production due to the harmful effect would be a cost for both parties.

Bass v. Gregory[12] will serve as an excellent final illustration of the problem. The plaintiffs were the owners and tenant of a public house called the Jolly Anglers. The defendant was the owner of some cottages and a yard adjoining the Jolly Anglers. Under the public house was a cellar excavated in the rock. From the cellar, a hole or shaft had been cut into an old well situated in the defendant's yard. The well therefore became the ventilating shaft for the cellar. The cellar "had been used for a particular purpose in the process of brewing, which, without ventilation, could not be carried on." The cause of the action was that the defendant removed a grating from the mouth of the well, "so as to stop or prevent the free passage of air from [the] cellar upwards through the well. . . ." What caused the defendant to take this step is not clear from the report of the case. Perhaps "the air . . . impregnated by the brewing operations" which "passed up the well and out into the open air" was offensive to him. At any rate, he preferred to have the well in his yard stopped up. The court had first to determine whether the owners of the public house could have a legal right to a current of air. If they were to have such a right, this case would have to be distinguished from *Bryant v. Lefever* (already considered). This, however, presented no difficulty. In this case, the current of air was confined to "a strictly defined channel." In the case of *Bryant v. Lefever*, what was involved was "the general current of air common to all mankind." The judge therefore held that the owners of the public house could have the right to a current of air whereas the owner of the private house in *Bryant v. Lefever* could not. An economist might be tempted to add "but the air moved all the same." However, all that had been decided at this stage of the argument was that there could be a legal right, not that the owners of the public house possessed it. But evidence showed that the shaft from the cellar to the well had existed for over forty years and that the use of the well as a ventilating shaft must have been known to the owners of the yard since the air, when it emerged, smelt of the brewing operations. The judge therefore held that the public house had such a right by the "doctrine of lost grant." This doctrine states "that if a legal right is proved to have existed and been exercised for a number of years the law ought to presume that it had a legal origin."[13] So the owner of the cottages and yard had to unstop the well and endure the smell.

[12] 25 Q.B.D. 481 (1890).

[13] It may be asked why a lost grant could not also be presumed in the case of the confectioner who had operated one mortar for more than 60 years. The answer is that until the doctor built the consulting room at the end of his garden there was no nuisance. So the nuisance had not continued for many years. It is true that the confectioner in his affidavit referred to "an invalid lady who occupied the house upon one occasion, about thirty years before" who "requested him if possible to discontinue the use of the mortars before eight o'clock in the morning" and that there was some evidence that the garden wall had been subjected to vibration. But the court had little difficulty in disposing of this line of argument: ". . . this vibration, even if it existed at all, was so slight, and the com-

The reasoning employed by the courts in determining legal rights will often seem strange to an economist because many of the factors on which the decision turns are, to an economist, irrelevant. Because of this, situations which are, from an economic point of view, identical will be treated quite differently by the courts. The economic problem in all cases of harmful effects is how to maximise the value of production. In the case of *Bass v. Gregory* fresh air was drawn in through the well which facilitated the production of beer but foul air was expelled through the well which made life in the adjoining houses less pleasant. The economic problem was to decide which to choose: a lower cost of beer and worsened amenities in adjoining houses or a higher cost of beer and improved amenities. In deciding this question, the "doctrine of lost grant" is about as relevant as the colour of the judge's eyes. But it has to be remembered that the immediate question faced by the courts is *not* what shall be done by whom *but* who has the legal right to do what. It is always possible to modify by transactions on the market the initial legal delimitation of rights. And, of course, if such market transactions are costless, such a rearrangement of rights will always take place if it would lead to an increase in the value of production.

VI. The Cost of Market Transactions Taken into Account

The argument has proceeded up to this point on the assumption (explicit in Sections III and IV and tacit in Section V) that there were no costs involved in carrying out market transactions. This is, of course, a very unrealistic assumption. In order to carry out a market transaction it is necessary to discover who it is that one wishes to deal with, to inform people that one wishes to deal and on what terms, to conduct negotiations leading up to a bargain, to draw up the contract, to undertake the inspection needed to make sure that the terms of the contract are being observed, and so on. These operations are often extremely costly, sufficiently costly at any rate to prevent many transactions that would be carried out in a world in which the pricing system worked without cost.

In earlier sections, when dealing with the problem of the rearrangement of legal rights through the market, it was argued that such a rearrangement would be made through the market whenever this would lead to an increase in the value of production. But this assumed costless market transactions. Once the costs of carrying out market transactions are taken into account it is clear that such a rearrangement of rights will only be undertaken when the increase in the value of production consequent upon the rearrangement

plaint, if it can be called a complaint, of the invalid lady . . . was of so trifling a character, that . . . the Defendant's acts would not have given rise to any proceeding either at law or in equity" (11 Ch.D. 863). That is, the confectioner had not committed a nuisance until the doctor built his consulting room.

is greater than the costs which would be involved in bringing it about. When it is less, the granting of an injunction (or the knowledge that it would be granted) or the liability to pay damages may result in an activity being discontinued (or may prevent its being started) which would be undertaken if market transactions were costless. In these conditions the initial delimitation of legal rights does have an effect on the efficiency with which the economic system operates. One arrangement of rights may bring about a greater value of production than any other. But unless this is the arrangement of rights established by the legal system, the costs of reaching the same result by altering and combining rights through the market may be so great that this optimal arrangement of rights, and the greater value of production which it would bring, may never be achieved. The part played by economic considerations in the process of delimiting legal rights will be discussed in the next section. In this section, I will take the initial delimitation of rights and the costs of carrying out market transactions as given.

It is clear that an alternative form of economic organisation which could achieve the same result at less cost than would be incurred by using the market would enable the value of production to be raised. As I explained many years ago, the firm represents such an alternative to organising production through market transactions.[14] Within the firm individual bargains between the various cooperating factors of production are eliminated and for a market transaction is substituted an administrative decision. The rearrangement of production then takes place without the need for bargains between the owners of the factors of production. A landowner who has control of a large tract of land may devote his land to various uses taking into account the effect that the interrelations of the various activities will have on the net return of the land, thus rendering unnecessary bargains between those undertaking the various activities. Owners of a large building or of several adjoining properties in a given area may act in much the same way. In effect, using our earlier terminology, the firm would acquire the legal rights of all the parties and the rearrangement of activities would not follow on a rearrangement of rights by contract, but as a result of an administrative decision as to how the rights should be used.

It does not, of course, follow that the administrative costs of organising a transaction through a firm are inevitably less than the costs of the market transactions which are superseded. But where contracts are peculiarly difficult to draw up and an attempt to describe what the parties have agreed to do or not to do (e.g. the amount and kind of a smell or noise that they may make or will not make) would necessitate a lengthy and highly involved document, and, where, as is probable, a long-term contract would be desir-

[14] See Coase, The Nature of the Firm, 4 Economica, New Series, 386 (1937). Reprinted in Readings in Price Theory, 331 (1952).

able;[15] it would be hardly surprising if the emergence of a firm or the extension of the activities of an existing firm was not the solution adopted on many occasions to deal with the problem of harmful effects. This solution would be adopted whenever the administrative costs of the firm were less than the costs of the market transactions that it supersedes and the gains which would result from the rearrangement of activities greater than the firm's costs of organising them. I do not need to examine in great detail the character of this solution since I have explained what is involved in my earlier article.

But the firm is not the only possible answer to this problem. The administrative costs of organising transactions within the firm may also be high, and particularly so when many diverse activities are brought within the control of a single organisation. In the standard case of a smoke nuisance, which may affect a vast number of people engaged in a wide variety of activities, the administrative costs might well be so high as to make any attempt to deal with the problem within the confines of a single firm impossible. An alternative solution is direct Government regulation. Instead of instituting a legal system of rights which can be modified by transactions on the market, the government may impose regulations which state what people must or must not do and which have to be obeyed. Thus, the government (by statute or perhaps more likely through an administrative agency) may, to deal with the problem of smoke nuisance, decree that certain methods of production should or should not be used (e.g. that smoke preventing devices should be installed or that coal or oil should not be burned) or may confine certain types of business to certain districts (zoning regulations).

The government is, in a sense, a super-firm (but of a very special kind) since it is able to influence the use of factors of production by administrative decision. But the ordinary firm is subject to checks in its operations because of the competition of other firms, which might administer the same activities at lower cost and also because there is always the alternative of market transactions as against organisation within the firm if the administrative costs become too great. The government is able, if it wishes, to avoid the market altogether, which a firm can never do. The firm has to make market agreements with the owners of the factors of production that it uses. Just as the government can conscript or seize property, so it can decree that factors of production should only be used in such-and-such a way. Such authoritarian methods save a lot of trouble (for those doing the organising). Furthermore, the government has at its disposal the police and the other law enforcement agencies to make sure that its regulations are carried out.

It is clear that the government has powers which might enable it to get some things done at a lower cost than could a private organisation (or at any

[15] For reasons explained in my earlier article, see Readings in Price Theory, n. 14 at 337.

rate one without special governmental powers). But the governmental administrative machine is not itself costless. It can, in fact, on occasion be extremely costly. Furthermore, there is no reason to suppose that the restrictive and zoning regulations, made by a fallible administration subject to political pressures and operating without any competitive check, will necessarily always be those which increase the efficiency with which the economic system operates. Furthermore, such general regulations which must apply to a wide variety of cases will be enforced in some cases in which they are clearly inappropriate. From these considerations it follows that direct governmental regulation will not necessarily give better results than leaving the problem to be solved by the market or the firm. But equally there is no reason why, on occasion, such governmental administrative regulation should not lead to an improvement in economic efficiency. This would seem particularly likely when, as is normally the case with the smoke nuisance, a large number of people are involved and in which therefore the costs of handling the problem through the market or the firm may be high.

There is, of course, a further alternative, which is to do nothing about the problem at all. And given that the costs involved in solving the problem by regulations issued by the governmental administrative machine will often be heavy (particularly if the costs are interpreted to include all the consequences which follow from the Government engaging in this kind of activity), it will no doubt be commonly the case that the gain which would come from regulating the actions which give rise to the harmful effects will be less than the costs involved in Government regulation.

The discussion of the problem of harmful effects in this section (when the costs of market transactions are taken into account) is extremely inadequate. But at least it has made clear that the problem is one of choosing the appropriate social arrangement for dealing with the harmful effects. All solutions have costs and there is no reason to suppose that government regulation is called for simply because the problem is not well handled by the market or the firm. Satisfactory views on policy can only come from a patient study of how, in practice, the market, firms and governments handle the problem of harmful effects. Economists need to study the work of the broker in bringing parties together, the effectiveness of restrictive covenants, the problems of the large-scale real-estate development company, the operation of Government zoning and other regulating activities. It is my belief that economists, and policy-makers generally, have tended to over-estimate the advantages which come from governmental regulation. But this belief, even if justified, does not do more than suggest that government regulation should be curtailed. It does not tell us where the boundary line should be drawn. This, it seems to me, has to come from a detailed investigation of the actual results of handling the problem in different ways. But it would be unfortunate if this investigation were undertaken with the aid of a faulty economic analysis. The aim of this article is to indicate what the economic approach to the problem should be.

VII. The Legal Delimitation of Rights and the Economic Problem

The discussion in Section V not only served to illustrate the argument but also afforded a glimpse at the legal approach to the problem of harmful effects. The cases considered were all English but a similar selection of American cases could easily be made and the character of the reasoning would have been the same. Of course, if market transactions were costless, all that matters (questions of equity apart) is that the rights of the various parties should be well-defined and the results of legal actions easy to forecast. But as we have seen, the situation is quite different when market transactions are so costly as to make it difficult to change the arrangement of rights established by the law. In such cases, the courts directly influence economic activity. It would therefore seem desirable that the courts should understand the economic consequences of their decisions and should, insofar as this is possible without creating too much uncertainty about the legal position itself, take these consequences into account when making their decisions. Even when it is possible to change the legal delimitation of rights through market transactions, it is obviously desirable to reduce the need for such transactions and thus reduce the employment of resources in carrying them out.

A thorough examination of the presuppositions of the courts in trying such cases would be of great interest but I have not been able to attempt it. Nevertheless it is clear from a cursory study that the courts have often recognized the economic implications of their decisions and are aware (as many economists are not) of the reciprocal nature of the problem. Furthermore, from time to time, they take these economic implications into account, along with other factors, in arriving at their decisions. The American writers on this subject refer to the question in a more explicit fashion than do the British. Thus, to quote Prosser on Torts, a person may

> make use of his own property or . . . conduct his own affairs at the expense of some harm to his neighbors. He may operate a factory whose noise and smoke cause some discomfort to others, so long as he keeps within reasonable bounds. It is only when his conduct is unreasonable, *in the light of its utility and the harm which results* [italics added], that it becomes a nuisance. . . . . As it was said in an ancient case in regard to candle-making in a town, "Le utility del chose excusera le noisomeness del stink."
>
> The world must have factories, smelters, oil refineries, noisy machinery and blasting, even at the expense of some inconvenience to those in the vicinity and the

plaintiff may be required to accept some not unreasonable discomfort for the general good.[16]

The standard British writers do not state as explicitly as this that a comparison between the utility and harm produced is an element in deciding whether a harmful effect should be considered a nuisance. But similar views, if less strongly expressed, are to be found.[17] The doctrine that the harmful effect must be substantial before the court will act is, no doubt, in part a reflection of the fact that there will almost always be some gain to offset the harm. And in the reports of individual cases, it is clear that the judges have had in mind what would be lost as well as what would be gained in deciding whether to grant an injunction or award damages. Thus, in refusing to prevent the destruction of a prospect by a new building, the judge stated:

> I know no general rule of common law, which . . . says, that building so as to stop another's prospect is a nuisance. Was that the case, there could be no great towns; and I must grant injunctions to all the new buildings in this town. . . .[18]

In *Webb v. Bird*[19] it was decided that it was not a nuisance to build a schoolhouse so near a windmill as to obstruct currents of air and hinder the working of the mill. An early case seems to have been decided in an opposite direction. Gale commented:

> In old maps of London a row of windmills appears on the heights to the north of London. Probably in the time of King James it was thought an alarming circumstance, as affecting the supply of food to the city, that anyone should build so near them as to take the wind out from their sails.[20]

In one of the cases discussed in section V, *Sturges v. Bridgman*, it seems clear that the judges were thinking of the economic consequences of alternative decisions. To the argument that if the principle that they seemed to be following

[16] See W. L. Prosser, The Law of Torts 398–99, 412 (2d ed. 1955). The quotation about the ancient case concerning candle-making is taken from Sir James Fitzjames Stephen, A General View of the Criminal Law of England 106 (1890). Sir James Stephen gives no reference. He perhaps had in mind *Rex. v. Ronkett*, included in Seavey, Keeton and Thurston, Cases on Torts 604 (1950). A similar view to that expressed by Prosser is to be found in F. V. Harper and F. James, The Law of Torts 67–74 (1956); Restatement, Torts §§826, 827 and 828.

[17] See Winfield on Torts 541–48 (6th ed. T. E. Lewis 1954); Salmond on the Law of Torts 181–90 (12th ed. R.F.V. Heuston 1957); H. Street, The Law of Torts 221–29 (1959).

[18] Attorney General v. Doughty, 2 Ves. Sen. 453, 28 Eng. Rep. 290 (Ch. 1752). Compare in this connection the statement of an American judge, quoted in Prosser, op. cit. supra n. 16 at 413 n. 54: "Without smoke, Pittsburgh would have remained a very pretty village," Musmanno, J., in Versailles Borough v. McKeesport Coal & Coke Co., 1935, 83 Pitts. Leg. J. 379, 385.

[19] 10 C.B. (N.S.) 268, 142 Eng. Rep. 445 (1861); 13 C.B. (N.S.) 841, 143 Eng. Rep. 332 (1863).

[20] See Gale on Easements 238, n. 6 (13th ed. M. Bowles 1959).

were carried out to its logical consequences, it would result in the most serious practical inconveniences, for a man might go—say into the midst of the tanneries of *Bermondsey*, or into any other locality devoted to any particular trade or manufacture of a noisy or unsavoury character, and by building a private residence upon a vacant piece of land put a stop to such trade or manufacture altogether,

the judges answered that

whether anything is a nuisance or not is a question to be determined, not merely by an abstract consideration of the thing itself, but in reference to its circumstances; What would be a nuisance in *Belgrave Square* would not necessarily be so in *Bermondsey;* and where a locality is devoted to a particular trade or manufacture carried on by the traders or manufacturers in a particular and established manner not constituting a public nuisance, Judges and juries would be justified in finding, and may be trusted to find, that the trade or manufacture so carried on in that locality is not a private or actionable wrong.[21]

That the character of the neighborhood is relevant in deciding whether something is, or is not, a nuisance, is definitely established.

He who dislikes the noise of traffic must not set up his abode in the heart of a great city. He who loves peace and quiet must not live in a locality devoted to the business of making boilers or steamships.[22]

What has emerged has been described as "planning and zoning by the judiciary."[23] Of course there are sometimes considerable difficulties in applying the criteria.[24]

An interesting example of the problem is found in *Adams v. Ursell*[25] in which a fried fish shop in a predominantly working-class district was set up near houses of "a much better character." England without fish-and-chips is a contradiction in terms and the case was clearly one of high importance. The judge commented:

It was urged that an injunction would cause great hardship to the defendant and to the poor people who get food at his shop. The answer to that is that it does not follow that the defendant cannot carry on his business in another more suitable place somewhere in the neighbourhood. It by no means follows that because a fried fish shop is a nuisance in one place it is a nuisance in another.

In fact, the injunction which restrained Mr. Ursell from running his shop did not even extend to the whole street. So he was presumably able to move to other premises near houses of "a much worse character," the inhabitants

[21] 11 Ch.D. 865 (1879).

[22] Salmond on the Law of Torts 182 (12th ed. R.F.V. Heuston 1957).

[23] C. M. Haar, Land-Use P' nning, A Casebook on the Use, Misuse, and Re-use of Urban Land 95 (1959).

[24] See, for example, Rushmer v. Polsue and Alfieri, Ltd. [1906] 1 Ch. 234, which deals with the case of a house in a quiet situation in a noisy district.

[25] [1913] 1 Ch. 269.

of which would no doubt consider the availability of fish-and-chips to outweigh the pervading odour and "fog or mist" so graphically described by the plaintiff. Had there been no other "more suitable place in the neighbourhood," the case would have been more difficult and the decision might have been different. What would "the poor people" have had for food? No English judge would have said: "Let them eat cake."

The courts do not always refer very clearly to the economic problem posed by the cases brought before them but it seems probable that in the interpretation of words and phrases like "reasonable" or "common or ordinary use" there is some recognition, perhaps largely unconscious and certainly not very explicit, of the economic aspects of the questions at issue. A good example of this would seem to be the judgment in the Court of Appeals in *Andreae v. Selfridge and Company Ltd.*[26] In this case, a hotel (in Wigmore Street) was situated on part of an island site. The remainder of the site was acquired by Selfridges which demolished the existing buildings in order to erect another in their place. The hotel suffered a loss of custom in consequence of the noise and dust caused by the demolition. The owner of the hotel brought an action against Selfridges for damages. In the lower court, the hotel was awarded £4,500 damages. The case was then taken on appeal.

The judge who had found for the hotel proprietor in the lower court said:

> I cannot regard what the defendants did on the site of the first operation as having been commonly done in the ordinary use and occupation of land or houses. It is neither usual nor common, in this country, for people to excavate a site to a depth of 60 feet and then to erect upon that site a steel framework and fasten the steel frames together with rivets. . . . Nor is it, I think, a common or ordinary use of land, in this country, to act as the defendants did when they were dealing with the site of their second operation—namely, to demolish all the houses that they had to demolish, five or six of them I think, if not more, and to use for the purpose of demolishing them pneumatic hammers.

Sir Wilfred Greene, M.R., speaking for the Court of Appeals, first noted

> that when one is dealing with temporary operations, such as demolition and re-building, everybody has to put up with a certain amount of discomfort, because operations of that kind cannot be carried on at all without a certain amount of noise and a certain amount of dust. Therefore, the rule with regard to interference must be read subject to this qualification. . . .

He then referred to the previous judgment:

> With great respect to the learned judge, I take the view that he has not approached this matter from the correct angle. It seems to me that it is not possible to say . . . that the type of demolition, excavation and construction in which the defendant company was engaged in the course of these operations was of such an abnormal and unusual nature as to prevent the qualification to which I have referred coming

[26] [1938] 1 Ch. 1.

into operation. It seems to me that, when the rule speaks of the common or ordinary use of land, it does not mean that the methods of using land and building on it are in some way to be stabilised for ever. As time goes on new inventions or new methods enable land to be more profitably used, either by digging down into the earth or by mounting up into the skies. Whether, from other points of view, that is a matter which is desirable for humanity is neither here nor there; but it is part of the normal use of land, to make use upon your land, in the matter of construction, of what particular type and what particular depth of foundations and particular height of building may be reasonable, in the circumstances, and in view of the developments of the day. . . . Guests at hotels are very easily upset. People coming to this hotel, who were accustomed to a quiet outlook at the back, coming back and finding demolition and building going on, may very well have taken the view that the particular merit of this hotel no longer existed. That would be a misfortune for the plaintiff; but assuming that there was nothing wrong in the defendant company's works, assuming the defendant company was carrying on the demolition and its building, productive of noise though it might be, with all reasonable skill, and taking all reasonable precautions not to cause annoyance to its neighbors, then the planitiff might lose all her clients in the hotel because they have lost the amenities of an open and quiet place behind, but she would have no cause of complaint. . . . [But those] who say that their interference with the comfort of their neighbors is justified because their operations are normal and usual and conducted with proper care and skill are under a specific duty . . . to use that reasonable and proper care and skill. It is not a correct attitude to take to say: 'We will go on and do what we like until somebody complains!' . . . Their duty is to take proper precautions and to see that the nuisance is reduced to a minimum. It is no answer for them to say: 'But this would mean that we should have to do the work more slowly than we would like to do it, or it would involve putting us to some extra expense.' All these questions are matters of common sense and degree, and quite clearly it would be unreasonable to expect people to conduct their work so slowly or so expensively, for the purpose of preventing a transient inconvenience, that the cost and trouble would be prohibitive. . . . In this case, the defendant company's attitude seems to have been to go on until somebody complained, and, further, that its desire to hurry its work and conduct it according to its own ideas and its own convenience was to prevail if there was a real conflict between it and the comfort of its neighbors. That . . . is not carrying out the obligation of using reasonable care and skill. . . . The effect comes to this . . . the plaintiff suffered an actionable nuisance; . . . she is entitled, not to a nominal sum, but to a substantial sum, based upon those principles . . . but in arriving at the sum . . . I have discounted any loss of custom . . . which might be due to the general loss of amenities owing to what was going on at the back. . . .

The upshot was that the damages awarded were reduced from £4,500 to £1,000.

The discussion in this section has, up to this point, been concerned with court decisions arising out of the common law relating to nuisance. Delimitation of rights in this area also comes about because of statutory enactments. Most economists would appear to assume that the aim of governmental action in this field is to extend the scope of the law of nuisance by designating as nuisances activities which would not be recognized as such by the common law. And there can be no doubt that some statutes, for example, the Public Health Acts, have had this effect. But not all Government enactments are of this kind. The effect of much of the legislation in this area is to protect businesses from the claims of those they have harmed by their actions. There is a long list of legalized nuisances.

The position has been summarized in *Halsbury's Laws of England* as follows:

> Where the legislature directs that a thing shall in all events be done or authorises certain works at a particular place for a specific purposes or grants powers with the intention that they shall be exercised, although leaving some discretion as to the mode of exercise, no action will lie at common law for nuisance or damage which is the inevitable result of carrying out the statutory powers so conferred. This is so whether the act causing the damage is authorised for public purposes or private profit. Acts done under powers granted by persons to whom Parliament has delegated authority to grant such powers, for example, under provisional orders of the Board of Trade, are regarded as having been done under statutory authority. In the absence of negligence it seems that a body exercising statutory powers will not be liable to an action merely because it might, by acting in a different way, have minimised an injury.

Instances are next given of freedom from liability for acts authorized:

> An action has been held not to be against a body exercising its statutory powers without negligence in respect of the flooding of land by water escaping from water-courses, from water pipes, from drains, or from a canal; the escape of fumes from sewers; the escape of sewage: the subsidence of a road over a sewer; vibration or noise caused by a railway; fires caused by authorised acts; the pollution of a stream where statutory requirements to use the best known method of purifying before discharging the effluent have been satisfied; interference with a telephone or telegraph system by an elctric tramway; the insertion of poles for tramways in the subsoil; annoyance caused by things reasonably necessary for the excavation of authorised works; accidental damage caused by the placing of a grating in a roadway; the escape of tar acid; or interference with the access of a frontager by a street shelter or safety railings on the edge of a pavement.[27]

The legal position in the United States would seem to be essentially the same as in England, except that the power of the legislatures to authorize what would otherwise be nuisances under the common law, at least without giving compensation to the person harmed, is somewhat more limited, as it is subject to constitutional restrictions.[28] Nonetheless, the power is there and cases more or less identical with the English cases can be found. The

[27] See 30 Halsbury, Law of England 690–91 (3d ed. 1960), Article on Public Authorities and Public Officers.

[28] See Prosser, op. cit. supra n. 16 at 421; Harper and James, op. cit. supra n. 16 at 86–87.

question has arisen in an acute form in connection with airports and the operation of aeroplanes. The case of *Delta Air Corporation v. Kersey, Kersey v. City of Atlanta*[29] is a good example. Mr. Kersey bought land and built a house on it. Some years later the City of Atlanta constructed an airport on land immediately adjoining that of Mr. Kersey. It was explained that his property was "a quiet, peaceful and proper location for a home before the airport was built, but dust, noises and low flying of airplanes caused by the operation of the airport have rendered his property unsuitable as a home," a state of affairs which was described in the report of the case with a wealth of distressing detail. The judge first referred to an earlier case, *Thrasher v. City of Atlanta*[30] in which it was noted that the City of Atlanta had been expressly authorized to operate an airport.

> By this franchise aviation was recognised as a lawful business and also as an enterprise affected with a public interest . . . all persons using [the airport] in the manner contemplated by law are within the protection and immunity of the franchise granted by the municipality. An airport is not a nuisance per se, although it might become such from the manner of its construction or operation.

Since aviation was a lawful business affected with a public interest and the construction of the airport was autorized by statute, the judge next referred to *Georgia Railroad and Banking Co. v. Maddox*[31] in which it was said:

> Where a railroad terminal yard is located and its construction authorized, under statutory powers, if it be constructed and operated in a proper manner, it cannot be adjudged a nuisance. Accordingly, injuries and inconveniences to persons residing near such a yard, from noises of locomotives, rumbling of cars, vibrations produced thereby, and smoke, cinders, soot and the like, which result from the ordinary and necessary, therefore proper, use and operation of such a yard, are not nuisances, but are the necessary concomitants of the franchise granted.

In view of this, the judge decided that the noise and dust complained of by Mr. Kersey "may be deemed to be incidental to the proper operation of an airport, and as such they cannot be said to constitute a nuisance." But the complaint against low flying was different:

> . . . can it be said that flights . . . at such a low height [25 to 50 feet above Mr. Kersey's house] as to be imminently dangerous to . . . life and health . . . are a necessary concomitant of an airport? We do not think this question can be answered in the affirmative. No reason appears why the city could not obtain lands of an area [sufficiently large] . . . as not to require such low flights. . . . For the sake of public convenience adjoining-property owners must suffer such inconvenience from noise and dust as result from the usual and proper operation of an airport, but their private rights are entitled to preference in the eyes of the law where the inconvenience is not one demanded by a properly constructed and operated airport.

[29] Supreme Court of Georgia. 193 Ga. 862, 20 S.E. 2d 245 (1942).

[30] 178 Ga. 514, 173 S.E. 817 (1934).

[31] 116 Ga. 64, 42 S.E. 315 (1902).

Of course this assumed that the City of Atlanta could prevent the low flying and continue to operate the airport. The judge therefore added:

From all that appears, the conditions causing the low flying may be remedied; but if on the trial it should appear that it is indispensable to the public interest that the airport should continue to be operated in its present condition, it may be said that the petitioner should be denied injunctive relief.

In the course of another aviation case, *Smith v. New England Aircraft Co.*,[32] the court surveyed the law in the United States regarding the legalizing of nuisances and it is apparent that, in the broad, it is very similar to that found in England:

It is the proper function of the legislative department of government in the exercise of the police power to consider the problems and risks that arise from the use of new inventions and endeavor to adjust private rights and harmonize conflicting interests by comprehensive statutes for the public welfare. . . . There are . . . analogies where the invasion of the airspace over underlying land by noise, smoke, vibration, dust and disagreeable odors, having been authorized by the legislative department of government and not being in effect a condemnation of the property although in some measure depreciating its market value, must be borne by the landowner without compensation or remedy. Legislative sanction makes that lawful which otherwise might be a nuisance. Examples of this are damages to adjacent land arising from smoke, vibration and noise in the operation of a railroad . . . ; the noise of ringing factory bells . . . ; the abatement of nuisances . . . ; the erection of steam engines and furnaces . . . ; unpleasant odors connected with sewers, oil refining and storage of naphtha. . . .

Most economists seem to be unaware of all this. When they are prevented from sleeping at night by the roar of jet planes overhead (publicly authorized and perhaps publicly operated), are unable to think (or rest) in the day because of the noise and vibration from passing trains (publicly authorized and perhaps publicly operated), find it difficult to breathe because of the odour from a local sewage farm (publicly authorized and perhaps publicly operated) and are unable to escape because their driveways are blocked by a road obstruction (without any doubt, publicly devised), their nerves frayed and mental balance disturbed, they proceed to declaim about the disadvantages of private enterprise and the need for Government regulation.

While most economists seem to be under a misapprehension concerning the character of the situation with which they are dealing, it is also the case that the activities which they would like to see stopped or curtailed may well be socially justified. It is all a question of weighing up the gains that would accrue from eliminating these harmful effects against the gains that accrue from allowing them to continue. Of course, it is likely that an extension of Government economic activity will often lead to this protection against

[32] 270 Mass. 511, 523, 170 N.E. 385, 390 (1930).

action for nuisance being pushed further than is desirable. For one thing, the Government is likely to look with a benevolent eye on enterprises which it is itself promoting. For another, it is possible to describe the committing of a nuisance by public enterprise in a much more pleasant way than when the same thing is done by private enterprise. In the words of Lord Justice Sir Alfred Denning:

> . . . the significance of the social revolution of today is that, whereas in the past the balance was much too heavily in favor of the rights of property and freedom of contract, Parliament has repeatedly intervened so as to give the public good its proper place.[33]

There can be little doubt that the Welfare State is likely to bring an extension of that immunity from liability for damage, which economists have been in the habit of condemning (although they have tended to assume that this immunity was a sign of too little Government intervention in the economic system). For example, in Britain, the powers of local authorities are regarded as being either absolute or conditional. In the first category, the local authority has no discretion in exercising the power conferred on it. "The absolute power may be said to cover all the necessary consequences of its direct operation even if such consequences amount to nuisance." On the other hand, a conditional power may only be exercised in such a way that the consequences do not constitute a nuisance.

> It is the intention of the legislature which determines whether a power is absolute or conditional. . . . [As] there is the possibility that the social policy of the legislature may change from time to time, a power which in one era would be construed as being conditional, might in another era be interpreted as being absolute in order to further the policy of the Welfare State. This point is one which should be borne in mind when considering some of the older cases upon this aspect of the law of nuisance.[34]

It would seem desirable to summarize the burden of this long section. The problem which we face in dealing with actions which have harmful effects is not simply one of restraining those responsible for them. What has to be decided is whether the gain from preventing the harm is greater than the loss which would be suffered elsewhere as a result of stopping the action which produces the harm. In a world in which there are costs of rearranging the rights established by the legal system, the courts, in cases relating to nuisance, are, in effect, making a decision on the economic problem and determining how resources are to be employed. It was argued that the courts are conscious of this and that they often make, although not always in a very explicit fashion, a comparison between what would be gained and what lost by preventing

33 See Sir Alfred Denning, Freedom Under the Law 71 (1949).

34 M. B. Cairns, The Law of Tort in Local Government 28–32 (1954).

actions which have harmful effects. But the delimitation of rights is also the result of statutory enactments. Here we also find evidence of an appreciation of the reciprocal nature of the problem. While statutory enactments add to the list of nuisances, action is also taken to legalize what would otherwise be nuisances under the common law. The kind of situation which economists are prone to consider as requiring corrective Government action is, in fact, often the result of Government action. Such action is not necessarily unwise. But there is a real danger that extensive Government intervention in the economic system may lead to the protection of those responsible for harmful effects being carried too far.

VIII. Pigou's Treatment in "The Economics of Welfare"

The fountainhead for the modern economic analysis of the problem discussed in this article is Pigou's *Economics of Welfare* and, in particular, that section of Part II which deals with divergences between social and private net products which come about because

> one person A, in the course of rendering some service, for which payment is made, to a second person B, incidentally also renders services or disservices to other persons (not producers of like services), of such a sort that payment cannot be exacted from the benefited parties or compensation enforced on behalf of the injured parties.[35]

Pigou tells us that his aim in Part II of *The Economics of Welfare* is

> to ascertain how far the free play of self-interest, acting under the existing legal system, tends to distribute the country's resources in the way most favorable to the production of a large national dividend, and how far it is feasible for State action to improve upon 'natural' tendencies.[36]

To judge from the first part of this statement, Pigou's purpose is to discover whether any improvements could be made in the existing arrangements which determine the use of resources. Since Pigou's conclusion is that improvements could be made, one might have expected him to continue by saying that he proposed to set out the changes required to bring them about. Instead, Pigou adds a phrase which contrasts "natural" tendencies with State action, which seems in some sense to equate the present arrangements with "natural" tendencies and to imply that what is required to bring about these improvements is State action (if feasible). That this is more or less Pigou's position is evident from Chapter I of Part II.[37] Pigou starts by referring to "optimistic

[35] A. C. Pigou, The Economics of Welfare 183 (4th ed. 1932). My references will all be to the fourth edition but the argument and examples examined in this article remained substantially unchanged from the first edition in 1920 to the fourth in 1932. A large part (but not all) of this analysis had appeared previously in Wealth and Welfare (1912).

[36] *Id.* at xii.

[37] *Id.* at 127–30.

followers of the classical economists"[38] who have argued that the value of production would be maximised if the Government refrained from any interference in the economic system and the economic arrangements were those which came about "naturally." Pigou goes on to say that if self-interest does promote economic welfare, it is because human institutions have been devised to make it so. (This part of Pigou's argument, which he develops with the aid of a quotation from Cannan, seems to me to be essentially correct.) Pigou concludes:

> But even in the most advanced States there are failures and imperfections. . . . there are many obstacles that prevent a community's resources from being distributed . . . in the most efficient way. The study of these constitutes our present problem. . . . its purposes is essentially practical. It seeks to bring into clearer light some of the ways in which it now is, or eventually may become, feasible for governments to control the play of economic forces in such wise as to promote the economic welfare, and through that, the total welfare, of their citizens as a whole.[39]

Pigou's underlying thought would appear to be: Some have argued that no State action is needed. But the system has performed as well as it has because of State action. Nonetheless, there are still imperfections. What additional State action is required?

If this is a correct summary of Pigou's position, its inadequacy can be demonstrated by examining the first example he gives of a divergence between private and social products.

> It might happen . . . that costs are thrown upon people not directly concerned, through, say, uncompensated damage done to surrounding woods by sparks from railway engines. All such effects must be included—some of them will be positive, others negative elements—in reckoning up the social net product of the marginal increment of any volume of resources turned into any use or place.[40]

The example used by Pigou refers to a real situation. In Britain, a railway does not normally have to compensate those who suffer damage by fire caused by sparks from an engine. Taken in conjunction with what he says in Chapter 9 of Part II, I take Pigou's policy recommendations to be, first, that there should be State action to correct this "natural" situation and, second, that the railways should be forced to compensate those whose woods are burnt. If this is a correct interpretation of Pigou's position, I would argue that the first recommendation is based on a misapprehension of the facts and that the second is not necessarily desirable.

[38] In Wealth and Welfare, Pigou attributes the "optimism" to Adam Smith himself and not to his followers. He there refers to the "highly optimistic theory of Adam Smith that the national dividend, in given circumstances of demand and supply, tends 'naturally' to a maximum" (p. 104).

[39] Pigou, op. cit. supra n. 35 at 129–30.

[40] *Id.* at 134.

Let us consider the legal position. Under the heading "Sparks from engines," we find the following in Halsbury's Laws of England:

> If railway undertakers use steam engines on their railway without express statutory authority to do so, they are liable, irrespective of any negligence on their part, for fires caused by sparks from engines. Railway undertakers are, however, generally given statutory authority to use steam engines on their railway; accordingly, if an engine is constructed with the precautions which science suggests against fire and is used without negligence, they are not responsible at common law for any damage which may be done by sparks. . . . In the construction of an engine the undertaker is bound to use all the discoveries which science has put within its reach in order to avoid doing harm, provided they are such as it is reasonable to require the company to adopt, having proper regard to the likelihood of the damage and to the cost and convenience of the remedy; but it is not negligence on the part of an undertaker if it refuses to use an apparatus the efficiency of which is open to bona fide doubt.

To this general rule, there is a statutory exception arising from the Railway (Fires) Act, 1905, as amended in 1923. This concerns agricultural land or agricultural crops.

> In such a case the fact that the engine was used under statutory powers does not affect the liability of the company in an action for the damage. . . . These provisions, however, only apply where the claim for damage . . . does not exceed £ 200, [£ 100 in the 1905 Act] and where written notice of the occurrence of the fire and the intention to claim has been sent to the company within seven days of the occurrence of the damage and particulars of the damage in writing showing the amount of the claim in money not exceeding £ 200 have been sent to the company within twenty-one days.

Agricultural land does not include moorland or buildings and agricultural crops do not include those led away or stacked.[41] I have not made a close study of the parliamentary history of this statutory exception, but to judge from debates in the House of Commons in 1922 and 1923, this exception was probably designed to help the smallholder.[42]

Let us return to Pigou's example of uncompensated damage to surrounding woods caused by sparks from railway engines. This is presumably intended to show how it is possible "for State action to improve on 'natural' tendencies." If we treat Pigou's example as referring to the position before 1905, or as being an arbitrary example (in that he might just as well have written "surrounding buildings" instead of "surrounding woods"), then it is clear that the reason why compensation was not paid must have been that the railway had statutory authority to run steam engines (which relieved it of liability for fires caused by sparks). That this was the legal position was

[41] See 31 Halsbury, Laws of England 474–75 (3d ed. 1960), Article on Railways and Canals, from which this summary of the legal position, and all quotations, are taken.

[42] See 152 H.C. Deb. 2622–63 (1922); 161 H.C. Deb. 2935–55 (1923).

established in 1860, in a case, oddly enough, which concerned the burning of surrounding woods by a railway,[43] and the law on this point has not been changed (apart from the one exception) by a century of railway legislation, including nationalisation. If we treat Pigou's example of "uncompensated damage done to surrounding woods by sparks from railway engines" literally, and assume that it refers to the period after 1905, then it is clear that the reason why compensation was not paid must have been that the damage was more than £100 (in the first edition of *The Economics of Welfare*) or more than £200 (in later editions) or that the owner of the wood failed to notify the railway in writing within seven days of the fire or did not send particulars of the damage, in writing, within twenty-one days. In the real world, Pigou's example could only exist as a result of a deliberate choice of the legislature. It is not, of course, easy to imagine the construction of a railway in a state of nature. The nearest one can get to this is presumably a railway which uses steam engines "without express statutory authority." However, in this case the railway would be obliged to compensate those whose woods it burnt down. That is to say, compensation would be paid in the absence of Government action. The only circumstances in which compensation would not be paid would be those in which there had been Government action. It is strange that Pigou, who clearly thought it desirable that compensation should be paid, should have chosen this particular example to demonstrate how it is possible "for State action to improve on 'natural' tendencies."

Pigou seems to have had a faulty view of the facts of the situation. But it also seems likely that he was mistaken in his economic analysis. It is not necessarily desirable that the railway should be required to compensate those who suffer damage by fires caused by railway engines. I need not show here that, if the railway could make a bargain with everyone having property adjoining the railway line and there were no costs involved in making such bargains, it would not matter whether the railway was liable for damage caused by fires or not. This question has been treated at length in earlier sections. The problem is whether it would be desirable to make the railway liable in conditions in which it is too expensive for such bargains to be made. Pigou clearly thought it was desirable to force the railway to pay compensation and it is easy to see the kind of argument that would have led him to this conclusion. Suppose a railway is considering whether to run an additional train or to increase the speed of an existing train or to install spark-preventing devices on its engines. If the railway were not liable for fire damage, then, when making these decisions, it would not take into account as a cost the increase in damage resulting from the additional train or the faster train or the failure to install spark-preventing devices. This is the source of the di-

[43] Vaughan v. Taff Vale Railway Co., 3 H. and N. 743 (Ex. 1858) and 5 H. and N. 679 (Ex. 1860).

vergence between private and social net products. It results in the railway performing acts which will lower the value of total production—and which it would not do if it were liable for the damage. This can be shown by means of an arithmetical example.

Consider a railway, which is *not* liable for damage by fires caused by sparks from its engines, which runs two trains per day on a certain line. Suppose that running one train per day would enable the railway to perform services worth $150 per annum and running two trains a day would enable the railway to perform services worth $250 per annum. Suppose further that the cost of running one train is $50 per annum and two trains $100 per annum. Assuming perfect competition, the cost equals the fall in the value of production elsewhere due to the employment of additional factors of production by the railway. Clearly the railway would find it profitable to run two trains per day. But suppose that running one train per day would destroy by fire crops worth (on an average over the year) $60 and two trains a day would result in the destruction of crops worth $120. In these circumstances running one train per day would raise the value of total production but the running of a second train would reduce the value of total production. The second train would enable additional railway services worth $100 per annum to be performed. But the fall in the value of production elsewhere would be $110 per annum; $50 as a result of the employment of additional factors of production and $60 as a result of the destruction of crops. Since it would be better if the second train were not run and since it would not run if the railway were liable for damage caused to crops, the conclusion that the railway should be made liable for the damage seems irresistable. Undoubtedly it is this kind of reasoning which underlies the Pigovian position.

The conclusion that it would be better if the second train did not run is correct. The conclusion that it is desirable that the railway should be made liable for the damage it causes is wrong. Let us change our assumption concerning the rule of liability. Suppose that the railway is liable for damage from fires caused by sparks from the engine. A farmer on lands adjoining the railway is then in the position that, if his crop is destroyed by fires caused by the railway, he will receive the market price from the railway; but if his crop is not damaged, he will receive the market price by sale. It therefore becomes a matter of indifference to him whether his crop is damaged by fire or not. The position is very different when the railway is *not* liable. Any crop destruction through railway-caused fires would then reduce the receipts of the farmer. He would therefore take out of cultivation any land for which the damage is likely to be greater than the net return of the land (for reasons explained at length in Section III). A change from a regime in which the railway is *not* liable for damage to one in which it *is* liable is likely therefore to lead to an increase in the amount of cultivation on lands adjoining the railway. It will also, of course, lead to an increase in the amount of crop destruction due to railway-caused fires.

Let us return to our arithmetical example. Assume that, with the changed rule of liability, there is a doubling in the amount of crop destruction due to railway-caused fires. With one train per day, crops worth $120 would be destroyed each year and two trains per day would lead to the destruction of crops worth $240. We saw previously that it would not be profitable to run the second train if the railway had to pay $60 per annum as compensation for damage. With damage at $120 per annum the loss from running the second train would be $60 greater. But now let us consider the first train. The value of the transport services furnished by the first train is $150. The cost of running the train is $50. The amount that the railway would have to pay out as compensation for damage is $120. It follows that it would not be profitable to run any trains. With the figures in our example we reach the following result: if the railway is not liable for fire-damage, two trains per day would be run; if the railway is liable for fire-damage, it would cease operations altogether. Does this mean that it is better that there should be no railway? This question can be resolved by considering what would happen to the value of total production if it were decided to exempt the railway from liability for fire-damage, thus bringing it into operation (with two trains per day).

The operation of the railway would enable transport services worth $250 to be performed. It would also mean the employment of factors of production which would reduce the value of production elsewhere by $100. Furthermore it would mean the destruction of crops worth $120. The coming of the railway will also have led to the abandonment of cultivation of some land. Since we know that, had this land been cultivated, the value of the crops destroyed by fire would have been $120, and since it is unlikely that the total crop on this land would have been destroyed, it seems reasonable to suppose that the value of the crop yield on this land would have been higher than this. Assume it would have been $160. But the abandonment of cultivation would have released factors of production for employment elsewhere. All we know is that the amount by which the value of production elsewhere will increase will be less than $160. Suppose that it is $150. Then the gain from operating the railway would be $250 (the value of the transport services) minus $100 (the cost of the factors of production) minus $120 (the value of crops destroyed by fire) minus $160 (the fall in the value of crop production due to the abandonment of cultivation) plus $150 (the value of production elsewhere of the released factors of production). Overall, operating the railway will increase the value of total production by $20. With these figures it is clear that it is better that the railway should not be liable for the damage it causes, thus enabling it to operate profitably. Of course, by altering the figures, it could be shown that there are other cases in which it would be desirable that the railway should be liable for the damage it causes. It is enough for my purpose to show that, from an economic point of view, a situation in which there is "uncompensated damage done to surrounding woods by sparks from railway engines" is not necessarily undesirable. Whether it is desirable or not depends on the particular circumstances.

How is it that the Pigovian analysis seems to give the wrong answer? The reason is that Pigou does not seem to have noticed that his analysis is dealing with an entirely different question. The analysis as such is correct. But it is quite illegitimate for Pigou to draw the particular conclusion he does. The question at issue is not whether it is desirable to run an additional train or a faster train or to install smoke-preventing devices; the question at issue is whether it is desirable to have a system in which the railway has to compensate those who suffer damage from the fires which it causes or one in which the railway does not have to compensate them. When an economist is comparing alternative social arrangements, the proper procedure is to compare the total social product yielded by these different arrangements. The comparison of private and social products is neither here nor there. A simple example will demonstrate this. Imagine a town in which there are traffic lights. A motorist approaches an intersection and stops because the light is red. There are no cars approaching the intersection on the other street. If the motorist ignored the red signal, no accident would occur and the total product would increase because the motorist would arrive earlier at his destination. Why does he not do this? The reason is that if he ignored the light he would be fined. The private product from crossing the street is less than the social product. Should we conclude from this that the total product would be greater if there were no fines for failing to obey traffic signals? The Pigovian analysis shows us that it is possible to conceive of better worlds than the one in which we live. But the problem is to devise practical arrangements which will correct defects in one part of the system without causing more serious harm in other parts.

I have examined in considerable detail one example of a divergence between private and social products and I do not propose to make any further examination of Pigou's analytical system. But the main discussion of the problem considered in this article is to be found in that part of Chapter 9 in Part II which deals with Pigou's second class of divergence and it is of interest to see how Pigou develops his argument. Pigou's own description of this second class of divergence was quoted at the beginning of this section. Pigou distinguishes between the case in which a person renders services for which he receives no payment and the case in which a person renders disservices and compensation is not given to the injured parties. Our main attention has, of course, centred on this second case. It is therefore rather astonishing to find, as was pointed out to me by Professor Francesco Forte, that the problem of the smoking chimney—the "stock instance"[44] or "classroom example"[45] of the second case—is used by Pigou as an example of the first case (services rendered without payment) and is never mentioned, at any rate explicitly, in connection with the second case.[46] Pigou points out that factory owners who devote resources to preventing their chimneys from smoking render services for which they receive no payment. The implication, in the light of Pigou's discussion later in the chapter, is that a factory owner with a smokey chimney should be given a bounty to induce him to install smoke-preventing devices. Most modern economists would suggest that the owner of the factory with the smokey chimney should be taxed. It seems a pity that economists (apart from Professor Forte) do not seem to have noticed this feature of Pigou's treatment since a realisation that the problem could be tackled in either of these two ways would probably have led to an explicit recognition of its reciprocal nature.

In discussing the second case (disservices without compensation to those damaged), Pigou says that they are rendered "when the owner of a site in a residential quarter of a city builds a factory there and so destroys a great part of the amenities of neighbouring sites; or, in a less degree, when he uses his site in such a way as to spoil the lighting of the house opposite; or when he invests resources in erecting buildings in a crowded centre, which by contracting the air-space and the playing room of the neighbourhood, tend to injure the health and efficiency of the families living there."[47] Pigou is, of course, quite right to describe such actions as "uncharged disservices." But he is wrong when he describes these actions as "anti-social."[48] They may or may not be. It is necessary to weigh the harm against the good that will result. Nothing could be more "anti-social" than to oppose any action which causes any harm to anyone.

The example with which Pigou opens his discussion of "uncharged disservices" is not, as I have indicated, the case of the smokey chimney but the case of the overrunning rabbits: ". . . incidental uncharged disservices are rendered to third parties when the game-preserving activities of one occupier involve the overrunning of a neighbouring occupier's land by rabbits. . . ." This example is of extraordinary interest, not so much because the economic

[44] Sir Dennis Robertson, I Lectures on Economic Principles 162 (1957).

[45] E. J. Mishan, The Meaning of Efficiency in Economics, 189 The Bankers' Magazine 482 (June 1960).

[46] Pigou, op. cit. supra n. 35 at 184.

[47] *Id.* at 185–86.

[48] *Id.* at 186 n.1. For similar unqualified statements see Pigou's lecture "Some Aspects of the Housing Problem" in B. S. Rowntree and A. C. Pigou, Lectures on Housing, in 18 Manchester Univ. Lectures (1914).

analysis of the case is essentially any different from that of the other examples, but because of the peculiarities of the legal position and the light it throws on the part which economics can play in what is apparently the purely legal question of the delimitation of rights.

The problem of legal liability for the actions of rabbits is part of the general subject of liability for animals.[49] I will, although with reluctance, confine my discussion to rabbits. The early cases relating to rabbits concerned the relations between the lord of the manor and commoners, since, from the thirteenth century on, it became usual for the lord of the manor to stock the commons with conies (rabbits), both for the sake of the meat and the fur. But in 1597, in *Boulston*'s case, an action was brought by one landowner against a neighbouring landowner, alleging that the defendant had made coney-burrows and that the conies had increased and had destroyed the plaintiff's corn. The action failed for the reason that

> . . . so soon as the coneys come on his neighbor's land he may kill them, for they are ferae naturae, and he who makes the coney-boroughs has no property in them, and he shall not be punished for the damage which the coneys do in which he has no property, and which the other may lawfully kill.[50]

As *Boulston*'s case has been treated as binding—Bray, J., in 1919, said that he was not aware that *Boulston*'s case has ever been overruled or questioned[51]—Pigou's rabbit example undoubtedly represented the legal position at the time *The Economics of Welfare* was written.[52] And in this case, it is not far from the truth to say that the state of affairs which Pigou describes came about because of an absence of Government action (at any rate in the form of statutory enactments) and was the result of "natural" tendencies.

Nonetheless, *Boulston*'s case is something of a legal curiousity and Professor Williams makes no secret of his distaste for this decision:

[49] See G. L. Williams, Liability for Animals—An Account of the Development and Present Law of Tortious Liability for Animals, Distress Damage Feasant and the Duty to Fence, in Great Britain, Northern Ireland and the Common Law Dominions (1939). Part Four, "The Action of Nuisance, in Relation to Liability for Animals," 236–62, is especially relevant to our discussion. The problem of liability for rabbits is discussed in this part, 238–47. I do not know how far the common law in the United State regarding liability for animals has diverged from that in Britain. In some Western States of the United States, the English common law regarding the duty to fence has not been followed, in part because "the considerable amount of open, uncleared land made it a matter of public policy to allow cattle to run at large" (Williams, *op. cit. supra* 227). This affords a good example of how a different set of circumstances may make it economically desirable to change the legal rule regarding the delimitation of rights.

[50] 5 Coke (Vol. 3) 104 b. 77 Eng. Rep., 216, 217.

[51] See Stearn v. Prentice Bros. Ltd., (1919) 1 K.B., 395, 397.

[52] I have not looked into recent cases. The legal position has also been modified by statutory enactments.

The conception of liability in nuisance as being based upon ownership is the result, apparently, of a confusion with the action of cattle-trespass, and runs counter both to principle and to the medieval authorities on the escape of water, smoke and filth. . . . The prerequisite of any satisfactory treatment of the subject is the final abandonment of the pernicious doctrine in *Boulston*'s case. . . . Once *Boulston*'s case disappears, the way will be clear for a rational restatement of the whole subject, on lines that will harmonize with the principles prevailing in the rest of the law of nuisance.[53]

The judges in *Boulston*'s case were, of course, aware that their view of the matter depended on distinguishing this case from one involving nuisance:

This cause is not like to the cases put, on the other side, of erecting a lime-kiln, dye-house, or the like; for there the annoyance is by the act of the parties who make them; but it is not so here, for the conies of themselves went into the plaintiff's land, and he might take them when they came upon his land, and make profit of them.[54]

Professor Williams comments:

Once more the atavistic idea is emerging that the animals are guilty and not the landowner. It is not, of course, a satisfactory principle to introduce into a modern law of nuisance. If A. erects a house or plants a tree so that the rain runs or drips from it on to B.'s land, this is A.'s act for which he is liable; but if A. introduces rabbits into his land so that they escape from it into B.'s, this is the act of the rabbits for which A. is not liable—such is the specious distinction resulting from *Boulston*'s case.[55]

It has to be admitted that the decision in *Boulston*'s case seems a little odd. A man may be liable for damage caused by smoke or unpleasant smells, without it being necessary to determine whether he owns the smoke or the smell. And the rule in *Boulston*'s case has not always been followed in cases dealing with other animals. For example, in *Bland v. Yates*,[56] it was decided that an injunction could be granted to prevent someone from keeping an *unusual and excessive* collection of manure in which flies bred and which infested a neighbour's house. The question of who owned the flies was not raised. An economist would not wish to object because legal reasoning sometimes appears a little odd. But there is a sound economic reason for supporting Professor Williams' view that the problem of liability for animals (and particularly rabbits) should be brought within the ordinary law of nuisance. The reason is not that the man who harbours rabbits is solely responsible for the damage; the man whose crops are eaten is equally responsible. And given that the costs of market transactions make a rearrange-

[53] Williams, op. cit. supra n. 49 at 242, 258.

[54] Boulston v. Hardy, Cro. Eliz., 547, 548, 77 Eng. Rep. 216.

[55] Williams, op. cit. supra n. 49 at 243.

[56] 58 Sol.J. 612 (1913–1914).

ment of rights impossible, unless we know the particular circumstances, we cannot say whether it is desirable or not to make the man who harbours rabbits responsible for the damage committed by the rabbits on neighbouring properties. The objection to the rule in *Boulston*'s case is that, under it, the harbourer of rabbits can *never* be liable. It fixes the rule of liability at one pole: and this is as undesirable, from an economic point of view, as fixing the rule at the other pole and making the harbourer of rabbits always liable. But, as we saw in Section VII, the law of nuisance, as it is in fact handled by the courts, is flexible and allows for a comparison of the utility of an act with the harm it produces. As Professor Williams says: "The whole law of nuisance is an attempt to reconcile and compromise between conflicting interests. . . ."[57] To bring the problem of rabbits within the ordinary law of nuisance would not mean *inevitably* making the harbourer of rabbits liable for damage committed by the rabbits. This is not to say that the sole task of the courts in such cases is to make a comparison between the harm and the utility of an act. Nor is it to be expected that the courts will always decide correctly after making such a comparison. But unless the courts act very foolishly, the ordinary law of nuisance would seem likely to give economically more satisfactory results than adopting a rigid rule. Pigou's case of the overrunning rabbits affords an excellent example of how problems of law and economics are interrelated, even though the correct policy to follow would seem to be different from that envisioned by Pigou.

Pigou allows one exception to his conclusion that there is a divergence between private and social products in the rabbit example. He adds: ". . . unless . . . the two occupiers stand in the relation of landlord and tenant, so that compensation is given in an adjustment of the rent."[58] This qualification is rather surprising since Pigou's first class of divergence is largely concerned with the difficulties of drawing up satisfactory contracts between landlords and tenants. In fact, all the recent cases on the problem of rabbits cited by Professor Williams involved disputes between landlords and tenants concerning sporting rights.[59] Pigou seems to make a distinction between the case in which no contract is possible (the second class) and that in which the contract is unsatisfactory (the first class). Thus he says that the second class of divergences between private and social net product

> cannot, like divergences due to tenancy laws, be mitigated by a modification of the contractual relation between any two contracting parties, because the divergence arises out of a service or disservice rendered to persons other than the contracting parties.[60]

[57] Williams, op. cit. supra n. 49 at 259.

[58] Pigou, op. cit. supra n. 35 at 185.

[59] Williams, op. cit. supra n. 49 at 244–47.

[60] Pigou, op. cit. supra n. 35 at 192.

But the reason why some activities are not the subject of contracts is exactly the same as the reason why some contracts are commonly unsatisfactory—it would cost too much to put the matter right. Indeed, the two cases are really the same since the contracts are unsatisfactory because they do not cover certain activities. The exact bearing of the discussion of the first class of divergence on Pigou's main argument is difficult to discover. He shows that in some circumstances contractual relations between landlord and tenant may result in a divergence between private and social products.[61] But he also goes on to show that Government-enforced compensation schemes and rent-controls will also produce divergences.[62] Furthermore, he shows that, when the Government is in a similar position to a private landlord, e.g. when granting a franchise to a public utility, exactly the same difficulties arise as when private individuals are involved.[63] The discussion is interesting but I have been unable to discover what general conclusions about economic policy, if any, Pigou expects us to draw from it.

Indeed, Pigou's treatment of the problems considered in this article is extremely elusive and the discussion of his views raises almost insuperable difficulties of interpretation. Consequently it is impossible to be sure that one has understood what Pigou really meant. Nevertheless, it is difficult to resist the conclusion, extroardinary though this may be in an economist of Pigou's stature, that the main source of this obscurity is that Pigou had not thought his position through.

IX. The Pigovian Tradition

It is strange that a doctrine as faulty as that developed by Pigou should have been so influential, although part of its success has probably been due to the lack of clarity in the exposition. Not being clear, it was never clearly wrong. Curiously enough, this obscurity in the source has not prevented the emergence of a fairly well-defined oral tradition. What economists think they learn from Pigou, and what they tell their students, which I term the Pigovian tradition, is reasonably clear. I propose to show the inadequacy of this Pigovian tradition by demonstrating that both the analysis and the policy conclusions which it supports are incorrect.

I do not propose to justify my view as to the prevailing opinion by copious references to the literature. I do this partly because the treatment in the literature is usually so fragmentary, often involving little more than a reference to Pigou plus some explanatory comment, that detailed examination would be inappropriate. But the main reason for this lack of reference is that the doctrine, although based on Pigou, must have been largely the product of an oral tradition. Certainly economists with whom I have discussed these problems have shown a unanimity of opinion which is quite

[61] *Id.* 174–75. [62] *Id.* 177–83. [63] *Id.* 175–77.

remarkable considering the meagre treatment accorded this subject in the literature. No doubt there are some economists who do not share the usual view but they must represent a small minority of the profession.

The approach to the problems under discussion is through an examination of the value of physical production. The private product is the value of the additional product resulting from a particular activity of a business. The social product equals the private product minus the fall in the value of production elsewhere for which no compensation is paid by the business. Thus, if 10 units of a factor (and no other factors) are used by a business to make a certain product with a value of $105; and the owner of this factor is not compensated for their use, which he is unable to prevent; and these 10 units of the factor would yield products in their best alternative use worth $100; then, the social product is $105 minus $100 or $5. If the business now pays for one unit of the factor and its price equals the value of its marginal product, then the social product rises to $15. If two units are paid for, the social product rises to $25 and so on until it reaches $105 when all units of the factor are paid for. It is not difficult to see why economists have so readily accepted this rather odd procedure. The analysis focusses on the individual business decision and since the use of certain resources is not allowed for in costs, receipts are reduced by the same amount. But, of course, this means that the value of the social product has no social significance whatsoever. It seems to me preferable to use the opportunity cost concept and to approach these problems by comparing the value of the product yielded by factors in alternative uses or by alternative arrangements. The main advantage of a pricing system is that it leads to the employment of factors in places where the value of the product yielded is greatest and does so at less cost than alternative systems (I leave aside that a pricing system also eases the problem of the redistribution of income). But if through some God-given natural harmony factors flowed to the places where the value of the product yielded was greatest without any use of the pricing system and consequently there was no compensation, I would find it a source of surprise rather than a cause for dismay.

The definition of the social product is queer but this does not mean that the conclusions for policy drawn from the analysis are necessarily wrong. However, there are bound to be dangers in an approach which diverts attention from the basic issues and there can be little doubt that it has been responsible for some of the errors in current doctrine. The belief that it is desirable that the business which causes harmful effects should be forced to compensate those who suffer damage (which was exhaustively discussed in section VIII in connection with Pigou's railway sparks example) is undoubtedly the result of not comparing the total product obtainable with alternative social arrangements.

The same fault is to be found in proposals for solving the problem of harmful effects by the use of taxes or bounties. Pigou lays considerable stress on this solution although he is, as usual, lacking in detail and qualified in his support.[64] Modern economists tend to think exclusively in terms of taxes and in a very precise way. The tax should be equal to the damage done and should therefore vary with the amount of the harmful effect. As it is not proposed that the proceeds of the tax should be paid to those suffering the damage, this solution is not the same as that which would force a business to pay compensation to those damaged by its actions, although economists generally do not seem to have noticed this and tend to treat the two solutions as being identical.

Assume that a factory which emits smoke is set up in a district previously free from smoke pollution, causing damage valued at $100 per annum. Assume that the taxation solution is adopted and that the factory owner is taxed $100 per annum as long as the factory emits the smoke. Assume further that a smoke-preventing device costing $90 per annum to run is available. In these circumstances, the smoke-preventing device would be installed. Damage of $100 would have been avoided at an expenditure of $90 and the factory-owner would be better off by $10 per annum. Yet the position achieved may not be optimal. Suppose that those who suffer the damage could avoid it by moving to other locations or by taking various precautions which would cost them, or be equivalent to a loss in income of, $40 per annum. Then there would be a gain in the value of production of $50 if the factory continued to emit its smoke and those now in the district moved elsewhere or made other adjustments to avoid the damage. If the factory owner is to be made to pay a tax equal to the damage caused, it would clearly be desirable to institute a double tax system and to make residents of the district pay an amount equal to the additional cost incurred by the factory owner (or the consumers of his products) in order to avoid the damage. In these conditions, people would not stay in the district or would take other measures to prevent the damage from occurring, when the costs of doing so were less than the costs that would be incurred by the producer to reduce the damage (the producer's object, of course, being not so much to reduce the damage as to reduce the tax payments). A tax system which was confined to a tax on the producer for damage caused would tend to lead to unduly high costs being incurred for the prevention of damage. Of course this could be avoided if it were possible to base the tax, not on the damage caused, but on the fall in the value of production (in its widest sense) resulting from the emission of smoke. But to do so would require a detailed knowledge of individual preferences and I am unable to imagine how the data needed for such a taxation system could be assembled. Indeed,

[64] *Id.* 192–4, 381 and Public Finance 94–100 (3d ed. 1947).

the proposal to solve the smoke-pollution and similar problems by the use of taxes bristles with difficulties: the problem of calculation, the difference between average and marginal damage, the interrelations between the damage suffered on different properties, etc. But it is unnecessary to examine these problems here. It is enough for my purpose to show that, even if the tax is exactly adjusted to equal the damage that would be done to neighboring properties as a result of the emission of each additional puff of smoke, the tax would not necessarily bring about optimal conditions. An increase in the number of people living or of business operating in the vicinity of the smoke-emitting factory will increase the amount of harm produced by a given emission of smoke. The tax that would be imposed would therefore increase with an increase in the number of those in the vicinity. This will tend to lead to a decrease in the value of production of the factors employed by the factory, either because a reduction in production due to the tax will result in factors being used elsewhere in ways which are less valuable, or because factors will be diverted to produce means for reducing the amount of smoke emitted. But people deciding to establish themselves in the vicinity of the factory will not take into account this fall in the value of production which results from their presence. This failure to take into account costs imposed on others is comparable to the action of a factory-owner in not taking into account the harm resulting from his emission of smoke. Without the tax, there may be too much smoke and too few people in the vicinity of the factory; but with the tax there may be too little smoke and too many people in the vicinity of the factory. There is no reason to suppose that one of these results is necessarily preferable.

I need not devote much space to discussing the similar error involved in the suggestion that smoke producing factories should, by means of zoning regulations, be removed from the districts in which the smoke causes harmful effects. When the change in the location of the factory results in a reduction in production, this obviously needs to be taken into account and weighed against the harm which would result from the factory remaining in that location. The aim of such regulation should not be to eliminate smoke pollution but rather to secure the optimum amount of smoke pollution, this being the amount which will maximise the value of production.

X. A Change of Approach

It is my belief that the failure of economists to reach correct conclusions about the treatment of harmful effects cannot be ascribed simply to a few slips in analysis. It stems from basic defects in the current approach to problems of welfare economics. What is needed is a change of approach.

Analysis in terms of divergencies between private and social products concentrates attention on particular deficiencies in the system and tends to nourish the belief that any measure which will remove the deficiency is necessarily desirable. It diverts attention from those other changes in the system which are inevitably associated with the corrective measure, changes which may well produce more harm than the original deficiency. In the preceding sections of this article, we have seen many examples of this. But it is not necessary to approach the problem in this way. Economists who study problems of the firm habitually use an opportunity cost approach and compare the receipts obtained from a given combination of factors with alternative business arrangements. It would seem desirable to use a similar approach when dealing with questions of economic policy and to compare the total product yielded by alternative social arrangements. In this article, the analysis has been confined, as is usual in this part of economics, to comparisons of the value of production, as measured by the market. But it is, of course, desirable that the choice between different social arrangements for the solution of economic problems should be carried out in broader terms than this and that the total effect of these arrangements in all spheres of life should be taken into account. As Frank H. Knight has so often emphasized, problems of welfare economics must ultimately dissolve into a study of aesthetics and morals.

A second feature of the usual treatment of the problems discussed in this article is that the analysis proceeds in terms of a comparison between a state of laissez faire and some kind of ideal world. This approach inevitably leads to a looseness of thought since the nature of the alternatives being compared is never clear. In a state of laissez faire, is there a monetary, a legal or a political system and if so, what are they? In an ideal world, would there be a monetary, a legal or a political system and if so, what would they be? The answers to all these questions are shrouded in mystery and every man is free to draw whatever conclusions he likes. Actually very little analysis is required to show that an ideal world is better than a state of laissez faire, unless the definitions of a state of laissez faire and an ideal world happen to be the same. But the whole discussion is largely irrelevant for questions of economic policy since whatever we may have in mind as our ideal world, it is clear that we have not yet discovered how to get to it from where we are. A better approach would seem to be to start our analysis with a situation approximating that which actually exists, to examine the effects of a proposed policy change and to attempt to decide whether the new situation would be, in total, better or worse than the original one. In this way, conclusions for policy would have some relevance to the actual situation.

A final reason for the failure to develop a theory adequate to handle the problem of harmful effects stems from a faulty concept of a factor of production. This is usually thought of as a physical entity which the businessman acquires and uses (an acre of land, a ton of fertiliser) instead of as a right to perform certain (physical) actions. We may speak of a person owning land and using it as a factor of production but what the land-owner in fact possesses is the right to carry out a circumscribed list of actions. The rights of a land-owner are not unlimited. It is not even always possible for him to remove the land to another place, for instance, by quarrying it. And although it may be possible for him to exclude some people from using "his" land, this may not be true of others. For example, some people may have the right to cross the land. Furthermore, it may or may not be possible to erect certain types of buildings or to grow certain crops or to use particular drainage systems on the land. This does not come about simply because of Government regulation. It would be equally true under the common law. In fact it would be true under any system of law. A system in which the rights of individuals were unlimited would be one in which there were no rights to acquire.

If factors of production are thought of as rights, it becomes easier to understand that the right to do something which has a harmful effect (such as the creation of smoke, noise, smells, etc.) is also a factor of production. Just as we may use a piece of land in such a way as to prevent someone else from crossing it, or parking his car, or building his house upon it, so we may use it in such a way as to deny him a view or quiet or unpolluted air. The cost of exercising a right (of using a factor of production) is always the loss which is suffered elsewhere in consequence of the exercise of that right—the inability to cross land, to park a car, to build a house, to enjoy a view, to have peace and quiet or to breathe clean air.

It would clearly be desirable if the only actions performed were those in which what was gained was worth more than what was lost. But in choosing between social arrangements within the context of which individual decisions are made, we have to bear in mind that a change in the existing system which will lead to an improvement in some decisions may well lead to a worsening of others. Furthermore we have to take into account the costs involved in operating the various social arrangements (whether it be the working of a market or of a government department), as well as the costs involved in moving to a new system. In devising and choosing between social arrangements we should have regard for the total effect. This, above all, is the change in approach which I am advocating.

[2]

An Overview of Methodological Approaches in the Analysis of Trade and Environment

Cees VAN BEERS* and Jeroen C.J.M. VAN DEN BERGH**

I. Introduction

Environmental problems have long been considered as occurring on a restricted spatial scale. Consequently, economic research has long been concentrated on local dimensions of pollution and resource use. In the 1960s, this resulted in a focus on the local air and water pollution. During the next decade, awareness of the importance of environmental problems increased and gave rise to the development of tools for environmental policy analysis. In the 1980s, a widespread concern for global issues and long-term environmental phenomena emerged, leading to the concept of sustainable development (WCED, 1987). Somewhat neglected in this pattern has been specific attention to repercussions of environmental policy on foreign trade flows, both from a theoretical and from an empirical point of view. Environmental economics seems to have mainly been concerned with policy analysis of closed economies (see Baumol and Oates, 1988). This is somewhat curious because of the openness of most economies. There have been some efforts since the beginning of the 1970s to investigate the link between international trade, environmental quality and pollution. Early contributions are Baumol (1971), GATT (1971), Siebert (1973, 1974), Markusen (1975) and Walter (1975, 1976). Recently, attention to trade and environment has increased significantly (see, amongst others Anderson and Blackhurst, 1992; Low, 1992; Ekins *et al.*, 1994; van Ierland, 1994; Carraro, 1994). This has led to the analysis of a number of specific issues which can be classified into:

— environmental determinants of trade;
— environmental effects of trade;
— effects of environmental policy on trade; and
— substitution or complementarity of trade and environmental policy measures.

The links between foreign trade and environmental quality can be analysed by means of formal methods based on specific theories. Environmental economists have mainly been concerned with environmental policy issues in closed economies, while trade economists have focused on imperfections other than environmental

* Department of Economics, Faculty of Law, Leiden University, Leiden, The Netherlands.
** Department of Spatial Economics, Faculty of Economics, Free University, Amsterdam, The Netherlands.

externalities, such as variations in market structures and economies-of-scale. Ultimately, some mix of externality and trade theories is unavoidable to answer the relevant fundamental and policy questions. Specific model analyses may, therefore, originate from foreign trade theory, growth theories, or externality theory.

One can distinguish between theories of foreign trade according to whether they are based on the notion of a general or a partial equilibrium. Trade theories of a general equilibrium nature (Ricardo, Heckscher-Ohlin) are implicitly based on a set of underlying micro-relations. The emphasis in such theories is on the determinants of foreign trade and their impact on the domestic income distribution and production structure. These theories will be discussed in the next section. Comparative static analysis in a partial equilibrium setting based on the assumption of perfect competition, is presented in Section III. Such an approach considers the factors that determine foreign trade from the perspective of isolated markets, and provides a clear view on how certain environmental policy interventions or environmental factors influence foreign trade directly. Section IV extends the discussion to imperfect competition, and discusses the implications of modern trade theory in terms of the relationship between trade and environmental policy. The main disadvantage of partial equilibrium models as in Sections III and IV is that they offer no insights about interactions between markets or distributional effects. Section V focuses on general equilibrium models which do explicitly include such effects, based on the perspective of multiple interactive markets. The difference with the general equilibrium type of approaches in Section II is that here the attention is focused on modelling economy-wide effects based on micro-economic relationships. Foreign trade in these models is therefore explicitly linked to the behaviour of individual agents in the economy, and likewise to environmental externalities in production and utility functions. Finally, Section VI contains some notes on empirical testing of theoretical results and Section VII provides concluding remarks.

II. General Trade Theories and Environmental Externalities: Comparative Advantage and Production Factors

A logical first step in understanding the mechanisms which describe the mutual influences between environmental quality and foreign trade is to extend traditional trade theories with environmental elements. International trade theories can be divided into two types: those emphasizing the importance of demand factors; and those focusing on supply factors. An example of the former are the analyses presented by Linder (1961). Two well-known supply-oriented theories are formalized in the Ricardian and the Heckscher-Ohlin models. The interface between foreign trade and environmental quality seems to be predominantly regarded as a matter of supply factors, as reflected by the current focus of general and environmental economic research. Therefore, the demand-oriented theories will not be discussed here. The trade theory of Ricardo implicitly uses differences in labour productivity as the cause of comparative advantage. The main contribution of Ricardo has been the revelation of the notion of comparative cost advantage *versus* absolute cost advantage. Other determinants of comparative advantage are not dealt with by this theory. Consideration of the interaction between foreign trade and environmental quality can focus on environmental quality and policy as determinants of foreign trade. This justifies a closer look at the Heckscher-Ohlin (H-O) model.

The factor-endowment theory of Heckscher and Ohlin focuses primarily on capital and labour endowments as the main causes of differences in comparative advantage, and therefore of the emergence of foreign trade. Attention to the domestic effects of the trade flows are revealed by the equalization of production factor prices among countries, like wages and capital rents.[1] The theory assumes the existence of perfectly competitive markets which implies an efficient allocation of economic resources. The main result of the H-O model is stated as:

> *A country has a comparative advantage in producing and exporting the commodity in the production of which, compared with other countries, relatively much is used of the relatively abundant production factor at home.*

The H-O result is based on the following assumptions:

(i) there are two countries producing n commodities with an endowment of m production factors that is different between the two countries;
(ii) there are no technological differences between countries, i.e. for a given commodity the production function is the same in all countries; furthermore, commodities are produced under constant returns to scale;
(iii) the supply of the production factors is completely inelastic, i.e. independent of the rewards of the production factors;
(iv) mobility of production factors is perfect among domestic industries but impossible internationally;
(v) there are no externalities in production, i.e. the output of the production process of the commodities are only determined by the quantity of the production factors;
(vi) the preferences of the consumers are the same and homothetic in all countries.

The central question now is how environmental elements can be included in this theory. There are two options:

(a) inclusion of environmental elements in the model with standard assumptions as mentioned above; or,
(b) relaxing the standard assumptions that are related to a treatment of the environment as a supply factor in international trade.

[1] Domestic effects are expressed more extensively in the Stolpher-Samuelson theorem (influence on factor prices) and the Rybczynski theorem (influence on quantities exported): see Falvey, 1994.

(a) *Standard Model with Environment*

With respect to the first option, introduction of environmental elements in the model is only possible along assumption (i). Siebert (1987, pp. 155–156) incorporates environmental elements in the H-O model by interpreting environmental scarcity—the availability of environmental assimilative capacities—as a factor of production that influences the comparative advantage of a country. A country that is rich in environmental resources will thus be expected to export pollution-intensive commodities. Two countries are distinguished: a home country and a foreign country. Assume the home country is richly endowed with environmental services. If z (z^*) represents the shadow price of environmental services in the home (foreign) country then the relative abundance of environmental services in the home country implies $z < z^*$. The use of environmental services, e.g. the possibility to pollute, bears therefore low cost as compared to the foreign country. As a result the environmentally sensitive (home) country will produce and export the relatively pollution-intensive commodity, while the other (foreign) country will produce and export the commodity that is relatively less pollution-intensive.

Suppose the home country government implements environmental policy by means of an emission tax t such that $z + t > z^*$. Such a measure would imply the reversal of comparative advantage, i.e. the home country will shift to exporting the relatively less pollution-intensive commodity.[2] The environmental quality of the home country improves, while that in the foreign nation deteriorates. In other words, environmental policy in the home country affects environmental quality abroad negatively through specialization and trade flows. Consequently, one may refer to this as "pollute-thy-neighbour" policy in the home country. It is possible that the foreign country adopts its own tax measures (subsidy) that stimulate production in commodities that are relatively less pollution-intensive. Such a retaliation is not desired as it will lead to erosion of the gains of trade. Foreign trade is assumed to generate welfare increases, since—according to the law of comparative advantage—every country produces and exports the commodities it can produce more efficiently than other countries. Incorporation of environmental elements will change the gains of trade a country achieves. Deterioration of environmental quality as a result of relatively pollution-intensive exports reduces the net gains from trade, which are defined as the sum of the direct welfare gain and the indirect welfare losses as a result of environmental degradation. An example of this are the gains of exporting timber. These are reduced as the endowment of forests decreases. This effect is stronger when the loss of forest area goes along with a decline of environmental quality and lower exports of timber in the future.

[2] This will go along with a re-location of the production of the pollution-intensive good to the foreign country, while total world production of the good may decrease because of decreased world demand as a result of increasing prices as compared with other (clean) commodities. A shift from dirty to clean final goods will be the result.

(b) *Changing Assumptions of the Standard Model*

The second possibility of incorporating environmental elements in the factor endowment model is changing the assumptions of the model. The assumptions (ii), (iv) and (v) are most essential here, whereas assumptions (i), (iii) and (vi) are necessary to retain the supply orientation. The relaxing of the latter three assumptions will require a more disaggregate approach, as in the general equilibrium models of Section V.

The second assumption can be relaxed by assuming the existence of technological differences. Trade models have been developed to explain trade patterns out of technology differences (see, e.g. Posner's technology gap model, 1961). Technology differences have their own influence on the pattern of trade even when factor-endowments would not be different. Falvey (1994) distinguishes two types of technology differences:

(1) Product-augmenting, i.e. one country can produce more output with the same factor inputs in a particular sector than another country.
(2) Factor-augmenting, i.e. one factor of production is more productive than the same factor in the other nation, independent of the sector in which the factor is employed.

It is especially this second type of technology difference between countries that offers an opportunity to introduce environmental aspects in the model, namely that based on the inclusion of environmental goods or services as a production factor in the H-O model. Suppose a country is relatively less well endowed with capital in comparison to another country. In the traditional H-O model, the country would have a comparative advantage in exports of labour-intensive commodities. However, if technology differences allow for, for example, a higher productivity of capital, it is possible that the country obtains a comparative advantage in the exports of relatively capital-intensive goods. Then the quantities of labour and capital will be measured in effective units, i.e. their productivity is taken into account. The central question is whether it is possible to combine this kind of technology difference with environment as a production factor. Now, the environment as a factor can be more productive in one country compared to another, since it is possible that technological differences are such that in one country the use of one "unit of environment" generates more output than another. There will then be a shift in the environmentally more productive country towards pollution-intensive products.

This result is very straightforward, however, a static model leaves unnoticed the fact that technological progress is a dynamic process. In the H-O model it is possible to analyse differences between technologies at a certain moment. If technological changes of the environment as a production factor are expressed in effective units, it is possible to analyse, by way of comparative statics, changes in this model as a change of the effective units.

According to assumption (iv), all factors of production have, internationally, a supply elasticity of zero—i.e. they are fixed, and internationally immobile. However, factors like capital and labour are mobile in the real world. It is important to note that environmental services, just like natural resources, are immobile. In a "Heckscher-Ohlin world", with one immobile factor inter-country equalization of the factor price of the immobile factor will result when either one of the other production factors is mobile, or when exchange of commodities occurs (see also Deardorff, 1984). However, this result is only valid when the mobility of the other production factors is independent of the endowment of the immobile factor. It is conceivable that the mobility of labour depends on the presence of environmental services. Indeed, labour will not only migrate to areas with higher wage rates but also where better environmental conditions prevail. This means that when the home country exports the pollution-intensive commodity, wages may need to rise substantially to compensate for the resulting lower level of environmental quality. The factor labour becomes more expensive and the wage level can be interpreted as a proxy for the price of environmental quality (i.e. it is a hedonic price). The question is, therefore, what wage should be paid to attract labour into "dirty" areas. Extension of the H-O model to incorporate the relationship between the mobile factor(s) and the immobile factor is not an easy task. It is necessary then to work out the underlying micro-relations more explicitly, possibly by means of general equilibrium models.

About assumption (v) we can be short. As environmental damage is an externality caused by the production of pollution-intensive commodities it is not incorporated in the standard H-O model. An extension by Siebert (1987) focuses on the incorporation of environmental quality as a separate factor of production. A larger availability of environmental assimilative services relative to other production factors will lead to the export of pollution-intensive goods.

Environment externalities can also be modelled via a production factor variable. However, not as an independent one. This would proceed through a negative influence on the "conventional" production factors, labour and capital. The productivity of labour and capital is dependent on the environmental production factor. Extension of the H-O model with an environmental externality therefore implies the incorporation of the dependence of the productivity of capital and labour on environmental quality which is used up by these production factors. Modelling these elements will give rise to all kinds of counteracting forces, which requires a more explicit treatment of the microeconomic relations underlying the H-O model structure. Also for this purpose, a general equilibrium treatment of the open economy seems to be more adequate.

III. Partial Equilibrium Models of International Trade and Environment: Externality Theories and Policies

The absence of externalities in trade theories presented in the previous Section is a drawback for analysing the relationship between trade and environment. Two alternative approaches are available to deal with environment in terms of externalities, namely the general equilibrium type of economic model (Section V) and partial equilibrium models in this and the next Section, in both cases using the method of comparative static analysis.

An important division of partial equilibrium trade models is based on the assumption regarding the market structure of the commodity considered, namely perfect or imperfect competition. The first category is part of standard welfare economics while the second one is often referred to as "modern trade theory". The models of both categories are of a partial equilibrium nature as they analyse only situations of a single, isolated market without taking into account interactions with other markets. This certainly restricts the relevance of the results, although the main advantage is that very clear conclusions can be derived about—supposedly—essential relationships between international trade and environmental externalities. It seems, thus, useful to consider the consequences of environmental policies on trade and trade policies on environment in a static, partial equilibrium context.

Anderson (1992) performs a partial comparative-static analysis to investigate how the social welfare and environment of a country are influenced by:

— opening up to or liberalizing its trade; and

— the implementation of appropriate environmental policies when opening up to or liberalizing trade.

Two types of externality may be distinguished, namely a production externality, i.e. in the country of production, and a consumption externality, i.e. in the country of consumption. In addition, a distinction is made between small-country and large-country cases, i.e. whether world prices are exogenous or can be influenced.

Only the cases of production externalities in small and large countries are considered below, since the analysis presented can easily be extended to many consumption externalities. This is graphically illustrated in Figures 1 and 2, where only a shift in supply S to S' is considered, and not in demand D.[3]

(a) *Small-Country Case*

Assuming the absence of environmental policy, opening up trade in a good whose production is pollutive will increase social welfare and improve the environment if the good is imported. If the good is exported, however, environmental quality decreases so that also a negative welfare effect results, in addition to the positive effect caused by a larger producer surplus. Therefore the direction of change in social welfare, which is equal to the sum of private welfare and the social or external benefits resulting from less pollution, is ambiguous.

[3] Besides these assumptions the regular assumptions necessary for a comparative-static analysis are also adopted, i.e. no changes in tastes and technology change, and no international factor mobility.

FIGURE 1: AN ENVIRONMENTAL EXTERNALITY AND AN IMPORTED COMMODITY IN A SMALL OPEN COUNTRY

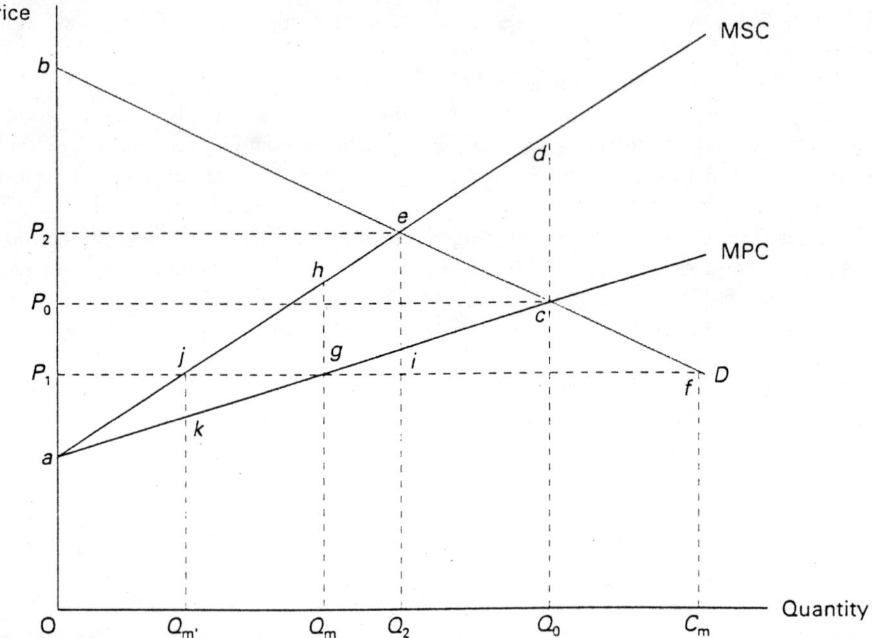

Increasing imports of a good whose production is pollutive will replace domestic production and therefore reduce environmental damage. In the case of exports, the increase in producer surplus is due to an international relative price that is higher than the domestic relative price. This works out positively on social welfare, but the increased domestic production reduces environmental quality and therefore decreases social welfare. The strongest of these two offsetting forces will determine whether social welfare will increase or decrease. In the case of exports, liberalizing trade will have ambiguous results on social welfare. If a socially optimal environmental policy were implemented (production tax), the result would be an increase of imports. Domestic production becomes more expensive and will decrease. So, pollution will decrease too, and environmental quality and social welfare will increase. If the good is exported, introduction of a production tax reduces producer surplus and improves environmental quality. The effect on social welfare is ambiguous again.

How can we find these conclusions in Figures 1 and 2? In Figure 1 the situation is shown for a commodity that is imported. The demand curve is D and the marginal cost curves are MPC (marginal private costs of production) and MSC (marginal social costs of production), where the latter is obtained by adding private production costs and external costs. The partial prices are relative to all other prices in the economy.

FIGURE 2: AN ENVIRONMENTAL EXTERNALITY AND AN EXPORTED COMMODITY IN A SMALL OPEN COUNTRY

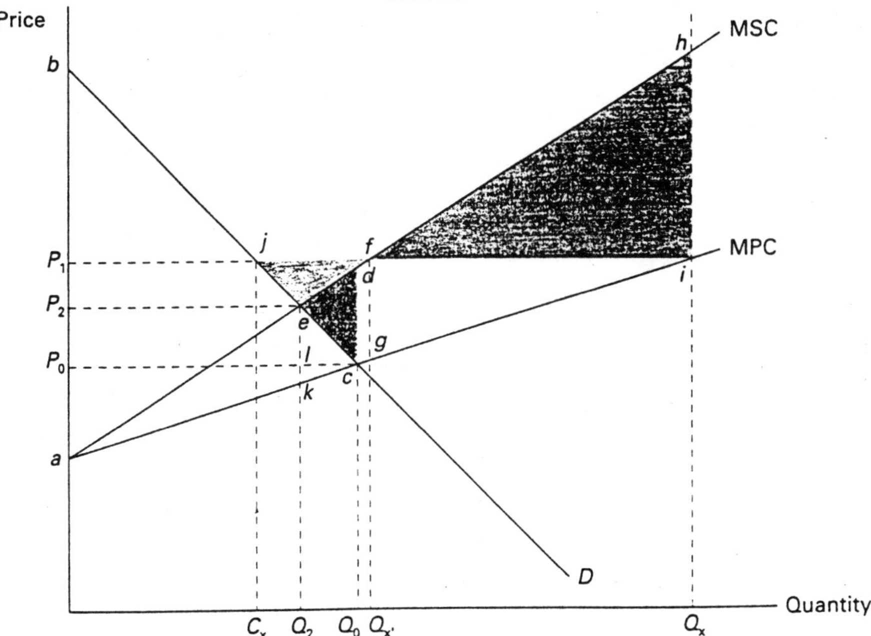

In the situation of autarky and no environmental policies Q_0 is produced and consumed at a relative price of P_0. If there is no externality, net social welfare is *abc* (= sum of producer and consumer surplus). In the case of pollution, net social welfare is lower, namely *abc* – *acd*, where *acd* is the external cost. Suppose that the relative price at which foreign countries offer the good is $P_1 < P_0$. Then imports are Q_mC_m. In that case net social welfare is *abfg* – *ahg*. The gain in social welfare (with respect to the autarky situation with no environmental policies) consists of *ghcd* (less pollution) and *cfg* (more consumer surplus).

Considering the autarky situation again, suppose that an environmental policy in the form of a production tax equal to "*ie*" per unit output is introduced. Welfare increases with *cdei* –/– *cei* = *dec*. The gain is *cdei*, resulting from lower pollution; *cei* = loss of producer and consumer surplus because of the increased marginal costs and therefore higher price to be paid by the consumers.[4] What happens when the country imports the commodity and a production tax is introduced? Then *jk* must be the tax. Compared with the situation of imports without a tax, welfare will increase as pollution will decline (*ghjk*). Imports increase from Q_mC_m to Q'_mC_m.

[4] The revenues of the production tax are collected by the government. As we are only interested in the effects on trade and environment of an environmental tax, we assume that the government re-distributes the tax revenues to producers and consumers.

Compared with the autarky situation with the tax, the net welfare gains is *eikj*. Therefore, opening up the import of a commodity that is produced in a pollutive way will increase net national social welfare.

Let us look at the situation of an exportable commodity in Figure 2. In case of autarky without pollution and a pollution tax, OQ_0 and OP_0 are the relevant quantities, and relative price of the good, respectively. Just like in the case of the importable good, net social welfare (in the absence of externality) equals *abc*. If there is pollution but no pollution tax, net welfare decreases and is: (area *abc* – area *acd*). Suppose the commodity can be exported because at the world market $P_1 > P_0$; exports are equal to C_xQ_s. Compared with the autarky situation with pollution but no tax, production has increased to Q_s and net social welfare is equal to (*abjf* – *fhi*). Therefore it cannot be stated generally whether net social welfare will increase or decrease. This depends on whether area *efj* is larger than, smaller than, or equal to area *dcih*. The increase of producer surplus (P_0P_1ic) results from a higher relative export price and the extra pollution cost (*dhic*) is caused by the increase in production for foreign markets.

A pollution tax of *fg* will decrease exports to $C_xQ'_x$. Net social welfare is then *abjf*. Compared with the situation of exports without environmental policy the increase in net social welfare is *fhi*. This consists of less pollution (*fhig*) minus loss of producer surplus (*fig*). Subsequently net social welfare increases. Therefore, compared with the autarky situation with environmental policy, net social welfare will increase with *jfe*. In other words, with international externalities opening up, the closed economy will improve net welfare. Now the effect of exporting the commodity whose production is pollutive gives rise again to ambiguous conclusions regarding welfare increase or decrease. Therefore, in spite of increased pollution as a result of export, it is still possible that net social welfare increases compared with the situation of autarky. The ultimate outcome depends, amongst others, on the steepness of the demand and supply curves. It is not possible to say anything in general about it.

In Table 1, four situations are shown which are being investigated in the above partial analysis. Now, in the context of trade and environment especially three comparisons between two situations are relevant. In the case of a shift from A to C, one is concerned with the welfare effect of opening up an autarkic economy with externalities. A change from B to D is similar, but in the presence of environmental policy. Finally, a shift from C to D means a focus on the welfare effect of environmental policy in an open economy. For each effect one can ask two questions:

TABLE 1: RELEVANT SITUATIONS IN COMPARATIVE-STATIC ANALYSIS OF TRADE AND ENVIRONMENT

	Environmental externalities and no policy	Environmental externalities and policy
Autarky	A	B
Open economy	C	D

TABLE 2: NET WELFARE DECOMPOSITION FOR THE FOUR SITUATIONS OF TABLE 1—THE EXPORT CASE

	1. Net Welfare = 4–5	2. Producer Surplus	3. Consumer Surplus	4. Total Surplus = 2+3	5. External Cost
A	$abe - edc$	ap_0c	bp_0c	abc	adc
B	abe	$ap_0c - klc + p_0p_1el$ $= ap_1ek$	p_1be	$abc - kec = abek$	$adc - edck = aek$
C	$abjf - fhi$	ap_1i	p_1bj	$abji$	ahi
D	$abjf$	$ap_1i - fig = ap_1fg$	p_1bj	$abji - fig = abjfg$	$ahi - fhig = afg$

Note: Combinations of letters *a* to *k* denote areas in Figure 2.

(i) may one determine the price range for which no sign switch in the effect occurs? and

(ii) can one establish whether an effect is unambiguous in terms of its sign?

The latter is summarized in Table 2. By combining the prices in Figures 1 and 2 with the signs in the Tables one can answer the first question for specific cases.

Table 2 summarizes the welfare effects for different situations. It shows that the shifts go along with the following total welfare effects: for A to B the area *edc*; for A to C the area *jfe* + *edc* – *fhi*; for B to D the area *jfe*; for C to D the area *fhi*; and for A to D the area *jfe* + *edc*. The results can easily be checked with Figure 2.

Finally, note that in Figure 2 a price equivalent to point *c*—i.e. the unregulated market equilibrium—represents the dividing line between import and export in the case of no environmental policy, while point *e*—i.e. the regulated market equilibrium—represents this for the case with environmental policy (given externalities MSC–MPC).

(b) *Large-Country Case*

What happens with the change of social welfare in the case of a large instead of a small country? Then two additional effects result. First, as a large country is able to influence world market prices, both its export supply and import demand curve will not be horizontal as in the small-country situation. Secondly, when a large country starts to import a pollutive commodity instead of producing it domestically, it will increase production abroad because of trade creation.

Some analyses also include international pollutive spill-overs which cause negative welfare effects. It is doubtful whether these spill-overs are a relevant factor. The same effects—but then the other way around—are valid when a large country exports a pollutive commodity and introduces a production tax at home.

The results of analyses of large-country cases can be summarized as follows (see Anderson, 1992):

— When a large country enters international trade by opening up the import of a pollutive commodity—rather than producing it domestically—then the gain in social welfare will be unambiguous but smaller than can be achieved in a small country. The main reason is that the import price will be higher, which decreases consumer surplus compared to the small-country case. This is the terms-of-trade effect.

— When a large country enters international trade by opening up the export of a pollutive commodity the gain in social welfare will be ambiguous as it depends on two opposite welfare effects;

— (i) a negative welfare impact resulting from a larger supply at the world market, depressing the export price and causing a loss of producer surplus, and an increased domestic production which stimulates domestic pollution; and

— (ii) less transfrontier pollution resulting from less foreign production may increase domestic welfare.

One of the rare studies dealing with large-country cases is Krutilla (1991). Krutilla considers the case of a large open country in which environmental policy can influence the economy's terms-of-trade.[5] In such a case, a comparison between regulatory impacts and comparative advantage is insufficient. Also offsetting terms-of-trade effects have to be included in a comparison. Optimal taxes will differ from the standard Pigouvian ones as a result of the terms-of-trade effect. This works in opposite directions for consumption and production taxes. The optimal consumption (production) tax is lower (higher) than the standard Pigouvian tax in the case of a net exporting (importing) country, in order to have the optimal trade-off between the second-order effects related to trade losses (gains) and the environmental benefits (costs) of lower consumption (higher production). An interesting idea mentioned by Krutilla is that the optimal environmental policy depends on the tariff parameter, so that one can vary this in order to find a zero environmental tax, i.e. trade policy is used as environmental policy. The resulting optimal tariff, a mix of the standard Pigouvian tax and standard optimal tariff, is, like other first-best optimal combinations, not generally attainable. The reason is that both instruments are generally chosen so as to maximize separate objectives, rather than maximizing social welfare of an open economy.

IV. Imperfect Competition in Domestic Markets: Modern Trade Theory

The analyses discussed in Sections II and III were based on perfectly operating domestic markets. The assumption of perfect competition seems restrictive for many product markets where the use of market power is present. A second category of partial equilibrium analysis—known as "modern trade theory"—is based on imperfect competitive markets. Since the beginning of the 1980s increasing attention

[5] According to Krutilla (1991) the assumption of a large country is similar to imperfect competition in international markets, since prices can be influenced. It should be clear that this is imperfect competition at the world market level and that no specific assumptions are made for competition in the domestic markets. This is explicitly done in the field of "modern trade theory", discussed in the next part of this Section.

has been given to imperfect competition in explaining foreign trade flows. There are many assumptions possible, often with (slightly) different implications. The most influential model of imperfect competition has been developed by Dixit and Stiglitz (1977). Helpman and Krugman (1985) and others have extended this work in different directions (see also Smith, 1994).

The major consequences of the introduction of environmental policy in open country models with imperfect competition are briefly indicated here. As in the case of the perfect competition models, we can distinguish between a commodity that can be imported or exported. We assume that the commodity is domestically produced by a firm with monopoly power. It is further assumed that there is perfect competition at the world market, so that the firm is a price-taker internationally.[6] Now, when the world market price is below the autarky price level (resulting under perfect competition in the domestic market), the commodity will be imported. In that case, in the absence of trade barriers against the commodity, the monopolist will lose its market power. Then the case of the monopolist will be analogous to that of perfect competition discussed in the previous Section.

The more interesting case is, therefore, to assume that the price at the world market (P_1) is higher than the autarky price in case of perfect competition P_{pf}. Then the monopolist will be an exporter in the competitive world market. Figure 3 shows the latter situation. The world market price here is assumed to be lower than the monopolist's price (P_0) under autarky. This shows that, even in this case, exports may result when the monopolist is a profit maximizer, namely up to the point where the marginal revenue (equal to world price P_1) equals the marginal costs (MPC or MSC). Furthermore, in the open economy the monopolist will then supply Q_{dom} at the domestic market (against price P_{dom}), where the marginal revenue in the domestic market (given by the MR curve) is equal to the marginal revenue abroad (namely P_1). It is profitable for the monopolist to export then $Q_3 - Q_{dom}$, with Q_3 being the total production. The firm maintains monopoly power in the domestic market in spite of a lower world market price, because it is still the only supplier.[7] Note that P_{dom} is higher than the autarky monopoly price P_0.

The external effects for the export case in the absence of environmental policy can be split up in *abc*—externalities via pollution caused by production for the domestic market—and *bdec*—externalities via pollution caused by producing for the world market.

Introducing an environmental tax in the autarkic situation would increase the domestic price from P_0 to P_1. The monopolist will reduce its supply in that case from Q_0 to Q_1. In the case of an open economy, the introduction of an environmental tax results in an unchanged domestic price P_{dom}, given that the intersection of MSC and

[6] See Dixit and Stiglitz (1977) for the case of imperfect competition internationally.

[7] Here it is assumed of course that the lower world market price does not give the domestic consumers the opportunity to import the commodity because of trade barriers that make the firm able to maintain its monopoly power.

FIGURE 3: IMPERFECT COMPETITION IN THE DOMESTIC MARKET OF A COMMODITY WHICH IS EXPORTED AND GENERATES ENVIRONMENTAL EXTERNALITIES

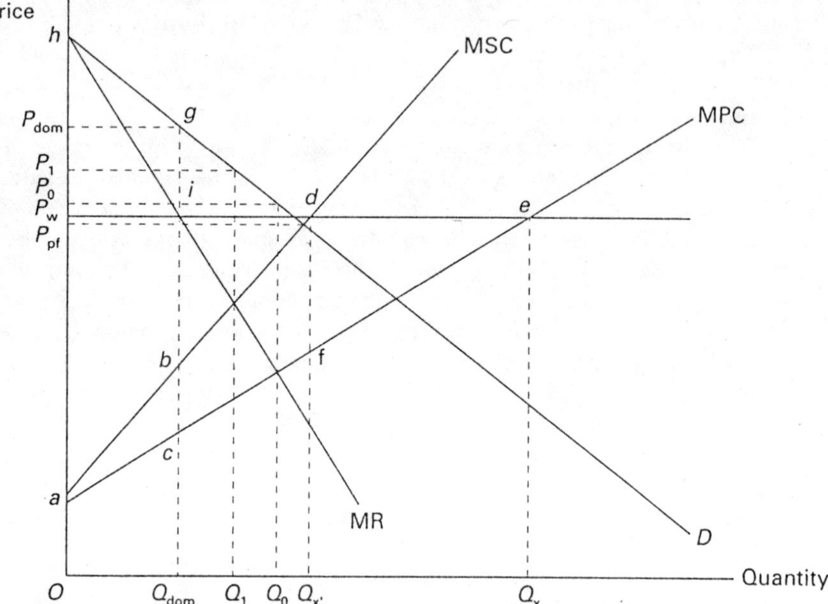

P_1 is not to the left of point i.[8] The monopolist will first cut on production for the export market, since marginal revenue in the domestic market is higher than in the export market. Exports will decrease to (Q'_x − Q_{dom}). Consequently, pollution will be reduced with *dgf*. Domestic consumer surplus hgP_{dom} remains unchanged. Only producer surplus will decrease by the area *ade*.

The example presented here has been kept tractable by assuming that the imperfect competition is of the monopoly type. Other kinds of imperfections, such as oligopolistic ones, can also be analysed, which would give rise to game theoretical models (see, for example, Dixit, 1984; and Eaton and Grossman, 1986). For both firms and governments, elements of strategic behaviour can be analysed. Examples of such analyses in the context of environmental policy and externalities are Ulph (1991 and 1992), Verdier (1993), Kennedy (1994a and b) and Conrad (1993 and 1994). Ulph concludes, in a model of strategic international trade, that there is a preference for pollution standards rather than pollution taxes as environmental policy instruments. Kennedy and Conrad show that imperfect competition in global markets is a reason for the strategic behaviour of governments in deciding about

[8] In the case where the intersection of MSC and P_w is to the left of i exports will disappear, the domestic supply is decreased, and the domestic price P_{dom} increases. In other words, only for very high externalities will the domestic market be affected by the introduction of (optimal) environmental policy measures.

domestic environmental regulation. This can lead to distortion of pollution taxes. Objectives in strategies may be focused on gaining competitive advantage or shifting pollution, and an equilibrium results from the trade-off between these. When transboundary pollution is included in a multicountry setting, this may change the outcome. For instance, with perfect transboundary pollution there is no shifting pollution effect.

V. General Equilibrium Analysis: Externalities, Environmental Factors, Multiple Sectors and Instruments

As already stated, foreign trade theories, such as discussed in the previous sections, do not take into account economy-wide effects based on explicit microeconomic relationships. In this Section, general equilibrium (GE) models that reflect the economy-wide perspective are discussed. They include models focusing on international trade, on environmental externalities or policies, or mixed types. First, a short introduction is given on the methodology. Subsequently, environmental policy models, trade models and combinations of these are discussed.

(a) *Theoretical and Applied General Equilibrium Models*

The standard GE framework is based on the interaction between various behavioural models, given that market clearing conditions are satisfied. Consumers are supposed to choose a consumption bundle in order to maximize welfare given income and prices. Producers are supposed to choose a cost-minimizing input mix and a profit-maximizing output, given input and output prices. In a competitive equilibrium without externalities, markets will be cleared for all factors and commodities, while every actor can achieve his objectives. If convexity conditions are satisfied, uniqueness of the equilibrium is guaranteed. Stability of an equilibrium means that no actor has an incentive to divert from the equilibrium (see, for example, Arrow and Hahn, 1971).

The potential advantages of the GE approach to trade and environment can be summarized by a number of effects of trade and environmental policies that can be analysed with it:

— resource allocation;
— distributional consequences in terms of households, income groups or sectors;
— welfare, income and employment effects;
— prices of commodities, wages, and capital rents;
— effects on the trade balance and the terms of trade;
— substitution effects between goods or between production factors;
— impact on public finance;
— impact of policy instruments.

Of course, not all of these potential advantages are realized in all applied studies, as this would give rise to complex, general-purpose models. For the issues involved here, the specific questions addressed will determine which elements will be useful. Examples are disaggregate income groups for dealing with ecological tax revision proposals, or disaggregation of energy products and a distinction between more and less energy-intensive goods in the context of carbon tax studies.

GE models are specifically useful for comparing trade and environmental policies with regard to their respective economic and distributive effects, as long as they realize the same environmental objective. Of course, there must be a caveat somewhere, and it is the increasing complexity that results from the fact that everything indirectly depends on everything else. In a theoretical analysis it is possible to add additional assumptions simplifying the analysis. The only alternative is to numerically solve (applied) general equilibrium models. Many of the applied models do not take the individual actors as the decision units—as would be according to the Arrow-Debreu theory—but instead adopt a multi-sectoral approach, which was originated by Johansen (1960).[9] The applied GE models are usually disaggregating sectors. From such a perspective they can be considered as an extension upon the traditional economy-wide framework for multi-sector analysis, i.e. the input/output model. This framework has been used in trade analysis (e.g. Moses, 1955; Leontief and Strout, 1963) as well as in environmental analysis (Leontief, 1970). However, combinations are rare (see Leontief *et al.*, 1977).

The equilibrium models are usually associated with neo-classical assumptions of smooth, monotonous, convex functions and competitive market assumptions which allow for a single equilibrium. Instead, one may, however, use model structures and functional specifications for which existence and uniqueness proof are not available. One may still find solutions then (see Dervis *et al.*, 1982, p. 170), but the interpretations are uncertain. One may also extend the GE approach to include rigid prices or quantity constraints for markets which do not clear, and imperfect market characteristics. The latter type of models are, because of analytical and numerical difficulties, still exceptions (see Harris, 1984; Norman, 1990; and Burniaux and Waelbroeck, 1992).

(b) *Trade General Equilibrium Models*

International trade is considered here as part of an open economy system, which includes a variety of commodity and production factor markets and price processes governing individual consumer and producer optimizing behaviour. Employment, income and inter-sectoral dependencies are simultaneously considered with trade and environmental policies. The GE analysis may be considered as more specific in the

[9] Bergman (1990) gives a typology and overview of Computable General Equilibrium (CGE) model applications: static models based on social accounting matrices; dynamic models based on econometric estimation using time-series data; and planning model formulations.

description of the microeconomic relationships underlying the assumptions of the traditional trade theories.[10]

Trade GE models are distinguished by an orientation to a single-country or multi-country system. As stated by Shoven and Whalley (1984, p. 1034) these models originate from different sources and have a more diffuse focus than the other important field of GE modelling, i.e. taxation analysis. Some models are general-purpose models of open countries, while others are exclusively oriented to trade-policy issues. Many of the empirical models apply to developing countries, and are oriented toward specific trade-policy questions (see Srinivasan and Whalley, 1986). The multi-country GE models differ from the standard theoretical trade model of Heckscher-Ohlin in that trade is not only determined by inter-country differences in relative factor-endowments, but also by differences in production and demand parameters. These multi-country models may be very suitable for dealing with global issues, for instance, for determination of effects of GATT agreements.

Many single-country GE models, although not explicitly focusing on trade issues, are concerned with small open economies. "Small" means that the economy is a price-taker on international markets. "Open" means that trade is relatively important, i.e. it requires to be dealt with in the GE formulation. The price-taking aspect may present inconsistency in a GE approach where prices are typically determined endogenously.[11] The perfect substitutability assumption usually employed in trade theory exaggerates the power of trade policy over the domestic price system and economic structure. Such an approximation is not a workable one in a GE context. An escape from both extreme specialization (with endogenous prices) and exogenous prices (i.e. smallness) is to assume that domestic and foreign products are imperfect substitutes. In general, for every open economy, one has to deal with substitution between inputs of the same kind supplied by different origins, both in utility and in production functions. Usually this is solved by some assumption of imperfect substitution (Armington assumption).

(c) *Environmental Policy in Closed and Open Economy GE Models*

General equilibrium analysis in the field of environmental economics has focused on the effects of environmental policy and abatement (investment) on distribution, factor rewards and public finance (see Comolli, 1977; Yohe, 1979; Steininger, 1994). The latter deals with a small open economy, in which labour is the only immobile factor, which turns out to be crucial for model results. Other

[10] Batra and Casas (1976) show that traditional trade theory and neo-classical models of international trade share a number of results. A variation on the GE approach is provided by Dixit and Norman (1980). Their framework is semi-general in the sense of focusing on the relationship between prices and quantities of production factors and produced commodities, and interactions between markets for traded and non-traded goods, while leaving out income effects.

[11] This inconsistency follows from the theoretical result established by Samuelson (1953) that with constant returns to scale in production and with domestic and foreign identical goods being perfect substitutes, the domestic economy will produce only as many different kinds of tradable goods as it has primary inputs.

examples of GE applications to environmental issues are Bovenberg and de Mooij (1994) focusing on the "double-dividend hypothesis", where the interaction between the public sector budget, taxation, environmental policy and employment is studied. Shifting the tax base from labour to environmental production factors would, according to the hypothesis, have two beneficial effects: more environmental quality and more employment. Although possible, this seems to hinge on a restrictive set of assumptions regarding production and utility parameters.

Some studies deal with energy, starting with Hudson and Jorgenson (1975). A number of recent studies look at the effects of environmental policies: country-specific (Hazilla and Kopp, 1990; Nestor and Pasurka, 1992; and Conrad and Schröder, 1991); acid-rain oriented (Boyd and Krutilla, 1992); CO_2 emissions (Burniaux *et al.*, 1991; Piggott *et al.*, 1992); long-run growth (Jorgenson and Wilcoxen, 1990). Bergman (1991) studies the economy-wide effects of tradable permits on energy use in the context of an applied Computable General Equilibrium (CGE) model. Often, interactions between production inputs receive a lot of attention via nested production relationships, usually represented by flexible constant elasticity of substitution (CES) functions. It should be noted that most applied models of environmental policy-impact analysis are concerned with open economies and are, therefore, of some relevance in the present context. However, it should also be clear that trade is not always dealt with explicitly or consistently in such models.

(d) *Environment and Trade in Theoretical GE Models*

GE models that address the relationship between trade and environmental policy are few in number. Some different approaches can be found in Pethig (1976), Asako (1979) McGuire (1982), and Merrifield (1988). Several attempts have been made to model the effects of environmental policies on foreign trade flows. Such models include environmental quality as a productive factor or a welfare determinant. Pethig and Asako deal with international trade of a polluting commodity in a GE framework. They both conclude that expansion of trade may be bad for the exporting country if the export good is the more polluting commodity, since additional pollution damages may offset the usual gains from trade. Another important conclusion is that with binding environmental policy constraints, the country with the least restrictive policy will export the pollution-intensive commodity.[12] Finally, an interesting result is that harmonization—i.e. striving for the same environmental quality—should not be interpreted as implying equally restrictive environmental controls.

Copeland (1994) considers quotas and mixed regimes in addition to taxes. Furthermore, he deals with the issue of multiple distortions, and states that:

[12] Restrictiveness of environmental policy is a relative notion, and is difficult to test (see, e.g., Tobey, 1990). Pethig (1976, p. 167) defines "more restrictive" in terms of relative emission standards or (not necessarily equivalent) relative emission prices in autarky.

"...if pollution and trade distortions are both important, then linkages between them cannot be ignored, and policy analysts must confront the spill-over effects that will result from piecemeal reform." (p. 63).

Finally, some studies deal with co-ordination of environmental policies in a GE frame. Uncoordinated regulation (McGuire, 1982) means that the shadow price of permitted polluting is not uniform over different countries. In this case, the link is destroyed between uniform world commodity prices and factor price equalization across trading countries. However, the relevance of such results is tempered by characteristics such as largeness of open countries, and local *versus* global or cross-boundary pollution. Unilateral environmental policy may lead to factor-re-location, which is efficient when a local pollution problem is at issue, but not necessarily when a global pollution issue is involved (see McGuire, 1982). Interaction between environmental and trade policies can be analysed by defining them both in one context. The optimum combination can be derived by comparing the GE results with a model optimizing social welfare (see van Beers and van den Bergh, 1994). In Siebert *et al.* (1980), a general equilibrium approach—an extension of Pethig (1976) with environmental production factors and inter-sectoral relationships—is used to analyse the multi-sectoral effects of an environmental tax on net emissions, resource allocation and trade flows. Many of their results are obtained by specifying various versions of a basic model.

In general, one can deal with two types of externalities in the GE context (see model specifications in van Beers and van den Bergh, 1994). First, there are externalities that only affect welfare. This is the type most commonly focused on. The other approach focuses on the production effects of environmental damage. Especially Siebert *et al.* (1980), have dealt with this issue very extensively. They analyse in detail, pollution as a joint output of production activities, for small-country and two-country models, two-sector and two-factor models, with or without abatement, recycling and capital mobility in open economies.

As a third approach, one may consider both types of effects simultaneously. Also the way the externality is modelled differs. Sometimes, emissions are explicitly modelled as part of production, i.e. leading away from the standard production function. Usually, emissions are regarded as an input with standard properties (substitution). However, one can expect very different outcomes when a more complex approach is adopted, namely dealing explicitly with complementarity between production levels and emissions (multi-product relationships). The same holds, however, for complementarity *versus* substitution of regular commodities and environmental quality in utility functions. In terms of having externalities between countries, one may develop models of trading countries which cause each other negative externalities by way of cross-boundary pollution. This, however, presents particular cases which are not at the heart of environment/trade issues.

It should be noted that empirical studies on the relationship between environment and trade have mainly focused on energy and carbon dioxide emissions, largely because these allow significant economy-wide effects to be found, as the required policy interventions are quite severe. Piggott *et al.* (1992, p. 115) study this by focusing on:

— production or consumption substitution across countries;

— terms-of-trade effects involving energy products; and

— terms-of-trade effects involving energy-intensive and other products.

Since environmental quality at the global level (typical of CO_2 emissions) has the character of a public-good, unilateral actions may generate benefits that also accrue to other countries. An example of effect-chains is that cutting production (consumption) in a country leads to higher producer (lower consumer) world prices, and increased production (consumption) in other countries, thus generating adverse spill-over effects in the country.

VI. A Note on Empirical Research

The trade theories of Section II and the partial-equilibrium models of Sections III and IV have not seen much application in the context of environmental factors, externalities and policies. They have mostly been used to obtain general, theoretical insights. Some GE models have been applied. It seems, thus, that theoretical research has received much more attention than empirical studies. Two explanations can be offered for this. First, not all theoretical models allow for immediate testing or application because of their abstract nature. Second, it is very difficult to link monetary with physical dimensions, and to define and measure unambiguous indicators for, for example, environmental effects, specific environmental measures, or strictness of environmental policy. This is partly a fundamental problem, and partly a matter of lacking data. It is, for instance, only recently that the World Bank Atlas started to publish national figures on the environment.

In order to alleviate such problems, one may use simple indicators such as ratios and trade variables to estimate the effects of, for instance, environmental policy on trade; this can be done by comparison of values of such indicators before and after implementation of policy in a specific country, or by country-wise comparison. An alternative is to adopt econometric or statistical (correlation) analysis based on single-country (time-series) or country-wise (cross-section) analysis as, for instance, in Tobey (1990).

Finally, one may note that statistical evidence on certain relationships between trade, environmental quality and policy may not be found when explanatory variation in the data is weak, which can be caused by unobserved technological processes, imperfectly operating markets, rigid prices, exogenous shocks, or just because policies have not been that strict. This is a problem that is also found in studies dealing with the question of the effect of environmental factors and regulation on location decisions (see, for example, Low and Yeats, 1992). And the mere choice of an indicator for strictness of environmental policy poses serious problems. One can choose, for instance, government outlays on environmental policy, participation in international agreements, or the number of environmental taxes and levies, as a basis for such an indicator. However, these will only be indirectly related to the strictness of the policy as it may affect private costs of production. The latter may be a good starting point for a search for indicators.

VII. Conclusions

The aim of this article was to discuss methodological approaches for investigating the diverse and multi-faceted relationship between international trade and environmental externalities. Although some authors argue that this relationship is not very important (see Palmeter, 1993), it is clear that a serious approach to environmental policy analysis should in any case take serious account of the open character and international dependence of most national economies. It is hoped that this overview has made it clear that each method can only generate a limited and partial insight, because of restrictive assumptions or analytical complexities. Table 3 summarizes some essential differences between the main approaches.

The Table shows that the main distinction between the trade, partial and general equilibrium models relates to the inclusion of externalities and environmental production factors. Whereas the first two approaches can only deal with one of these, the GE approach allows both to be considered simultaneously. The most important difference between the partial analysis and the economy-wide analysis (GE models) is that the first comes with firm conclusions based on a simple model, while the second focuses on the significance of various effects operating within a complex system. A disadvantage of GE models is that everything is related to everything, which means that these models are very difficult to make operational and validate.

Table 3: A rough comparison between three methods for environment/trade analysis

Model Type	Externality	Environmental Production Factors	Number of Goods	Market Structure	Policy Options
General trade models	no	yes	>1(2)	perfect	environmental policy = trade policy
Partial equilibrium	yes	no	1	perfect or imperfect	environmental policy ≠ trade policy
General equilibrium	yes	yes	≥1 (>>)	mainly perfect	whole set of specific policies; distinction environmental/ trade policies

The advantage is that the effect of various demand and production parameters on the allocation of factors and goods and the (factor or sectoral) distribution of welfare effects can be analysed. In a way, the partial and general equilibrium approaches can be regarded as complementary, although it is also interesting to see where they overlap and are consistent. The consistency has been noted also for open economy GE models and general trade theories *à la* Heckscher-Ohlin, which focus on trade-offs between different activities, given availability of primary resources.

Other criteria which may be relevant are dimensions and market structure. The dimensions of models are determined by the number of production factors, households and production sectors. In a GE model, typically all dimensions can be chosen freely, whereas this is more difficult, albeit possible, in general trade models and partial equilibrium models. Models incorporating imperfect competition throw light on the relationship between market structure, foreign trade and environmental policy. These analyses may play an important role in future research. The effects of environmental policy on foreign trade patterns are dependent on the kind of competition present in domestic and foreign markets. Also the combination of imperfect domestic and international markets may lead to interesting insights about optimal policies.

It is clear that international co-ordination of environmental policy is a necessity for maintaining, as much as possible, elements of free trade. Such issues, although not given much attention here, are increasingly attracting attention from economists. In this context also, formal modelling, often based on game theory, is used to deal with relevant questions. Although not always directly concerned with trade issues, the interaction with these is sometimes important, and relates most strongly to analyses such as referred to in Section IV.

Finally, formal models for studying the interface of environment and trade are always the result of abstractions and simplifications. Therefore, one may never directly translate the conclusions obtained from model exercises to implications for policy, but instead try to combine results from separate model studies, each throwing a specific light on the issue. Therefore, it is necessary to know which alternatives are available and how they are related to each other. This has been the purpose of the present article.

References

Anderson, K., and R. Blackhurst (eds.), 1992: *The Greening of World Trade Issues*, Harvester Wheatsheaf, London/New York.

Anderson, K., 1992: *The Standard Welfare Economics of Policies Affecting Trade and the Environment* in Anderson and Blackhurst (eds.), *op. cit.*, Chapter 2.

Arrow, K.J., and F.H. Hahn, 1971: *General Competitive Analysis*, Holden-Day, San Francisco.

Asako, K., 1979: *Environmental Pollution in an Open Economy*, The Economic Record, Vol. 55, 359–367.

Barna, T. (ed.), 1963: *Structural Interdependence and Economic Development*, St. Martin's Press, New York.

Batra, R.N., and F.R. Casas, 1976: *A Synthesis of the Heckscher-Ohlin and the Neo-Classical Models of International Trade*, Journal of International Economics, Vol. 6, 21–38.

Baumol, W.J., and W.E. Oates, 1988: *The Theory of Environmental Policy*, 2nd edition, Cambridge University Press, Cambridge.

Baumol, W.J., 1971: *Environmental Protection, International Spillovers and Trade*, Almqvist and Wiksell, Stockholm.

Beers, C. van, and J.C.J.M. van den Bergh, 1994: *Environmental and Foreign Trade Policies in a Small Open Economy* in de Mooij and Vollebergh (eds.), *op. cit.*

Bergman, L., 1990: *The Development of Computable General Equilibrium Modelling*, in Bergman, Jorgenson and Zalai, *op. cit.*

Idem, 1991: *General Equilibrium Effects of Environmental Policy: A CGE-Modelling Approach*, Environmental and Resource Economics, Vol. 1, 43–61.

Bergman, L., D.W. Jorgenson, and E. Zalai, 1990: *General Equilibrium Modelling and Economic Policy Analysis*, Basil Blackwell, Oxford.

Bovenberg, A.L., and R.A. de Mooij, 1994: *Environmental Policy in a Small Open Economy with Distortionary Labour Taxes: A General Equilibrium Analysis*, in van Ierland (ed.), *op. cit.*

Boyd, R., and K. Krutilla, 1992: *Controlling Acid Deposition: A General Equilibrium Assessment*, Environmental and Resource Economics, Vol. 2, 307–322.

Burniaux, J.M., J.P. Martin, G. Nicoletti, and J. Oliveira-Martins, 1991: *GREEN – A Multi-Region Dynamic General Equilibrium Model for Quantifying the Costs of Curbing CO_2 Emissions: A Technical Manual*, Working Paper 89, OECD, Dept. of Economics and Statistics, Paris.

Burniaux, J.M., and J. Waelbroeck, 1992: *CGE and Imperfect Competition Model for EC*, Journal of Policy Modelling, Vol. 14, 65–92.

Carraro, C., 1994: *Trade, Innovation, Environment*, Kluwer Academic Publishers, Dordrecht.

Comolli, P., 1977: *Pollution Control in a Simplified General Equilibrium Model with Production Externalities*, Journal of Environmental Economics and Management, Vol. 4, 289–304.

Conrad, K., 1993: *Trade Policy under Taxes and Subsidies for Pollution-Intensive Industries*, Journal of Environmental Economics and Management, Vol. 25, 121–135.

Idem, 1994: *Emission Taxes and International Market-Share Rivalry*, in van Ierland (ed.), *op. cit.*

Conrad, K., and M. Schröder, 1991: *The Control of CO_2 Emissions and its Economic Impact*, Environmental and Resource Economics, Vol. 1.

Copeland, B.R., 1994: *International Trade and the Environment: Policy Reform in a Polluted Small Open Economy*, Journal of Environmental Economics and Management, Vol. 26, 44–65.

Deardorff, A.V., 1984: *Testing Trade Theories and Predicting Trade Flows*, in Jones and Kenen (eds.), *op. cit.*

de Mooij, R., and H. Vollebergh (eds.), 1994: *Quantitative Economics for Environmental Policy*, OCFEB, Erasmus University, Rotterdam.

Dervis, K., J. de Melo, and S. Robinson, 1982: *General Equilibrium Models for Development Policy*, Cambridge University Press, Cambridge.

Dixit, A., 1984: *International Trade Policy for Oligopolistic Industries*, Economic Journal, Supplement, 1–15.

Dixit, A.K., and J.E. Stiglitz, 1977: *Monopolistic Competition and Optimum Product Diversity*, American Economic Review, Vol. 67, No. 3, 297–308.

Dixit, A., and V. Norman, 1980: *Theory of International Trade: A Dual General Equilibrium Approach*, Cambridge University Press, Cambridge.

Eaton, J., and G.M. Grossman, 1986: *Optimal Trade and Industrial Policy under Oligopoly*, The Quarterly Journal of Economics, Vol. CI, 383–406.

Ekins, P., R. Costanza, and C. Folke, 1994: *Trade and Environment*, Ecological Economics, Vol. 9, special issue.

Falvey, R.E., 1994: *The Theory of International Trade*, in Greenaway and Winters, *op. cit.*, Chapter 2.

GATT, 1971: *Industrial Pollution Control and International Trade*, GATT Studies in International Trade No. 1, General Agreement on Tariffs and Trade, Geneva.

Greenaway, D., and L.A. Winters, 1994: *Surveys in International Trade*, Blackwell Publications, Oxford.

Harris, R.G., 1984: *Applied General Equilibrium Analysis of Small Open Economies and Imperfect Competition*, American Economic Review, Vol. 74, 1016–1032.

Hazilla, M., and R.J. Kopp, 1990: *Social Cost of Environmental Quality Regulations: A General Equilibrium Analysis*, Journal of Political Economy, Vol. 98, 853–873.

Helpman, E., and P.R. Krugman, 1985: *Market Structure and Foreign Trade: Increasing Returns, Imperfect Competition, and the International Economy*, MIT Press, Cambridge, Mass.

Hudson, E.A., and D.W. Jorgenson, 1975: *U.S. Energy and Economic Growth 1975–2000*, Bell Journal of Economics and Management Science, Vol. 5, 461–514.

Johansen, L., 1960: *A Multisectoral Study of Economic Growth*, North-Holland, Amsterdam.

Jones, R.W., and P.B. Kenen (eds.), 1984: *Handbook of International Economics*, Elsevier Science Publishers, Amsterdam.

Jorgenson, D.W., and J. Wilcoxen, 1990: *Intertemporal General Equilibrium Modelling of U.S. Environmental Policy*, Journal of Policy Modeling, Vol. 12, 715–744.

Kennedy, P., 1994a: *Equilibrium Pollution Taxes in Open Economies with Imperfect Competition*, Journal of Environmental Economics and Management, Vol. 27, 49–63.

Idem, 1994b: *Environmental Policy and Trade Liberalization under Imperfect Competition*, in van Ierland (ed.), *op. cit.*

Krutilla, K., 1991: *Environmental Regulation in an Open Economy*, Journal of Environmental Economics and Management, Vol. 20, 127–142.

Leontief, W.W., 1970: *Environmental Repercussions and the Economic Structure: An Input-Output Approach*, Review of Economic Studies, Vol. 52, 262–271.

Leontief, W.W., and A. Strout, 1963: *Multi-regional Input-Output Analysis*, in Barna (ed.), *op. cit.*

Leontief, W.W., A.P. Carter, and P.A. Petri, 1977: *The Future of the World Economy*, Oxford University Press, New York.

Linder, S.B., 1961: *An Essay on Trade and Transformation*, Almquist & Wiksell, Upsala.

Low, P. (ed.), 1992: *International Trade and Environment*, World Bank Discussion Papers, 159, World Bank, Washington, D.C.

Low, P., and A. Yeats, 1992: *Do "Dirty" Industries Migrate?* in Low (ed.), *op. cit.*

Markusen, J.R., 1975: *International Externalities and Optimal Tax Structures*, Journal of International Economics, Vol. 5, 15–29.

McGuire, M.C., 1982: *Regulation, Factor Rewards, and International Trade*, Journal of Public Economics, Vol. 17, 335–354.

Merrifield, J.D., 1988: *The Impact of Selected Abatement Strategies on Transnational Pollution, the Terms of Trade and Factor Rewards: A General Equilibrium Approach*, Journal of Environmental Economics and Management, Vol. 15, 259–284.

Moses, L.N., 1955: *The Stability of Interregional Trading Patterns and Input-Output Analysis*, American Economic Review, Vol. 45, 803–832.

Nestor, D.V., and C.A. Pasurka, 1992: *General Equilibrium Model of German Environmental Regulation*, U.S. Environmental Protection Agency, Economic Analysis and Research Branch, Washington, D.C.

Norman, V.D., 1990: *Assessing Trade and Welfare Effects of Trade Liberalization: A Comparison of Alternative Approaches to CGE Modelling with Imperfect Competition*, European Economic Review, Vol. 34, 725–751.

Palmeter, D., 1993: *Environment and Trade: Much Ado About Little?* 27 Journal of World Trade 3, June, 55–70.

Pethig, R., 1976: *Pollution, Welfare and Environmental Policy in the Theory of Comparative Advantage*, Journal of Environmental Economics and Management, Vol. 2, 160–169.

Idem, (ed.), 1992: *Conflicts and Co-operation in Managing Environmental Resources*, Springer-Verlag, Berlin, 111–128.

Piggott, J., J. Whalley, and R. Wigle, 1992: *International Linkages and Carbon Reduction Initiatives*, in Anderson and Blackhurst (eds.), *op. cit.*, Chapter 6.

Posner, M.V., 1961: *International Trade and Technical Change*, Oxford Economic Papers, 323–341.

Samuelson, P.A., 1953: *Prices of Factors and Goods in General Equilibrium*, Review of Economic Studies 21, 1–20.

Shoven, J.B., and J. Whalley, 1984: *Applied General-Equilibrium Models of Taxation and International Trade: An Introduction and Survey*, Journal of Economic Literature, Vol. 22, 1007–51.

Siebert, H., 1973: *Comparative Advantage and Environmental Policy: A Note*, Zeitschrift für Nationalökonomie, Vol. 34, 397–402.

Idem, 1974: *Environmental Protection and International Specialization*, Weltwirtschaftliches Archiv, Vol. 110, 494–508.

Idem, 1987: *Economics of the Environment: Theory and Policy*, Springer-Verlag, Berlin.

Siebert, H., J. Eichberger, R. Gronych, and R. Pethig, 1980: *Trade and Environment: A Theoretical Enquiry*, Studies in Environmental Science 6, Elsevier Science Publishers, Amsterdam.

Smith, A., 1994: *Imperfect Competition and International Trade*, in Greenaway and Winters, *op. cit.*, Chapter 3.

Srinivasan, T.N., and J. Whalley, 1986: *General Equilibrium Trade Policy Modelling*, MIT Press, Cambridge, Mass.

Steininger, K., 1994: *Trade and Environment: A Computable General Equilibrium for Austria*, Physica-Verlag, Vienna.

Tobey, J.A., 1990: *The Effects of Domestic Environmental Policies on Patterns of World Trade: An Empirical Test*, Kyklos, Vol. 43, 191–209.

Ulph, A., 1991: *The Choice of Environmental Policy Instruments and Strategic International Trade*, in Pethig (ed.), *op. cit.*, 111–128.

Idem, 1992: *The Choice of Environmental Policy Instruments and Strategic International Trade*, in Pethig, *op. cit.*, Chapter 5.

van Ierland, E.C. (ed.), 1994: *International Environmental Economics: Theories, Models and Applications to Global Warming, International Trade and Acidification*, Elsevier Science Publications, Amsterdam.

Verdier, T., 1993: *Strategic Trade and the Regulation of Pollution by Performance or Design Standards*, Nota di Lavoro della Fondazione Eni Enrico Mattei, University of Venice, No. 58.

Walter, I., 1975: *The International Economics of Pollution*, Macmillan, London.

Idem, 1976: *Studies in International Environmental Economics*, Wiley, New York.

WCED, 1987: *Our Common Future*, World Commission on Environment and Development, Oxford University Press, Oxford/New York.

Yohe, G.W., 1979: *The Backward Incidence of Pollution Control – Some Comparative Statistics in General Equilibrium*, Journal of Environmental Economics and Management, Vol. 6, 187–198.

The Economic Journal, **101** (*March* 1991), 180–189
Printed in Great Britain

THE INTERFACE BETWEEN ENVIRONMENTAL AND TRADE POLICIES*

John Whalley

Last March I gave the Frank Paish Lecture to the Society under the title 'Economic Life in a Greenhouse'. In my lecture, I tried both to survey professional opinion as to some of the possible climatic implications of the greenhouse effect, and also to draw out the economic consequences which might follow.[1] Towards the end of my talk, I made reference to some preliminary joint work with Randy Wigle,[2] a colleague at Wilfrid Laurier University in Canada, on the global consequences of carbon tax schemes designed to limit and/or reduce the build-up of CO_2 emissions, a key element underlying the greenhouse effect.

The written version of the lecture consciously does not reproduce the survey material which made up the first part of the lecture. Instead, it elaborates on the issues raised towards the end. It incorporates the work by Randy Wigle and myself, and offers some thoughts on what seems to be a growing issue for the 1990s; namely, the consequences for the international trading system of interactions between trade issues and both future global and current national environmental policies.

What follows emphasises that, if they occur in the next few decades, global policy responses[3] (carbon taxes, tradeable permit schemes) to environmental concerns will almost certainly have large economic effects. Among these are likely to be significant effects on trade patterns and trade volumes. Large interregional effects will also accompany such policies, depending upon how such policies are implemented. Also, the 1990s may see a growing use of trade measures to achieve objectives set for environmental policies. Environmental policies towards such countries as Brazil, the Philippines and others where deforestation is a concern may increasingly take the form of threatened trade sanctions unless compliance with global environmental policy objectives occurs.[4]

* This paper is based on a broader talk 'Economic Life in a Greenhouse', given as the Frank Paish Lecture to the annual meetings of the Royal Economic Society held in Nottingham in March 1990. It draws heavily on joint work with Randy Wigle, to whom I am grateful for repeated discussion on the issues covered. I am indebted to Ngee-Choon Chia for research support.

[1] The discussion of the possible scientific dimensions of the greenhouse effect was, in part, based on Schneider (1989). A range of the economic consequences discussed are set out in Cline (1989).

[2] See Whalley and Wigle (1989).

[3] See Robertson (1990) for a recent discussion of negotiation and treaty aspects of such responses.

[4] While no formal trade sanctions linked to environmental objectives have yet been used against these countries, a regional development grant made by the World Bank to Brazil in 1985 was interrupted in 1985 because of concerns expressed by environmental groups in OECD countries that the loan to develop Northern Brazil would result in significant deforestation (see Le Prestre (1989, p. 181), and Repetto and Gillis (1988, p. 281)). The same policy approach is reflected through the recent creation of the UN Environmental Fund through which the World Bank, the UN Environmental Programme, and the UN Developmental Programme will jointly provide \$1 billion to countries in Asia, Africa and Latin American

There may also be growing pressures to link fairness in trade to environmental policies. Thus, in countries where there are more stringent environmental standards than in neighbouring states, the argument will be that imports are relatively favourably treated by their neighbours' environmental policies because their production is not subject to the higher costs associated with stronger environmental regulation. The logical next step will be the argument that because such trade was unfair, protection should be granted to domestic producers.

The present structure of international trade arrangements seems neither to make allowance for such pressures, nor to indicate how they could be accommodated. The GATT, with its present thirty-eight articles, makes no explicit reference to environmental matters.[5] Thus, trade measures justified on arguments about unfair trade linked to environmental considerations are unlikely to have a foundation under GATT. They would almost certainly be ruled as GATT-incompatible by GATT panels if complaints were brought.

Threats of trade measures against countries who do not comply with global environmental policies would face much the same difficulty. No GATT justification for the use of such measures exists. Either increases would occur in remaining unbound tariffs, or other trade measures would come into play, such as anti-dumping and countervailing duties (with some reinterpretation). Either way, there would be yet further erosion in the global system of trade rules beyond that which has already occurred in the 1970s and 1980s.[6]

Given the quantitative orders of magnitude involved the argument made here is that the interaction of these two sets of policies made in the 1990s may well yield turbulence, conflict and confusion.[7]

I. POLICY RESPONSES TO GLOBAL ENVIRONMENTAL ISSUES

One key element of the emerging interface between environmental policies and trade is possibly policy responses to global warning. Some of the proposals made thus far (carbon taxes, tradeable permits) aim to reduce consumption of

---

to ensure 'that their development programs are undertaken in a manner which protects their global environment'. (See *Wall Street Journal*, Tuesday, September 18, 1990.)

[5] The coverage of environmental concerns in the GATT is both remote and tangential, and nowhere in the General Agreement is the word 'environment' used. Article 20-B which allows Contracting Parties to use import restrictions to protect human life and health, including measures against toxic substances (see GATT (1986) p. 37). The standards code which emerged from the Tokyo Round in 1979 directs Contracting Parties not to use product standards (including environmental standards) in such a way as to create unnecessary obstacles to trade. See Rubin and Graham (eds) (1982), p. 169. A new GATT working group has also been established on Domestically Prohibited Goods and Hazardous Substances (see Sankey (1989)). None of these, however, deals with environmental issues in a central way.

[6] The term 'erosion' of the global system of trade rules refers to unchecked deviations from the GATT principles of trade measures being non-discriminatory, transparent, and based on tariffs. Erosion of these principles was present in agriculture in the 1940s when the GATT was signed, spread to textiles and clothing in the early 1960s, spread further into steel and voluntary export restraint arrangements in the 1970s, and continued with increased use of contingent trade protection measures (anti-dumping and countervailing duties) and unilateral actions (Section 301 of the 1988 Trade Act in the United States) in the 1980s. For more discussion, see Low (1990) and Whalley (1989).

[7] Furthermore, as discussed in Leonard (1988), there are linkages between investment flows and environmental policies with certain inward investment to developing countries being driven, in part, by relatively lax environmental standards. These issues seem likely to also grow in prominence in the 1990s.

carbon-based energy products (oil, coal, natural gas) and thus slow (or even stabilise) the build-up of atmospheric carbon dioxide.[8]

The approach suggested here is to tax (or quota restrict) the carbon content of individual fuels; hence different tax rates would apply to coal, natural gas, and oil.[9] Such taxes are seen as meeting a specified target for global reduction in carbon emission levels. Targets commonly discussed lie between 20 and 50% of projected levels by some specified date.[10] Taxes are usually proposed as a fixed dollar (or currency) amount on a physical unit basis; say, $250 per ton of carbon embodied in each fuel.[11] Ad valorem equivalent carbon tax rates (which vary by fuel) are in the region of 50–100% (higher in some cases). The rate needed in any given carbon tax scheme is thus dependent on a variety of factors, including the target emission reduction and assumed elasticity values for energy demand and supply functions. The latter will, in part, determine how closely the emission reduction target will be met by any given tax rate.

As can be seen from Table 1, carbon use around the globe is highly concentrated, suggesting that significant intercountry effects may accompany the introduction of such a tax. Emissions per capita in developed countries are on average around 20–30 times those of developing countries; three countries (United States, U.S.S.R., and China) account for over 50% of emissions. On the other hand, carbon use per dollar of GNP is typically much higher in developing countries, reflecting the use of relatively inefficient energy conversion technologies.

It is the size of some of the potential inter-country effects which might accompany such taxes which I have tried to quantify in recent joint work with Randy Wigle (Whalley and Wigle, 1989, 1990). We use a global equilibrium model and produce a number of counterfactual calculations which provide an indication of what could happen to the global economy if carbon taxes of various kinds were introduced. The models we have used incorporate trade, production and consumption of both energy and non-energy products for a number of countries (or groups of countries). To keep the models manageable, we do not identify fuel types within the broader carbon-based energy category, even though the various elements within this category (oil, coal, natural gas) would, in practice, be taxed at different rates. The model also does not incorporate existing taxes on energy products (such as excise taxes on gasoline), even though these vary by region, and could also affect results.

[8] Those proposals have generated a number of country responses already in European countries. Although much smaller than the globally proposed taxes, taxes in Sweden, Finland and Denmark already exist, with planned taxes under way in Italy, the Netherlands and Norway (see *The Economist*, March 17, 1990, pp. 45–57).

[9] Edmunds and Reilly (1983), for instance, consider taxes at rates of 100% on coal, 78% on oil, 56% on gas, and 115% on shale oil. Flavin (1990, fn. 45) suggests tax rates proportional to the carbon content of fuels; with coal average 24·12 kilograms of carbon per gigajoule, oil 19·94 (82% of coal), and natural gas 13·78 (57% of coal).

[10] Manne and Richels (1990), for instance, consider a target of a 20% reduction from base line emission levels by 2020, with a stabilised level of emissions thereafter, until 2100. See also Nordhaus (1977, 1990).

[11] Tax rates of this order are considered by Manne and Richels (1990) and Nordhaus (1990). They imply more than a five fold increase in the price of coal, and a doubling or more in gasoline prices.

Table 1*

Country Characteristics of Fossil Fuel Carbon Emissions, 1987

	Emissions per capita in tons/year	Country emissions as % of world total	Grams of carbon per $ of GNP
U.S.	5·03	21·9	276
Canada	4·24	1·9	247
Australia	4·00	1·1	320
Soviet Union	3·68	18·5	436
Saudi Arabia	3·60	0·8	565
Poland	3·38	2·3	492
W. Germany	2·98	3·3	223
U.K.	2·73	2·8	224
Japan	2·12	4·5	156
Italy	1·78	1·8	147
France	1·70	1·7	133
S. Korea	1·14	0·8	347
Mexico	0·96	1·4	609
China	0·56	10·7	2,024
Egypt	0·41	0·4	801
Brazil	0·38	0·9	170
India	0·19	2·7	655
Indonesia	0·16	0·5	403
Nigeria	0·09	0·2	359
Zaire	0·03	0·01	183
Average for the world	1·08		327

* Information reported in this table has been extracted from table 2-1, p. 19 of Flavin (1990) who, in turn, uses a variety of primary sources in his calculations.

In the simpler of these two models (Whalley and Wigle, 1989), the world is divided into three regions. The first is the developed world (all countries with per capita income in 1986 above US$2,000 and with less than 25% of exports in fossil fuels). The second is the developing world (all countries with per capita income in 1986 below US$2,000, and with less than 25% of exports in fossil fuels). The third is oil exporters, which includes all OPEC countries and major non-OPEC energy exporters.

Nested CES functions are used in the model to represent production and demand in each region, as shown in Table 2. Each region is endowed with three non-traded primary factors: (i) primary factors, exclusive of energy resources, (ii) carbon-based energy resources (deposits of oil, gas and coal), and (iii) other energy resources (hydro-electric capacity and nuclear). Both energy resources are converted into the relevant energy products through a refining/extraction process, which uses other resources (primary factors). There are three internationally traded commodities: carbon-based energy products, energy-intensive goods, and other goods (all other GNP). Energy-intensive goods, other goods, and the composite energy product (carbon-based and non-carbon-based energy) are the commodities which enter final demands.

Carbon-based and non-carbon-based energy products use the respective energy resources and primary factors. Non-carbon-based energy products are

Table 2

Production and Demand Structures Used by Whalley and Wigle (1989) to Evaluate Carbon Tax Options to Achieve Reductions in CO_2 Emissions

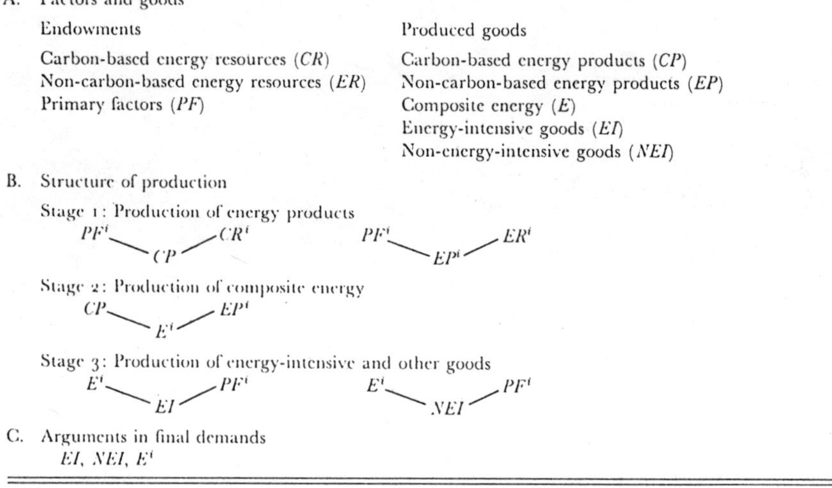

A. Factors and goods

Endowments	Produced goods
Carbon-based energy resources (*CR*)	Carbon-based energy products (*CP*)
Non-carbon-based energy resources (*ER*)	Non-carbon-based energy products (*EP*)
Primary factors (*PF*)	Composite energy (*E*)
	Energy-intensive goods (*EI*)
	Non-energy-intensive goods (*NEI*)

B. Structure of production

Stage 1: Production of energy products

Stage 2: Production of composite energy

Stage 3: Production of energy-intensive and other goods

C. Arguments in final demands

EI, NEI, E^i

i denotes good which is distinguished by country of production.

non-traded, since hydro-electric, solar and nuclear power are not traded in significant quantities between the regions they consider. A domestic energy composite is produced by a third (energy conversion) industry, using inputs of the two energy products. The two final-goods (energy-intensive goods, and other goods) use primary factors and the composite energy product as inputs. Perfect competition is assumed throughout for all sectors and in all regions.

Equilibrium in this model involves full global market clearing in all three traded goods (carbon-based energy products, energy-intensive manufactures, and other goods). For the two non-traded goods (non-carbon energy products, and composite energy) there is domestic market clearing within each economy. Since prices in this system are treated as completely flexible, they will adjust to the levels required to clear the relevant international and domestic markets.

Whalley and Wigle (1989) use their model in counterfactual mode[12] to evaluate international incidence effects of alternative carbon tax schemes for the three regions. This involves constructing base (or reference) case data for 1986 to which the equilibrium model is calibrated[13] (i.e., the parameters are chosen such that the model will reproduce the base case data as a full equilibrium solution prior to any policy change being introduced). The base case data thus fully describes a no-policy-change model solution. Different

[12] This is a technical term used in the applied general equilibrium modelling literature; see Shoven and Whalley (1984, and forthcoming) for more details.

[13] See Whalley and Wigle (1990) for a more complete discussion of data and elasticity parameters used in the model, and Mansur and Whalley (1984) for a discussion of calibration.

Table 3
Whalley and Wigle's (1989) Analyses of Carbon Tax Options

A. Target reduction in carbon use — 50% reduction in global carbon use relative to base case

B. Tax options considered:
1. National production based tax
2. National consumption based tax
3. Global tax

C. Carbon tax rates needed to meet emission reduction targets

Option	Tax rate/rates* (range by region)
1	80·42–80·78%
2	79·51–83·41%
3	80·59%

D. Gain or loss by region under each option (Hicksian EVs $billion 1986; figures in parentheses are % of GDP)

Region	Tax option 1	2	3
Developed countries	−179·7	−67·3	−252·92
	(−1·68)	(−0·63)	(−2·36)
Oil exporters	46·99	−108·13	−122·84
	(10·80)	(−24·85)	(−28·73)
Developing countries	−151·23	−120·60	+93·98
	(−4·76)	(−3·80)	(+2·96)
World	−283·94	−269·12	−281·78
	(−1·98)	(−2·07)	(−1·97)

* These are gross tax rates, i.e. an 80% tax rate means that for each $ spent by consumers, 80 cents is collected in tax. The equivalent net tax rate is 400% (i.e. 80/20%).

carbon tax schemes can then be introduced, with a new equilibrium (counterfactual equilibrium) solution computed for each. Using a pair-wise comparison (base case versus counterfactual), impacts on regions are calculated.

Table 3 reports Whalley and Wigle's (1989) central case results based on 1986 annual data. They consider three alternative forms of carbon tax: a national production-based tax, a national consumption-based tax, and a global tax. In each case, the target emission reduction is 50% relative to the base case model solution.

As Table 3 indicates, their central case estimates of the annual gains or losses for the regions identified in the model under each of the carbon tax options are large. In making these estimates, they calculate Hicksian equivalent variations (EVs) in $ billions (expressed in 1986 prices). These measures capture the combined gains or losses to regions from the production and sale of carbon-based products, as well as the consumption side gains associated with price changes. They also capture the economy-wide effects of energy price changes as they feed through the model. Their results suggest the global economic cost of carbon taxes to be in the range of $280 billion per year. This represents a cost in the region of 2% of world product.

Effects by region differ dramatically across the various tax options. Developed countries lose \$250 billion per year, or approximately 2·4% of the value of income, under a global tax; whereas their loss under a national consumption-based carbon tax is substantially smaller, \$67 billion or 0·6% of income. Developing countries lose over \$150 billion (or 4% of income) under a national production-based carbon tax, whereas they gain \$95 billion (or 3% of national income) under a global tax. Oil exporters gain substantially from a national production-based tax, while they lose from either a global tax or a national consumption-based tax.

These results, therefore, underline the point emphasised above; namely, that any carbon limitation initiatives will have major implications for the international economy. Under a national production-based tax, energy producers will collect tax revenues; hence oil exporters will gain. Under a national consumption tax, oil importers will collect revenues, and hence developed countries lose less. Under a global tax, the revenues are redistributed on a per capita basis and developing countries and centrally planned gain substantially. And effects on trade flows between regions (reported in Whalley and Wigle (1989) will be substantial).

II. TRADE POLICY AS AN INSTRUMENT OF ENVIRONMENTAL POLICY, AND ENVIRONMENTAL POLICY AS A SOURCE OF TRADE POLICY TENSIONS

A second element of the emerging interface between environmental and trade policies which seems likely to become more prominent in the 1990s is the use of trade policies as an enforcement machine for environmental policies, and the related issue of pressures on trade policies created by differing environmental regulation across countries.

The notion that trade policies may ultimately be used to enforce global environmental policies is something that has been little considered by those who have been active in debates on global environmental policy, but lurks as a major concern among trade policy practitioners.[14] It has commonly been assumed that what was necessary to deal with such problems as global warming, CFCs, and other matters was to negotiate an international treaty which would bind all signatories to reductions in levels of emissions. The assumption was that some form of enforcement procedure would automatically follow. Moral commitment to emission reduction would hopefully be sufficient to implement the treaty.

It has become apparent, however, that such an approach neglects many elements of interaction between environmental and other policies. Typically, global environmental action involves a large public good element, since one's country's decision to reduce emissions confers benefits on all other countries. To rely on sanctions within the environmental area as the enforcement device simply does not seem practicable. In theory, it is conceivable that a global

[14] See the recent discussion of possible levies on 'dirty trade' within the U.N. Environmental Program (see *The Economist*, pp. 24–25, Sept. 8–14, 1990).

treaty on carbon emission reduction could specify a penalty system which would allow other countries to deviate from carbon emission reduction targets if particular countries did not meet their own commitments. What seems more likely, however, is that large countries would use threats of actions in other non-environmental policy areas to enforce environmental treaty commitments.

The instrument which is most commonly suggested for this purpose is trade threats. Thus, it is not inconceivable in the next ten years that with concerns over deforestation in Brazil, the Philippines, Costa Rica, and elsewhere, commitments in these areas agreed upon either globally or by a subset of larger developed countries, may in part be policed through trade threats used against these countries. This would involve the use of threatened increases in trade barriers or actual trade retaliatory measures, until compliance with environmental goals occurred.

If growth should resume in China and continue through the 1990s and into the next century, given current emission levels in China, it is not inconceivable that trade policies in OECD countries might be linked to the adoption of more energy-efficient energy conversion technologies in China. The effect would be to use trade sanctions to encourage China to reduce coal burning and move to oil, gas, or even nuclear power. Even for localised problems, such as trans-border pollution problems between the United States and Mexico, or acid rain issues involving the European countries, trade threats could be part of the interaction of policies linking enforcement to environmental objectives.

The difficulty for the trading system in all of this is that the GATT has little to say about environmental policies and their impact on trade, and the potential further erosion of already frail trading rules through such actions is significant and by itself impedes economic performance. All that countries are entitled to do under GATT is ban imports of hazardous or toxic substances on health and safety grounds. Any use of trade threats seeking to achieve environmental objectives, would run full-square into the disciplines contained in the General Agreement. Environmentally motivated trade measures executed in a manner which was GATT-compatible could not involve complaint to a GATT panel, with a dispute settlement procedure ultimately sanctifying retaliatory measures. Any increase in barriers, to be GATT-compatible, would have to take the form of increases in GATT unbound tariffs.

In reality, environmentally motivated trade threats from larger countries would, in all probability, involve unilateral actions, such as we now see in Section 301 of the 1988 Trade Act, or threats of anti-dumping or other contingent trade-restricting measures. The severity of these would be likely to increase with concerns over environmental issues. The pressures such developments would create for the trading system are obvious, as are the new difficulties potentially facing global trade out into the 1990s and beyond.

Beyond the issues raised by enforcement of global environmental policies through trade sanctions come a further set of trade-related issues reflecting differing environmental regulations across countries and possible uses of trade remedy measures justified by such differences. North American economies and a number of the European countries have already adopted stringent environmental standards. Producers within these countries have long complained that they operate in a relatively unfair trade environment, since their costs are significantly higher than those of comparable producers in neighbouring countries.[15] The danger in the 1990s is that these political pressures may eventually be translated into more focused pressures for trade remedy actions justified on these grounds. This could involve attempts to reinterpret dumping law in such a way that they capture cost differences due to differing environmental standards, and possible attempts to reinterpret the definition of subsidy under countervailing duty law with a similar aim in mind.[16]

The GATT, as with environment-driven trade threats, has nothing to say on these matters. But to the extent that their severity increases in the decade of the 1990s, so the potential wider problems for the global trading system will also come to the fore. Attempts to introduce environmental considerations into future GATT rounds or other trade negotiating fora may occur. And the vocabulary within which trade policy is debated could well swing towards discussion of 'green' and 'dirty' trade.

III. SUMMARY AND CONCLUDING REMARKS

This paper suggests that in the 1990s we may well see an emerging interface between environmental and trade policies. I suggest in the paper that it may come more to the fore in the 1990s, and in ways which were little anticipated at the birth of the environmental movement in the 1960s and 70s. If indeed global policy responses to issues such as global warming are enacted, the consequences for both regional imbalances and the patterns of trade between regions, is likely to be severe. In addition, the pressures within the trading system which would accompany attempts to use trade policy as an instrument of enforcement of environmental policies, and the further pressures created by differing environmental policies in countries seem likely to be of substantial importance in the years ahead.

How all of this plays out remains to be seen. As the paper emphasises, our global trade institutions (especially the GATT) have evolved as if there were no environmental linkages to trade; and recent environmental arrangements (such as the Montreal Protocol on CFCs) seem, from a trade policy viewpoint, to have given little thought to implementation and enforcement, suggesting non-environmental instruments may be resorted to in order to achieve environmental objectives. Global institutional evolution to reflect these linkages thus seems to be in its infancy, and the 1990s may well see institutional adaptation in this area, in addition to simply a heightened focus on issues.

University of Western Ontario

[15] Rubin and Graham (1982), p. 174, for instance, report cost differentials across countries for compliance with air pollution standards in different countries. These are based on a U.S. Commerce Department study published in 1975. For wood pulp, costs per ton may range from \$494 for U.S. firms, to \$13 for Canadian firms, and zero for Finnish firms. For copper, smelting costs are 6·6¢ per pound in the United States, as against 0·5¢ per pound in Peru and Chile.

[16] See the discussion in Rubin and Graham (1982), p. 165.

References

Cline, W. R. (1989). 'Political economy of the greenhouse effect.' Mimeo, Institute for International Economics, Washington, D.C. August.

Economist, The. March 17, 1990, pp. 45–7.

Economist, The. September 8–14, 1990, pp. 24–5.

Edmunds, J. and Reilly, J. (1983). 'Global energy and CO_2 to the year 2050.' *The Energy Journal*, vol. 4, no. 3, pp. 21–47.

GATT (1986). *The Text of The General Agreement on Tariffs and Trade*, p. 37. July, Geneva.

Flavin, C. (1990). 'Slowing global warming.' In *State of the World* (ed. Lester R. Brown). New York: W. W. Norton.

Leonard, H. J. (1988). *Pollution and the Struggle for the World Product*. Cambridge: Cambridge University Press.

Le Prestre, Philippe (1989). *The World Bank and the Environmental Challenge*, p. 181. Cranbury, New Jersey: Associated University Presses, Inc.

Low, Patrick (1990). 'United States Trade Policy and the future of the multilateral trading system.' Mimeo (July).

Manne, A. S. and Richels, R. G. (1990). 'Global CO_2 emission reductions – the impacts of rising energy costs.' Revised version of a paper presented to the International Association of Energy Economics, New Delhi (February). Mimeo.

Mansur, A. and Whalley, J. (1984). 'Numerical specification of applied general equilibrium models: estimation, calibration and data.' In *Applied General Equilibrium Analysis* (ed. J. B. Shoven and H. Scarf), pp. 69–127. Cambridge: Cambridge University Press.

Nordhaus, W. D. (1977). 'Economic growth and climate: the carbon dioxide problem.' *American Economic Review*, Papers and Proceedings (February), pp. 341–6.

—— (1990). 'A survey of estimates of the cost of reduction of greenhouse gas emissions.' Mimeo.

—— and Yohe, G. W. (1983). 'Future paths of energy and carbon dioxide emissions.' In *Changing Climate: Report of the Carbon Dioxide Assessment Committee*. National Research Council. Washington: National Academy Press.

Repetto, Robert and Gillis, Malcolm (eds) (1988). *Public Policies and the Misuse of Forest Resources*. Cambridge: Cambridge University Press.

Robertson, D. (1990). 'The global environment: are international treaties a distraction?' *The World Economy*, vol. 13, no. 1.

Rubin, S. J. and Graham, T. R. (1982). 'Summary and conclusions.' In *Environment and Trade* (ed. S. J. Rubin and T. R. Graham), p. 169. New Jersey: Allanheld, Osmun and Co. Publishers Inc.

Sankey, John (1989). 'Domestically prohibited goods and hazardous substances – a new GATT working group is established.' *Journal of World Trade*, vol. 23, no. 6, pp. 99–108.

Schneider, Stephen (1989). 'The greenhouse effect: science and policy.' *Science*, vol. 243 (February), pp. 771–81.

Shoven, J. and Whalley, J. (1984). 'Applied general equilibrium models of taxation and international trade: an introduction and survey.' *Journal of Economic Literature* (September), pp. 1007–51.

—— and —— (forthcoming). *Applying General Equilibrium*. Cambridge: Cambridge University Press.

Whalley, J. (1989). *The Uruguay Round and Beyond: The Final Report from the Ford Foundation Project on Developing Countries and the Global Trading System*. London: Macmillan.

—— and Wigle, R. (1989). 'Cutting CO_2 emissions: the effects of alternative policy approaches.' A paper presented to a conference on Applied General Equilibrium Modelling in San Diego, on September 8–9, 1989.

—— and —— (1990). 'The international incidence of carbon taxes.' Paper prepared for a conference on Economic Policy Responses to Global Warming organised by the Istituto Bancario Sao Paolo di Torino, to be held at Palazzo Colonna, Rome, October 4–6, 1990.

[4]

Trade Measures for Environment: A Nearly Empty Box?

Arvind Subramanian

1. INTRODUCTION

EVENTS in recent months have appeared to pitch trade and environment as antagonists in mutually destructive competition for the attention of policy makers. Of the forty-eight bills on environmental matters introduced in the 101st Congress in the United States, thirty-three contained provisions affecting international trade of which thirty-one took the form of restrictive trade measures, the implication clearly being that trade contraction rather than expansion is the appropriate means of advancing environmental objectives.[1]

With hindsight, however, the confluence of these twin concerns seems to have been inevitable. On the one hand, multilateral efforts at cooperation and negotiation have progressively embraced a number of internal (or non-border) policy instruments, which were hitherto regarded as somehow outside the purview of international trade policy. In the last ten years, for example, the GATT has gone much beyond addressing tariffs, quotas and other border measures to internal instruments such as standards, intellectual property rights, production subsidies, investment measures, etc.[2] Globalisation and the concomitant concern with international competitiveness, especially with the loss of it from allegedly unfair practices, have motivated this search for cooperative

---

ARVIND SUBRAMANIAN is an Economic Affairs Officer in the GATT Secretariat in Geneva. The views expressed in this paper are those of the author and should not be attributed to his employing organisation. This paper has benefited from discussions with Kym Anderson, Richard Blackhurst, Vijay Kelkar, Patrick Low, Adrian Otten and especially David Hartridge and Aaditya Mattoo.

[1] The perceived unfriendliness of freer trade to the cause of the environment is also reflected in proposals calling for a re-writing of GATT rules. See Shrybman (1989) and Arden-Clarke (1991).

[2] Strictly speaking the view that internal instruments are not regulated by the GATT is fallacious. Under the national treatment obligation — possibly the most important aspect of the 'non-discrimination principle' — every conceivable policy instrument is constrained so as to prevent protection from being accorded to domestically produced goods. What has not been regulated, but progressively being done is the *level* at which these instruments can be set — levels of production subsidies, of intellectual property protection, of standards etc.

solutions encompassing a wider range of policy instruments.[3] It was inevitable that environmental issues, given their intrinsically emotive nature, would be a prime candidate for espousal by the practitioners of the unfair trade rhetoric.

On the other hand, increasing scientific work brought squarely into the popular domain awareness of certain environmental problems which were truly global in nature and potentially far-reaching, even catastrophic, in their consequences. It was also inevitable that the search for multilateral solutions in the environmental area would rely on the use of trade measures as an inducement mechanism, given the track record of their effectiveness in areas ranging from human rights, workers' rights and arms control to services, intellectual property and competition policy. Thus the internationalisation of the environmental agenda and 'greenification' of the trade agenda have been parallel, though intimately related processes, where denouement will be the focus of attention in the years to come.

The purposes of this paper is two-fold. First, to ouline an exhaustive taxonomy of the interactions between trade policy and environmental problems; and second, on the basis of this taxonomy, to analyse the role that trade measures can play. The analysis will be both positive and normative.

2. TRADE AND ENVIRONMENT: A TAXONOMY

It is imperative to make the distinction, even though it may be impractical to operationalise it in all instances, between environmental problems whose effects are localised within the country where they arise — domestic environmental problems (DEPs), and others whose effects cross national boundaries — transborder environmental problems (TEPs).[4] The distinction is important to make because, as will become evident below, it will enable the protectionist use of environmental arguments to be distinguished from their more legitimate use. In other words, the distinction facilitates the identification and analysis of two distinct categories of issues — those related to competitiveness and others related to the environment *per se*.

The distinction between purely domestic environmental problems and those with cross-border effects can be attacked on at least two levels. First, it is argued that even physical pollution is never confined to one country, since the biosphere is an individual whole — an argument for which, in the moral sphere, John

[3] See Bhagwati (1990) for an analysis in relation to United States trade policy.

[4] The latter can in turn be bilateral (Mexican pollution spilling over into the United States), regional (the acid rain problem) or global (ozone layer, global warming). See Mäler (1990) for a taxonomy of transborder environmental problems. The discussion below suggests that this category encompasses the majority of problems currently being discussed.

Donne provides high authority but which offers a dangerously tenuous basis for intervention by a foreign government. A more powerful objection is that even where there is no physical spillover onto other countries, environmental problems or policies often have non-physical spillover effects, giving rise to aesthetic, ethical or moral concerns strong enough to compel attention and response from governments. Examples include destruction of animal species and perceived cruelty to animals. Nevertheless, I believe there is a valid distinction between problems which impact on other countries' environment and those which do not.

Table 1 summarises the various interactions between trade and environment in terms of the *types* of trade measures that can be taken. These are described under each of the two categories identified above and examples are provided for each situation. Trade measures broadly fall under three categories which are called *direct trade interventions*, *supporting trade provisions*, and *trade inducements* respectively. In turn, actions taken under each of these categories can be unilateral or multilateral. Although these categories are not always mutually exclusive and overlap in terms of the effect of trade measures, it is nevertheless useful to make the distinction for analytical purposes.[5]

a. Direct Trade Interventions

I have chosen to characterise as 'direct trade interventions' trade measures which impact directly on the perceived environmental problem. In TEP situations such measures are taken to correct environmental externalities, which may be non-physical; examples would be the anticipated trade restrictions against fur and related products caught in leghold traps (unilateral action) and the ban on ivory trade under the CITES Convention (multilateral action). In DEP situations such measures may be taken to compensate for loss of competitiveness caused, for example, by lower environmental standards in an exporting country. Examples of trade interventions to correct for environment-related competitiveness effects include the Boren proposal[6] for the automatic levying of countervailing duties on imports from countries with allegedly low pollution standards (alleged to be *de facto* subsidies) (unilateral action) and the border tax adjustment rules (multilateral action) under the GATT permitting the levying of tariffs on products on the domestic production of which an environment tax has been levied. Trade interventions will also have sanctions-like effects and often these might be important as they will be directed at the very actions which create the externality (see Section 4 below).

[5] See Blackhurst and Subramanian (1991) for an earlier attempt at a similar taxonomy.
[6] See Senator Boren's proposed Pollution Deterrence Act of 1991.

TABLE 1

Type of measure	Features	Transborder	Domestic
1. *Direct Trade Interventions*			
(a) Unilateral	Aimed to impact directly on the substantive problem: either the loss in competitiveness or the environmental externality; restrictive action will have penalising effects (incidental or otherwise) on actions creating the pollution.	(a) US import ban on Mexican Tuna, EC's threatened ban against exports of tropical timber and against fur products produced from animals caught in leghold traps.	(a) Countervailing duty against products produced under alleged 'low standards' (e.g. Boren Initiative). Export subsidies for pollution equipment.
(b) Multilateral		(b) Trade ban on Ivory and on several other endangered species under the CITES Convention. Trade restrictions in Basel Convention on Hazardous Wastes.	(b) Proposals in the Uruguay Round to exempt certain kinds of production subsidies for pollution abatement from countervailing action. Multilaterally sanctioned use of trade measures to offset production taxes imposed on environmental grounds as in the Superfund Panel Case.
2. *Supporting Trade Provisions*			
(a) Unilateral	Intended to enforce *other* actions or interventions, which address the substantive problem or externality; action by its nature will be in the related area and could have incidental penalising effects.	(a) Circle of Poison Act intended to stop exports of harmful pesticides on the grounds that they may be used in products which are reimported; import ban to enforce domestic consumption ban or domestic standards (e.g. Danish beer beer bottles case).	
(b) Multilateral		(b) Trade restrictions against non-signatories of Montreal Protocol. National actions that are sanctioned multilaterally.	
Trade Inducements			
3A. *Sanctions*:			
(a) Unilateral	Actions intended to change environmental behaviour and taken in *unrelated* areas: hence substitutable in principle by equivalent actions, e.g. financial sanctions for trade sanctions and technology transfer for trade incentives. Often sanctions will only be threatened and, if credible and effective, need not be taken.	(a) Pelly Amendment to US Fisherman's Protective Act of 1967 and Packward-Magnuson Amendment to the US Fisherman's Protective Act of 1967 under which imports of fish products in general can be restricted or prohibited. (e.g. Recent US action against Japan for policies endangering the sea turtle.)	(a) Use of trade restrictions to *raise* pollution standards abroad; use of trade restrictions to *lower* standards, e.g. threatened US action in Beef Hormone case.
(b) Multilateral		(b) None so far.	
3B. *Incentives*			
(a) Unilateral			
(b) Multilateral		(b) US-Mexico NAFTA negotiations for of market access in return for reduced transborder pollution.	(b) US-Mexico NAFTA negotiations for provision of market access in return for higher standards.

b. Supporting Trade Provisions

A trade measure can be characterised as a supporting trade provision when its function is to enforce another action, which is itself the substantive intervention; or in other words a trade provision is itself not the substantive intervention. A good example in the TEP category is the Montreal Protocol which provides for trade restrictions on CFC-related products against non-signatories. The substantive obligations or policy interventions envisaged under the Protocol are production and/or consumption related. The monitoring and restriction of trade with non-signatories ensures that the objectives of the agreement, namely the production and consumption obligations on signatories, are not circumvented or undermined.[7]

An example of a unilateral trade provision is the use of an import ban in order to enforce a domestic consumption ban. The law adopted by Denmark banning imports of soft drink bottled in non-reusable containers would thus be a trade provision used to enforce a domestic consumption ban. Similarly, the 'Circle of Poison Prevention Act', a proposal seeking to block exports of domestically banned pesticides on the grounds that they would be used on food grown abroad and re-imported, would also constitute a trade provision.

c. Trade Inducements (Carrot and Stick)

In their function as means, trade measures serve merely as instruments to induce (in a positive) (carrot) or negative (stick) sense) changes in environmental behaviour of other countries. In this role, trade actions are taken in *unrelated* products. By definition trade action under the other two categories has to be directed at the product in question. Here trade measures serve as punishments and/or rewards to induce others to participate in and subsequently comply with international environmental agreements or to change their environmental standards on competitiveness grounds. What is often not sufficiently recognised (or at least not translated into practice) is that in their role as inducements, trade measures are in principle substitutable by other measures — financial, technological, diplomatic, military etc. and it is not always evident as to why one form ought to be preferred to another. Another feature of trade

[7] The distinction between trade provisions and interventions is highlighted if we consider the trade ban on ivory. Several authors have argued that the optimal policy intervention to preserve the elephant population is a series of measures by ivory producing countries including the formation of a producers' cartel combined with better design of property rights to create the right incentives to invest in the maintenance of elephants as an asset. They envisage, however, that consuming countries would not import from those producers which did not follow the policy interventions envisaged. Such import restrictions would constitute trade provisions as their primary role would be to enforce other optimal policy interventions; the current ban on ivory trade is, however, seen by some as the optimal intervention. See Barbier et al. (1990).

inducments is that they need not always be used: often the *threatened* use of sanctions is sufficient to alter behaviour if this is seen as credible, and effective in the sense that it would impose costs on the victim which are sufficiently high to induce the desired change in behaviour.

Trade inducements can be further divided into trade *sanctions* and trade *incentives*. An example of trade sanctions under the TEP category is the Pelly Amendment which authorises trade restrictions in a whole range of unrelated products for failure by a country to observe United States' standards for tuna fishing methods. Similarly, the United States' threat to impose trade restrictions against Japan for its over-use of hawksbill sea turtles is another example of the role of trade sanctions. Sanctions could equally be used in cases not involving transborder spillovers. Countries might use sanctions to change the pollution standards of others because they are considered to be too low thus conferring competitive advantage. Alternatively, sanctions might be used on grounds that standards are too high as happened when the United States threatened to withdraw concessions against the EC for its standards on hormone in beef products which the United States alleged to be a non-tariff barrier to trade.[8]

However, inducements to change behaviur could also take the form of *trade incentives*: although few examples spring to mind, it could plausibly be argued that the NAFTA exercise involves, albeit implicitly, the use of incentives in the form of increased market access to Mexico in return for raising its environmental standards.[9]

A final distinction, one that will not be discussed, is worth bearing in mind in relation to the category of trade inducements. Trade sanctions can be used to *induce* participation in multilateral rule-making, but they could also be used to *sustain* it in the event of deviation from the agreed rules. Where incentives are used to secure cooperation, sanctions would consist of the withdrawal of such incentives. Under the GATT the possibility of retaliation in the form of withdrawal of existing concessions might be thought of as a means of sustaining cooperation by penalising defectors from the agreement. However, examples of

---

[8] Supporting trade provisions (category 2 above) may also have a sanctions-like effect. The trade restrictions against non-signatories envisaged by the Montreal Protocol have a penalising function. Non-signatories are worse off as a result of the trade restrictions because as importers and exporters of CFC products they are denied respectively, access to cheapest sources of supplies and to markets. However, the trade restrictions in the original protocol were not strong enough as sanctions to induce participation by at least two of the major consumers of CFC products; other inducements (in the form of the technology transfer fund) were required to achieve this objective.

[9] There are more examples of non-trade incentives being used in the environment area. An example of the provision of multilateral financial incentives is the creation in 1990 of the United Nations Environmental Fund through which certain international agencies would ensure that globally appropriate environmental policies would be pursued in developing countries. Similarly, the technology fund in the Montreal Protocol is an incentive mechanism.

trade sanctions to sustain cooperation in the environment area are more difficult to come by.[10]

3. DOMESTIC ENVIRONMENTAL PROBLEMS

As argued earlier, it was inevitable that differences in standards of pollution and pollution control or rate of exploitation of environmental resources would become causes for remedial trade action on grounds of unfair competition. As the taxonomy shows there are several possible trade responses to this 'problem'. However, before examining each it is worth asking what the alleged problem is which needs action. Comparative advantage is predicated on the existence of *differences* between countries — differences in factor endowments, preferences and technology. The familiar gains from trade or from international specialisation derive from this difference. In this picture.the environment is one element of possible difference between countries. A country could have a greater endowment of environmental resources or a greater pollution assimilation capacity than another. Equally its social preferences could be different from the others leading to a lower valuation of environmental goods (including for example through high rates of time preference) or even of human resources (in the form of lower health and safety standards). In the eyes of the proponents of unfair trade these differences constitute 'problems' because they give rise to differences in competitiveness and far from being celebrated as creating opportunities for international specialisation are sought to be nullified through remedial action. The logical culmination of this line of thought would be to attack *any* difference in endowment, technology or preference as being symptomatic of unfair competitive advantage and to eradicate any trade created therefrom.[11]

Apart from being protectionist *per se*, it is also vulnerable to the slippery slope argument: with equal consistency arguments could be advanced for remedial action against lax population policy (as this might be seen as leading to low wages and increased competitiveness), differing standards on workers' rights, education and health. The more disconcerting question that is not posed, but which ought to be, is whether, on this line of reasoning, technological advantage should not also be seen as conferring unfair competitive advantage thus warranting trade action by the technological laggards? The risks and the costs in national and global welfare terms of going down this path are immense.

[10] However, non-trade punishment mechanisms can be found in some international environmental agreements such as the North Pacific Fur Seal Treaty under which deviation by one signatory can elicit withdrawal by another leading to the eventual termination of the agreement.

[11] A recent safeguard action was justified with appealing frankness on the grounds that the price of imports was lower than that of domestic competitors!

Thus where there are no physical spillovers, and this is an important caveat, there ought to be a serious presumption against the use of trade restrictive action — be it in the form of contingent protection action (e.g. countervailing or anti-dumping duty), competitive subsidisation *or* attempts to harmonise pollution standards.

However, even if it were admitted that differential environmental policies were a source of unfair competitive advantage, the empirical picture is not very supportive of the need for trade action. A number of studies show that even in the most pollution intensive industries, pollution abatement costs constitute a very small fraction (between one and three per cent) of total industry costs — hardly the sort of margin by which competitive advantage is conferred or 'injury' caused.[12]

Table 1 shows that there are several ways in which action on environment-related competitiveness grounds can be taken: first, to impose countervailing duties on products alleged to have been subsidised abroad either directly through the provision of environment-related subsidies or through the institution of a regime of low environmental standards or to provide offsetting environment-related subsidies to domestic producers in competition with such products: second, to change the other country's standard through the use of sanctions; and finally, where environmental action in one's own country is being taken, trade action to offset any consequent loss in competitiveness in the home market or in third country markets.

In terms of attaining the 'desired' objective of nullifying loss in competitiveness, a welfare ranking of the alternative instruments is possible: countervailing action is likely to be most distortionary as it raises domestic prices and does not help domestic producers in third country markets. Production subsidies would avoid these problems but would entail budgetary costs. From a national welfare viewpoint a first-best situation would result if the other country changed its standards especially if this can be accomplished costlessly, without resource transfers. But, from a global welfare point of view the main question is whether the *objectives* of such actions are justifiable given that they are predicated on notions of unfairness which are questionable and whose logical extension would lead to the negation of the very basis of international trade.

One of the ironies in the current view that existing trade arrangements somehow impede the pursuit of sensible environmental policies is that a closer

[12] Tobey (1990) finds, for example, that strict environmental regulations imposed in the 1960s and 1970s by industrialised countries have not measurably affected trade patterns in the *most polluting industries*, which are defined as those for which direct and indirect abatement costs account for greater than 1.85 per cent of total costs. The most polluting industry — chemicals — faced abatement costs equal to 2.89 per cent of total costs. For similar results in the case of Mexico, see Low (1991).

scrutiny might well point to the opposite conclusion. This is illustrated in the ruling of the GATT Superfund dispute which sanctioned the levying of an equivalent border tax on products the domestic production of which had been subject to a tax on environmental grounds. The implications of this ruling are two-fold. First, it suggests that any purely domestic objectives, in this instance an environmental objective, can be pursued without having to suffer the adverse international competitiveness implications because the latter can be neutralised, at least partially by an equivalent tax on the imported product. The important condition for access to the border-tax instrument is that the domestic tax be on a *product*. A second implication is that if the pollution is caused by a process rather than a product, domestic industry would lobby in favour of a *product* tax because of the attractiveness that it would offer in blunting the adverse competitiveness consequences. An inefficiency results, namely that of the choice of the second-best instrument — product rather than process tax — in relation to the given environmental externality.[13]

4. TRANSBORDER ENVIRONMENTAL PROBLEMS

In this section it will be argued that allegations regarding the incompatibility of freer trade and desirable environmental outcomes are misplaced. To anticipate the arguments, trade interventions especially when taken unilaterally are *inefficient* in attaining globally superior environmental outcomes; to put it another way, there are more efficient ways of achieving the same result. Furthermore, the use of unilateral trade sanctions is an *inequitable* way of pursuing what may well be desirable outcomes. Their availability might militate against the search for cooperative solutions, and also bias the nature of such solutions in terms of adversely affecting resource flows to low-income countries. Here again the opposition between trade and environment is a false one. The distinction is rather between unilateral and cooperative approaches to solving environmental problems. There might be a role for trade measures but only in the context of sustaining cooperative outcomes.

a. Trade Interventions and Environmental Externalities

All environmental externalities be they domestic or transborder arise from some kind of market failure which includes imperfectly functioning markets or their very absence.[14] The choice of appropriate policy instruments to correct externalities in a domestic context is the subject of a growing body of

[13] See also Sorsa in this issue.
[14] See Dasgupta (1990).

literature.[15] The relevant instruments range from Pigouvian taxes and subsidies, to assignment of property rights, regulatory instruments and emissions trading.

From the point of view of *global efficiency*, and leaving aside equity considerations, optimum intervention or the choice of appropriate intervention to correct the market failure is independent of whether the problem is domestic or transborder. The intuition underlying the theory of domestic distortions is that, in the absence of other distortions, the further removed the intervening instrument is from the source of the distortion the less efficient it is likely to be. Thus trade-based interventions are generally likely to be second-best instruments to correct the market failure relative to the production and consumption-based instruments mentioned above. (See Anderson, 1991; and Snape, 1991.)

The *extent* of the inappropriateness of trade interventions, i.e. the extent to which they are removed from the source of market failure arising in the context of environmental problems can be gauged from the following examples. Where the cause of the pollution is a process, a trade tax is at least twice removed from the optimum intervention. In the case of pollution stemming from carbon emissions a trade intervention is even further removed (a trade tax on carbon-containing products would be dominated by a production or consumption tax on such products; in turn this would be inferior to a tax on carbon emissions from factories, with the optimum instrument being a tax on the carbon content of fuel). Similarly, problems relating to *stocks* require intervention which corrects the relevant intertemporal externalities — imperfect or incorrect assignment of property rights, high rates of time preference leading to excessive depletion.[16] For some resources the problem may be a lack of markets. Existence value, the value attached by consumers to the knowledge that certain species exist even though they may never see them, is often not marketable. Over-exploitation, therefore, results because resource owners are not remunerated for some of the benefits they confer on others. Here too, trade actions will be an inappropriate instrument. Finally, in relation to environmental resources such as species of plants whose future value is unknown and which once destroyed cannot be recovered (irreversible), optimal intervention would require a mixture of proper assignment of property rights and even macroeconomic policy.[17] In the absence of a common identification or recognition of a problem, either because of conflicting social preferences or of lack of agreement on the scientific evidence,

[15] See Muzando, Miranda and Bovenberg (1990).

[16] See Barbier et al. (1990) for an analysis of the problem of depletion of elephant stocks in which the case against the desirability of trade interventions in an intertemporal context is argued.

[17] See Binswanger (1991) who argues that Brazilian deforestation is attributable largely to bad macroeconomic policy.

unilateral trade actions notably in relation to the more complex problems are likely to have very uncertain effects.[18]

The foregoing analysis has assumed away what might be seen as the key problem in relation to transborder externalities, namely that of distinct sovereignties trying to gain advantage, through the use of trade actions, at the expense of others. In other words, a concern with global efficiency or welfare neglects the fact that the allocation of that welfare amongst countries might lead to a situation less advantageous for some than what might be achieved through the use of trade actions. It is in relation to this question that trade sanctions play a key role.

b. Trade Sanctions

It has been one of the singular features of recent trade policy that the threatened or actual use of trade sanctions has been an important instrument to secure bilateral or multilateral cooperation in several areas of international policy making — in services, intellectual property, competition policy etc. At the outset a clear distinction needs to be made between trade sanctions used to induce cooperation, where such cooperation in the form of multilateral agreements governing environmental action does not already exist (*unilateral* trade sanctions — the main focus of this section) and sanctions which are needed to sustain such agreements and serve the role of securing compliance with actions agreed upon (*multilateral* trade sanctions).

With increasing evidence and recognition that environmental problems involve more than one country, attention is turning to finding cooperative solutions to these problems. The absence of a supranational enforcement authority implies that national jurisdiction and sovereignty must be respected. Consequently, any mechanism for securing cooperation must be self-enforcing in the sense that compliance with rules must be forthcoming voluntarily. This, however, may not always be easy, as there may be inherent contradictions between the individual (national) good and the collective (international) good exemplified in the famous prisoner's dilemma.[19]

In general, there are two ways of improving the incentives for countries to cooperate on international environmental issues. The first is by providing compensation to countries for their cooperation, and the second by threatening

[18] If the assumption that there are no other distortions does not hold, the inappropriateness of trade intervention cannot be presumed. A case-by-case determination would have to be made, but even then, given the enormous complexity of many environmental problems, trade interventions are unlikely to be the most appropriate instruments. See Anderson (1991). As Low and Safadi (1991) point out, in the hasty search for 'new' trade-based solutions, the environmental unfriendliness of prior non-trade interventions is inadequately examined.

[19] See Dasgupta (1990). The discussion in this section draws on the analysis in Blackhurst and Subramanian (1991).

coercive action in the event of non-cooperation — the sanctions approach.[20] The most important difference between these two is the effect on the distribution of welfare. The compensation route results in a higher level of welfare for the country whose cooperation is sought (and secured) than the level which would have prevailed had cooperation been secured through the threat of sanctions. Mcmillan (1990) shows that in a bargaining game a bargainer's payoff is higher, *ceteris paribus*, the worse is the opponent's alternative in the event of a breakdown in the bargain (formally described as the 'outside option'). The threat of sanctions affects the terms of agreement by worsening the opponent's payoffs in the event of non-cooperation rendering him in a 'weaker' bargaining position and allowing the user of the threat to appropriate a larger share of the cake. The import of this result is that if *unilateral* trade sanctions were permitted as a legitimate response to TEPs, in the subsequent *multilateral bargain*, their user could appropriate a larger share of the cake from, or alternatively could transfer a lower amount of resources to, the country whose cooperation is being secured. Therefore the greatest fear of unilateral trade sanctions is not necessarily that it would lead to protectionism (often it does not as sanctions are more often threatened than used), but that it might affect significantly the flow of resources especially to those developing countries whose cooperation would be important in securing viable and efficient multilateral environmental agreements.[21]

These two approaches seem, at first glance, to have analogies in the literature on the environment in terms of the polluter pays principle (PPP) and the victim pays principle (VPP). In an international context they imply respectively that the polluting and polluted (victim) nation should bear the costs of controlling or preventing the transborder pollution.

But the PPP/VPP distinction is very problematic to apply at the multilateral level. In relation to environmental flow problems such as the pollution of a river crossing borders it might be easy to distinguish the polluter and the victim. But in relation to several environmental problems such as the depletion of the ozone layer and greenhouse gas build up, which involve stocks, and those involving non-physical spillovers such as species preservation, 'cruelty' to animals, the very determination of polluter and victim becomes difficult. Indeed, the search for cooperative solutions through international negotiations involves decisions

[20] It is somewhat surprising to see that the environmental literature appears to take for granted that cooperation would require the payment of compensation (see e.g. Mäler, 1990; and Barrett, 1990) to polluting countries while appearing to ignore the recent history (which trade policy analysts are more aware of) of the use of sanctions to promote cooperation. On the latter, see Mcmillan (1990).

[21] This ignores the adverse effects of threatened sanctions on the *efficiency* of bargaining outcomes which could include counter-retaliation and the breakdown of cooperative bargaining and the weaker incentives that a country would have in abiding by the bargain if it feels that its cooperation has been secured through coercive means. See Bhagwati (1990) and Mcmillan (1990).

regarding the appropriate allocation of the costs of pollution abatement between countries based in part on a prior collective determination as to who is the polluter and who the victim and who should be accorded property rights.

A look at the current controversy in relation to the greenhouse gas problem clarifies this point. Alternative proposals have been put forward for the obligations — in terms of carbon emission reductions — that countries should be expected to assume.[22] On a static, marginal view of net carbon emissions, China and India would rank high among the category of polluters and an application of PPP might require greater reduction by these countries (or alternatively a smaller initial allocation of tradeable carbon permits). On the other hand, in the same situation, an application of VPP would require either lower levels of environmental obligations or greater levels of net resource flows to these countries. Here the application of VPP would stem from extraneous considerations, i.e. *despite* their being deemed to be polluters, global equity or population considerations might justify such resource flows.

However, if an intertemporal view were taken of the carbon emission problem, i.e. viewing the pollution of the atmosphere as a *stock* problem due to the emission of greenhouse gases over several hundred years, an application of PPP itself would necessitate net resource flows accruing to the countries mentioned above. In other words, compensation need not always reflect VPP: it might equally reflect PPP depending on the definition of polluter.[23]

A similar problem arises as regards flows of environmental services from certain environmental resources located within national boundaries, on which there are differences of opinion about the obligations of the rest of the world to pay for those services. A good example is the Amazon forest, which Brazil views as a national resource rendering environmental services to the rest of the world in the form of carbon absorption and species variety. Accordingly, Brazil could ask to be paid by the rest of the world for these international flows of services (or, in what amounts to the same thing, it could ask for compensation for the preservation of the forest). The other view is that these services of the

[22] In the context of the possible institution of a system of internationally tradable permits for carbon emissions, for example, it has been suggested that such permits be allocated on a *per capita* basis. Another approach advocated by some countries is that the allocation of future property rights in the context of the global warming problem should be inversely related to a country's cumulative contribution to the stock of greenhouse gases over the last hundred or more years. The argument in this case is that there should be some intertemporal equity in the right to emit sustainable amounts of waste into the atmosphere and hence in the right to future growth opportunities. A third option would be for each country to reduce current carbon emissions by an equal percentage — a proposal which implicitly allocates rights to discharge carbon into the atmosphere on a first come, first served basis. The income distributional implications of these various proposals — between different groups within a country, as well as between countries — are sizeable and thus could be expected to have a major impact on the willingness of particular countries to participate in an agreement to reduce the emission of greenhouse gases.

[23] Mäler (1990) and Low and Safadi (1991) for example tend to equate compensation with VPP.

Amazon forest are a universal resource. On this view, the world has a right to the forest's preservation and conversely its destruction should result in the rest of the world being compensated by Brazil.

Species preservation and allegations of cruelty to animals raise conflicts arising from differing societal valuations and preferences. Here too, international cooperation is meant to address the question of property rights. Is there a right to kill or not to kill dolphins, a right to catch animals in leghold traps or not? Should Mexican fisherman be penalised or threatened with penalties for *purse seine* net fishing or be compensated for having to desist from the activity or to use more expensive alternative technologies? The magnitude and direction of resource flows depends crucially on answers to these questions.

What the foregoing has illustrated is that in relation to transborder problems: (a) the use of sanctions or compensation determines crucially the resource flows or the share of the global welfare cake accruing to different countries; (b) this share depends on resolving questions relating to who is the polluter or victim or free-rider and as to who should have the property rights? This latter should be determined through cooperative means. Legitimising unilateral sanctions would amount to allowing unilateral determination as to who is the polluter and also as to who should have the property rights.

An important point which should not be overlooked is the effect that resource transfers themselves will have on global environmental quality. Evidence suggests that environmental quality and income levels are highly correlated; poverty and low incomes have been shown to crucially determine environmental degradation especially in relation to forest resources. The sanctions route thus carries with it the heavy cost that smaller resource transfers to low income developing countries would lead to further environmental degradation.

There is a parallel between the role of ecological arguments in relation to DEPs and to TEPs. In the former, several coalitions, including domestic industries and labour groups, are likely to hitch their wagon to the ecological star to secure or legitimise protectionist outcomes. In the case of TEPs, ecological arguments by tending to elevate the sanctity of certain outcomes — not to kill dolphins, not to burn forests — implicitly shape the determination of the international allocation of property rights by deeming the perpetrators of these acts as polluters. This favours the use of the sanctions rather than the compensation route to securing cooperation, adversely affecting the flow of resources to certain low-income environmentally abundant countries.[24] The risk of protectionism in relation to DEPs thus has a counterpart in eco-imperialism in relation to TEPs. In the former, groups with economic interests capture ecological arguments and in the latter, groups with environmental interests

[24] Thus, even if greater resources are transferred, it is seen as happening *despite* 'bad' environmental behaviour.

capture (the phenomenon of 'reverse capture') trade instruments to secure their objectives.

However, the foregoing discussion should not be interpreted as ruling out the use of sanctions altogether. There are, at least, two examples of situations where the use of trade sanctions might be appropriate. First, to induce cooperation where it has been established in the course of multilateral efforts to attain such cooperation that some countries are 'genuinely' free-riding. Establishing who is a true free-rider would probably be difficult, given the necessarily subjective nature of such judgements,[25] but a stronger case can be made for such an evaluation if the cooperative route has been explored than if it has not. Second, sanctions are probably necessary to enforce or sustain multilateral agreements — a credible threat of punishment (which would take the form of the withdrawal of the benefits of cooperation) would be effective in securing compliance with any agreement.

Nothing in the foregoing discussion has suggested that the threat of sanctions to induce changes in environmental behaviour should necessarily take the form of *trade* sanctions. And yet recent history shows that trade sanctions are the most often used instruments. The attractiveness of directed trade sanctions in the form of restrictions on the very product that creates the externality (import restrictions in tuna, import restrictions on tropical timber), is easy to see. They can be directed at the very economic agents who are responsible for creating the externality and the larger the import market the greater the magnitude of the penalty faced by such agents. The country taking the action does not have to rely on the intermediary services of the other government to influence the externality-creating agents as it would if financial sanctions were to be used.

But often trade sanctions take the form of restrictions on unrelated products which are therefore no different from, say, financial sanctions in terms of their effect. Indeed, in a welfare comparison between the use of financial sanctions and trade sanctions on unrelated products, the former may well be superior as they would not create the by-product distortions that trade sanctions would.[26] The revealed attractiveness of trade sanctions reflects, therefore, political economy according disproportionate influence to the pressure of sectional interests. In other words, the supply of trade sanctions is only too readily forthcoming and the threat of their use is seen to be credible despite its welfare consequences. This facilitates 'reverse' capture: the very ease of supply of trade

[25] This is related to the point about how 'multilateral' participation in an agreement should be, in order to decide whether non-participants are 'free-riding'. Sanctions against non-participants must always be somewhat arbitrary but are more defensible if membership is wide enough to establish a credible international consensus.

[26] More recently, there have been signs of use of the aid mechanism as sanctions: for example, Japan has begun to attach environmental guidelines to aid-funded projects. Similarly, a World Bank loan to Brazil in 1985 was interrupted because of fears expressed by environmental groups that it might aggravate deforestation.

sanctions leads to their use in furthering environmental objectives and creates a bias against the search for other forms (including through compensation) of securing cooperation.

On the other hand, it has to be admitted that if the success of trade sanctions or other forms of unilateralism diminishes interest in reaching negotiated solutions on the part of countries able to use them, they have been effective in bringing other countries to the negotiating table, even though, as suggested above, the results of such negotiations under the threat of sanctions may be less than optimal in equity terms.

c. *Supporting Trade Provisions*

As defined above, trade provisions serve the purpose of enforcing rules — national or multilateral, and are not intrinsic to correcting the given environmental externality. At the national level, import restrictions are often used to enforce domestic consumption bans or domestic standards.[27] For example, it is clear that a ban on domestic smoking would require the prohibition of imported cigarettes and that compliance with domestic emission standards would require a ban on cars not fitted with the appropriate catalytic convertor. But such unilateral actions are permitted under existing trading rules because they would meet the national treatment standard requiring equivalent treatment of domestic and imported products.[28] Similarly, trade provisions in multilateral agreements serve the function of ensuring their effectiveness as has been argued in the case of the Montreal Protocol. As long as the substantive

---

[27] Of course, there are cases, arising notably in relation to packaging requirements, where there might be concerns regarding standards becoming *de facto* restrictions despite their consonance with the non-discrimination principle.

[28] At the national level, measures that attempt to enforce domestic *process* standards by action against imported goods produced abroad under similar conditions might run foul of trading rules as the recent case between the United States and Mexico on the use of 'purse seine nets' has shown. However, it could be contended that there is a grey area of uncertainty arising in connection with certain kinds of trade provisions used to enforce domestic process standards. Consider the case where certain processes for the killing of animals in the production of meat for consumption (clearly therefore production methods) are disallowed domestically on grounds that they offend religious sentiments. A prohibition on the import of such meat might well be defended on the grounds that it is necessary to protect public morals in the country of importation and Article XX(a) of the General Agreement (a much overlooked provision) could be invoked. A case could be made that the logic of this example should be extended to other activities — chicken rearing, methods of catching animals or preparing products — that similarly offended aesthetic, ethical or religious sentiments. In such cases the problem arises as to how to circumscribe the domain of what constitutes legitimate grounds for offence. The slippery slope argument looms in the background — another country's health and labour standards might also be argued as offending a society's morals or sentiments and safeguards against the protectionist abuse of these arguments might be difficult to specify. A less contentious approach to these problems might be the use of labelling requirements which would allow consumers the freedom to exercise their preference against eco-unfriendly products or processes if they so wished.

interventions designed to correct the externality are appropriate and collectively agreed upon, the use of supporting trade provisions might have a useful role to play.

5. CONCLUSION

This paper has characterised the nature of trade policy measures which can be employed in relation to environmental problems. The conclusions that might be derived are the following. First, in relation to domestic environmental problems (i.e. where there are no spillovers across countries) the use of trade measures is flawed because it is largely protectionist in intent. They are aimed at negating the very source of comparative advantage which could legitimately be conferred by differences in environmental endowments, pollution assimilation capacities or social preferences regarding environmental outcomes. There is also the attendant risk captured in the 'slippery slope' argument: what source of comparative advantage is legitimate and not actionable under the garb of unfair trade? Would any outcome other than the eradication of trade or managed trade be immune to the accusation of unfairness?

Second, in relation to transborder environmental problems it was seen that trade interventions were *inefficient* instruments in correcting the market failures creating the environmental problem. Production or consumption interventions, creation of markets and proper assignment of property rights are likely to be more appropriate instruments of corrective action. It was also seen that unilateral trade sanctions were *inequitable* when used in the context of transborder problems as they permit unilateral determination of the international allocation of property rights and hence of the magnitude and direction of resource flows in a manner which is likely to be adverse for low-income countries. Insofar as there are strong and proven links between levels of income and environmental quality, the use of sanctions to secure cooperation may have further undesirable effects on environmental quality. However, the use of trade restrictive measures need not be entirely precluded: they might serve a useful role in securing compliance with multilateral agreements or even in inducing 'true' free-riders to assume greater obligations. Thus the opposition is not between freer trade and desirable environmental outcomes, but rather between unilateralism and multilateralism. Trade restrictions can be necessary or even desirable but only in the latter context, which allows truly cooperative solutions to be explored and secured.

REFERENCES

Anderson, K. (1991), 'Effects of Trade and Environmental Policies on the Environment and Welfare' in K. Anderson and R. Blackhurst (ed.), *The Greening of World Trade Issues* (Harvester-Wheatsheaf).

Arden-Clarke, C. (1991), 'The General Agreement on Tariffs and Trade, Environmental Protection and Sustainable Development', *World Wildlife Fund Discussion Paper.*

Barbier, E., J. Burgess, T. Swanson and D. Pearce (1990), *Elephants, Economies and Ivory* (London).

Barrett, S. (1990), 'The Problem of Global Environmental Protection', *Oxford Review of Economic Policy* 6, 68-79.

Barrett, S. (1991), 'The Paradox of International Environmental Agreements', mimeo (London Business School, January).

Bhagwati, J.N. (1990), 'Aggressive Unilateralism: An Overview', *Aggressive Unilateralism: America's 301 Trade Policy and the World Trading System*, J.N. Bhagwati and H.T. Patrick (eds.) (London: Harvester-Wheatsheaf).

Binswanger, H.P. (1991), 'Brazilian Policies that Encourage Deforestation in the Amazon', *World Development*, 19, 7, 821-830.

Blackhurst, R. and A. Subramanian (1991), 'Promoting Multilateral Cooperation on the Environment' in *The Greening of World Trade Issues*, K. Anderson and R. Blackhurst (eds.) (Harvester-Wheatsheaf).

Dasgupta, P.S. (1990), 'The Environment as a Commodity', *Oxford Review of Economic Policy* 6, 51-67.

GATT (1986), *The Text of The General Agreement on Tariffs and Trade* (Geneva).

Low, P. (1991), 'Trade Measures and Environmental Quality: The Implications for Mexico's Exports', mimeo (World Bank).

Low, P. and R. Safadi (1991), 'Trade Policy and Pollution', mimeo (World Bank, Washington DC).

Mäler, K.-G. (1990), 'International Environmental Problems', *Oxford Review of Economic Policy* 6, 80-108.

Mcmillan, J. (1990), 'Strategic Bargaining and Section 301' in *Aggressive Unilateralism: America's 301 Trade Policy and the World Trading System*, J.N. Bhagwati and H.T. Patrick (eds.) (London, Harvester-Wheatsheaf).

Muzando, T.R., K.M. Miranda and A.L. Bovenberg (1990), 'Public Policy and the Environment: A Survey of the Literature', *IMF Fiscal Affairs Department Working Paper 56.*

Shrybman, S. (1989), 'International Trade and the Environment: An Environmental Assessment of Present GATT Negotiations', Canadian *Environmental Law Association* (October).

Snape, R. (1991), 'The Environment, International Trade, and Competitiveness', forthcoming in K. Anderson and R. Blackhurst (ed.) *The Greening of World Trade Issues*, Harvester-Wheatsheaf.

Sorsa, P. (1992), 'GATT and Environment', *The World Economy*, 15, 1,

Tobey, J.A. (1990), 'The Effects of Domestic Environmental Policies on Patterns of World Trade: An Empirical Test', *Kyklos*, 43, 2, 191-210.

Journal of Economic Perspectives—Volume 9, Number 4—Fall 1995—Pages 97–118

Toward a New Conception of the Environment-Competitiveness Relationship

Michael E. Porter and Claas van der Linde

The relationship between environmental goals and industrial competitiveness has normally been thought of as involving a tradeoff between social benefits and private costs. The issue was how to balance society's desire for environmental protection with the economic burden on industry. Framed this way, environmental improvement becomes a kind of arm-wrestling match. One side pushes for tougher standards; the other side tries to beat the standards back.

Our central message is that the environment-competitiveness debate has been framed incorrectly. The notion of an inevitable struggle between ecology and the economy grows out of a static view of environmental regulation, in which technology, products, processes and customer needs are all fixed. In this static world, where firms have already made their cost-minimizing choices, environmental regulation inevitably raises costs and will tend to reduce the market share of domestic companies on global markets.

However, the paradigm defining competitiveness has been shifting, particularly in the last 20 to 30 years, away from this static model. The new paradigm of international competitiveness is a dynamic one, based on innovation. A body of research first published in *The Competitive Advantage of Nations* has begun to address these changes (Porter, 1990). Competitiveness at the industry level arises from superior productivity, either in terms of lower costs than rivals or the ability to offer products

■ *Michael E. Porter is the C. Roland Christensen Professor of Business Administration, Harvard Business School, Boston, Massachusetts. Claas van der Linde is on the faculty of the International Management Research Institute of St. Gallen University, St. Gallen, Switzerland.*

with superior value that justify a premium price.[1] Detailed case studies of hundreds of industries, based in dozens of countries, reveal that internationally competitive companies are not those with the cheapest inputs or the largest scale, but those with the capacity to improve and innovate continually. (We use the term innovation broadly, to include a product's or service's design, the segments it serves, how it is produced, how it is marketed and how it is supported.) Competitive advantage, then, rests not on static efficiency nor on optimizing within fixed constraints, but on the capacity for innovation and improvement that shift the constraints.

This paradigm of dynamic competitiveness raises an intriguing possibility: in this paper, we will argue that properly designed environmental standards can trigger innovation that may partially or more than fully offset the costs of complying with them. Such "innovation offsets," as we call them, can not only lower the net cost of meeting environmental regulations, but can even lead to absolute advantages over firms in foreign countries not subject to similar regulations. Innovation offsets will be common because reducing pollution is often coincident with improving the productivity with which resources are used. In short, firms can actually benefit from properly crafted environmental regulations that are more stringent (or are imposed earlier) than those faced by their competitors in other countries. By stimulating innovation, strict environmental regulations can actually enhance competitiveness.

There is a legitimate and continuing controversy over the social benefits of specific environmental standards, and there is a huge benefit-cost literature. Some believe that the risks of pollution have been overstated; others fear the reverse. Our focus here is not on the social benefits of environmental regulation, but on the private costs. Our argument is that whatever the level of social benefits, these costs are far higher than they need to be. The policy focus should, then, be on relaxing the tradeoff between competitiveness and the environment rather than accepting it as a given.

The Link from Regulation to Promoting Innovation

It is sometimes argued that companies must, by the very notion of profit seeking, be pursuing all profitable innovations. In the metaphor economists often cite, $10 bills will never be found on the ground because someone would have already picked them up. In this view, if complying with environmental regulation can be profitable, in the sense that a company can more than offset the cost of compliance, then why is such regulation necessary?

[1] At the industry level, the meaning of competitiveness is clear. At the level of a state or nation, however, the notion of competitiveness is less clear because no nation or state is, or can be, competitive in everything. The proper definition of competitiveness at the aggregate level is the average *productivity* of industry or the value created per unit of labor and per dollar of capital invested. Productivity depends on both the quality and features of products (which determine their value) and the efficiency with which they are produced.

The possibility that regulation might act as a spur to innovation arises because the world does not fit the Panglossian belief that firms always make optimal choices. This will hold true only in a static optimization framework where information is perfect and profitable opportunities for innovation have already been discovered, so that profit-seeking firms need only choose their approach. Of course, this does not describe reality. Instead, the actual process of dynamic competition is characterized by changing technological opportunities coupled with highly incomplete information, organizational inertia and control problems reflecting the difficulty of aligning individual, group and corporate incentives. Companies have numerous avenues for technological improvement, and limited attention.

Actual experience with energy-saving investments illustrates that in the real world, $10 bills are waiting to be picked up. As one example, consider the "Green Lights" program of the Environmental Protection Agency. Firms volunteering to participate in this program pledge to scrutinize every avenue of electrical energy consumption. In return, they receive advice on efficient lighting, heating and cooling operations. When the EPA collected data on energy-saving lighting upgrades reported by companies as part of the Green Lights program, it showed that nearly 80 percent of the projects had paybacks of two years or less (DeCanio, 1993). Yet only after companies became part of the program, and benefitted from information and cajoling from the EPA, were these highly profitable projects carried out. This paper will present numerous other examples of where environmental innovation produces net benefits for private companies.[2]

We are currently in a transitional phase of industrial history where companies are still inexperienced in dealing creatively with environmental issues. The environment has not been a principal area of corporate or technological emphasis, and knowledge about environmental impacts is still rudimentary in many firms and industries, elevating uncertainty about innovation benefits. Customers are also unaware of the costs of resource inefficiency in the packaging they discard, the scrap value they forego and the disposal costs they bear. Rather than attempting to innovate in every direction at once, firms in fact make choices based on how they perceive their competitive situation and the world around them. In such a world, regulation can be an important influence on the direction of innovation, either for better or for worse. Properly crafted environmental regulation can serve at least six purposes.

First, regulation signals companies about likely resource inefficiencies and potential technological improvements. Companies are still inexperienced in measuring their discharges, understanding the full costs of incomplete utilization of resources and toxicity, and conceiving new approaches to minimize discharges or

[2] Of course, there are many nonenvironmental examples of where industry has been extremely slow to pick up available $10 bills by choosing new approaches. For example, total quality management programs only came to the United States and Europe decades after they had been widely diffused in Japan, and only after Japanese firms had devastated U.S. and European competitors in the marketplace. The analogy between searching for product quality and for environmental protection is explored later in this paper.

eliminate hazardous substances. Regulation rivets attention on this area of potential innovation.[3]

Second, regulation focused on information gathering can achieve major benefits by raising corporate awareness. For example, Toxics Release Inventories, which are published annually as part of the 1986 Superfund reauthorization, require more than 20,000 manufacturing plants to report their releases of some 320 toxic chemicals. Such information gathering often leads to environmental improvement without mandating pollution reductions, sometimes even at lower costs.

Third, regulation reduces the uncertainty that investments to address the environment will be valuable. Greater certainty encourages investment in any area.

Fourth, regulation creates pressure that motivates innovation and progress. Our broader research on competitiveness highlights the important role of outside pressure in the innovation process, to overcome organizational inertia, foster creative thinking and mitigate agency problems. Economists are used to the argument that pressure for innovation can come from strong competitors, demanding customers or rising prices of raw materials; we are arguing that properly crafted regulation can also provide such pressure.

Fifth, regulation levels the transitional playing field. During the transition period to innovation-based solutions, regulation ensures that one company cannot opportunistically gain position by avoiding environmental investments. Regulations provide a buffer until new technologies become proven and learning effects reduce their costs.

Sixth, regulation is needed in the case of incomplete offsets. We readily admit that innovation cannot always completely offset the cost of compliance, especially in the short term before learning can reduce the cost of innovation-based solutions. In such cases, regulation will be necessary to improve environmental quality.

Stringent regulation can actually produce greater innovation and innovation offsets than lax regulation. Relatively lax regulation can be dealt with incrementally and without innovation, and often with "end-of-pipe" or secondary treatment solutions. More stringent regulation, however, focuses greater company attention on discharges and emissions, and compliance requires more fundamental solutions, like reconfiguring products and processes. While the cost of compliance may rise with stringency, then, the potential for innovation offsets may rise even faster. Thus the *net* cost of compliance can fall with stringency and may even turn into a net benefit.

How Innovation Offsets Occur

Innovation in response to environmental regulation can take two broad forms. The first is that companies simply get smarter about how to deal with pollution

[3] Regulation also raises the likelihood that product and process in general will incorporate environmental improvements.

once it occurs, including the processing of toxic materials and emissions, how to reduce the amount of toxic or harmful material generated (or convert it into salable forms) and how to improve secondary treatment. Molten Metal Technology, of Waltham, Massachusetts, for example, has developed a catalytic extraction process to process many types of hazardous waste efficiently and effectively. This sort of innovation reduces the cost of compliance with pollution control, but changes nothing else.

The second form of innovation addresses environmental impacts while simultaneously improving the affected product itself and/or related processes. In some cases, these "innovation offsets" can exceed the costs of compliance. This second sort of innovation is central to our claim that environmental regulation can actually increase industrial competitiveness.

Innovation offsets can be broadly divided into product offsets and process offsets. Product offsets occur when environmental regulation produces not just less pollution, but also creates better-performing or higher-quality products, safer products, lower product costs (perhaps from material substitution or less packaging), products with higher resale or scrap value (because of ease in recycling or disassembly) or lower costs of product disposal for users. Process offsets occur when environmental regulation not only leads to reduced pollution, but also results in higher resource productivity such as higher process yields, less downtime through more careful monitoring and maintenance, materials savings (due to substitution, reuse or recycling of production inputs), better utilization of by-products, lower energy consumption during the production process, reduced material storage and handling costs, conversion of waste into valuable forms, reduced waste disposal costs or safer workplace conditions. These offsets are frequently related, so that achieving one can lead to the realization of several others.

As yet, no broad tabulation exists of innovation offsets. Most of the work done in this area involves case studies, because case studies are the only vehicle currently available to measure compliance costs and both direct and indirect innovation benefits. This journal is not the place for a comprehensive listing of available case studies. However, offering some examples should help the reader to understand how common and plausible such effects are.

Innovation to comply with environmental regulation often improves product performance or quality. In 1990, for instance, Raytheon found itself required (by the Montreal Protocol and the U.S. Clean Air Act) to eliminate ozone-depleting chlorofluorocarbons (CFCs) used for cleaning printed electronic circuit boards after the soldering process. Scientists at Raytheon initially thought that complete elimination of CFCs would be impossible. However, they eventually adopted a new semiaqueous, terpene-based cleaning agent that could be reused. The new method proved to result in an increase in average product quality, which had occasionally been compromised by the old CFC-based cleaning agent, as well as lower operating costs (Raytheon, 1991, 1993). It would not have been adopted in the absence of environmental regulation mandating the phase-out of CFCs. Another example is the move by the Robbins Company (a jewelry company based in Attleboro,

Massachusetts) to a closed-loop, zero-discharge system for handling the water used in plating (Berube, Nash, Maxwell and Ehrenfeld, 1992). Robbins was facing closure due to violation of its existing discharge permits. The water produced by purification through filtering and ion exchange in the new closed-loop system was 40 times cleaner than city water and led to higher-quality plating and fewer rejects. The result was enhanced competitiveness.

Environmental regulations may also reduce product costs by showing how to eliminate costly materials, reduce unnecessary packaging or simplify designs. Hitachi responded to a 1991 Japanese recycling law by redesigning products to reduce disassembly time. In the process, the number of parts in a washing machine fell 16 percent, and the number of parts on a vacuum cleaner fell 30 percent. In this way, moves to redesign products for better recyclability can lead to fewer components and thus easier assembly.

Environmental standards can also lead to innovation that reduces disposal costs (or boost scrap or resale value) for the user. For instance, regulation that requires recyclability of products can lead to designs that allow valuable materials to be recovered more easily after disposal of the product. Either the customer or the manufacturer who takes back used products reaps greater value.

These have all been examples of product offsets, but process offsets are common as well. Process changes to reduce emissions frequently result in increases in product yields. At Ciba-Geigy's dyestuff plant in New Jersey, the need to meet new environmental standards caused the firm to reexamine its wastewater streams. Two changes in its production process—replacing iron with a different chemical conversion agent that did not result in the formation of solid iron sludge and process changes that eliminated the release of potentially toxic product into the wastewater stream—not only boosted yield by 40 percent but also eliminated wastes, resulting in annual cost savings of $740,000 (Dorfman, Muir and Miller, 1992).[4]

Similarly, 3M discovered that in producing adhesives in batches that were transferred to storage tanks, one bad batch could spoil the entire contents of a tank. The result was wasted raw materials and high costs of hazardous waste disposal. 3M developed a new technique to run quality tests more rapidly on new batches. The new technique allowed 3M to reduce hazardous wastes by 10 tons per year at almost no cost, yielding an annual savings of more than $200,000 (Sheridan, 1992).

Solving environmental problems can also yield benefits in terms of reduced downtime. Many chemical production processes at DuPont, for example, require start-up time to stabilize and bring output within specifications, resulting in an initial period during which only scrap and waste is produced. Installing higher-quality monitoring equipment has allowed DuPont to reduce production interruptions and the associated wasteful production start-ups, thus reducing waste generation as well as downtime (Parkinson, 1990).

[4] We should note that this plant was ultimately closed. However, the example described here does illustrate the role of regulatory pressure in process innovation.

Regulation can trigger innovation offsets through substitution of less costly materials or better utilization of materials in the process. For example, 3M faced new regulations that will force many solvent users in paper, plastic and metal coatings to reduce its solvent emissions 90 percent by 1995 (Boroughs and Carpenter, 1991). The company responded by avoiding the use of solvents altogether and developing coating products with safer, water-based solutions. At another 3M plant, a change from a solvent-based to a water-based carrier, used for coating tablets, eliminated 24 tons per year of air emissions. The $60,000 investment saved $180,000 in unneeded pollution control equipment and created annual savings of $15,000 in solvent purchases (Parkinson, 1990). Similarly, when federal and state regulations required that Dow Chemical close certain evaporation ponds used for storing and evaporating wastewater resulting from scrubbing hydrochloric gas with caustic soda, Dow redesigned its production process. By first scrubbing the hydrochloric acid with water and then caustic soda, Dow was able to eliminate the need for evaporation ponds, reduce its use of caustic soda, and capture a portion of the waste stream for reuse as a raw material in other parts of the plant. This process change cost $250,000 to implement. It reduced caustic waste by 6,000 tons per year and hydrochloric acid waste by 80 tons per year, for a savings of $2.4 million per year (Dorfman, Muir and Miller, 1992).

The Robbins Company's jewelry-plating system illustrates similar benefits. In moving to the closed-loop system that purified and recycled water, Robbins saved over $115,000 per year in water, chemicals, disposal costs, and lab fees and reduced water usage from 500,000 gallons per week to 500 gallons per week. The capital cost of the new system, which completely eliminated the waste, was $220,000, compared to about $500,000 for a wastewater treatment facility that would have brought Robbins' discharge into compliance only with current regulations.

At the Tobyhanna Army Depot, for instance, improvements in sandblasting, cleaning, plating and painting operations reduced hazardous waste generation by 82 percent between 1985 and 1992. That reduction saved the depot over $550,000 in disposal costs, and $400,000 in material purchasing and handling costs (PR Newswire, 1993).

Innovation offsets can also be derived by converting waste into more valuable forms. The Robbins Company recovered valuable precious metals in its zero discharge plating system. At Rhone-Poulenc's nylon plant in Chalampe, France, diacids (by-products that had been produced by an adipic acid process) used to be separated and incinerated. Rhone-Poulenc invested Fr 76 million and installed new equipment to recover and sell them as dye and tanning additives or coagulation agents, resulting in annual revenues of about Fr 20.1 million. In the United States, similar by-products from a Monsanto Chemical Company plant in Pensacola, Florida, are sold to utility companies who use them to accelerate sulfur dioxide removal during flue gas desulfurization (Basta and Vagi, 1988).

A few studies of innovation offsets do go beyond individual cases and offer some broader-based data. One of the most extensive studies is by INFORM, an environmental research organization. INFORM investigated activities to prevent waste generation—so-called source reduction activities—at 29 chemical plants in California, Ohio and New Jersey (Dorfman, Muir and Miller, 1992). Of the 181 source-reduction activities identified in this study, only one was found to have resulted in a net cost increase. Of the 70 activities for which the study was able to document changes in product yield, 68 reported yield increases; the average yield increase for the 20 initiatives with specific available data was 7 percent. These innovation offsets were achieved with surprisingly low investments and very short payback periods. One-quarter of the 48 initiatives with detailed capital cost information required no capital investment at all; of the 38 initiatives with payback period data, nearly two-thirds were shown to have recouped their initial investments in six months or less. The annual savings per dollar spent on source reduction averaged $3.49 for the 27 activities for which this information could be calculated. The study also investigated the motivating factors behind the plant's source-reduction activities. Significantly, it found that waste disposal costs were the most often cited, followed by environmental regulation.

To build a broader base of studies on innovation offsets to environmental regulation, we have been collaborating with the Management Institute for Environment and Business on a series of international case studies, sponsored by the EPA, of industries and entire sectors significantly affected by environmental regulation. Sectors studied include pulp and paper, paint and coatings, electronics manufacturing, refrigerators, dry cell batteries and printing inks (Bonifant and Ratcliffe, 1994; Bonifant 1994a,b; van der Linde, 1995a,b,c). Some examples from that effort have already been described here.

A solid body of case study evidence, then, demonstrates that innovation offsets to environmental regulation are common.[5] Even with a generally hostile regulatory climate, which is not designed to encourage such innovation, these offsets can sometimes exceed the cost of compliance. We expect that such examples will proliferate as companies and regulators become more sophisticated and shed old mindsets.

Early-Mover Advantage in International Markets

World demand is moving rapidly in the direction of valuing low-pollution and energy-efficient products, not to mention more resource-efficient products with higher resale or scrap value. Many companies are using innovation to command price premiums for "green" products and open up new market segments. For example, Germany enacted recycling standards earlier than in most other

[5] Of course, a list of case examples, however long, does not prove that companies can always innovate or substitute for careful empirical testing in a large cross-section of industries. Given our current ability to capture the true costs and often multifaceted benefits of regulatory-induced innovation, reliance on the weight of case study evidence is necessary. As we discuss elsewhere, there is no countervailing set of case studies that shows that innovation offsets are unlikely or impossible.

countries, which gave German firms an early-mover advantage in developing less packaging-intensive products, which have been warmly received in the marketplace. Scandinavian pulp and paper producers have been leaders in introducing new environmentally friendly production processes, and thus Scandinavian pulp and paper equipment suppliers such as Kamyr and Sunds have made major gains internationally in selling innovative bleaching equipment. In the United States, a parallel example is the development by Cummins Engine of low-emissions diesel engines for trucks, buses and other applications in response to U.S. environmental regulations. Its new competence is allowing the firm to gain international market share.

Clearly, this argument only works to the extent that national environmental standards anticipate and are consistent with international trends in environmental protection, rather than break with them. Creating expertise in cleaning up abandoned hazardous waste sites, as the U.S. Superfund law has done, does little to benefit U.S. suppliers if no other country adopts comparable toxic waste cleanup requirements. But when a competitive edge is attained, especially because a company's home market is sophisticated and demanding in a way that pressures the company to further innovation, the economic gains can be lasting.

Answering Defenders of the Traditional Model

Our argument that strict environmental regulation can be fully consistent with competitiveness was originally put forward in a short *Scientific American* essay (Porter, 1991; see also van der Linde, 1993). This essay received far more scrutiny than we expected. It has been warmly received by many, especially in the business community. But it has also had its share of critics, especially among economists (Jaffe, Peterson, Portney and Stavins, 1993, 1994; Oates, Palmer and Portney, 1993; Palmer and Simpson, 1993; Simpson, 1993; Schmalensee, 1993).

One criticism is that while innovation offsets are theoretically possible, they are likely to be rare or small in practice. We disagree. Pollution is the emission or discharge of a (harmful) substance or energy form into the environment. Fundamentally, it is a manifestation of economic waste and involves unnecessary, inefficient or incomplete utilization of resources, or resources not used to generate their highest value. In many cases, emissions are a sign of inefficiency and force a firm to perform non-value-creating activities such as handling, storage and disposal. Within the company itself, the costs of poor resource utilization are most obvious in incomplete material utilization, but are also manifested in poor process control, which generates unnecessary stored material, waste and defects. There are many other hidden costs of resource inefficiencies later in the life cycle of the product. Packaging discarded by distributors or customers, for example, wastes resources and adds costs. Customers bear additional costs when they use polluting products or products that waste energy. Resources are also wasted when customers discard products embodying unused materials or when they bear the costs of product disposal.[6]

As the many examples discussed earlier suggest, the opportunity to reduce cost by diminishing pollution should thus be the rule, not the exception. Highly toxic materials such as heavy metals or solvents are often expensive and hard to handle, and reducing their use makes sense from several points of view. More broadly, efforts to reduce pollution and maximize profits share the same basic principles, including the efficient use of inputs, substitution of less expensive materials and the minimization of unneeded activities.[7]

A corollary to this observation is that scrap or waste or emissions can carry important information about flaws in product design or the production process. A recent study of process changes in 10 printed circuit board manufacturers, for example, found that 13 of 33 major changes were initiated by pollution control personnel. Of these, 12 resulted in cost reduction, eight in quality improvements and five in extension of production capabilities (King, 1994).

Environmental improvement efforts have traditionally overlooked the systems cost of resource inefficiency. Improvement efforts have focused on *pollution control* through better identification, processing and disposal of discharges or waste, an inherently costly approach. In recent years, more advanced companies and regulators have embraced the concept of *pollution prevention,* sometimes called source reduction, which uses material substitution, closed-loop processes and the like to limit pollution before it occurs.

But although pollution prevention is an important step in the right direction, ultimately companies and regulators must learn to frame environmental improvement in terms of *resource productivity,* or the efficiency and effectiveness with which companies and their customers use resources.[8] Improving resource productivity within companies goes beyond eliminating pollution (and the cost of dealing with it) to lowering true economic cost and raising the true economic value of products. At the level of resource productivity, environmental improvement and competitiveness come together. The imperative for resource productivity rests on the private costs that companies bear because of pollution, not on mitigating pollution's social costs. In addressing these private costs, it highlights the opportunity costs of pollution—wasted resources, wasted efforts and diminished product value to the customer—not its actual costs.

[6] At its core, then, pollution is a result of an intermediate state of technology or management methods. Apparent exceptions to the resource productivity thesis often prove the rule by highlighting the role of technology. Paper made with recycled fiber was once greatly inferior, but new de-inking and other technologies have made its quality better and better. Apparent tradeoffs between energy efficiency and emissions rest on incomplete combustion.

[7] Schmalensee (1993) counters that NO_X emissions often result from thermodynamically efficient combustion. But surely this is an anomaly, not the rule, and may represent an intermediate level of efficiency.

[8] One of the pioneering efforts to see environmental improvement this way is Joel Makower's (1993) book, *The E-Factor: The Bottom-Line Approach to Environmentally Responsible Business.*

This view of pollution as unproductive resource utilization suggests a helpful analogy between environmental protection and product quality measured by defects. Companies used to promote quality by conducting careful inspections during the production process, and then by creating a service organization to correct the quality problems that turned up in the field. This approach has proven misguided. Instead, the most cost-effective way to improve quality is to build it into the entire process, which includes design, purchased components, process technology, shipping and handling techniques and so forth. This method dramatically reduces inspection, rework and the need for a large service organization. (It also leads to the oft-quoted phrase, "quality is free.") Similarly, there is reason to believe that companies can enjoy substantial innovation offsets by improving resource productivity throughout the value chain instead of through dealing with the manifestations of inefficiency like emissions and discharges.

Indeed, corporate total quality management programs have strong potential also to reduce pollution and lead to innovation offsets.[9] Dow Chemical, for example, has explicitly identified the link between quality improvement and environmental performance, by using statistical process control to reduce the variance in processes and lower waste (Sheridan, 1992).

A second criticism of our hypothesis is to point to the studies finding high costs of compliance with environmental regulation, as evidence that there is a fixed tradeoff between regulation and competitiveness. But these studies are far from definitive.

Estimates of regulatory compliance costs prior to enactment of a new rule typically exceed the actual costs. In part, this is because such estimates are often self-reported by industries who oppose the rule, which creates a tendency to inflation. A prime example of this type of thinking was a statement by Lee Iacocca, then vice president at the Ford Motor Company, during the debate on the 1970 Clean Air Act. Iacocca warned that compliance with the new regulations would require huge price increases for automobiles, force U.S. automobile production to a halt after January 1, 1975, and "do irreparable damage to the U.S. economy" (Smith, 1992). The 1970 Clean Air Act was subsequently enacted, and Iacocca's predictions turned out to be wrong. Similar dire predictions were made during the 1990 Clean Air Act debate; industry analysts predicted that burdens on the U.S. industry would exceed $100 billion. Of course, the reality has proven to be far less dramatic. In one study in the pulp and paper sector, actual costs of compliance were $4.00 to $5.50 per ton compared to original industry estimates of $16.40 (Bonson, McCubbin and Sprague, 1988).

Early estimates of compliance cost also tend to be exaggerated because they assume no innovation. Early cost estimates for dealing with regulations concerning emission of volatile compounds released during paint application held everything

[9] A case study of pollution prevention in a large multinational firm showed those units with strong total quality management programs in place usually undertake more effective pollution prevention efforts than units with less commitment to total quality management. See Rappaport (1992), cited in U.S. Congress, Office of Technology Assessment (1994).

else constant, assuming only the addition of a hood to capture the fumes from paint lines. Innovation that improved the paint's transfer efficiency subsequently allowed not only the reduction of fumes but also paint usage. Further innovation in water-borne paint formulations without any VOC-releasing solvents made it possible to eliminate the need for capturing and treating the fumes altogether (Bonifant, 1994b). Similarly, early estimates of the costs of complying with a 1991 federal clean air regulation calling for a 98 percent reduction in atmospheric emissions of benzene from tar-storage tanks used by coal tar distillers initially assumed that tar-storage tanks would have to be covered by costly gas blankets. While many distillers opposed the regulations, Pittsburgh-based Aristech Chemical, a major distiller of coal tar, subsequently developed an innovative way to remove benzene from tar in the first processing step, thereby eliminating the need for the gas blanket and resulting in a saving of $3.3 million instead of a cost increase (PR Newswire, 1993).

Prices in the new market for trading allowances to emit SO_2 provide another vivid example. At the time the law was passed, analysts projected that the marginal cost of SO_2 controls (and, therefore, the price of an emission allowance) would be on the order of $300 to $600 (or more) per ton in Phase I and up to $1000 or more in Phase II. Actual Phase I allowance prices have turned out to be in the $170 to $250 range, and recent trades are heading lower, with Phase II estimates only slightly higher (after adjusting for the time value of money). In case after case, the differences between initial predictions and actual outcomes—especially after industry has had time to learn and innovate—are striking.

Econometric studies showing that environmental regulation raises costs and harms competitiveness are subject to bias, because net compliance costs are over-estimated by assuming away innovation benefits. Jorgenson and Wilcoxen (1990), for example, explicitly state that they did not attempt to assess public or private benefits. Other often-cited studies that solely focus on costs, leaving out benefits, are Hazilla and Kopp (1990) and Gray (1987). By largely assuming away innovation effects, how could economic studies reach any other conclusion than they do?

Internationally competitive industries seem to be much better able to innovate in response to environmental regulation than industries that were uncompetitive to begin with, but no study measuring the effects of environmental regulation on industry competitiveness has taken initial competitiveness into account. In a study by Kalt (1988), for instance, the sectors where high environmental costs were associated with negative trade performance were ones such as ferrous metal mining, nonferrous mining, chemical and fertilizer manufacturing, primary iron and steel and primary nonferrous metals, industries where the United States suffers from dwindling raw material deposits, very high relative electricity costs, heavily subsidized foreign competitors and other disadvantages that have rendered them uncompetitive quite apart from environmental costs.[10] Other sectors identified by Kalt

[10] It should be observed that a strong correlation between environmental costs and industry competitiveness does not necessarily indicate causality. Omitting environmental benefits from regulation, and

as having incurred very high environmental costs can actually be interpreted as supporting our hypothesis. Chemicals, plastics and synthetics, fabric, yarn and thread, miscellaneous textiles, leather tanning, paints and allied products, and paperboard containers all had high environmental costs but displayed positive trade performance.

A number of studies have failed to find that stringent environmental regulation hurts industrial competitiveness. Meyer (1992, 1993) tested and refuted the hypothesis that U.S. states with stringent environmental policies experience weak economic growth. Leonard (1988) was unable to demonstrate statistically significant offshore movements by U.S. firms in pollution-intensive industries. Wheeler and Mody (1992) failed to find that environmental regulation affected the foreign investment decisions of U.S. firms. Repetto (1995) found that industries heavily affected by environmental regulations experienced slighter reductions in their share of world exports than did the entire American industry from 1970 to 1990. Using U.S. Bureau of Census Data of more than 200,000 large manufacturing establishments, the study also found that plants with poor environmental records are generally not more profitable than cleaner ones in the same industry, even controlling for their age, size and technology. Jaffe, Peterson, Portney and Stavins (1993) recently surveyed more than 100 studies and concluded there is little evidence to support the view that U.S. environmental regulation had a large adverse effect on competitiveness.

Of course, these studies offer no proof for our hypothesis, either. But it is striking that so many studies find that even the poorly designed environmental laws presently in effect have little adverse effect on competitiveness. After all, traditional approaches to regulation have surely worked to stifle potential innovation offsets and imposed unnecessarily high costs of compliance on industry (as we will discuss in greater detail in the next section). Thus, studies using actual compliance costs to regulation are heavily biased toward finding that such regulation has a substantial cost.[11] In no way do such studies measure the potential of well-crafted environmental regulations to stimulate competitiveness.

A third criticism of our thesis is that even if regulation fosters innovation, it will harm competitiveness by crowding out other potentially more productive investments or avenues for innovation. Given incomplete information, the limited

reporting obvious (end-of-pipe) costs but not more difficult to identify or quantify innovation benefits can actually obscure a reverse causal relationship: industries that were uncompetitive in the first place may well be less able to innovate in response to environmental pressures, and thus be prone to end-of-pipe solutions whose costs are easily measured. In contrast, competitive industries capable of addressing environmental problems in innovative ways may report a lower compliance cost.

[11] Gray and Shadbegian (1993), another often-mentioned study, suffers from several of the problems discussed here. The article uses industry-reported compliance costs and does not control for plant technology vintage or the extent of other productivity-enhancing investments at the plant. High compliance costs may well have been borne in old, inefficient plants where firms opted for secondary treatment rather than innovation. Moreover, U.S. producers may well have been disadvantaged in innovating given the nature of the U.S. regulatory process—this seems clearly to have been the case in pulp and paper, one of the industries studied by the Management Institute for Environment and Business (MEB).

attention many companies have devoted to environmental innovations and the inherent linkage between pollution and resource productivity described earlier, it certainly is not obvious that this line of innovation has been so thoroughly explored that the marginal benefits of further investment would be low. The high returns evident in the studies we have cited support this view. Moreover, environmental investments represent only a small percentage of overall investment in all but a very few industries.[12]

A final counterargument, more caricature than criticism, is that we are asserting that any strict environmental regulation will inevitably lead to innovation and competitiveness. Of course, this is not our position. Instead, we believe that if regulations are properly crafted and companies are attuned to the possibilities, then innovation to minimize and even offset the cost of compliance is likely in many circumstances.

Designing Environmental Regulation to Encourage Innovation

If environmental standards are to foster the innovation offsets that arise from new technologies and approaches to production, they should adhere to three principles. First, they must create the maximum opportunity for innovation, leaving the approach to innovation to industry and not the standard-setting agency. Second, regulations should foster continuous improvement, rather than locking in any particular technology. Third, the regulatory process should leave as little room as possible for uncertainty at every stage. Evaluated by these principles, it is clear that U.S. environmental regulations have often been crafted in a way that deters innovative solutions, or even renders them impossible. Environmental laws and regulations need to take three substantial steps: phrasing environmental rules as goals that can be met in flexible ways; encouraging innovation to reach and exceed those goals; and administering the system in a coordinated way.

Clear Goals, Flexible Approaches

Environmental regulation should focus on outcomes, not technologies.[13] Past regulations have often prescribed particular remediation technologies—like catalysts or scrubbers to address air pollution—rather than encouraging innovative approaches. American environmental law emphasized phrases like "best available technology," or "best available control technology." But legislating as if one par-

[12] In paints and coatings, for example, environmental investments were 3.3 percent of total capital investment in 1989. According to Department of Commerce (1991) data (self-reported by industry), capital spending for pollution control and abatement outside of the chemical, pulp and paper, petroleum and coal, and primary metal sectors made up just 3.15 percent of total capital spending in 1991.

[13] There will always be instances of extremely hazardous pollution requiring immediate action, where imposing a specific technology by command and control may be the best or only viable solution. However, such methods should be seen as a last resort.

ticular technology is always the "best" almost guarantees that innovation will not occur.

Regulations should encourage product and process changes to better utilize resources and avoid pollution early, rather than mandating end-of-pipe or secondary treatment, which is almost always more costly. For regulators, this poses a question of where to impose regulations in the chain of production from raw materials, equipment, the producer of the end product, to the consumer (Porter, 1985). Regulators must consider the technological capabilities and resources available at each stage, because it affects the likelihood that innovation will occur. With that in mind, the governing principle should be to regulate as late in the production chain as practical, which will normally allow more flexibility for innovation there and in upstream stages.

The EPA should move beyond the single medium (air, water and so on) as the principal way of thinking about the environment, toward total discharges or total impact.[14] It should reorganize around affected industry clusters (including suppliers and related industries) to better understand a cluster's products, technologies and total set of environmental problems. This will foster fundamental rather than piecemeal solutions.[15]

Seeding and Spreading Environmental Innovations

Where possible, regulations should include the use of market incentives, including pollution taxes, deposit-refund schemes and tradable permits.[16] Such approaches often allow considerable flexibility, reinforce resource productivity, and also create incentives for ongoing innovation. Mandating outcomes by setting emission levels, while preferable to choosing a particular technology, still fails to provide incentives for continued and ongoing innovation and will tend to freeze a status quo until new regulations appear. In contrast, market incentives can encourage the introduction of technologies that exceed current standards.

The EPA should also promote an increased use of preemptive standards by industry, which appear to be an effective way of dealing with environmental

[14] A first step in this direction is the EPA's recent adjustment of the timing of its air rule for the pulp and paper industry so that it will coincide with the rule for water, allowing industry to see the dual impact of the rules and innovate accordingly.

[15] The EPA's regulatory cluster team concept, under which a team from relevant EPA offices approaches particular problems for a broader viewpoint, is a first step in this direction. Note, however, that of the 17 cluster groups formed, only four were organized around specific industries (petroleum refining, oil and gas production, pulp and paper, printing), while the remaining 13 focused on specific chemicals or types of pollution (U.S. Congress, Office of Technology Assessment, 1994).

[16] Pollution taxes can be implemented as effluent charges on the quantity of pollution discharges, as user charges for public treatment facilities, or as product charges based on the potential pollution of a product. In a deposit-refund system, such product charges may be rebated if a product user disposes of it properly (for example, by returning a lead battery for recycling rather than sending it to a landfill). Under a tradable permit system, like that included in the recent Clean Air Act Amendments, a maximum amount of pollution is set, and rights equal to that cap are distributed to firms. Firms must hold enough rights to cover their emissions; firms with excess rights can sell them to firms who are short.

regulation. Preemptive standards, agreed to with EPA oversight to avoid collusion, can be set and met by industry to avoid government standards that might go further or be more restrictive on innovation. They are not only less costly, but allow faster change and leave the initiative for innovation with industry.

The EPA should play a major role in collecting and disseminating information on innovation offsets and their consequences, both here and in other countries. Limited knowledge about opportunities for innovation is a major constraint on company behavior. A good start can be the "clearinghouse" of information on source-reduction approaches that EPA was directed to establish by the Pollution Prevention Act (PPA) of 1990. The Green Lights and Toxics Release Inventories described at the start of this paper are other programs that involve collecting and spreading information. Yet another important initiative is the EPA program to compare emissions rates at different companies, creating methodologies to measure the full internal costs of pollution and ways of exchanging best practices and learning on innovative technologies.

Regulatory approaches can also function by helping create demand pressure for environmental innovation. One example is the prestigious German "Blue Angel" eco-label, introduced by the German government in 1977, which can be displayed only by products meeting very strict environmental criteria. One of the label's biggest success stories has been in oil and gas heating appliances: the energy efficiency of these appliances improved significantly when the label was introduced, and emissions of sulfur dioxide, carbon monoxide and nitrogen oxides were reduced by more than 30 percent.

Another point of leverage on the demand side is to harness the role of government as a demanding buyer of environmental solutions and environmentally friendly products. While there are benefits of government procurement of products such as recycled paper and retreaded tires, the far more leveraged role is in buying specialized environmental equipment and services.[17] One useful change would be to alter the current practice of requiring bidders in competitive bid processes for government projects to only bid with "proven" technologies, a practice sure to hinder innovation.

The EPA can employ demonstration projects to stimulate and seed innovative new technologies, working through universities and industry associations. A good example is the project to develop and demonstrate technologies for super-efficient refrigerators, which was conducted by the EPA and researchers in government, academia and the private sector (United States Environmental Protection Agency, 1992). An estimated $1.7 billion was spent in 1992 by the federal government on environmental technology R&D, but only $70 million was directed toward research on pollution prevention (U.S. Congress, Office of Technology Assessment, 1994).

Incentives for innovation must also be built into the regulatory process itself. The current permitting system under Title V of the Clean Air Act Amendments, to

[17] See Marron (1994) for a demonstration of the modest productivity gains likely from government procurement of standard items, although in a static model.

choose a negative example, requires firms seeking to change or expand their production process in a way that might impact air quality to revise their permit extensively, *no matter how little the potential effect on air quality may be.* This not only deters innovation, but drains the resources of regulators away from timely action on significant matters. On the positive side, the state of Massachusetts has initiated a program to waive permits in some circumstances, or promise an immediate permit, if a company takes a zero-discharge approach.

A final priority is new forums for settling regulatory issues that minimize litigation. Potential litigation creates enormous uncertainty; actual litigation burns resources. Mandatory arbitration, or rigid arbitration steps before litigation is allowed, would benefit innovation. There is also a need to rethink certain liability issues. While adequate safeguards must be provided against companies that recklessly harm citizens, there is a pressing need for liability standards that more clearly recognize the countervailing health and safety benefits of innovations that lower or eliminate the discharge of harmful pollutants.

Regulatory Coordination

Coordination of environmental regulation can be improved in at least three ways: between industry and regulators, between regulators at different levels and places in government, and between U.S. regulators and their international counterparts.

In setting environmental standards and regulatory processes to encourage innovation, substantive industry participation in setting standards is needed right from the beginning, as is common in many European countries. An appropriate regulatory process is one in which regulations themselves are clear, who must meet them is clear, and industry accepts the regulations and begins innovating to address them, rather than spending years attempting to delay or relax them. In our current system, by the time standards are finally settled and clarified, it is often too late to address them fundamentally, making secondary treatment the only alternative. We need to evolve toward a regulatory regime in which the EPA and other regulators make a commitment that standards will be in place for, say, five years, so that industry is motivated to innovate rather than adopt incremental solutions.

Different parts and levels of government must coordinate and organize themselves so that companies are not forced to deal with multiple parties with inconsistent desires and approaches. As a matter of regulatory structure, the EPA's proposed new Innovative Technology Council, being set up to advocate the development of new technology in every field of environmental policy, is a step in the right direction. Another unit in the EPA should be responsible for continued reengineering of the process of regulation to reduce uncertainty and minimize costs. Also, an explicit strategy is needed to coordinate and harmonize federal and state activities.[18]

[18] The cluster-based approach to regulation discussed earlier should also help eliminate the practice of sending multiple EPA inspectors to the same plant who do not talk to one another, make conflicting

A final issue of coordination involves the relationship between U.S. environmental regulations and those in other countries. U.S. regulations should be in sync with regulations in other countries and, ideally, be slightly ahead of them. This will minimize possible competitive disadvantages relative to foreign competitors who are not yet subject to the standard, while at the same time maximizing export potential in the pollution control sector. Standards that lead world developments provide domestic firms with opportunities to create valuable early-mover advantages. However, standards should not be too far ahead of, or too different in character from, those that are likely to apply to foreign competitors, for this would lead industry to innovate in the wrong directions.

Critics may note, with some basis, that U.S. regulators may not be able to project better than firms what type of regulations, and resultant demands for environmental products and services, will develop in other nations. However, regulators would seem to possess greater resources and information than firms for understanding the path of regulation in other countries. Moreover, U.S. regulations influence the type and stringency of regulations in other nations, and as such help define demand in other world markets.

Imperatives for Companies

Of course, the regulatory reforms described here also seek to change how companies view environmental issues.[19] Companies must start to recognize the environment as a competitive opportunity—not as an annoying cost or a postponable threat. Yet many companies are ill-prepared to carry out a strategy of environmental innovation that produces sizable compensating offsets.

For starters, companies must improve their measurement and assessment methods to detect environmental costs and benefits.[20] Too often, relevant information is simply lacking. Typical is the case of a large producer of organic chemicals that retained a consulting firm to explore opportunities for reducing waste. The client thought it had 40 waste streams, but a careful audit revealed that 497 different

demands and waste time and resources. The potential savings from cluster- and multimedia-oriented permitting and inspection programs appear to be substantial. During a pilot multimedia testing program called the Blackstone Project, the Massachusetts Department of Environmental Protection found that multimedia inspections required 50 percent less time than conventional inspections—which at that time accounted for nearly one-fourth of the department's operating budget (Roy and Dillard, 1990).

[19] For a more detailed perspective on changing company mindsets about competitiveness and environmentalism, see Porter and van der Linde (1995) in the *Harvard Business Review*.

[20] Accounting methods that are currently being discussed in this context include "full cost accounting," which attempts to assign all costs to specific products or processes, and "total cost accounting," which goes a step further and attempts both to allocate costs more specifically and to include cost items beyond traditional concerns, such as indirect or hidden costs (like compliance costs, insurance, on-site waste management, operation of pollution control and future liability) and less tangible benefits (like revenue from enhanced company image). See White, Becker and Goldstein (1991), cited in U.S. Congress, Office of Technology Assessment (1994).

waste streams were actually present (Parkinson, 1990). Few companies analyze the true cost of toxicity, waste, discharges and the second-order impacts of waste and discharges on other activities. Fewer still look beyond the out-of-pocket costs of dealing with pollution to investigate the opportunity costs of the wasted resources or foregone productivity. How much money is going up the smokestack? What percentage of inputs are wasted? Many companies do not even track environmental spending carefully, or subject it to evaluation techniques typical for "normal" investments.

Once environmental costs are measured and understood, the next step is to create a presumption for innovation-based solutions. Discharges, scrap and emissions should be analyzed for insights about beneficial product design or process changes. Approaches based on treatment or handling of discharges should be accepted only after being sent back several times for reconsideration. The responsibility for environmental issues should not be delegated to lawyers or outside consultants except in the adversarial regulatory process, or even to internal specialists removed from the line organization, residing in legal, government or environmental affairs departments. Instead, environmental strategies must become a general management issue if the sorts of process and product redesigns needed for true innovation are to even be considered, much less be proposed and implemented.

Conclusion

We have found that economists as a group are resistant to the notion that even well-designed environmental regulations might lead to improved competitiveness. This hesitancy strikes us as somewhat peculiar, given that in other contexts, economists are extremely willing to argue that technological change has overcome predictions of severe, broadly defined environmental costs. A static model (among other flaws) has been behind many dire predictions of economic disaster and human catastrophe: from the predictions of Thomas Malthus that population would inevitably outstrip food supply; to the *Limits of Growth* (Meadows and Meadows, 1972), which predicted the depletion of the world's natural resources; to *The Population Bomb* (Ehrlich, 1968), which predicted that a quarter of the world's population would starve to death between 1973 and 1983. As economists are often eager to point out, these models failed because they did not appreciate the power of innovations in technology to change old assumptions about resource availability and utilization.

Moreover, the static mindset that environmentalism is inevitably costly has created a self-fulfilling gridlock, where both regulators and industry battle over every inch of territory. The process has spawned an industry of litigators and consultants, driving up costs and draining resources away from real solutions. It has been reported that four out of five EPA decisions are currently challenged in court (Clay, 1993, cited in U.S. Congress, Office of Technology Assessment, 1994). A study by the Rand Institute for Civil Justice found that 88 percent of the money paid out between 1986 and 1989 by insurers on Superfund claims went to pay for legal and administrative costs, while only 12 percent were used for actual site cleanups (Acton and Dixon, 1992).

The United States and other countries need an entirely new way of thinking about the relationship between environment and industrial competitiveness—one closer to the reality of modern competition. The focus should be on relaxing the environment-competitiveness tradeoff rather than accepting and, worse yet, steepening it. The orientation should shift from pollution control to resource productivity. We believe that no lasting success can come from policies that promise that environmentalism will triumph over industry, nor from policies that promise that industry will triumph over environmentalism. Instead, success must involve innovation-based solutions that promote both environmentalism and industrial competitiveness.

■ *The authors are grateful to Alan Auerbach, Ben Bonifant, Daniel C. Esty, Ridgway M. Hall, Jr., Donald B. Marron, Jan Rivkin, Nicolaj Siggelkow, R. David Simpson and Timothy Taylor for extensive valuable editorial suggestions. We are also grateful to Reed Hundt for ongoing discussions that have greatly benefitted our thinking.*

References

Acton, Jan Paul, and Lloyd S. Dixon, *Superfund and Transaction Costs: The Experiences of Insurers and Very Large Industrial Firms.* Santa Monica: Rand Institute for Civil Justice, 1992.

Amoco Corporation and United States Environmental Protection Agency, "Amoco-U.S. EPA Pollution Prevention Project: Yorktown, Virginia, Project Summary," Chicago and Washington, D.C., 1992.

Basta, Nicholas, and David Vagi, "A Casebook of Successful Waste Reduction Projects," *Chemical Engineering,* August 15, 1988, *95*:11, 37.

Berube, M., J. Nash, J. Maxwell, and J. Ehrenfeld, "From Pollution Control to Zero Discharge: How the Robbins Company Overcame the Obstacles," *Pollution Prevention Review,* Spring 1992, *2*:2, 189–207.

Bonifant, B., "Competitive Implications of Environmental Regulation in the Electronics Manufacturing Industry," Management Institute for Environment and Business, Washington, D.C., 1994a.

Bonifant, B., "Competitive Implications of Environmental Regulation in the Paint and Coatings Industry," Management Institute for Environment and Business, Washington, D.C., 1994b.

Bonifant, B., and I. Ratcliffe, "Competitive Implications of Environmental Regulation in the Pulp and Paper Industry," Management Institute for Environment and Business, Washington, D.C., 1994.

Bonson, N. C., Neil McCubbin, and John B. Sprague, "Kraft Mill Effluents in Ontario." Report prepared for the Technical Advisory Committee, Pulp and Paper Sector of MISA, Ontario Ministry of the Environment, Toronto, Ontario, Canada, March 29, 1988, Section 6, p. 166.

Boroughs, D. L., and B. Carpenter, "Helping the Planet and the Economy," *U.S. News & World Report,* March 25, 1991, *110*:11, 46.

Clay, Don, "New Environmentalist: A Cooperative Strategy," *Forum for Applied Reserch and Public Policy,* Spring 1993, *8,* 125–28.

DeCanio, Stephen J., "Why Do Profitable Energy-Saving Investment Projects Languish?" Paper presented at the Second International Research Conference of the Greening of Industry Network, Cambridge, Mass., 1993.

Department of Commerce, "Pollution Abatement Costs and Expenditures," Washington, D.C., 1991.

Dorfman, Mark H., Warren R. Muir, and Catherine G. Miller, *Environmental Dividends: Cutting More Chemical Wastes.* New York: INFORM, 1992.

Ehrlich, Paul, *The Population Bomb.* New York: Ballantine Books, 1968.

Freeman, A. Myrick, III, "Methods for Assessing the Benefits of Environmental Programs." In Kneese, A. V., and J. L. Sweeney, eds., *Handbook of Natural Resource and Energy Economics.* Vol. 1. Amsterdam: North-Holland, 1985, pp. 223–70.

Gray, Wayne B., "The Cost of Regulation: OSHA, EPA, and the Productivity Slowdown," *American Economic Review,* 1987, *77*:5, 998–1006.

Gray, Wayne B., and Ronald J. Shadbegian, "Environmental Regulation and Productivity at the Plant Level," discussion paper, U.S. Department of Commerce, Center for Economic Studies, Washington, D.C., 1993.

Hartwell, R. V., and L. Bergkamp, "Eco-Labelling in Europe: New Market-Related Environmental Risks?," *BNA International Environment Daily,* Special Report, Oct. 20, 1992.

Hazilla, Michael, and Raymond J. Kopp, "Social Cost of Environmental Quality Regulations: A General Equilibrium Analysis," *Journal of Political Economy,* 1990, *98*:4, 853–73.

Jaffe, Adam B., S. Peterson, Paul Portney, and Robert N. Stavins, "Environmental Regulations and the Competitiveness of U.S. Industry," Economics Resource Group, Cambridge, Mass., 1993.

Jaffe, Adam B., S. Peterson, Paul Portney, and Robert N. Stavins, "Environmental Regulation and International Competitiveness: What Does the Evidence Tell Us," draft, January 13, 1994.

Jorgenson, Dale W., and Peter J. Wilcoxen, "Environmental Regulation and U.S. Economic Growth," *Rand Journal of Economics,* Summer 1990, *21*:2, 314–40.

Kalt, Joseph P., "The Impact of Domestic Environmental Regulatory Policies on U.S. International Competitiveness." In Spence, A. M., and H. Hazard, eds., *International Competitiveness,* Cambridge, Mass: Harper and Row, Ballinger, 1988, pp. 221–62.

King, A., "Improved Manufacturing Resulting from Learning-From-Waste: Causes, Importance, and Enabling Conditions," working paper, Stern School of Business, New York University, 1994.

Leonard, H. Jeffrey, *Pollution and the Struggle for World Product.* Cambridge, U.K.: Cambridge University Press, 1988.

Makower, Joel, *The E-Factor: The Bottom-Line Approach to Environmentally Responsible Business.* New York: Times Books, 1993.

Marron, Donald B., "Buying Green: Government Procurement as an Instrument of Environmental Policy," mimeo, Massachusetts Institute of Technology, 1994.

Massachusetts Department of Environmental Protection, Daniel S. Greenbaum, Commissioner, interview, Boston, August 8, 1993.

Meadows, Donella H., and Dennis L. Meadows, *The Limits of Growth.* New York: New American Library, 1972.

Meyer, Stephen M., *Environmentalism and Economic Prosperity: Testing the Environmental Impact Hypothesis.* Cambridge, Mass.: Massachusetts Institute of Technology, 1992.

Meyer, Stephen M., *Environmentalism and Economic Prosperity: An Update.* Cambridge, Mass.: Massachusetts Institute of Technology, 1993.

National Paint and Coatings Association, *Improving the Superfund: Correcting a National Public Policy Disaster.* Washington, D.C., 1992.

Palmer, Karen L., and Ralph David Simpson, "Environmental Policy as Industrial Policy," *Resources,* Summer 1993, *112,* 17–21.

Parkinson, Gerald, "Reducing Wastes Can Be Cost-Effective," *Chemical Engineering,* July 1990, *97*:7, 30.

Porter, Michael E., *Competitive Advantage: Creating and Sustaining Superior Performance.* New York: Free Press, 1985.

Porter, Michael E., *The Competitive Advantage of Nations.* New York: Free Press, 1990.

Porter, Michael E., "America's Green Strategy," *Scientific American,* April 1991, *264,* 168.

Porter, Michael E., and Claas van der Linde, "Green *and* Competitive: Breaking the Stalemate," *Harvard Business Review,* September-October 1995.

PR Newswire, "Winners Announced for Governor's Waste Minimization Awards," January 21, 1993, State and Regional News Section.

Oates, Wallace, Karen L. Palmer, and Paul Portney, "Environmental Regulation and International Competitiveness: Thinking About the Porter Hypothesis." Resources for the Future Working Paper 94–02, 1993.

Rappaport, Ann, "Development and Transfer of Pollution Prevention Technology Within a Multinational Corporation," dissertation, Department of Civil Engineering, Tufts University, May 1992.

Raytheon Inc., "Alternate Cleaning Technology." Technical Report Phase II. January-October 1991.

Raytheon Inc., J. R. Pasquariello, Vice President Environmental Quality; Kenneth J. Tierney, Director Environmental and Energy Conservation; Frank A. Marino, Senior Corporate Environmental Specialist; interview, Lexington, Mass., April 4, 1993.

Repetto, Robert, "Jobs, Competitiveness, and Environmental Regulation: What are the Real Issues?," Washington, D.C.: World Resources Institute, 1995.

Roy, M., and L. A. Dillard, "Toxics Use in Massachusetts: The Blackstone Project," *Journal of Air and Waste Management Association,* October 1990, *40*:10, 1368–71.

Schmalensee, Richard, "The Costs of Environmental Regulation." Massachusetts Institute of Technology, Center for Energy and Environmental Policy Research Working Paper 93–015, 1993.

Sheridan, J. H., "Attacking Wastes and Saving Money . . . Some of the Time," *Industry Week,* February 17, 1992, *241*:4, 43.

Simpson, Ralph David, "Taxing Variable Cost: Environmental Regulation as Industrial Policy." Resources for the Future Working Paper ENR93–12, 1993.

Smith, Zachary A, *The Environmental Policy Paradox.* Englewood Cliffs, N.J.: Prentice Hall, 1992.

United States Environmental Protection Agency, "Multiple Pathways to Super Efficient Refrigerators," Washington, D.C., 1992.

U.S. Congress, Office of Technology Assessment, "Industry, Technology, and the Environment: Competitive Challenges and Business Opportunities," OTA-ITE-586, Washington, D.C., 1994.

van der Linde, Claas, "The Micro-Economic Implications of Environmental Regulation: A Preliminary Framework." In *Environmental Policies and Industrial Competitiveness.* Paris: Organization of Economic Co-Operation and Development, 1993, pp. 69–77.

van der Linde, Claas, "Competitive Implications of Environmental Regulation in the Cell Battery Industry," Hochschule St. Gallen, St. Gallen, forthcoming 1995a.

van der Linde, Claas, "Competitive Implications of Environmental Regulation in the Printing Ink Industry," Hochschule St. Gallen, St. Gallen, forthcoming 1995b.

van der Linde, Claas, "Competitive Implications of Environmental Regulation in the Refrigerator Industry," Hochschule St. Gallen, St. Gallen, forthcoming 1995c.

Wheeler, David, and Ashoka Mody, "International Investment Location Decisions: The Case of U.S. Firms," *Journal of International Economics,* August 1992, *33*, 57–76.

White, A. L., M. Becker, and J. Goldstein, "Alternative Approaches to the Financial Evaluation of Industrial Pollution Prevention Investments," prepared for the New Jersey Department of Environmental Protection, Division of Science and Research, November 1991.

[6]

Environmental Regulations and International Competitiveness: Strategies for Canada's Forest Products Industry

Alan M. Rugman

INTRODUCTION

This article describes a case study of the manner in which environmental regulations in one country can affect the competitiveness of an industry from another country. An existing analytical base (Rugman and Verbeke, 1990, 1992) will be extended and applied to assess the impact of environmental regulations on the strategic management and competitiveness of Canadian firms, especially in the forestry sector. The work is generalizable because most industries from small, open, trading economies (like Canada's) need access to a triad market, like that of the United States.

The author is on the Faculty of Management, University of Toronto, 105 St. George Street, Toronto, Ontario, M5S 3E6, Canada.

A previous version of this article was first presented at the Academy of Management Division, Social Issues in Management, Dallas, August 1994 at the session on "Trade, Technology and the Environment." The author thanks participants at the session for their helpful comments and he also acknowledges the comments of participants at a seminar at the University of Toronto's Centre for International Business. Research support for this work on competitiveness was provided as part of a strategic grant by the Social Sciences and Humanities Research Council of Canada.

The International Executive, Vol. 37(5) 451–465 (September/October 1995)
 CCC 0020-6652/95/050451-15

ENVIRONMENTAL REGULATIONS AND COMPETITIVENESS STRATEGY

The thesis of this study is that environmental regulations by large triad groups such as the European Community (EC) and the United States can pose nontariff barriers to entry to firms from small, open economies like Canada. The "asymmetry" in size between the triad markets, where economies of scale and scope are possible, and small, open economies, means that access to a triad market is required for a Canadian firm to develop a global strategy (see Rugman, 1994b). Knowing this, rival firms in the EC or United States can lobby for tighter environmental regulations within their regimes, thereby forcing outsiders to incur costs in conforming to triad-based measures, because the outsiders cannot afford to lose access to these critical markets. In other words, there is a potential incentive for US and EC firms to attempt to "capture" the administration of environmental laws and use them as entry barriers.

A related issue is that international trade law, with its emphasis on national treatment, does not fully compensate for the size asymmetry problem. The North American Free Trade Agreement (NAFTA) contains environmental provisions based on the principle of national treatment (see Rugman, 1994a), meaning that Canadian-based firms have an equal opportunity to adapt to new US environmental regulations along with their US rivals. Under NAFTA and the GATT, US-based environmentalists have no international trade rights to establish the extraterritoriality of domestic US environmental laws, because the principle of national treatment means that US laws cannot be applied to the sovereign jurisdictions of Canada and Mexico. Under NAFTA an environmental commission has been set up to ensure no lowering of environmental standards in the three member countries and to monitor policies designed to increase standards, but its entire operation is subject to the national treatment principle.

From the viewpoint of a Canadian firm selling its products to the large US market (such as in the lumber, fish, pork, wheat, or even steel sectors), a domestic US environmental regulation can affect its trade strategy. If domestic US laws are enforced against Canadian imports, entry could be denied Canadian produced products that do not comply with US environmental standards. Note that it is the US regulations that matter here, not the Canadian ones.

However, if US laws are tightened it can affect the strategy of Canadian firms. Because US market access is vital for most Canadian firms to achieve basic economies of scale in a globalized industry, denial of entry to Canadian exports will require a substitution of exports from Canada toward foreign direct investment in the United

States. Thus US environmental laws could force Canadian firms to take over US rival firms, or to open up new business behind the US environmental shield. Then, of course, the Canadian multinational enterprises (MNEs) would operate according to US practices, so US environmentalists would be happy. But Canadians may be unhappy at the forced transfer of business out of Canada and consumers in both Canada and the United States would suffer due to the loss of efficiency gains as the true comparative advantages of such Canadian—US industries are distorted by new US environmental regulations.

THEORETICAL LITERATURE

To analyze the use of environmental regulations as a strategy with asymmetric differences between firms in the triad and outsiders, it is useful to build upon the mainstream literature in strategic management. According to Porter (1990), a strong "home base" diamond is required to develop successful corporate strategies for national competitiveness. Furthermore, in an analysis of Canadian competitiveness, Porter and Armstrong (1992) argue that Canadian firms can only "tap into" the US market and its diamond characteristics and, at best, achieve parity with US rivals but never beat them. The principle of national treatment does, indeed, permit parity but parity is not a competitive advantage; the latter requires the ability to beat the average competitor.

In a related article Rugman (1994b), building on Rugman and Verbeke (1993b) and Rugman and D'Cruz (1991), argued that a "double diamond" approach to corporate strategy is required for Canadian managers. They need to understand both the Canadian and US diamonds and then they need to develop a North American strategy in order to have a chance of beating their US rivals. In developing a Canadian corporate strategy to deal with US environmental regulations, it is apparent that the double diamond approach offers very useful insights and guidelines. Indeed, Canadian managers who can move quickly to respond to such change are engaging in a form of "national responsiveness" (see Rugman and Verbeke, 1993b; and Rugman, 1994b).

This viewpoint, however, is not widely accepted, and has been explicitly rejected by Porter and Armstrong (1992). Instead, Porter and Monitor (1991) have been interpreted as advocating strong environmental regulations in Canada, the home base, so that its firms can embody these strengths in their sales abroad. This is the so-called "Porter Hypothesis." To be precise, in Porter and Monitor (1991) it is stated that:

> Stringent standards and regulations for product performance and environmental impact can create and upgrade competitive advantage by pressuring firms to improve product and process quality. Further, standards that anticipate international trends often have particularly beneficial benefits.

This is not a good recommendation for the two reasons discussed above. First, there is an asymmetry of market access to a triad market for Canadian-based firms with the small size of the "domestic" market not providing a strong enough base for new environmental strategies relative to the large US "foreign" market. Second, the double diamond framework suggests that it is difficult to build a supportive institutional framework in the Canadian diamond alone and that an understanding of US economic regulations is just as important as Canadian ones. Thus environmental policies in Canada's triad customers (the United States and EC) are much more relevant benchmarks for competitiveness strategies than are purely Canadian environmental policies.

Although the Porter policy recommendation may be relevant for a triad economy, it is entirely wrong for Canada, because over 70 percent of Canadian trade and investment is with the United States and the host country environmental regulations are much more important, for strategy, than Canadian home-based ones. In other words, the Porter hypothesis of tight, home-based environmental regulations completely ignores the asymmetry trap and the related issue of the need for triad market access for companies from smaller nations.

These issues of competitiveness, home and host country diamonds, national treatment, national size asymmetry, and market access are explored in this article, all as they relate to environmental regulations. The case example taken is the West Coast Canadian forest products cluster. For discussion of the institutional differences between the British Columbia (provincially owned) forestry system and the US Pacific Northwest "market-based" system, see Hoberg (1994). The international competitiveness of Canada's West Coast Forest Products Cluster has been analyzed in Rugman and D'Cruz (1991, 1993). The concept of "clusters" is found in Porter (1990) and has been adapted in a Canadian context by Rugman and D'Cruz (1991, 1993) and Rugman and Verbeke (1993a). Indeed, a distinction has been made between the competitiveness of regions, clusters, and business networks, in the discussion of the "five partners" framework of international competitiveness (see D'Cruz and Rugman, 1992, 1993). In the next sections this work on market access and asymmetry is reviewed; then it is applied to the issue of the impact of environmental regulations on competitiveness, using the double diamond framework.

TRIAD MARKET ACCESS STRATEGIES FOR CANADIAN FOREST PRODUCTS

The Canadian forest products industry consists of two distinct clusters. First is the West Coast forest products cluster based in the province of British Columbia (BC) and led by large MNEs like MacMillan Bloedel and Fletcher Challenge. Second is the Eastern Canada forest product cluster, including the Atlantic provinces, Quebec, and Ontario. This cluster is led by paper and newsprint firms like Abitibi Price, Stone Container, and Repap. The majority of sales of the BC cluster goes to Asia and the United States, whereas the Eastern Canadian cluster has a much bigger proportion of sales to Europe.

The Eastern Canada forest products cluster is potentially much more affected by EC trade and environmental regulations than is the West Coast cluster, although some recent measures also affect the latter. For example, for many years there has been an EC quota on newsprint sales from Canada, as well as other nontariff barriers to trade such as discriminatory watermark requirements for paper products. Recently the EC has pursued a series of environmental and health regulations to shelter European business from Canadian competitors. One example, over the 1992–1994 period, has been the pinewood nematode regulation. This is designed to keep out Canadian green lumber and force it to be kiln dried, thereby increasing the relative costs of Canadian compared to Scandinavian lumber. Other environmental regulations are proposed, especially in Germany, for example, to enforce the end of chlorine bleaching for pulp and paper products (due to chemical side affects in Canadian waterways). Another environmental barrier to trade is the proposed ban against sales of Canadian West Coast paper products in the EC due to the adverse environmental affects of clear cutting (which led the British subsidiaries of two firms, Scott Paper and Kimberly Clark, to terminate contracts in 1993 with Canadian suppliers of paper products, specifically in response to threats from Greenpeace to boycott their products).

Perhaps the most important example of environmental regulations affecting Canadian firms is state level newspaper recycling laws, especially in California. This can be considered as such a significant factor that it may require a switch from exporting to foreign direct investment by Canadian MNEs such as MacMillan Bloedel and Noranda Forest Products. This subnational regulation could have a major impact on the global strategy of Canada's West Coast forest products cluster. The competitiveness issue is that a state level requirement for 50 percent recycled fiber in newsprint runs up against the logistical impossibility for Canadian firms in transporting old newspapers and magazines back to their "home base" newsprint mills in Canada. It is a regulation that discriminates in favor of US based mills against foreign ones. Given that approximately 80 percent of all newsprint produced in Canada is exported to the United States, it is too costly to transport enough of the used newsprint back to Canada and convert it for use in the Canadian mills. Instead, Canadian firms will need to access the "urban forest" of large American cities instead of the natural forest in British Columbia. To do so in an efficient manner they will need to make major capital investments in new deinking plants in California and other states with these environmental regulations. (This actually shifts the location of environmental pollution from Canada to California, because a deinking plant is basically a huge amount of chemical sludge close to a city.)

Such state level environmental laws will have profound repercussions on the strategic management of the forest products industry and it will benefit local US firms at the expense of foreign (Canadian) firms. The state laws are discriminatory in an international context. This occurs despite NAFTA giving Canadian firms national treatment because the California type laws are applied equally to Canadian and US firms. Yet the size asymmetry effect will force Canadian firms out of their home base and destroy Canada's comparative advantage in resources. To survive in this global business, Canadian firms are forced to switch from exporting from British Columbia to foreign direct investment in California.

The legality, or illegality, of such laws is not the issue. What matters is the impact on Canadian firms of denying them market access to a triad economy. When subnational levels of government impose such indirect barriers to international trade and commerce, these laws effectively discriminate against foreign producers and protect domestic producers. This is an example of the theory of "shelter," as developed by Rugman and Verbeke (1990, 1992). Given that shelter exists, how can Canadian firms react? The next sections outline a strategic rationale for Canadian firms to be nationally responsive to US environmental regulations.

THE DOUBLE DIAMOND AND CANADIAN COMPETITIVENESS IN FOREST PRODUCTS

The relevant conceptual tool for Canadian managers to employ when developing a global competitive advantage is that of a North American double diamond. Strategies for Canadian businesses need to be designed across both the US and Canadian diamonds (see Rugman and D'Cruz, 1991, 1993). For an American business, the US market is large enough to provide rivalry, customers, and supporting infrastructure and demand conditions to the extent that the home nation diamond tests and hones the ability of its firms to compete successfully. Yet, the Canadian market has not and does not offer such rigors and opportunity. It is for this key reason of asymmetry that Canadian firms should not in theory (and do not in practice) consider the US market as an export market but as an extension of the domestic (Canadian) market. More specifically, Canadian managers look to North America as a regional home base and do not use a single Canadian home base diamond. This double diamond thinking is illustrated in Figure 1.

For US-based MNEs, Porter's (1990) single diamond model makes conceptual sense but it is made operational due to the special case of the United States as a triad market. US-based multinationals have grown up in a large domestic market that provided opportunity for product development and economies of scale (Rugman, 1992). The size and attractiveness of the US market is reflected in the fact that US-based multinationals typically garner 20–40 percent of their revenues from foreign sales versus 60–90 percent for Canadian-based multinationals (see Globerman, 1994). Another ex-

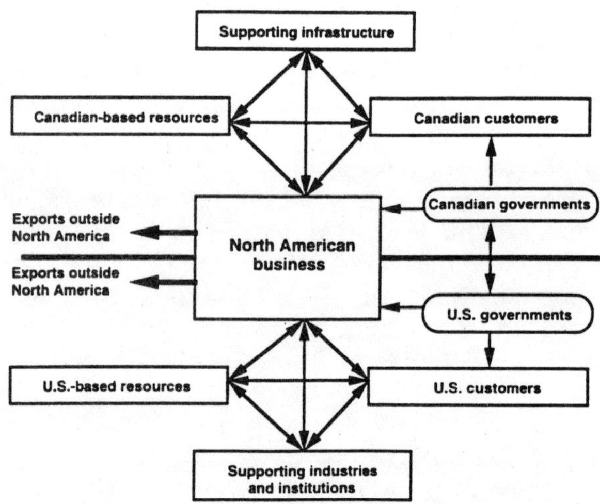

Figure 1 Double diamond framework

Source: Adapted from Alan M. Rugman and Joseph R. D'Cruz, *Fast Forward: Improving Canada's International Competitiveness* (Toronto: Kodak Canada, 1991).

ample of a Canadian-type company with too small a domestic national diamond is Nestlé, which obtains 95 percent of its revenues from outside Switzerland. (This latter point was also made by Dunning, 1993).

The relevance of the North American double diamond for Canadian strategic management has been discussed elsewhere (see Rugman, 1992; Rugman and D'Cruz, 1993; Rugman, 1994b; Rugman and Verbeke, 1993a). To build a global business, Canadian firms need access to a triad market. Companies in the forest products industry on Canada's West Coast benefit from relative nearness to two of these triad markets, the United States and Japan. Across Canada, there are clusters of industries in which firms face competition from close rivals, draw inputs from supporting industries and infrastructure, and depend upon the close availability of physical and human resources. In work by Rugman and D'Cruz (1991) building on Porter's (1990) use of strategic clusters, several such clusters of industries are readily identifiable in Canada. The competitiveness of the West Coast forest products cluster can be analyzed using Figure 1. This is a straightforward application of Porter (1990) as modified by Rugman and D'Cruz (1991, 1993).

Resource Base

The widespread forests of British Columbia and parts of western Alberta offer a close and easily accessible physical resource/input for the cluster. Within the cluster, low value-added processing or raw product opens firms to the risks of the cyclicality of world demand and prices. The competitiveness of this cluster is affected by trade sanctions arising from disputes with the United States over alleged industry subsidies (for further discussion see Governments below). The cluster must compete with the equally well-forested US Pacific Northwest states and the US South with its faster growing trees. Increasingly, environmental concerns and interest group lobbying are affecting the ability of the cluster to exploit and process/refine this resource base which impacts costs. Forest products firms have heavily unionized work forces that affects cost structures and the ability to change to remain globally competitive.

Supporting Industries and Infrastructure

This part of the cluster is not as widely developed as is necessary for international competitiveness. The relatively small economies of British Columbia and Alberta hinder the depth of this infrastructure.

Customers

The domestic market of Western Canada does not provide a large enough base of demanding customers to support the development of new, globally competitive products and services. The United States has served this purpose in some product lines and continued focus on the North American customer will improve product development. Demanding customers, like those in more competitive markets such as the United States and where consumer demands for quality are paramount such as Japan, help push firms to focus on the production of higher value-added products. This focus is necessary to reduce dependence on the depth of the resource base (the forests) and public subsidies.

Leading Firms

MacMillan Bloedel is the largest company in the cluster and has been recognized as a leader in the industry. Continued growth of competitors should enhance the ability of the cluster to develop internationally competitive products and advantages.

Governments

Both Canadian government policy (at provincial level of course) and US government policy is important. The BC government from 1990–1994 increased the taxation of BC-based forest product companies through changes in the stumpage rates and other methods. The Canadian Federal Government has helped to organize legal defense against ongoing US countervailing duty cases (see Stranks, 1994). US use of countervailing duty and the abusive use of this type of administered protection has meant that Canadian exporters have been forced to participate in legal cases before the US International Trade Commission and the US Department of Commerce on an almost continual basis since 1983 when three major countervail cases were heard (see Anderson, 1995). The direct legal costs of the 1991–1994 case and appeals has run to over Cdn $40 million for Canadian firms. Elements of a nationally responsive strategy are beginning to appear, for example when a Canadian firm persuaded the US home builders association to file an intervention on their behalf stating that a countervail duty on imports of Canadian softwood lumber would increase US house prices. But, in general, Canadian firms have been slow to adopt a full double diamond strategy and they have relied too much on the Canadian government to carry the ball instead of making a US play themselves.

Clusters

Porter (1990) also says that a nation's industries tend to cluster for synergistic purposes and that national competitiveness depends upon success in clusters of industries, not just in isolated industries. This clustering occurs in the home base single diamond and competitiveness is measured by exports or outward foreign direct investment. According to Porter, successful industries develop both vertical (buyer and supplier) and horizontal (customers, distribution channels, technology sharing) relationships that, combined with the "systemic" nature of the diamond, help to create other successful and competitive industries. Moreover, this replication of success is alleged by Porter to occur in both large and small countries, although the nature of the clusters varies according to national/regional-specific factors like legislation and industrial/union history.

Porter's view of clustering needs to be modified to take account of the double diamond. The West Coast forest products cluster will not evolve toward a more efficient and competitive system within its home base. The increase in US environmental, and other protectionist, regulations means that its cluster is now transborder. Several good examples of clustering in economies similar in nature to Canada's highlight this double diamond process. Sweden has a competitive pulp and paper industry and draws on the forest resource much like British Columbia does. However, unlike Canada, Sweden has preferential access to the EC triad market, and this helps it to be internationally competitive in related industries such as sulfur boilers, paper making machinery, paper drying machinery, wood handling machinery, etc. The reinforcing nature of a cluster in developing competitiveness in related industries is illustrated sharply by the fact that Sweden is competitive in chemicals required for pulp and paper making but not in chemicals in general (Porter, 1990: 149). But Porter fails to note that if Sweden did not have secure market access to the EC, its competitiveness and cluster development would have been slower, as is the danger in British Columbia.

While Porter's views on the single home diamond of competitiveness and the clustering of industries are necessary background (and relevant for triad-based clusters), they need to be modified and adapted in Canada for the asymmetry reasons given earlier. Canadian corporate strategy must necessarily be less nationalist and home-country oriented than Porter implies. Canadian forest products firms are competing not just against other Canadian or American or Swedish forest product firms; they are competing with US firms and clusters who can exploit US laws and environmental regulations and deny market access. If Swedish pulp and paper firms (who have secure access to the EC) benefit from equipment innovation, chemical process improvement, etc. derived from cluster relationships, then they are likely to gain cost and/or product advantages over Canadian firms (who are being denied access to the EC and the United States). In any case, Canadian firms are finding it harder to get their products into protected US and EC markets. Thus the vital amendment to Porter's home base, single diamond cluster thinking is the critical issue of market access. To achieve this requires a strategy of national responsiveness (see Rugman, 1994b).

ENVIRONMENTAL REGULATIONS AND CORPORATE STRATEGY

Figure 2 brings together these issues of firm-level strategy with and without a firm's interaction with government. This is a simple variation of the Bartlett and Ghoshal (1989) framework of globalization and national responsiveness. On the horizontal axis is depicted the firm's responsiveness to environmental regulations, low and high. (No distinction needs to be made on this axis between domestic and foreign firms, although the matrix will be used later to illustrate the arguments developed in this article.) On the vertical axis is shown the firm's commitment to pure globalization (such as increased market share and/or profitability), that is, ignoring any environmental considerations.

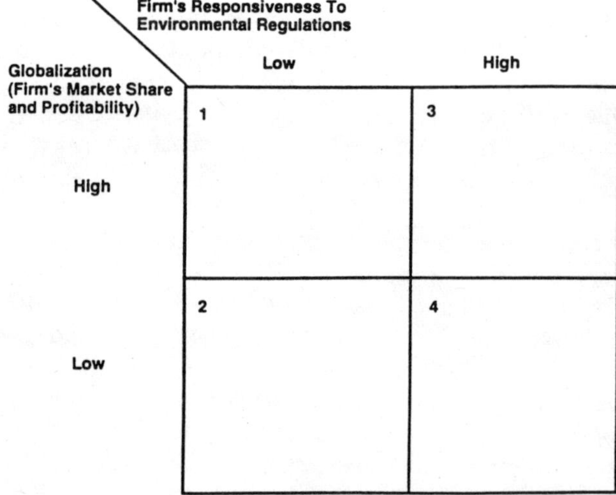

Figure 2 Environmental regulations and corporate strategy

There are some firms that are potentially concerned with both globalization and environmental responsiveness. These are in quadrant 3, and will be discussed in detail below. There are other firms who ignore environmental regulations and have a single minded focus on globalization. These are the traditional "business first" efficiency-driven firms in quadrant 1. These are the firms identified by environmentalists as ignoring environmental issues, which is quite true in quadrant 1, because a competitive advantage can be achieved by efficiency-driven strategies alone, such as price competition. In contrast, conceptually at least, there can be firms in quadrant 4 that are so highly responsive to environmental regulations that they can ignore the firm's objective of globalization. In quadrant 4 the firm can beat other firms solely on its environmental responsiveness strategy. While both quadrants 1 and 4 have potentially viable strategies, the unfortunate firms in quadrant 2 whose globalization and environmental commitment are both low, are losers. This indicates the need to change strategies in order to move out of quadrant 2.

Potentially the most interesting quadrant to consider is number 3. The significance of a quadrant 3 strategy is that it suggests that a firm can beat other firms by combining managerial skills in globalization and environmental responsiveness. This, of course, is not easy to accomplish. The firm must make a major investment in the development of green management skills, such as the ability to adapt quickly to government imposed regulations; indeed, it is the ability to anticipate such changes in policy that will give the firm a competitive edge over rivals slower to respond to environmental pressures. Examples of high environmental responsiveness would be firms that develop the ability to negotiate with government officials and with non-government organizations (NGOs), perhaps by developing a special team that can provide reliable and relevant scientific information about the environmental impact of the firm's operations, where this information can be unbundled from the company's proprietary firm-specific know-how. A quadrant 3 strategy means that the firm must make a credible commitment to overcome the environmentalists' viewpoint that the firm can be opportunistic in its dealings with them. Thus, the implementation of strategies in quadrant 3 requires transaction cost reducing behavior by the firm.

EXAMPLES OF MATRIX STRATEGIES

To help illustrate the Figure 2 framework, the following examples may be useful. In quadrant 1 the forestry firm follows the generic strategies of cost, differentiation, or finding a global niche. In the case of newsprint and paper producers the firm can be a "low cost polluter," that is, its competitive advantage is derived from price competition and it ignores environmental issues. Many environmentalists simply assume that all producers are in quadrant 1, following economic, efficiency-driven strategies that ignore environmental externalities. For example, the Canadian forest products sector has been accused of ignoring the effects of chlorine bleaching in the production of BC newsprint.

In quadrant 4 the opposite strategy is followed, that is, the firm ignores efficiency-driven globalization issues and concentrates only on being responsive to environmental regulations; indeed the firm tries to anticipate new environmental thinking. This is a "green alone" strategy. Here firms can beat the average competitor by having firm-specific advantages in responsiveness to environmental regulations. There are few firms today in quadrant 4, which is a pity from the viewpoint of Greenpeace, as it would like regulations to be stringent enough to force firms into quadrant 4. Some firms may develop environmental technologies at home due to stringent domestic environmental regulations and then export such products or services. This is a green alone export strategy, and there are a few examples of such companies doing business in Mexico since NAFTA.

Quadrant 2 deals with local products and services where environmental issues are ignored, that is, a "local polluter." Many observers allege that some of Mexico's manufacturing sector is in quadrant 2.

Quadrant 3 is theoretically attractive but practically difficult to achieve. It is desirable because both economic efficiency and environmental responsiveness is achieved but this dual focus requires a mixed (or matrix) organizational structure that few firms can develop. To implement a quadrant 3 strategy would require combining the talents of efficiency-driven accountants, economists, and production managers with the sensitivity and responsiveness skills of marketing and government relations managers.

One interesting potential difference between quadrants 3 and 4 in terms of environmental strategies is that firms in quadrant 3 could possibly succeed with *compliance* to environmental regulations whereas, in quadrant 4, a more proactive strategy is required. In other words, to beat the average competitor on environment alone requires the anticipation of new environmental regulations and the design of a firm-specific advantage.

Canadian firms that pursue quadrant 1 strategies in Figure 2 are in danger, and they need to develop quadrant 3 strategies. In the long run, perhaps Canadian firms in quadrant 3 can even beat US rivals. There is little evidence of much movement from quadrant 1 to 3 in industries such as lumber, steel, pork, and others where the FTA and NAFTA dispute settlement panels have been used frequently as nation to nation conflicts are pushed along by corporate rivalry.

To summarize, for sensible reasons of corporate survival, Canadian firms must adopt strategies to comply with the increased environmental regulations of larger triad countries like the United States. The size asymmetry of the small open trading economy versus the large triad market means that the larger market's environmental standards become the norm for strategic decision making when there are adverse repercussions in global consumer welfare. From this perspective environmental regulations are economically inefficient, but need to be dealt with through corporate strategy.

REFERENCES

Anderson, A. (1995) *Seeking Common Ground: An Analysis of the Canada–U.S. Dispute Settlement Cases,* Boulder, CO: Westview Press.

Bartlett, C.A. and Ghoshal, S. (1989) *Managing Across Borders: The Transnational Solution,* Boston, MA: Harvard Business School Press.

D'Cruz, J.R. and Rugman, A.M. (1992) "Business Networks for International Competitiveness," *Business Quarterly,* 56, 101–107.

D'Cruz, J.R. and Rugman, A.M. (1993) "Developing International Competitiveness: The Five Partners Model," *Business Quarterly,* 58, 60–72.

Dunning, J.H. (1993) *The Globalization of Business: The Challenge of the 1990s,* London: Routledge.

Globerman, S. (Ed.) (1994) *Canadian-Based Multinationals,* Calgary: University of Calgary Press.

Hoberg, G. (1994) *Regulating Forestry: A Comparison of British Columbia and the U.S. Pacific Northwest,* Discussion paper, School of Policy Studies, Queen's University, 94–107.

Porter, M.E. (1990) *The Competitive Advantage of Nations,* New York: The Free Press.

Porter, M.E. and Armstrong, J. (1992) "Canada at the Crossroads: Dialogue," *Business Quarterly,* Spring, 8–12.

Porter, M.E. and Monitor (1991) *Canada at the Crossroads,* Business Council on National Issues, Ottawa, Canada.

Rugman, A.M. (1992) "Porter Takes the Wrong Turn," *Business Quarterly,* 56, 59–64.

Rugman, A.M. (Ed.) (1994a) *Foreign Investment and NAFTA,* Columbia SC: University of South Carolina Press.

Rugman, A.M. (1994b) "Strategic Management and Canadian Multinational Enterprises," in S. Globerman (Ed.), *Canadian-Based Multinationals,* Calgary: University of Calgary Press, 241–262.

Rugman, A.M. and D'Cruz, J.R. (1991) *Fast Forward: Improving Canada's International Competitiveness,* Canada: Kodak Canada Inc.

Rugman, A.M. and D'Cruz, J.R. (1993) "The 'Double Diamond' Model of International Competitiveness," *Management International Review,* 33, 17–40.

Rugman, A.M. and Verbeke, A. (1990) *Global Corporate Strategy and Trade Policy,* London: Routledge.

Rugman, A.M. and Verbeke, A. (1992) "Shelter, Trade Policy and Strategies for Multinational Enterprises," in A.M. Rugman and A. Verbeke (Eds.), *Research in Global Strategic Management, Vol. 3, Corporate Response to Global Change,* Greenwich, CT: JAI Press, 3–25.

Rugman, A.M. and Verbeke, A. (1993a) "Foreign Subsidiaries and Multinational Strategic Management: An Extension and Correction of Porter's Single Diamond Framework," *Management International Review,* 33 (Special Issue 2), 71–84.

Rugman, A.M. and Verbeke, A. (1993b) "Generic Strategies in Global Competition," in *Research in Global Strategic Management, Vol. 4, Beyond the Three Generics,* Greenwich, CT: JAI Press, 3–16.

Stranks, R.T. (1994) *Pandora's Box?: Countervailing Duties and the Environment,* Department of Foreign Affairs and International Trade, Ottawa, Canada.

[7]

Journal of Economic Literature
Vol. XXXIII (March 1995), pp. 132–163

Environmental Regulation and the Competitiveness of U.S. Manufacturing: What Does the Evidence Tell Us?

By

ADAM B. JAFFE
Brandeis University and National Bureau of Economic Research

STEVEN R. PETERSON
Economics Resource Group

PAUL R. PORTNEY
Resources for the Future

and

ROBERT N. STAVINS
Harvard University and Resources for the Future

The authors thank Lawrence Goulder, Raymond Kopp, William Nordhaus, Richard Schmalensee, Martin Weitzman, David Wheeler, and participants in seminars at Harvard University and Resources for the Future for helpful comments. Funding for previous work on this subject from the U.S. Department of Commerce is gratefully acknowledged. The authors alone are responsible for any omissions or other errors.

1. *Introduction*

MORE THAN TWO DECADES ago, the first Earth Day in 1970 marked the beginning of the modern environmental movement. Since that time, the United States has spent more than $1 trillion to prevent or reduce environmental damages created by industrial and commercial activities. During the latter part of this period, the U.S. economy has moved from a position of approximate trade balance on a long-term basis to a position of chronic trade deficit. The coincidence of these two major trends has led many to suspect that environmental regulation may be playing a major causal role in impairing the "competitiveness" of U.S. firms.[1]

The conventional wisdom is that environmental regulations impose significant costs, slow productivity growth, and thereby hinder the ability of U.S. firms to compete in international markets. This loss of competitiveness is believed to be reflected in declining exports, increasing imports, and a long-term movement of manufacturing capacity from the United States to other countries, particularly in "pollution-intensive" industries.[2]

Under a more recent, revisionist view, environmental regulations are seen not only as benign in their impacts on international competitiveness, but actually as a net *positive* force driving private firms and the economy as a whole to become more competitive in international markets.[3] During the past few years, a heated debate has arisen in the United States revolving around these two views.[4] This paper assembles and assesses the evidence on these hypothetical linkages between environmental regulation and competitiveness.

The terms of the debate and the nature of the problems have not always been clear, but it is possible to sketch the general nature of the concerns. Much of the discussion has revolved around the fear that environmental regulation may reduce net exports in the manufacturing sector, particularly in "pollution-intensive" goods. Such a change in our trade position could have several effects. First, in the short run, a reduction in net exports in manufacturing will exacerbate the overall trade imbalance. Although we are likely to return toward trade balance in the long run, one of the mechanisms through which this happens is a decline in the value of the dollar. This means that imported goods become more expensive, thus reducing the standard of living for many people. Second, if those industries most affected by regulation employ less educated workers, then this portion of the labor force will be particularly hard hit, because those workers may have an especially hard time finding new jobs at comparable wages. Third, a diminishing U.S. share of world capacity in petroleum-refining, steel, autos, and other industries could endanger economic security. Finally, even in the absence of these income distribution or economic security concerns, the rearrangement of production from pollution-intensive to other industries creates a broader set of social costs, at least in the short run. Because the "short run" could last for years or even decades, these transition costs are also a legitimate policy concern.

[1] This argument is related but not identical to expressed concerns about the loss of "competitiveness" of the U.S. as a whole. For a trenchant criticism of the notion that countries "compete" in the same ways that individual firms do, see Paul Krugman (1994).

[2] The theoretical argument that ambitious environmental regulations could harm a nation's comparative advantage is well established, but our focus is exclusively on empirical evidence. On the former, see Rudiger Pethig (1975); Horst Siebert (1977); Gary W. Yohe (1979); and Martin C. McGuire (1982).

[3] These ideas, generally associated most with Michael E. Porter (1991), have become widely disseminated among policy makers. For example, a U.S. Environmental Protection Agency (EPA) conference recently concluded that environmental regulations induce "more cost-effective processes that both reduce emissions and the overall cost of doing business. . ." (U.S. Environmental Protection Agency 1992b).

[4] For an overview of the dimensions of this debate, see Richard B. Stewart (1993). Unfortunately, this debate has often been clouded by the very criteria chosen by proponents of alternative views. For example, there has been substantial debate *and* confusion among policy makers about whether environmental regulations create new jobs and whether such "job creation" ought to be considered a regulatory benefit or cost (if either). See Thomas D. Hopkins (1992).

TABLE 1
U.S. EMISSIONS OF SIX MAJOR AIR POLLUTANTS, 1970–1991[a]

Year	SO_2	NO_x	VOCs	CO	TSPs	Lead
1970	100[b]	100	100	100	100	100
1975	90	107	82	85	58	72
1980	84	124	79	81	48	34
1981	79	113	77	79	45	27
1982	75	107	71	73	40	26
1983	73	104	74	75	41	22
1984	76	106	77	71	43	19
1985	76	102	72	67	41	9
1986	74	99	67	62	38	3
1987	74	100	68	61	39	3
1988	75	104	68	61	42	3
1989	76	102	63	55	40	3
1990	74	102	64	55	39	3
1991	73	99	62	50	39	2

Source: U.S. Environmental Protection Agency (1992a).
[a] The six "criteria air pollutants" listed are: sulfur dioxide (SO_2); nitrogen oxides (NO_x); reactive volatile organic compounds (VOCs); carbon monoxide (CO); total suspended particulates (TSPs); and lead.
[b] Indexed to 1970 emissions, set equal to 100. Note that these are aggregate national emissions, not emissions per capita or emissions per unit of GNP; the latter two statistics would, of course, exhibit greater downward trends.

There are a number of reasons to believe that the link between environmental regulation and competitiveness could be significant. First, environmental regulation has grown significantly in the United States since 1970, and substantial gains have been achieved in reducing pollutant emissions (Table 1).

But according to the U.S. Environmental Protection Agency (EPA), the annual cost of complying with environmental regulation administered by EPA now exceeds $125 billion in the United States, or about 2.1 percent of gross domestic product (GDP).[5] Furthermore, EPA has projected that annual environmental compliance spending may reach $190 billion by the end of this decade. If that happens, the United States will be devoting nearly 2.6 percent of its GDP to environmental compliance by the year 2000.[6]

It is extremely difficult to compare this compliance cost burden with that borne by competing firms in other countries. Environmental requirements throughout most of the developing world are less stringent than ours, and related compliance costs are hence generally lower. On the other hand, some data suggest that other countries, such as Germany, have regulatory programs that give rise to regulatory costs roughly comparable to those imposed on U.S. firms (Table 2).[7]

Putting aside the potential effect of differences in regulatory stringency, there are other ways in which environmental regulations may affect competi-

[5] As we discuss later in some detail, these direct compliance costs represent only a share of the overall social costs of environmental regulation. For example, Weitzman (1994) estimates that the total "environmental drag" on the U.S. economy may be two to three times greater than these fractions of GNP dedicated to compliance spending would suggest.

[6] Figures are in constant 1992 dollars (throughout the paper, unless otherwise specified), assuming a seven percent cost of capital (U.S. Environmental Protection Agency 1990). These estimates include both capital and operating costs. Projections for compliance costs of existing regulations are based on historical extrapolations. Projections for the costs of new and proposed regulations are based on EPA regulatory analyses. EPA actually makes its projections in terms of gross national product (GNP), rather than gross domestic product (GDP), but any difference between the two is small compared to uncertainty over compliance costs.

[7] It is indicative of the data problems in this area that the OECD numbers in Table 2 differ in both level *and* trend from the EPA numbers cited above and presented in Table 4. It is our view that the data in the latter table more accurately reflect annual expenditures in the United States to comply with federal environmental regulations. It would be helpful if the environmental agencies of other nations made the same effort as the U.S. Environmental Protection Agency to keep track of and regularly report estimated compliance expenditures.

TABLE 2
POLLUTION ABATEMENT AND CONTROL EXPENDITURES FOR SELECTED OECD COUNTRIES AS A PERCENTAGE OF GROSS DOMESTIC PRODUCT

	1981	1982	1983	1984	1985	1986	1987	1988	1989	1990
United States	1.5	1.5	1.5	1.4	1.4	1.4	1.4	1.3	1.4	1.4
France	0.9	0.9	0.9	0.8	0.9	0.8	1.0	1.0	1.0	1.0
West Germany	1.5	1.5	1.4	1.4	1.5	1.5	1.6	1.6	1.6	1.6
Netherlands	—	1.2	—	—	1.3	1.5	1.5	—	1.5	—
United Kingdom	1.6	—	—	—	1.3	1.3	—	—	—	1.5

Sources: Organization for Economic Cooperation and Development (1990, p. 40), for years 1981–1985; Organization for Economic Cooperation and Development (1993b, p. 11) for years 1986–1990.

tiveness. Holding constant the *stringency* of environmental standards, the *form* these rules take can potentially affect business location. For instance, U.S. environmental regulations often go beyond specifying numerical discharge standards for particular sources or source categories, and mandate, instead, specific control technologies or processes. If other countries tend to avoid such technological mandates and thus allow more flexibility in compliance, manufacturing abroad may be relatively attractive because sources will have the ability to use new, innovative, and low-cost ways to meet discharge standards.

Another difference between U.S. and foreign environmental regulation should also be recognized: namely, the adversarial approach to regulation typically taken in the United States. Regulatory decisions in the United States are time-consuming and characterized by litigation and other legal wrangling. By way of contrast, a more cooperative relationship is said to exist between regulator and regulatee in some other countries, with the United Kingdom offered as the definitive example (David Vogel 1986). Unfortunately, data on these aspects of respective costs are essentially unavailable.

In general, the studies that attempt to analyze directly the effects of environmental regulations on trade and competitiveness are limited in number. If one casts a wide enough net, however, by defining competitiveness rather broadly and by searching for indirect as well as direct evidence, it is possible to identify more than one hundred studies potentially capable of shedding some light on the relationship.[8] It is nearly the case, however, that no two of these studies ask the same question or even examine the same problem. This is one of the challenges of trying to assess the competing hypotheses of the environment-competitiveness linkage.

Despite our relatively broad focus with regard to competitiveness, the scope of this review is somewhat limited in another respect. Specifically, we limit our attention here to studies shedding light on the effects of environmental regulation on manufacturing firms. This is not because of an absence of such regulation in natural resource industries such as forestry, agriculture, mining, and com-

[8] For a comprehensive review of the literature, see Jaffe et al. (1993). An earlier survey is provided by Judith M. Dean (1992). See, also U.S. Office of Technology Assessment (1992).

mercial fishing. Indeed, the controversy over the Northern Spotted Owl, the Endangered Species Act in general, and the effects of habitat preservation on the location of timber production is among the most visible U.S. environmental issues of recent times. Similarly, regulations pertaining to pesticide use in agriculture, the reclamation of land mined for coal or non-fuel minerals, or the equipment that can be used by commercial fishing fleets can clearly affect the costs faced by (and hence the international competitiveness of) U.S. firms in these industries.

Rather, we concentrate our attention on manufacturing industries for two reasons. First, that is where the research has been done. With a few exceptions, economists have paid little attention to the effects of environmental regulation on competitiveness in the natural resources sector. By way of contrast, there is a substantial and growing literature focused on the manufacturing sector, as suggested above. Second, the political and policy debate has centered around the possible "flight" of manufacturing from the U.S. to other countries with less stringent environmental standards.

To some extent, this distinction is a peculiar one. To be sure, environmental restrictions on pesticide use or habitat destruction cannot induce someone to move a farm or commercial forest to another country. Such natural capital is immobile, even in the long run. But if concern about competitiveness is primarily a "jobs" issue—and, to many, at least, it is—then it is relevant that environmental regulations pertaining to natural resource industries can affect *where* crops are grown, timber is harvested, fish are caught, or minerals are mined. Nevertheless, because the overwhelming share of attention by policy makers and academics has been devoted to the competitiveness of manufacturing, we concentrate our attention there, as well.

The remainder of this paper is organized as follows. Section 2 outlines an analytical framework for identifying the effects of environmental regulation on international trade in manufactured goods, discusses how different notions of competitiveness fit into that framework, and examines the major categories of environmental regulatory costs. In Section 3, we draw on the available evidence to examine the effects of environmental regulations on international trade in manufacturing. In Section 4, we turn to the empirical evidence regarding the linkage between environmental regulation and investment; and in Section 5, we look at links between regulation and more broadly defined economic growth. Finally, in Section 6, we draw some conclusions.

2. *Framework for Analyzing Regulation and Competitiveness*

2.1 *A Theoretically Desirable Indicator of Competitiveness*

The standard theory of international trade is based on the notion that trade is driven by comparative advantage—that countries export those goods and services that they make relatively (but not necessarily absolutely) more efficiently than other nations, and import those goods and services they are relatively less efficient at producing. Because of the anticipated international adjustments that occur when relative costs change, we could measure—in theory, at least—the real effects of regulation (or any other policy change, for that matter) on competitiveness by identifying the effect that the policy would have on net exports *holding real wages and exchange rates constant*.[9] We would wish to measure the

[9] This definition is closely related to those suggested by Laura D'Andrea Tyson (1988), and Organization of Economic Cooperation and Development (1993a).

reduction in net exports "before" any adjustments in the exchange rate (and hence in net exports of other goods) have taken place, because other industries whose net exports increase to balance a fall in exports should not be thought of as having become more competitive if their export increase is brought about solely by a fall in exchange rates. Similarly, we should not construe an increase in exports brought about solely by a fall in real wages as an increase in "competitiveness."

The unfortunate problem with this analytically clean definition of competitiveness is that it is essentially impossible to implement in practice. We simply are not presented with data generated by the hypothetical experiment in which regulations are imposed while everything else is held constant. In principle, one could formulate a structural econometric model in which net exports by industry, wages, and exchange rates are determined jointly as a function of regulatory costs and resource endowments. We have identified no study that has attempted to do so, and it is not clear that available data would support such an effort.[10] As a result, we are left with indicators of the effects on competitiveness that are not wholly satisfactory because they fail to take account of the complicated adjustment mechanisms that operate when regulations are imposed. Nevertheless, these indicators can be useful to sort through many of the policy debates regarding the environment-competitiveness linkage.

2.2 *Alternative Indicators of "Competitiveness"*

The indicators of "competitiveness" that are used in the existing literature can be classified into three broad categories.[11] One set of measures has to do with the change in net exports of certain goods, the production of which is heavily regulated, and with comparisons between net exports of these goods and others produced under less regulated conditions. For example, stringent environmental regulation of the steel industry should, all else equal, cause the net exports of steel to fall *relative* to the net exports of goods the production of which is more lightly regulated. Thus, the magnitude and significance of an econometric parameter estimate that captures the effect of regulatory stringency in a regression explaining changes in net exports across industries could be taken as an indicator of the strength of the effects of regulation on competitiveness.

A second potential indicator is the extent to which the locus of *production* of pollution-intensive goods has shifted from countries with stringent regulations toward those with less. After all, the policy concern about competitiveness is that the United States is losing world market share in regulated industries to countries with less stringent regulations. If this is so, then there should be a general decrease in the U.S. share of world production of highly regulated goods and an increase in the world share of production of these goods by countries with relatively light regulation.

Third, if regulation is reducing the attractiveness of the United States as a locus for investment, then there should be a relative increase in investment by U.S. firms overseas in highly regulated industries. Similarly, all else equal, new plants in these industries would be more likely to be located in jurisdictions with lax regulation.

Finally, in addition to research focusing on these aspects of competitiveness,

[10] Later we discuss the quantity and quality of available cross-country compliance-cost data.

[11] We henceforth drop the quotation marks around our use of the term "competitiveness" for convenience of presentation.

there exists one other set of important analytical approaches that can shed light on the environment-competitiveness debate. These are analyses focused on the more fundamental link between environmental compliance costs, productivity, investment, and the ultimate social costs of regulation. These analyses, including investigations of the productivity effects of regulation as well as general-equilibrium studies of long-term, social costs of regulation, have implications for both the conventional and the revisionist hypotheses concerning environmental regulation and competitiveness.

Because the economic adjustment to regulation is highly complex, and because there are a multiplicity of issues wrapped up in the term "competitiveness," it is not possible to combine estimates of these different aspects of the process into a single, overall quantification of the effects of regulation on competitiveness.[12] The best that can be done is to assess somewhat qualitatively the magnitude of estimated effects, based on multiple indicators. We return to that assessment shortly.

2.3 *A Framework for Analysis*

These diverse sets of indicators reflect the various routes through which regulation can conceivably affect competitiveness. First, environmental regulations affect a firm's costs of production, both directly through its own expenditures on pollution reduction and indirectly through the higher prices it must pay for certain factors of production that are affected by regulation. Both direct and indirect costs will affect competitiveness, including measures of trade and investment flows.[13]

It is also true that environmental regulations can reduce costs for some firms or industries, by lowering input prices or by increasing the productivity of their inputs. Such "benefits to industry" could take the form, for example, of reduced costs to the food processing industry when its supplies of intake water are less polluted; likewise, workers may become more productive if health-threatening air pollution is reduced (see Bart D. Ostro 1983). Such benefits would have positive effects on U.S. trade and investment through the same mechanisms by which increased costs would have negative effects. Additionally, firms in the environmental services sector typically benefit from stricter regulations affecting their clients and/or potential clients.[14]

In any case, the degree to which domestic regulatory costs (and benefits) affect trade will depend also on the magni-

[12] Having highlighted a theoretically desirable measure and a set of empirically practical means of assessing the link between environmental protection and economic competitiveness, we should also note the multiplicity of *inappropriate* means of examining this link. Indeed, the amount of published, muddled thinking on this subject seems to exceed the norm. Numerous studies have focused exclusively on "jobs created in the environmental services sector" and taken this to be a measure of net positive economic benefits of regulation (apart from any environmental benefits). A recent example of this approach is provided by Roger H. Bezdek (1993), with numerous citations to other such studies. See Hopkins (1992) and Portney (1994) for critiques of this approach.

[13] For the economy as a whole, there is, of course, no distinction between direct and indirect costs. To measure total industry expenditures for pollution compliance, it would be incorrect to add the increased costs of the steel industry and the increased costs in the auto industry resulting from higher steel prices; to do so would result in obvious double-counting. The necessity of tracking indirect costs arises, however, when the analyst wishes to estimate the impact of regulation on a particular industry, or to compare effects on different industries. We postpone discussion of another notion of "indirect costs," including transition costs and reduced investment, which we refer to for semantic clarity as "other social costs" of regulation. See Section 5, below.

[14] There are, of course, additional benefits of environmental regulation that accrue to society at large rather than to industry. We exclude these here, not because they are unimportant, but because they do not bear on the issue of competitiveness.

tude of the costs (and benefits) that other countries impose on the firms operating within their borders. Likewise, other nations' policies will also affect the investment decisions of their indigenous firms and of foreign firms, as well. Any changes in investment patterns that do occur ultimately affect trade flows as well, and both trade and investment effects interact with exchange rates.

2.4 *Measuring the Costs of Environmental Regulation*

In Table 3, we provide a taxonomy of the costs of environmental regulation, beginning with the most obvious and moving toward the least direct.[15] First, many policy makers and much of the general public would identify the on-budget costs to government of administering (monitoring and enforcing) environmental laws and regulations as *the* cost of environmental regulation. Most analysts, on the other hand, would identify the capital and operating expenditures associated with regulatory compliance as the fundamental part of the overall costs of regulation, although a substantial share of compliance costs for some federal regulations fall on state and local governments rather than private firms—the best example being the regulation of contaminants in drinking water. Additional direct costs include legal and other transaction costs, the effects of refocused management attention, and the possibility of disrupted production.

Next, one should also consider potential "negative costs" (in other words, nonenvironmental benefits) of environmental regulation, including the productivity impacts of a cleaner environment and the potential innovation-stimulating effects of regulation (linked with the so-called Porter hypothesis, which we discuss later). General equilibrium effects associated with product substitution, discouraged investment,[16] and retarded innovation constitute another important layer of costs, as do the transition costs of real-world economies responding over time to regulatory changes. Finally, there is a set of potential social impacts that is given substantial weight in political forums, including impacts on jobs and economic security.

TABLE 3
A TAXONOMY OF COSTS OF ENVIRONMENTAL REGULATION

Government Administration of Environmental Statutes and Regulations
Monitoring
Enforcement
Private Sector Compliance Expenditures
Capital
Operating
Other Direct Costs
Legal and Other Transactional
Shifted Management Focus
Disrupted Production
Negative Costs
Natural Resource Inputs
Worker Health
Innovation Stimulation
General Equilibrium Effects
Product Substitution
Discouraged Investment
Retarded Innovation
Transition Costs
Unemployment
Obsolete Capital
Social Impacts
Loss of Middle-Class Jobs
Economic Security Impacts

[15] For a very useful decomposition and analysis of the full costs of environmental regulation, see Schmalensee, (1994). Conceptually, the cost of an environmental regulation is equal to "the change in consumer and producer surpluses associated with the regulations and with any price and/or income changes that may result" (Maureen L. Cropper and Wallace E. Oates 1992, p. 721).

[16] For example, if a firm chooses to close a plant because of a new regulation (rather than installing expensive control equipment), this would be counted as zero cost in typical compliance-cost estimates.

TABLE 4
TOTAL COSTS OF POLLUTION CONTROL[a]
(millions of 1992 dollars)

	1972	1973	1974	1975	1976	1977	1978	1979	1980	1981	1982
Toatl Air & Radiation	9,915	11,995	12.725	13,942	15,854	18,071	19,993	21,413	22,313	22,992	23,550
Total Water	12,387	14,352	16,795	18,940	21,769	24,234	26,342	28,707	30,925	33,149	34,832
Total Land	10,543	11,120	11,683	12,235	12,984	14,160	14,897	16,223	17,011	17,660	16,502
Total Chemicals	115	179	229	226	436	510	729	1,066	1,111	989	890
Multi-Media	135	174	576	734	911	1,149	1,129	1,107	1,085	869	757
Total Costs	33,094	37,818	42,009	46,043	51,954	58,124	63,089	68,516	72,446	75,658	76,530
Percentage of GNP	0.88	0.96	1.07	1.19	1.28	1.37	1.41	1.49	1.58	1.62	1.68
	1983	**1984**	**1985**	**1986**	**1987**	**1988**	**1989**	**1990**	**1991**	**1992**	**2000**
Toatl Air & Radiation	25,970	27,899	31,885	31,782	33,751	34,482	35,326	35,029	36,852	37.763	46,859
Total Water	37,199	39,099	41.418	44,197	46,904	48,104	50,317	52,604	55,114	57,277	72,705
Total Land	17,034	18,711	19,881	21,884	23,860	25,392	28,760	33,177	37,184	41,186	57,673
Toatl Chemicals	762	856	966	1,027	1,024	1,137	1,531	1,973	2,356	2.662	3,614
Multi-Media	865	821	859	1,147	1,052	1,475	1,853	2,003	2,493	2,486	2,872
Total Costs	81,829	87,388	92,507	100,037	106,590	110,590	117,826	124,787	133,999	141,375	184,842
Percentage of GNP	1.74	1.74	1.78	1.87	1.92	1.91	1.98	2.13	2.24	2.32	2.61

Source: U.S. Environmental Protection Agency (1990, pp. 8–20 to 8–21).
[a] Assuming present implementation annualized at 7 percent.

Within the category of direct compliance costs, expenditures for pollution abatement in the United States have grown steadily over the past two decades, both absolutely and as a percentage of GNP (Table 4), reaching $125 billion (2.1 percent of GNP) by 1990. EPA estimates these costs will reach 2.6 percent of GNP by 2000.[17]

Even estimates of direct, compliance expenditures vary greatly. For example, Gary L. Rutledge and Mary L. Leonard (1992) estimate that pollution abatement costs for 1990 were $94 billion, rather than $125 billion as estimated by EPA.[18]

There are a number of potential problems of interpretation associated with these data. The questionnaire used by the U.S. Department of Commerce (1993) to collect data for its *Pollution Abatement Costs and Expenditures* (*PACE*) survey asks corporate or government officials how capital expenditures

[17] Recall that these estimates capture, at most, only what we have labelled private sector compliance expenditures in Table 4. As is shown in Table 5, business pollution-abatement expenditures represented about 61 percent of total *direct* costs in 1990. The remainder consisted of: personal consumption abatement (11%); government abatement (23%); government regulation and monitoring (2%); and research and development (3%).

[18] The primary difference between the estimates is due to the fact that EPA includes the cost of all solid waste disposal, while Rutledge and M. L. Leonard exclude some of these costs. See, also: Rutledge and Leonard 1993. The EPA data, however, exclude a significant portion of other expenditures mandated at the state and local level.

TABLE 5
EXPENDITURES FOR POLLUTION ABATEMENT AND CONTROL BY SECTION[a]
(millions of 1992 dollars)

Sector	1981	1982	1983	1984	1985	1986	1987	1988	1989	1990
Personal Consumption Abatement	10,278	10,307	12,119	13,270	14,254	15,349	13,159	14,316	12,278	10,485
Business Abatement	48,969	45,726	46,031	49,825	51,314	52,994	53,846	55,615	57,784	60,122
Government Abatement	16,446	15,912	15,504	16,760	17,684	18,974	20,727	20,559	21,560	23,122
Regulation & Monitoring	2,190	2,068	1,946	1,823	1,647	1,923	1,838	1,988	2,005	1,980
Research & Development	2,626	2,484	3,115	2,998	3,017	3,186	3,204	3,216	3,303	3,303
Total	80,509	76,495	78,713	84,677	87,914	92,425	92,773	95,694	96,928	99,024

Source: Rutledge and Leonard (1992), pp. 35–38.
[a] Excludes expenditures for solid waste collection and disposal; excludes agricultural production except feedlot operations.

compared to what they would have been in the absence of environmental regulations. This creates two problems. The first involves the determination of an appropriate baseline. Absent any regulation, firms might still engage in some—perhaps a great deal of—pollution control to limit tort liability, stay on good terms with communities in which they are located, maintain a good environ-

TABLE 6
POLLUTION ABATEMENT EXPENDITURES FOR SELECTED INDUSTRIES, 1991
(Monetary amounts are in millions of 1992 dollars.)

Industry	Total Capital Expenditures	Pollution Abatement Cap. Exp. (PACE)	PACE as Percentage of Total Cap. Exp.	Total Value of Shipments	Abatement Gross Annual Cost (GAC)	GAC as Percentage of Value of Shipments
All Industries	$101,773	$7,603	7.47%	$2,907,848	$17,888	0.62%
Industries with High Abatement Costs						
Paper and Allied Products	$9,269	$1,269	13.68%	$132,545	$1,682	1.27%
Chemical and Allied Products	$16,471	$2,126	12.91%	$300,770	$4,164	1.38%
Petroleum and Coal Products	$6,066	$1,505	24.81%	$162,642	$2,931	1.80%
Primary Metal Industries	$6,049	$692	11.45%	$136,674	$2,061	1.51%
Industries with Moderate Abatement Costs						
Furniture and Fixtures	$750	$25	3.29%	$41,183	$140	0.34%
Fabricated Metal Products	$4,190	$182	4.35%	$161,614	$867	0.54%
Electric, Electronic Equipment	$8,356	$241	2.88%	$203,596	$857	0.42%
Industries with Low Abatement Costs						
Printing and Publishing	$5,187	$38	0.73%	$161,211	$235	0.15%
Rubber, Misc. Plastics Products	$4,337	$84	1.95%	$103,576	$454	0.44%
Machinery, except Electrical	$7,546	$132	1.75%	$250,512	$591	0.24%

Source: U.S. Department of Commerce (1993), pp. 12–13.

mental image, etc. Should such expenditures be included or excluded in the no-regulation baseline?

Second, when additional capital expenditures are made for end-of-the-pipe abatement equipment, respondents have relatively little difficulty in calculating these expenditures. But when new capital equipment is installed, which has the effect of both reducing emissions and improving the final product or enhancing the efficiency with which it is produced, it is far more difficult to calculate how much of the expenditures are attributable to environmental standards. Furthermore, it is not always clear whether a regulation is an "environmental regulation." The *PACE* data do not include expenditures for worker health and safety (U.S. Department of Commerce 1993, p. A4), but some expenditures for health and safety essentially control the working environment. Determining precisely which regulatory costs should be included in the costs of environmental regulations is ultimately somewhat arbitrary.[19]

The most striking feature of either annual capital or annual total expenditures for pollution abatement is the degree of variation across industries.[20] For all manufacturing industries combined, 7.5 percent of new capital expenditures in 1991 were for pollution control equipment, and gross annual operating costs for pollution control were 0.62 percent of the total value of shipments. For the highest abatement-cost industries, however, the costs of complying with environmental regulations were dramatically higher (Table 6).

[19] For a detailed discussion of environmental compliance cost measurement problems, see U.S. Congressional Budget Office (1985).

[20] Gross annual costs for pollution abatement are equal to the sum of operating costs attributable to pollution abatement and payments to the government for sewage services and solid waste collection and disposal.

In particular, for the chemicals, petroleum, pulp and paper, and primary metals industries, new capital expenditures for pollution abatement ranged from 11 to 25 percent of overall capital expenditures, and annual abatement (operating) costs ranged from 1.3 to 1.8 percent of the total value of shipments.

3. *Environmental Regulations and International Trade*

3.1 *Effects of Regulation on Net Exports*

Natural resource endowments have been a particularly important determinant of trading patterns (see, for example, Edward E. Leamer 1984). Having recognized this, we note that when a firm pollutes, it is essentially using a natural resource (a clean environment), and when a firm is compelled or otherwise induced to reduce its pollutant emissions, that firm has, in effect, seen its access to an important natural resource reduced. Industries that lose the right to pollute freely may thus lose their comparative advantage, just as the copper industry in developed countries lost its comparative advantage as copper resources dwindled in those regions. The result is a fall in exports.

This suggests an analytical approach to investigating the environmental protection-competitiveness connection. The primary difficulty in implementing this approach, however, is the limited availability of data on environmental regulatory compliance expenditures, particularly for foreign (and especially for developing) countries. Because such comparative data are generally unavailable, we must rely instead on studies that either examine the effect of environmental controls on U.S. net exports (without considering more general trading patterns) or those that examine international trading patterns (but rely

TABLE 7
EFFECTS OF ENVIRONMENTAL REGULATIONS ON NET EXPERTS

Study	Time Period of Analysis	Industrial Scope	Geographic Scope	Results[a]
Grossman and Krueger 1993	1987	Manufacturing	U.S.-Mexico Trade	Insignificant
Kalt 1988	1967–1977	78 industry categories	U.S. Trade	Insignificant
		Manufacturing		Significant
		Manufacturing w/o Chemicals		More Significant
Tobey 1990	1977	Mining, Paper, Chemicals, Steel, Metals	23 Nations	Insignificant

[a] See the text for descriptions of the results of each study.

on qualitative measures of environmental control costs in different countries).

First, we can ask whether (all else equal) net exports have been systematically lower in U.S. industries subject to relatively stringent environmental regulations. The evidence pertaining to this question is not conclusive (Table 7). Employing a Heckscher-Ohlin model of international trade, Joseph P. Kalt (1988) regressed changes in net exports between the years 1967 and 1977 across 78 industrial categories on changes in environmental compliance costs and other relevant variables, and found a statistically insignificant inverse relationship. On the other hand, when the sample was restricted to manufacturing industries, the predicted negative effect of compliance costs on net exports became significant. It is troubling, however, that the magnitude and significance of the effect was increased even further when the chemical industry was excluded from the sample, because this is an industry with relatively high environmental compliance costs (Table 6).[21]

Gene M. Grossman and Alan B. Krueger (1993) found that pollution abatement costs in industries in the United States have apparently not affected imports from Mexico or activity in the maquiladora sector[22] along the U.S.-Mexico border.[23] Using 1987 data across

[21] The explanation appears to be the relatively strong net export performance of the chemical industry (at the same time that it was heavily regulated).

[22] The maquiladora program was established by Mexico in the 1960s to attract foreign investment. Under the program, qualified firms are exempt from national laws that require majority Mexican ownership and prohibit foreign ownership of border and coastline property. Also inputs for production processes can be imported duty-free, as long as 80 percent of the output is re-exported. For further discussion of the maquiladoras sector in the context of the environmental protection—competitiveness debate, see Robert K. Kaufmann, Peter Pauly, and Julie Sweitzer (1993).

[23] As Grossman and Krueger (1993) point out, however, there is evidence from one government survey suggesting that a number of U.S. furniture manufacturers relocated their California factories across the Mexican border as a result of increases in the stringency of California state air pollution

industry categories and three different measures of economic impacts—total U.S. imports from Mexico, imports under the offshore assembly provisions of the U.S. tariff codes, and the sectoral pattern of maquiladora activity—they examined possible statistical relationships with: industry factor intensities, tariff rates, and the ratio of pollution abatement costs to total value-added in respective U.S. industries. With all three performance measures, they found that "traditional determinants of trade and investment patterns"—in particular, labor intensity—were very significant, but that cross-industry differences in environmental costs were both quantitatively small and statistically insignificant.[24] Given the physical proximity of Mexico, the large volume of trade between the two countries, and the historically significant differences between Mexican and U.S. environmental laws, these findings cast doubt on the hypothesis that environmental regulations have significant adverse effects on net exports.

Finally, environmental regulations in other nations are, of course, also important in determining trade patterns, but here the available evidence again indicates that the relative stringency of environmental regulations in different countries has had no effect on net exports (James A. Tobey 1990). Using a qualitative measure of the stringency of national environmental policies (Ingo Walter and J. Ugelow 1979), Tobey applied what is otherwise a straightforward Hecksher-Ohlin framework to test empirically for the sources of international comparative advantage. In an examination of five pollution-intensive industries—mining, paper, chemicals, steel, and metals—Tobey found that environmental stringency was in no case a statistically significant determinant of net exports. The results could theoretically be due to no more than the failure of the ordinal measure of environmental stringency to be correlated with true environmental control costs,[25] but Tobey's results are essentially consistent with those from other, previous analyses that employed direct cost measures (Walter 1982; Charles S. Pearson 1987; and H. Jeffrey Leonard 1988).

3.2 *International Trade in Pollution-Intensive Goods*

We can also search for evidence on the impact of environmental regulations on international competitiveness by examining temporal shifts in the overall pattern of trade in pollution-intensive goods.[26] Defining such goods as those produced by industries that incur the highest levels of pollution abatement and control expenditures in the United States, shifts in trade flows can be examined to determine whether a growing proportion of these products in world trade originate in developing countries, where regulatory standards are often (but not always) relatively lax (Patrick Low and Alexander Yeats 1992). The results for the period 1965–1988 show that: (i) the share of pollution-intensive products in total

standards affecting paints and solvents (U.S. General Accounting Office 1991).

[24] As we discuss later, this result is consistent with something else the data reveal—international differences in environmental costs (as a fraction of total production costs) are trivial compared with apparent differences in labor costs and productivity.

[25] For example, a nation might have strict regulations but not enforce them.

[26] Unfortunately, a major constraint faced by any such analysis is a lack of sufficient data on environmental costs and regulations in foreign countries to permit a direct link to be established between observed changes in trade flows and differences in environmental regulations across various countries. Not only are data on environmental regulations sparse, but a further difficulty is separating the impact of environmental costs on trade from shifts in natural resource advantages or other factor endowments, such as labor costs.

world trade fell from 19 to 16 percent; (ii) the share of pollution-intensive products in world trade originating in North America fell from 21 to 14 percent;[27] (iii) the share of pollution-intensive products originating in Southeast Asia rose from 3.4 to 8.4 percent; and (iv) developing countries gained a comparative advantage in pollution-intensive products at a greater rate than developed countries.[28]

These results may be less meaningful than they may seem at first glance. First of all, Low and Yeats found that industrialized countries accounted for the lion's share of the world's exports of pollution-intensive goods from 1965 to 1988, contradicting the notion that pollution-intensive industries have fled to developing countries. Second, to the extent pollution-intensive industries *have* moved from industrialized to industrializing countries, this may be due simply to increased demand within the latter for the products of pollution-intensive industries. Third, natural resource endowments may partly or largely explain the pattern of pollution-intensive exports.[29]

In general, it would be preferable to examine individual nations' production of pollution-intensive goods relative to world production rather than their share of world trade or the proportion of their exports that are pollution intensive. This is because as world demand grows for pollution-intensive goods, production facilities will be built in new locations close to sources of product demand, and trade in these goods may shrink. A declining volume of world trade in such goods would result in a drop in U.S. exports, even if the United States maintained its *share* of such trade. The drop in overall trade could indicate that other countries were developing expertise in making these goods for domestic consumption, and that the U.S. competitive advantage was shrinking.

The evidence that developing countries are more likely to gain a comparative advantage in the production of pollution-intensive goods than in clean ones[30] is consistent with the change in U.S. trading patterns identified by H. David Robison (1988; see also Ralph D'Arge 1974 and Organization for Economic Cooperation and Development 1985). He found that the abatement content of U.S. imports[31] has risen more rapidly than the abatement content of exports as U.S. environmental standards have grown relatively more stringent than those in the rest of the world. However, the U.S.-Canadian trade pattern has not shifted in this way, presumably because of the similarity of Canadian and U.S. environmental standards and costs. While this result suggests that U.S. environmental regulations have had an affect on trading patterns, Robison's model indicates that, relative to domestic consumption, the effects of increased abatement costs of U.S. trade are quite small, even when no mitigating general equilibrium effects are taken into account.

[27] This result is consistent with a parallel finding by Kalt (1988) that in 1967 U.S. exports were more pollution-intensive than its imports while the opposite was true by 1977.

[28] These results are consistent with the findings of Robert E. B. Lucas, Wheeler, and Hemamala Hettige (1992), who also found evidence that pollution-intensive industries had migrated from the United States to developing countries, in a study of 15,000 plants (from Census Bureau data) for the period, 1986–1987.

[29] The data suggest that countries that export a high proportion of pollution-intensive goods may do so because their natural resource base makes them efficient producers of particular pollution-intensive products. Finland exports paper products, while Venezuela and Saudi Arabia export refined petroleum products.

[30] This result is based primarily on an analysis of one industry, iron and steel pipes and tubes (Low and Yeats 1992).

[31] The abatement content of imported goods is the cost of abatement that would be embodied in those goods had they been produced in the United States.

TABLE 8
EFFECTS OF ENVIRONMENTAL REGULATIONS ON TRADE PATTERNS IN ABATEMENT-INTENSIVE GOODS

Study	Time Period of Analysis	Industrial Scope	Geographic Scope	Results[a]
Low and Yeats 1992	1965–1988	"Dirty" Industries[b]	World Trade	Generally consistent with migration of dirty industries
Robison 1988	1973–1982	78 Industry categories	U.S. Trade	Increased U.S imports of relatively abatement-intensive goods
			Canadian Trade	No change in relative abatement-intensity of trade

[a] See the text for descriptions of the results of each study.
[b] Dirty industries are those incurring the highest level of abatement expenditure in the U.S.

Observed changes in international trading patterns over the past thirty years thus indicate that pollution-intensive industries have migrated, but the observed changes are small in the overall context of economic development (Table 8). Furthermore, it is by no means clear that the changes in trade patterns were caused by increasingly strict environmental regulations in developed countries. The observed changes in international trading patterns are consistent with the general process of development in the Third World. As countries develop, manufacturing accounts for a larger portion of their economic activity.

4. *Environmental Regulations and Investment*

The spatial pattern of economic activity is partly a function of resource endowments and the location of markets; but, to some degree, it is also an accident of history. Although firms may locate where production costs are low and market access is good, there are benefits to firms that locate where other firms have previously located (in terms of existing infrastructure, a trained work force, potential suppliers, and potential benefits from specialization).[32] Under this latter view, productivity and competitiveness arise, at least in part, from the existence of a large industrial base; the ability to attract capital is also an important determinant of competitiveness.

In any case, the choice of a new plant location is obviously a complex one. When choosing between domestic and foreign locations, firms consider the market the plant will serve, the quality of the work force available, the risks associated with exchange rate fluctuations, the political stability of foreign governments, and the available infrastructure, among other factors. Hence, isolating the effect of environmental regulations on the decision will inevitably be difficult. Two sources of evidence can be used to investigate the sensitivity of firms' investment patterns to environmental regulations:

[32] See Wheeler and Ashoka Mody (1992) for a brief discussion of these issues in the context of the effects of regulation. For a more general discussion of agglomeration effects, see Krugman (1991).

changes in direct foreign investment and siting decisions for domestic plants.

4.1 *Direct Foreign Investment*

Although there has been little focus on the direct effects of environmental regulations on foreign investment decisions,[33] the results from more general studies can be informative. Wheeler and Mody (1992) found that multinational firms appear to base their foreign investment decisions primarily upon such things as labor costs and access to markets, as well as upon the presence of a developed industrial base. On the other hand, corporate tax rates appear to have little or no appreciable effect on these investment decisions. To the extent that environmental regulations impose direct costs similar to those associated with taxes, one could infer that concerns about environmental regulations will be dominated by the same factors that dominate concerns about taxes in these investment decisions.[34]

General trends in direct investment abroad (DIA) can also provide insights into the likely effects of environmental regulations. If environmental regulations cause industrial flight from developed countries, then direct foreign investment by pollution-intensive industries should increase over time, particularly in developing nations. In fact, from 1973 to 1985, overall direct foreign investment by the U.S. chemical and mineral industries *did* increase at a slightly greater rate than that for all manufacturing industries.[35] Over the same period, however, there was an increase in the proportion of DIA made by all manufacturing industries in developing countries, while the proportion of DIA made by the chemicals industry in developing countries actually fell.[36]

Information is also available on the capital expenditures of (majority-owned) foreign affiliates of U.S. firms. The evidence indicates that those affiliates in pollution intensive industries, such as chemicals, did not undertake capital expenditures at a rate greater than manufacturing industries in general. Majority-owned affiliates in pollution-intensive industries in developing countries, however, did increase their capital expenditures at a slightly greater rate than did all manufacturing industries (H. J. Leonard 1988).[37] Overall, the evidence

[33] There is abundant anecdotal evidence in the press and at least one survey of 1,000 North American and Western European corporations regarding their attitudes toward investing in Eastern and Central Europe (Anthony Zamparutti and Jon Klavens 1993).

[34] Wheeler and Mody (1992) included a composite variable in their analysis designed to measure the effects of a variety of risks associated with various countries. One of the ten components of this composite variable reflects the bureaucratic "hassle" associated with doing business in the countries examined. If this variable had been entered separately, the analysis might have shed more light on the nonpecuniary effects of regulation on location decisions.

[35] Direct investment abroad (DIA) made by the chemical and mineral industries as a proportion of DIA by all manufacturing industries increased from 25.7 percent to 26.5 percent between 1973 and 1985 (H. J. Leonard 1988). Of course, this statistic may simply indicate that markets for these products were growing in developing countries.

[36] The proportion of DIA made by mineral processing industries in developing countries increased from 22.8 to 24.4 percent between 1973 and 1985. This shift could have been caused by changes in comparative advantage due to natural resource endowments (Leonard 1988).

[37] A preliminary study by Charles D. Kolstad and Yuqing Xing (1994) has examined the relationship between the laxity of various countries' environmental regulations and the level of investment by the U.S. chemical industry in those nations. The authors used two proxies for the laxity of environmental regulation: emissions of sulphur dioxide (SO_2) per dollar of GDP, and the growth rate of SO_2 emissions. They found that both measures were positively and significantly related to the amount of inbound direct investment by the chemical industry, and they interpreted this as evidence that strict regulation discourages investment. It seems equally likely, however, that these empirical results are due to omitted variables or causality running in the opposite direction, from investment to pollution.

of industrial flight to developing countries is weak, at best.[38]

4.2 *Domestic Plant Location*

As suggested above, data on required pollution-control expenditures in foreign countries are insufficient to permit plant-level analyses of the effects of environmental regulations on international siting of plants. Nevertheless, such analyses have been conducted for plant location decisions in the United States in an effort to link such decisions to environmental regulatory factors. Despite the fact that new environmental regulations typically will not cause firms to relocate *existing* plants (due to significant relocation costs), firms have more flexibility in making decisions about the siting of new plants. Indeed, some environmental regulations are particularly targeted at new plants—so-called, "new source performance standards."

There appears to be widespread belief that environmental regulations have a significant effect on the siting of new plants in the United States. The public comments and private actions of legislators and lobbyists, for example, certainly indicate that they believe that environmental regulations affect plant location choices. Indeed, there is evidence that the 1970 Clean Air Act and the 1977 Clean Water Act Amendments were designed in part to limit the ability of states to compete for businesses through lax enforcement of environmental standards (Portney 1990). The House Committee Report on the 1970 Clean Air Act amendments claims that "the promulgation of Federal emission standards for new sources . . . will preclude efforts on the part of States to compete with each other in trying to attract new plants and facilities without assuming adequate control of large scale emissions therefrom" (U.S. Congress 1979). Likewise, environmental standards became a major obstacle to ratification of the North American Free Trade Agreement (NAFTA) in 1993, largely because of concerns that U.S. companies would move to Mexico to take advantage of relatively lax environmental standards there.

The evidence from U.S. studies suggests that these concerns may not be well founded. Timothy J. Bartik (1985) examined business location decisions as influenced by a variety of factors. While he did not take the stringency of states' environmental regulations into account, his findings are helpful in identifying factors that can affect business location decisions. First, Bartik found that both state taxes and public services are important determinants of location choice;[39] second, he found that unionization of a state's labor force has a strongly negative effect on the likelihood that firms will locate new plants within a given state. Third, he found that the existing level of manufacturing activity in a state seems to have a positive effect on the decision to locate a new plant, consistent with other findings in the international context (Low and Yeats 1992).

While these results indicate that firms are sensitive, in general, to cost variations among states when deciding where to locate new facilities, there is little direct evidence of a relationship

[38] It has been suggested in the popular press that multinational companies install pollution control equipment in their foreign plants for a variety of reasons—including public relations and stockholders demands—even where and when not required by local laws and regulations (see, for example, "The Supply Police," *Newsweek*, Feb. 15, 1993, pp. 48–49). If true, this could help explain why investment patterns have been relatively unaffected by regulatory stringency.

[39] The effect of state taxes was statistically significant, but not particularly large in Bartik's (1985) analysis. A 10 percent increase in the corporate tax rate (from 5 to 5.5%, for example) will cause a 2 to 3 percent decline in the number of new plants.

TABLE 9
EFFECTS OF ENVIRONMENTAL REGULATIONS ON DOMESTIC PLANT LOCATION DECISIONS

Study	Time Period of Analysis	Industrial Scope	Results[a]
Bartik 1988	1972–1978	Manufacturing branch plants of Fortune 500 companies	No Significant Effects[b]
Bartik 1989	1976–1982	New small businesses in 19 manufacturing industries	Significant but Small Effects[c]
Friedman, Gerlowski, and Silberman 1992	1977–1988	Foreign multinational corporations	No Significant Effects[d]
Levinson 1992	1982–1987	U.S. Manufacturing	No Significant Effects[e]
McConnell and Schwab 1990	1973, 1975, 1979, 1982	Motor-Vehicle Assembly Plants (SIC 3711)	Mostly Insignificant Effects[f]

[a] See the text for descriptions of the results of each study.
[b] In a previous study, Bartik (1985) found significant impacts of state corporate tax rates, suggesting that differences in the costs of doing business matter.
[c] A one standard deviation change in environmental stringency yielded a 0.01 standard deviation change in the start-up rate of small businesses.
[d] An exception is that when the sample was restricted to new branch plants built by Japanese firms alone, the environmental variable was both negative and significant.
[e] Although the results are insignificant when the entire sample is considered, state-level environmental regulations exhibit significant effects when the sample is restricted to firms in the most pollution-intensive industries (chemicals, plastics, and electronics).
[f] The insignificance of regional differences in environmental regulation held across a substantial number of alternative measures of environmental regulatory strinency. They found significant effects in the case of countries that were exceptionally far out of compliance with air quality standards.

between stringency of environmental regulations and plant location choices (although the fact that state taxes were significant could be taken to infer that environmental regulations ought to be significant as well).[40] In a more recent analysis that included measures of environmental stringency, Bartik (1988) found that state government air and water pollution control expenditures, average costs of compliance, and allowed particulate emissions all had small[41] and insignificant effects on plant location decisions.[42] In a subsequent analysis, Bartik (1989) detected a significant, negative impact of state-level environmental regulations on the start-up rate of small businesses, but the effect was substantively small.[43] These results are essentially consistent with those of Arik Levinson (1992), who found that large differences in the stringency of environ-

[40] In any event, the magnitude of the two effects could be dramatically different, because state taxes may impose a burden that is large relative to the monetary-equivalent regulatory burden.

[41] In the case of highly polluting industries, Bartik (1988) could not reject the possibility of a substantively large effect of environmental regulation, although the estimated effect was statistically not significant.

[42] State spending on pollution control is meant to be a proxy for the likelihood that a plant will face inspection. Bartik experimented with a variety of variables and specifications, and the general results were quite robust to these changes.

[43] A change of one standard deviation in the environmental stringency variable—the Conservation Foundation's rating of state environmental laws and regulations (from Christopher Duerksen 1983)—yielded a 0.01 standard deviation change in the state start-up rate of small businesses.

mental regulations among states had no effect on the locations of most new plants; but the locations of new branch plants of large multi-plant companies in pollution-intensive industries were found to be somewhat sensitive to differences in pollution regulations.[44]

In another plant-location study, Virginia D. McConnell and Robert M. Schwab (1990) found no significant effects of regional differences in environmental regulation on the choice of location of automobile industry branch plants.[45] This finding held across a variety of alternative measures of environmental stringency. Finally, Joseph Friedman, Daniel A. Gerlowski, and Jonathan Silberman (1992) analyzed the determinants of new manufacturing branch plant location in the United States by foreign multinational corporations. Among the independent variables they used to explain location choice was a measure of regulatory intensity—the ratio of pollution abatement capital expenditures in a state to the gross product in the state originating in manufacturing. When the investment decisions of all foreign companies were considered together, the measure of environmental stringency—while negative—did not exert a statistically significant effect on new plant investment (Table 9).[46]

5. *Environmental Regulations and Economic Growth*

The evidence reviewed above does not provide much support for the proposition that environmental regulation has significant adverse effects on competitiveness. This can be placed in perspective by scrutinizing what may be more fundamental, though possibly less direct, evidence related to the overall social costs of environmental regulation.[47]

5.1 *Productivity Effects*

If firms are operating efficiently before environmental regulations are imposed, new regulations will theoretically cause firms to use more resources in the production process. We can posit five ways in which environmental regulations could negatively affect productivity (see Robert H. Haveman and Gregory B. Christiansen 1981; Robert W. Crandall 1981; and U.S. Office of Technology Assessment 1994). First, by definition, the *measured* productivity of the affected industry will fall because measured inputs of capital, labor, and energy are being diverted to the production of an additional output—environmental quality—that is not included in conventional measures of output and hence productivity (Robert

[44] In work in progress, Wayne B. Gray (1993) uses data from six Censuses of Manufacturing between 1963 and 1987 to examine how the births and deaths of plants are related to a set of state characteristics, including: factor prices, population density, unionization, taxes, education, and various measures of environmental regulation, such as enforcement activity by state and federal regulators, pollution abatement costs, and indices of state-level environmental policy stringency. In this preliminary work, Gray finds significant effects for two of his measures of regulatory stringency—air pollution enforcement and state-level laws—but the respective parameters have opposite signs.

[45] An exception was found in the case of counties that were exceptionally far out of compliance with air quality standards.

[46] When the sample was restricted to new branch plants built by Japanese firms alone, however, the environmental variable was both negative and significant. In other words, ceteris paribus, states with more stringent regulation were less likely to attract new Japanese-owned branch plants in manufacturing.

[47] One way to gain a perspective on this issue is to ask: Are environmental regulations more costly to a society with an open economy or one with a closed economy? On the simplest possible level, the existence of trade *reduces* the social cost of regulation. Rather than invest in pollution control equipment for its pollution-intensive industries, a country might specialize in the production of cleaner goods and stop producing pollution-intensive goods, choosing to import these goods rather than produce them domestically. Essentially, a country open to international trade has available a means of cleaning up its environment that is not available to countries closed to trade.

TABLE 10
EFFECTS OF ENVIRONMENTAL REGULATIONS ON TOTAL FACTOR PRODUCTIVITY DECLINE[a]

Study	Time Period of Analysis	Industrial Scope	Results:[b] Percentage Share Due to Environmental Regulation
Barbera and McConnell 1990	1970–1980	Chemicals; stone, clay, and glass; iron and steel	10%–12%
Barbera and McConnell 1990	1970–1980	Paper	30%
Dension 1979	1972–1975	Business sector	16%
Gallop and Roberts 1983	1973–1979	Electric utilities	44%
Gray 1987	1973–1978	240 manufacturing sectors	12%
Haveman and Christainsen 1981	1973–1975	Manufacturing	8%–12%
Norsworthy, Harper, and Kunze 1979	1973–1978	Manufacturing	12%[c]

[a] Based upon Table A-1 in U.S. Office of Technology Assessment 1994.
[b] See the text for descriptions of the results of each study.
[c] Share of labor productivity decline due to environmental regulation.

Repetto 1990; Robert M. Solow 1992). Second, when and if firms undertake process or management changes in response to environmental regulations, the new practices may be less efficient than old ones (although, as we discuss below, there are those who suggest that this factor operates in the opposite direction, i.e., regulation-induced process and management shake-ups may increase productive efficiency). Third, environmental investments could conceivably crowd out other investments by firms.[48] Fourth, many environmental regulations exempt older plants from requirements, in effect mandating higher standards for new plants. This "new-source bias" can be particularly harmful by discouraging investment in new, more efficient facilities. Fifth, requirements that firms use the "best available control technology" for pollution abatement may increase the adoption of these new technologies *at the time* regulations go into effect, but subsequently blunt firms' incentives to develop new pollution control or prevention approaches over time. This is because their emission standard may be tightened each time the firm innovates with a cost-saving approach.

Empirical analyses of these productivity effects have found modest adverse impacts of environmental regulation. A number of studies focused on the 1970s, a period of productivity decline in the United States (Table 10), attempting to determine what portion of the decline in productivity growth rates could be attributed to increased regulatory costs. When the scope of the analysis is most or all manufacturing sectors, the estimates of the fraction of the decline in the total factor productivity growth rate due to environmental regulations range from 8 percent to 16 percent (Edward Denison 1979; Gray 1987; Haveman and Christiansen 1981;[49] and J. R. Norsworthy,

[48] The empirical evidence here is mixed. Adam Rose (1983) finds that pollution-control investments reduce other investments by firms, but on less than a one-for-one basis; Gray and Ronald J. Shadbegian (1993) actually found a positive correlation of environmental investments and "productive investments" for some sectors, such as pulp and paper mills.

[49] Haveman and Christiansen (1981) examine the contribution of environmental regulation to the observed decline in labor productivity, not total factor productivity.

Michael J. Harper, and Kent Kunze 1979). Thus, regulation cannot be considered the primary cause of the productivity slowdown. There is, however, substantial variation by industrial sector: 10 percent for the chemical industry; 30 percent percent for paper producers (Anthony J. Barbera and McConnell 1990); and 44 percent for electric utilities (Frank M. Gallop and Mark J. Roberts 1983).

Gray and Shadbegian (1993) merged plant-level input and output data from the Census and Survey of Manufactures with plant-level data from the PACE surveys. They estimated equations for productivity at the plant level as a function of pollution control expenditures. If the only effect of pollution control expenditures on productivity were that they do not contribute to measured output, then their coefficient in such a regression ought to be minus one, because, holding inputs (including pollution control expenditures) constant, there ought to be $1 less output for every $1 diverted to pollution control. They found, however, that output fell by $3–$4 for every dollar of PACE spending, suggesting extremely large adverse productivity effects. In subsequent work (Gray and Shadbegian 1994), however, the same authors showed that these results were extremely sensitive to econometric specification, and that the large negative effects in the first paper were largely an artifact of measurement error in output.[50] In a specification that is robust to the measurement error problem, they found that the coefficient on PACE expenditures fell to about 1.5 in pooled time-series/cross section regressions, and was not significantly greater than one in fixed-effect regressions. Thus, there remains some evidence of a productivity penalty, but it has to be regarded as weak because the pooled regression is likely to be subject to spurious negative correlation between productivity levels and pollution control expenditures.[51]

Any discussion of the productivity impacts of environmental protection efforts should recognize that not all environmental regulations are created equal in terms of their costs or their benefits.[52] So-called market-based or economic-incentive regulations, such as those based on tradeable permits or pollution charges, will tend to be more cost-effective than regulations requiring technological adoption or establishing conventional performance standards. This is because under the market-based regulatory regime, firms are likely to abate up to the point they find it profitable, and firms that find it cheapest to reduce their levels of pollution will clean up the most. With such incentive-based regulatory systems, regulators can thus achieve a given level of pollution control more cheaply than by imposing fixed technological or performance standards on firms (Robert W. Hahn and Stavins 1991). Furthermore, market-based environmental policy instruments provide ongoing incentives for firms to adopt new and better technologies and processes, because under these systems, it always pays to clean up more if a suffi-

[50] The specification in Gray and Shadbegian (1993) is to regress productivity levels (the ratio of value-added to a weighted average of inputs) on the ratio of PACE expenditures to value-added. If value-added is measured with error, this introduces a downward bias in the coefficient on the PACE/Value-added ratio.

[51] If some plants are generally inefficient relative to others, then it would not be surprising if they had both higher control costs and lower productivity, even if there were no causal relationship between the two.

[52] Stewart (1993) attributes observed differences in the productivity effects of environmental regulations in the U.S., Canada, and Japan (U.S. Congressional Budget Office 1985) to differences in legal and administrative systems, although he notes that the CBO study did not attempt to control for regulatory stringency.

ciently cheap way of doing so can be identified and adopted.[53]

5.2 *General Equilibrium Effects*

To quantify the overall, long-run social costs of regulation (where costs are measured by the compensation required to leave individuals as well off after a regulation as before—ignoring environmental benefits), a general equilibrium perspective is essential, in order to incorporate interindustry interactions and cumulative effects of changes in investment levels. In general, the overall social costs of environmental regulation will exceed direct compliance costs because regulations can cause reductions in output, inhibit investments in productive capital, reduce productivity, and bring about transitional costs (Schmalensee 1994).

Michael Hazilla and Kopp (1990) compared projected costs for compliance with the Clean Air and Clean Water Acts, with and without allowing for general equilibrium adjustments in labor input and investment by industry. They found that the annual social costs allowing for general equilibrium adjustments were smaller than projected pollution control expenditures in early years, but eventually came to exceed greatly the partial equilibrium projection (because of reductions in investment and labor supply).

Dale W. Jorgenson and Peter J. Wilcoxen (1990) used a model with 35 industry sectors (including government enterprises), a representative consumer, and an exogenous current account balance. Each sector's demand for inputs responds to prices according to econometrically estimated demand functions. There is a single malleable capital good, whose quantity is based on past investment and whose service price is determined endogenously. Investment is determined by the consumer's savings, which is given by the solution to a perfect foresight intertemporal optimization of consumption. They model the dynamic effects of operating costs associated with pollution control, pollution control investment, and compliance with motor vehicle emissions standards. They find that over the period 1974–1985, the combined effect of these mandated costs was to reduce the average growth rate of real GNP by about 0.2 percentage points per year, with required investment having the biggest effect and operating costs the smallest.[54] By 1985, the cumulative effect of this reduced growth is that simulated GNP without environmental regulation would be about 1.7 percent more than the actual historical value. This lost output is of roughly the same magnitude as the direct costs of compliance (Table 4).[55]

The results of any simulation model are, of course, somewhat sensitive to the structure and parameter values employed. This can be a particular concern with computable general equilibrium models because of their size and complexity. Nevertheless, the results examined in this section suggest that there are significant dynamic impacts of environmental regulation in the form of costs associated with reduced investment.

5.3 *Economic Growth Enhancement*

The vast majority of economic analyses of regulation and competitiveness are

[53] See Jaffe and Stavins, forthcoming. Some types of market-based instruments can raise special problems in the context of international trade, however, if the policy instruments are not harmonized across nations (Harmen Verbruggen 1993).

[54] Because the compliance expenditures are included in GNP, this reduction in growth is a cost over and above the direct costs.

[55] Jorgenson and Wilcoxen (1992) estimate that the 1990 amendments to the Clean Air Act will impose incremental losses in economic growth that are approximately one-fifth as large as the losses they estimated for regulation in place during the 1974–1985 period.

based upon the assumption that regulations increase production costs. Nevertheless, there have been some recent suggestions in the literature that regulations may actually stimulate growth and competitiveness. This argument—articulated recently by Porter (1991)[56]—has generated a great deal of interest and enthusiasm among some influential policy makers (see, for example, Senator Al Gore 1992).

There are several levels on which the so-called Porter hypothesis may be interpreted. First of all, it can be taken simply to mean that some sectors of private industry, in particular, environmental services, will benefit directly from more stringent environmental regulations *on their customers* (but not on themselves). Thus, the acid-rain reduction provisions of the Clean Air Act amendments of 1990, which call for significant reductions in sulfur dioxide (SO_2) emissions from electric utilities, are unambiguously good news for the manufacturers of flue-gas purification equipment (scrubbers) and producers of low-sulfur coal.

To push this argument slightly further, it would also not be surprising if environmental regulation induced innovation with respect to technologies to achieve compliance. Surely, catalytic converter technology today is superior to what it would have been if auto emissions had never been regulated. Internationally, it has been suggested that German firms possess some competitive advantage in water-pollution control technology and U.S. firms dominate hazardous waste management, because of relatively stricter regulations (Organization for Economic Cooperation and Development 1992; U.S. Environmental Protection Agency 1993). Jean Lanjouw and Mody (1993) looked at patents originating from inventors in different countries, in patent classes deemed to be environmental technologies, and found that increases in environmental compliance costs were related to increases in patenting of such technologies with a one to two year lag. The existence of such "induced innovation" suggests that projections of compliance costs made *before* regulatory implementation may be biased upwards, because they will inevitably take existing technology as given to some extent. On the other hand, this effect does *not* necessarily suggest that measured compliance costs overstate actual costs, because measured costs will reflect technology as it actually evolved.[57]

Second, putting aside the obvious gainers in the environmental services sector, the Porter hypothesis can be taken to imply that, under stricter environmental regulations, *some* regulated firms will benefit competitively, at the expense of *other* regulated firms. If, for example, larger firms find it less costly to comply than smaller firms, then the former might actually benefit from regulation, if higher prices from reduced competition more than offset *their* increased costs. Similarly, the Chrysler Corporation may have benefitted—relative to General Motors and Ford—from the imposition of automobile fuel-efficiency standards[58] in 1975, because its fleet consisted of smaller-sized models. Somewhat related to this, the hypothesis can be thought of as referring dynamically to the reality that environmental regulation

[56] The idea goes back, at least, to Nicholas A. Ashford, C. Ayers, and R.F. Stone (1985). For a recent explication, see Claas van der Linde (1993).

[57] One could argue that measured costs understate the social cost, because they generally do not include the cost of R&D to develop new control technologies. On the other hand, if, as discussed further below, R&D has large positive externalities, then the net mismeasurement is ambiguous.

[58] Energy Policy and Conservation Act of 1975 (89 Stat. 902), amending the Motor Vehicle Information and Cost Savings Act (86 Stat. 947).

can provide some firms with "early mover" advantages by pushing them to produce products that will in the future be in demand in the marketplace.

The proponents of the Porter hypothesis—in public policy circles—have asserted some significantly stronger interpretations, however, namely that the competitiveness of the U.S. as a whole can be enhanced by stricter regulation.[59] It has been suggested that induced innovation can create lasting comparative advantage for U.S. firms, if other countries eventually follow our lead to stricter regulations and there are strong "first-mover" advantages enjoyed by the first firms to enter the markets for control equipment (see, for example, David Gardiner 1994). Even ignoring export possibilities, it has been suggested that environmental regulation can increase domestic efficiency, either by wringing inefficiencies out of the production process as firms struggle to meet new constraints or by spurring innovation in the long term through "outside-of-the-box thinking."[60] The notion is that the imposition of regulations impels firms to reconsider their production processes, and hence to discover innovative approaches to reduce pollution *and* decrease costs or increase output. If this happened widely enough, total social costs of regulation could be no greater than measured compliance costs. Indeed, if the innovation-stimulating effect of regulation were large enough, then regulation would offer the possibility of a "free lunch," that is, improvements in environmental quality without any costs.[61]

Economists generally have been unsympathetic to these stronger arguments, because they depend upon firms being systematically ignorant of profitable production improvements or new technologies that regulations bring forth. (For a more detailed explication of economists' skepticism, see Karen L. Palmer and R. David Simpson 1993, and Oates, Palmer, and Portney 1993.) Nevertheless, specific instances of "cheap" or even "free lunches" may occur. For example, Barbera and McConnell (1990) found that lower production costs in the nonferrous metals industry were brought about by new environmental regulations that led to the introduction of new, low-polluting production practices that were also more efficient.[62] One way in which environmental regulation could theoretically have a positive impact on measured productivity at the industry level is by forcing exceptionally inefficient plants to close. To the degree that production is shifted to other domestic plants with higher productivity, the industry's overall productivity could actually increase. One study suggests that this is what happened when environmental regulations in the 1970s unintentionally accelerated

[59] Scott Barrett (forthcoming) calls this notion "strategic standard-setting."

[60] Porter (1990) emphasizes that a number of industrial sectors subject to the most stringent domestic environmental regulations have become more competitive internationally: chemicals, plastics, and paints.

[61] Note that the suggestion of proponents of the Porter hypothesis is *not* that the benefits of environmental regulation (in terms of reduced health and ecological damages) exceed the costs of environmental protection. This is obviously possible, and it is an empirical issue. Rather, the notion of a "free lunch" is that—putting aside the benefits of environmental protection—the costs of regulatory action can be zero or even negative (a "paid lunch"). For an example of "free lunch" arguments —both theoretical and empirical—in the context of energy efficiency and global climate change, see Robert Ayers (1993).

[62] Two of five industries studied experienced induced savings in conventional capital costs and operating costs as a result of stricter environmental regulations and consequent increases in environmental capital investment. But, even for these two industries, the indirect effects were not sufficient to offset the direct cost increases. In the other three industries studied, environmental regulations caused both direct increases in environmental capital investments *and* increases in conventional capital costs and operating costs.

the "modernization" of the U.S. steel industry (U.S. Office of Technology Assessment 1980).[63]

Even if firms are systematically ignorant of potential new processes that are both cleaner and more profitable than current methods of production, there is considerable doubt as to whether regulators would know more about these better methods of production than firm managers, or that continually higher regulatory standards would lead firms regularly to discover new clean and profitable technologies.[64] Moreover, one must be careful when claiming that firms are not operating on their production frontiers: if there are managerial costs to investigating new production technologies, then firms may be efficient even if they do not realize that new, more efficient processes exist until regulations necessitate their adoption.[65] In other words, there may be many efficiency-enhancing ideas that firms could implement if they invested the resources required to search for them. If firms do successfully search in a particular area for beneficial ideas, it will appear ex post that they were acting suboptimally by not having investigated this area sooner. But with limited resources, the real question is not whether searching produces new ideas, but whether particular searches that are generated by regulation systematically lead to more or better ideas than searches in which firms would otherwise engage.[66]

Finally, one could argue that regulation, by forcing a re-examination of products and processes, will induce an overall increase in the resources devoted to "research," broadly defined. Even if firms were previously choosing the (privately) optimal level of research investment, this inducement could be (socially) desirable, if the social rate of return to research activities is significantly greater than the private return.[67] Jaffe and Palmer (1994) examined the PACE expenditure data, R&D spending data, and patent data, in a panel of industries between 1976 and 1989. They found some evidence that increases in PACE spending were associated with increases in R&D spending,

[63] While the premature scrapping of "obsolete" capital will raise measured industry productivity, this does not mean that it is socially beneficial. Such plants were, presumably, producing output whose value exceeded variable production costs.

[64] The optimal timing of the adoption of a new technology is obviously a complicated issue. Although early adoption can be better than waiting, if technology advances quickly, it may be optimal for firms to wait to invest until even better processes are available. Regulation may cause firms to invest in clean technologies today, but then discourage investment in still cleaner technologies later. See Jaffe and Stavins (1994).

[65] As contrary anecdotal evidence, we should recognize that many business people find economists' skepticism about businesses not operating on their frontiers to be, at best, an indication of the naivete of academic economists, and, at worst, a special case of the joke about the economist who fails to pick up a twenty-dollar bill from the sidewalk because he assumes that if it were not counterfeit someone else would surely have taken it.

[66] As noted above, environmental regulations may lower some firms' costs and increase their productivity by cleaning the environment. Some studies find that environmental regulations are productive when one takes into account the cost of the "environmental inputs" into the production process (Repetto 1990). Studies of this type are tangential to the "Porter hypothesis," because such studies focus on situations where the benefits of environmental regulations are not sufficient to make individual firms undertake cleanup, but are substantial enough that industry as a whole may benefit. For example, it is unlikely that any single firm has an incentive to reduce its smokestack emissions solely to improve its own workers' health, but if every firm lowered its emissions, industry might find that, as a result of the change, fewer work days were lost due to illness. See Lester B. Lave and Eugene Seskin (1977); U.S. Environmental Protection Agency (1982); and Douglas W. Dockery et al. (1993).

[67] A priori, private incentives to engage in research could be either too low (because research generates knowledge externalities enjoyed by other firms) or too high (because research creates negative externalities by destroying quasi-rents being earned by other firms). Empirical evidence seems to confirm that social returns exceed private returns (Edward Mansfield et al. 1977; Jaffe 1986; and Zvi Griliches 1990).

but no evidence that this increased spending produced greater innovation as measured by successful patent applications.

One empirical analysis that is frequently cited in support of the Porter hypothesis is Stephen M. Meyer (1992), which examines whether states with strict environmental laws demonstrate poor economic performance relative to states with more lax standards. Meyer (1992, p. iv) finds that

> *at a minimum* the pursuit of environmental quality does not hinder economic growth and development. Furthermore, there appears to be a moderate yet consistent positive association between environmentalism and economic growth.

Unfortunately, his statistical analysis sheds very little light on a possible causal relationship between regulation and economic performance.[68] His approach does not control for factors other than the stringency of a state's environmental laws that could affect the state's economic performance. Consequently, it is quite possible that he has merely found a spurious positive correlation between the stringency of a state's environmental standards and its economic performance. His results are consistent with the hypothesis that poor states with no prospect for substantial growth will not enact tough environmental regulations, just as developing countries are less likely than rich countries to enact tough environmental regulations.[69]

Thus, overall, the literature on the "Porter hypothesis" remains one with a high ratio of speculation and anecdote to systematic evidence. While economists have good reason to be skeptical of arguments based on nonoptimizing behavior where the only support is anecdotal, it is also important to recognize that if we wish to persuade others of the validity of our analysis we must go beyond tautological arguments that rest solely on the postulate of profit-maximization. Systematic empirical analysis in this area is only beginning, and it is too soon to tell if it will ultimately provide a clear answer.

6. *Conclusions*

Overall, there is relatively little evidence to support the hypothesis that environmental regulations have had a large adverse effect on competitiveness, however that elusive term is defined. Although the long-run social costs of environmental regulation may be significant, including adverse effects on productivity, studies attempting to measure the effect of environmental regulation on net exports, overall trade flows, and plant-location decisions have produced estimates that are either small, statistically insig-

[68] This has not kept a number of authors from describing Meyer's analysis as absolutely conclusive: "Meyer's study does repudiate the hypothesis that environmental regulations reduce economic growth and job creation" (Bezdek 1993, p. 10).

[69] For some environmental problems, such as inadequate sanitation and unsafe drinking water, there is a monotonic and *inverse* relationship between the level of the environmental threat and per capita income (International Bank for Reconstruction and Development 1992). This relationship holds both cross-sectionally (across nations) and for single nations over time. For other environmental problems, the relationship with income level is not monotonic at all, but an inverted *u*-shaped function in which at low levels of income, pollution increases with per capita income, but then at some point begins to decline with further increases in income. This is true of most forms of air and water pollution (Grossman and Krueger 1994), some types of deforestation, and habitat loss. Pollution increases from the least developed agricultural countries to those beginning to industrialize fully—such as Mexico and the emerging market economies of Eastern Europe and parts of the former Soviet Union. After peaking in such nations, pollution is found to decline in the wealthier, industrialized nations that have both the demand for cleaner air and water and the means to provide it. Finally, for another set of environmental pollutants, including carbon dioxide emissions, there is an *increasing* monotonic relationship between per capita income and emission levels, at least within the realm of experience.

nificant, or not robust to tests of model specification.

There are a number of reasons why the effects of environmental regulation on competitiveness may be small and difficult to detect. First, the existing data are severely limited in their ability to measure the relative stringency of environmental regulation, making it difficult to use such measures in regression analyses of the effects of regulation on economic performance. Second, for all but the most heavily regulated industries, the cost of complying with federal environmental regulation is a relatively small fraction of total cost of production. According to EPA, that share for U.S. industry as a whole averages about two percent, although it is certainly higher for some industries, such as electric utilities, chemical manufacturers, petroleum refiners, and basic metals manufacturers. This being the case, environmental regulatory intensity should not be expected to be a significant determinant of competitiveness in *most* industries. Labor cost differentials, energy and raw materials cost differentials, infrastructure adequacy, and other factors would indeed overwhelm the environmental effect.

Third, although U.S. environmental laws and regulations are generally the most stringent in the world, the difference between U.S. requirements and those in other western industrial democracies is not great, especially for air and water pollution control.[70] Fourth, even where there are substantial differences between environmental requirements in the United States and elsewhere, U.S. firms (and other multinationals, as well) are reluctant to build less-than-state-of-the-art plants in foreign countries. If such willingness existed before the accident at the Union Carbide plant in Bhopal, India, it does not now. Thus, even significant differences in regulatory stringency may not be exploited. Fifth and finally, it appears that even in developing countries where environmental standards (and certainly enforcement capabilities) are relatively weak, plants built by indigenous firms typically embody more pollution control—sometimes substantially more—than is required. To the extent this is true, even significant *statutory* differences in pollution control requirements between countries may not result in significant effects on plant location or other manifestations of competitiveness.

Having stated these conclusions, it is important to emphasize several caveats. First, in many of the studies, differences in environmental regulation were measured by environmental control costs as a percentage of value-added, or some other measure that depends critically on accurate measurement of environmental spending. Even for the United States, where data on environmental compliance costs are relatively good, compliance expenditure data are notoriously unreliable. The problem is more pronounced in other OECD countries, whose environmental agencies have not typically tracked environmental costs. Thus, we may have found little relationship between environmental regulations and competitiveness simply because the data are of poor quality.

In an era of increasing reliance on incentive-based and other performance-based environmental regulations, accurate accounting for pollution control will become an even more pronounced problem. This is because pollution control expenditures increasingly are taking the form of process changes and product reformulations, rather than installation of end-of-pipe control equipment. It will be

[70] See Kopp, Diane Dewitt, and Portney (1990) for empirical evidence, and Barrett (1992) for a theoretical argument of why governments should *not* be expected to adopt relatively weak pollution standards for competitive reasons.

increasingly difficult (perhaps even impossible) to allocate accurately that part of the cost of a new plant that is attributable to environmental control (Hahn and Stavins 1992). Ironically, in ten years we may know less about total annual pollution control costs than we do now, in spite of increased concern about these expenditures and their possible effects on competitiveness.

A second caveat is that only two of the studies we reviewed controlled for differences in "regulatory climate" between jurisdictions. If the delays and litigation surrounding regulation are the greatest impediments to exporting or to new plant location, these effects will not be picked up by studies that look exclusively at source discharge standards or traditional spending for pollution control equipment as measures of regulatory intensity, unless these direct compliance costs are highly correlated with the costs of litigation and delay.

A third factor that tempers our findings is the difficulty of measuring the effectiveness of enforcement efforts. Subtle differences in enforcement strategies are very difficult to measure, but these differences can lead to variations from country to country that *could* influence competitiveness. Finally, it is important to recall that any comprehensive effort to identify the competitiveness effects associated with regulation must look at both the costs *and* benefits of regulation. To the extent that air or water pollution control efforts reduce damages, they may reduce costs for some businesses and thus make them more competitive. Similarly, pollution control can reduce labor costs and enhance competitiveness in some locations under certain conditions.

Just as we have found little consistent empirical evidence for the conventional hypothesis regarding environmental regulation and competitiveness, there is also little or no evidence supporting the revisionist hypothesis that environmental regulation stimulates innovation and improved international competitiveness. Given the large direct and indirect costs that regulation imposes, economists' natural skepticism regarding this free regulatory lunch is appropriate, though further research would help to convince others that our conclusions are well grounded in fact.

Overall, the evidence we have reviewed suggests that the truth regarding the relationship between environmental protection and international competitiveness lies in between the two extremes of the current debate. International differences in environmental regulatory stringency pose insufficient threats to U.S. industrial competitiveness to justify substantial cutbacks in domestic environmental regulations. At the same time, such regulation clearly imposes large direct and indirect costs on society, and there is no evidence supporting the enactment of stricter domestic environmental regulations to stimulate economic competitiveness. Instead, policy makers should do what they can to establish environmental priorities and goals that are consistent with the real tradeoffs that are inevitably required by regulatory activities; that is, our environmental goals should be based on careful balancing of benefits and costs. At the same time, policy makers should seek to reduce the magnitude of these costs by identifying and implementing flexible and cost-effective environmental policy instruments, whether they be of the conventional type or of the newer breed of market-based approaches.

REFERENCES

AYRES, ROBERT U. "On Economic Disequilibrium and Free Lunch." Working Paper, Centre for the Management of Environmental Resources, INSEAD, Fontainebleau, France, June 1993.

ASHFORD, NICHOLAS A.; AYERS, C. AND STONE, R. F. "Using Regulation to Change the Market for Innovation," *Harvard Environ. Law Rev.*, 1985, *9*, pp. 419–66.

BARBERA, ANTHONY J. AND MCCONNELL, VIRGINIA D. "The Impact of Environmental Regulations on Industry Productivity: Direct and Indirect Effects," *J. Environ. Econ. Manage.*, Jan. 1990, *18*(1), pp. 50–65.

BARRETT, SCOTT. "Strategy and Environment," *Columbia J. World Bus.*, Fall/Winter 1992, *27*, pp. 202–08.

———. "Strategic Environmental Policy and International Trade," *J. Public Econ.*, forthcoming.

BARTIK, TIMOTHY J. "Business Location Decisions in the United States: Estimates of the Effects of Unionization, Taxes, and Other Characteristics of States," *J. Bus. Econ. Statist.*, Jan. 1985, *3*(1), pp. 14–22.

———. "The Effects of Environmental Regulation on Business Location in the United States," *Growth Change*, Summer 1988, *19*(3), pp. 22–44.

———. "Small Business Start-Ups in the United States: Estimates of the Effects of Characteristics of States," *Southern Econ. J.*, Apr. 1989, *55*(4), pp. 1004–18.

BEZDEK, ROGER H. "Environment and Economy: What's the Bottom Line?" *Environment*, Sept. 1993, *35*(7), pp. 7–11, 25–32.

CRANDALL, ROBERT W. "Pollution Controls and Productivity Growth in Basic Industries," in *Productivity measurement in regulated industries*. Eds.: THOMAS G. COWING AND RODNEY F. STEVENSON. New York, NY: Academic Press, Inc., 198, pp. 347–68.

CROPPER, MAUREEN L. AND OATES, WALLACE E. "Environmental Economics: A Survey," *J. Econ. Lit.*, June 1992, *30*(2), pp. 675–740.

D'ARGE, RALPH. "International Trade, Domestic Income, and Environmental Controls: Some Empirical Estimates" in *Managing the environment: International economic cooperation for pollution control*. Ed.: ALLEN KNEESE. New York: Praeger, 1974, pp. 289–315.

DEAN, JUDITH M. "Trade and the Environment: A Survey of the Literature," in *International trade and the environment*. Ed.: PATRICK LOW. Washington, DC: International Bank for Reconstruction and Development/World Bank, 1992.

DENISON, EDWARD F. *Accounting for slower economic growth: The U.S. in the 1970's*. Washington, DC: Brookings Institution, 1979.

DOCKERY, DOUGLAS W. ET AL. "An Association Between Air Pollution and Mortality in Six U.S. Cities," *New Eng. J. Medicine*, 1993, *329*, pp. 1753–59.

DUERKSEN, CHRISTOPHER. *Environmental regulation of industrial plant siting*. Washington, DC: Conservation Foundation, 1983.

FRIEDMAN, JOSEPH; GERLOWSKI, DANIEL A. AND SILBERMAN, JONATHAN. "What Attracts Foreign Multinational Corporations? Evidence from Branch Plant Location in the United States," *J. Reg. Sci.*, Nov. 1992, *32*(4), pp. 403–18.

GALLOP, FRANK M. AND ROBERTS, MARK J. "Environmental Regulations and Productivity Growth: The Case of Fossil-Fueled Electric Power Generation," *J. Polit. Econ.*, 1983, *91*, pp. 654–74.

GARDINER, DAVID. "Does Environmental Policy Conflict with Economic Growth?" *Resources*, Spring 1994, (115), pp. 20–21.

GORE, SENATOR AL. *Earth in the balance: Ecology and the human spirit*. New York: Houghton Mifflin Company, 1992.

GRAY, WAYNE B. "The Cost of Regulation: OSHA, EPA, and the Productivity Slowdown," *Amer. Econ. Rev.*, Dec. 1987, *77*(5), pp. 998–1006.

———. "Cross-State Differences in Environmental Regulation and the Births and Deaths of Manufacturing Plants," 1993, work in progress.

GRAY, WAYNE B. AND SHADBEGIAN, RONALD J. "Environmental Regulation and Manufacturing Productivity At The Plant Level." Discussion Paper, U.S. Department of Commerce, Center for Economic Studies, Washington, DC, 1993.

———. "Pollution Abatement Costs, Regulation, and Plant-Level Productivity." Forthcoming working paper, National Bureau of Economic Research, Cambridge, MA, July 1994.

GRILICHES, ZVI. "Patent Statistics as Economic Indicators: A Survey," *J. Econ. Lit.*, Dec. 1990, *28*(4), pp. 1661–1707.

GROSSMAN, GENE M. AND KRUEGER, ALAN B. "Environmental Impacts of a North American Freed Trade Agreement," in *The U.S.-Mexico free trade agreement*. Ed.: PETER GARBER. Cambridge, MA: MIT Press, 1993, pp. 13–56.

———. "Economic Growth and the Environment." Working Paper No. 4634. Cambridge, MA: National Bureau of Economic Research, 1994.

HAHN, ROBERT W. AND STAVINS, ROBERT N. "Incentive-Based Environmental Regulation: A New Era from an Old Idea," *Ecology Law Quart.*, 1991, *18*, pp. 1–42.

———. "Economic Incentives for Environmental Protection: Integrating Theory and Practice," *Amer. Econ. Rev.*, May 1992, *82*(2), pp. 464–68.

HAVEMAN, ROBERT H. AND CHRISTIANSEN, GREGORY B. "Environmental Regulations and Productivity Growth," in *Environmental regulation and the U.S. economy*. Eds.: HENRY M. PESKIN, PAUL R. PORTNEY, AND ALLEN V. KNEESE. Washington, DC: Resources for the Future, 1981, pp. 55–75.

HAZILLA, MICHAEL AND KOPP, RAYMOND J. "Social Cost of Environmental Quality Regulations: A General Equilibrium Analysis," *J. Polit. Econ.*, Aug. 1990, *98*(4), pp. 853–73.

HOPKINS, THOMAS D. "Regulation and Jobs—Sorting Out the Consequences." Prepared for the American Petroleum Institute, Washington, DC, Oct. 1992.

International Bank for Reconstruction and Development/the World Bank. *World development report 1992: Development and the environment*. New York: Oxford U. Press, 1992.

JAFFE, ADAM B. "Technological Opportunity and Spillovers of R&D: Evidence from Firms' Patents, Profits, and Market Value," *Amer. Econ. Rev.*, Dec. 1986, *76*(5), pp. 984–1001.

JAFFE ADAM B. AND PALMER, KAREN L. "Environmental Regulation and Innovation: A Panel Data Study." Paper prepared for the Western Economic Association Meetings, June 1994.

JAFFE, ADAM B. ET AL. "Environmental Regulations and the Competitiveness of U.S. Industry." Report prepared for the Economics and Statistics Administration, U.S. Department of Commerce. Cambridge, MA: Economics Resource Group, 1993.

JAFFE, ADAM B. AND STAVINS, ROBERT N. "The Energy Paradox and the Diffusion of Conservation Technology," *Resource Energy Econ.*, May 1994, *16*(2), pp. 91–122.

———. "Dynamic Incentives of Environmental Regulation: The Effects of Alternative Policy Instruments on Technology Diffusion," *J. Environ & Econ. Manage.* July 1995, *29*(1), forthcoming.

JORGENSON, DALE W. AND WILCOXEN, PETER J. "Environmental Regulation and U.S. Economic Growth," *Rand J. Econ.*, Summer 1990, *21*(2), pp. 314–40.

———. "Impact of Environmental Legislation on U.S. Economic Growth, Investment, and Capital Costs," in *U.S. environmental policy and economic growth: How do we fare?* Ed.: DONNA L. BRODSKY. Washington, DC: American Council for Capital Formation, 1992.

KALT, JOSEPH P. "The Impact of Domestic Environmental Regulatory Policies on U.S. International Competitiveness," in *International competitiveness*. Eds.: A. MICHAEL SPENCE AND HEATHER A. HAZARD. Cambridge, MA: Harper and Row, Ballinger, 1988, pp. 221–62.

KAUFMANN, ROBERT K.; PAULY, PETER AND SWEITZER, JULIE. "The Effects of NAFTA on the Environment," *Energy J.*, 1993, *14*(3), pp. 217–40.

KOLSTAD, CHARLES D. AND XING, YUQING. "Do Lax Environmental Regulations Attract Foreign Investment?" Working Paper, Department of Economics and Institute for Environmental Studies, U. of Illinois, Urbana, Illinois, February 1994.

KOPP, RAYMOND J., DEWITT, DIANE AND PORTNEY, PAUL R. "International Comparison of Environmental Regulation," in *Environmental policy and the cost of capital*. Washington, DC: American Council for Capital Formation, 1990.

KRUGMAN, PAUL. *Geography and trade*. Cambridge, MA: MIT Press, 1991.

———. "Competitiveness: A Dangerous Obsession," *Foreign Affairs*, Mar./Apr. 1994, *73*(2), pp. 28–44.

LANJOUW, JEAN AND MODY, ASHOK. "Stimulating Innovation and the International Diffusion of Environmentally Responsive Technology: The Role of Expenditures and Institutions." mimeo, World Bank, 1993.

LAVE, LESTER B. AND SESKIN, EUGENE. *Air pollution and human health*. Washington, DC: Johns Hopkins U. Press for Resources for the Future, 1977.

LEAMER, EDWARD E. *Sources of international comparative advantage*. Cambridge: MIT Press, 1984.

LEONARD, H. JEFFREY. *Pollution and the struggle for the world product*. Cambridge, UK: Cambridge U. Press, 1988.

LEVINSON, ARIK. "Environmental Regulations and Manufacturers' Location Choices: Evidence from the Census of Manufactures." New York: Columbia U., 1992.

VAN DER LINDE, CLAAS. "The Micro-Economic Implications of Environmental Regulation: A Preliminary Framework," in *Environmental policies and industrial competitiveness*. Paris: Organization of Economic Cooperation and Development (OECD), 1993, pp. 69–77.

LOW, PATRICK AND YEATS, ALEXANDER. "Do 'Dirty' Industries Migrate?" in *International trade and the environment*. Washington, DC: The World Bank, 1992.

LUCAS, ROBERT E.B.; WHEELER, DAVID AND HETTIGE, HEMAMALA. "Economic Development, Environmental Regulation and the International Migration of Toxic Industrial Pollution: 1960–1988," in *International trade and the environment*. Ed.: PATRICK LOW. Washington, DC: World Bank, 1992, pp. 67–86.

MANSFIELD, EDWIN ET AL. "Social and Private Rates of Return from Industrial Innovations," *Quart. J. Econ.*, May 1977, *91*(2), pp. 221–40.

MCCONNELL, VIRGINIA D. AND SCHWAB, ROBERT M. "The Impact of Environmental Regulation on Industry Location Decisions: The Motor Vehicle Industry," *Land Econ.*, Feb. 1990, *66*(1), pp. 67–81.

MCGUIRE, MARTIN C. "Regulation, Factor Rewards, and International Trade," *J. Public Econ.*, Apr. 1982, *17*(3), pp. 335–54.

MEYER, STEPHEN M. "Environmentalism and Economic Prosperity: Testing the Environmental Impact Hypothesis." M.I.T. Mimeo, 1992. Cambridge, MA, Updated 1993.

NORSWORTHY, J. R.; HARPER, MICHAEL J. AND KUNZE, KENT. "The Slowdown in Productivity Growth: Analysis of Some Contributing Factors," *Brookings Pap. Econ. Act.*, 1979, 2, pp. 387–421.

OATES, WALLACE; PALMER, KAREN AND PORTNEY, PAUL. "Environmental Regulation and International Competitiveness: Thinking About The Porter Hypothesis." Mimeo, 1993.

ORGANIZATION FOR ECONOMIC COOPERATION AND DEVELOPMENT. *The macro-economic impacts of environmental expenditures*. Paris, France: Organization for Economic Cooperation and Development, 1985.

———. *OECD environment data compendium*. Paris, France: Organization for Economic Cooperation and Development, 1990.

———. *The OECD environment industry: Situation, prospects, and government policies*. Paris,

France: Organization of Economic Cooperation and Development. 1992.

———. *Summary report of the workshop on environmental policies and industrial competitiveness, 28–29 January 1993*. Paris, France: Organization of Economic Cooperation and Development, 1993a.

———. *Pollution abatement and control expenditure in OECD countries*. OECD Environment Monograph No. 75. Paris, France: Organization of Economic Cooperation and Development, 1993b.

OSTRO, BART D. "The Effects of Air Pollution on Work Loss and Morbidity," *J. Environ. Econ. Manage.*, Dec. 1983, *10*(4), pp. 371–82.

PALMER, KAREN L. AND SIMPSON, R. DAVID. "Environmental Policy as Industrial Policy," *Resources*, Summer 1993, (112), pp. 17–21.

PEARSON, CHARLES S., ed. *Multinational corporations, environment, and the Third World*. Durham, NC: Duke U. Press and World Resources Institute, 1987.

PETHIG, RUDIGER. "Pollution, Welfare, and Environmental Policy in the Theory of Comparative Advantage," *J. Environ. Econ. Manage.*, 1975, *2*, pp. 160–69.

PORTER, MICHAEL E. *The competitive advantage of nations*. New York: Free Press, 1990.

———. "America's Green Strategy," *Sci. Amer.*, Apr. 1991, p. 168.

PORTNEY, PAUL R. "Economics and the Clean Air Act," *J. Econ. Perspectives*, Fall 1990, *4*(4), pp. 173–81.

———. "Does Environmental Policy Conflict with Economic Growth?" *Resources*, Spring 1994, (115), pp. 21–23.

REPETTO, ROBERT. "Environmental Productivity and Why It Is So Important," *Challenge*, Sept.-Oct. 1990, *33*(5), pp. 33–38.

ROBISON, H. DAVID. "Industrial Pollution Abatement: The Impact on Balance of Trade," *Can. J. Econ.*, Feb. 1988, *21*(1), pp. 187–99.

ROSE, ADAM. "Modeling the Macroeconomic Impact of Air Pollution Abatement," *J. Reg. Sci.*, Nov. 1983, *23*(4), pp. 441–59.

RUTLEDGE, GARY L. AND LEONARD, MARY L. "Pollution Abatement and Control Expenditures, 1972–90," *Surv. Curr. Bus.*, June 1992, *72*(6), pp. 25–41.

———. "Pollution Abatement and Control Expenditures, 1987–91," *Surv. Curr. Bus.*, May 1993, *73*(5), pp. 55–62.

SCHMALENSEE, RICHARD. "The Costs of Environmental Protection," in *Balancing economic growth and environmental goals*. Ed.: MARY BETH KOTOWSKI. Washington, DC: American Council for Capital Formation Center for Policy Research, 1994, pp. 55–75.

SIEBERT, HORST. "Environmental Quality and the Gains from Trade," *Kyklos*, 1977, *30*(4), pp. 657–73.

SOLOW, ROBERT M. *An almost practical step toward sustainability*. Washington, DC: Resources for the Future, 1992.

STEWART, RICHARD B. "Environmental Regulation and International Competitiveness," *Yale Law J.*, June 1993, *102*(8), pp. 2039–2106.

TOBEY, JAMES A. "The Effects of Domestic Environmental Policies on Patterns of World Trade: An Empirical Test," *Kyklos*, 1990, *43*(2), pp. 191–209.

TYSON, LAURA D'ANDREA. "Competitiveness: An Analysis of the Problem and a Perspective on Future Policy," in *Global competitiveness: Getting the U.S. back on track*. Ed.: MARTIN K. STARR. New York, NY: Norton, 1988, pp. 95–120.

U.S. CONGRESS. *Legislative history of the Clean Air Act*. Part 3. Washington, DC: U.S. GPO, 1979.

U.S. CONGRESSIONAL BUDGET OFFICE. *Environmental regulation and economic efficiency*. Washington, DC: U.S. GPO, 1985.

U.S. DEPARTMENT OF COMMERCE. *Pollution abatement costs and expenditures, 1991*. Economics and Statistics Administration, Bureau of the Census. Washington, DC: U.S. GPO, 1993.

U.S. ENVIRONMENTAL PROTECTION AGENCY. *Air quality criteria for particulate matter and sulfur oxides*. Research Triangle Park, North Carolina: U.S. Environmental Protection Agency, 1982.

———. *Environmental investments: The cost of a clean environment*. Washington, DC: U.S. Environmental Protection Agency, 1990.

———. *National air quality and emissions trends report*. Office of Air Quality Planning and Standards, EPA-450-R-92-001. Research Triangle Park, North Carolina: U.S. Environmental Protection Agency, 1992a.

———. "The Clean Air Marketplace: New Business Opportunities Created by the Clean Air Act Amendments—Summary of Conference Proceedings." Washington, DC, Office of Air and Radiation, July 24, 1992b.

———. *International trade in environmental protection equipment*. Washington, DC: U.S. Environmental Protection Agency, 1993.

U.S. GENERAL ACCOUNTING OFFICE. *U.S.—Mexico Trade: Some U.S. wood furniture firms relocated from Los Angeles area to Mexico*. Report Number GAO/NSIAD-91-191. Washington, DC: U.S. General Accounting Office, 1991.

U.S. OFFICE OF TECHNOLOGY ASSESSMENT. *Technology and steel industry competitiveness*. OTA-M-122. Washington, DC: U.S. GPO, 1980.

———. *Trade and the environment: Conflicts and opportunities*. Washington, DC: U.S. GPO, 1992.

———. *Industry, technology, and the environment: Competitive challenges and business opportunities*. OTA-ITE-586. Washington, DC: U.S. GPO, 1994.

VERBRUGGEN, HARMEN. "The Trade Effects of Economic Instruments," in *Environmental policies and industrial competitiveness*. Paris: Organization of Economic Cooperation and Development (OECD), 1993, pp. 55–62.

VOGEL, DAVID. *National styles of regulation: Environmental policy in Great Britain and the United States*. Ithaca, NY: Cornell U. Press, 1986.

WALTER, INGO. "Environmentally Induced Industrial Relocation to Developing Countries," in *Environment and trade: The relation of international trade and environmental policy*. Eds.: SEYMOUR J. RUBIN AND THOMAS R. GRAHAM. Totowa, NJ: Allanheld, Osmun, 1982, pp. 67–101.

WALTER, INGO AND UGELOW, J. "Environmental Policies in Developing Countries," *Ambio*, 1979, *8*, pp. 102–09.

WEITZMAN, MARTIN L. "On the 'Environmental' Discount Rate." *J. Environ. Econ. Manage.*, Mar. 1994, *26*(2), pp. 200–09.

WHEELER, DAVID AND MODY, ASHOKA. "International Investment Location Decisions: The Case of U.S. Firms," *J. Int. Econ.*, Aug. 1992, *33*(1,2), pp. 57–76.

YOHE, GARY W. "The Backward Incidence of Pollution Control—Some Comparative Statics in General Equilibrium," *J. Environ. Econ. Manage.*, Sept. 1979, *6*(3), pp. 187–98.

ZAMPARUTTI, ANTHONY AND JON KLAVENS. "Environment and Foreign Investment in Central and Eastern Europe: Results from a Survey of Western Corporations," in *Environmental policies and industrial competitiveness*. Paris: Organization of Economic Cooperation and Development (OECD), 1993, pp. 120–27.

Part II
Legal Perspectives

[8]

Trade, Environment, and Sustainable Development: A Primer

By ROBERT HOUSMAN *and* DURWOOD ZAELKE*

I. INTRODUCTION

Free trade policy is designed to let markets allocate resources to their most efficient uses, while environmental policy seeks to manage and maintain the earth's resources efficiently. Conflicts can and do arise where the same resources are subject to both trade efforts to allocate and environmental efforts to manage and maintain. This conflict must be reconciled; both trade and environmental policies are too important to let conflicts persist. Yet many environmentalists still believe that the economic system, including trade, is the enemy, and many trade and development experts still believe that the environment is not a fundamental part of the economy, but rather a luxury to be added on later, when and if it can be afforded.

The trade and environmental communities have different backgrounds and professional "cultures." Economic principles, such as efficiency and comparative advantage, guide trade experts while environmental experts are informed more by the biological sciences and ecological principles.

On the other hand, most environmental professionals appreciate the need to internalize environmental costs. Many now see that market-based strategies often may be more efficient than command and control strategies in achieving this goal. In addition to the common language of cost internalization, both the trade and environmental cultures use law to help implement their goals and to resolve disputes.

---

* Mr. Housman is an attorney with the Center for International Environmental Law—U.S. and Adjunct Professor of Law, the Washington College of Law, the American University. Mr. Zaelke is the President and founder of the Center for International Environmental Law—U.S. and Adjunct Professor of Law, the Washington College of Law, the American University. This article grew out of a report for the EPA's Committee on Trade and the Environment, prepared by Mr. Housman, Mr. Zaelke and Mr. Gary Stanley. The authors wish to thank David Downes, Chris Wold, Margaret Spring, Don Goldberg, Gary Stanley, Claudia Saladin, Hal Kane, Doug Arnold, Steve Heller, and Patti Goldman for their assistance in this effort. Any remaining errors are the sole property of the authors.

Given time, it seems reasonable to expect that both trade and environmental policy makers will adopt sustainable development as a legitimate goal. As the Environmental Protection Agency's Trade and Environment Committee noted last summer, "On the most fundamental level, trade and environmental policy must meet in the concept of sustainable development. Both trade policy and environmental policy must serve that concept as their ultimate goal."[1]

The problem, of course, is that time is running out. By the middle of the twenty-first century world population is expected to double to ten billion people, and the world economy of sixteen trillion dollars may reach eighty trillion dollars.[2] Scientists have detected record levels of the ozone-depleting chemical chlorine monoxide over the New England region of the United States and Canada. This discovery raises fears that a new hole in the ozone layer may be opening, exposing large numbers of people to harmful levels of ultraviolet radiation.[3] Assuming that the present rate of growth in greenhouse gases remains constant, we may have already committed the earth to a mean global warming of between 3 degrees and 8 degrees Farenheit (1.5 degrees to 4.5 degrees Celsius).[4]

Even with the most optimistic projections of technological advancement, these growth trends in population and the economy almost certainly cannot be sustained. Still more troubling is that the scale of today's development already appears to be overextending the ecosystem that sustains us all. "Further growth beyond the present scale," according to World Bank senior economist Herman Daly, "is overwhelmingly likely to increase costs more rapidly than it increases benefits, thus ushering in a new era of uneconomic growth that impoverishes rather than

1. *See* EPA Trade and Environment Committee, Minutes of Aug. 5, 1991 Meeting, Aug. 6, 1991, at 1 (unpublished minutes on file with CIEL-US). The GATT Secretariat has, however, denied any linkage between trade and the achievement of sustainable development. *See* GATT Secretariat, Trade and the Environment 3 (undated advance copy on file with the authors) [hereinafter GATT Secretariat, Trade and the Environment]. The GATT Secratariat views trade as a mere "magnifier" of the existing policies. *Id.* Thus, if a country has sustainable policies in place, trade will promote them. *Id.* "Alternatively, if such policies are lacking, the country's international trade may contribute to a skewing of the country's development in an environmentally damaging direction, but then so will most of the other economic activities in the country." *Id.* The Secretariat does not view this "magnifier" effect as a direct causal relationship between trade and the goal of sustainable development. *Id.*

2. *See* GEORGE HEATON ET AL., TRANSFORMING TECHNOLOGY: AN AGENDA FOR ENVIRONMENTALLY SUSTAINABLE GROWTH IN THE 21ST CENTURY 1 (1991).

3. *See* Cathy Sawyer, *Ozone-Hole Conditions Spreading*, WASH. POST, Feb. 4, 1992, at A1.

4. *See* Dean Edwin Abrahamson, *Global Warming: The Issue, Impacts, Responses*, *in* THE CHALLENGE OF GLOBAL WARMING 10 (Dean Edwin Abrahamson ed., 1989).

enriches."[5] Daly believes that "[t]his is the fundamental wild fact that so far has not found expression in words sufficiently feral to assault successfully the civil stupor of economic discourse."[6]

As the critical scientific and policy debate about the limits of the ecosystem continues, it is necessary to reconcile the legal relationships between trade agreements and environmental agreements. They cannot remain at odds if we are to achieve sustainable development and long-term international economic prosperity. Accordingly, this Article surveys provisions within the General Agreement on Tariffs and Trade (GATT)[7] and other trade agreements relevant to environmental concerns. It then reviews several international environmental agreements and U.S. laws for possible friction with those trade provisions. The Article concludes by briefly discussing issues and options for reducing or eliminating such friction.

II. PROVISIONS WITHIN TRADE AGREEMENTS RELEVANT TO ENVIRONMENTAL AGREEMENTS AND CONCERNS

The GATT provides the legal framework under which almost all trade among nations occurs. A number of regional (e.g., the European Free Trade Association) and bilateral trade agreements (e.g., the United States-Canada Free Trade Agreement) co-exist with the GATT.

GATT and these other agreements seek to provide a secure and predictable international trading environment while fostering greater economic efficiency and growth through trade liberalization. The GATT's preamble accordingly recognizes "that . . . trade and economic endeavor

5. HERMAN DALY & JOHN COBB, FOR THE COMMON GOOD: REDIRECTING THE ECONOMY TOWARDS COMMUNITY, THE ENVIRONMENT, AND A SUSTAINABLE FUTURE 2 (1989).

6. *Id.*

7. General Agreement on Tariffs and Trade, *opened for signature* Oct. 30, 1947, 61 Stat. A3, 55 U.N.T.S. 187 [hereinafter GATT]. GATT was signed in 1947 by 23 countries and its rules, which provide the basic structural framework in which trade and environment issues interact, went into force on January 1, 1948. The United States became a contracting party to GATT by executive agreement and proclamation. *See* Protocol of Provisional Application of the General Agreement on Tax on Tariffs and Trade, Oct. 30, 1947, 61 Stat. pt. 6, at A2051, 55 U.N.T.S. 308; Proclamation No. 2761A, 12 Fed. Reg. 8863 (1947). Despite the fact that the Senate has never explicitly consented to GATT, nor has Congress formally approved or implemented the agreement, GATT is generally accepted as a binding treaty obligation of the United States. *See* John H. Jackson, Changing GATT Rules (Nov. 7, 1991) (memorandum to the Trade and Environment Committee of the EPA); Robert Hudec, *The Legal Status of GATT in the Domestic Law of the United States*, *in* THE EUROPEAN COMMUNITY AND GATT 187, 199 (Meinhard Hilf et al. ed., 1986).

should be conducted with a view to raising standards of living, . . . developing the full use of the resources of the world and expanding the production and exchange of goods . . . ."[8] Free trade proponents argue that utilizing the "comparative advantage" of individual countries maximizes the welfare of all. The economic activity spawned by trade, however, has both positive and negative consequences for the environment when viewed in the context of sustainable development.

A. GATT

The GATT consists of three major parts: Part I (articles I to III) which contains the most-favored-nation and tariff concession obligations; Part II (articles III to XXIII), sometimes referred to as the "code of conduct," which contains the majority of the GATT's substantive provisions and the exceptions to its obligations; and Part III (articles XXIX to XXXVIII), which contains the procedural mechanisms for implementing the other obligations and provisions contained within the GATT.[9]

1. GATT's General Trade Principles and Their Environmental Implications

a. *The Most-Favored-Nation-Principle*

Article I's most-favored-nation principle (MFN) ensures that the contracting parties do not discriminate among imported products on the basis of their national origin. The MFN obligation requires that each contracting party extend immediately and unconditionally any privilege or advantage it provides to a product to like products from, or destined for, all GATT contracting parties. The MFN obligation applies to: 1) customs, duties, and charges related to imports and exports; 2) the methods of levying all such duties and charges; 3) rules, regulations, and procedures connected with importation and exportation; and 4) internal taxes, charges, laws, regulations, restrictions, and rules affecting the internal sale or offering for sale, purchase, transportation, warehousing or storage, distribution, or use of a product.[10]

Because the MFN principle requires that the parties treat all like products equally, it seemingly prohibits a contracting party from using trade restrictions to address the differences in environmental soundness.

---

8. GATT, *supra* note 7, pmbl., 61 Stat. at A11.

9. *See* JOHN H. JACKSON, THE WORLD TRADING SYSTEM: LAW AND POLICY OF INTERNATIONAL ECONOMIC RELATIONS 40 (1989).

10. *See* GATT, *supra* note 7, art. I, 61 Stat. at A12; *see also* Jeanne J. Grimmett, *Environmental Regulation and the GATT*, Aug. 1991, at 3-4 Cong. Res. Service, No. 91-285-A (1991).

Such differences may be caused by differences in production process methods (PPMs) that exist between like products originating from nations with high environmental standards and from nations with low environmental standards or lax enforcement.[11] Thus, an importation ban—such as the European Community's ban on animal furs caught with leghold traps—or a tax on a product of one contracting party, imposed because the PPM used in creating that product was environmentally harmful, would appear to run afoul of the MFN.[12]

Additionally, the MFN obligation has been found to apply to labeling schemes that are not marks of origin, including "eco-labeling" regimes.[13] Therefore, government labeling requirements relating to PPMs that grant market access or indirectly provide market advantages may also conflict with this GATT provision.

b. *The National Treatment Principle*

Article III's national treatment principle requires that a contracting party treat like foreign and domestic products equally once they have met tariffs and other import requirements.[14] Additionally, article III requires that any measure taken under its guise may not be applied to protect the domestic industry.

As the GATT Secretariat has noted so eloquently:

> Production and consumption activities in other countries can also be a source of domestic environmental concern. Pollution may be spilling over borders and harming either the regional environment (acid rain)

11. *See* GATT Secretariat, Trade and the Environment, *supra* note 1, at 10 ("In principle, it is not possible under GATT's rules to make access to one's own domestic market dependent on the domestic environmental policies or practices of the exporting country."); Grimmett, *supra* note 10, at 16; WORLD WILDLIFE FOUNDATION, THE GENERAL AGREEMENT ON TARIFFS AND TRADE, ENVIRONMENTAL PROTECTION AND SUSTAINABLE DEVELOPMENT 12 (1991) [hereinafter WWF]; ROBERT REPETTO, ENVIRONMENTAL ISSUES IN RELATION TO GATT 1 (1991).

12. *See supra* note 11; Council Regulation 3254/91, 1991 O.J. (L 308) 1-2.

13. *United States—Restrictions on Imports of Tuna*, 50-51, GATT Doc. DS21/R (Sept. 3, 1991) (finding *inter alia* that certain provisions of U.S. law that protect dolphin in the Eastern Tropical Pacific Ocean, as applied to imports of Mexican tuna, violated the United States obligations under GATT) [hereinafter *Tuna/Dolphin Panel Report*]; *see also generally* Robert Housman & Durwood Zaelke, *The Collision of the Environment and Trade: The GATT Tuna/Dolphin Decision*, 22 ENVTL. L. REP. 10,268, 10,273-74 (1992). The Tuna/Dolphin Panel upheld the particular labeling provisions before the panel because the provisions allowed suppliers of dolphin-safe tuna the option of disclosing its environmental character, but did not require unsafe or safe tuna to bear certain labeling to be sold. *Tuna/Dolphin Panel Report*, *supra*, at 51. The panel implied that if the labeling requirements had required certain PPM labeling, they would have violated the GATT. *Id.*

14. *See* GATT, *supra* note 7, art. III, 61 Stat. at A18.

> or the global commons (ozone depletion). Or land development projects may be threatening the extinction of an animal or plant species, and uncontrolled fishing may be depleting fish stock in the high seas. It is not unreasonable that the government of a country concerned by such practices would seek to see them changed—and that it would find it difficult to accept that this would not be possible. . . . *In principle it is not possible under GATT's rules to make access to one's own market dependent on the domestic environmental policies or practices of the exporting country.*[15]

Article III as applied appears to prohibit a nation from applying tariffs, levies, or other import restrictions to protect the competitiveness of a domestic industry that internalizes environmental costs in its product cost. Foreign competitors whose product costs do not reflect the environmental costs associated with the production of their products may gain a competitive advantage over the domestic products.[16]

While article III restricts a contracting party from imposing different regulations on imported products than on domestic products, article III does allow a contracting party to impose the same internal regulations applying to domestic products upon imported products at their point of importation. In order to qualify as a "point of importation regulation," the regulation must further apply directly to the product (i.e., it must alter or affect the physical or chemical makeup of the product).[17] A restriction failing to qualify as a point of importation regulation is a quantitative restriction and thus violates GATT's general obligations. Thus, a contracting party that distinguishes among imported products based on the environmental soundness of the exporting party's PPMs is vulnerable to attack under article III.[18]

While article III allows point of importation regulations, it has been read narrowly to permit only those restrictions that apply directly to, or affect the physical and/or chemical composition of, the product in question.[19] It is as yet unclear as to what level of effect article III would require a regulation to make in the product. For example, must a regula-

15. GATT Secretariat, Trade and the Environment, *supra* note 1, at 8-10 (emphasis in the original).

16. GATT Secretariat, Trade and the Environment, *supra* note 1, at 11; *Tuna/Dolphin Panel Report*, *supra* note 13, at 50; *see also* Grimmett, *supra* note 10, at 16; WWF, *supra* note 11, at 12.

17. *See supra* note 14 and accompanying text. This provision raises the issue as to whether required product content labeling requirements, that relate to, but do not affect the content of a product, could violate article III.

18. Housman & Zaelke, *supra* note 13, at 10,276.

19. *Tuna/Dolphin Panel Report*, *supra* note 13, at 41.

tion affect the content, appearance, value, or performance of a product in order to fall within article III? If a content difference is required, it is unclear whether, and to what degree, the difference must be discernable. This limitation appears to exclude from article III point of importation regulations all environmental regulations that govern the PPM of a product, as opposed to the product itself.[20] Even those environmental production process standards that encourage efficiency and free trade, such as Canadian regulations requiring paper products to contain a certain percentage of recycled materials, could be found to violate the prohibition on PPM regulations.[21] Because Canada lacks a sufficient supply of recyclable wastes, these paper product regulations would actually encourage increased free trade.[22]

Similarly, to qualify for article III treatment, a point of importation regulation must apply equally to "like" domestic and imported products.[23] But there is no guide as to how to determine when similar products are "like" products. For example, the European Community's ban on beef produced using hormones restricted the importation of both beef produced with natural hormones and beef produced with synthetic hormones.[24] Beef produced with synthetic hormones may not be "like" beef made without hormones. Beef made with artificially-provided natural hormones, however, has no chemicals not found in beef made without

20. *See* Grimmett, *supra* note 10, at 16; Frederick L. Kirgis Jr., *Effective Pollution Control in Industrialized Countries: International Economic Disincentives, Policy Responses, and the GATT*, 70 MICH. L. REV. 860, 893-901 (1972); WWF, *supra* note 11, at 12; Durwood Zaelke et al., Frictions Between International Trade Agreements and Environmental Protections 3 (1992) (paper prepared for the Trade & Env't Comm., Nat'l Advisory Council on Env't Policy & Technology, EPA) [hereinafter Frictions Between International Trade Agreements and Environmental Protections]. If, however, a PPM has an effect on the product, then the PPM may be GATT consistent. PPMs that do not actually effect the product are not, unless otherwise provided for, consistent with GATT.

21. *Imposition of Recycled Paper Regulations Would Force Imports From U.S., Industry Says*, 14 Int'l Envtl. Rep. (BNA) 462, 462-63 (1991) [hereinafter *Imposition of Recycled Paper Regulations*]. While the Canadian regulation appears to regulate the content of the paper, i.e. it requires a certain percentage of the material to be derived from recycled materials, unless there is a discernable difference between paper made from recycled materials and that made from virgin materials, the regulation will be deemed a production process regulation. *See also* Joint Session of Trade and Environment Experts, Organization for Economic Cooperation & Development, *The Applicability of the GATT to Trade and Environmental Concerns* 13, COM/ENV/EC/TD (91) 66 (Oct. 24, 1991) [hereinafter OECD, Joint Session] (noting the distinction between PPMs that affect the product and those PPMs that do not affect the product is often times a difficult, yet seminal, distinction). If a content difference is required, it is unclear to what extent that difference must be discernable.

22. *See Imposition of Recycled Paper Regulations*, *supra* note 21.

23. *See* GATT, *supra* note 7, art. III, 62 Stat. at 3680.

24. *See* Council Directive 88/146, 1988 O.J. (L 70) 16.

hormones. The only differences between the natural hormone-fortified beef and the all-natural beef is the level of hormones present and the way these hormones came to be present. Whether natural hormone-fortified beef and all-natural beef are "like" products and must be regulated similarly or are not "like" products and may be regulated differently, is unclear.

c. *The Prohibition of Quantitative Restrictions*

GATT article XI prohibits quantitative restrictions such as quotas, bans, and licensing schemes on imported or exported products. Article XI contains several narrow exceptions that allow departure from this general proscription, such as the application of standards to internationally-sold commodities and agricultural products.[25] Even when the exceptions permit a quantitative restriction, the contracting parties must still observe the MFN and national treatment obligations in implementing it.[26]

Applying the strict prohibition against quantitative restrictions can hamper environmental initiatives that are not directly intended to be protectionist devices in the common sense of the term. By broadly prohibiting non-tariff barriers, the ban on quantitative restrictions also prohibits a contracting party from instituting environmental restrictions such as a conservation ban or limit imposed on exports of resources (unless the ban can be justified as an article XX exception).[27] Examples of environmental protections that could conflict with the prohibition of quantitative measures include the United States law banning the exportation of old growth timber harvested from federal lands.[28]

While the quantitative restriction prohibition may restrict the policy options available to a contracting party, such constraints sometimes pro-

25. *See* GATT, *supra* note 7, art. XI(2), 61 Stat. at A33. Other than through article XI's specific exemptions, the only way a quantitative restriction can conform with the GATT is by falling within one of the public policy exceptions set out in article XX.

26. *See* GATT, *supra* note 7, art. XIII, 61 Stat. at A40, art. XIV, 61 Stat. at A43 for extensive prescriptions regarding the non-discriminatory administration of quantitative restrictions.

27. *See* Grimmett, *supra* note 10, at 19; WWF, *supra* note 11, at 14. Article XX's exceptions are discussed *infra* at notes 42-43 and accompanying text.

28. 16 U.S.C. §§ 620(a), (c), (e), 489(a), 491(a), 493(5) (Supp. I 1990); *see also Logging on Protectionism*, WALL ST. J., Sept. 6, 1990, at A14; Dori Jones Yung, *Weyerhauser's Exports: An Endangered Species*, BUS. WK., July 16, 1990, at 51. The Forest Resources Conservation and Shortage Relief Act of 1990, Pub. L. No. 101-382, (codified at 16 U.S.C. § 488(b)(3), (5) (Supp. I 1990)) is intended "to ensure sufficent supplies of certain forest resources or products which are essential to the United States" while simultaneously requiring that actions taken to meet this objective conform with the obligations of the U.S. under GATT.

vide an environmental benefit. In some instances the trade distortions caused by imposing quantitative restrictions can exacerbate the very environmental harms the trade measures were intended to minimize or eliminate. The Indonesian ban on exports of unprocessed timber provides an illustration. The intent of the Indonesian ban was to remove development pressures causing the unsustainable use of dwindling forest resources. In practice, the export ban has been cited as having caused a discriminatory preference to accrue to local, inefficient sawmills, yielding a lower rate of output per unit of log input, resulting in increased levels of environmental degradation.[29]

2. Other GATT Articles and Their Impact on Environmental Agreements and Concerns

In addition to the GATT's general principles, many of the GATT's other articles could cause friction between trade and environmental policies.

a. *Article II: Maximum Tariff Barriers*

Article II establishes the negotiated maximum tariff levels, as provided in the accompanying annexes to the GATT, for national products.[30] This article also prohibits the imposition of import surcharges by exempting the scheduled items from all other duties and/or charges imposed in connection with importation. Article II(2)(a), however, provides exceptions to the maximum tariff levels for: 1) any charge imposed

29. *See* Carlos Alberto Primo Braga, Tropical Forests and Trade Policy: The Cases of Indonesia and Brazil 19 (1991) (paper presented at the Symposium on Int'l Trade & the Env't, sponsored by Int'l Trade Division, Int'l Economics Dep't, World Bank). Despite the quantifiable short-term environmental harms from the Indonesian export ban, the long-term environmental effects—including the environmental gains made through the reduction of poverty from increased profits to the local areas of production—of the ban are difficult to quantify. *See* ROBERT REPETTO, THE FOREST FOR THE TREES? GOVERNMENT POLICIES AND THE MISUSE OF FOREST RESOURCES (World Resources Institute ed., 1988).

From the Indonesian experience, one scholar argues that the failure of trade policies to create environmental protections in Indonesia demonstrates that trade policies are, generally, not an appropriate vehicle for creating environmental protections. *See* Braga, *supra*. Factual nuances, however, make it difficult to extrapolate the overall effectiveness of trade restrictions in creating environmental protections from this one example and work against this scholar's conclusion. Whether or not trade policies are actually appropriate mechanisms for crafting environmental protections, the ability of the author to draw this conclusion from the isolated example of Indonesia's ban on unfinished timber exports must be questioned. The Indonesian example involved the unilateral use of export bans that resulted in protections being given to inefficent local industries that, in the absence of any domestic conservation intiatives, had no incentive to increase their long-term sustainable production capabilities. *See id.*

30. *See* GATT, *supra* note 7, art. II, 61 Stat. at A13.

on an import, consistent with the national treatment principle, that is equivalent to an internal tax imposed on the like domestic product or articles from which the like domestic and imported products are derived; 2) antidumping or countervailing duties applied consistent with the GATT; and 3) fees or charges, in accordance with article VII (valuations for customs purposes), commensurate with the costs of services rendered.[31]

In essence, article II in its current form is environmentally neutral. While article II does not provide a mechanism that would allow environmental regulations to satisfy the GATT's other obligations, article II does not prohibit the use of antidumping measures or countervailing duties to equalize the environmental standards subsidy provided to the industries of nations with lower environmental standards, nor does it bar the application of internal environmental regulations to imported products at the point of importation.[32]

The only deviation from the environmental neutrality of article II occurs in the case of products that appear on the article's annexed lists of scheduled items. If a product is listed, such as tropical timber, then a contracting party cannot levy new import taxes or other charges on the products, such as a sustainable use tax, that does not conform with the listed negotiated charges.[33]

b. *Article VI: Antidumping and Countervailing Duties*

Article VI condemns the practice of dumping—when one contracting party introduces products into the markets of another contracting party at less than the normal value of the products—if it causes or threatens material harm to a domestic industry or retards the establishment of a domestic industry.[34] Article VI also sets the ground rules by which contracting parties may impose antidumping duties on imported products and may apply countervailing duties to offset bounties or subsidies relating to imported products.[35] The Subsidies Code negotiated in the Tokyo Round of Multilateral Trade Negotiations significantly elaborates upon the scope and details of article VI.[36]

31. *See id.* art. II(2), 61 Stat. at A13.

32. As has been explained, however, other provisions of GATT, such as the MFN and article II, would likely bar such environmental regulation.

33. *See* REPETTO, *supra* note 11, at 1.

34. *See* GATT, *supra* note 7, art. VI, 61 Stat. at A23.

35. *Id.*

36. An analysis of the environmental implications of article VI and article XVI regarding subsidies can be found *infra* in section II.3.b.

c. *Article X: Transparency and Equal Access to Review Processes*

Article X requires transparency (that is, public access) in publishing and administering all regulations affecting trade.[37] This requirement applies to all laws, regulations, rules, judicial and administrative rulings of general or precedential application to requirements, restrictions or prohibitions, on imports or exports, or affecting the sale, offering for sale, purchase, distribution, transportation, insurance, warehousing, inspection, exhibition, processing, mixing or other use, of such imports or exports.[38] In addition, article X requires transparency and equal access to judicial and administrative review procedures related to such actions and/or requirements.

Article X grants importers and exporters equal access to information and review processes of contracting parties with regard to trade. Article X does not, however, provide affected citizens or consumers access to information or recourse to review procedures when imports or exports allegedly cause them environmental harm. Moreover, the transparency requirements in article X do not apply to the GATT's own information and review processes.

d. *Article XII and Article XIII: Developing Countries Balance of Payment*

Article XII, as elaborated in the Declaration on Trade Measures Taken for Balance of Payment Purposes from the Tokyo round, and article XIII provide certain limited exceptions to the other GATT obligations for import restrictions imposed by developing countries as a result of their concern over their balance of payments.[39]

The developing country allowances in articles XII and XIII give developing nations greater leeway in enacting measures to protect nascent industries. This increased leeway can assist these nations in achieving sustainable patterns of growth by minimizing pressures on fledgling industries to overutilize natural resources in order to ensure their short-term survival.

e. *Article XVI: Subsidies*

Article XVI embodies the GATT's general aversion to trade-distorting subsidies. While article XVI does not itself prohibit the use of such subsidies, its provisions form the basis of the challenge and counter-

37. *See* GATT, *supra* note 7, art. X, 61 Stat. at A30-31.
38. *See id.*
39. *See id.* art. XII, 61 Stat. at A34, art. XIII, 61 Stat. at A40.

vailing duties provisions developed in the GATT Subsidies Code.[40]

f. *Article XIX: Emergency Measures Provisions*

Article XIX allows a contracting party to impose emergency trade restrictions to protect a domestic industry that is seriously threatened by imports.[41] If an environmental regulation so burdens a domestic industry as to place it in jeopardy, article XIX allows the contracting party to adopt measures to protect its industry. The procedural and political burdens of invoking article XIX, however, significantly diminish its value as a bridge between trade and environmental concerns.

g. *Article XX: Policy Exceptions*

Article XX establishes limited exceptions to the contracting parties' general obligations under the GATT for measures based on national policy considerations.[42] These exceptions do not exempt measures that constitute arbitrary or unjustifiable discrimination between countries or that are disguised restrictions on international trade. In a challenge to a contracting party's action, the party seeking to invoke article XX to justify a departure from the GATT's general obligations bears the burden of proving that the action: 1) was justified and not arbitrarily applied; and 2) was proportional in scope (i.e., "necessary") to the concern giving rise to the action so as to meet the objectives of the exceptions.[43]

i. Article XX(b): Human, Animal, and Plant Life or Health

Article XX(b) provides an exception for measures "necessary to protect human, animal or plant life or health."[44] The Tuna/Dolphin Panel held that article XX(b)'s exception is available only for health, safety, and preservation initiatives within a contracting party's jurisdiction, and not within the global commons (or within the jurisdiction of a third party state).[45]

---

40. *See id.* art. XVI, 61 Stat. at A51. The provisions of the Subsidies Code, and their environmental implications, are further elaborated on *infra* section II.3.b.

41. *Id.* art. XIX, 61 Stat. at A58.

42. *Id.* art. XX, 61 Stat. at A60-61.

43. *Id.* art. XX, 61 Stat. at A60-61; *see also* Piritta Sorsa, GATT and Environment: Basic Issues and Some Developing Country Concerns (1991) (paper presented at the Symposium on Int'l Trade & the Env't, sponsored by Int'l Trade Division, Int'l Economics Dep't, World Bank).

44. *Id.* art. XX(1)(b), 61 Stat. at A61.

45. *See Tuna/Dolphin Panel Report, supra* note 13, at 45-46. It is, however, unclear from the Panel's report whether this jurisdictional limitation applies to the scope of the party's action, or to the location of the individual or species protected. The Panel based its finding that article XX(1)(b) did not extend "extrajurisdictionally" upon a somewhat erroneous un-

The GATT dispute panel report addressing Thai restrictions and taxes on imported cigarettes interpreted the term "necessary" as used in article XX(b) to require that: 1) no reasonably available alternative measure consistent with the GATT existed, and 2) the measure taken was the least trade restrictive measure of all available alternatives.[46] Elaborating on these requirements, the Tuna/Dolphin Panel Report noted that the United States had not demonstrated to the Panel—as required of a party invoking an article XX exception—that it had exhausted all options reasonably available to it to pursue its dolphin protection objectives through measures consistent with the GATT, including, in particular, the negotiation of international cooperative arrangements relating to dolphin protection.[47] Moreover, even assuming that an import prohibition was the only measure reasonably available to the United States, the panel felt that the United States' measure could not be considered necessary within the meaning of article XX(b) because of its unpredictable application.[48]

The limitations that recent GATT dispute panel reports have placed on the use of article XX(b) negatively impact many measures currently proposed by environmental groups. The goal of article XX(b) is to provide the contracting parties with the ability to take measures they feel are necessary to preserve and protect the lives of humans, animals, and plant

---

derstanding of the negotiating history of the article. *Cf.* Steve Charnovitz, *Exploring the Environmental Exceptions in GATT Article XX*, 25 J. OF WORLD TRADE 37, 38-47 (1991) (providing an excellent discussion of the negotiating history of article XX). Because the *Tuna/Dolphin Panel Report* has not, as yet, been adopted by the contracting parties, the decision is not binding. Absent any changes to the GATT, it is likely, however, that if a future panel was confronted with similar issues, the panel would apply the same reasoning as the Tuna/Dolphin Panel.

46. *Thailand - Restrictions on Importation of and Internal Taxes on Cigarettes, Report of the Panel adopted 7 November 1990*, BISD (37th Supp.) 200-23 para. 74 (1990) (in a dispute concerning Thai prohibitions on the importation or exportation of tobacco and tobacco products the panel held that, although smoking constituted a serious risk to human health, Thailand's measures were not necessary for protecting human life because alternative measures, consistent with the GATT, could have been adopted instead).

47. *See Tuna/Dolphin Panel Report*, *supra* note 13, at 46. Unfortunately, the Tuna/Dolphin Panel failed to recognize that the United States and the other ETP nations have been involved in ongoing efforts to reach an agreement on the conservation of dolphin since the 1970s. *See* INTER-AMERICAN TROPICAL TUNA COMMISSION, 1977 ANNUAL REPORT 8-9 (1978); INTER-AMERICAN TROPICAL TUNA COMMISSION, 1987 ANNUAL REPORT 8-9 (1988).

48. *Tuna/Dolphin Panel Report*, *supra* note 13, at 46. The United States had linked the maximum incidental dolphin taking rate which the Mexican tuna fleet had to meet during a particular period to be able to export tuna to the United States to the taking rate actually recorded for U.S. tuna fleet during the same period. Consequently, the Panel believed that Mexican authorities could not know whether, at a given point of time, their policies conformed to the United States' dolphin protection standards. The Panel considered that a limitation on trade based on such unpredictable conditions could not be regarded as "necessary" to protect the health or life of dolphins. *Id.*

species. Thus, article XX(b) would allow a ban, for example, on importing a product that was hazardous to life or health.[49] Although article XX(b) still allows a safe haven for many important environmental initiatives by limiting the application of the exception to domestic restrictions and by placing added requirements on the term "necessary," recent panel decisions have diminished the ability of article XX(b) to reconcile environmental and international trade policies and laws. First, for a restriction to be "necessary" under article XX(b), according to the Tuna/Dolphin Panel, the restriction must be preceded by an effort to forge an international agreement to create the environmental protection desired.[50] This requirement creates an obstacle to environmental protections because it substantially hinders the ability of the contracting parties to take unilateral actions, actions which frequently serve an important role in forcing the evolution of environmental protections gained from international agreements.[51] Moreover, the Tuna/Dolphin Panel decision's requiring what is essentially a good faith attempt to enter into an agreement restricts the ability of contracting parties to act quickly when they perceive a developing environmental threat, given the typically lengthy period of time needed to negotiate an international agreement.

Second, the Tuna/Dolphin Panel's decision creates uncertainties as to the extent to which a contracting party's environmental standard-setting must be justified. One reading provides that by forcing contracting parties to set their environmental measures at a fixed level of protection "necessary" to achieve the goal of the exception, which is the preservation and protection of the species, the panel implicitly equates some degree of scientific certainty with "necessity." Adopting this approach obviously would limit the ability of the contracting parties to take precautionary actions in the face of the scientific uncertainty that often tempers early analyses of environmental threats.[52] This limitation appears to

49. *See* Grimmett, *supra* note 10, at 19. Such a ban could still be challenged as a disguised restriction on trade and would receive careful scrutiny under the necessity standards discussed in this section. *Id.*; *see also* GATT, GATT ACTIVITIES 1989, at 100-01 (1990) (discussing Chile's response to a United States ban on certain Chilean grapes and grape products).

50. *See Tuna/Dolphin Panel Report*, *supra* note 13, at 46.

51. *See* GATT Secretariat, Trade and the Environment, *supra* note 1, at 25 (discussing the success of unilateral environmentally-based trade restrictions, such as the U.S. threatened ban on Japanese imports of hawksbill sea turtles shells, in affecting other nations' behavior).

52. A prime example of a threat whose abatement could be hindered by a required degree of scientific uncertainty is global warming. Despite general scientific agreement that global warming is occurring, the sheer complexity of the problem makes uncertain what results or threats global warming will produce. *See generally* Durwood Zaelke & James Cameron, *Global Warming and Climate Change: An Overview of the International Legal Process*, 5 AM. U. J. INT'L L. & POL'Y 249 (1990) If a high degree of scientific certainty is required to meet article

conflict with the internationally recognized precautionary principle that has developed in the field of international environmental law.[53]

An alternative, and somewhat less restrictive, reading of the panel's "necessity" standard provides that the panel primarily based its concern with the U.S. standard on the arbitrary nature of the trade measure and not on the underlying environmental protection.[54] Under this reading, as long as the trade measure effectuating an environmental protection is not arbitrary, i.e., is set at a definitive and predictable level, article XX(b) is not concerned with the scientific justifications for the underlying environmental policy.

Third, the panel found that article XX(b) did not extend to the "extrajurisdictional" measures of a contracting party.[55] This jurisdictional

---

XX's necessity requirement, contracting parties will find it difficult to make such showings and will be hindered in their ability to combat global warming and other problems that require a precautionary approach.

53. *See* Lothar Gündling, *The Status in International Law of the Principle of Precautionary Action*, 5 INT'L J. OF ESTUARINE & COASTAL L. 23 (1990); Margaret Spring, Fish or Famine: International Fisheries Management and the Precautionary Principle (1992) (paper prepared for CIEL-US).

54. *See Tuna/Dolphin Panel Report*, *supra* note 13, at 45.

55. *See id.* The panel conspicuously fails to use the term "territorial" in describing the parameters of article XX(1)(b). While the Panel's decision on the limits of a party's jurisdictional ability to act is unclear, it is possible that an action taken extraterritorially, but within the jurisdiction of a contracting party, falls within article XX. This raises the significant issue as to what are the "jurisdictional" limitations on a nation's actions. There are a number of different bases that provide a state with the jurisdiction to prescribe law. *See* RESTATEMENT (THIRD) OF THE FOREIGN RELATIONS LAW OF THE UNITED STATES §§ 402 (basis of jurisdiction to prescribe), 404 (universal jurisdiction) (1990). Section 402 of the *Restatement* provides:

> Subject to [the limitations on a state's jurisdiction set out in] § 403 a state has the jurisdiction to prescribe law with respect to
>
> (1)(a) conduct that, wholly or in substantial part, takes place within its territory;
>
> (b) the status of persons, or interests in things, present within its territory;
>
> (c) conduct outside its territory that has or is intended to have substantial effect within its territory;
>
> (2) the activities, interests, status, or relations of its nationals outside as well as within its territory; and
>
> (3) certain conduct outside its territory by persons not its nationals that is directed against the security of the state or against a limited class of security interests.

Id. § 402.

Section 403 limits these jurisdictional bases in cases where the exercise of jurisdiction is unreasonable based on a list of factors, including, for example, the extent of the link between the territory of the state and the act in question, and "the likelihood of conflicts with regulations of another state." *Id.* § 403(1), (2)(a)-(h).

In addition to the jurisdictional basis for regulation set out in section 402, all states have universal jurisdiction, without limitation, to regulate certain types of conduct, such as piracy, slave trade, genocide, certain acts of terrorism, and war crimes. *See id.* § 404. These areas of universal jurisdiction have developed as a matter of customary law and additional acts subject

limitation imposed on the exception further restricts the scope of article XX(b)'s exception. Most importantly, this jurisdictional limitation constrains a contracting party from unilaterally protecting the at-risk resources of the global commons, such as the ozone, ocean water quality, and at-risk species inhabiting common areas such as the high seas.[56]

ii. Article XX(g): Conservation of Exhaustible Natural Resources

Article XX(g) provides an exception to GATT obligation for measures "relating to the conservation of exhaustible natural resources if such measures are made effective in conjunction with restrictions on domestic production or consumption."[57] The GATT dispute panel in its report on "Canada—Measures Affecting Exports of Unprocessed Herring and Salmon" stated that any trade measure taken under article XX(g) must be "primarily aimed at" conserving the resource.[58] Under this standard, trade measures aimed at preserving a resource need not be necessary to preserve the resource, but instead need only to be: 1) primarily aimed at preserving the resource; 2) taken in conjunction with domestic restrictions on the use of the resource; and 3) primarily aimed at rendering the domestic restriction effective.[59]

As with article XX(b), prior to the Tuna/Dolphin Panel Report,

to universal jurisdiction (including protection of the environment) can be added in similar fashion. *Id.* § 404 cmt. a.

As applied, these principles give a state the jurisdiction to prescribe laws with respect to the conduct of foreign branches of domestic corporations and in limited circumstances, the extraterritorial acts of affiliated foreign entities. This is the case where the regulation is essential to further major national interests of the regulating state, or where the national program of which the regulation is a part can only be successful if it is applied to foreign subsidiaries. *Id.* § 414. The United States also recognizes the jurisdiction of a state to regulate anti-competitive agreements or conduct occurring outside the territory of a state if the intent of the agreement or conduct is to affect commerce and some effect results, or where the conduct has a substantial effect on the commerce of a state and the exercise of jurisdiction is not unreasonable. *Id.* § 415.

In the sphere of the environment, states are obligated to take measures to ensure that acts within their jurisdiction or control conform with accepted international standards and norms, and are conducted so as not to cause significant injury to the environment of another state or beyond the limits of national jurisdiction. *Id.* § 601. The obligations imposed on states by section 601 implies, at least indirectly, that states have the jurisdiction to prescribe laws to meet these obligations.

56. *See* WWF, *supra* note 11, at 29.

57. *See* GATT, *supra* note 7, art. XXI(g), 61 Stat. at A61.

58. *Canada - Measures Affecting Exports of Unprocessed Herring and Salmon, Report of the Panel adopted 22 March 1988*, Gatt Doc. L/6268, BISD (35th Supp.) 98, 114, para. 4.6 (1988).

59. *Id.*

many viewed article XX(g) as a mechanism for allowing contracting parties environmental protection actions that would otherwise be in conflict with their obligations under other provisions of the GATT. The Tuna/Dolphin Panel Report, however, interpreted the scope of article XX(g) much more narrowly, finding that article XX(g), like article XX(b), does not apply to measures extending beyond a party's jurisdiction.[60] Additionally, the Panel narrowed the scope of article XX(g) by reading article XX(g)'s "primarily aimed at" test to require many of the more stringent requirements that the Panel applied under article XX(b)'s "necessary" test. By merging to a certain extent article XX(g)'s "primarily aimed at" requirements with article XX(b)'s stricter "necessity" requirements, the tuna dolphin panel diminished the ability of the contracting parties to use article XX(g) to harmonize environmental restrictions with their GATT obligations.[61]

iii. Article XX(h): Intergovernmental Commodity Agreements

Article XX(h) provides an exception to GATT liability for the actions of the contracting parties taken pursuant to obligations incurred under any international commodity agreement.[62] Article XX(h) may provide a precedential model for the creation of a similar exception for actions taken to accomplish obligations incurred under international environmental agreements. Because article XX(h) only allows actions taken in accordance with international agreements, the creation of an environmental XX(h) would not allow the contracting parties to act unilaterally.

h. *Article XXII and Article XXIII: Dispute Resolution Procedures*

Articles XXII and XXIII provide the basis for the GATT's dispute resolution procedures. Article XXII allows the parties in dispute to consult informally without needing to invoke a formal GATT proceeding.[63] Article XXIII sets forth two alternative methods for the formal resolution of GATT disagreements: subsection (1) provides for a process of exchanging written representations, while subsection (2) provides for a

60. As with the Tuna/Dolphin Panel's decision on article XX(1)(b), it is, however, unclear from the decision whether this limits the exception to domestic actions to protect domestic resources, or whether an extraterritorial action taken to protect a domestic resource is still allowed under article XX(1)(g).

61. *See* Frictions Between International Trade Agreements and Environmental Protections, *supra* note 20, at 7 (discussing interplay of "primarily aimed at" and "necessary" standards).

62. *See* GATT, *supra* note 7, art. XX(1)(h), 61 Stat. at A61.

63. *See id.* art. XXII, 61 Stat. at A64.

process of submission to the contracting parties to establish a dispute panel.[64]

While these dispute resolution mechanisms have been enhanced by the Tokyo Round's Understanding Regarding Notification, Consultation, Dispute Settlement and Surveillance,[65] both the formal and informal dispute resolution mechanisms contained in articles XXII and XXIII are quite opaque, precluding affected interests from overseeing the dispute resolution process.[66] This is of considerable concern to environmentalists, who traditionally have sought standing to challenge environmentally-related government actions in domestic courts and otherwise to participate in the shaping of environmental policies.

i. *Article XXIV: State and Local Laws*

Article XXIV:12 mandates that each contracting party take "all reasonable measures" to ensure that the obligations provided in the GATT are complied with at sub-national levels, including the actions of regional, state, and local governments.[67] The "reasonable measures" test has been interpreted to require that a contracting party must take all available measures except those that are outside its "jurisdiction under the constitutional distribution of power," to bring the sub-national regulations into compliance with the contracting party's GATT obligations.[68]

A great number of environmental laws and regulations, especially within the United States, exist at the sub-national level. Local, state, and regional environmental laws and regulations that do not comply with the GATT cause a contracting party to violate its GATT obligations.[69] In the United States, such a conflict raises constitutional questions; federal attempts to enforce GATT obligations that trespass on local or state environmental regulations could be challenged on the grounds that they exceed the constitutional limits of federal power. While the recent articulation of the "reasonable measures" test appears to avoid the potential

64. *Id.* art. XXIII, 61 Stat. at A64.

65. The Tokyo Round is discussed in section III.3.d. *infra.*

66. *See* WWF, *supra* note 11, at 19.

67. *See* GATT, *supra* note 7, art. XXIV(6), 61 Stat. at A67-68.

68. *See* GATT, *United States—Measures Affecting Alcoholic and Malt Beverages, Report of the Panel* 97 (Feb. 7, 1992).

69. Before the recent GATT panel decision upholding Canada's challenge of U.S. state laws that place non-tariff barriers to imports of Canadian beer, it was clear that GATT imposed obligations at the sub-federal level, although the extent of these obligations was not clear. *See* Clyde H. Farnsworth, *U.S.-Canada Rifts Grow Over Trade*, N.Y. TIMES, Feb. 18, 1992, at A1; Territory v. Ho, 41 Haw. 565 (1957) (GATT applicable to state law); Hudec, *supra* note 7, at 219-25; JACKSON, *supra* note 9, at 68 (discussing GATT's obligations at the sub-national level).

for constitutional conflict, it does establish a very broad scope for the terms "all reasonable measures." For example, the federal government can make aid money normally provided to the states contingent upon the states adopting certain policies.[70] Presumably, if a state or local environmental measure violated the GATT obligations of the U.S. to meet the "reasonable measures" test, the federal government would have to attempt measures including, but not limited to, conditioning aid to the sub-federal government entity's compliance with GATT. The heightened burden imposed on federal contracting parties to bring their sub-federal environmental measures into line with the contracting party's GATT obligations could not only jeopardize existing sub-federal environmental laws but also could have a significant chilling effect, preventing the enactment of important new protections.[71]

j. *Article XXV: Waiver of Obligations*

Under article XXV, a contracting party's specific GATT obligations may be waived by a two-thirds majority of the votes cast.[72] Article XXV's waiver provision potentially could be a means for ensuring the GATT-compatibility of some, if not all, of the existing international agreements on the protection of the environment.[73] The "prevailing view," however, is that article XXV waivers do not substitute for revising the GATT's rules when necessary.[74] Thus, waivers for existing environmental agreements are "not a ready way around GATT obligations."[75]

Even if an article XXV waiver did function as a ready way of bringing the GATT and existing environmental agreements into accord and thereby reconciling trade and the environment, a number of serious issues concerning the impact of such a waiver on environmental protections must be addressed. For example if such a waiver is viewed as a "one shot deal," waiving existing agreements could hamper the creation of effective and enforceable environmental agreements in the future. Moreover, the waiver of the GATT's obligations as to these treaties implies that environmental rules are somehow subservient to those of international trade—a conclusion that the discussion of conflict of treaties rules in section IV.A.B of this article shows may be inappropriate.

70. The federal government used such a funding device to encourage the states to raise their drinking ages to twenty-one years of age.

71. *See accordingly* Letter from James E. Doyle, Attorney General of Wisconsin, to the Honorable Stanley Gruzynski, State Representative 3-5 (Oct. 3, 1991) (on file with author).

72. *See* GATT, *supra* note 7, art. XXV.

73. *See* GATT Secretariat, Trade and the Environment, *supra* note 1, at 12.

74. *Id.*

75. *Id.*

3. Tokyo Instruments and Their Impact on Environmental Agreements and Concerns

a. *The Agreement on Technical Barriers to Trade: The Standards Code*

The Agreement on Technical Barriers to Trade,[76] commonly known as the "Standards Code," is intended to ensure that the testing and adoption of technical regulations or standards relating to health, safety, consumer and environmental protection, and other police power type purposes do not create unnecessary barriers to trade. In accordance with GATT article X's transparency mandates, the Standards Code requires contracting parties to notify other parties of such standards and regulations where they differ from international standards or are adopted in the absence of any international standard and are expected to have an impact on trade.[77] After notification, the other parties may comment on the measures.

Signatories confronted with a challenge to a regulation may choose between justifying the regulation under GATT or under the code. There has never been a formal dispute resolution under the Standards Code. Consequently it is difficult to determine how the Code's procedures and substantive terms would apply, although the United States did use the *threat* of a Standards Code challenge to cause the European Community to soften its import ban on beef produced with hormones.[78]

Nevertheless, the Standards Code generally follows article XX and thus incorporates many of the same difficulties now being faced by environmental regulations seeking to come within article XX. For instance, despite the fact that contracting parties may invoke the Code's dispute resolution mechanisms to examine PPMs, the Code is silent as to whether trade restrictions based on PPMs fall within it.

While the Standards Code generally follows GATT's article XX, the environmental scope of the Code allowances are arguably broader than those of GATT article XX's exceptions. The Code explicitly mentions the environment; thus environmental regulations that might fall outside article XX's purview may come within the Code's allowances. For example, if it is determined that the Standards Code regulates PPMs, the

76. GATT Doc. L/4907, BISD (26th Supp.) 8 (1980).

77. Between 1980 and 1990, 211 notifications took place in which the acting party stated the objective of the standard was protection of the environment. GATT Secretariat Report on Trade and the Environment, *supra* note 1, at 23. 167 other notifications have been justified under similar grounds such as the protection of health, safety, and consumer protection. *Id.*

78. *See* Werner P. Meng, *The Hormone Conflict Between the EEC and the United States Within the Context of GATT*, 11 MICH. J. INT'L L. 819, 824-27, 835-39 (1990).

Code's broader environmental scope might allow for a wider range of environmental PPM regulations.

b. *The Agreement on Interpretation and Application of Articles VI, XVI, and XXIII of the GATT: The Subsidies Code*

The Agreement on Interpretation and Application of articles VI, XVI, and XXIII of the General Agreement on Tariffs and Trade,[79] or the "Subsidies Code," substantively expands GATT article XVI's provisions to encourage the parties more forcefully to eliminate subsidies as a form of domestic trade regulation. The Subsidies Code requires signatories to ensure that their use of subsidies does not harm the trading interests of other signatories and authorizes countervailing duties where subsidized imports threaten material harm to domestic industries.[80]

Pursuant to the GATT, as expanded upon by the Subsidies Code, a contracting party that subsidizes a domestic industry to reduce any additional costs its domestic industry must bear because of stricter environmental standards will likely violate its GATT obligations.[81] If a contracting party subsidizes its industries to mitigate internalized environmental costs, the industries' exports could be subject to the imposition of countervailing duties by other contracting parties seeking to eliminate the subsidy. The Canadian Government's subsidizing reforestation efforts and the development of sustainable forestry practices, for example, might conflict with the Code.[82]

In addition to effectively precluding contracting parties from subsidizing their industries for the costs of complying with higher environmental standards (at least where the industries are export-oriented), the Subsidies Code also makes it difficult for a contracting party to institute countervailing measures under article VI to combat the subsidies resulting from lower environmental standards.[83]

Although the language of article VI does not explicitly bar counter-

---

79. BISD (26th Supp.) 56 (1980).

80. *See id.*

81. *See* GATT, INDUSTRIAL POLLUTION CONTROL AND INTERNATIONAL TRADE, (1971); Grimmett, *supra* note 10, at 16; JACKSON, *supra* note 9, at 209.

82. *Five Year Development Agreement Reached*, 14 Int'l Envtl. Rep. (BNA) 185, 207 (1991).

83. OECD, Joint Session, *supra* note 21, at 17. Three rationales are offered against countervailing measures for environmental standard subsidies: 1) the subsidy is put in place at the production level and thus should be removed at the production level and not by measures at the trade level that will only cause further distortions; 2) allowing countervailing measures for environmental standards subsidies makes the continuation of a party's GATT "rights" contingent on certain environmental behaviors and thus contradicts the unconditional nature of the party's GATT "rights"; and 3) allowing a party to countervail for environmental standards

vailing measures, the Subsidies Code limits a party's ability to impose such countervailing measures.[84] Pursuant to the Subsidies Code, to commence a countervailing measure against a party subsidizing its domestic industry, the challenging party must show that a subsidy exists which causes harm to the industry of the challenging party. This provision has two important implications for the use of countervailing duties and anti-dumping rules to address differences in environmental protections between contracting parties.

First, whether a contracting party's failure to regulate adequately a domestic industry is an implicit subsidy to that industry is not fully answered.[85]

Second, a party seeking to prove an implicit environmental subsidy or "eco-dumping" would have a difficult task establishing the necessary elements to impose measures in compliance with the Code.[86] For a harm to be considered an "injury," allowing the aggrieved party to institute a counter-measure, the harm must fall within the the Subsidies Code's definition of "injury." It is unclear whether harm that stems from environmental standards subsidies falls within the Subsidies Code's definition of injury. For example, the Subsidies Code defines "injury" as relating to certain types of economic harms felt by a specific industry of one contracting party as a result of a subsidy provided by another contracting party to its domestic industry. This definition fails to take into account the many non-economic and attenuated economic harms which environmental standard subsidies may inflict on populations outside of the industrial realm.

Moreover, the GATT Secretariat has indicated that for a contracting party to prevail on a claim that another party's lower environmental standards are a subsidy to its industries, the challenging party would have to prove not only that the environmental standards were low, causing a cognizable injury to the challenging party's industries, but that the standards were too low given the other party's per capita income and

subsidies allows that party to unilaterally determine the appropriate level of environmental protections for another party. *Id.*

84. *See* GATT Secretariat, Trade and the Environment, *supra* note 1, at 19.

85. *See* Piritta Sorsa, Environment—A New Challenge to GATT? 28 (June 1991) (manuscript prepared for the *1992 World Development Report*) [hereinafter Sorsa, Environment—A New Challenge to GATT?]; *see also* Kenneth S. Komoroski, *The Failure of Governments to Regulate Industry: A Subsidy Under GATT*, 10 HOUS. J. INT'L L. 189, 209 (1988).

86. *See* Sorsa, Environment—A New Challenge to GATT?, *supra* note 85, at 28; *see also infra* section II.B.2.c. (discussing the U.S.'s proposed S.984, known as the International Pollution Deterrence Act (1991)).

its environment's physical characteristics.[87] This balancing test fails to conform with the GATT's usual method of finding a subsidy, which does not look to mitigating factors. Additionally, the Secretariat's balancing formula for environmental subsidies is slanted towards allowing developing nations to maintain even lower environmental standards. This bias fails to comport with the Uruguay Round's efforts to eliminate preferences to developing countries.[88]

c. *The Agreement on Import Licensing Procedures*

The Agreement on Import Licensing Procedures[89] seeks to ensure that contracting parties do not use import licensing and registration schemes to erect protectionist barriers to free trade. The Agreement establishes requirements that parties must follow in their national procedures for submitting, reviewing, and granting importation licenses for products entering their markets. The Agreement also limits the penalties that may be administered for violations (including omissions and misstatements) of such national licensing requirements.

A number of national and international environmental protections that attach to import licenses, such as the United States' Resources Conservation and Recovery Act,[90] arise from stringent information and documentation regimes that must be followed strictly to avoid substantial penalties. There have been no challenges to such programs under the Agreement on Import Licensing Procedures that would shed light on applying the Agreement in an environmental context.

d. *The Understanding Regarding Notification, Consultation, Dispute Settlement, and Surveillance*

One of the GATT's most important goals is to provide a forum for peacefully resolving trade conflicts. The Understanding Regarding Notification, Consultation, Dispute Settlement, and Surveillance[91] establishes the procedural framework for handling disputes between contracting parties arising under the terms of the GATT. Because these procedures place a priority on easing the political difficulties that can arise in a mul-

87. *See* GATT Secretariat, Trade and the Environment, *supra* note 1, at 19.

88. *See supra* section II.4.g.

89. GATT Doc. BISD (26th Supp.) 154 (1980) (open for signature Apr. 12, 1979).

90. *See* 40 C.F.R. § 262.20 (1990) (imports of hazardous waste). The Department of Transportation licensing schemes for the transportation of wastes in the United States work in conjunction with the Environmental Protection Agency's regulations under RCRA and are equally applicable. *See* 49 C.F.R. §§ 171-179 (1990).

91. GATT Doc. L/4907, BISD (26th Supp.) 210-18 (1980) (adopted on Nov. 18, 1979).

tinational dispute, they include a number of provisions geared towards allowing the parties to negotiate freely, unbridled by the spotlight of public attention and oversight.

Because the Understanding cloaks its dispute resolution procedures, its process contrasts sharply with the American system of citizen access to information and public participation and oversight. Areas of friction between these two systems arise from: 1) the closed nature of the GATT dispute resolution process, including its exclusion of interested citizens and non-governmental organizations from presenting information to GATT dispute panels; 2) the embargo of papers submitted by the parties to GATT panels; and 3) the embargo of panel decisions for a period of time to allow for negotiations to take place.

Moreover, decisions resulting from the dispute resolution processes are based solely on the terms of the GATT. Therefore, the dispute resolution process and the ensuing decisions suffer from the environmental limitations embodied within the GATT as a whole.[92]

4. Instruments Under Negotiation in the Uruguay Round and Their Impact on Environmental Agreements and Concerns

Now in its fifth year, the Uruguay Round of the GATT has been called the "most ambitious effort ever to reorganize the world's trading system."[93] The ambitious goals of the Round have jeopardized its ability to come to an agreement, leading some to characterize the GATT as the "General Agreement to Talk and Talk."[94]

The underlying intent of the Uruguay Round is to liberalize trade by removing the remaining barriers to free and fair trade. There is no link between liberalization *per se* and either environmental degradation or environmental preservation and remediation. Rather, the processes and mechanisms by which trade is liberalized implicate the environment. The one hundred and five parties (GATT's one hundred and two will be joined by three developing nations) participating in the Uruguay Round are discussing fifteen primary negotiating goals, of which at least ten implicate the environment.[95] The latest expression of the Uruguay Round's progress towards an agreement among the parties is the GATT Secreta-

92. *See* Konrad von Moltke, International Trade and Environmental Imperatives: Dispute Resolution and Transparency 2 (Jan. 20, 1992) (unpublished manuscript on file with author).

93. *GATT Bargaining Goes Down to the Wire*, WALL ST. J. Mar. 6, 1992, at A6.

94. *Id.*

95. *See generally* Lori Wallach, The Dec. 20, 1991 Uruguay Round "Final Act" Text is

riat's *Draft Final Act Embodying the Results of the Uruguay Round of Multilateral Trade Negotiations*, commonly known as the "Dunkel draft."[96]

a. *Tariff Reductions*

The tariff reductions being negotiated in the Uruguay Round apply exclusively to imports. During the course of these negotiations, emphasis also has been placed on "tariffication," the replacement of quotas in the agricultural sector with tariffs.[97]

Reducing tariffs effectively decreases the price of commodities and products in the importing nation. In certain instances, tariff reductions could cause the cost of products at market to reflect their true costs more accurately, including their environmental and natural resource costs, reducing the competitiveness of environmentally unsound products and increasing consumer-based environmental protections.[98] However, price reductions that cause the cost of the imported product to fall below that of competing products, can cause an increase in demand for the resource, increasing, in turn, incentives to exploit the resource in an unsustainable fashion.[99] This is perhaps best exemplified by the reductions in tropical timber tariffs currently being negotiated: if the tariffs on unprocessed logs are abolished (as appears probable) then the demand for these goods in timber-consuming nations could create increased pressure to over-utilize already dwindling areas of remaining tropical forests.[100]

Reducing tariffs, however, also could increase access for products from developed countries to the markets of developing countries, thereby potentially alleviating some of the development pressure on developing countries' natural resources.[101] Additionally, tariff reductions that eliminate escalating tariff schemes—schemes that place higher tariffs on value-added products—could encourage developing countries to shift production from unfinished raw goods (such as uncut logs) to value-added prod-

Worse Than Expected on Environmental, Health and Consumer Issues (Dec. 26, 1991) (memorandum to Environmental, Health and Consumer Advocates, on file with *Public Citizen*).

96. GATT Secretariat, *Draft Final Act Embodying the Results of the Uruguay Round of Multilateral Trade Negotiations*, Dec. 20, 1991, at C.1, L.2-11, 23, MTN/TNC/W/FA (1991) [hereinafter Draft Final Act]; *see also* Keith Bradsher, *Trade Plan Criticized, Stalling World Talks*, N.Y. TIMES, Dec. 24, 1991, at D2.

97. Draft Final Act, *supra* note 96, at C.1, L.2-11, 23; *see also* Bradsher, *supra* note 96, at D2.

98. *See* WWF, *supra* note 11, at 25.

99. *Id.*

100. *Id.*

101. *Id.*

ucts (such as tables and chairs) that require less natural resources to provide the same amount of economic value.[102]

b. *Reduction of Agricultural Subsidies*

One of the top priorities of the United States and certain other developed countries in the Uruguay Round is to reduce agricultural price supports, export subsidies, and border controls.[103] Agricultural subsidies, like all other forms of subsidies, create trade distortions that lead to inefficient use of resources.

In developed countries, specific area agricultural subsidies have been a major factor in their specialization of agricultural activities. Specialization has caused distortions in the natural development of agricultural markets because of preferences to development within those subsidized sectors that have caused environmental harms.[104] Thus, assuming that unanticipated negative environmental results do not outweigh anticipated benefits, eliminating agricultural subsidies in developed nations should have a positive environmental effect.

In developing nations, the effects of agricultural subsidies cuts are more uncertain and will vary to a large extent from country to country, depending on the manner in which each nation removes such subsidies. Generally speaking, however, environmentalists have expressed fears that if demand remains constant, eliminating agricultural subsidies will increase prices and give farmers added incentive to till greater amounts of marginal lands.[105]

The overall environmental balance of eliminating agricultural subsidies will be decided to a large extent by the treatment the Round affords

102. *Id.*

103. Draft Final Act, *supra* note 96, at L.2-11, 31-34. While the United States and other developed countries are seeking reductions in agricultural subsidies, the split among the nations of the European Community with regard to such reductions has been one of the major sticking points in the Round. *See GATT Bargaining Does Down to the Wire, supra* note 93; Bradsher, *supra* note 96, at D2.

104. *See* GATT Secretariat, Trade and the Environment, *supra* note 1, at 32-33. Traditional commodity support programs:

> encourage monocultural, chemical-intensive cropping of . . . a handfull of . . . 'program' commodities. These rules penalize beneficial, multi-year crop rotations that provide natural sources of fertilizer and biological means of pest control. With limited exceptions, subsidized crop insurance and credit programs impose no environmental conditions, and often make heavy agrichemical use a pre-condition of assistance.

CENTER FOR RESOURCE ECONOMICS ET AL, FARM BILL 1990, at 8 (1991). The environmental effects of these farming practices include increased soil erosion, poisoning of water tables and waterways, and the increased use of marginal lands. *Id.* at 8-15.

105. *See* WWF, *supra* note 11, at 27.

to domestic agricultural support measures taken to reduce the degrading effects of current agricultural production methods.[106] Examples of such support measures include the United States' conservation reserve program, which provides subsidies to retire vast amounts of farmland as a soil conservation measure,[107] and the European Community's Common Agricultural Policy provisions granting subsidies to set aside environmentally sensitive farmlands.[108] Many Uruguay Round participants have expressed the view that such measures, provided they meet certain criteria, should be excluded from the agricultural subsidies the Round is considering eliminating.[109] In this vein, the Draft Uruguay Round Decision on Sanitary and Phytosanitary Measures now under negotiation draws a parallel to article XX's exceptions and establishes guidelines to ensure that contracting parties' sanitary and phytosanitary measures are both necessary for the protection of human, animal, or plant life and are not arbitrary or unjustified barriers to trade.[110]

c. *Liberalized Trade in Natural Resource Products*

Another major goal of the developed nations in the Uruguay Round is to remove trade barriers to the free flow of natural resources and natural resource-derived products. Ongoing negotiations in the natural resource-derived products group have focused on liberalized trade in fisheries, forestry, minerals, and non-ferrous metals.[111] The developed nations in this group have aimed their efforts at eliminating developing countries' domestic export controls. Meanwhile, the developing nations' agenda in this group has focused on increasing access for their products in the markets of the developed countries.[112]

106. *Id.* at 28.

107. *See* Food Security Act of 1985, Pub. L. No. 99-198, § 1231, 99 Stat. 1354, 1509 (1985). Subject to certain limited exceptions, the conservation reserve program prohibits the production of commodities on highly erodible lands and pays farmers for setting aside these lands for a ten year period. *See* 16 U.S.C. §§ 3811-36 (Supp. 1991). The conservation reserve program currently protects more than 34 million acres of the United States' most fragile lands. *See* CENTER FOR RESOURCE ECONOMICS ET AL., *supra* note 104, at 14.

108. *See* 1985 O.J. (L 93) 1, *as amended* 1990 O.J. (L 353) 12; 1991 O.J. (C 104) 1 (proposed arable land set asides); *see also* D. BALDLOCK & D. CONDOR, REMOVING LAND FROM AGRICULTURE: THE IMPLICATIONS FOR FARMING AND THE ENVIRONMENT (1987).

109. *GATT, The Uruguay Round and the Environment*, GATT FOCUS, Oct. 1991, at 3, 5 [hereinafter *Uruguay Round and the Environment*].

110. *See* Draft Final Act, *supra* note 96, at L.36-7; GATT Secretariat, Trade and Environment, *Factual Note by the Secretariat* 14-15 GATT Doc. L/6896 (Aug. 1991) [hereinafter *Factual Note*].

111. *See Ministerial Declaration*, GATT Doc. L/5424, BISD (29th Supp.) 9, 20-21 (1983) (adopted Nov. 29, 1982); WWF, *supra* note 11, at 26.

112. *See* WWF, *supra* note 11, at 26.

If this group is successful in forging an agreement that removes export controls and/or increases market access for developing nations' natural resource-derived products, it is possible that demand for these products will increase creating disincentives to sustainably managing these natural resources.[113]

d. *Technical Barriers*

Yet another goal of the Uruguay Round is the curtailing of non-tariff, or technical, barriers to trade.[114] Increased emphasis on removing technical barriers to trade, including labeling requirements, could adversely affect the ability of the contracting parties to adopt environmental or conservation-oriented policies and laws. Under the rules now being discussed in the Uruguay Round, where international technical standards exist, parties are obligated to adopt these standards subject to certain narrow exceptions.[115] Even where no international standard exists, the rules now proposed in the Uruguay Round would require that all technical standards be "not-more trade restrictive than necessary."[116] This "not-more restrictive than necessary" requirement would limit the ability of the parties to adopt appropriate environmental policies substantially.[117]

The agreement now being negotiated further would require federal governments to take affirmative action to bring standards adopted at the sub-federal level into compliance with the GATT.[118] By exposing the contracting party to countervailing measures for the sub-federal GATT violation, this proposed rule could severely limit the ability of states and municipal governments to regulate local environmental concerns. Moreover, the Uruguay Round's proposed rules on technical barriers would also require the parties to take steps to ensure that non-governmental organizations, such as those that certify products with a "green seal of approval," also function in conformity to the rules against technical barriers that the parties adopt.[119] The proposed rules also would subject technical barriers to full GATT enforcement mechanisms, including countervailing duties and dispute resolution procedures.[120]

113. *Id.*

114. *See* Draft Final Act, *supra* note 96, at G.1-27; *Factual Note*, *supra* note 110, at 10-11.

115. *See* Draft Final Act, *supra* note 96, at G.1-5.

116. *Id.* at G.2.2.

117. *See* Steve Charnovitz, *Trade Negotiations and the Environment*, 15 Int'L. Envt. Rep. (BNA) 144, 145 (1992) [hereinafter *Trade Negotiations*].

118. Draft Final Act, *supra* note 96, at G.5.

119. *Id.* at G.5.

120. *Id.* at G.18.

e. *Trade in Tropical Products*

Beyond the Uruguay Round's general attention to eliminating barriers to trade in natural resource-derived products and to agricultural subsidies, the participants are negotiating similar proposals in the specific context of tropical products and resources.[121] The negotiations on tropical products, focusing mainly on plant-derived foods, but also including tropical timber, tobacco, and natural rubber, seek to reduce tariffs on these products and eliminate non-tariff barriers to their trade.[122]

As discussed above,[123] the expected environmental effects of tariff reductions are somewhat mixed. These reductions ultimately may produce benefits to the environment. The environmental effects of tariff reductions, however, may not be as benign in tropical regions where many of the food products—coffee and coconut palms, for example—that could experience demand-driven production intensification are grown on cleared forest lands.[124]

f. *Trade Related Aspects of Intellectual Property Rights*

The negotiation of Trade Related Intellectual Property Rights (TRIPS) has been one of the more contentious areas under consideration in the Uruguay Round.[125] Developed countries, recognizing the trade distorting effects resulting from the lack of effective intellectual property protections, are looking to the TRIPS negotiations to provide international protections against widespread "pirating" of intellectual property from these countries' research organizations and industries.[126] Developing nations, many of which continue to lack effective domestic intellectual property protection mechanisms, have sought to trade concessions on a TRIPS agreement for greater access to developed nations' markets for their TRIPS products, as well as for concessions in other areas of the Round.[127] Additionally, some developing countries have argued that the need to stimulate domestic development justifies lower levels of intellectual property rights protection in developing countries and have sought to distinguish intellectual property rights and trade issues.[128]

121. *See* WWF, *supra* note 11, at 28.

122. *Id.*

123. *See supra* section II.4.a.

124. WWF, *supra* note 11, at 28.

125. Draft Final Act, *supra* note 96, at 57-90; *see also* Frank Emmert, *Intellectual Property in the Uruguay Round Negotiating Strategies of the Western Industrialized Countries*, 11 MICH. J. INT'L L. 1317, 1319-21, 1354-56, 1372 (1990).

126. Draft Final Act, *supra* note 96, at 57-90.

127. *See* WWF, *supra* note 11, at 29-30.

128. *See* Emmert, *supra* note 125, at 1354-56.

The TRIPS agreement could have two significant environmental ramifications. First, certain environmental organizations fear that stronger intellectual property protections will hamper the transfer of environmentally-sound technologies to developing countries, especially in light of the transfer goals of the Montreal Protocol and the global warming agreement currently being negotiated.[129] It is likely, however, that such protections would actually assist the development and transfer of such technologies, although developing countries may find themselves in need of financial assistance to pay for the costs of such technologies. In general, evolving environmentally-friendly technologies are owned by private entities. Unless these technologies are secure from "piracy," the private parties investing in their development will be reluctant to supply these technologies to much of the developing world.

Second, industries in developed countries are increasingly turning to biodiverse ecosystems, such as tropical rain forests, as resource warehouses and to the indigenous peoples who live in these ecosystems for their knowledge about the resources these ecosystems hold.[130] Whether or not the contributions of indigenous discoverers, preservers, and users, and national governments that preserve these ecosystems, will receive some form of intellectual property recognition to give economic value to their efforts is at issue in the Uruguay Round's negotiations.[131] A trade agreement providing tangible benefits to these indigenous peoples and national governments would encourage the preservation of these ecosystems and indigenous cultures, whereas the failure of the Round to come to such an agreement could frustrate ongoing conservation and preservation efforts substantially.[132]

Under the current Dunkel draft text, life forms, including plants and animals, may be patented; however, countries may elect to limit patent protection to only microorganisms.[133] Countries can also elect to exclude inventions from intellectual property protections for reasons of morality or of endangering human, animal, or plant life or health.[134] By not requiring intellectual property protections for biotechnology discov-

---

129. *See* WWF, *supra* note 11, at 30 (discussing the view that intellectual property protections could hinder environmental technology transfer). Additionally, it is difficult to determine how many of the environmental technologies that must be transferred to assist countries in developing sustainably are protected by intellectual property regimes.

130. *See* Robert Weissman, *Prelude to a New Colonialism*, THE NATION, Mar. 18, 1991, at 336, 336-38.

131. *See Factual Note*, *supra* note 110, at 17; Weissman, *supra* note 130, at 336-38.

132. *See* Weissman, *supra* note 130; WWF, *supra* note 11, at 29.

133. *See* Draft Final Act, *supra* note 96, at Y, Annex III.

134. *Id.* at 69.

eries, the Dunkel draft fails to ensure the protection of the contributions of indigenous peoples. Similarly, the Dunkel draft leaves a substantial loophole for countries to continue to "pirate" technologies by allowing for the denial of intellectual property protections for moral, life, health, safety, and conservation goals. While this loophole may allow developing countries to obtain existing environmentally friendly technologies less expensively, it does little to ensure the international availability of these technologies and stifles the competitive impetus for companies to invest in developing new technologies that may be environmentally beneficial.

g. *The "Development Policy"*

Throughout its history, the GATT has accorded developing nations special privileges to accommodate their development needs. This commitment, called the "Development Policy," permits developing nations to use trade restrictions, including import curbs and export limits, that are unavailable to other contracting parties.[135] Developed countries are using the Uruguay Round to encourage developing countries to relinquish many, if not all, of these special privileges.[136]

While reducing the barriers to trade can have certain environmental benefits,[137] if the Development Policy is rescinded, the inability of these nations to provide protections to fledgling industries could cause these industries to adopt practices aimed at short-term survival as opposed to long-term sustainability.[138] The ultimate environmental effect of this proposal is difficult to discern at this time.

h. *Subsidies and Countervailing Measures*

In an effort to provide greater clarity and to reduce international trade conflicts, early negotiations in the Uruguay Round attempted to classify a range of subsidies into three general categories: permissive subsidies, "proceed at the risk of domestic countervailing duty proceedings" subsidies, and prohibited subsidies.[139] Subsidies for environmental purposes were placed in the permissive, or "no-action" category—the so called "green box."[140]

Acquiescing to the United States' demands to eliminate what the

135. *See* WWF, *supra* note 11, at 29. The Development Policy appears in the balance of payment provisions of GATT articles XII and XIII.

136. *See* Draft Final Act, *supra* note 96, at B.1, R.1-4.

137. *See supra* section II.A.4.a.

138. *See* WWF, *supra* note 11, at 29.

139. *See* Draft Final Act, *supra* note 96, at I.1, 3, 5; *Factual Note*, *supra* note 110, at 16-17.

140. *See* Draft Final Act, *supra* note 96, at 92-94; *see also* WWF, *supra* note 11, at 29.

U.S. perceived to be an overly permissive loophole for subsidies, the Dunkel draft deletes the green box, rendering virtually all environmental subsidies vulnerable to challenge.[141] Only subsidies for "clearly defined" environmental and conservation programs that provide public payments to agricultural producers would be classified as unactionable.[142]

Approving the Dunkel draft's text on subsidies would impede the ability of the contracting parties to assist their industries in becoming more environmentally sustainable. The types of programs made vulnerable by the draft's text include Canada's program of subsidizing the development of sustainable forestry practices.

i. *Harmonization of Environmental, Health, and Safety Standards*

One of the most environmentally important negotiations underway in the Uruguay Round is the negotiation of harmonized health and environmental standards.[143] The Uruguay Round's negotiations on harmonizing standards have been premised on three principles: 1) parties must adopt strict principles of national treatment in standard-setting and enforcement; 2) parties' decisions to permit or restrict the availability of a new product or technology may only be based upon "sound scientific evidence;"[144] and 3) international agencies, such as Codex Alimentarius,[145] are the only legitimate sources of scientific information.[146]

Harmonization of standards could produce either more stringent or

141. *See Trade Negotiations, supra* note 117, at 146-47.

142. *See* Draft Final Act, *supra* note 96, at L, pt. A, Annex 2; *see also Trade Negotiations, supra* note 117, at 147.

143. *See* Draft Final Act, *supra* note 96, at G.1-27; *see generally* Wallach, *supra* note 95.

144. Although sound science is an important part of setting appropriate environmental, health, and safety standards, even with the most reliable scientific information, standard setting still relies heavily upon extrapolation from existing data. Thus, sound science cannot eliminate the need for policy decisions to be made based upon scientific evidence. Because even with sound science countries must still make risk assessment and management decisions, sound science is not a panacea for the conflicts between trade and environmental policies. *See Trade Negotiations, supra* note 117, at 146.

145. Codex Alimentarius Commission is the primary international standard-setting body dealing with food products. *See* Daphne Wysham, *The Codex Connection: Big Business Hijacks GATT*, 251 THE NATION 770, 770-72 (1990); WWF, *supra* note 11, at 30-31. Codex's aim is the development of harmonized regulations pertaining to animal, vegetable, and other food products. Codex is administered by the United Nations Food and Agriculture Organization and is co-financed by the World Health Organization. *See* Wysham, *supra*. Membership within the Codex Commission is made up of officials appointed by member-nation governments. *Id.* For example, the United States delegation is headed up by a White House appointee from the Department of Agriculture. *Id.* Codex delegations also, generally, include appointees drawn from the respective regulated industry sectors. *Id.*

146. *See* Draft Final Act, *supra* note 96, at G.1-5.

lenient standards.[147] If existing levels of protection do not diminish in the process, harmonizing environmental, health, and safety standards could have significant environmental and trade benefits. By providing unified standards, harmonization would diminish the burdens that the plethora of sometimes widely divergent national standards have imposed on internationally-traded products.[148] Moreover, harmonized standards that raise the environmental, health, and safety standards of nations with lower levels of existing protections would bring much needed protections to many nations.

Additionally, whether or not industries actually migrate to nations with lower environmental standards,[149] harmonized standards would remove the incentive for industries to do so. Developing nations, however, fear that raising standards to the level of the developed world would impede increased market access for their products and would deprive them of the ability to choose increased levels of development as opposed to higher levels of environmental quality.[150]

In contrast, if harmonized standards are set at the level of the country with the lowest standard—the least common denominator approach—environmental protection in countries with higher standards will suffer.[151] And the strict harmonization of standards could hamper the evolution of environmental protections by removing the ability of individual contracting parties to push environmental standards forward.[152]

The harmonization provisions of the Dunkel draft, with their strong bias towards international standards (and consequently, against domestic standards that are more stringent than international standards) appear to

147. Affidavit of Joan Claybrook at 29-30, Public Citizen v. Office of the United States Trade Representative, 782 F. Supp. 139 (D.D.C. 1992) (No. 91-1916).

148. *See* U.S. COUNCIL FOR INTERNATIONAL BUSINESS, AN INTEGRATED APPROACH TO ENVIRONMENT AND TRADE ISSUES (statement presented to Carla A. Hills, U.S. Trade Representative and William W. Reilly, Administrator, Environmental Protection Agency) 1, 6 (Mar. 27, 1991). *Cf.* David Robertson, Trade and the Environment Harmonization and Technical Standards, Oct. 10, 1991 (paper presented at the symposium on Int'l Trade & the Env't, sponsored by Int'l Trade Division, Int'l Economics Dep't, World Bank) (noting that harmonization is not necessary for increased trade efficiencies and may not provide environmental benefits).

149. *See generally* Patrick Low & Alexander Yeats, Do Dirty Industries Migrate (Nov. 1991) (unpublished manuscript, on file with author); Robert Lucas, et al., Economic Development, Environmental Regulation and International Migration of Toxic Industrial Pollution: 1960-1988 (Nov. 1991) (unpublished manuscript, on file with author). *See also infra* note 189.

150. *See* Gene Grossman, *In Poor Regions Environmental Law Should Be Appropriate*, N.Y. TIMES, Mar. 1, 1992, at C11 ("Attention to environmental issues is a luxury poor countries can't afford").

151. WWF, *supra* note 11, at 30-31; Frictions Between International Trade Agreements and Environmental Protections, *supra* note 20, at 9.

152. *See* WWF, *supra* note 11, at 30.

adopt an approach that more closely resembles a lowest common denominator approach.[153] This raises serious concern that if the Dunkel draft is accepted, the harmonizing that will occur under the draft's procedures will compromise existing environmental protections. For example, the United States' Delaney Clause[154] prohibits the use of any food additives that have a cancer risk level greater than zero. The Delaney Clause's zero risk factor is substantially more stringent than both international standards and other United States cancer risk standards and could be jeopardized by the proposed Uruguay Round provisions on harmonization.[155]

Another problem with the Dunkel draft is that its delegation of environmental, health, and safety standard-setting to international appointees rather than to democratically elected representatives could undermine developing democratic processes in many nations. It also conflicts with the traditional processes of public participation and accountability in nations (including the United States) with established democratic schemes of governance.[156] Additionally, there are concerns over procedural obstacles to effective peer review of these internationally set standards, such as the lack of a "paper trail" of the decision-making process. For example, environmentalists note that the Canadian pesticide standards, which were harmonized under the United States-Canada Free Trade Agreement, would not have been so compromised if the process of harmonization had gone through the democratic parliamentary process.[157]

j. *Trade in Services*

Article XIV in the draft Agreement on Trade in Services contains exceptions to the general obligations set out in the agreement.[158] To a large extent these exceptions parallel the public policy exceptions to GATT's general obligations contained in GATT article XX.[159] Certain

153. *See Trade Negotiations*, *supra* note 117, at 146.

154. 21 U.S.C. § 348(c).

155. *See Trade Negotiations*, *supra* note 117, at 146.

156. *See* WWF, *supra* note 11, at 30-31; Wysham, *supra* note 145, at 770-72. For example, Codex panels are heavily lobbied by national constituencies that include disproportionate representation from the industrial sectors the panels regulate. *See id.* Codex panel decisions are not exposed to external peer review and do not provide a paper record that discloses the "sound science" behind the decision so as to allow independent evaluation of the decision. *See id.*

157. *See* Steven Shrybman, *Trading Away the Environment*, 9 WORLD POL'Y J. 93, 106 (1992).

158. *See* Draft Final Act, *supra* note 96, at 18, art. XIV, 103 Annex II.

159. *See supra* notes 42-43 and accompanying text.

countries have proposed that article XIV should not only allow the parties to take measures necessary to protect human, animal, and plant life and health but should also allow for measures which are necessary for "sustainable development and environment," "cultural values," and "conservation of exhaustible natural resources."[160] These expanded definitions would allow a wider range of environmental measures to conform with the GATT in the services area and would provide a precedent for future efforts aimed at minimizing the frictions between trade and environmental concerns. These expanded definitions are, however, not reflected in the Uruguay Round's proposed final agreement on trade in services.[161] Moreover, although the Dunkel Draft's services text includes an exception for life and health that parallels the GATT's article XX(b) exception, the Draft does not provide a conservation exception paralleling the GATT's article XX(g).

k. *Dispute Resolution*

The dispute resolution rules being negotiated in the Uruguay Round would change the existing GATT dispute resolution framework significantly. First, under the proposed rules, unless a consensus of the parties votes against adopting the report of a dispute resolution panel, all panel reports are automatically adopted sixty days after publication.[162] This change would reverse the current rule, which requires a consensus of the parties to adopt the decision of a dispute resolution panel. By making the adoption of panel reports virtually automatic, the proposed rule would minimize the ability of the parties to block such an adoption, thereby exacerbating the potential for direct conflicts between GATT obligations and environmental protections.

Second, the Uruguay Round dispute resolution proposal would expand the reach of the GATT's dispute resolution mechanisms, including the application of countervailing sanctions and the availability of dispute panels, to include sub-federal level trade restrictions explicitly.[163] This proposal would expose a host of sub-federal level environmental regulations to potential GATT challenges.

Third, the proposed dispute resolution rules strengthen the enforcement of GATT obligations by: 1) increasing the burden on parties defending against a GATT challenge by requiring them to rebut the inference that a breach of a GATT obligation entails an injury to chal-

160. *See Factual Note, supra* note 110, at 18.
161. *See* Draft Final Act, *supra* note 96, at 18 art. XIV, 102 Annex II.
162. *See id.* at S.12.
163. *See id.* at S.18.

lenging parties;[164] and 2) affirmatively charging parties that violate GATT obligations with either complying with their GATT obligations or facing trade sanctions.[165] Strengthening the GATT's enforcement powers would exacerbate the already existing potential for direct conflict between the GATT and environmental initiatives.

1. *Multilateral Trading Organization*

The final proposed text of the Uruguay Round would establish a Multilateral Trading Organization (MTO).[166] The proposed MTO would adopt the GATT as it exists after the Tokyo and Uruguay Rounds as its rules and would have in all territories of the member states the legal capacity, privileges, and immunities as needed to carry out its functions under these rules.[167] By expanding the obligations of all the GATT parties to include the obligations contained in the Tokyo and Uruguay Round agreements and understandings, creating an MTO as now proposed would expand the powers and scope of GATT significantly, increasing the GATT's ability to trump environmental regulations. Additionally, the creation of an MTO might re-start the GATT's clock, making the GATT later-in-time than most environmental laws and agreements.[168] Finally, some scholars have noted that institutionalizing GATT without mentioning the environment represents a waste of a substantial opportunity to bring about the overall greening of GATT.[169] Proponents of the MTO regard it as too late in the negotiation of the Uruguay Round to begin discussing the environment. A compromise view that would make a "Green Round" of the GATT the first item on the MTO's agenda currently is being discussed.[170]

5. Other GATT Activities

a. *The Working Group on the Export of Domestically Prohibited Goods and Other Hazardous Substances*

In 1982, the contracting parties agreed to examine measures to con-

---

164. *See id.* at S.3.

165. *See id.* at S.16.

166. *See id.* at 95.

167. *See id.* at 92, 95.

168. For a discussion of the effects of the "later in time rule" *see supra* section IV.A. While the adoption of the MTO might make GATT later-in-time, it would not necessarily make GATT more specific than these environmental laws and treaties. Under conflicts of laws and conflicts of treaties analyses, if an earlier treaty or law is more specific than a later law or treaty, then the earlier treaty is not trumped by the later treaty.

169. *See Trade Negotiations, supra* note 117, at 147-48.

170. *Id.*

trol the export of products that are prohibited from sale in domestic markets yet are allowed to continue as exports.[171] This agreement evolved into the GATT Council's creation of the Working Group on the Export of Domestically Prohibited Goods and Other Hazardous Substances in 1989. This working group examines the trade-related aspects of ongoing international work, such as the Basel Convention,[172] to regulate the flow of such goods and substances among the contracting parties.[173]

The working group currently is considering a Draft Decision on Products Banned or Severely Restricted in the Domestic Markets.[174] This draft covers all products (including hazardous wastes) that a contracting party determines present a serious and direct danger to human, animal, or plant life or health, or the environment within the contracting party's territory, and which are banned or severely restricted within the contracting party's domestic markets.[175] The draft also includes notice provisions requiring the contracting parties to notify the GATT Secretariat of all such banned or restricted products for which no similar control of exports have occurred.[176] In an effort to avoid conflict and duplication, the draft does not apply to substances covered under other international regimes (such as the Basel Convention) to which a contracting party is a signatory.[177]

An agreement allowing the contracting parties to make efforts to regulate trade in hazardous and otherwise restricted substances could provide substantial environmental protections, as well as allowing international environmental agreements pertaining to similar matters greater ability to conform with GATT's mandates. If the working group cannot assist the contracting parties in forging such an understanding, however, then domestic initiatives, such as the ban on exporting domestically prohibited pesticides Congress considered in the 1990 farm bill, would appear to violate the GATT.[178]

---

171. *See Uruguay Round and the Environment, supra* note 109, at 3.

172. *See* section III.A.3. *infra*.

173. BISD (36th Supp.) 402, 403 (1990).

174. *See Uruguay Round and the Environment, supra* note 109, at 4.

175. *See Factual Note, supra* note 110, at 9.

176. *Id.*

177. *Id.*

178. Grimmett, *supra* note 10, at 19. *See also* S. 2830, 101st Cong. 2d Sess. (1990); H.R. 3950, 102d Cong. 1st Sess. (1990). The provisions in both the House and Senate bills that would have banned the export of domestically prohibited pesticides were dropped in conference.

b. *The Group on Environmental Measures and International Trade*

The Group on Environmental Measures and International Trade was established at the November 1971 GATT Council meeting. In the ensuing twenty years, the group has been dormant. However, as a result of pressure from European Free Trade Association member states and other countries, the group has recently convened.[179] The group's current agenda is to consider: 1) trade provisions contained in existing multilateral environmental agreements; 2) multilateral transparency of national environmental laws and regulations that are likely to have effects on trade; and 3) trade effects of newly developing domestic and international "eco" packaging and labeling requirements.[180] Additionally, the group is discussing a GATT contribution to the 1992 United Nations Conference on Environment and Development.[181] Believing that the GATT is not the appropriate forum for such discussions, certain GATT parties, most notably the developing nations, were against convening the group.[182]

Given the group's early emphasis on the impact of environmental protection on trade, environmental groups have expressed fears that the group will focus on subjugating environmental protections to trade's regimes as opposed to finding some way of reconciling the concerns of both trade and environmental interests. At this time, it is unclear to what extent these fears are justified.

B. The Environmental Implications of the NAFTA and the CFTA

Although the vast majority of trade occurs under the umbrella of GATT, a wide range of additional regional and bilateral trade agreements have a hand in determining patterns of national and international resource use. With the emergence of rival trading blocs, including a more integrated European Community and the possibility of an Association of South East Asian Nations free trade area, bilateral and multilateral trade agreements increasingly will play a major role in determining the competitiveness of domestic industries in world markets.[183] In the

179. *See Factual Note*, *supra* note 110, at 4-6; *GATT to Focus on Trade and Environment Link*, GATT FOCUS, Oct. 1991, at 1.

180. *See* GATT Secretariat, Trade and the Environment, *supra* note 1, at 10; *GATT to Focus on Trade and Environment Link*, *supra* note 179, at 1.

181. *GATT to Focus on Trade and Environment Link*, *supra* note 179, at 1.

182. *Id.*

183. *See* Stuart Auerbach, *Bush Stresses U.S. Commitment to Asia*, WASH. POST, Jan. 5, 1992, at A23; *ASEAN Endorses Free-Trade Area*, WALL ST. J., Oct. 9, 1991, at A-12.

context of resource consumption patterns in the Americas, the most important of these agreements are the United States/Canadian Free Trade Agreement (CFTA) and the ongoing negotiation of a trilateral North American free trade agreement among the United States, Canada, and Mexico (NAFTA).

1. NAFTA

Joint efforts between President Bush and Mexico's President Salinas to craft a Mexico/United States free trade agreement began in September of 1990.[184] On February 5, 1991, after Canada expressed a desire to be included in the Mexico/United States negotiations, the bilateral United States/Mexico talks became the current trilateral NAFTA negotiations.[185]

The creation of a trilateral trade agreement between the United States, Canada, and Mexico would form the world's largest market, incoporating 360 million consumers and a total output of $6 trillion.[186] NAFTA seeks to eliminate trade barriers and to reduce market distortions and hence economic inefficiencies between the United States first- and third-largest trading partners, enabling a free and fair trade block.[187]

Environmentalists have subjected NAFTA to intense scrutiny. Proponents of NAFTA argue that NAFTA and its negotiations will provide Mexico with both the impetus and the resources to address its environmental difficulties.[188] But its critics argue that absent significant changes in Mexico's environmental practices, NAFTA will open the way for U.S. industries to escape U.S. environmental requirements by moving their

184. *See* Arlene Wilson et. al, *North American Free Trade Agreement: Issues for Congress*, Mar. 25, 1991, at 1, Cong. Res. Service, No. 91-282-E (1991). Official dialogue between the Bush and Salinas administrations concerning a potential MFTA commenced in June of 1990 with the issuance of a joint statement in support of negotiation of an MFTA. *Id.* In a letter of Aug. 21, 1990, President Salinas proposed that negotiations commence. *Id.* In response to the Mexican President's letter, President Bush notified the Senate Finance Committee and the House Ways and Means Committee of the intent to enter into negotiations. *Id.* at 1-2.

185. *See* Executive Office of the President, Response of the Administration to Issues Raised in Connection with the Negotiation of a North American Free Trade Agreement, May 1, 1991, at 1 [hereinafter May 1 Plan].

186. *Id.*

187. *Id.* Taking Mexico as an example, in 1989 Mexico was the United States' third largest trading partner with a turnover (exports plus imports) of approximately $52 billion. *See Mexico-U.S. Free Trade Agreement?*, Jan. 7, 1991, at 5. In the same year, the United States was Mexico's largest trading partner, accounting for 66% of all Mexican exports and 62% of all imports. *Id.*

188. *See* William K. Reilly, *Mexico's Environment Will Improve With Free Trade*, WALL ST. J., Apr. 19, 1991, at A15 (Mr. Reilly is the administrator of the U.S. EPA); May 1 Plan, *supra* note 185, at 1-3.

operations to Mexico.[189] They also argue that increasing economic activity in Mexico without proper environmental controls will only exacerbate Mexico's environmental problems.[190] Mexico's environmental problems are already surfacing in the Southwestern region of the United States.[191] Additionally, they criticize the U.S. decision to deal with environmental issues on a parallel track rather than as an integrated part of NAFTA.[192] Environmentalists point out that both the United States and Canada, for the most part, have lived up to their obligations under the CFTA because of the CFTA's trade enforcement provisions; in contrast, the United States and Canada both have failed to live up to their obligations under the Great Lakes Water Quality Agreement because it lacks effective enforcement provisions.[193]

In an effort to reassure environmentalists from all three NAFTA

---

189. *See* Bruce Stokes, *Greens Talk Trade*, NAT'L J., Apr. 13, 1991, at 862, 864-66; CRS: *North American Free Trade Agreement: Issues for Congress*, July 12, 1991, at 47-48. While comprehensive data regarding the potential flight of U.S. businesses south of the border to avoid more stringent U.S. environmental regulation is lacking, such pollution migration may already be occurring. There have been reports that at least forty Southern California furniture makers have relocated all or part of their operations to Mexico to avoid the Southern California Air Quality District's standards that require the use of low-emission paints, varnishes and solvents. *See* Robert Reinhold, *Mexico Proclaims an End to Sanctuary for Polluters*, N.Y. TIMES, Apr. 18, 1991, at A20; GENERAL ACCOUNTING OFFICE, U.S.-MEXICO TRADE: SOME U.S. WOOD FURNITURE FIRMS RELOCATED FROM LOS ANGELES AREA TO MEXICO, *Report to the Chairman, Comm. on Energy and Commerce, House of Representatives*, GAO/NSIAD-91-191, 1-4 (Apr. 1991).

In addition to the environmental questions raised by the NAFTA, labor groups argue that the NAFTA will cause a migration of American jobs to Mexico and will hurt U.S. industries as Mexican industries become more competitive. *See* Gary Lee, *Lobbyists Clash Over Free Trade Accord*, WASH. POST, Apr. 28, 1991, at A4, A6; Geroge W. Grayson *Mexico's Pemex Begins to Act Like a Competitor*, WALL ST. J., Sept. 27, 1991, at A11.

190. *See* Stokes, *supra* note 189, at 864-66.

191. *See* LESLIE KOCHAN, THE MAQUILADORAS AND TOXICS: THE HIDDEN COSTS OF PRODUCTION SOUTH OF THE BORDER 7 (1989). *Issues Relating to a Bilateral Free Trade Agreement with Mexico: Hearings Before the Subcomm. on Western Hemisphere and Peace Corps Affairs of the Senate Comm. on Foreign Relations*, 102d Cong., 1st Sess. 117 (1991) (Statement of Micheal McCloskey, Chairman, Sierra Club [hereinafter McCloskey]). The aquifers that supply water to communities on both sides of the U.S./Mexican border are being seriously depleted and poisoned by the improper disposal of wastes, largely from the Mexican maquiladora industries. *Id.* Liver and gall bladder cancer incidence rates from communities that get their drinking water from the Rio Grande have been found to be significantly higher than the U.S. national averages. KOCHAN, *supra* at 7. Santa Cruz County, Arizona was forced, on at least one occasion, to declare a state of emergency after millions of gallons of raw sewage from Mexico were released into its water treatment system. *Mexico's Maquiladoras: Free Trade, or Foul Play?*, E: ENVIRONMENT MAGAZINE, July/Aug., 1991, at 36-37. The hepatitis rate in Nogales, Arizona, a community downstream of certain Mexican maquiladoras, has shot up to 20 percent over the national average. *Id.*

192. *See* Stokes, *supra* note 189, at 865.

193. Shrybman, *supra* note 157, at 107.

participant countries, the United States Trade Representative, in conjunction with other American and Mexican governmental agencies, has released a comprehensive review of U.S-Mexican environmental issues predicated upon the assumption that "increased economic activity is likely to translate into greater environmental protection."[194] Environmentalists point out that economic growth in the U.S.-Mexican border region, caused by the expansion of the *maquiladora* industry, has failed to bring about environmental benefits and in fact has caused increased environmental degradation.[195] To ensure that the environmental effects of NAFTA are known and addressed, environmentalists have also commenced litigation to have an environmental impact statement prepared for the NAFTA negotiations.[196]

2. CFTA

The concerns over NAFTA have been heightened by problems arising from CFTA. Challenges to domestic environmental laws as nontariff trade barriers and harmonization by reducing environmental standards under CFTA have underscored the weaknesses of negotiating trade agreements without regard to environmental issues.

The CFTA has functioned both as a sword to attack more stringent domestic environmental regulation and as a shield to protect less stringent environmental and health standards. For instance, both U.S. and Canadian entities have used the CFTA and GATT prohibitions on nontariff trade barriers to challenge the other nation's domestic environmental laws. In the CFTA's first dispute resolution panel decision, the panel found the provisions of the Canadian Fisheries Act, which required that all fish caught for commercial purposes in Canadian waters must be landed first in Canada for biological sampling, to violate the CFTA.[197] While the biological sampling requirement clearly restricted trade, the requirement was intended to provide accurate and reliable data to ensure adequate fisheries management over already-depleted stocks of herring and salmon in Canada's Pacific coast waters.[198] The U.S. Non-Ferrous

194. *Id.*

195. *Id.*

196. *See* Public Citizen v. United States Trade Representative, 782 F. Supp. 139 (D.D.C. 1992), *appeal docketed*, No. 92-5010 (D.C. Cir. Feb. 14, 1992) (dismissing litigation requesting an environmental impact statement for the NAFTA and Uruguay Round negotiations for plaintiff's lack of standing).

197. *In re* Canada's Landing Requirement for Pacific Coast Salmon and Herring, Canada-U.S. Trade Commission Panel, Oct. 16, 1989, 2 TCT 7162; *see also* Shrybman, *supra* note 157, at 99.

198. *See* Shrybman, *supra* note 157, at 99.

Metal Producers Committee has challenged Canadian environmental and safety programs in lead, zinc, and copper smelters as unfair trade practices under the CFTA.[199] Conversely, in U.S. Federal court, both the Canadian asbestos industry and the Canadian government challenged EPA regulations that would phase out production, importation, and use of asbestos as violations of CFTA and GATT.[200]

Moreover, harmonization as required under CFTA arguably has resulted in lower environmental standards and reduced import protections at the border.[201] For example, Canadian pesticide regulations now are set using the U.S. risk-benefit model rather than the more stringent precautionary model previously used in the Canadian regulations.[202] In ad-

199. *See* PUBLIC CITIZEN, FACT SHEET #3—TRADE DISPUTES, at 2. Acid rain, caused largely by the mixing of sulfur dioxide emissions from human sources with water in the air to create rain showers high in sulfuric acid content, has been linked to damage to soil, trees, streams and fisheries in Canada. *See* Drew Lewis & Williams Davis, Joint Report of the Special Envoys on Acid Rain 26 (Jan. 1986). The principal sources of Canada's acid rain problem are non-ferrous metal smelting plants in Ontario and Quebec, however, Canada receives significant "exports" of sulfur dioxide emissions from U.S. based industries as well. *Id.*; John M. Sibley, *A Canadian Perspective on the North American Acid Rain Problem*, 4 N.Y.L. SCH. J. INT'L & COMP. L. 529, 530 (1983). To combat its acid rain problems Canada offers financial incentives to to lead zinc and copper smelters for the purchase and installation of scrubbers which collect sulfur dioxide emissions. The U.S. Non-Ferrous Metals Producers Committee has challenged this Canadian program under the CFTA as a non-tariff barrier to trade. *See* PUBLIC CITIZEN, FACT SHEET #3—TRADE DISPUTES, *supra* at 2.

200. *See* Corrosion Proof Fittings v. EPA, 947 F.2d 1201, 1209, (5th Cir. 1991) (finding that Canadian parties lacked standing, despite their GATT rights, to assert substantive claim that U.S. asbestos regulations violated U.S.'s binding obligations under GATT); *see also* Brief of Amicus Curiae for the Government of Canada at 16-19, Corrosion Proof Fittings v. EPA, 947 F.2d 1201 (5th Cir. 1991).

201. *See* Shrybman, *supra* note 157, at 105; PUBLIC CITIZEN, FACT SHEET #3—TRADE DISPUTES, *supra* note 199, at 2.

202. *See* Shrybman, *supra* note 157, at 105; PUBLIC CITIZEN, FACT SHEET #3—TRADE DISPUTES, *supra* note 199, at 2. Schedule 7 of Chapter 7 of the CFTA deals specifically with pesticides. The schedule provides that the U.S. and Canada must "work toward equivalent guidelines, technical regulations, standards and test methods for pesticide regulation." Canada follows the precautionary principle in licensing pesticides under the Pest Control Products Act, and requires the pesticides to be demonstrated as safe prior to registration. *See* Toby Vigod, *The Canada-U.S. Free Trade Agreement: Selling the Environment Short*, ENVIRONMENT (forthcoming 1992) (on file with CIEL-US). In contrast the United States licenses pesticides under the Federal Insecticide, Fungicide and Rodenticide Act, which provides a risk-benefit approach to registration decisions. *Id.* The parties also committed to working together to achieve equivalence in "the process for risk-benefit assessment." Moving away from proven safety towards risk-benefit has weakened Canadian pesticide regulations. *See* PUBLIC CITIZEN, FACT SHEET #3—TRADE DISPUTES, *supra* note 199, at 3; Vigod, *supra*. Prior to the CFTA, Canada had registered twenty percent fewer active pesticide ingredients and seven times fewer pesticide products than the U.S. *See* PUBLIC CITIZEN, FACT SHEET #3—TRADE DISPUTES, *supra* note 199, at 3. Now Canada finds itself having to increasingly accept imports of pesticide products made from compounds that were not among those listed prior to the CFTA. *See id.*

dition, a "streamlined" random meat inspection system to further the CFTA goal of reducing trade restrictions replaced inspection of Canadian meat at the U.S. border.[203] A 1990 U.S. Department of Agriculture proposal to end U.S. meat inspections along the Canadian border as part of the CFTA[204] was abandoned in 1991.[205]

Perhaps the most environmentally devastating effect of the CFTA has been its elimination of Canadian controls over the exportation of energy to the United States.[206] Under chapter 9 of the CFTA, both the United States and Canada have agreed to eliminate regulatory controls over energy development and trade. To further facilitate the development of energy for export markets, chapter 9 also accords special status to subsidies for oil and gas exploration and development. While energy development subsidies are protected from challenge, programs that provide subsidies for energy conservation remain vulnerable to challenge.

The energy development incentives set out in the CFTA run counter to the intent, if not the letter, of previously-negotiated international agreements, specifically those concerning ozone depletion and air pollution.[207] Moreover, these incentives pose obstacles to ongoing international efforts to address the threat of global warming. The CFTA's bias towards increased energy development to meet rising U.S. consumption demands has spawned the development of a number of environmentally destructive Canadian-based energy mega-projects.[208]

203. 54 Fed. Reg. 273 (1989) (to be codified at 9 CFR pts. 327 & 381); *see also* U.S. GENERAL ACCOUNTING OFFICE, REPORT TO CONGRESSIONAL REQUESTERS: FOOD SAFETY: ISSUES USFDA SHOULD ADDRESS BEFORE ENDING CANADIAN MEAT INSPECTIONS, GAO/RCED-90-176, 1-2 (1990) [hereinafter FOOD SAFETY].

204. 55 Fed. Reg. 26,695 (1990) (to be codified at 9 CFR pts. 312, 322, 327 & 381); *see also* FOOD SAFETY, *supra* note 203, at 1-2.

205. 56 Fed. Reg. 52,218 (1991) (to be codified at 9 CFR pts. 312, 322, 327 & 381).

206. Shrybman, *supra* note 157, at 98.

207. *Id.*

208. *See id.* The two most destructive mega-projects are the Arctic Gas Project and the James Bay Hydroelectric Project. The Arctic Gas Project entails the construction of a 1,200 mile long natural gas pipeline traversing the arctic perma frost—one of the world's most rare and fragile ecosystems. *Id.* The James Bay Project involves the extension of hydroelectric dams that will "reshape a territory the size of France and flood an area the size of the state of Vermont." *Id.* The James Bay Project threatens to destroy the culture of the Northern Cree and Innuit peoples and will have a devastating effect on whales, seals, birds, caribou and other species. *Id.* at 98-99. In the past, projects like James Bay and the Arctic Gas Project might have been prevented by Canada's National Energy Board. Today, however, The National Energy Board's regulatory mandate has been virtually eliminated by the CFTA. *Id.* at 98.

III. THE EFFECTS OF ENVIRONMENTAL PROTECTIONS ON TRADE

A. Trade Aspects of International Environmental Protections

1. The Montreal Protocol on Substances That Deplete the Ozone Layer[209]

The Montreal Protocol on Substances That Deplete the Ozone Layer[210] (the Protocol), first negotiated in 1987 and substantially revised in June of 1990,[211] provides for eliminating, by the year 2000, CFCs and other chemicals harmful to the ozone layer. The consequences of ozone depletion range from health effects, such as increased incidence of skin cancer and cataracts, to reductions in yield of food crops.[212]

The Protocol controls both the production and consumption of CFCs and other ozone-depleting substances. Several of the Protocol's key enforcement provisions directly implicate trade.[213] First, the Protocol restricts parties from trading in CFCs and CFC-related products with non-parties.[214] Second, the Protocol restricts trade in CFCs and CFC-related products between parties.[215] Third, the Protocol contains a number of provisions assisting developing countries in meeting their obligations under the Protocol, including lengthened timetables for the phase-out of controlled substances, financial assistance, and technology transfer incentives.[216]

a. *Trade with Non-Parties*

To encourage countries to participate in the Protocol and to discourage industries that produce and use CFCs from migrating to non-party states, the Protocol establishes three tiers of trade regulation in restricted products between parties and non-parties. The first tier of restrictions applies directly to trade in the controlled substances, banning parties from importing controlled substances from non-parties. As of

209. This section is substantially derived from Donald M. Goldburg, Provisions of the Montreal Protocol Affecting Trade (Jan. 16, 1992), CIEL-US Working Paper.

210. The Montreal Protocol on Substances That Deplete the Ozone Layer, adopted and opened for signature Sept. 16, 1987, *entered into force* Jan. 1, 1989, 26 I.L.M. 1541 (1987) [hereinafter Protocol].

211. *See* Dale A. Bryk, *The Montreal Protocol and Recent Developments to Protect the Ozone Layer*, 15 HARV. ENVTL. L. REV. 275, 283-297 (1991).

212. *See* WORLD RESOURCES INSTITUTE, WORLD RESOURCES 1990-1991, at 62-63 (1990).

213. *See* Goldburg, *supra* note 209.

214. *See* Protocol, *supra* note 210, art. 4, 26 I.L.M. at 1554-55.

215. *Id.* art. 2, 26 I.L.M. at 1553.

216. *Id.* art. 5, 26 I.L.M. at 1555-56.

January 1, 1993, parties to the Protocol also may not export controlled substances to non-parties.[217] The Protocol's second tier of restrictions applies to products that contain controlled substances.[218] In June of 1991, the parties adopted an annex, which lists products containing controlled substances.[219] This annex became effective in December of 1991, and those parties that did not object must ban import of such products by June 1992. The third tier of restrictions envisioned by the Protocol would apply to products made with, but not containing, controlled substances. The Protocol requires the parties to conduct a feasibility study on banning imports from non-parties of substances made with, but not containing, controlled substances by January 1, 1994.[220]

Because the Protocol phases out trade in controlled substances among the member states while simultaneously banning the import of "like" products from non-party states, there is a period during which non-party states will be precluded from exporting products containing controlled substances to party states that continue to be able to trade such products among themselves. Thus, if the GATT contracting parties apply the Protocol's import restrictions against imports from other contracting parties that are not parties to the Protocol, these import provisions would appear to violate GATT's non-discrimination obligations.[221] Similar GATT non-discrimination issues arise from the Protocol's ban on exports of controlled substances to non-parties. Moreover, should the parties enact restrictions that apply to imported products made with, but not containing, controlled substances, such restrictions would be PPM restrictions that could violate GATT's article III (governing national treatment) and article XI (prohibiting quantitative restrictions).[222]

Using these trade restrictions to accomplish the Protocol's goals was discussed extensively during the Protocol's negotiation in 1987.[223] The parties agreed to use trade restrictions because they feared that the parties' industries could not internalize the costs of complying with the agreement while competing with industries in non-party countries that did not have to bear these costs. In practice, however, efforts to elimi-

217. *Id.* art. 4(2), 26 I.L.M. at 1554.

218. *Id.* art. 4(3), 26 I.L.M. at 1554.

219. Montreal Protocol on Substances that Deplete the Ozone Layer, London 1990, Annexes A, B, UNEP/OzL.Pro.2/3 at 31.

220. *See* Protocol, *supra* note 210, art. 4(4); 26 I.L.M. at 1555.

221. *See* GATT Secretariat, Trade and the Environment, *supra* note 1, at 11; OECD, Joint Session, *supra* note 21, at 23; Goldburg, *supra* note 209.

222. *See supra* note 164.

223. *See Report of the Ad Hoc Workup Group on the Work of its Third Session*, U.N. Environment Program, at 17-18, UNEP/WG.172/2 (1987).

nate the use of CFCs and other controlled substances in many instances have led to the discovery of less expensive and more efficient substitutes for these products. Nevertheless, at the time of the agreement, these trade restrictions were deemed essential incentives to encourage countries to join the Protocol, and they continue to play a major role in preserving the integrity of the Protocol.

These discussions also addressed the compatibility of these trade restrictions with the GATT.[224] A legal expert from the GATT Secretariat advised the Protocol's negotiators that these measures would be compatible with the GATT by virtue of article XX's exceptions because the conditions present in the party nations would be substantially different from those in non-party nations—allowing the parties to draw non-arbitrary distinctions between products from party nations and non-party nations.[225] In light of the findings of the Tuna/Dolphin Panel Report, this conclusion may have to be reexamined.

b. *Special Provisions for Developing Countries*

The Protocol contains a number of provisions with trade implications to assist developing countries in meeting their obligations under the Protocol. First, the Protocol permits developing countries to delay by ten years their phase-out of controlled substances.[226] Second, the Protocol establishes a Multilateral Fund to provide developing countries and their industries with technical and financial assistance necessary for compliance with the Protocol.[227]

These special provisions for developing countries could run afoul of certain GATT obligations, especially in view of the Uruguay Round emphasis on eliminating preferences to developing countries.[228] For example, a developing nation receiving financial assistance from the Multilateral Fund and then passing it on to its industries to purchase "clean" technologies could be in violation of the GATT's provisions against subsidies.

2. Convention on International Trade in Endangered Species of Wild Fauna and Flora

In recognition of global threats to the world's biodiversity, the Con-

224. *Id.* at 18.
225. *Id.*
226. *See* Protocol, *supra* note 210, art. 5(1), 26 I.L.M. at 1555.
227. *See id.*, art. 5(3), 26 I.L.M. at 1555.
228. *See* Frictions Between International Trade Agreements and Environmental Protections, *supra* note 20, at 20.

vention on International Trade in Endangered Species of Wild Fauna and Flora[229] (CITES) seeks to control or eliminate trade in plant and animal species which are now, or may become, threatened with extinction. Because the intent of CITES is to alleviate trade-driven pressures on a species, its trade-related provisions are necessary to the achievement of its goal.

The level of the trade restriction CITES places on trade in a species is proportional to the degree of the threat to the species. CITES classifies each regulated species by its degree of "endangeredness" and establishes corresponding levels of trade restrictions through a listing system consisting of three Appendices.[230] Parties may propose changes to the categorization of a species as well as additions and deletions to the Appendices.[231]

Appendix I includes species that currently are threatened with extinction.[232] The threat of extinction to an Appendix I species need not be linked with trade demands on the species. CITES defines commercial trade broadly to include transactions in the species and species-derived products that have even nominal commercial aspects.[233] Such commercial trade is prohibited.[234] Noncommercial trade is allowed only if moving the species will not be detrimental to the survival of the species.[235] Before an export country may grant a permit for non-commercial trade in a species, the import country must issue an import permit.[236]

Appendix II lists species which are not currently threatened with extinction but may become threatened unless trade in the species is strictly regulated.[237] The exporting country may grant export permits for Appendix II species where the country's scientific authorities determine that the export will not be detrimental to the survival of the species.[238]

Appendix III consists of those species that any party has identified as requiring protection to prevent the species' demise from trade-driven

229. Convention on International Trade in Endangered Species of Wild Fauna and Flora, Mar. 3, 1973, 27 U.S.T. 1087, 993 U.N.T.S. 243, [hereinafter CITES]. CITES currently has 113 parties. *See* Fish & Wildlife Service, U.S. Dept. of Interior, *CITES Update #12: February 1992*, at 1, FWS/OMA TRE 1-02g (Feb. 1992).

230. *See* CITES art. II.

231. *See id.* arts. XV, XVI.

232. *Id.* art. II(1).

233. *Id.* art. I(b),(c).

234. *Id.* art. III(3).

235. *Id.*

236. *Id.* art. III(3).

237. *Id.* art. II(2).

238. *Id.* art. IV(2).

overexploitation and for which the co-operation of the other parties is needed to control the threat to the species.[239] Appendix III listing applies to only those populations of a species found within those countries that have classified the species as an Appendix III species.[240] Appendix III listing enables the contracting parties to address localized threats of extinction to sub-populations of species where these threats do not effect other sub-populations of the species. Trade in Appendix III species between parties that have not listed the species as Appendix III species is allowed so long as a certificate of origin accompanies the species or product.[241]

While parties must conform to these mandates, the agreement does not limit the ability of a party to adopt unilaterally stricter protection standards. Parties are required to enforce the provisions of CITES in their dealings with non-parties.[242]

A number of CITES provisions pose potential areas of friction with the GATT's obligations.[243] Because CITES allows a party to protect non-domestic species through trade restrictions, such trade restrictions, in light of the Tuna/Dolphin Panel Report, would not appear to qualify for article XX's exceptions for conservation of exhaustible natural resources and protection of species health and life. If the provisions would not qualify for an article XX exception, then a CITES party imposing trade restrictions against products of a GATT party that is not a CITES party could be violating the GATT's prohibition against quantitative restrictions.[244]

3. The Basel Convention on the Control of Transboundary Movements of Hazardous Wastes and Their Disposal

To avoid the high costs of domestic disposal of hazardous wastes caused by stringent environmental laws and regulations, industries in developed countries increasingly have sought to export these wastes to developing countries with lower environmental standards. International negotiations to address the environmental and social implications of this practice led to the Basel Convention on the Control of Transboundary Movements of Hazardous Wastes and Their Disposal[245] (the Basel Con-

239. *Id.* art. II(3).

240. *Id.*

241. *Id.* art. V(3).

242. *Id.* art. X.

243. *See* Frictions Between International Trade Agreements and Environmental Protections, *supra* note 20, at 21.

244. *Id.*

245. Convention on the Control of Transboundary Movements of Hazardous Wastes and

vention). The Basel Convention seeks to control international trade in hazardous wastes so that baseline health and safety standards are met in all countries. Because the Convention is intended to restrict trade in wastes, the trade provisions are central to achieving the Convention's goals.

The Basel Convention permits the parties' transboundary movement of hazardous wastes in only three circumstances: (1) where the exporting party lacks the technical capacity, necessary facilities, or siting capacity to ensure the environmentally sound disposal of the wastes in question; (2) where the wastes in question are required as a raw material for recycling and recovery industries in the importing nation; or (3) where the party performs transboundary shipment and disposal in accordance with the particular requirements established in the convention.[246]

The Basel Convention prohibits the export of wastes to nations that have prohibited the import of such hazardous wastes, to non-parties, and to the Antarctic region. Parties that choose to prohibit the import of hazardous wastes must inform the other parties of this decision.[247] Parties may only permit the shipment of hazardous wastes if the shipment is authorized in writing by the importing country.[248] The exporting parties must provide prior notification of any shipment.[249] A party that chooses instead to allow the import of such wastes must not allow the import of any wastes that it has reason to believe will not be managed in an environmentally-sound manner.[250] The exporting party has the burden of ensuring that any exports of wastes that it permits are, in fact, managed in an environmentally-sound manner.[251]

If a shipment of hazardous waste is found to have violated the Convention's terms, then the exporting country must either return the waste itself or ensure that the exporter or generator returns the waste. If the return of the waste is impracticable, the exporting country must provide for its disposal in accordance with the requirements of the convention.[252]

The requirements that the Basel Convention places on trade in hazardous and toxic wastes impose conditions on trade in such wastes that

Their Disposal, *opened for signature* Mar. 22, 1989, 28 I.L.M. 649 (1989) (The agreement will enter into force May 1992) [hereinafter Basel].

246. *Id.* art. 4(9)(a).

247. *Id.* art. 4(1)(a).

248. *Id.* art. 4(1),(5),(6).

249. *Id.* art. 6(1).

250. *Id.* art. 4(2)(g).

251. *Id.* art. 4(2)(e),(8).

252. *Id.* art. 9(2).

appear to violate the GATT's trade obligations.[253] Additionally, because many of the conditions imposed on exporting countries are designed to protect the welfare of individuals and the environment in importing countries "extrajurisdictionally," they would appear to fall outside the scope of the article XX exceptions. Similarly, the prohibition on exports to the Antarctic region may not be justifiable under article XX. The ban on trade with non-parties is most troublesome. For this provision to come within article XX, the discrimination against non-parties would need to be justified on the basis of domestic health, safety, or conservation concerns in the exporting country.

4. Proposed International Agreements[254]

The interaction between the spheres of international trade and environmental protection is becoming a topic of discussion in a number of international fora, including the United Nations Conference on Environment and Development (UNCED) and the inter-governmental negotiations on climate change and protection of biodiversity. This section summarizes the current discussions within the biodiversity and climate change negotiations and UNCED, which will culminate at the June, 1992 conference in Rio de Janeiro.

a. *The United Nations Conference on Environment and Development*

The UN General Assembly uses UNCED to devise strategies for reversing environmental degradation while promoting "sustainable and environmentally sound development in all countries." Envisioned as a follow-up to the landmark 1972 UN Conference on the Human Environment in Stockholm, the conference is intended to produce two non-binding comprehensive documents to guide the world towards environmental clean-up and sustainable development. "Agenda 21" is to be a plan of action—covering a panoply of topics from desertification to environmental accounting—for dealing with environmental degradation and promoting sustainable development over the next twenty years. The parties also planned to draft an "Earth Charter" that would serve as a set of basic principles governing human behavior in the biosphere. Discussion of trade issues in the UNCED process has been limited. Only in the fourth and final Preparatory Committee (PrepCom IV) meeting, held in New

253. *See* Frictions Between International Trade Agreements and Environmental Protections, *supra* note 20, at 22.

254. This section was substantially derived from a research memorandum prepared by David Downes, General Counsel, CIEL-US.

York from March 2 to April 3, 1992, did the parties attempt to deal with the issues in draft decision documents.

At PrepCom IV, delegates still could not come up with unbracketed texts. Indeed, delegates could not even agree on "Earth Charter" as a title for the statement of principles; the draft is entitled the "Rio Declaration." Many major issues remain unsettled. Among the biggest obstacles to agreement is conflict over the extent to which developed countries should provide additional financial resources and should take special measures for transferring environmentally appropriate technology to the developing world.

In the closing sessions of PrepCom IV, language explicitly dealing with the interrelationship of trade and environment made its way into the proposed texts. This language may yet be revised, since informal discussions of the contents of documents will continue sporadically through April and May and since delegations will continue to negotiate during their first days in Rio.

i. UN Background Studies Prepared for UNCED

Two UNCED background studies explicitly discuss trade and environment.[255] The first is a briefing text prepared for government delegations by the UNCED Secretariat on the international economy and environment and development, which includes discussions of the relationship of international trade and sustainable development, as well as several of the major areas of potential conflict between international trade and environmental law.[256] The report begins by acknowledging the "underlying presumption of trade theory" that trade "at prices which reflect real resource cost" leads to the most efficient allocation of resources and the maximization of economic welfare generally.[257] As an aside, it notes that there are exceptions to this rule, including trade in hazardous products, but it does not assess the validity of measures restraining the export of hazardous substances under the GATT.[258]

The report notes that it is unclear whether provisions in interna-

255. A third background report, focusing on the impact of international environmental regulation on trade, is being prepared by C&M International Ltd. of Washington D.C., but was not yet available as of this writing. *See* LEGAL TIMES, Jan. 13, 1992, at 5; Telephone Interview with Offices of C&M International Ltd. (Feb. 5, 1992).

256. *The International Economy and Environment and Development: Report of the Secretary-General of the Conference*, Preparatory Committee for United Nations Conference on Environment and Development, 3d Sess., UN Doc. A/CONF.151/PC/47 (1991) [hereinafter UNCED Sec't Int'l Econ. Report].

257. *Id.* at 4.

258. *Id.*

tional environmental agreements for trade measures against non-parties—aimed at discouraging "free riders" who benefit from the agreement's success without paying the costs of compliance—are consistent with GATT obligations.[259] It also acknowledges the related issue of determining "the appropriate forum for the resolution of trade related disputes arising from the application of such global agreements."[260] It concludes that at least one issue appears settled: that the GATT requires such trade measures to be "proportional to the environmental objectives which are sought to be achieved."[261]

Regarding domestic environmental laws, the report states that it is a "generally accepted proposition" that environmental standards may differ among countries and that therefore "differences in standards per se cannot be a basis for valid trade restraint."[262] It supports this view by arguing that differences in environmental "conditions" make up part of international specialization in production and thus contribute to efficiency and to "sustainability."[263] Obviously, this argument does not take into account the externalization of environmental costs under one country's environmental standards that could result in a production process which, although it produces products that appear to be cheaper, is overall more costly and less efficient than production in a country with stricter environmental standards.

In discussing the trade implications of national standards that regulate the process by which a product is produced, however, the report concludes that it is reasonable to impose such standards on imports, at least where the production process degrades common resources and thus affects the importing as well as the exporting country.[264] As to whether such measures are consistent with GATT, the report merely notes that GATT does not "explicitly" allow them.[265]

The second UNCED background study discussing trade and the environment was prepared at the request of the UN General Assembly by the United Nations Conference on Trade and Development (UNCTAD) for the UNCED PrepCom.[266] The report states that "trade liberalization will induce shifts in production, leading to a more efficient and sustaina-

259. *Id.* at 7.
260. *Id.*
261. *Id.*
262. *Id.* at 6.
263. *Id.*
264. *Id.* at 7.
265. *Id.* at 8.
266. *Report of the Secretary-General of the UNCTAD, submitted to the Secretary-General of the Conference Pursuant to General Assembly Resolution 45/210*, Preparatory Committee for

ble use of environmental resources throughout the world," *if* "in *all* countries production and end-use prices incorporate the full cost of resource use (the Polluter-Pays and User-Pays Principles)."[267] Thus, a rational trade policy ultimately may include, for example, increased intervention in energy markets in order to address global warming.[268] By the same token, it will mandate removing some trade barriers that prevent allocating the real costs of resource use, such as the agricultural protectionism of developed countries.[269]

The UNCTAD trade report urges further study of the interrelationship of trade and environment, including both "the effects of trade liberalization on the environment," particularly with regard to removing developed countries' agricultural subsidies, and the "impact of environmental regulations on trade," including trade-related provisions of international environmental agreements, particularly in light of developing countries aspiring to further development.[270] The report tentatively concludes that trade measures based on environmental grounds should conform to three principles. First, they should not result in arbitrary discrimination between countries "where the same conditions prevail" and should not serve as disguised trade barriers.[271] Second, trade-restrictive measures should be "proportional" to the environmental objectives of those measures.[272] Third, the "precautionary principle"—"tighten[ing] acceptable risk margins"—should guide the setting of environmental standards and "corresponding trade measures" so that the "lack of full scientific certainty" does not hinder "the prevention of environmental hazards."[273]

ii. General Positions of Governments

Although trade policy is an aspect of the "cross-sectoral" issue of the international economy which PrepCom IV is to consider, in the early stages, governmental delegations to UNCED have devoted relatively little attention to the interrelationship of international trade and environmental policy.[274] Developed countries, especially the United States, have

the U.N. Conference on Environment and Development, 3d Sess., Agenda Item 2B, U.N. Doc. A/Conf.151/PC/48 (1991).

267. *Id.* at 14 (emphasis added).

268. *Id.*

269. *Id.*

270. *Id.* at 15.

271. *Id.* at 16.

272. *Id.*

273. *Id.* at 7, 16.

274. Telephone interview with Tahar Sadoc, UNCED Secretariat (Jan. 3, 1991).

tended to argue that trade issues should be addressed at GATT. Thus, the United States has stated that, "We look to the GATT to define how trade measures can properly be used for environmental purposes."[275] To the extent that they have addressed the issue, developing countries— in particular, countries sometimes termed "newly industrialized countries"—have expressed concern that stringent environmental regulation may function as protectionist trade barriers, with a particularly negative effect on the exports of developing countries.[276]

India, for instance, has argued for strict limits on the imposition of trade restrictions on environmental grounds, stating that even "global" environmental considerations "cannot justify restrictive trade practices, except when these are introduced in terms of specific provisions in a globally accepted environmental convention."[277] A UN General Assembly resolution on UNCED reflects this concern, stating that incorporating environmental considerations into development policy should not "serve as a pretext for creating unjustified barriers to trade."[278]

At PrepCom IV, language was inserted into draft documents that, if approved, would significantly implicate the interrelationship of international trade policy and measures for environmental protection. Among the twenty-seven principles enunciated in the "Rio Declaration," which was pushed through in the closing hours of the session, was Principle 12 on trade and environment, which expresses a viewpoint with ominous consequences for global environmental protection.[279] Principle 12 begins uncontroversially by noting that "[t]rade policy measures for environmental purposes should not constitute a means of arbitrary or unjustifiable discrimination or a disguised restriction on international trade."[280]

---

275. Preparatory Committee for the 1992 UN Conference on Environment and Development, Statement by the U.S. Delegation on International Economics and Trade, Integrated Economic-Environmental Accounting, and Economic Instruments (Aug. 1991) (on file with authors).

276. *See, e.g., Principles on General Rights and Obligations: Chairman's Consolidated Draft*, Preparatory Committee for the United Nations Conference on Environment and Development, ¶¶ 86, 89, U.N. Doc. A/Conf.151/PC/WG.III/L.8 (1991) (statements of South Korea and Singapore).

277. *Id.* ¶ 85.

278. *See* G.A. Res. 228, U.N. GAOR, 44th Sess., U.N. Doc. (1989).

279. Late drafts of some sections of Agenda 21 contained similar proposed language. *See, e.g., Protection of Oceans, All Kinds of Seas Including Enclosed and Semi-Enclosed Seas, Coastal Areas and the Protection, Rational Use and Development of Their Living Resources*, Preparatory Committee for the United Nations Conference on Environment and Development, 4th Sess., Agenda Item 2, at 35, U.N. Doc. A/Conf. 151/PC/WG.II/L.25/Rev.1 (1992) (including handwritten amendments "as adopted at Plenary April 3, 1992, 9:30 p.m.").

280. *Principles on General Rights and Obligations: Draft Principles Proposed by the Chairman: Rio Declaration on Environment and Development*, Preparatory Committee for the

The next sentence reflects the holding of the GATT panel in the Tuna/Dolphin Panel decision, stating that "[u]nilateral actions to deal with environmental challenges outside the jurisdiction of the importing country should be avoided."[281] Similarly, the final sentence, drawing once again from the Tuna/Dolphin Panel's rationale, states that "[e]nvironmental measures addressing transboundary or global environmental problems should, as far as possible, be based on an international consensus." This language, taken literally, places an almost impossible burden on the proponents of international environmental agreements containing trade-related enforcement measures since it is almost impossible to achieve an international consensus.[282] Indeed, even the United Nations does not include every nation-state.

iii. General Comments of Non-Governmental Organizations (NGOs)

A number of NGOs involved in UNCED from both North and South strongly criticize the ramifications of current trade policy trends for environmental protection and sustainable development. The World Wide Fund for Nature complained that GATT's "narrow focus" on "liberalization of world trade" blinds it to environmental and natural resource costs of traded products that are currently externalized.[283] It called on the PrepCom to analyze the GATT's potential impact on current and future international agreements for environmental protection and to suggest GATT reforms that will ensure that GATT provisions do not hamper countries' ability to protect the environment and develop sustainably.[284] The Poverty and Affluence Working Group, a coalition of seventy NGOs, has also urged that UNCED analyze "how trade practices distort the environment and development . . . [and] ensure that environmental and development policy [supersede] trade policy" so as to correct current trade practices that encourage uneconomic and environmentally destructive exploitation of the natural resources of the South.[285]

United Nations Conference on Environment and Development, 4th Sess., Agenda Item 3, at 4, U.N. Doc. A/Conf. 151/PC/WG.III/L.33/Rev.1 (1992).

281. *Id.*

282. Although the sentence by its terms includes *all* environmental measures, whether or not they pertain to trade, the context within Principle 12 suggests that it is intended to restrict only those environmental measures that relate to trade.

283. *See UNCED Must Recognize Role of Trade* (Sept. 3, 1991) (press release from World Wildlife Fund).

284. *Id.*

285. *See* Third World Resurgence, No. 14/15 at 34 (1991). The term "south" is used to refer to developing countries and the term "north" refers to developed countries.

Similarly, in a statement to UNCED, thirty-eight environment and development NGOs from twenty-five countries ask that any decisions taken at the Uruguay Round conform to "the principles of sustainable development which will hopefully [sic] be elaborated at the UNCED meeting."[286]

iv. Forestry Principles

Originally, delegations to the PrepCom were to negotiate a convention to preserve forests, to be ready for UNCED's consideration in Rio in June, 1992. It is extremely unlikely, however, that anything more than a non-binding statement of general principles on forests will be ready by that time. While the discussion of timber trade has raised the issue of the interrelation of trade and environment more explicitly than in most other contexts, mutually inconsistent provisions on trade policy in a heavily-bracketed draft text that came out of the third PrepCom meeting demonstrate that there is as yet no agreement on how to deal with trade issues with regard to forests.[287] Some proposed language would, for instance, encourage "subsidies or incentives encouraging sound practices," while another proposed clause would provide that "[t]rade on forest products must be consistent with international trade law and practices as embodied for example in [GATT] and its subsidiary agreements."[288] Some NGOs have commented on trade-related issues, with one Malaysia-based group arguing that UNCED "must ensure that countries reserve the right and freedom to ban the export of forest products for conservation purposes, and not support efforts to label such moves as an obstacle to trade."[289]

v. Technology Transfer and Intellectual Property Rights

The terms for transfer of environmentally appropriate technology from North to South have been intensely debated in the UNCED process, with little progress toward agreement so far. Developing countries

286. *See* Third World Network, NGO Statement on Some Key Issues for UNCED 7 (Aug. 1991) (statement to UNCED from 38 environment and development NGOs from 25 countries, drafted at a meeting in Penong, Malaysia, 25-30 July 1991).

287. *See, e.g., Land Resources: Deforestation, A non-legally binding authoritative statement of principles for a global consensus on the management, conservation and sustainable development of all types of forests*, Preparatory Committee for the United Nations Conference on Environment and Development, 3d Sess., Agenda Item 3, ¶ 14 U.N. Doc. A/Conf. 151/PC/WG.I/CRP/14/Rev.1 (1991) [hereinafter *Land Resources: Deforestation*].

288. *See id.*

289. *See* Ling & Khor, Principles for an UNCED Consensus on Forests, Third World Network Briefing Papers for UNCED No. 4, at 16 (1991).

insist that developed countries must help them obtain the technology needed to comply with obligations under any new international agreements for environmental protection. In general, they ask that developed countries make special efforts to transfer appropriate technology by providing funds and by transferring such technology on preferential and non-commercial terms.[290] Developed countries are reluctant to make commitments to any more funding, especially in the absence of developing countries clearly committing to new environmental protection measures. And preferential technology transfer or funding potentially conflicts with GATT obligations barring discriminatory treatment in the form of subsidies.

In this context, developing countries are concerned that protecting intellectual property rights (IPR), an issue now under discussion in the Uruguay Round's TRIPS negotiations, may hamper the transfer of environmentally appropriate technology. These concerns implicitly conflict with the United States' effort in GATT negotiations and in bilateral relations to strengthen IPR protection worldwide,[291] an effort reflected in the United States' comments in the UNCED process.[292] A number of developing countries, as well as many NGOs, also are increasingly concerned that genetic resources from wild and domesticated tropical ecosystems

290. *See, e.g.*, *Draft Decision proposed by the Vice-Chairman, Mr. B.S. Utheim (Norway) on the basis on informal consultations: Transfer of Technology*, Preparatory Committee for the United Nations Conference on Environment and Development, 3d Sess., Agenda Item 2, ¶¶ 2(a):(d), 2(a):(g), 8, U.N. Doc. A/Conf. 151/PC/L.53 (1991) (bracketed text calling for various measures to transfer patents on environmentally sound technology to developing countries on non-commercial terms); *China and Ghana: Draft decision: Financial resources*, Preparatory Committee for the United Nations Conference on Environment and Development, 3d Sess., Agenda Item 2(c), ¶¶ (b), (g), U.N. Doc. A/Conf. 151/PC/L.41 (1991) (G-77 proposal on provision of financial resources and transfer of technology).

291. *See* Keith Bradsher, *U.S. and China Reach Accord on Copying*, N.Y. TIMES, Jan. 17, 1992, at D1, D14 (reporting that China agreed to United States demands for strengthened intellectual property protection); Hans Peter Kunz-Hallstein, *The United States Proposal for a GATT Agreement on Intellectual Property and the Paris Convention for the Protection of Industrial Property*, 22 VAND. J. TRANSNAT'L L. 265, 267 (1989); Richard A. Morford, *Intellectual Property Protection: A United States Priority*, 19 GA. J. INT'L & COMP. L. 336, 337-39 (1989) (describing United States pursuit of improved protection of intellectual property in foreign countries through bilateral consultations and Section 301 actions under United States international trade law).

292. *See* Preparatory Committee for the 1992 UN Conference on Environment and Development, Statement by the U.S. Delegation on Technolology Cooperation (Aug. 30, 1991) (stating that "[t]echnology has been adapted most successfully in those countries where the business environment . . . offer[s] adequate protection for intellectual property"); UN Conference on Environment and Development, U.S. Statement on UNGA U.N. Doc. A/Conf. 151/ PC/67 "Environmentally Sound Management of Biotechnolology: Background and Issues" (Aug. 22, 1991) (stating that "intellectual property rights have been key to advances in biotechnology . . . [and] must be respected").

are transferred freely to developed countries, while commercially valuable substances and technology derived from those resources by Northern industry are rendered expensive or unaffordable for developing countries by IPR. Some developing countries are calling for the reduction or elimination of IPR, at least in the South, over products derived from Southern genetic resources.[293]

On the other hand, legal and economic scholars, as well as environmental and human rights NGOs and representatives of indigenous peoples, have called for the creation of property rights over biological resources that would enable governments or individuals with biologically diverse territory to earn some return from the use of that biodiversity to create new products—a creative use of IPR-like concepts that many believe could stimulate preservation of natural resources that are currently imperilled. Advocates for indigenous peoples also have urged governments to recognize some form of intellectual property rights in their traditional knowledge of the biological resources of their natural environment—so far without success.[294]

b. *Negotiations on a Biodiversity Convention*

In a process paralleling the preparations for UNCED, an Inter-Governmental Negotiating Committee with a Secretariat staffed through UNEP is overseeing negotiations on a convention to protect biological diversity. These negotiations were supposed to result in a draft convention ready for the consideration of delegates in Rio in June, 1992, but the betting is fifty-fifty that a convention of any significance will be drafted by that time.[295] In large part, negotiations appear to have snagged on the same two issues that have hampered progress at UNCED: transfering technology (although its relevance in the context of conservation of biodiversity is less clear than in other areas) and allocating financial resources for conservation measures.

So far, there has been little discussion of trade issues in the negotiations.[296] Trade policy has arisen only implicitly in discussions of protect-

293. *See Land Resources: Deforestation*, *supra* note 287, ¶ 8(h) (draft of forest principles including bracketed text calling for "sharing of technology and profits of bio-technology products, for example pharmaceutical, derived from [biological resources of forests]").

294. *See, e.g.*, Intellectual Property Rights for Indigenous Peoples in the Context of Sustainable Development, Trade, and Conservation of Biodiversity (1991) (proposed resolution to be presented to UNCED PrepCom III in Geneva).

295. Interview with UNEP Inter-Governmental Negotiating Committee for a Convention on Biological Diversity Secretariat for Working Group II (January 6, 1992).

296. Telephone Interview with Eleanor Savage, Department Negotiator, United States Department of State (Dec. 12, 1991); Interview with UNEP Inter-Governmental Negotiating

ing or compensating for the use of developing countries' genetic resources, i.e., the genetic variety found in wild and domesticated plant and animal species which may have commercial value in pharmaceutical, agricultural, and other applications. For instance, the Mexican delegation has suggested that the rights to any product derived from the biological resources of a developing country should be in the public domain, at least in the source country. The fourth draft convention, dated December 16, 1991, reflects this view, providing that "countries of origin of genetic material or providing genetic material subject to biotechnological research [should] be exempted from royalties on patents relating to the products of such research."[297] As such a rule would create different levels of IPR protection for similar imports from different countries, its validity in light of GATT's prohibition of discriminatory treatment is unclear. The fifth draft of the convention takes a more ambiguous position, including bracketed language providing that contracting parties shall promote "priority access" to biotechnology for the countries upon whose genetic resources that biotechnology is based. Whether providing for such priority access violates the GATT's trade rules would depend on the nature of the measures taken.[298]

There are several other provisions in the fifth draft convention which implicate trade. Article 16 provides that contracting parties shall facilitate other parties' access to natural genetic resources on mutually agreed-upon terms and conversely that parties shall promote access for countries that are sources of natural genetic resources to commercial derivatives of those resources. This language appears to provide for free trade in biological resources and their derivatives. Bracketed language in article 17, which covers technology transfer, provides for "preferential and concessional" transfer of technology—an approach which, as mentioned above,[299] raises questions under GATT standards.

In past years, a number of developing countries have attempted to restrict the export of plant samples from developing countries to the de-

---

Committee for a Convention on Biological Diversity Secretariat for Working Group II (January 6, 1992).

297. *Fourth Revised Draft Convention on Biological Diversity*, UNEP Inter-Governmental Negotiating Committee for a Convention on Biological Diversity, Art. 17 bis, ¶ 1 [hereinafter 4th Draft Biol. Diversity Conv.]. This draft was prepared for use in the negotiations in Nairobi on Feb. 6-15, 1992.

298. *See Fifth Revised Draft Convention on Biological Diversity*, UNEP Inter-Governmental Negotiating Committee for a Convention on Biological Diversity, UNEP/Bio.Div./N7-INC.5/2, art. 20, ¶ 2 [hereinafter 5th Draft Biol. Diversity Conv.]. This draft was prepared for use in the negotiations in Nairobi in May 1992.

299. *See supra* Part I.E.

veloped world. These countries are concerned that such exports are being used to create improved strains of commercially valuable crops that are then sold back to developing countries at a vastly higher price—without compensing the contributor of the genetic resources.[300] Developed as well as developing countries have imposed both de jure and de facto restrictions on export of plant genetic resources.[301] As yet, these trade-related issues have been addressed through little more than general language requiring parties to "facilitate access [for other parties] to genetic resources for environmentally sound purposes."[302]

c. Negotiations on a Climate Change Convention

Like the biodiversity convention negotiations, the goal of these negotiations (organized by an Intergovernmental Negotiating Committee for a Framework Convention on Climate Change) is to produce a convention ready for delegates' consideration at Rio in June. As in other UNCED-related contexts, little explicit discussion of trade has occurred so far. Trade has been implicated for the most part only in the context of requests for technology transfer on "preferential, concessional and non-commercial terms," including the waiver of patents as against developing countries—policies which would raise questions under GATT's prohibition of discrimination and subsidies.[303] Of particular interest, however, is that the draft negotiating text includes language drastically curtailing the possibility of enforcing a climate change control agreement through trade-related sanctions of the kind employed by the Montreal Protocol. Article II, Principle 6 of the draft would allow "barriers to trade on the basis of claims related to climate change" only if based on a decision by the Conference of the Parties and only if "consistent with GATT."[304] Even broader is the language of draft Principle 7, which provides that "[m]easures taken to combat climate change should not introduce trade distortions inconsistent with GATT or hinder the promotion of an open and multilateral trading system."[305] In light of the GATT bureacracy's

300. *See* Eric Christensen, *Genetic Ark: A Proposal to Preserve Genetic Diversity for Future Generations*, 40 STAN. L. REV. 279, 301 (1987) (quoting Mooney, *The Law of the Seed: Another Development and Plant Genetic Resources*, 1983: DEV. DIALOGUE 24, 39).

301. *See* C. FOWLER & PAT MOONEY, SHATTERING: FOOD, POLITICS & THE LOSS OF GENETIC DIVERSITY 193-96 (1990).

302. *See* 5th Draft Biol. Diversity Conv., *supra* note 298, art. 16, ¶ 2.

303. *See Revised Consolidated Text Under Negotiation*, Intergovernmental Negotiating Committee for a Framework Convention on Climate Change, 5th Sess., Agenda Item 3, art. IV.2.3, U.N. Doc. No. A/AC.237/Misc.20 (1992).

304. *See id.* at art. II, ¶ 6.

305. *Id.* art. II, ¶ 7.

current interpretation of the GATT, such language could seriously hamper international efforts to control global warming.[306]

B. Unilateral Environmental Protections

Many domestic environmental protections in the United States and other countries rely heavily upon trade measures to ensure their effectiveness or to ensure that domestic industries that must meet more stringent environmental standards are not disadvantaged competitively by these standards.[307] Certain of these measures are summarized below.

1. Current Environmental Laws

a. *The Endangered Species Act*

To friend and foe alike, the Endangered Species Act[308] (ESA) is one of the strongest U.S. laws protecting the environment. The ESA is best known for its provisions proscribing the domestic "taking" of an endangered species or the destruction of such species' habitat.[309] The ESA also bars any person or entity subject to U.S. jurisdiction from importing or exporting any species listed by the Secretary of the Interior as endangered or any product derived from such a species.[310] While the ESA's prohibitions applying to endangered species generally apply to threatened species as well, the Secretary of the Interior, through the Fish and Wildlife Service, may promulgate special rules excepting threatened species from some or all of these provisions.[311] Listing of a species for the purposes of the ESA does not necessarily correspond to the international listing of a species under CITES. Species listed as endangered or threatened include both domestic and extraterritorial species, and a species need not be protected in its habitat country for the species to receive protection under the ESA.[312]

The ESA's import and export bans may conflict with the GATT's non-discrimination obligations in terms of the ESA's treatment of distinct population segments. For these provisions to comply with the GATT, they would have to be justified under article XX. If, however,

306. *See* Donald Goldberg, *INC: Watch Out for GATTzilla*, ECO, Feb. 27, 1992 at 4.

307. *See* Melinda Chandler, *Recent Developments in the Use of International Trade Restrictions as a Conservation Measure for Marine Reources, in* FREEDOM FOR THE SEAS IN THE 21ST CENTURY: A NEW LOOK AT OCEAN GOVERNANCE AND ENVIRONMENTAL HARMONY (John Van Dyke et al. eds., forthcoming 1992).

308. Endangered Species Act of 1973, 16 U.S.C. §§ 1531-1534 (1988).

309. *Id.* § 1538(a).

310. *Id.* § 1538(d).

311. *Id.* § 1533(a)(3).

312. *Id.* § 1533(b).

the species being protected is not found in the United States, these provisions would seem to violate the United States' GATT obligations since article XX has been read as not extending "extrajurisdictionally."

b. *The Marine Mammal Protection Act*

One of the primary goals of the Marine Mammal Protection Act[313] (the MMPA) is to reduce the incidental killing of marine mammals, particularly dolphins, during commercial fishing operations. To achieve this goal, the MMPA establishes a regulatory program that sets industry-wide standards for U.S. tuna fleet fishing practices.[314] This regulatory program is strictest in the Eastern Tropical Pacific Ocean (ETP), where schools of tuna tend to swim in the waters below pods of dolphin. Under this program, foreign tuna fishing fleets operating in the ETP must meet similar standards to be able to import their tuna to the United States. For a foreign tuna fleet to be able to export its tuna and tuna products to the United States, the Secretary of Commerce must certify: one, that the foreign fleet operates under a regulatory program that is comparable to that of the United States and two, that during a given period of time the foreign fleet's adjusted average rate of incidental taking of marine mammals did not exceed 1.25 times the unweighted average of the U.S. fleet for that same period of time.[315] Additionally, intermediary nations that import tuna from nations that have not obtained comparability findings cannot import their tuna and tuna products into the United States.[316]

The recent Tuna/Dolphin Panel Report found these MMPA import and intermediary restrictions to violate the GATT's prohibitions contained in article III (national treatment) and article XI (quantitative restrictions). Additionally, the Panel Report held the MMPA's provisions to fall outside the scope of article XX because they were both extrajurisdictional in nature and not "necessary" within the meaning of article XX.[317]

c. *The Magnuson Fishery Conservation and Management Act*

The Magnuson Fishery Conservation and Management Act[318] (the Magnuson Act) establishes a national program for conserving and man-

313. Marine Mammal Protection Act of 1972 (current version at 16 U.S.C. §§ 1361-1407 (1988)).

314. *Id.* § 1374(h).

315. *Id.* § 1371(a)(2)(B)(II).

316. *Id.* § 1371(a)(2)(C).

317. *See* Housman & Zaelke, *supra* note 13, at 10,272-73.

318. 16 U.S.C. §§ 1801-1882 (1988).

aging fisheries resources, including domestic, migratory, and anadromous stocks. To a large extent, the Magnuson Act was motivated by fears that foreign fishing fleets were depleting U.S. fisheries.[319] The Act establishes for the United States a 197-mile-wide exclusive fishery zone abutting the United States' territorial sea.[320]

Under the Magnuson Act, trade figures most directly in the provisions govern foreign fleets' access to fishery stocks claimed by the U.S.. No foreign vessel may fish in U.S. waters unless it has obtained a permit to do so.[321] Foreign vessels operating in United States waters are required to, *inter alia*: 1) have a U.S. observer on board the vessel during their time in these waters; 2) reimburse the United States for the cost of the observers; 3) take no more than their allocated share of the fisheries resource; and, 4) abide by all other rules and regulations applying to them promulgated under the Act.[322] The Act requires the Secretary of Commerce to establish total allowable levels for foreign fishing fleet catches from U.S. fisheries.[323] In establishing these levels, the Secretary is to look at several factors, including the extent to which the foreign government helps or hinders the United States' development of export markets for its fishery products.[324] Foreign fleets that violate the Act's provisions may be subject to an embargo on all fishery imports to the United States pursuant to section 8 of the Fishermen's Protective Act.[325]

The Magnuson Act appears to establish conditions for trade that violate GATT's non-discrimination obligations and quantitative restriction prohibition. While these measures at first glance would seem to qualify for article XX's exception for measures to conserve a domestic exhaustible resource, to qualify for article XX a measure must not be applied in a discriminatory or arbitrary manner. Because the Act links certain of its conservation conditions with what seem to be trade protectionist standards, these provisions may not come within article XX and thus may violate the GATT.

d. *The Dolphin Protection Consumer Information Act*

In an effort to encourage consumer-driven, market-based protection

319. *Id.* § 1801(a)(4); *see also* MICHEAL BEAN, THE EVOLUTION OF NATIONAL WILDLIFE LAW 387-88 (1983).
320. 16 U.S.C. § 1811.
321. *Id.* § 1821(a).
322. *Id.* § 1821(c)(2)(D).
323. *Id.* § 1821(e)(1).
324. *Id.*
325. *Id.* § 1821(e)(2).

of dolphins, the Dolphin Protection Consumer Information Act[326] (the DPCIA) specifies labeling standards that allow qualifying tuna products to carry the terms "dolphin safe" on their packaging. The DPCIA makes it a violation of section 5 of the Federal Trade Commission Act for any producer, importer, distributor, or seller of tuna products to include on its label the terms "dolphin safe" or any equivalent statement unless the manner in which the tuna was harvested meets certain standards for dolphin protection.[327]

The recent Tuna/Dolphin Panel Report decision found that the DPCIA complied with the GATT because the DPCIA established voluntary standards that did not restrict a product's access to the market and did not provide a government-supplied market advantage.[328] In contrast, labeling provisions that require an imported product to carry a label that can only be obtained by meeting certain standards that do not apply directly to the product but instead to the product's PPM would appear to violate the GATT's obligations.[329]

e. *The Pelly Amendment*

The Pelly Amendment,[330] also known as section 8 of the Fishermen's Protective Act,[331] seeks, *inter alia*, to provide a means to ensure that the unsustainable fishing practices of foreign fishing fleets do not jeopardize American fishery stocks or harm American fishing fleets. To provide added protection to American fishing fleets and fisheries, the Pelly Amendment works in conjunction with certain other American laws, such as the MMPA and the Magnuson Act, which are designed to ensure the use of sustainable fishing practices by enabling the President to increase the trade sanctions against foreign fishing fleets that continually violate these laws. Under the Pelly Amendment, the President of the United States has the discretionary authority to embargo all fishery imports from another nation upon notice from the Secretary of Commerce that that nation has violated one or more of these American laws for a certain period of time.[332]

The Tuna/Dolphin Panel Report found that the Pelly Amendment complied with the GATT's provisions only because the President had

326. *Id.* §§ 1361, 1385 (Supp. 1991).
327. *Id.* § 1385(d).
328. *Tuna/Dolphin Panel Report, supra* note 13, at 49-50.
329. *See* Housman & Zaelke, *supra* note 13, at 10,271.
330. *codified at* 22 U.S.C. § 1978 (1988).
331. Fishermen's Protective Act of 1967, 22 U.S.C. §§ 1971-1980 (1988).
332. *Id.* § 1978.

not invoked his powers under the Amendment.[333] Actually applying the Pelly Amendment's embargo provisions to another party's fisheries imports, however, would appear to violate GATT nondiscrimination obligations.

2. Pending Environmental Legislation

In addition to existing United States environmental laws that impact trade, a number of pending bills and resolutions raise trade concerns. Certain of these measures are summarized below.

a. *The General Agreement on Tariffs and Trade for the Environment Act of 1991 (S.59)*

The General Agreement on Tariffs and Trade for the Environment Act of 1991 (S.59) was introduced by Senator Moynihan. It would require a comprehensive study of the impact of international trade on international environmental agreements. S.59 would also require a study of foreign environmental laws, foreign governments' compliance with international environmental agreements, and foreign environmental laws that restrict trade. Further, S.59 would require the United States Trade Representative to provide a statement of the efforts being undertaken to make the GATT more environmentally sound. Additionally, S.59 requires that foreign trade practices diminishing the effectiveness of international agreements aimed at preserving species be treated as unjustifiable trade practices under the Trade Act of 1974, and it allows the United States to adopt measures to retaliate against the foreign party's practices.

The study provisions of S.59 would in no way conflict with GATT obligations. S.59's provisions with regard to the justifiability of foreign actions that diminish international protections of species, however, would appear to conflict with the GATT's obligations if adopted.

b. *House Concurrent Resolution 246*

House Concurrent Resolution 246 (H.Con.Res. 246), introduced by Representative Waxman for himself and 25 other representatives, would express the will of the House and Senate regarding the relationship between trade agreements and U.S. health, safety, labor, and environmental laws. H.Con.Res. 246 calls upon the President to initiate and complete discussions within the Uruguay Round to make GATT compatible with the MMPA and other American health, safety, labor, and environmental

333. *Tuna/Dolphin Panel Report*, *supra* note 13, at 43.

laws. H.Con.Res. 246 also expresses Congress' resolve to reject legislation implementing any trade agreement, including both the Uruguay Round and the NAFTA, if such agreement jeopardizes U.S. health, safety, labor, or environmental laws.

Because H.Con.Res. 246 is merely a statement of congressional resolve, it cannot conflict with the GATT. Nevertheless, H.Con.Res. 246's provisions do raise substantial implications for the GATT and for trade policy generally. H.Con.Res. 246 calls upon the President to expand the scope of the debate in the Uruguay Round negotiations, which are well along and already fraught with difficulty. Moreover, this statement from Congress that it will not adopt any trade legislation that could undermine American social protections places additional burdens on the negotiation of NAFTA and the Uruguay Round instruments. Despite the concerns of the trade community, adopting H.Con.Res. 246 would be an important statement that Congress does not intend to allow free trade to jeopardize the U.S.' commitment to environmental protection at home or abroad.

c. *International Pollution Deterrence Act of 1991 (S.984)*

The International Pollution Deterrence Act of 1991 (S.984), introduced by Senator Boren, seeks to level the playing field for international trade by removing what many perceive to be subsidies to foreign industries in the form of lower national environmental standards. The goal of S.984 is to ensure that all products sold in U.S. markets fully reflect their environmental costs, at least to the extent that U.S. laws require such internalization.

S.984 amends the countervailing duty provisions of U.S. trade law to establish that the failure to impose and enforce effective environmental protections amounts to a subsidy which can be subjected to a countervailing duty. The costs the manufacturer or producer would have to bear to comply with the U.S. environmental laws imposed on like domestic products would determine the amount of the subsidy provided by lower environmental standards. Additionally, S.984 would allocate fifty percent of the monies paid through the countervailing duty provisions to a fund that would be distributed by the Agency for International Development to assist developing countries in purchasing U.S. pollution control equipment. The other fifty percent of the countervailing revenues would be allocated to a fund administered by the Environmental Protection Agency ("EPA") that would assist U.S. companies researching and developing pollution control technologies. S.984 would require the EPA to create an index for the top fifty U.S. trading partners to compare each country's pollution control standards to U.S. standards.

S.984 would have a number of trade ramifications. Using countervailing duties to mitigate environmental standards subsidies appears to violate GATT articles I, II, and III, as well as the countervailing duty provisions of the GATT and the Subsidies Code. And subsidies paid both to U.S. companies to create environmental technologies and to developing countries to purchase U.S. environmental technologies could allow other parties to institute countervailing measures to mitigate these subsidies.

3. Sub-National Level Environmental Laws

In addition to the national-level environmental protections implicating trade, the United States system of governance reserves a wide latitude of powers to state and local governments to legislate environmental protections. Certain of these sub-national level protections implicate trade as well. For example, at least nine states and twenty-five municipalities have adopted legislation that restricts the sale and use of CFCs as products or in consumer products.[334] A number of states have introduced legislation to control the flow of agricultural research information and products, including ten states that have enacted controls over Bovine somatropin (BST) or beef hormones.[335] Hawaii has enacted legislation to provide funds to help establish and operate small business medical incubator research facilities.[336]

Many of these sub-national provisions seem to be inconsistent with the GATT's obligations. As discussed above,[337] a recent GATT panel found that U.S. state laws regulating imported beer violated GATT.[338] It would appear that state environmental laws conflicting with the GATT's obligations would suffer the same fate.

334. *See* Special Committee on Global Climate, *1990 Annual Report on Global Climate, in* ABA SECTION ON NATURAL RESOURCES, ENERGY AND ENVIRONMENTAL LAW, NATURAL RESOURCES, ENERGY AND ENVIRONMENTAL LAW: 1990 THE YEAR IN REVIEW 237 (1991).

335. *See* Biotechnology Special Committee, *1990 Annual Report on Biotechnology, in* ABA SECTION ON NATURAL RESOURCES, ENERGY AND ENVIRONMENTAL LAW, *supra* note 334, at 203, 207-10 (1991) [hereinafter *Biotechnology Report*].

336. H.B. 1144, 15th Leg., 1990 Sess., 1990 Haw. Sess. Laws Act 290 (to be codified at Haw. Rev. Stat. §§ 137-93; *see also Biotechnology Report, supra* note 335, at 209.

337. *See supra* section II.A.2.i.

338. *See supra* note 69 and accompanying text.

IV. OPTIONS FOR REDUCING OR ELIMINATING FRICTION BETWEEN ENVIRONMENTAL PROTECTIONS AND TRADE AGREEMENTS

Again, the goal of free trade policy is to allow markets to allocate the use of resources, while the general goal of environmental policy is to manage and maintain the earth's resources efficiently. This article has demonstrated that when the same resources are the subject of both trade and environmental policies, conflict often results. Yet the ability of both free trade and environmental policy to accomplish their respective goals largely depends on their mutual ability to reconcile these conflicts. In the long term, if economic development from expanded trade endangers the world's resource base, trade may find itself with no natural resources left to allocate. Contemporaneously, improving environmental quality and the standard of living around the globe in many instances requires economic resources that economic growth attended by expanded free trade can provide. Moreover, the ability of the global community to adopt international agreements that encourage state participation and discourage "free riders" appears at this time to depend on the use of trade measures within these agreements.

What follows is a brief discussion of certain options to reconcile trade and environmental concerns and to move each of these disciplines closer to the mutually reinforcing goal of sustainable development. This discussion focuses on the legal predicates for and ramifications of these options.

A. Application of Treaty Law

Perhaps the most obvious question that arises regarding how to reduce or eliminate the friction described above is whether there is any way to reconcile conflicting terms of international trade agreements and international environmental agreements.[339]

339. This analysis assumes that GATT is an international treaty. *See* RESTATEMENT (THIRD) OF FOREIGN RELATIONS LAW OF THE UNITED STATES, *supra* note 55, § 301(1) (defining international agreement). If the GATT is not, in fact, an international treaty obligation, then the most that could be said for the GATT's role in international law is that its terms, to the extent that states abide by them, are customary law. *See id.* § 102 (1)(a), (2); *id.* cmt. b. If frictions arise between a customary law, GATT, and an international environmental agreement, the agreement would modify the customary law among the parties. *Id.* reporter's note 4. Moreover, because the United States, and other states have repeatedly refused to strictly comply with the GATT, its status as customary law, especially as to these dissenting states, is also unclear. *Id.* cmt. d. Regardless of whether or not GATT is customary law, unless the GATT

Article 30 of the Vienna Convention on the Law of Treaties provides general rules governing the relationship of successive treaties.[340] Under article 30, when the provisions of two treaties conflict, the later-in-time provision prevails as between parties to both unless one treaty expressly specifies otherwise.[341] If a State is party to only one treaty, then under article 30(4)(b) only that treaty governs.[342]

Thus, as between States that are parties to both the GATT and the Montreal Protocol, paragraphs 4 and 4 *bis* of the Montreal Protocol, which ban the import of substances produced with, but not containing, the controlled substances listed in Annexes A and B of the Protocol, would prevail over inconsistent provisions of the GATT. (This ignores, of course, the legal opinion the negotiators of the Montreal Protocol obtained from the member of the GATT Secretariat regarding the consistency of the proposed provisions of the Protocol with the GATT.) Note that paragraphs 1 through 3 *bis* of the Protocol presumably would not be inconsistent with the GATT even when applied against States that are not parties to the Protocol because the paragraphs pertain to products rather than processes.

This leaves the problem of non-parties. Specifically, the issue is whether a party to the GATT can be bound by a subsequent environmental agreement to which it is not a party that contains inconsistent trade provisions. Article 34 of the Vienna Convention states that a subsequent treaty cannot bind non-party States without their consent.[343] Article 38 recognizes a limited exception to article 34 if the treaty rule becomes customary international law.[344] Thus, a GATT contracting party that has not signed the Montreal Protocol very well may have a legitimate dispute under the GATT if another contracting party that is

is an international treaty, it would occupy a lower place on the totem pole of international law than an international environmental agreement.

340. Vienna Convention on the Law of Treaties, *opened for signature* May 23, 1969, U.N.Doc. A/CONF.39/27, 8 I.L.M. 679 (entered into force Jan. 27, 1980), art. 30, 8 I.L.M. at 691 [hereinafter Vienna Convention]. For a discussion of the problem of reconciling conflicts between interrelated trade agreements, see Henry R. Zheng, *Defining Relationships and Resolving Conflicts Between Interrelated Multinational Trade Agreements: The Experience of the MFA and the GATT*, 25 STAN. J. INT'L L. 45 (1988).

341. *See* Vienna Convention, *supra* note 340, art. 30, 8 I.L.M. at 691. This rule applies where the two treaties address the same subject matter—which is generally the only situation in which conflicts would arise. The date of a treaty for conflicts purposes is determined by the effective date of the treaty.

342. *Id.* art. 30(4)(b), 8 I.L.M. at 691.

343. *Id.* art. 34, 8 I.L.M. at 693.

344. *Id.* art. 38, 8 I.L.M. at 695; *see also* RESTATEMENT (THIRD) OF THE FOREIGN RELATIONS LAW OF THE UNITED STATES, *supra* note 55, § 102, cmt. j (discussing treaty incorporation into customary law can bind non-signatories).

also a party to the Protocol bans its products made with CFCs (unless the Montreal Protocol has become customary law).

B. Application of International Law: Extrajurisdictional Actions

Because the GATT's article XX exceptions now only allow for jurisdictional actions, there is concern as to who has the jurisdictional ability to take actions to preserve the global commons. Under principles of international law, such as the Law of the Sea and the Law of Space, jurisdiction over the commons areas is *sui generis* to the international community; the international community has reserved jurisdiction over these commons areas.[345] Thus, actions taken pursuant to multilateral agreements to protect resources in the global commons should fall within article XX. The Tuna/Dolphin Panel Report recognized this principle in a very limited sense by allowing parties to act "jointly to address international environmental problems which can only be resolved through measures in conflict with the present rules of the General Agreement."[346]

Additionally, it may be argued under international law that unilateral trade actions not specifically provided for in an international agreement are permitted under article XX if they are necessary for the party to meet its general obligations under an international agreement.[347] For example, although the Law of the Sea III does not specifically authorize or provide for trade restrictions, if a party adopts a trade restriction to fulfill its obligations to preserve the sea, this trade restriction should not conflict with article XX's jurisdictional requirements.

C. Advancing the Discourse

Obviously, the foregoing analysis is not an adequate long-term solu-

345. *See, e.g.*, United Nations Convention on the Law of the Sea, Dec. 20, 1982, U.N. Doc.A/CONF 62/122, 21 I.L.M. 1261 (1982) (noting all rights to the sea are vested in mankind on whose behalf the international community acts) [hereinafter the Law of the Sea] (while the Law of the Sea has not been entered into force, it is accepted by most countries including the United States as customary international law, with the exception of Part XI governing the deep seabed); Treaty on Principles Governing the Activities of States in the Exploration and Use of Outer Space, Including the Moon and Other Celestial Bodies, Jan. 27, 1967, 18 U.S.T. 2410, 610 U.N.T.S. 205, arts. I-III (noting that states acting within outer space are subject to the principles of international law) [hereinafter Space Treaty]. This argument might also be more broadly phrased to provide that the international community not only has jurisdiction over the global commons, but also has jurisdiction over the global environment.

346. *See Tuna/Dolphin Panel Report*, *supra* note 13, at 50.

347. *See, e.g.*, Law of the Sea, *supra* note 345 (placing responsibilities for preserving and developing the high seas on the parties); Space Treaty, *supra* note 345, art. IX (placing responsibility on parties to conduct their activities in outer space so as to avoid "adverse changes to the environment of Earth").

tion. The law of treaties applies only after two treaties or other international agreements have come into conflict and so does not help in avoiding those conflicts in the first place. Moreover, it offers no mechanism for reconciling the legitimate goals of prior treaties with those conflicting treaties coming later in time. Finally, and perhaps most important, it leaves open the question of what to do in disputes where the States are not parties to both treaties or agreements.

Some individuals have called for a reexamination of various terms, assumptions, and principles relating to trade and the environment as a way of at least advancing the discourse, if not reconciling the two policy areas. A change in any of the following terms, assumptions, and principles would radically reshape views of trade and environment issues.

1. Internalization of Environmental Costs

Many of the options proposed to date to reduce or eliminate friction between trade and environmental concerns have focused on modifying the GATT to permit greater use of trade restrictions to force countries to internalize environmental costs. Any modification to the GATT must overcome considerable procedural and substantive obstacles.[348] United States' environmental laws however, increasingly are turning to environmental cost internalization for both foreign and domestic products. Unless changes are made to the GATT, these U.S. initiatives could precipitate additional conflicts.

a. *"Like Products"*

As noted earlier, GATT articles I, III, XI, and XX pose obstacles to using discriminatory tariffs and quantitative restrictions against other countries' PPMs that are perceived to be environmentally unsound.[349] These obstacles could be overcome by reinterpreting the concept of "like products" in the GATT to allow product standards based on PPMs. Environmentalists, who are in favor of allowing environmental PPMs, argue that the contemporary meaning of "product" includes the product's life cycle and thus that products with different PPMs are not "like products." For such a reinterpretation to occur, the GATT would have to be amended, or a side agreement or understanding to GATT adopted, setting out the extensive procedural and substantive requirements necessary to implement such a program.[350]

348. *See generally* Changing GATT Rules, *supra* note 7.
349. *See supra* notes 10-34, 42-61, and accompanying text.
350. *See generally* Changing GATT Rules, *supra* note 7.

b. *Countervailing Duties or Antidumping Duties*

The GATT in its current form does not view a party's application of lower standards of domestic environmental protections, allowing the party's industries to externalize their environmental costs, as a subsidy (or dumping when the product is exported). As a subsidy, it could be countervailed by another party whose industries are harmed by the subsidy (or dumping).[351] A number of options have been presented to modify or interpret GATT articles VI and XVI and the Subsidies Code to permit the imposition of countervailing duties or antidumping duties to counter such practices.[352] Quantifying the effect of differing environmental standards, however, could pose additional administrative problems beyond those already associated with countervailing and antidumping statutes.

2. "Necessary" Under GATT Article XX(b)

As noted earlier, GATT article XX(b) provides a general exception only to those trade measures that are *necessary* to protect human, animal or plant life or health. One way to permit greater use of trade restrictions to enforce internalization of environmental costs might be to give greater consideration to whether a trade restriction is proportional to its environmental benefit in determining whether it is "necessary" under article XX(b).[353] Many trade specialists argue that this approach represents a "slippery slope" that would likely spawn a flood of disguised protectionist measures.[354] At the very least, it would likely sharpen the debate over whether import restrictions based on "consumer preference" rather than "sound science" are ever legitimate. Environmentalists counter that requiring environmental protections to be justified as "necessary" places too high a burden on environmental actions and could diminish the ability of nations under the precautionary principle to act proactively in the face of scientific uncertainty.[355]

3. Harmonization of Standards

The GATT Standards Code clearly demonstrates that harmonizing standards is a very important goal of the GATT process. Negotiations in

351. *See supra* notes 34-35 and accompanying text; *see also* Komoroski, *supra* note 85.

352. *See* GATT Secretariat, Trade and the Environment, *supra* note 1, at 12; OECD, Joint Session, *supra* note 21, at 14.

353. *See* OECD, JOINT REPORT ON TRADE AND ENVIRONMENT 11 (June 1991).

354. *See* GATT Secretariat, Trade and the Environment, *supra* note 1, at 5.

355. *See* Eliza Patterson, *International Trade and the Environment: Institutional Solutions*, 21 E.L.R. 10,599, 10,602-03 (1991).

the Uruguay Round have also made harmonization a high priority, particularly with respect to phytosanitary and sanitary regulations and measures. As discussed above, the effects of harmonizing environmental standards on international trade and the environment largely will be determined by the manner in which harmonization occurs.[356]

If environmental standards are harmonized towards more stringent levels of protection it is possible that certain U.S. domestic laws might not meet these standards. This would require U.S. environmental protections to be strengthened. Should harmonization adopt international standards or a "least common denominator" approach, the United States would have to weaken many of its environmental laws, a path the U.S. Congress and state legislatures may find difficult and undesirable.

4. Procedure

a. *Dispute Resolution*

There have been a number of proposals for improving GATT's dispute resolution procedures, including expanding GATT dispute resolution panels to include experts from other disciplines such as environmental scientists and law scholars; creating a "cut-out" mechanism to move trade and environment disputes to an alternative forum for dispute resolution; and improving the ability of trade panels to take into account other areas of concern that relate to trade policy, such as the environment.[357] Expanding the membership of dispute resolution panels to include other disciplines could be achieved under the existing GATT framework and would provide input as to the non-trade effects of GATT decisions. Existing GATT rules, however, would bind these multidisciplinary panels in formulating decisions. Creating new procedures for dispute resolution that would allow GATT panels to take into account other areas of concern, such as the environment, could turn GATT's dispute resolution panels into international overcourts—a role their creators never envisioned for them and to which they consequently are not well-suited. Establishing a "cut-out" mechanism for environmental trade disputes would require an agreement of the parties and the creation of a new international tribunal—a difficult process, to say the least.

356. *See supra* notes 143-56, and accompanying text; *see generally* Charles Pearson & Robert Repetto, Reconciling Trade and Environment: The Next Steps (1991) (paper prepared for the Trade and Environment Committee of the EPA); Wallach, *supra* note 95.

357. *See generally* von Moltke, *supra* note 92; Patterson, *supra* note 355, at 10,600; STEWART HUDSON, TRADE, ENVIRONMENT AND THE PURSUIT OF SUSTAINABLE DEVELOPMENT 5-6 (1991).

b. *Transparency and Public Participation*

The relative secrecy and isolation in which GATT officials make decisions concerns many critics. They argue that the GATT decisionmaking process should be more open to the international public so that individuals and NGOs can participate in GATT decisionmaking by having timely access to GATT documents and decisions[358] and by presenting evidence and arguments to the GATT Council and to dispute resolution panels. Environmentalists view transparency and public participation as integral to the democratic process and to rational decisionmaking.[359] On the other hand, traditional GATT proponents argue with great force that nations have a significant interest in preserving world order through negotiated settlements of international disputes insulated from the influence of publicity. To provide for increased transparency and public participation, the Parties would have to either amend GATT or agree to a new understanding or side agreement.[360]

5. Trade Restrictions as a Tool for Enforcing Environmental Protections

Many policymakers see trade restrictions as a legitimate tool for enforcing international environmental agreements and even for pursuing unilateral environmental objectives. Free trade advocates, on the other hand, argue that trade restrictions are ill-suited as environmental protection devices.[361] They point out that imposing trade restrictions increases international tensions and skews the efficient allocation of resources just as failing to internalize environmental costs does.[362] Both, they argue, reduce overall welfare. They cannot see using one economic distortion to fight another. Moreover, they find no guarantee that imposing a trade restriction to force internalization of environmental costs will not have a greater distortive effect than the lack of cost internalization. Among the alternatives they suggest are using side payments and trade concessions to induce adherence to international environmental agreements.[363]

Environmental advocates respond that the effectiveness of environ-

---

358. *See* von Moltke, *supra* note 92, at 26.

359. *See* Hudson, *supra* note 357, at 5-6.

360. For a more complete discussion of the options for increasing transparency and public participation in GATT's decisionmaking see von Moltke, *supra* note 92.

361. GATT Secretariat, Trade and the Environment, *supra* note 1, at 16, 34 ("judged on the basis of economic efficency, there are almost no circumstances in which such a trade policy measure would be the 'first best' tool for dealing with such problems.")

362. *See* Pearson & Repetto, *supra* note 356, at 44-49.

363. *See* GATT Secretariat, Trade and the Environment, *supra* note 1, at 30-31.

mental restrictions is a highly complex question that usually is determined on a case-by-case basis and which does not lend itself well to generalizations. They note that relatively few methods are available to nations to influence the behavior of other nations and conclude that absent substantial changes to the central principles of the international law and the international order of nation-states, trade measures offer the most cost-effective means of securing compliance with international agreements.[364] Moreover, they note that compensation schemes requiring the international community to purchase protections effectively in all developing countries are not appropriate in every instance, and that relying too much on these schemes could prohibit environmental protections from developing effectively.

In an effort to reconcile the trade and environment perspectives, several proposals seek to provide frameworks for determining when trade restrictions are appropriate mechanisms for securing environmental objectives. These frameworks focus on delineating certain factors, such as how integral the trade measure is to the environmental protection and the proportionality of the trade measure to the environmental protection sought, to help make such determinations.[365]

Over the past twenty years, a number of alternative proposals that do not focus upon trade sanctions as the primary enforcement device have been advanced for the enforcement of environmental obligations. Perhaps the most ambitious of these proposals is creating an international environmental court, with all nations submitting to its jurisdiction.[366] A more recent proposal seeks to facilitate the ability of domestic and foreign parties to bring suit in domestic courts of all nations for violations of national and international environmental laws and obligations.[367] These proposals lack substantial backing within the international community, and so trade restrictions continue to be one of the more, if not the most, attractive mechanisms for enforcing environmental obligations.

364. *See* Shrybman, *supra* note 157, at 108.

365. *Id.*

366. *See generally* Amadeo Postiglione, *A More Efficient International Law on the Environment and Setting up an International Court for the Environment Within the United Nations*, 20 ENVT'L L. 321 (1990).

367. *See Gephardt Proposes Enforcement of Foreign Environmental Laws in U.S. Courts*, INSIDE U.S. TRADE, Sept. 13, 1991, at 3; Convention for the Protection of the Environment, Feb. 19, 1974, 1092 U.N.T.S. 279 (establishing equal access and remedy legal regime between Denmark, Finland, Norway and Sweden); Joel Gallob, *Birth of the North American Transboundary Environmental Plaintiff: Transboundary Pollution and the 1979 Draft Treaty for Equal Access and Remedy*, 15 HARV. ENVTL. L. REV. 85 (1991).

6. Mutually Reinforcing Market-Based Protections

Both the trade and environment communities embrace cost internalization through the "polluter pays" principle and through eliminating subsidies, particularly those that directly and negatively affect the environment. Allowing greater opportunity in the GATT for the parties to adopt such market-based measures and increasing the reliance on environmental policies that utilize market-based strategies may be the most immediate means to begin reconciling trade and environment concerns. Caution should be exercised, however, in placing too great a reliance upon market-based strategies.[368] Environmentalists stress that while market-based strategies are effective for addressing conventional environmental threats, markets are not effective in dealing with uncertainties, such as setting values for natural resources that do not have readily apparent economic uses; in dealing with the risk of irreversible losses that cannot be countered through the use of economic resources; or in setting the costs of unconventional threats whose real harms cannot be established scientifically with sufficent certainty.

Weighing the need for increased reliance upon market-based strategies against the limitations of such strategies, developing market-based strategies probably should be facilitated where they apply to conventional environmental threats, such as conventional nontoxic pollutants, and to the protection of species that are not threatened with extinction. Where, however, environmental protections apply to unconventional threats (such as the Montreal Protocol or the Basel Convention on Hazardous Wastes), to irreversible effects (such as CITES), or to resources that cannot be easily valued in economic terms (such as wetlands or species), other protections designed to protect against harms caused by market failures should complement market-based strategies.

While market-based strategies increasingly are being incorporated into domestic and international environmental law, full incorporation of these strategies in even conventional areas will require substantial change to United States environmental laws and to the frameworks of international agreements. Furthermore, for market-based environmental protections to be altogether compatible with the GATT, the GATT will have to be changed to provide the Parties with mechanisms to ensure environmental costs internalization.

---

368. *See generally* Joel Mintz, *Economic Reform of Environmental Protection: A Brief Comment on a Recent Debate*, 15 HARV. ENVT'L L.REV. 149, 156-60 (1991).

V. CONCLUSION

The rate of ozone layer loss is now believed to be occurring twice as fast as scientists estimated only a few years ago. It is estimated that every year over 50,000 species—over 140 per day—vanish from the face of the earth.[369] Over 17 million hectares of forests, an area equivalent to half the size of Finland, are lost each year.[370] Meanwhile, the world's population increases at a rate of approximately 92 million people per year—roughly the population of Mexico—with 88 million of these new inhabitants born into the developing world.[371] It is estimated that between 500 million and 1 billion people are under-nourished.[372]

As these figures demonstrate, the world is currently ill-equipped to suffer either environmental policies that diminish the economic resources necessary to meet the needs and aspirations of its burgeoning human population or trade policies that jeopardize the survival of the planet and its natural resources. Thus, the ongoing and largely polarized debate over whether trade policies should serve environmental goals or whether the environment protections must conform to the goals of free trade is woefully misguided. Both trade and the environment must be disciplined to serve the overarching goal of sustainable development.

Past efforts at free trade have paid little attention to the goal of sustainable development. Now free trade must become synonymous with "sustainable trade."[373] In principle, free trade seeks to address social concerns, such as environmental degradation, by applying expanded economic resources gained through increased and more efficient economic activity. But this is no longer sufficent. As World Bank economist Herman Daly has noted, "[F]urther growth beyond the present scale is overwhelmingly likely to increase costs more rapidly than it increases benefits, thus ushering in a new era of 'uneconomic growth' that impoverishes rather than enriches."[374] Any growth, including growth from trade, that is not sustainable must be rejected.

While environmentalists have only recently begun to study trade law and policy, they are mastering the subject and offering constructive

369. *See* Sandra Postel, *Denial in the Decisive Decade*, *in* LESTER BROWN, STATE OF THE WORLD 1992, at 3 (1991).

370. *Id.*

371. *Id.*

372. *Id.* at 4.

373. Sustainable trade, as a sub-part of sustainable development, is trade and trade policies that meet the needs of the current generation without jeopardizing the resource base for future generations.

374. DALY & COBB, *supra* note 5, at 2.

suggestions for moving trade into the parameters of sustainable development. If the experience in the U.S. is any example, however, many in the trade community are resisting the need to learn environmental economics, policy, and law. Yet until the trade community makes the effort to understand environmental imperatives and until they embrace sustainable development, trade and the environment will remain at odds and the world will suffer for it.

[9]

WORLD TRADE RULES AND ENVIRONMENTAL POLICIES: CONGRUENCE OR CONFLICT?

JOHN H. JACKSON*

TABLE OF CONTENTS

ANNEXES:

INTRODUCTION[1]

Proposition 1: Protection of the environment has become exceedingly important, and promises to be more important for the benefit of future generations. Protecting the environment involves rules of international co-

---

* Hessel E. Yntema Professor of Law, University of Michigan.

1. In connection with the subject of this paper, readers may want to examine the following other works by this same author. *See* JOHN H. JACKSON, RESTRUCTURING THE GATT SYSTEM (1990) [hereinafter JACKSON, RESTRUCTURING GATT]; JOHN H. JACKSON, WORLD TRADE AND GATT (1969) [hereinafter JACKSON, WORLD TRADE AND GATT]; JOHN H. JACKSON, THE WORLD TRADING SYSTEM: LAW AND POLICY OF INTERNATIONAL ECONOMIC RELATIONS (1989) [hereinafter JACKSON, WORLD TRADING SYSTEM]; JOHN H. JACKSON & WILLIAM J. DAVEY, LEGAL PROBLEMS OF INTERNATIONAL ECONOMIC RELATIONS (2d ed. 1986); JOHN H. JACKSON ET AL., IMPLEMENTING THE TOKYO ROUND: NATIONAL CONSTITUTIONS AND INTERNATIONAL ECONOMIC RULES (1984) [hereinafter JACKSON ET AL., IMPLEMENTING THE TOKYO ROUND].

operation, sanction, or both, so that some government actions to enhance environmental protection will not be undermined by the actions of other governments. Sometimes such rules involve trade restricting measures.

Proposition 2: Trade liberalization is important for enhancing world economic welfare and for providing a greater opportunity for billions of individuals to lead satisfying lives. Measures that restrict trade often will decrease the achievement of this goal.

These two propositions state the opposing policy objectives that currently pose important and difficult dilemmas for governments. This type of "policy discord" is not unique; there are many similar policy discords, at both the national and the international levels, that governments must confront.[2] Indeed, there is some evidence that environmental policy and trade policy are complementary, at least in the sense that increasing world welfare can lead to citizen demands and governmental actions to improve protection for the environment. The poorest nations in the world cannot afford such protection, but as welfare increases protection becomes more affordable.[3]

An unfortunate development in public and interest group attention to trade and the environment is the appearance of hostility between proponents of the two different propositions stated above. The hostility is misplaced because both groups will need the assistance and cooperation of the other group in order to accomplish their respective policy objectives. Of course, some of this tension is typical of political systems. Political participants often seek to achieve opposing objectives and goals. Each side may endorse legitimate goals, but when the goals clash, accommodation is necessary.

To some extent, the conflicts between the trade liberalization proponents and the environmental protection proponents derive from a certain "difference in cultures" between the trade policy experts and the environmental policy experts. Oddly enough, even when operating within the framework of the same society, these different "policy cultures" have developed different attitudes and perceptions of the political and policy processes, and these different outlooks create misunderstandings and conflict between the groups.[4]

These problems are part of a broader trend of international economic relations that is posing a number of perplexing and troublesome situations for statesmen and policy leaders. Part of the difficulty inevitably results from the growth of international economic interdependence.[5] Such interde-

---

2. An example of policy discord is the conflicting goals of providing adequate medical coverage while minimizing budget expenditures.

3. Gene M. Grossman & Alan B. Krueger, *Environmental Impacts of a North American Free Trade Agreement*, 158 DISCUSSION PAPERS ECON. (Woodrow Wilson School of Public and International Affairs, Princeton, N.J.), Nov. 1991.

4. The "culture of difference" is well described in Robert W. Jerome, *Traders and Environmentalists*, J. COM., Dec. 27, 1991, at 4A.

5. *See* JACKSON, WORLD TRADING SYSTEM, *supra* note 1, at 2; John H. Jackson, *Transnational Enterprises & International Codes of Conduct: Introductory Remarks for Experts*, Address Before International Bar Association Meeting in Berlin (Aug. 27, 1980), *in Law Quadrangle Notes* 19, 19-24.

pendence increases trade in both products and services across national borders and brings many benefits to participating countries. International interdependence also results in efficiencies and economies of scale that can raise world welfare (but not necessarily *everyone's* welfare, because some groups will be required to adjust in the face of increased competition).[6] This trend towards increased international economic interdependence requires a different sort of attitude towards government regulation. Within a nation, government regulations in such areas as consumer protection, competition policy, prudential measures (of banking and financial institutions), health and welfare (for example, alcohol and abortion control), and human rights (for example, prohibiting discrimination), are all designed by governments to promote worthy policies that sometimes clash with market oriented economic policies. When economic interdependence moves a number of these issues to the international scene, they become (at least in today's defective international system) much more difficult to manage. The circumstances and the broader scope of the international system create in many contexts (not just those concerning environmental policies) a series of problems and questions including:

— General questions of effectiveness of national "sovereignty" in the face of a need to cooperate with other countries to avoid some aspects of the "prisoners dilemma"[7] or "free rider"[8] problems. Unless there is cooperation, individual countries can profit from the efforts of other countries without contributing to those efforts, but in the longer run all may suffer;

— Perplexing questions of how new international rules should be made, questions that often involve voting procedures;

— General questions of the appropriateness and degree to which national sovereignty will submit to international dispute settlement procedures to resolve differences on various policy matters;

— Problems of a single national sovereign using the extraterritorial

---

6. *See, e.g.*, PETER B. KENEN, THE INTERNATIONAL ECONOMY 167-92 (1985).

7. "Prisoners dilemma" refers to the hypothetical economic paradigm where two persons have partially opposing goals and might achieve a better result from cooperation than competition. The example often used is two prisoners being interrogated separately by a police official who is offering each one some advantage in return for confessing to a joint crime, or for giving information about the other's involvement in the crime. If the two cooperate and refuse to give any information, it is suggested that they may be in a better situation than if each tells on the other. In economic terms, countries, firms, or individuals could pursue competitive policies which, when pursued by everyone, cause aggregate damage to all (for example, competitive subsidization). The question then arises what would be the case if they cooperate so as to prevent the incentive to compete against each other with damaging policies.

8. "Free rider" refers to the situation where a group of countries agree to some discipline such as a restraint on using certain trade barriers. Under Most-Favored-Nation (MFN) they may be required to give the advantages of that discipline to other countries including countries that have not entered the specific agreement. Consequently, those countries that have not joined the agreement enjoy a benefit without submitting themselves to the discipline and are "free riders."

reach of its regulation (sometimes termed unilateralism) to impose its will on the actions of other nations, or the citizens of other nations;

— Significant legitimate differences of view between nations as to economic structure, level of economic development, forms of government, appropriate role of government in economic activities, etc. Developing countries, for example, will have different views than on many "trade-off" matters, with developing countries generally arguing that environmental regulations unfairly restrain their economic development. They note that rich countries have benefitted from decades or centuries of freedom from environmental protection rules, and that even today the rich countries are responsible for most of the world's pollution. Furthermore, poor countries argue that the imposition of environmental regulations threatens their economies with stagnation and populations with starvation.

All these circumstances and arguments occur in the context of a relatively chaotic and unstructured international system, which in many ways has not evolved adequately to keep up with the implications of growing international economic interdependence. This paper will probe the more specific issues of the relationship of international trade policy rules to environmental policies and rules,[9] primarily in the context of the General Agreement on Tariffs and Trade (GATT)[10] (which is the most important set of international trade policy rules). This will be done in the eight parts. Part I surveys the policies and certain rules of the GATT system and is followed by five parts that discuss areas of conflict between GATT policies and environmental policies. Part VII discusses institutional and dispute settlement issues and Part VIII draws conclusions about the relationship between trade policies and environmental policies.

The term "environmental policies" is defined very broadly for purposes of this paper. It includes, for example, measures relating to health or health risks. The phrases "trade policies" and "trade liberalization" also are defined broadly to include not only trade in goods, but also trade in services.

I. Objectives of Trade Rules and Relation to Environmental Policy

The most significant and widespread rule system for international trade is the GATT system, which includes the GATT and over 200 ancillary

9. The literature and documents discussing environmental policy are so voluminous and numerous that it is pointless to cite very much. Obviously the drafts for "Agenda 21" for the Rio June 1992 conference are an important expression of environmental policies, as are the 27 "Principles" set forth in a document for "Agenda item 9." The rather high generality of these expressions leave many questions open for further analytical works on detail.

10. General Agreement on Tariffs and Trade, Oct. 30, 1947, 61 Stat. All, 55 U.N.T.S. 187 [hereinafter GATT].

treaties, as well as a number of other related arrangements and decisions. The GATT may soon be modified by the Uruguay Round,[11] so this paper will refer to the GATT/MTO system as broadly embracing the system as it is now and as it may emerge within a year or two. Of course, a number of other treaties or arrangements, such as regional blocs like the proposed North American Free Trade Agreement (NAFTA),[12] are relevant to this discussion of "trade-environment policy discord," but most of the essential principles of the discord can be discussed in the context of GATT. Consequently, this paper will focus on the GATT/MTO rules and policies as worthy generic examples of problems that also occur in other contexts.

The basic policy underlying the GATT (and the broader "Bretton Woods System" established in 1944-1948) is well known.[13] The objective is to liberalize trade that crosses national boundaries, and to pursue the benefits described in economic theory as "comparative advantage." The notion of comparative advantage relates partly to the theories of economies of scale. When nations specialize, they become more efficient in producing a product (and possibly also a service). If they can trade their products or services for the different products or services that other countries specialize in producing, then all parties involved will be better off because countries will not waste resources producing products that other countries can produce more efficiently. The international rules are designed to restrain governmental interference with this type of trade.

There are exceptions to the general policy of liberalizing trade, one of which arises from the problem of "externalities," a concept that is closely associated with environmental protection. If a producer pollutes a stream during its manufacturing process, and there are no laws prohibiting such pollution, then it has imposed an "externality cost" on the world. The externality cost is the difference between the values of the unpolluted stream and the polluted stream. Because there is no law against polluting the stream, the cost is not recouped from the producer or passed on to the consumers of the product. This concept appears to be one of the most important core dilemmas or policy problems of the relationship between trade and environmental policies. Thus, much of the relationship is concerned with how environmental protection costs can be "internalized," to follow what is sometimes termed the "polluter pays principle."

The problem often boils down to the need to provide certain kinds of governmental rules or incentives that in certain ways either clash with the

---

11. Draft Final Act Embodying the Results of the Uruguay Round of Multilateral Trade Negotiations, GATT Doc. MTN.TNC/W/FA (Dec. 20, 1991) [hereinafter Dunkel Draft]. An Agreement Establishing the Multilateral Trade Organization (MTO) is proposed in a Draft Charter in the Dunkel Draft, Annex IV. *See* Dunkel Draft, *supra*, at 91-101.

12. North America Free Trade Agreement, Sept. 6, 1992, U.S.-Can.-Mex., *available in* LEXIS, GENFED-EXTRA Database; WL, NAFTA Database (awaiting ratification as this article went to press).

13. *See* Jackson, World Trade and GATT, *supra* note 1; Jackson, World Trading System, *supra* note 1.

basic trade liberalization rules, or that alter them significantly. As soon as this occurs, however, there is a risk of undermining the GATT liberalization policies and rules. It is this "policy discord" that raises the difficult question of how to accommodate the competing values of trade liberalization on the one hand, and environmental protection on the other hand, without undermining the basic principles of both policy sets.

The GATT trade liberalization policies that have been deemed fundamental for almost one-half of a century include:

— Tariff reduction: Originally the basic goal of the GATT was to reduce tariffs. In this respect the GATT has been most successful (particularly with respect to tariffs on industrial products imported into industrial nations).[14] Indeed, in the last several years this goal has had a profound influence on a number of countries that are not industrialized.[15] (GATT Article II).

— National treatment: The national treatment rule requires that nations, when applying their domestic taxes and regulations, treat imports no less favorably than they treat their domestically produced goods (and services). (GATT Article III).

— Most-Favored-Nation (MFN): Nations are required to treat other nation participants in the system (GATT members) equally with respect to imports (or exports). Thus, under the GATT rules a nation cannot discriminate (with some exceptions) between bicycle imports from Japan and bicycle imports from Italy. (Article I).

— Non-Tariff Barriers: As the decades of GATT history passed, it became increasingly clear that tariffs were no longer the major problem of trade barriers. Instead, so-called "non-tariff barriers (NTBs)" became much more important, and were addressed systematically for the first time in the Tokyo Round of the 1970s which produced a series of "codes" (special side treaties or agreements) that attempted to address some of the key NTB issues.[16] In the current Uruguay Round Negotiation, this process is being extended even further, and of course new issues involving intellectual property and trade in services are being added (with considerable complexity).[17] NTBs are very numerous, and new trade restriction and distortion techniques are constantly arising.[18]

Arguably the current GATT system is not capable of handling the trade liberalization problems of the forthcoming decades, and improvement will be necessary. One major emerging problem is the effect of differences in economic structures and cultures. Issues formerly thought to be well within

14. JACKSON, WORLD TRADING SYSTEM, *supra* note 1, at 115-31.

15. *See, e.g.*, Richard E. Feinberg, *Latin America: Back on the Screen*, INT'L ECON. INSIGHTS, July-Aug. 1992, at 2, 2-6.

16. JACKSON ET AL., IMPLEMENTING THE TOKYO ROUND, *supra* note 1.

17. Dunkel Draft, *supra* note 11.

18. JACKSON, WORLD TRADING SYSTEM, *supra* note 1, at 130.

the exclusive terrain of national sovereignties, such as exchange rates and taxing policies, now must be examined for their impact on trade liberalization or barriers.

The GATT has established a new program to systematically look at governmental trade policies, called the Trade Policy Review Mechanism (TPRM).[19] In addition, the United States and Japan have bilaterally entered into a discussion process called Structural Impediments Initiative (SII)[20] that has probed very deeply into the two different societies and the systemic problems that affect trade flows between them. (SII could very well be generalized gradually to include other groups of countries, and ultimately become part of the GATT TPRM). These procedures are part of a trend for the future, and while environmental discussions could become a part of these procedures, further evolution will be needed.

Several recent important studies have tried to inventory some of the particular GATT system rules and clauses that have implications for environmental policy. Rather than repeat those inventories here, I refer to them in the footnotes,[21] and include some text in an Annex.[22] Needless to say, this area is very complex and important work needs to be done on understanding the particular relationship between a number of the GATT/MTO system rules on the one hand, and the environmental policies on the other hand.

A few "hypothetical" cases will demonstrate some of the possible policy clashes. In the cases below I use the initials "ENV" to indicate the environmentally "correct" country that imports (or exports), and the initials "EXP" to indicate the exporting country, and "IMP" to indicate an importing country.

— ENV establishes a rule that requires a special deposit or tax on packaging which is not biodegradable, arguing that such packages are a danger for the environment. It so happens that ENV producers use a different package that is not so taxed. Only the packages from EXP are effected. (In some cases it can be established that the tax imposed is in excess of that needed for the environmental protection.)

— ENV establishes a rule that requires any business firm which sells a product in the ENV market to establish a center that will

19. *See* GATT Doc. Series C/RM/. . ., and recent reports such as GATT Doc. C/RM/S/26A&B (June 12, 1992) (regarding Uruguay) and GATT Doc. C/RM/S/23A&B (Nov. 7, 1991) (regarding United States).

20. Mitsuo Matsushita, *The Structural Impediments Initiative: An Example of Bilateral Trade Negotiations*, 12 MICH. J. INT'L L. 436 (1991).

21. GENERAL AGREEMENT ON TARIFFS AND TRADE, INTERNATIONAL TRADE 90-91, at 19-39 (1992) [hereinafter GATT REPORT 90-91]; U.S. CONGRESS OFFICE OF TECHNOLOGY ASSESSMENT, TRADE AND ENVIRONMENT: CONFLICTS AND OPPORTUNITIES (1992) [hereinafter OTA REPORT]; Robert F. Housman & Durwood J. Zaelke, *Trade, Environment, and Sustainable Development: A Primer*, 15 HASTINGS INT'L & COMP. L. REV. 535 (1992).

22. See Annex A, which includes the text of some of the relevant GATT provisions.

recycle, or appropriately dispose of the product when the ENV consumer is finished with the product's useful life. Such centers are relatively easy for domestic producers to establish, but much more difficult for importers (or exporters in EXP), and particularly difficult for EXP sellers of small quantities (which is often the case for new market entrants) to establish.

— ENV establishes a subsidy for machinery purchased and used by domestic producers to assist in environmental protection (such as smoke stack cleaners). The subsidy could be in the form of special income tax depreciation deductions. When products from plants benefitting from the subsidy are exported, foreign countries such as IMP apply a countervailing duty to the exports to offset the benefits of the "subsidy."

— ENV establishes a border tax (countervailing duty) on any electronics product that is imported from a country that does not have an environmental rule required by ENV. ENV argues that the lack of such a rule is in effect a "subsidy" when measured by economic principles of internalization and "polluter pays," and that the subsidy should be off-set by a countervailing duty. EXP argues that while its own method of pollution control is different, it is fully adequate and more efficient than ENV's and is also cheaper. Consequently, EXP argues either that its products should not incur the clean up duty or that its environment can better withstand pollution activity.

— ENV prohibits the importation of tropical hardwoods on the ground that imports of tropical hardwood products tend to induce deforestation in important tropical forest areas, and that such deforestation damages the world environment. ENV is a temperate zone nation with temperate forests, but does not apply any rule against temperate forest products, domestic or imported.

— ENV has an important fishing fleet that captures salmon and herring. It also has an important fish processing industry. ENV establishes a rule against the exportation of the unprocessed salmon or herring caught within its territorial and protected zone area, arguing that landing those fish at its ports is necessary for an appropriate count of the fish supply. This count is needed for economic and environmental models designed to assist regulators in limiting the catch and promoting the growth of the fish supply. Local ENV fish processing plants enjoy the benefit of avoiding competition for purchase of the fish by foreign processors in IMP.

— ENV prohibits the sale of domestic or imported vegetables that have been genetically engineered to achieve certain characteristics, such as longer shelf life and better color. Its domestic industry does not use these genetically engineered plants, while certain foreign countries do. The foreign countries wish to export to ENV, arguing that the genetically engineered products are equal in every respect, and better in some respects, to the safety and other characteristics of products that are not so engineered.

— IMP establishes a rule against the importation of products from any producer in a foreign country that utilizes women in its factory. IMP argues that it is culturally offensive to its domestic producers to utilize women in their factories. Furthermore, because IMP prohibits the employment of women in factories, it feels obliged to prohibit the importation of goods that were produced from female labor.

A number of different trade policy problems are posed by the examples above and some of these will be discussed further under specific parts below. As a logical exercise one can use an unrealistic hypothetical to illustrate the conflict between trade policy and environmental policy. Imagine a country, ENV, establishing a rule that prohibits the importation of products from "any country that pollutes." Presumably that would cause virtually all trade to cease, totally undermining the GATT/MTO policies of liberalization. Although the example is extreme, one thing seems reasonably clear: The GATT/MTO system, and its policy and government specialists, need to change so as to better accommodate environmental policies. All too often during the past decade, it has appeared that the trade policy specialists have feared the incursion of the environmental policies on their terrain (partly because the environmental policies can be so easily used as an excuse for protectionism), and this fear has led to a certain attitude of "fending off," or other "lack of friendliness" towards environmental policies. Likewise, there has been a certain "unfriendliness" on the part of some of the environmental policy experts towards trade policies, reflected in large newspaper advertisements and "anti-GATT-zilla" posters![23]

The purpose of this paper is to probe the differences between the two policy sets, and to identify ways in which some of those differences can be narrowed. It is not possible to cover all of the problems that are involved in this clash, so I will focus on a selected number of key legal and institutional issues: particularly the problem of national treatment and its relation to product standards (Part II); the problem of the general exceptions in GATT Article XX (Part III); the related problem of the "process-product" characteristics that have been involved in the tuna/dolphin case, and concern with what is sometimes called the global commons (Part IV); the intricate and elaborate problem of subsidies (Part V); the subject of "competitiveness" (Part VI); and finally, a certain group of institutional problems related to the GATT/MTO system, including dispute settlement, transparency, and jurisprudence (Part VII).

II. National Treatment and Product Standards

One of the core principles of the GATT/MTO system of trade liberalization is the rule known as "national treatment," found in GATT Article

23. *See SABOTAGE! of America's Health, Food Safety and Environmental Laws*, N.Y. Times (Midwest ed.), Apr. 20, 1992, at B5; *see also* Nancy Dunne, *Fears Over "GATT-Zilla the Trade Monster,"* Fin. Times, Jan. 30, 1992, at 3.

III. The national treatment clause can be traced far back into treaties of centuries ago, and is applied to a number of different governmental activities.[24] For purposes of a variety of governmental actions, it obligates a government to treat foreign products or persons the same as it treats its domestic products or persons. Before World War II, the national treatment clause was perhaps most commonly found in the Treaties of Friendship Commerce and Navigation (FCN Treaties), and in that context called for nondiscriminatory treatment by treaty parties with respect to citizens or firms of the other party to a treaty, operating within the territory of a treaty party. This principle has been applied extensively to issues of arrest and criminal process, and human rights.

In traditional international law practice there were two possible dimensions of national treatment. On the one hand, national treatment was deemed to be a rule of "nondiscrimination," requiring a government to treat aliens in a manner no less favorable than it treats its own citizens. However, under that approach, if its treatment of its own citizens was very bad (for example arbitrary arrest, or very poor jail conditions) similar treatment of foreigners would comply with the clause. Thus, there developed a second aspect of national treatment under phraseology and customary practice of certain treaty clauses that requires a certain minimum standard of treatment.

In general, the GATT national treatment clause (expressed in ten paragraphs of Article III, with certain exceptions built in) opted primarily for the nondiscrimination standard.[25] Thus it has been said that while GATT requires a nation to tax and regulate imports from other GATT parties in a manner no less favorable than it treats its domestic product, if a government imposed a regulation on its domestic product that is utterly foolish, it could also impose such a regulation on imported products. The government, for example, could prohibit the sale of both domestic and imported shampoo when the container showed a picture of a blond woman. Likewise, it could arguably prohibit the sale of domestic and imported products if the label contained any words in a language other than that of the importing country. Thus, the latter regulation often requires specialized labels on imports.

The GATT, however, does contain some language in paragraph 1 of Article III which states that regulations and taxes shall not be imposed in a way "so as to afford protection" against import competition. Thus, GATT contains some element of minimum standard that is related to principles of liberal trade. This type of minimum standard has resulted in an interpretation of Article III that prohibits government regulation even when it appears "on its face" to be nondiscriminatory, if in fact it is "de

24. *See* JACKSON, WORLD TRADE AND GATT, *supra* note 1, at 273-303; JACKSON & DAVEY, *supra* note 1, at 266, 483-537.

25. *See* GATT, *supra* note 10, art. III, 61 Stat. at A18, 55 U.N.T.S. at 204; *see also* sources cited *supra* note 23.

facto" discriminatory. An important case in United States jurisprudence of some decades ago struggled with this concept[26] and GATT panel cases and other discussions have made references to the problem of government regulation that affords effective protection, even though on its face it appears neutral.[27]

One example of a de facto discriminatory regulation would be a regulation that imposed a higher tax on automobiles with greater horse power and speed, when the importing country knew that its own automobile production tended to concentrate heavily in automobiles with lesser horse power and speed. Likewise, a less favorable tax treatment for automobiles priced in excess of a certain amount of money, say $25,000, in circumstances where domestic production tended not to produce such higher priced autos while imports tended to concentrate in them, could be suspect. Clearly there are some difficult issues in these circumstances, particularly because governments may have a legitimate regulatory interest in classifying goods in certain ways, for example, taxing luxury goods more heavily than daily staples. Thus, there are some delicate decisions that have to be made in interpreting the GATT Article III.

Similar issues of interpretation arise in a number of "environmental" type cases. For example, an Ontario regulation[28] imposing a higher tax on the sale of beverages in aluminum containers than on other types of containers is arguably designed to help environmental matters. On the other hand, when it is discovered that very few Ontario-made beverages are sold in aluminum cans, while imports from the United States are very frequently sold in those containers, the regulation becomes suspect as a "de facto discrimination." The key issue then becomes one of determining who should decide whether the regulation is appropriate.

Even if a regulation is both *facially* nondiscriminatory and also *de facto* nondiscriminatory, some important issues about a "minimum standard" arise. The Beef Hormone Case, a current significant case between the United States and the European Community (EC) raised this issue.[29] In that case the EC had prohibited the sale of beef that had been grown with the assistance of artificial hormone infusions. The United States argued that it applied hormones by a method that was totally safe for human ingestion, and that the EC had no scientific basis for its regulation, which incidentally happened to hurt U.S. exports of beef products to the EC. The EC replied that it had no obligation to provide a scientific justification for its regulation.

---

26. JACKSON & DAVEY, *supra* note 1, at 496; *see Report of the GATT Panel, United States—Section 337 of the Tariff Act of 1930*, para. 3.18, GATT Doc. L/6439 (Nov. 7, 1989), BASIC INSTRUMENTS AND SELECTED DOCUMENTS [hereinafter BISD] 36th Supp. 345, 360 [hereinafter *Section 337 Panel Report*].

27. JACKSON & DAVEY, *supra* note 1, at 483-537; *Report of the GATT Panel, United States—Alcoholic Beverages*, GATT Doc. DS23/R (Mar. 16, 1992).

28. *See, e.g.*, *Beer Blast*, WALL ST. J., Aug. 4, 1992, at A14.

29. *See* Janice Castro, *Why the Beef Over Hormones*, TIME, Jan. 16, 1989, at 44.

This dispute has festered. The United States pointed to a clause in the Tokyo Round Standards Code[30] that might have given some opportunity to require scientific justification for a product regulation. However, negotiators in the Uruguay Round have developed a draft phyto-sanitary text designed to provide some minimum standards for government regulation requiring "scientific principles" as justification.[31] This draft text has raised some serious concerns on the part of environmental policy experts in the United States and elsewhere. The experts worry that this text would inhibit national governments, or sub-federal governmental units, from determining the appropriateness of a regulation that went beyond some minimum international standard. The language of the text itself does not seem to call for this, but the implication is that there will be an opportunity for exporting countries to challenge regulations of importing countries and to require importing countries to justify their regulations on the basis of "sound science." This raises substantial fears that GATT panels will tend to rule against regulations that go beyond a lowest common denominator of national environmental regulations in the GATT/MTN system.[32] This concern pushes the discourse into the question of institutions.

In summary, the GATT relatively easily accommodates national government environmental regulations that concern the characteristics of imported products. Thus, if a nation wishes to prohibit the sale of domestic and imported croissants which have a high cholesterol content, presumably this would be consistent with the GATT obligations of Article III. Under the Tokyo Round Standards Code and the Uruguay Round phyto-sanitary draft text approach there might be some opportunity to challenge the regulation. Nevertheless, it would seem that the national treatment standard would not be a major impediment or a major conceptual problem for environmental regulation, unless a requirement of scientific justification was interpreted to require such a high degree of justification as to unreasonably inhibit governments from imposing environmental standards. To ensure against that, it might be useful to have some interpretive notes for the Uruguay Round text.[33]

---

30. *Agreement on Technical Barriers to Trade*, GATT Doc. L/4812 (Nov. 12, 1979), BISD 26th Supp. 8, 8. Article 2, paragraph 2.1 states that "[p]arties shall ensure that technical regulations and standards are not prepared, adopted or applied with a view to creating obstacles to international trade." *Id.* para. 2.1, at 9. The Agreement also provides "technical expert groups" to assist dispute settlement panels. *Id.* annex 2, at 31.

31. Dunkel Draft, *supra* note 11. *See* Text on Agriculture, Part C, which at paragraph 6 reads: "Contracting parties shall ensure that sanitary and phyto-sanitary measures are applied only to the extent necessary to protect human, animal or plant life or health, are based on scientific principles and are not maintained against available scientific evidence." *Id.* § L, para. 6, at L.36.

32. *See* Stewart Hudson, *Trade, Environment, and the Pursuit of Sustainable Development*, Paper Prepared for World Bank Symposium on International Trade and Environment, Washington, D.C. (Nov. 1991) (transcript available from author). Stewart Hudson is with the National Wildlife Federation, Washington, D.C.

33. Some text in the October 7, 1992 NAFTA draft is interesting in connection with the

The minimum standard scientific justification approach can be very significant for the future of trade rules in the GATT/MTN system. For certain interests within a large country like the United States to argue that there should never be an international "second guess" (such as a tribunal process) of any national regulations in the environmental, or other area, could prevent important international cooperative measures to allow the trading system to evolve in a way to meet the new challenge. But there are some legitimate concerns on the part of the environmental policy advocates, and further work needs to be taken in the GATT/MTO context, some of which will extend over the next decade, to address those concerns. Briefly, the major concerns include:

1) The question of how difficult it will be to justify national or sub-federal governmental unit regulations on environmental matters, in the context of international dispute settlement processes and a new treaty text that requires certain minimum standards of scientific justification for such regulations;
2) The amount of latitude that will be granted to nation-states to impose environmental regulations that require higher standards than some international minimum.

III. General Exceptions in Article XX: Health & Conservation

The GATT contains an Article XX entitled "General Exceptions" which includes important provisions that override other obligations of the GATT, under certain circumstances defined in the Article. Again it is not practical or appropriate in this paper to deal with all of Article XX, but there are certain key measures that should be addressed. Quite often, concern for environmental matters focuses on paragraphs (b) and (g) of Article XX:[34] (See Annex A).

> (b) necessary to protect human, animal or plant life or health
> . . .
> (g) relating to the conservation of exhaustible natural resources if such measures are made effective in conjunction with restrictions on domestic production or consumption . . .

The exceptions of Article XX are subject to some important qualifications in the opening paragraph of Article XX, however, which reads as follows:

> Subject to the requirement that such measures are not applied in a manner which would constitute a means of arbitrary or unjustifiable

---

burdens of scientific proof. For example, articles 904(3), 905(3), and 907, which are quoted in Annex C. The language specifies a right of governments to use a "higher level of protection" for the environmental international standards.

34. GATT, *supra* note 10, art. XX, 61 Stat. at 1460, 55 U.N.T.S. at 262; *see* Jackson & Davey, *supra* note 1, at 514 (Doc. Supp. 1989); OTA Report, *supra* note 21, at 32.

discrimination between countries where the same conditions prevail, or a disguised restriction on international trade, nothing in this Agreement shall be construed to prevent the adoption or enforcement by any contracting party of measures.

To a large degree, these provisions provide a softened measure of "national treatment," and MFN obligations. They require governments that take measures which arguably qualify for the exceptions of Article XX to do so in such a way as to minimize the impacts mentioned in the opening paragraph. This has led some panel reports to interpret Article XX[35] to require nations to use the "least restrictive alternative" reasonably available to it as measures designed to support the goals of the exceptions of Article XX.

There are a number of important interpretive problems with respect to Article XX, and some of them are key to the environmental-trade liberalization clash. Two interpretive questions in particular stand out, namely the interpretation of the word "necessary," and the question of *whose health*, or *which exhaustible natural resources* can be the object of an acceptable national government regulation.

The word "necessary" clearly needs interpretive attention. It is partly interpreted by the "least restrictive alternative" jurisprudence mentioned above. Thus, if there are two or more alternatives that a government could use to protect human life or health, it is not "necessary" to choose the one that places more restrictions on trade, when an alternative that is equally efficient in protecting human life or health exists. This will obviously impose some restraint on the latitude that nations, or sub-federal governments have to impose regulations for environmental purposes.[36] On the other hand, it is considered important to prevent Article XX from becoming a large loop hole that governments can use to justify almost any measures that are motivated by protectionist considerations. It is this slippery slope problem that worries many in connection with Article XX. The problem arises in a number of cases, including the packaging and fish examples that were discussed in the introduction.

The other interpretive problem is conceptually more difficult. When GATT Article XX provides an exception for measures necessary to protect human, animal or plant life or health, should it be interpreted to mean only the life or health of humans within the importing country, or extend to the life or health of humans throughout the world? This interpretive problem is intimately related to the process-product characteristic difficulty. As far as this author can determine, Article XX has not been interpreted

---

35. *Section 337 Panel Report*, *supra* note 26, para. 5.26, BISD 36th Supp. at 393; General Agreement on Tariffs and Trade: Disupe Settlement Panel Report on Thai Restrictions on Importation of and Internal Taxes on Cigarettes, 30 I.L.M. 1122 (1991).

36. General Agreement on Tariffs and Trade: Dispute Settlement Panel Report on United States Restrictions on Imports of Tuna, 30 I.L.M. 1594 (1991) [hereinafter Tuna/Dolphin Panel Report].

to allow a government to impose regulations to protect the life or health of humans, animals, or plants that exist outside of the government's own territorial borders. This problem was addressed, although somewhat ambiguously, in the tuna/dolphin case.[37] The problem is that of the typical slippery slope danger, combined with the concern that powerful and wealthy countries will impose their own views regarding environmental or other social or welfare standards on other parts of the world, even where such views may not be entirely appropriate. The term "eco-imperialism" has been coined for this problem.[38]

If a nation can prohibit the importation of goods from a poor third world country where the method of production is moderately dangerous to humans, why would a nation not also be able to prohibit the importation of goods produced in an environment that differs in many social or cultural attributes from its own society? Why should one country be able to use its trade laws to depart from the general liberal trade rules of the GATT/MTO system, to enforce its own view of how plant or animal life in the oceans (beyond territorial sea, or other jurisdictional limits), or to protect the ozone layer (as suggested in the tropical hardwoods hypothetical case)?

Other countries may have a somewhat different view of the trade-off between economic and welfare values of production, and human life or health. Even in the industrial countries, there is tolerance of certain kinds of economic activity that almost inevitably will result in human deaths or injuries, an example being major construction projects for dams or bridges. These are tough issues, and ones that will require a lot of close and careful attention, presumably in the context not only of new rule making or treaty drafting, but also in the processes of interpretation through the dispute settlement mechanisms. Thus, once again, institutional questions become significant.

It has been argued by one author[39] that the drafting history of the GATT would lead to an interpretation of Article XX that would permit governments to take a variety of environmental measures and justify them under the general exceptions of GATT. While this view is interesting, and the research is apparently thorough, it is not entirely persuasive and overlooks important issues of treaty interpretation. Under typical international law, elaborated by the Vienna Convention on the Law of Treaties,[40] preparatory work history is an ancillary means of interpreting treaties. In the

37. *Id.*

38. Gijs M. DeVries, *How to Banish Eco-Imperialism*, J. COM., Apr. 30, 1992, at 8A.

39. Steve Charnovitz, *Exploring the Environmental Exceptions in GATT Article XX*, 25 J. WORLD TRADE 37, 37-55 (1991). A more recent article by Charnovitz, which has just come to the attention of this author and with which this author substantially agrees, is Steve Charnovitz, *Environmental and Labor Standards in Trade*, 15 WORLD ECON. 335, 335-56 (1992).

40. Vienna Convention on the Law of Treaties, *opened for signature* May 23, 1969, U.N. Doc. A/CONF.39/27, arts. 31, 32, 8 I.L.M. 679, 691-97 (entered into force Jan. 27, 1980).

context of interpreting the GATT, we have more than forty years of practice since the origin of GATT, and we also have some very important policy questions raised by the "slippery slope arguments" mentioned above. Thus, unlike certain schools of thought concerning United States Supreme Court interpretation of the United States Constitution, it is this author's view that one cannot rely too heavily on the original drafting history.[41]

IV. The Process-Product Problem: The Tuna Dolphin Case & The Global Commons Questions

An important conceptual "difficulty" of GATT is the so-called process-product characteristic problem, which relates closely to the Article XX exceptions and also to the national treatment obligations and other provisions of GATT.[42] This issue is central to the so-called tuna/dolphin case[43] and needs to be explained.

Suppose that an importing country wishes to prohibit the sale of domestic or imported automobiles that emit more pollutants in their exhaust than permitted by a specified standard. Subject to the discussion in Part II, there seems to be little difficulty with this regulation. It relates to the characteristics of the product itself. If the product itself is polluting, then on a nondiscriminatory basis the government may prohibit its sale (or also prohibit its importation, as a measure to prohibit its sale).[44]

Suppose, on the other hand, that the government feels that an automobile plant in a foreign country is operated in such a way that it poses substantial hazards to human health, possibly through dangers of accidents from the machinery, pollutants or unduly high temperatures in the factory. On an apparently nondiscriminatory basis, the government may wish to impose a prohibition on the sale of domestic or imported automobiles that are produced in factories with certain characteristics. However, in this case it should be noted that the imported automobiles themselves are perfectly appropriate and do not have dangerous or polluting characteristics. Thus, the target of the importing country's regulation is the production "process." The key question under the GATT/MTO system is whether the importing country is justified either under national treatment rules of nondiscrimination, or the exceptions of Article XX (which do not require strict national

41. The criticism regarding some theories of interpretation refers to various doctrines of "original intent" in connection with theories of U.S. Constitutional interpretation.

42. Jackson & Davey, *supra* note 1, at 448, 514; Frederic L. Kirgis, Jr., *Effective Pollution Control in Industrialized Countries: International Economic Disincentives, Policy Responses and the GATT*, 70 Mich. L. Rev. 859 (1972); *see also supra* note 25.

43. Tuna/Dolphin Panel Report, *supra* note 36; *see* Jackson, World Trading System, *supra* note 1, at 197-99; GATT Report 90-91, *supra* note 21, at 27; OTA Report, *supra* note 21, at 49; *see also supra* note 37.

44. *See supra* notes 24-33 and accompanying text (discussing national treatment and product standards); *see also* Jackson & Davey, *supra* note 1, at 448 (citing to GATT Report on Belgian Family Allowances adopted by GATT Contracting Parties on November 7, 1952); GATT, *supra* note 10, annex I, 61 Stat. at A85-90, 55 U.N.T.S. at 292-305.

treatment nondiscrimination as was discussed above). Trade policy experts are concerned that if a nation is allowed to use the process characteristic as the basis for trade restrictive measures, then the result would be to open a pandora's box of problems that could open large loopholes in the GATT. The following are some hypothetical illustrations of potential "process" problems further down the road:[45]

— An importing country prohibits the sale of radios, whether domestic or imported, that are produced by workers who are paid less than a minimum amount of wages specified by the importing country. This minimum amount might be the importing country's own minimum wage, or it might be an amount considerably less but still substantial (in deference to poor countries).
— An importing country that prohibits women from working in certain types of manufacturing plants also prohibits the importation of goods produced in similar plants that utilize women employees.
— An importing country that specifies a weekly religious holiday, for example, Saturday or Sunday, prohibits the importation of goods produced by work on the specified religious holiday.
— An importing country has strong political interests regarding the threat to marine mammals from certain fishing practices on the high seas, and thus prohibits the sale of products from both its domestic fishing industry and from foreign fishing if the products come from countries that permit the destructive fishing practices.

Obviously the tuna/dolphin case[46] relates to these issues. Although the GATT panel report is not entirely clear on this matter, it seems fair to say that there were two important objections to the U.S. embargo on the importation of tuna. First, there is the question of "eco-imperialism," where one nation unilaterally imposes its fishing standards (albeit for environmental purposes) on other nations in the world without their consent or participation in the development of the standard. Second, there is the problem that the import embargo is inconsistent with the GATT rules unless there is some GATT exception that would permit the embargo. Of course, that exception relates to the "process-product" interpretation problem and therefore also to the problem in the national treatment rule (Article III) and the general exceptions of GATT (Article XX).

The approach in the GATT system so far has given great weight to this slippery slope concern, and thus tilted towards interpreting both the Article III (including some Article XI questions) and the Article XX exceptions to apply to the product standards and to life and health within the importing country, but not to extend these concepts and exceptions to "processes" outside the territorial limits of jurisdiction. The alternative which threatens to create the great loop hole is a serious worry. The theories of comparative

45. *See* sources cited *supra* note 20, 38-40.
46. *See* Tuna/Dolphin Panel Report, *supra* note 36.

advantage which drive the policy of liberal trade, suggest that differences among nations are an important reason for trade. These can be differences of natural resources, as well as differences of cultural and population characteristics such as education, training, investment, and environment. To allow an exception to GATT to permit some governments to unilaterally impose standards on production processes as a condition of importation would substantially undermine these policy objectives of trade liberalization. On the other hand, trade sanctions, which include embargoes, are a very attractive and potentially useful means of providing enforcement of international cooperatively developed standards, including environmental standards.

Thus, there is an important trade-off that the GATT must face. It is not adequate, in this writer's view, for the GATT simply to say that trade should never be used as a sanction for environmental (or human rights, or anti-prison labor) purposes. There are already a number of situations in which the GATT has at least tolerated, if not explicitly accepted, trade sanction type activity for what is perceived to be valid overriding international objectives.[47] What are the implications of this problem? To this writer, it seems clear that the GATT/MTO system must give specific and significant attention to this trade-off in order to provide for exceptions for environmental purposes. The exceptions should have well-established boundaries so as to prevent them from being used as excuses for a variety of protectionist devices or unilateral social welfare concerns. Possibly these exceptions should be limited to the situation where governments are protecting matters that occur within their territorial jurisdiction.

It may be feasible to develop an explicit exception in the GATT/MTO system, possibly by the waiver process which is reasonably efficient,[48] for a certain list of specified broad-based multilateral treaties. One of the concerns expressed about the tuna/dolphin case in GATT is the implications that it might have for the so-called "Montreal Protocol" concerning chlorofluorocarbons (CFCs) and the danger to the Earth's ozone layer. The Montreal Protocol[49] provides a potential future authorization of trade sanction measures against even nonsignatories for processes, not product characteristics, that violate the norms of the treaty. If the current rules of the GATT are

---

47. Instances where the GATT has tolerated such uses include the imposition of trade sanctions on South Africa and Southern Rhodesia. Article XXI of GATT provides an exception for national security, and for measures in pursuance of a Contracting Parties "obligations under the United Nations Charter for the maintenance of international peace and security." GATT, *supra* note 23, art. XXI, 61 Stat. at A63, 55 U.N.T.S. at 266. The GATT Analytical Index to Article XXI reports various practices that have been tolerated by the GATT system, including an Egyptian boycott against Israel, an EC action during the Falkland/Malvinas situation, and United States measures prohibiting trade involving Nicaragua.

48. *See* JACKSON, WORLD TRADE AND GATT, *supra* note 1, at 541-52; *see also* Annex B.

49. Montreal Protocol on Substances That Deplete the Ozone Layer, Sept. 16, 1987, 26 I.L.M. 1550 (entered into force Jan. 1, 1989) [hereinafter Montreal Protocol]. See a description of this problem in OTA REPORT, *supra* note 21, at 43-46.

interpreted to exclude exceptions for the process situation, the Montreal Protocol Measures, except as among the signatories to the Montreal Protocol, would be contrary to GATT obligations.[50] It may take some time and study to develop the precise wording of an appropriate amendment or treaty exception for the GATT/MTO system for these environmental treaty cases, but in the short run for a limited period of years, it could be efficient to use a GATT waiver to clarify the issue as to specifically named treaties.[51]

In all likelihood, there are a sufficient number of signatories to the Montreal Protocol that are also GATT members so that a GATT waiver authorizing the trade measures contemplated in the Montreal Protocol could be adopted. Adoption of a waiver requires approval by two-thirds vote of the GATT contracting parties. But at the same time, it might be wise to go a few steps further and include in such a waiver several other specified treaties.[52] Obviously the waiver can also be amended in the future to add more specifically named treaties.

Even under such a waiver approach, there are still some important policy and treaty drafting questions that must be faced. For example, should the exception to the GATT be worded to apply only to the mandatory trade measures required by the specified environmental treaties? Or should it also be extended to those measures that are deemed discretionary but "authorized" by the environmental treaties? Or, would the GATT waiver even go one step further and authorize GATT members to take trade measures unilaterally to help enforce the substantive environmental norms contained in the environmental treaties, even when such environmental treaties do not have trade measures or sanctions indicated in the their treaty texts?

V. Subsidies

The problem of subsidies in international trade policy is perhaps the single most perplexing issue of the current world trading system, and one that is very complex. Some of the major controversies and negotiation impasses, such as the question of agriculture, relate to this problem. The GATT rules have become increasingly elaborate, and contain several different dimensions. Not only are there provisions in the GATT itself (Articles VI and XVI), but there is also the Tokyo Round "Code" on subsidies and

50. Montreal Protocol, *supra* note 49. *See* OTA Report, *supra* note 21, at 44. The OTA Report notes that the Montreal Protocol has seventy nine members. GATT has more than one hundred members, and a waiver requires two-thirds of those voting, which must include at least one-half of the total membership.

51. Some language used in the NAFTA text suggests the possibility of a GATT waiver along the same lines as the NAFTA article 104. *See* Annex C, art. 104.

52. Apart from the Montreal Protocol, other treaties mentioned as candidates for a GATT waiver include: The Basel Convention on the Control of Transboundary Movements of Hazardous Wastes and their Disposal, Mar. 27, 1989, U.N. Doc. UNEP/IG. 80-3 (1989), *reprinted in* 28 I.L.M. 657 and The Convention on International Trade in Endangered Species of Wild Fauna and Flora, Mar. 3, 1973, 27 U.S.T. 1087, 993 U.N.T.S. 243 [hereinafter CITES].

countervailing duties which provides obligations to the signatories of that code.[53] It is not feasible in this paper to go into great detail about the subsidies question. Indeed, the subsidies question in relation to environmental policies may be one of the most intricate and difficult issues facing the world trading system during the next decade. Here I will only outline some of the major characteristics and problems of the potential clash between trade policies and environmental policies in relation to subsidies.

First, to look briefly at the subsidy trade rules,[54] the trade system has traditionally divided subsidies into two types: export subsidies (subsidies that apply only to exported products), and general subsidies (subsidies that apply to all products produced in the country, whether exported or not). The international system has imposed considerably more restraint on the use of export subsidies, thus deeming them to be particularly suspect.

Subsidies can have at least three different kinds of impacts on international trade. Two of these relate to exports from a subsidizing country regardless of whether the subsidies are general or export subsidies. First, the subsidized exports can have an impact on an importing country, and the rules will often allow the importing country to impose a so-called "countervailing duty" to offset the effect of the subsidized imports. Second, subsidized exports may be introduced into a third country market to which a nonsubsidizing country is also exporting. In that case, the countervailing duty remedy is not available. The international system (GATT and the Subsidies Code) imposes specific international obligations on the use of certain kinds of subsidies, and it is this international obligation and its enforcement procedures (through dispute settlement) that is almost the only available remedy to the competing nonsubsidizing country in its complaint against that country that subsidizes. This international rule enforcement mechanism and dispute settlement process has been one of the most troublesome areas in the GATT, and there is considerable thought that the Tokyo Round Subsidies Code has largely failed in this respect. It should also be noted that the United States is the only major user of countervailing duties, although there is some evidence that other countries are now interested in increasing their use of them.

The third influence of subsidies on trade is to inhibit imports into a subsidizing country. If an importing country subsidizes its domestic producers, these producers can often reduce their prices and thus inhibit imports that are not equally subsidized simply through increased price, quality, or other forms of competition. Indeed, the system is tilted against imports in that it permits a subsidizing importing country to subsidize its domestic

---

53. *Agreement on Interpretation and Application of Articles VI, XVI and XXIII*, GATT Doc. L/4812 (Nov. 12, 1979), BISD 26th Supp. 56. The current number of signatories to this Convention is approximately twenty-five (25). *See* GATT Doc. L/6453 and addenda (through Mar. 12, 1992).

54. Jackson, World Trading System, *supra* note 1, at 249-73; Jackson, World Trade and GATT, *supra* note 1, at 365-99; Jackson & Davey, *supra* note 1, at 723-89.

product, and yet impose a countervailing duty on imports that are equally subsidized!

An underlying problem for all of these complex rules concerning subsidies is the definition of "subsidy" itself. The definition is often stated in very broad terms such that it would include governmental measures such as fire and police protection, roads, and schools. If the subsidy definition is so broad, the various trade response rules, particularly the countervailing duty, could totally undermine the liberal trading system. Thus, it has been necessary either to use a restricted definition of subsidy, or to define a "subset" of the broader set which subset is called "actionable" and thus subject to trade response measures.[55]

Having presented this all too brief outline of the general trade subsidies rules in the GATT/MTO system, it is now important to turn to how they might apply in the environmental context. The following hypothetical cases can illustrate some of the problems that could occur:

— Suppose an exporting country establishes a subsidy for certain of its manufacturing companies that allows them to receive grants or tax privileges for establishing environmental enhancement measures (such as machinery to clean up smoke or water emissions, or other capital goods for environmental or safety and health purposes). When those producers export their goods, the goods could be vulnerable to foreign nations imposing countervailing duties. Is this appropriate or should a special exception for environmental measures be carved out?

— Suppose an exporting country lacks meaningful environmental rules, and exports goods into an importing country that has strict environmental rules for its manufacturers. The importing country's domestic industry will likely complain about what it perceives to be "unfair import competition." Can the importing country argue that the lack of environmental rules in the exporting country is the equivalent of a "subsidy" and impose a countervailing duty? Again this poses a slippery slope problem. Could such an importing country likewise impose countervailing duties against imports based on the argument that the imports were produced in a country that lacked competition policy (antitrust laws)? Or lacked minimum standards of safety and health in the factories? This is a problem that closely relates to the process-product characteristic problem discussed in Part IV.

— Similarly, suppose a nation lacks environmental rules such that its domestic producers can produce goods cheaper than its competitors and thus compete to keep out goods that are imported from other countries that have substantial environmental rules. In that

55. Jackson, World Trading System, *supra* note 1, at 249-73; Dunkel Draft, *supra* note 11 (Draft Agreement on Subsidies and Countervailing Measures).

situation, the lack of environmental rules becomes an effective protectionist device.

Obviously these hypotheticals are not so "hypothetical." A good part of the discourse about the proposed NAFTA treaty expresses the concern that if Mexico lacks environmental rules it will have a competitive advantage vis-á-vis American or Canadian producers.[56] These problems illustrate the need for careful examination of the subsidy rules so as to design appropriate environmental exceptions or rules without destroying the advantages of the subsidy rules. These environmental exceptions or rules should probably include:

1) A modification to the definition of "actionable subsidy" to allow certain types of environment enhancing government benefits and to exempt them from countervailing duties or other trade obligations.
2) A provision allowing trade restrictions, whether called "countervailing" or not, under authority of other multilateral treaties designed to enforce certain international agreements.
3) A recognition that just because the environmental rules of an exporting nation are not as stringent as those of an importing nation, the latter should not apply "countervailing duties" based on a subsidy theory. On the other hand, international minimum standards might be formulated over time, possibly creating a benchmark required for goods to move freely in international trade.

VI. Exports and Competitiveness

Apart from the problems of the various technical rules of the GATT discussed above, there are also some important additional considerations for the relationship and possible effect of trade liberalization on environmental policies. One of those can be characterized as the question of "competitiveness." The situation is as follows: an exporting country has important environmental rules and standards, which its producers meet. These environmental efforts obviously have a cost, and the producers must bear those costs and build them into the price structure of the products that they export. These products compete in other countries with products from countries that do not have such environmental standards or efforts. This could be the case when the environmentalist country exports to a relatively nonenvironmentalist country, or when the two countries compete in some third market. Because the producers in the nonenvironmentalist country escape the cost of the environmental regulations, presumably they can produce at a lower cost and thus offer their product at a lower price.

56. *The Trade Accord*, N.Y. Times, Aug. 13, 1992, at A2, C3. See also the reports of discussions on the environment in the July 10, 1992 issue of relation to the NAFTA agreement in Inside U.S. Trade.

The concern of the producers in the environmentalist country is that this will be a form of competition for them that will be hard to meet and, thus, in their minds, is "unfair" because they are contributing to the world environment by their compliance with environmental standards.

This problem was touched on in the previous section when we discussed subsidies, but even apart from the rules of subsidies it can be an important problem, especially as it relates to political perceptions. Furthermore, because it is primarily a question of "export competitiveness," it does not get discussed in connection with many of the problems of national treatment, or the general exceptions to the GATT, which have been previously expressed. There are some GATT rules that cover exports, but they are not closely related to the problem posed here.

To some extent, this problem is similar to many other problems resulting from differences among societies. Some societies will have more stringent rules with respect to plant worker safety. Other societies will have stringent rules regarding family allowances or holidays. Still other societies will have minimum wages, and many other social measures can differ from society to society. As indicated earlier in this paper, attempts to use trade rules to make the world uniform in this regard could be futile and very damaging to the underlying policies of trade liberalization. Thus, the questions posed are whether environmental policies are substantially different than some of the other policies mentioned, and if so, do they deserve a different kind of treatment in the world trading system.

First, it might be conceptually feasible to separate the environmental problems that affect only the environment of the country concerned (within its borders), from other problems that have an effect either across borders, or, even more broadly, on the world's environment (the global commons). It could be, and has been, argued that because different countries vary in their degrees of environmental quality, and in the extent to which they tolerate environmental problems as a trade-off to gaining other benefits (such as eating better), that these issues can and should be left to the national sovereign states. Consequently, the international trading system ought not to try to redress or "harmonize" the different environmental approaches. Obviously there are many intricacies in this argument, and some of them have already been subjects of full papers elsewhere.[57]

Perhaps the more important question relates to the situation where the environmental degradation is of a type that impacts on the world as a whole, or at least on countries other than the acting or exporting nation. Here we have something of the "free rider" problem, or "prisoner's dilemma" issue, that points towards the need for international cooperation. Given the imperfections of the international system, and particularly its

57. *See, e.g.*, Jagdish Bhagwati, *Why The Sins of One Economist Should Not Be Visited On All*, FIN. TIMES, Feb. 18, 1992, at 21; *A Greener Bank*, ECONOMIST, May 23, 1992, at 79 (talking about World Bank's *World Development Report*, and mentioning provocative memo by Lawrence Summers, the Bank's Chief Economist).

system for developing new rules (with its least common denominator constraints) environmental policy experts can legitimately argue that there must be some room for unilateral nation state actions designed to support the world environment. This is perhaps the trickiest area for which to develop appropriate policy. It relates closely to the process-product characteristic question discussed above. Certainly the optimal approach would seem to be through broad based multilateral treaties and rules, which then in turn raises the question of how to make such rules effective. This latter question quite often leads to a focus on trade sanctions as a means to make such rules effective, and as indicated earlier, an argument can be made that there should be an explicit exception in the GATT for certain kinds of trade actions to help enhance the effectiveness of international environmental rules, while preventing misuse of the exception.

Let us return for a moment to the first category of problems, those in which the environmental issues involve the environment only within the producing country, or the importing country which has competing producers that will benefit from lack of environmental rules. In some of these cases, the importing country's political system would in fact desire some additional pressures on its decision making processes to help induce the development of environmental rules. This is a common feature of the relationship of international action, particularly in the area of economic affairs, but also in the human rights area. In many cases, domestic leaders find it politically difficult to implement a preferred course of action unless there is some external pressure that helps them in their domestic advocacy, and also in some cases gives them an "excuse" for taking that action.

Some of this attitude certainly exists in the context of environmental rules,[58] and may in fact justify a broader approach in the GATT/MTO trading system. Thus, it could well be feasible and worthwhile, although time-consuming, to develop some rules in the trading system that impose certain kinds of harmonizing minimum level standards for environmental protection. In the alternative, rules that impose certain kinds of trade detriments, such as compensatory duties, on countries that do not adopt or enforce the harmonized or minimal environmental rules, might also be worthwhile.

VII. The Institutional Problems: Dispute Settlement, Transparency, and Jurisprudence

The GATT is a rather strange and troubled institution. It was born with several birth defects because it was never meant to be an organization. Instead, it was intended that an International Trade Organization (ITO) Charter would come into effect that would provide the institutional framework, in which the GATT would be one part. Because of this troubled

58. These views on external pressure are expressed in private conversations with various foreign government officials, but are not generally stated in public, or in publications.

birth history, the GATT has always been deficient in the institutional clauses normally found in a treaty establishing an international organization.[59] These problems have become increasingly troublesome as world economic developments have gone beyond the rules provided by the GATT system. Some of these problems are being addressed in the current Uruguay Round GATT negotiation, and if that is ultimately successful, it may help improve the institutional situation. Other GATT issues include problems of accepting new members, particularly those with different economic structures; the problem of assisting developing countries; the difficulty of facing up to some of the more newly appreciated issues that are effecting international trade flows, such as cultural and economic structural differences; questions of competition policy (antitrust); and, of course, environmental policies.

More broadly, the GATT generally suffers from institutional deficiencies in the two essential ingredients for an effective international organization, namely the making of new rules, and the provisions for making those rules effective through dispute settlement procedures. With respect to rule making, the GATT basically relies heavily on a consensus treaty making process. With a membership that now exceeds one hundred countries, this becomes extremely difficult. This difficulty is accentuated by the MFN obligations that give rise to a potential "free rider" problem of nonsigning countries receiving the benefits of new agreements. This in turn tends to force negotiations towards a consensus for a new rule, into a "least common denominator" approach.

Likewise, the dispute settlement procedures of the GATT have been troubled. The actual GATT clauses setting them up are extremely sketchy. Nevertheless, through trial and error and general practice over four decades, the GATT dispute settlement procedures have now developed into a remarkably full procedure that has been largely, but not totally, effective. Its effectiveness has been such, however, as to attract various interests who see in the GATT dispute settlement procedures an important attribute for subject matters that they would like to see placed under the GATT, such as the area of intellectual property.[60] Likewise, other trading arrangements, particularly some of the arrangements for trading blocs or free trade areas, have followed some of the general outlines of the GATT dispute settlement procedure, paying it the compliment of emulation.

The Uruguay Round Negotiation currently sponsored by the GATT (the eighth since its origin) has been troubled. It was launched in September 1986, but is not yet complete. Nevertheless, in December 1991, the negotiating groups, through the coordination of the Secretariat and the Director-General, Arthur Dunkel, issued a tentative draft text of an entire package of agreements which could form the basis of the final negotiations towards a complete package to be approved. This is commonly called the "Dunkel

59. *See supra* note 1, and particularly JACKSON, RESTRUCTURING GATT, *supra* note 1.

60. *See Symposium: Trade Related Aspects of Intellectual Property*, 22 VAND. J. TRANSNAT'L L. 223 (1989); Dunkel Draft, *supra* note 11, annex III at 57.

Draft," and it contains two important institutional texts that relate to the problems discussed above. First, there is a charter for a Multilateral Trade Organization (MTO), which will provide some measure of improvement in the basic institutional structure of the GATT. It will not change such things as the structure of rule making, but it does provide, for the first time, a definitive legal treaty text to establish the organization, and put it on a sounder footing for future evolution. The existence of this text has been criticized by some interests in various participating countries, including some of the environmental interests. Some of this criticism is, I think, due to misunderstanding of the specific draft charter provisions and their relation to broader international law principles. Indeed, the draft charter is very minimal, and in many ways will result in no differences in the normal work of the organization, as compared to the existing organizational structure.[61]

Another important text in the Dunkel Draft is a draft agreement concerning revised dispute settlement procedures in the GATT. It should be noted that these dispute settlement procedures could exist independently of an MTO, if an MTO failed to come into being. However, an MTO does facilitate and help administer a broadened dispute settlement system that would now apply, not only to trade in goods, but also to intellectual property and trade in services. This procedure would provide a more effective "umbrella" for a single dispute settlement procedure and avoid some of the contentious problems of competing procedures that existed after the various Tokyo Round texts came into force.

Of course, there are those who would prefer not to have a more effective dispute settlement procedure, or for that matter, a more effective organization. They see any such organization, or procedure at the international level as a threat to their ability to achieve the results which they wish within a particular country. There is not much that can be said in response to that desire. In the view of this author, such a desire is somewhat irresponsible because the basic trends of world economic interaction, regardless of what happens in connection with new treaties, are such that some kinds of international cooperation and coordination are essential to avoid the rancorous and damaging disputes that are constantly arising between nations. International cooperation also provides the measure of predictability and stability that is essential for individual entrepreneurs and firms to act effectively. Often the action desired is investment, which depends on decisions that need a predictable rule system.

Several particular aspects of the legal effects of international actions should be clarified because there have been statements by various interest groups that suggest some misunderstanding about them. The first of these is the question of the domestic law application of international decisions of a GATT/MTO system. For the United States, it is very unlikely that any international GATT/MTO decision as to new rules (such as a new treaty) or a dispute settlement procedure result, would have direct application (self-

61. Dunkel Draft, *supra* note 11, at 92.

executing effect) in United States law. Although some treaties can have self-executing effect in the United States, in recent years Congress has rather consistently negated such effect by provisions in its legislation approving the international trade treaties.[62] This result, incidentally, differs from country to country.

Many other countries are in the same position as the United States, such that the international treaty or international decisions will not automatically become part of their domestic law.[63] Instead, there must be an "act of transformation," which is some sort of domestic legal action that would implement the international rules or decisions. In the United States this could be an Act of Congress, or in cases where the power is delegated to the President, an action by the President or his delegatees. If the domestic law institutions fail to enact the appropriate transformation, the United States or other country may be placed in contravention of international obligations. Such a situation, however, will not result in automatic domestic law change. To some extent this provides a certain escape hatch from inappropriate and overreaching international decisions. Needless to say this is a matter of considerable discussion and literature.[64]

A second potential misunderstanding of the legal situation relates to the effect of the GATT dispute settlement panel decisions. Under the current and proposed procedure, a "panel" will make its ruling in a report, and this report must be approved by the GATT Council. Under the new proposed procedures, this approval would be fairly automatic, subject to an appeal to a higher tribunal.[65] The GATT panel report is not binding until it is approved. After such approval, it is binding on the participant nations as a matter of international law, even though it does not directly become domestic law. In the case of the Canada-U.S. Free Trade Agreement (FTA), and possibly some new FTA arrangements, there is one portion of the dispute settlement procedures available that does provide for direct, or nearly direct, application of the decisions of the tribunal. This is relatively rare and quite novel.[66]

Even with respect to international law obligations, the general international law rule is that the doctrine of precedent, or "stare decisis," does

62. Trade Agreements Act of 1979, § 3(a), (f), 19 U.S.C. § 2119(a), (f) (1988); S. REP. No. 249, 96th Cong., 1st Sess. 4, 36 (1979); JACKSON ET AL., IMPLEMENTING THE TOKYO ROUND, *supra* note 1, at 169-72; JACKSON, WORLD TRADING SYSTEM, *supra* note 1, at 68, 75.

63. *See generally* John H. Jackson, *Status of Treaties in Domestic Legal Systems: A Policy Analysis*, 86 AM. J. INT'L L. 310, 310-40 (1992). The United Kingdom and Canada are generally considered "dualist" nations where treaties do not apply in domestic law, but must be implemented through parliamentary or other governmental acts of transformation. R. Higgins, *United Kingdom*, *in* THE EFFECT OF TREATIES IN DOMESTIC LAW 123 (Francis G. Jacobs & Shelley Roberts, eds., 1987).

64. *See supra* note 60.

65. Dunkel Draft, *supra* note 11, §§ S (Understanding on Rules and Procedures on Dispute Settlement), T (Elements of an Integrated Dispute Settlement System).

66. Free Trade Agreement, Jan. 2, 1988, U.S.-Can., 27 I.L.M. 293; H.R. Doc. No. 216, 100th Cong., 2d Sess. 512 (1988).

not apply to rulings of international tribunals. Thus, the result of a panel report as between countries A & B, for example, is not technically a rule that obligates countries C & D, or even A & D. This leaves open the possibility that through general international negotiating processes, or actions in a council of the GATT or MTO, the results of a panel report, even when approved, could be modified when applied to future cases. Nevertheless, it is true that panels do tend to follow prior panel decisions as a matter of persuasiveness and logical consistent reasoning. In some cases, however, the panels have expressly departed from prior panel reports.[67]

What are the implications of all of this for environmental policy? First, as is fairly frequently noted in the text discussion in prior sections, many of the policy clashes that environmental policy has with trade policy point towards institutional questions. This is most importantly the case for the dispute settlement processes of the GATT. It is in those processes that some of the interstitial decisions involving interpretation of current or future GATT/MTO treaties will be fought out. One example of that was the tuna/dolphin case, in which the panel itself noted that it would be inappropriate for the panel to make the requested interpretation of the GATT general exceptions of Article XX. It stated that such decisions should be made by the negotiators or the appropriate GATT bodies as a matter of treaty law alteration, rather than simply an interpretation of a panel.[68] In that sense, the tuna/dolphin case was praiseworthy, and in a broader sense should be praised even by the environmentalists who dislike the outcome. It suggests a certain amount of "judicial restraint." A contrary approach, with the panel seizing the issue and going forward with it, might in some future case be severely contrary to the interests of environmental policy.

---

67. *See Report of the GATT Panel, European Economic Community Restrictions on Imports of Dessert Apples*, para 12.1, GATT Doc. L/6491 (June 22, 1989), BISD 36th Supp. 93, 124. The Report states that "[t]he Panel . . . did not feel it was legally bound by all the details and legal reasoning of the 1980 Panel report." *Id.* This is generally consistent with international law. *See, e.g.*, Ian Brownlie, Principles of Public International Law 21 (4th ed. 1990).

68. Tuna/Dolphin Panel Report, *supra* note 36, at para. 6.3, at 1623 reads:

> The Panel further recalled its finding that the import restrictions examined in this dispute, imposed to respond to differences in environmental regulation of producers, could not be justified under the exceptions in Articles XX(b) or XX(g). These exceptions did not specify criteria limiting the range of life or health protection policies, or resource conservation policies, for the sake of which they could be invoked. It seemed evident to the Panel that, if the CONTRACTING PARTIES were to permit import restrictions in response to differences in environmental policies under the General Agreement, they would need to impose limits on the range of policy differences justifying such responses and to develop criteria so as to prevent abuse. If the CONTRACTING PARTIES were to decide to permit trade measures of this type in particular circumstances it would therefore be preferable for them to do so not by interpreting Article XX, but by amending or supplementing the provisions of the General Agreement or waiving obligations thereunder. Such an approach would enable the CONTRACTING PARTIES to impose such limits and develop such criteria.

Nevertheless, the environmentalists, apart from the question of precedent, have several legitimate complaints about the GATT dispute settlement procedures, among others. First, they note appropriately that the GATT lacks a certain amount of transparency. By that, we can understand that the GATT tends too often to try to operate in secrecy, attempting to avoid public and news media accounts of its actions. In recent years, this has become almost a charade, because many of the key documents, most importantly the early results of a GATT dispute settlement panel report, leak out almost immediately to the press. For purposes of gaining a broader constituency among the various policy interested communities in the world, gaining the trust of those constituencies, enhancing public understanding, as well as avoiding the "charade" of ineffective attempts to maintain secrecy, the GATT could go much further in providing "transparency" of its processes.

Secondly, there is criticism and concern that the GATT lacks the kind of expertise that would help it to make better decisions in dispute settlement processes. In particular, it is believed that the GATT lacks expertise in environmental issues. Again, there is considerable room for improvement in this regard, perhaps with procedures that would give panels certain technical assistance.

Finally, there is criticism of the GATT panel processes in that they (while operating in secret) fail to make provisions for the transmittal of arguments, information, and evidence from a variety of interested groups including nongovernment environmental policy groups. Once again, there should be ways that the GATT can improve on this problem.

Apart from the dispute settlement procedures, the overall institutional set up of a GATT and a possible MTO could be likewise improved. In particular, transparency could be enhanced, perhaps by Non-Governmental Organizations (NGOs) as well as Inter-Governmental Organizations (IGOs) gaining some share of participation in the GATT processes, possibly through an annual open meeting. Furthermore, as the GATT or MTO continue to evolve, procedures such as the already set up TPRM might build in provisions for explicit attention to environmental concerns. It is clear that some of the GATT rules need to be changed. There are a variety of ways for them to be changed, some discussion on which is provided in Annex B.[69]

VIII. Some Conclusions

The discussions of this paper cover only the tip of the iceberg regarding the problematic relationship between world trade system policies and environmental policies. But in the light of those discussions, what can we say about the relationship of two policy sets? Are they congruent or conflicting? The answer obviously is a bit of both.

---

69. *See* Jackson, World Trade and GATT, *supra* note 1; John H. Jackson, *Changing GATT Rules* (Nov. 7, 1991) (appended as Annex B).

In the broader long term perspective there would seem to be a great deal of congruence. Some of that congruence derives from the economic and welfare enhancement of trade liberalization policies. Such welfare enhancement can in turn lead to enhancement of environmental policy objectives, as mentioned at the outset of this paper.

On the other hand, it is clear that the world trade policies and environmental policies do provide a certain amount of conflict. This conflict is not substantially different from a number of other areas where governmental policies have to accommodate conflicting aims and goals of the policy makers and their constituents. Thus, to some degree it is a question of where the line will be drawn, or how the compromises will be made. In that sense, institutions obviously become very important because the decision making process can tilt the decision results. If the world trade rules are pushed to their limit, for example, free trade with no exceptions for problems raised by environmental policies and actions effecting environments, clearly the trade rules will cause damage to environmental objectives. Likewise, if the environmental policies are pushed to their limit at the expense of the trading rules, so that governments will find it convenient and easy to set up a variety of restrictive trade measures, in some cases under the excuse of environmental policies, world trade will suffer.

Furthermore, there is no doubt that the "cultures" of the two policy communities: that of trade, and that of environment, differ in important ways. The trade policy experts have tended, over decades and perhaps centuries, to operate more under the practices of international diplomacy, which often means secrecy, negotiation, compromise, and to some extent behind the scenes catering to a variety of special economic interests. In addition, at the international level, because there is no over-arching "sovereign leader," the processes are slow, faltering, and lend themselves to lowest common denominator results, or to diplomatic negotiations that agree to language without real agreement on substance.

On the other hand, the environmental policy groups, perhaps partly because they primarily operate on the national scene, have become used to using the processes of publicity and lobbying pressure on Congress or Parliaments, to which they have considerable access. There is, thus, a much broader sense of "participation" in the processes, which the international processes have not yet accommodated. Furthermore, the environmental policy groups, like many other groups working on the domestic level, have a sense of power achieved through successes in the legislative and public discussion processes. They feel somewhat frustrated with the international processes because those are sufficiently different to pose puzzling obstacles to the achievement of environmental goals.

This difference in culture is not inevitably permanent, and indeed the international processes need to accommodate more transparency and participation. This is true not only of the environmental case, but it is increasingly an important consideration for the broader way that international economic interdependence is managed. As more and more decisions that effect firms, citizens, and other groups, are made at the international level, it will be necessary for the international decision making process to accommodate the goals of transparency, adequate expertise, and participation in the advocacy and rule making procedures.

To some extent, the rhetoric of some environmental policy advocates has been the rhetoric of antagonism to international organizations and procedures altogether. This, I suggest, is not constructive. The notion that the United States, for example, can, or should impose unilaterally its environmental views and standards on other parts of the world, without any constraint from international rules or international dispute settlement procedures, is not likely to be a viable approach in the longer run. This means that in some cases when the United States submits (as it must, partly so as to reciprocally get other countries to submit) to international dispute settlement procedures, it will sometimes lose, and find itself obliged to alter its own domestic policy preferences. This has already been the case, and the United States has a mixed record of compliance with GATT rulings, although for a large powerful nation that record is not too bad.[70]

Apart from these longer run and institutional issues, there are matters that can be undertaken jointly by the trade and environmental policy communities, in the context of the GATT/MTO system. By way of reviewing some of the discussion in sections above, there seem to be two groups of actions that would be called for, the near term, and the longer term.

Focusing first on the near term actions: it seems feasible for the international trading system to accommodate some of the following actions or goals:

1) Greater transparency both in the rule making and in the dispute settlement procedures of the trading system. This would call for more participation, greater opportunity for policy advocacy inputs, and for more openness in terms of publication of the relevant documents faster and in a way more accessible to interested parties;
2) Greater access to participation in the processes,
3) Some clarification is needed about the degree to which the international process will be allowed to intrude upon the scope of

70. In a number of not too recent GATT panel cases that were brought by complaints against the United States, and in which the panel ruled that the U.S. measures were inconsistent with GATT, the United States subsequently revised its legislation or other measures in order to comply with the GATT panel report. *See, e.g.*, *Report of the GATT Panel, United States—Customs User Fee*, GATT Doc. L/6264 (Feb. 2, 1988), BISD 35th Supp. 245; *United States Manufacturing Clause*, GATT Doc. L/5609 (May 5, 1984), BISD 31st Supp. 74; *Report of the GATT Panel, United States—Taxes on Petroleum and Certain Imported Substances*, GATT Doc. L/6175 (June 17, 1987), BISD 34th Supp. 136; *Report of the GATT Panel, United States—Tax Legislation (DISC)*, GATT Doc. L/4422 (Nov. 12, 1976), BISD 23rd Supp. 98. On the other hand, the United States has not complied with several other panel reports. In some cases the United States has announced that it will accept the panel report and ultimately comply, but will wait until after the end of the Uruguay Round in case the Uruguay Round modifies the rule. *See, e.g.*, *Section 337 Panel Report*, *supra* note 24; *Report of the Committee on Anti-Dumping Practices*, GATT Doc. L/6609, BISD 36th Supp. 435, 438 (addressing complaint of Sweden).

decision making of national and sub-national governments. For example, the "scope of review" of international GATT/MTO panels over national government regulatory decisions concerning environment needs to be better defined. This is not an easy question, and it will not be solved quickly, but there probably needs to be some near term accommodation through interpretive notes or otherwise in the Dunkel Draft texts, for example. Some of the NAFTA text approach can be an useful example; and

4) Finally, there will have to be some near-term rule accommodation by the GATT, by which I mean some adjustments or changes in those rules through one or another of the techniques for changing GATT rules (probably focusing on the waiver procedure) to establish a reasonably clear set of exceptions for certain multilateral environmental treaty provisions that call for trade action that would otherwise be inconsistent with the GATT/MTO rules.

Looking at the longer term, it is clear that there is a substantial agenda that must be addressed with regard to the intersection and potential clash of trade policies and environmental policies. The GATT/MTO system must develop mechanisms, including working parties and negotiations, to address these, and they will take time. The long term agenda includes the following actions and goals:

1) The subsidies area will need substantial study and some kind of rule alteration to accommodate the respective interest;

2) Some type of more permanent exception will be needed either as an amendment or waiver embellishment of the Article XX exceptions of the GATT system, or possibly in the context of the national treatment rules. This can build upon the short term rule alterations (for example, by waiver) mentioned above, with particular reference to the process-product characteristic question, so as to accommodate the broadly agreed international environmental policy provisions, such as those now contained in some treaties;

3) Undoubtedly the GATT/MTO dispute settlement procedure will continue to evolve, in the light of experience. Even if near term provision is made for policy advocacy inputs from environmental policy experts, as time goes on and experience is obtained, there will need to be further adjustments in that procedure, possibly with some added limitations on the scope of review of international panels over domestic national environmental provisions; and

4) In particular, there needs to be some clarification about the rules and exceptions to accommodate national government unilateral imposition of environmentally justified rules that require or provide incentive for a higher standard of environmental protection than that for which the international community is able to develop a consensus.

It would be tragic if increased antagonism between the two policy groups occurred in such a way that the essential policy goals of both groups would be damaged unnecessarily. Hopefully, with some of the clarifications of the policies outlined in this paper, combined with some of the institutional measures suggested, such antagonism can be largely avoided, or creatively channeled to promote a constructive accommodation of the discordant policy objectives.

ANNEX A: SELECTED PROVISIONS OF GATT

PART I

Article I

General Most-Favoured-Nation Treatment

1. With respect to customs duties and charges of any kind imposed on or in connection with importation or exportation or imposed on the international transfer of payments for imports or exports, and with respect to the method of levying such duties and charges, and with respect to all rules and formalities in connection with importation and exportation, and with respect to all matters referred to in paragraphs 2 and 4 of Article III,* any advantage, favour, privilege or immunity granted by any contracting party to any product originating in or destined for any other country shall be accorded immediately and unconditionally to the like product originating in or destined for the territories of all other contracting parties.

2. The provisions of paragraph 1 of this Article shall not require the elimination of any preferences in respect of import duties or charges which do not exceed the levels provided for in paragraph 4 of this Article and which fall within the following descriptions:

(*a*) Preferences in force exclusively between two or more of the territories listed in Annex A, subject to the conditions set forth therein;
(*b*) Preferences in force exclusively between two or more territories which on July 1, 1939, were connected by common sovereignty or relations of protection or suzerainty and which are listed in Annexes B, C and D, subject to the conditions set forth therein;
(*c*) Preferences in force exclusively between the United States of America and the Republic of Cuba ;
(*d*) Preferences in force exclusively between neighbouring countries listed in Annexes E and F.

3. The provisions of paragraph 1 shall not apply to preferences between the countries formerly a part of the Ottoman Empire and detached from it on July 24, 1923, provided such preferences are approved under paragraph 5 of Article XXV, which shall be applied in this respect in the light of paragraph 1 of Article XXIX.

4. The margin of preference* on any product in respect of which a preference is permitted under paragraph 2 of this Article but is not specifically set forth as a maximum margin of preference in the appropriate Schedule annexed to this Agreement shall not exceed:

(*a*) in respect of duties or charges on any product described in such Schedule, the difference between the most-favoured-nation and preferential rates provided for therein; if no preferential rate is provided for, the preferential rate shall for the purposes of this paragraph be taken to be that in force on April 10, 1947, and, if no most-favoured-nation rate is provided for, the margin shall not exceed the difference between the most-favoured-nation and preferential rates existing on April 10, 1947;

(*b*) in respect of duties or charges on any product not described in the appropriate Schedule, the difference between the most-favoured-nation and preferential rates existing on April 10, 1947.

In the case of the contracting parties named in Annex G, the date of April 10, 1947, referred to in sub-paragraphs (*a*) and (*b*) of this paragraph shall be replaced by the respective dates set forth in that Annex.

PART II

Article III*

National Treatment on Internal Taxation and Regulation

1. The contracting parties recognize that internal taxes and other internal charges, and laws, regulations and requirements affecting the internal sale, offering for sale, purchase, transportation, distribution or use of products, and internal quantitative regulations requiring the mixture, processing or use of products in specified amounts or proportions, should not be applied to imported or domestic products so as to afford protection to domestic production.*

2. The products of the territory of any contracting party imported into the territory of any other contracting party shall not be subject, directly or indirectly, to internal taxes or other internal charges of any kind in excess of those applied, directly or indirectly, to like domestic products. Moreover, no contracting party shall otherwise apply internal taxes or other internal charges to imported or domestic products in a manner contrary to the principles set forth in paragraph 1.*

3. With respect to any existing internal tax which is inconsistent with the provisions of paragraph 2, but which is specifically authorized under a trade agreement, in force on April 10, 1947, in which the import duty on the taxed product is bound against increase, the contracting party imposing the tax shall be free to postpone the application of the provisions of paragraph 2 to such tax until such time as it can obtain release from the obligations of such trade agreement in order to permit the increase of such duty to the extent necessary to compensate for the elimination of the protective element of the tax.

4. The products of the territory of any contracting party imported into the territory of any other contracting party shall be accorded treatment no less favourable than that accorded to like products of national origin in respect of all laws, regulations and requirements affecting their internal sale,

offering for sale, purchase, transportation, distribution or use. The provisions of this paragraph shall not prevent the application of differential internal transportation charges which are based exclusively on the economic operation of the means of transport and not on the nationality of the product.

5. No contracting party shall establish or maintain any internal quantitative regulation relating to the mixture, processing or use of products in specified amounts or proportions which requires, directly or indirectly, that any specified amount or proportion of any product which is the subject of the regulation must be supplied from domestic sources. Moreover, no contracting party shall otherwise apply internal quantitative regulations in a manner contrary to the principles set forth in paragraph 1.*

6. The provisions of paragraph 5 shall not apply to any internal quantitative regulation in force in the territory of any contracting party on July 1, 1939, April 10, 1947, or March 24, 1948, at the option of that contracting party; *Provided* that any such regulation which is contrary to the provisions of paragraph 5 shall not be modified to the detriment of imports and shall be treated as a customs duty for the purpose of negotiation.

7. No internal quantitative regulation relating to the mixture, processing or use of products in specified amounts or proportions shall be applied in such a manner as to allocate any such amount or proportion among external sources of supply.

8. (*a*) The provisions of this Article shall not apply to laws, regulations or requirements governing the procurement by governmental agencies of products purchased for governmental purposes and not with a view to commercial resale or with a view to use in the production of goods for commercial sale.

(*b*) The provisions of this Article shall not prevent the payment of subsidies exclusively to domestic producers, including payments to domestic producers derived from the proceeds of internal taxes or charges applied consistently with the provisions of this Article and subsidies effected through governmental purchases of domestic products.

9. The contracting parties recognize that internal maximum price control measures, even though conforming to the other provisions of this Article, can have effects prejudicial to the interests of contracting parties supplying imported products. Accordingly, contracting parties applying such measures shall take account of the interests of exporting contracting parties with a view to avoiding to the fullest practicable extent such prejudicial effects.

10. The provisions of this Article shall not prevent any contracting party from establishing or maintaining internal quantitative regulations relating to exposed cinematograph films and meeting the requirements of Article IV.

Article VI

Anti-dumping and Countervailing Duties

1. The contracting parties recognize that dumping, by which products of one country are introduced into the commerce of another country at less than the normal value of the products, is to be condemned if it causes or threatens material injury to an established industry in the territory of a contracting party or materially retards the establishment of a domestic industry. For the purposes of this Article, a product is to be considered as being introduced into the commerce of an importing country at less than its normal value, if the price of the product exported from one country to another

(*a*) is less than the comparable price, in the ordinary course of trade, for the like product when destined for consumption in the exporting country, or,

(*b*) in the absence of such domestic price, is less than either

(i) the highest comparable price for the like product for export to any third country in the ordinary course of trade, or

(ii) the cost of production of the product in the country of origin plus a reasonable addition for selling cost and profit.

Due allowance shall be made in each case for differences in conditions and terms of sale, for differences in taxation, and for other differences affecting price comparability.*

2. In order to offset or prevent dumping, a contracting party may levy on any dumped product an anti-dumping duty not greater in amount than the margin of dumping in respect of such product. For the purposes of this Article, the margin of dumping is the price difference determined in accordance with the provisions of paragraph 1.*

3. No countervailing duty shall be levied on any product of the territory of any contracting party imported into the territory of another contracting party in excess of an amount equal to the estimated bounty or subsidy determined to have been granted, directly or indirectly, on the manufacture, production or export of such product in the country of origin or exportation, including any special subsidy to the transportation of a particular product. The term "countervailing duty" shall be understood to mean a special duty levied for the purpose of offsetting any bounty or subsidy bestowed, directly or indirectly, upon the manufacture, production or export of any merchandise.*

4. No product of the territory of any contracting party imported into the territory of any other contracting party shall be subject to anti-dumping or countervailing duty by reason of the exemption of such product from duties or taxes borne by the like product when destined for consumption in the country of origin or exportation, or by reason of the refund of such duties or taxes.

5. No product of the territory of any contracting party imported into the territory of any other contracting party shall be subject to both anti-

dumping and countervailing duties to compensate for the same situation of dumping or export subsidization.

6. (*a*) No contracting party shall levy any anti-dumping or countervailing duty on the importation of any product of the territory of another contracting party unless it determines that the effect of the dumping or subsidization, as the case may be, is such as to cause or threaten material injury to an established domestic industry, or is such as to retard materially the establishment of a domestic industry.

(*b*) The CONTRACTING PARTIES may waive the requirement of sub-paragraph (*a*) of this paragraph so as to permit a contracting party to levy an anti-dumping or countervailing duty on the importation of any product for the purpose of offsetting dumping or subsidization which causes or threatens material injury to an industry in the territory of another contracting party exporting the product concerned to the territory of the importing contracting party. The CONTRACTING PARTIES shall waive the requirements of sub-paragraph (*a*) of this paragraph, so as to permit the levying of a countervailing duty, in cases in which they find that a subsidy is causing or threatening material injury to an industry in the territory of another contracting party exporting the product concerned to the territory of the importing contracting party.*

(*c*) In exceptional circumstances, however, where delay might cause damage which would be difficult to repair, a contracting party may levy a countervailing duty for the purpose referred to in sub-paragraph (*b*) of this paragraph without the prior approval of the CONTRACTING PARTIES; *Provided* that such action shall be reported immediately to the CONTRACTING PARTIES and that the countervailing duty shall be withdrawn promptly if the CONTRACTING PARTIES disapprove.

7. A system for the stabilization of the domestic price or of the return to domestic producers of a primary commodity, independently of the movements of export prices, which results at times in the sale of the commodity for export at a price lower than the comparable price charged for the like commodity to buyers in the domestic market, shall be presumed not to result in material injury within the meaning of paragraph 6 if it is determined by consultation among the contracting parties substantially interested in the commodity concerned that:

> (*a*) the system has also resulted in the sale of the commodity for export at a price higher than the comparable price charged for the like commodity to buyers in the domestic market, and
> (*b*) the system is so operated, either because of the effective regulation of production, or otherwise, as not to stimulate exports unduly or otherwise seriously prejudice the interests of other contracting parties.

Article XI*

General Elimination of Quantitative Restrictions

1. No prohibitions or restrictions other than duties, taxes or other charges, whether made effective through quotas, import or export licenses or other measures, shall be instituted or maintained by any contracting party on the importation of any product of the territory of any other contracting party or on the exportation or sale for export of any product destined for the territory of any other contracting party.

2. The provisions of paragraph 1 of this Article shall not extend to the following:

(*a*) Export prohibitions or restrictions temporarily applied to prevent or relieve critical shortages of foodstuffs or other products essential to the exporting contracting party;
(*b*) Import and export prohibitions or restrictions necessary to the application of standards or regulations for the classification, grading or marketing of commodities in international trade;
(*c*) Import restrictions on any agricultural or fisheries product, imported in any form,* necessary to the enforcement of governmental measures which operate:
(i) to restrict the quantities of the like domestic product permitted to be marketed or produced, or, if there is no substantial domestic production of the like product, of a domestic product for which the imported product can be directly substituted; or
(ii) to remove a temporary surplus of the like domestic product, or, if there is no substantial domestic production of the like product, of a domestic product for which the imported product can be directly substituted, by making the surplus available to certain groups of domestic consumers free of charge or at prices below the current market level; or
(iii) to restrict the quantities permitted to be produced of any animal product the production of which is directly dependent, wholly or mainly, on the imported commodity, if the domestic production of that commodity is relatively negligible.

Any contracting party applying restrictions on the importation of any product pursuant to sub-paragraph (*c*) of this paragraph shall give public notice of the total quantity or value of the product permitted to be imported during a specified future period and of any change in such quantity or value. Moreover, any restrictions applied under (i) above shall not be such as will reduce the total of imports relative to the total of domestic production, as compared with the proportion which might reasonably be expected to rule between the two in the absence of restrictions. In determining this proportion, the contracting party shall pay due regard to the proportion prevailing during a previous representative period and to any special factors* which may have affected or may be affecting the trade in the product concerned.

Article XVI*

Subsidies

Section A—Subsidies in General

1. If any contracting party grants or maintains any subsidy, including any form of income or price support, which operates directly or indirectly to increase exports of any product from, or to reduce imports of any product into, its territory, it shall notify the CONTRACTING PARTIES in writing of the extent and nature of the subsidization, of the estimated effect of the subsidization on the quantity of the affected product or products imported into or exported from its territory and of the circumstances making the subsidization necessary. In any case in which it is determined that serious prejudice to the interests of any other contracting party is caused or threatened by any such subsidization, the contracting party granting the subsidy shall, upon request, discuss with the other contracting party or parties concerned, or with the CONTRACTING PARTIES, the possibility of limiting the subsidization.

Section B—Additional Provisions on Export Subsidies*

2. The contracting parties recognize that the granting by a contracting party of a subsidy on the export of any product may have harmful effects for other contracting parties, both importing and exporting, may cause undue disturbance to their normal commercial interests, and may hinder the achievement of the objectives of this Agreement.

3. Accordingly, contracting parties should seek to avoid the use of subsidies on the export of primary products. If, however, a contracting party grants directly or indirectly any form of subsidy which operates to increase the export of any primary product from its territory, such subsidy shall not be applied in a manner which results in that contracting party having more than an equitable share of world export trade in that product, account being taken of the shares of the contracting parties in such trade in the product during a previous representative period, and any special factors which may have affected or may be affecting such trade in the product.*

4. Further, as from 1 January 1958 or the earliest practicable date thereafter, contracting parties shall cease to grant either directly or indirectly any form of subsidy on the export of any product other than a primary product which subsidy results in the sale of such product for export at a price lower than the comparable price charged for the like product to buyers in the domestic market. Until 31 December 1957 no contracting party shall extend the scope of any such subsidization beyond that existing on 1 January 1955 by the introduction of new, or the extension of existing, subsidies.*

5. The CONTRACTING PARTIES shall review the operation of the provisions of this Article from time to time with a view to examining its effectiveness, in the light of actual experience, in promoting the objectives of this Agreement and avoiding subsidization seriously prejudicial to the trade or interests of contracting parties.

Article XX

General Exceptions

Subject to the requirement that such measures are not applied in a manner which would constitute a means of arbitrary or unjustifiable discrimination between countries where the same conditions prevail, or a disguised restriction on international trade, nothing in this Agreement shall be construed to prevent the adoption or enforcement by any contracting party of measures:

(*a*) necessary to protect public morals;
(*b*) necessary to protect human, animal or plant life or health;
(*c*) relating to the importation or exportation of gold or silver;
(*d*) necessary to secure compliance with laws or regulations which are not inconsistent with the provisions of this Agreement, including those relating to customs enforcement, the enforcement of monopolies operated under paragraph 4 of Article II and Article XVII, the protection of patents, trade marks and copyrights, and the prevention of deceptive practices;
(*e*) relating to the products of prison labour;
(*f*) imposed for the protection of national treasures of artistic, historic or archaeological value;
(*g*) relating to the conservation of exhaustible natural resources if such measures are made effective in conjunction with restrictions on domestic production or consumption;
(*h*) undertaken in pursuance of obligations under any intergovernmental commodity agreement which conforms to criteria submitted to the CONTRACTING PARTIES and not disapproved by them or which is itself so submitted and not so disapproved;*
(*i*) involving restrictions on exports of domestic materials necessary to ensure essential quantities of such materials to a domestic processing industry during periods when the domestic price of such materials is held below the world price as part of a governmental stabilization plan; *Provided* that such restrictions shall not operate to increase the exports of or the protection afforded to such domestic industry, and shall not depart from the provisions of this Agreement relating to non-discrimination;
(*j*) essential to the acquisition or distribution of products in general or local short supply; *Provided* that any such measures shall be consistent with the principle that all contracting parties are entitled to an equitable share of the international supply of such products,

and that any such measures, which are inconsistent with the other provisions of this Agreement shall be discontinued as soon as the conditions giving rise to them have ceased to exist. The CONTRACTING PARTIES shall review the need for this sub-paragraph not later than 30 June 1960.

ANNEX B: JOHN H. JACKSON MEMO, "CHANGING GATT RULES"

(NOVEMBER 7, 1991)
The University of Michigan
Law School
MEMORANDUM
By: John H. Jackson
Hessel E. Yntema Professor of Law
University of Michigan
School of Law
Ann Arbor, MI 48109-1215
Tel: (313)764-2359
Tel: (313)764-8309
Re: Changing GATT Rules
Date: November 7, 1991

I have been asked to review the various techniques by which governments may be able to change GATT rules, perhaps to provide that these rules better accommodate some of the important environmental concerns and objectives of GATT Contracting Parties.

The following is a brief review of this subject. I have appended a list of some of the published works by this author, which can be consulted for greater detail.

I. INTRODUCTION.

Despite some occasional misguided or misinformed statements to the contrary, the GATT is a binding treaty obligation accepted by the nations which are Contracting Parties. Because of the odd beginnings of the GATT, however, there is considerable confusion about this and other matters concerning it.[71] The GATT was not originally intended to be an international organization, nor to be the central international institution for facilitating international trade. That role was to be for an ITO—International Trade Organization, as embodied in the so-called Havana Charter of 1948 which never came into force. Because it never came into force, the GATT has had to fill that role. Because of the structure of the drafting of the GATT agreement, the GATT treaty as such has never come into a force either, but it is nevertheless applied by the 1947 Protocol of Provisional Application (PPA), which is a binding treaty obligation. The practice of nations in GATT since this treaty came into force on January 1, 1948, entirely confirms the treaty nature. There is very little doubt expressed among the people who have looked at this issue closely, that the GATT has this binding treaty status.

71. *See* JACKSON, WORLD TRADE AND GATT, *supra* note 1; JACKSON, WORLD TRADING SYSTEM, *supra* note 1.

However, because of this peculiar history of origin, the GATT has a number of institutional weaknesses, what I have sometimes called "birth defects." I will not elaborate on these, but reference can be made to some of my other works where I have given this detail.[72] One example, has been the difficulty of amending the GATT, and this has led to approaches other than amendments, such as the various separate treaty "side-codes" resulting from the Tokyo Round. Furthermore, ambiguities in the GATT treaty relating to institutional procedures such as powers of the contracting parties, or voting, have provided a number of risks to the contracting parties, risks that have been felt particularly important to large trading powers. Thus, although the language in some cases might be deemed loose enough to authorize certain kinds of procedural ways to change the GATT, the contracting parties have been understandably and appropriately reluctant to exercise these procedures to their fullest scope.

II. Changing the GATT Rules.

The following is a quick summary outline of most of the various possibilities:

1) Formal Amendments to the GATT Treaty.

Article XXX of the GATT provides for amendment. Of course, the GATT is applied through the Protocol of Provisional Application, and one must look first to that protocol, but the practice in GATT has been to utilize the provisions of GATT as applied by the PPA, including Article XXX regarding amendments. In technical legal terms, the Protocol of Provisional Application applying the GATT is amended through the procedure of Article XXX, as incorporated in the PPA.

The provisions of Article XXX, however, are very stringent. This article requires unanimous consent to amend certain portions of the GATT (particularly Articles I & II on MFN and tariff concessions), and two-thirds approval to amend other provisions of the GATT. The practice has been that approval must be through a treaty ratification process of a protocol of amendment. Thus, many national governments find it necessary to submit amendments to their parliaments. When the "membership" numbered in the thirties, this procedure of amendment was more feasible. However, a unanimous amendment has never succeeded. As the membership has enlarged, and now exceeds 100, it appears to be increasingly difficult to fulfill the amending requirements. The Council of GATT was set up in the late 1950's by resolution of the Contracting Parties (there is no provision in the treaty for such a body), and the Council was formulated to be open to any Contracting Party which is interested. Yet, only about two-thirds of the GATT Contracting Parties have established membership in the Council as

72. *See* JACKSON, WORLD TRADE AND GATT, *supra* note 1; JACKSON, RESTRUCTURING GATT, *supra* note 1.

"interested." This can possibly be a signal of relative lack of interest of the other one-third, which could make it very difficult to achieve a two-thirds vote, especially if among the two-thirds "interested" parties there were even a small number who oppose an amendment.

Even if an amendment procedure succeeds, GATT Article XXX provides that those countries that do not accept the amendment are not bound by it. Thus, even an amendment has a certain "GATT à la carte" characteristic, with some countries bound and others not. In the Uruguay Round, there is some discussion of a fairly radical new technique for changing the GATT, by substituting a whole new treaty. I will refer to this below.

2) Waivers.

Article XXV paragraph 5 of GATT, provides that the Contracting Parties can adopt a "waiver" of the GATT, in circumstances not otherwise provided for, by two-thirds of votes cast (which must include at least a majority of the total membership). Waivers have been used for a variety of circumstances in GATT, including even waivers from Article I & II (thus somewhat undermining the amending unanimity requirement). Some waivers have been open ended without a termination date, and there is considerable discussion about a) whether that is appropriate; and b) whether even such waivers can be terminated by later vote of the Contracting Parties. Nevertheless, a waiver can be a very important and flexible means of changing GATT rules, at least for a temporary period of time. For example, a five year waiver could be adopted by the Contracting Parties that would specifically refer to certain listed multilateral environmental agreement (such as the Montreal Protocol) and provide that actions under them would not be deemed inconsistent with other GATT rules.

3) Decisions of Article XXV.

The language of Article XXV provides that the Contracting Parties acting jointly can "meet from time to time for the purpose of giving effect to those provisions of this agreement which involve joint action and, generally, with a view to facilitating the operation and furthering the objectives of this agreement." Article XXV provides for one nation, one vote, and unless otherwise specified, actions by a majority of the votes cast.

This is extraordinarily broad and flexible language, and thus could be subject to abuse. A large number of small countries could theoretically adopt new binding rules in the GATT to achieve an advantage for themselves at the expense of a minority of even very large and powerful trading countries, although such rules would not likely be followed. However, during the history of GATT it appears that there has never been a Contracting Party vote that imposed a new obligation on GATT Contracting Parties (except sometimes as a condition, or prerequisite to a waiver opportunity).

4) Interpretations of the GATT Agreement.

The language of GATT Article XXV is broad enough to conclude that the Contracting Parties have the power to definitively interpret the GATT provisions. By definitive interpretation, I mean an interpretation which would be binding as a matter of treaty law on all parties to the agreement including those which oppose the interpretation. Such is explicitly provided for in the charters of a number of other organizations including the IMF and the World Bank. There is no such explicit provision in GATT, and thus it could be contrarily argued that the intent of the draftsman was to exclude this power. However, the language of Article XXV is so broad, and there have been a number of instances of GATT practice consistent with the notion of GATT Contracting Party interpretations of the agreement, that in my judgment it can be successfully argued that Contracting Parties have this power of interpretation.

However, this raises a number of additional legal issues. An important first consideration is how to draw the line between an "interpretation," and a "new rule, or new obligation." There is no easy way, except in general an interpretation implies that the structure of the *existing language* reasonably permits a legal body, or tribunal to conclude that that language shall have the implications decided by the "interpretation." In instances of interpretation practice of the GATT, this has been the case.

Under general international law regarding treaties, as expressed, inter alia, in the Vienna Convention on the Law of Treaties, the practice of an international organization's bodies and organs over a period of time, is an important source of interpreting the charter, at least when that practice implies the agreement of the parties in the organization. Thus, the practice of GATT, including practice which interprets the provisions of GATT (whether by chairman's rulings, formal resolutions, waivers, etc.) all becomes part of the source material on which to base interpretations.

5) Dispute Settlement Panel Interpretations.

In the light of the previous section, dispute settlement panel reports which almost always include interpretations of the GATT rules become an important element of GATT practice. This is also the case for various dispute settlement bodies of the other related GATT treaties or side codes.

In fact there are several different ways to interpret the impact of a GATT dispute panel report. The practice of GATT, is that these reports must be approved by the Council. Thus, it can be successfully argued that without approval, the panel reports do not have any legal binding status (but they may still be persuasive as the opinion of important experts.)

Assuming that a panel report is adopted by the Council, however, there is still considerable ambiguity about its impact. There are at least two possibilities for that impact: 1) That the adoption by the Council is an exercise of the Contracting Parties authority under Article XXV to issue a definitive interpretation of the GATT binding on all; or 2) a decision by the Contracting Parties to adopt the panel report is a statement of how the particular dispute between the disputing parties involved in the case shall be resolved, thus imposing a binding international law obligation on those disputing parties (and only those disputing parties), to carry out the recommendation, decisions, or implications of the panel report.

It seems reasonably clear to me that the general practice of GATT supports the second but not the first interpretation. Indeed, arguably if the first were intended, a formal vote (at least a mail or telegraph ballot) should be taken of the Contracting Parties, and action should not merely be by Council decision. Furthermore, if one were to ask delegates at a Council meeting which adopted a panel report, if they intended that to be definitive in the broader binding sense, I feel secure in saying that most would indicate they had not thought of that question, but did not intend such an important impact.

If the second interpretation is the correct one about the result of an adopted GATT panel report, then we must understand that under international law there is no formal doctrine of "stare decisis" or precedent. Thus, the panel report legally binds only the disputants in the particular case, and even then only for that case (not even for a future case between the same disputants). This is the impact of explicit provisions in the statute governing the world court (the International Court of Justice, statute Article 59), which is also generally deemed to be the rule in international law (and indeed in most legal systems of the world, excepting the common law systems such as the UK and the United States). Nevertheless, such a GATT panel report is now "practice" of the organization, and becomes part of the source materials for interpreting the agreement. Furthermore, the panels themselves often use "precedent," by referring to prior panel reports, and certainly after a period of time, panel reports are relied and acted upon in a way that reinforces their impact as definitive interpretations through practice. Nevertheless, it must be understood, that the Contracting Parties (and thus the Council) do have the authority to depart from prior panel reports, and indeed subsequent panels themselves have departed from the conclusions of prior panel reports.

Of course, again, a panel's work engages the issue of when is a recommendation/decision an "interpretation," or really an exercise in "law making," of new rules. This issue is always involved in legal systems, and is certainly prominent among those debated in the context of national courts such as the U.S. Supreme Court. At the international level, there are likewise similar issues, and one can find in GATT panel reports language which is criticized because of the alleged overreach of a panel, encroaching upon the authority of the nation-state contracting parties to negotiate new rules.

6) Separate Treaties.

Another way to effectively change the significance and impact of GATT rules, is for those countries that are willing to undertake such change to enter into a separate treaty agreement embodying that change. This was the technique heavily used in the Tokyo Round Negotiation, developing a series of side "stand alone" treaties, sometimes called codes (such as those for customs valuation, antidumping, subsidies, government procurement, product standards, aircraft, etc.). This can be an effective legal device, particularly if such a treaty agreement is accepted by a large number of Contracting Parties, representing a very large proportion of world trade. Such treaties, of course, only bind those that accept it, so that those that refuse to accept it can argue that they are entitled to continue to rely upon the GATT agreement. Since the GATT agreement includes MFN—Most Favored Nation, some of those hold-out countries can argue they are entitled to the benefits of a side agreement even though they do not accept the side agreement, or its obligations. This has been an important limitation—sometimes termed the "free rider" or "foot dragger" problem of MFN. In the GATT, among the Tokyo Round codes, the one most widely accepted is that of product standards, and the number of countries which have accepted that is only about 40. Because this approach fragmented the rules system, it is termed "GATT à la carte" and has been heavily criticized, particularly in the context of Uruguay Round plans.

Treaties can have an impact on GATT, even though they are not negotiated or concluded in the GATT context. For example, if a number of GATT Contracting Parties in a totally different context (such as a multilateral environmental conference) enter into a treaty, that latter treaty will prevail in the event of conflict with GATT, as to the Contracting Parties which have accepted the latter treaty. Thus, for example, the Montreal Protocol dealing with CFC's, would be deemed to prevail as among those countries which have accepted it, even if inconsistent with GATT provisions. However, once again, it would not be deemed as a matter of law to prevail over the GATT obligations owed to GATT Contracting Parties which have *not* accepted the later treaty, or Montreal Protocol. Sometimes, a sufficiently large number of important trading countries have accepted a later treaty such that those members have felt that the risk of complaint by GATT Contracting Parties who have not accepted the later treaty making is minimal. This is legally a bit messy, but may be pragmatically acceptable.

7) Replacement Treaty Concepts and the Uruguay Round.

An additional way to change GATT rules, probably only available in the context of a very broad based reform or negotiation, such as the result of a major trading round, is in effect to replace the GATT with a totally new GATT agreement. Under the Protocol of Provisional Application of GATT, countries can withdraw from the protocol and GATT by only sixty days notice. It is possibly that a large number of GATT Contracting Parties, embodying an overwhelmingly large part of world trade, could come to a new GATT agreement, and agree to offer the benefits of the new agreement only to those countries which accept it. At the same time (or after a delay) these countries would exercise their right to terminate their obligations in the old GATT. If the numbers of new GATT followers were sufficiently large, this could effectively establish a new GATT, and put such heavy pressure on the hold out countries that they would deem it virtually essential to go along with the new GATT, thus abandoning the old GATT entirely.

This is not an approach to be lightly or repeatedly undertaken. It is probably available only in major reform circumstances, such as embodying the results of the end of the Uruguay Round. It would not be useful for time to time adjustments in the rules to keep abreast of rapidly changing international trade circumstances. It is also likely not to be available at this stage of the Uruguay Round for rather new subjects that could be acrimoniously controversial and thus a threat to the success of the Round as a whole.

III. Concluding Remarks

To summarize, there are a number of different ways to effectively change the GATT rules. It is likely that the most flexible for time limited and short term changes may be the "waiver" at least when the result is not to impose a new obligation on GATT Contracting Parties. But overall, the institutional defects and ambiguities of the GATT legal structure, while apparently providing a number of different options for changing the GATT rules, do not easily accommodate permanent change of a nature requiring new affirmative obligations. To slide by the legal requirements of GATT, or to rely on ambiguous clauses such as those of Article XXV, can raise considerable risks at least for major trading countries. These risks arise from the vulnerability to a one-nation, one-vote system in the context of more than 100 nation participants. It is thus likely that the United States, Europe, and Japan among others, would be reluctant to endorse a procedure that would provide a precedent for such future risks.

ANNEX C: SELECTED TEXT FROM NORTH AMERICAN FREE TRADE AGREEMENT (October 7, 1992)

ARTICLE 104: RELATION TO ENVIRONMENTAL AND CONSERVATION AGREEMENTS

1. In the event of any inconsistency between this Agreement and the specific trade obligations set out in:

(a) the *Convention on the International Trade in Endangered Species of Wild Fauna and Flora*, done at Washington, March 3, 1973, as amended June 22, 1979;
(b) the *Montreal Protocol on Substances that Deplete the Ozone Layer*, done at Montreal, September 16, 1987, as amended June 29, 1990;
(c) the *Basel Convention on the Control of Transboundary Movements of Hazardous Wastes and Their Disposal*, done at Basel, March 22, 1989, upon its entry into force for Canada, Mexico and the United States; or
(d) the agreements set out in Annex 104.1,

such obligations shall prevail to the extent of the inconsistency, provided that where a Party has a choice among equally effective and reasonably available means of complying with such obligations, the Party chooses the alternative that is the least inconsistent with the other provisions of this Agreement.

ANNEX 104.1

BILATERAL AND OTHER ENVIRONMENTAL AND CONSERVATION AGREEMENTS

1. The *Agreement Between the Government of Canada and the Government of the Untied States of America Concerning the Transboundary Movement of Hazardous Waste*, signed at Ottawa, October 28, 1986.

2. The *Agreement Between the United States of America and the United Mexican States on Cooperation for the Protection and Improvement of the Environment in the Border Area*, signed at La Paz, Baja California Sur, August 14, 1983.

ARTICLE 903:AFFIRMATION OF AGREEMENT ON TECHNICAL BARRIERS TO TRADE AND OTHER AGREEMENTS

Further to Article 103 (Relation to Other Agreements), the Parties affirm with respect to each other their existing rights and obligations relating to standards-related measures under the *GATT Agreement on Technical Barriers to Trade* and all other international agreements, including environmental and conservation agreements, to which those Parties are party.

ARTICLE 904:BASIC RIGHTS AND OBLIGATIONS *Non-Discriminatory Treatment*

3. Each party shall, in respect of its standards-related measures, accord to goods and service providers of another Party:

(a)national treatment in accordance with Article 301 (Market Access) or Article 1202 (Cross-Border Trade in Services); and

(b)treatment no less favorable than that it accords to like goods, or in like circumstances to service providers, or any other country.

ARTICLE 905:USE OF INTERNATIONAL STANDARDS

3. Nothing in paragraph 1 shall be construed to prevent a Party, in pursuing its legitimate objectives, from adopting, maintaining or applying any standards-related measure that results in a higher level of protection than would be achieved if the measure were based on the relevant international standard.

ARTICLE 907:ASSESSMENT OF RISK

1. A Party may, in pursuing its legitimate objectives, conduct an assessment of risk. In conducting such assessment, a Party may take into account, among other factors relating to a good or service:

(a) available scientific evidence or technical information;

(b) intended end uses ;

(c) processes or production, operating, inspection, sampling or testing methods; or

(d) environmental conditions.

2. Where pursuant to Article 904(2) a Party establishes the level of protection that it considers appropriate and conducts an assessment of risk, it should avoid arbitrary or unjustifiable distinctions between similar goods or services in the level of protection it considers appropriate, where the distinctions:

(a) result in arbitrary or unjustifiable discrimination against goods or service providers of another Party;

(b) constitute a disguised restriction on trade between the Parties; or

(c) discriminate between similar goods or services for the same use under the same conditions that pose the same level of risk and provide similar benefits.

3. Where a Party conducting an assessment of risk determines that available scientific evidence or other information is insufficient to complte the assessment, it may adopt a provisional technical regulation on the basis of available relevant information. The Party shall, within a reasonable period after information sufficient to complete the assessment of risk is presented to it, complete its assessment, review and, where appropriate, revise the provisional technical regulation in the light of that assessment.

[10]

Colorado Journal of International Environmental Law and Policy

Volume 5, Number 2 Summer 1994

NAFTA and the North American Agreement on Environmental Cooperation: A New Model for International Collaboration on Trade and the Environment

J. Owen Saunders†

I. INTRODUCTION

The North American Free Trade Agreement[1] (NAFTA) has both been attacked by environmentalists for its insensitivity to environmental issues and hailed as a breakthrough example of a "green" trade agreement. However one evaluates these conflicting views, the NAFTA is significant in that it represents an example of concerted, and at least to some degree effective, action by the environmental community to place environmental issues on the international trade agenda, as evidenced by the separate side agreement on the environment which became part of the political price exacted for gaining assent to the NAFTA proper. Moreover, the NAFTA experience has potentially wider applicability than merely in the North American context. At a minimum, of course, the approach will certainly

† Executive Director, Canadian Institute of Resources Law, and Adjunct Professor, Faculty of Law, The University of Calgary. The author would like to thank Lee Lau, a University of Victoria law student visiting the Institute as a Research Assistant, for his research assistance with this article.

1. North American Free Trade Agreement Between The Government of Canada, The Government of the United Mexican States, and The Government of the United States of America, Dec. 17, 1992 (*entered into force* Jan. 1, 1994) [hereinafter NAFTA].

prove important with respect to the question of admitting additional Parties to the Agreement. It is virtually impossible to imagine the terms of accession for such Parties not including environmental provisions similar to those in the NAFTA and its side agreement on the environment.

The NAFTA approach may, however, have even wider precedential value owing to the nature of the Parties involved. The NAFTA is a North-South trade agreement very unlike those concluded in the past. Previous trade agreements between developed and developing countries have involved largely nonreciprocal trade concessions from developed countries towards developing states; in sum, they were typically regarded as a form of development assistance. The NAFTA, however, provides an arrangement that was bargained for on a reciprocal basis, with both North and South making concessions. Indeed, it could be argued strongly that it was the developing state that made the bulk of the concessions.

The possible interest in the NAFTA approach as a precedent may prove especially high with respect to the environment. The concerns that were reflected with regard to the environment in the NAFTA negotiations are not unique to the North American experience. More and more they permeate the trade agenda, both among developed states and between developed and developing blocs. They cut to the heart of issues such as how one balances development and environmental objectives and how one reconciles traditional international legal concepts of sovereignty with the need to establish supranational environmental norms. While this article focuses on the North American experience, it may nevertheless have broader implications.

This article begins with a brief description of the background to the environmental provisions of the NAFTA, focusing on the growing interest in trade-environment issues, especially on the part of environmentalists. It then gives a brief overview of some of the major environmental provisions of the NAFTA. In this respect it will be suggested that the NAFTA does make at least some modest contributions towards "greening" international trade law; some of these are built on the negotiations undertaken in the context of the General Agreement on Tariffs and Trade[2] (GATT) Uruguay Round, while others are original to the NAFTA. Arguably, however, the greater contribution in the long run to resolving trade-environment problems (or, for that matter, environmental problems alone) is found in the side agreement on environmental cooperation. Accordingly, it is this agreement, rather than the NAFTA as such, to which the article turns for the bulk of the discussion. Finally, some brief conclusions are included.

2. General Agreement on Tariffs and Trade, *opened for signature* Jan. 1, 1948, T.I.A.S. No. 1700, 55 U.N.T.S. 194, *as amended* [hereinafter GATT].

II. BACKGROUND

The past five years have seen the growth of a voluminous legal literature on issues relating to the intersection of trade and the environment.[3] The increased and, in a sense, renewed,[4] interest in trade and environment reflects both global and regional factors. As to the former, the interest in the GATT and the environment is due partly to a number of environment-related trade disputes that have arisen under the GATT in recent years[5] and partly to the realization that the Uruguay Round of the GATT did not seem to be effectively addressing environmental concerns.[6]

Regionally, although the interest in the environment-trade nexus was not a major focus of the Canada-United States Free Trade Agreement[7] (FTA)—either in the negotiation of the Agreement or in the substance of the text finally agreed to—the FTA did act as the catalyst, at least in Canada, for discussing a number of environment-related issues. The particular emphasis on environmental issues in Canada was initiated not only by environmental groups, but also by a strong, and to a significant extent

---

3. *See, e.g.*, Ralf Buckley, *International Trade, Investment and Environmental* Regulation, J. WORLD TRADE, Aug. 1993, at 101; Steve Charnovitz, *Environmentalism Confronts GATT Rules*, J. WORLD TRADE, Apr. 1993, at 37; John H. Jackson, *World Trade Rules and Environmental Policies: Congruence or Conflict?*, 49 WASH. & LEE L. REV. 1227 (1992); Ernst-Ulrich Petersmann, *International Trade Law and International Environmental Law*, J. WORLD TRADE, Feb. 1993, at 43; Christopher Thomas & Greg A. Tereposky, *The Evolving Relationship Between Trade and Environmental Regulation*, J. WORLD TRADE, Aug. 1993, at 23.

4. There was considerable interest in trade-environment issues in the 1970s among trade theorists, especially economists. The early work in this area, beginning in the 1970s and continuing through the 1980s, was centered especially in the Organisation for Economic Cooperation and Development, focusing particularly on pollution-related issues (most notably the so-called polluter-pays principle). However, the interest of lawyers and environmentalists in such issues is of much more recent vintage. For a history of the interest in trade-environment issues, *see* J. Owen Saunders, *Legal Aspects of Trade and Sustainable Development*, *in* THE LEGAL CHALLENGE OF SUSTAINABLE DEVELOPMENT 370 (J. Owen Saunders ed., 1990).

5. Some of these disputes have been the subject of GATT panels—most notably, the highly visible dispute over the incidental killing of dolphins associated with tuna fishing: *United States Restrictions on Imports of Tuna*, GATT Doc. DS21/R (August 16, 1991), *reproduced in* 30 I.L.M. 1594 (1991) [hereinafter *Tuna Dolphin Case*]. Others, such as the dispute between the United States and the European Union regarding the use of hormones in the production of beef, while not going to a GATT panel, have nevertheless proved to be serious irritants in international trade relations. *See* John H. Jackson, *Dolphins and Hormones: GATT and the Legal Environment for International Trade After the Uruguay Round*, 14 U. ARK. LITTLE ROCK L.J. 429 (1992).

6. The general unhappiness with the GATT on this score has led to proposals for a new "green round" of GATT negotiations to deal with environmental issues. Gijs M. De Vries, *How to Banish Eco-Imperialism*, J. COM., Apr. 30, 1992, at 8A.

7. Canada-United States Free Trade Agreement, Dec. 10, 1987, *entered into force* Jan. 1, 1989 (implemented in Canada by the Canada-United States Free Trade Agreement Implementation Act, ch. 65, 1988 S.C. 1999 (Can.), and in the United States by the United States-Canada Free Trade Agreement Implementation Act of 1988, Pub. L. No. 100-449, 102 Stat. 26 (1988)) [hereinafter FTA].

overlapping, nationalist constituency which was opposed to the Agreement for a number of reasons. This constituency has no real equivalent in the United States,[8] although it bears some striking resemblance to movements that have played an influential role in Mexican political life.[9]

In the case of the FTA, this coalition of environmentalists and nationalists, together with other groups such as organized labor, found common cause in the issue of whether or not Canada had effectively surrendered its sovereignty with respect to management of its natural resources. In this latter respect, two concerns achieved particular visibility. First, there was intense debate over the "energy chapter" of the FTA,[10] which arguably instituted a continental energy market, in striking contradistinction to much of Canadian energy policy of the previous decade.[11] Second, suggestions were advanced that the Agreement would negatively affect Canada's ability to prevent the export of its water resources to the United States, echoing fears that, especially in the event of climate change, there might be a revival of schemes for major diversions of Canadian northern rivers southwards.[12]

Against this backdrop, it was not surprising that environmentalists in both Canada and the United States should concentrate their attention on the NAFTA negotiations. On the one hand, many US environmentalists were clearly frustrated with the treatment of environmental issues by the GATT,

---

8. This is not to suggest that the United States does not have powerful voices in favor of advancing—or protecting—the interests of American industry. However, such voices differ qualitatively from those that have characterized the nationalist constituency in Canada, which historically has been directed at broader issues of political and cultural sovereignty, and which has had as its primary focus (at least since World War II) the threat of US cultural and economic hegemony.

9. For a discussion of the similarities between Mexican and Canadian political history in this respect, focusing especially on historical distrust of US designs on continental energy resources, *see* J. Owen Saunders, *The Mexico Factor in North American Free Trade: A Canadian Perspective*, 9 J. ENERGY & NAT. RESOURCES L. 239, 240-48 (1991).

10. FTA, *supra* note 7, ch. 9. The essential elements of this chapter have since been affirmed for Canada and the United States (but not, in some important respects, for Mexico) in Chapter 6 of the NAFTA. NAFTA, *supra* note 1, ch. 6.

11. For a discussion of the transformation of Canadian policy in this respect, *see* Albert J. Hudec & John J. Quinn, *Energy Aspects of the Canada–United States Free Trade Agreement*, 2 CAN. PET. TAX J. 1 (1989); J. Owen Saunders, *Energy, Natural Resources and the Canada–United States Free Trade Agreement*, 8 J. ENERGY & NAT. RESOURCES L. 1 (1990).

12. For a survey of the issues on water export and free trade from varying perspectives, *see* CANADIAN WATER EXPORTS AND FREE TRADE (A.L.C. de Mestral & D.M. Leith eds., Rawson Academy Occasional Paper No. 2, Dec. 1989). The issue was revived again, following the signing of the NAFTA and the side deals, as part of the Canadian federal election campaign in the fall of 1993. As part of its election platform to "fix" the NAFTA

and especially the treatment of such issues in the *Tuna Dolphin* case.[13] This frustration reflected a wider suspicion of the willingness of trade institutions generally to give full credit to environmental concerns. On the other hand, for Canadian environmentalists, the NAFTA negotiations were seen as an opportunity to redress some of the unresolved concerns flowing out of the FTA, or at least as a challenge to prevent further "losses." In addition to these background issues, a new dimension was introduced by the inclusion of Mexico.

The possible addition of Mexico to a free trade area raised directly the problem of dealing with the trade consequences of environmental policies, owing to a widespread assumption that enforcement of environmental laws in Mexico was substantially more relaxed than in either Canada or the United States.[14] In the view of many environmental and labor groups in Canada and the United States, this held at least three important implications for both trade and investment flows in North America. First, Mexican products would enjoy an "unfair" competitive advantage because of the lower costs of environmental compliance in Mexico. Second, the existence of such an advantage would inevitably draw investment—again "unfairly"—away from the other two partners to seek a pollution haven in Mexico. Finally, there would inevitably be downward pressure on domestic environmental standards in both Canada and the United States as businesses demanded relaxation of these standards in order to remain internationally competitive.

This was not the first time that these considerations had been raised in the context of North American free trade. Indeed, all of these factors had been advanced previously in Canada—but vis-à-vis the United States, and focusing particularly on certain southern states—as reasons for rejecting

---

in a number of respects as a condition of implementing it, the Liberal Party undertook, inter alia, to make it clear that Canada would not be forced to export water as a consequence of the Agreement (a consequence that had always been denied by the then-ruling Progressive Conservative government, which had negotiated both the FTA and the NAFTA). Following the election of the Liberal Party, a number of statements were issued by the Parties which were taken by the incoming Liberal government as satisfying its election commitments. One of these was a joint statement with respect to water exports, which included the statement, "in order to correct false interpretations," that "[t]he NAFTA creates no rights to the natural water resources of any Party to the Agreement." *Statement by the Governments of Canada, Mexico and the United States*, Dec. 1, 1993 (on file with the COLO. J. INT'L ENVTL. L. & POL'Y). Other statements released simultaneously with this were the triparty statement on *Future Work on Antidumping Duties, Subsidies and Countervail*, and a unilateral *Declaration of the Government of Canada on Energy and the NAFTA* (both on file with the COLO. J. INT'L ENVTL. L. & POL'Y).

13. *Tuna Dolphin Case*, *supra* note 5.

14. It seems generally conceded that enforcement, rather than the substance of Mexican environmental laws, is the real problem to be addressed.

the FTA. However, they had special appeal in the case of the NAFTA because of the much greater disparity in effective (as opposed to de jure) environmental protection among the parties. The following section addresses briefly some of the major provisions of the NAFTA designed to deal with these environmental issues. As will be discussed, these provisions ultimately were not enough to satisfy political sentiment in the United States; however, they represent the first part of an environmental package that was eventually completed with the conclusion of a separate side agreement on the environment.

III. NAFTA AND THE ENVIRONMENT: AN OVERVIEW

As with the FTA, the NAFTA is preeminently a trade agreement. While it does have significant environmental provisions and indeed goes well beyond previous trade agreements in this respect, the fundamental character of the NAFTA as a treaty on trade must underlie any analysis of its implications for the environment. Since the focus of this article is not the NAFTA per se, but rather the separate agreement on environmental cooperation, the following discussion will merely outline the major environmental aspects of the NAFTA.[15] Three of these are of particular interest: (1) the relationship between the NAFTA and international environmental obligations, (2) the implications of the NAFTA standards chapter with respect to setting environmental standards, and (3) the NAFTA provision dealing with the issue of pollution havens for investment.[16]

---

15. For more detail on the environmental provisions of the NAFTA, *see* Steve Charnovitz, *NAFTA: An Analysis of Its Environmental Provisions*, [1993] 23 Envtl. L. Rep. (Envtl. L. Inst.) 10067 (Feb. 1993); Christopher Thomas & Gregory A. Tereposky, *The NAFTA and the Side Agreement on Environmental Co-operation*, J. WORLD TRADE, Dec. 1993, at 5; Bradly John Condon, Making Environmental Protection Trade Friendly Under the North American Free Trade Agreement (1993) (unpublished M. Thesis, University of Calgary).

16. GATT, *supra* note 2, art. XX. While these aspects are the most important ones, they are not the only provisions with possible implications for the environment. At least one other provision with direct bearing on trade and the environment is the interpretation of GATT Article XX, which creates exceptions from the normal application of GATT rules in the case of measures: "(b) necessary to protect human, animal or plant life or health [and] . . . (g) relating to the conservation of exhaustible natural resources if such measures are made effective in conjunction with restrictions on domestic production or consumption . . . ." There has been some concern on the part of environmentalists that the wording of these exceptions was not broad enough to create a full "environmental" exception. While some would argue that the provisions as now interpreted by the GATT are adequate to this task, the NAFTA clarifies the situation by incorporating GATT Article XX with respect to trade in goods and technical barriers to trade, and specifying that "[t]he Parties understand that the measures referred to in GATT Article XX(b) include environmental measures necessary to protect human, animal or plant life or health, and that GATT Article XX(g) applies to measures relating to the conservation of living and non-living natural exhaustible resources." *Id.*, art. 2101(1).

A. International Environmental Concerns

With respect to international environmental obligations, the NAFTA attempts to address the fundamental concern of many environmentalists that trade obligations should be made to give way to international environmental obligations. This was an issue raised in the wake of the *Tuna Dolphin* decision,[17] although that case did not itself raise an instance of a state in violation of its international environmental commitments. The NAFTA does not entirely resolve the question of the possible inconsistency of international trade and environmental commitments; however, it does take one step in this direction by spelling out the consequences of such inconsistency for certain specified agreements. For such agreements, the environmental obligations "shall prevail to the extent of the inconsistency, provided that where a Party has a choice among equally effective and reasonably available means of complying with such obligations, the Party chooses *the alternative that is the least inconsistent with the other provisions of [the NAFTA].*"[18]

17. *Tuna Dolphin Case*, *supra* note 5. The case involved, inter alia, the question of whether US legislation designed to protect the incidental killing of dolphin associated with purse-seine tuna fishing in the eastern tropical Pacific, and which had the effect of prohibiting imports of Mexican tuna into the United States, placed the United States in violation of its GATT obligations. The GATT panel decided in favor of Mexico on the major points (although finding in favor of the United States with respect to a separate issue of labelling requirements). In rejecting the US attempts to rely on two GATT exceptions relating to protection of animal health, GATT, *supra* note 2, art. XX(b), and conservation, *id.*, art. XX(g), the panel held that these exceptions were aimed at production or consumption within the jurisdiction of the importing country. It rejected the notion that the United States had the right to "unilaterally determine" the health protection or conservation policies of other states. The ruling, while never adopted because of a political settlement of the dispute between the United States and Mexico, infuriated many environmentalists in the United States. Interestingly, however, there was no serious contention that Mexico had violated international fisheries laws by its practices. Rather the case represented a situation where a nation (the United States) unhappy with the state of international law attempted to apply its domestic law in such a way as to influence fishing practices beyond its own borders. For a discussion of the US legislative initiatives in this respect, and their intersection with GATT norms, *see* Ted L. McDorman, *The GATT Consistency of U.S. Fish Import Embargoes to Stop Driftnet Fishing and Save Whales, Dolphins and Turtles*, 24 GEO. WASH. J. INT'L L. & ECON. 477 (1991). A reaction to the case typical of the US environmental community can be found in Robert F. Housman & Durwood J. Zaelke, *The Collision of Environment and Trade: The GATT Tuna/Dolphin Decision*, [1992] 22 Envtl. L. Rep. (Envt. L. Inst.) 10271 (Apr. 1992). For a more general argument that unilateralism (and US unilateralism specifically) has worked to the benefit of the environment, *see* Steve Charnovitz, *GATT and the Environment, Examining the Issues*, 4 INT'L ENVTL. AFF. 203, 206-08 (1992). For a perspective less sympathetic to the use of unilateral measures, *see* J. Owen Saunders, *Trade and Environment: The Fine Line Between Environmental Protection and Environmental Protectionism*, 47 INT'L J. 723 (1992).

18. NAFTA, *supra* note 1, art. 104(1) (emphasis added). Article 104 includes specifically as such agreements the Convention on International Trade in Endangered Species of Wild Fauna and Flora, Mar. 3 1973, 993 U.N.T.S. 243 (amended June 22, 1979, T.I.A.S. 11079) [hereinafter CITES]; the Montreal Protocol on Substances That Deplete the Ozone

There remains of course the question of the possible inconsistency between the NAFTA and other international agreements not included under this provision.[19] To an extent, some of the potential problems in this respect can be dealt with by established rules of treaty interpretation.[20] However, these will not always provide satisfactory or even clear answers. Moreover, such rules would not address the even more vexing question of the conflict between the NAFTA and possible rules of customary international environmental law. However, the challenge faced by the NAFTA in this respect is not unique. Similar problems exist with respect to the GATT, where indeed they are more serious given the large and diverse membership of the latter. In practice, though, the conflicts, at least between treaty obligations, may prove more theoretical than actual. For example, no GATT panel (nor any panel established under the FTA) has yet held that international environmental treaty obligations would have to yield to obligations under international trade law, and, as a practical matter, a state making such a claim might well face intense political pressures (not to mention embarrassment). In summary, while the NAFTA has not resolved this problem, it certainly represents a first useful step beyond the status quo.

B. Standards

With respect to the question of environmental standards, the NAFTA (following the Uruguay Round of the GATT in this regard) deals separately with sanitary and phytosanitary (SPS) measures[21] and other standards-related measures[22] (SRMs). In negotiating these sections of the NAFTA, the negotiators were heavily influenced by the work that had already been accomplished in preliminary drafts emerging from the Uruguay Round of the GATT negotiations. Accordingly, although the NAFTA predates the

---

Layer, Sept. 16, 1987, 28 I.L.M. 657 (amended June 29, 1990); the Basel Convention on the Control of Transboundary Movements of Hazardous Wastes and Their Disposal, Mar. 20–22, 1989, 28 I.L.M. 657 (on its entry into force for all three Parties; currently Canada and Mexico are Parties to the Basel Convention, while the United States has yet to ratify it); as well as any agreements included in Annex 104.1 (two bilateral agreements were included at the time of negotiation), which pursuant to Article 104(2) may be added to by agreement of the Parties.

19. There also remains the requirement of meeting the "least inconsistent" test, which some environmentalists would suggest is unduly restrictive of a state's ability to act in protection of the environment.

20. *E.g.*, the Vienna Convention on the Law of Treaties, May 23, 1969, S. EXEC. DOC. L, 92d Cong., 1st Sess., 1155 U.N.T.S. 331 (*entered into force* Jan. 27, 1980).

21. NAFTA, *supra* note 1, ch. 7 (Agriculture and Sanitary and Phytosanitary Measures). Sanitary and phytosanitary measures refer to those measures designed to protect human, animal, or plant life from risks related to additives, contaminants, pests, or disease (for a definition, which follows the text of the Uruguay Round, *see* NAFTA art. 724).

22. *Id.*, ch. 9, including specifically environmental protection (art. 904, para. 1). For a detailed discussion of the NAFTA's treatment of SRMs, *see* Irene Erika McConnell, Treatment of Standards Under the North American Free Trade Agreement: Integrating Trade and the Environment (1993) (unpublished M. Thesis, University of Calgary).

final text of the Uruguay Round, many of its provisions are strikingly similar to those found in the latter.[23]

As to SPS measures, the NAFTA establishes the right of each Party to take such measures, even if they are more stringent than international standards;[24] concomitantly, it is the right of each Party to establish the level of protection that it deems appropriate.[25] However, this right is subject to constraints. The measure shall be based on "scientific principles"[26] and "based on a risk assessment, *as appropriate to the circumstances*."[27] Furthermore, there are prohibitions on discriminatory treatment with respect to the goods of all Parties,[28] on the creation of unnecessary obstacles,[29] and on the creation of disguised restrictions on trade.[30] Despite the affirmation of sovereignty with regard to SPS measures, the NAFTA nevertheless encourages the reliance on international standards "as a basis for" such measures[31] and commits the Parties "to the greatest extent practicable . . . [to] pursue equivalence of their respective sanitary or phytosanitary measures."[32] More generally, there are a number of provisions—again largely based on the Uruguay Round negotiations—designed to increase the transparency of SPS provisions and to further cooperation between the Parties.[33]

Regarding the issue of other standards-related measures, including environmental measures, there is again established a general right to take such measures, including a right in each Party to establish the level of protection it deems appropriate in the pursuance of "its legitimate objectives of safety or the protection of human, animal or plant life or health, *the*

---

23. For the relevant final texts of the Uruguay Round negotiations with respect to SPS measures, *see Agreement on the Application of Sanitary and Phytosanitary Measures*, GATT Doc. MTN/FA/Corr.5-Annex 1A (Mar. 11, 1994); and with respect to SRMs, *see Agreement on Technical Barriers to Trade*, GATT Doc. MTN/FA/Corr.5-Annex 1a (Mar. 11, 1994).

24. NAFTA, *supra* note 1, art. 712(1).

25. *Id.*, art. 712(2).

26. *Id.*, art. 712(3)(a).

27. *Id.*, art. 712(3)(c) (emphasis added). Factors to take into account in conducting a risk assessment are set out in Article 715. In setting the level of protection each Party is further to take into account certain specified economic factors "where relevant" (art. 715(2)), as well as other factors such as "the objective of minimizing negative trade effects" (art. 715(3)(a)).

28. *Id.*, art. 712(4).

29. *Id.*, art. 712(5).

30. *Id.*, art. 712(6).

31. *Id.*, art. 713(1).

32. *Id.*, art. 714(1).

33. *See, e.g.*, *id.*, art. 717 ("Control, Inspection and Approval Procedures"), art. 718 ("Notification, Publication and Provision of Information"), art. 719 ("Inquiry Points"), art. 720 ("Technical Cooperation") and art. 722 ("Committee on Sanitary and Phytosanitary Measures").

environment or consumers."[34] Also, these rights are coupled with duties to provide nondiscriminatory treatment[35] and to ensure that unnecessary obstacles to trade are not created.[36] Each Party is also required both to use international standards as a basis for its SRMs, "except where [they] would be an ineffective or inappropriate means to fulfill its legitimate objectives,"[37] and to work towards compatibility and equivalence in SRMs.[38] In line with the chapter on SPS measures (and following the Uruguay Round of the GATT), there are additional provisions designed to emphasize the scientific basis of standards and to promote transparency and cooperation with respect to SRMs.

In summary, the environmental provisions of the NAFTA relating to standards are strongly influenced by the negotiations in the Uruguay Round of the GATT. As such, they emphasize the sovereign rights of each Party to set its own standards (even though they may be more stringent than international standards), but at the same time attempt to ensure that such standards are scientifically based and do not merely serve as disguised protectionism. While it has been suggested that the NAFTA language is in some respects more environmentally friendly than that of the Uruguay Round with respect to standards,[39] the general tenor of the NAFTA and the Uruguay Round final text is very similar.

---

34. *Id.*, art. 904(2) (emphasis added). "Legitimate objective" is defined as including:

> (a) safety,
>
> (b) protection of human, animal or plant life or health, *the environment* or consumers, including matters relating to quality and identifiability of goods or services, and
>
> (c) *sustainable development*,
>
> considering, among other things, where appropriate, fundamental climatic or other geographical factors, technological or infrastructural factors, or scientific justification *but does not include the protection of domestic production*.

Id., art. 915(1) (emphasis added).

35. *Id.* art. 904(3). This provision differs from that established for SPS measures, especially in its affirmation of a right to national treatment in accordance with Article 301; Article 710 explicitly provides, inter alia, that the national treatment obligations of Article 301 do not apply to SPS measures.

36. *Id.*, art. 904(4).

37. *Id.*, art. 905(1).

38. *Id.*, art. 906.

39. *See* Charnovitz, *supra* note 15. Charnovitz was directing his comments to the earlier "Dunkel Draft" of Dec. 20, 1991. Admittedly, the wording of the final agreement on SPS measures differs to some extent from that of the Dunkel Draft—most notably in changing the requirement that SPS measures be the "least restrictive to trade" to a requirement that such measures be "not more trade-restrictive than required to achieve their appropriate level of sanitary or phytosanitary protection" (where it is further noted in an interpretive footnote that "a measure is not more trade-restrictive than required unless there is another measure, reasonably available taking into account technical and economic

C. Environment and Investment

Where the NAFTA does depart significantly from the GATT is in its provision concerning environment and investment. This provision is directed primarily at the concern on the part of the United States and Canada that the NAFTA could give rise to pollution havens.[40] In this respect, the NAFTA Parties "*recognize* that it is inappropriate to encourage investment by relaxing domestic health, safety or environmental measures" and agree that "a Party *should not* waive or otherwise derogate from . . . such measures as an encouragement for . . . investment . . . ."[41] Clearly, this provision is not worded as strongly as it might be; moreover, the only remedy provided where one Party feels that another is indeed offering such encouragement is consultations.[42] However, given the reluctance of the GATT until recently even to deal with investment measures, this provision is at least a modest step forward.

D. Conclusion

In summary, the NAFTA does address some important environmental issues, although the response will not be far-reaching enough to satisfy many environmentalists. While many of the provisions with respect to standards are modeled on the negotiations of the Uruguay Round of the GATT, there are also provisions where the NAFTA moves unambiguously—albeit modestly—beyond existing trade treaties. These include especially the provisions relating to the treatment of conflicts between the NAFTA and certain international environmental agreements and the provision relating to environment and investment.

Precisely because these provisions were somewhat modest, especially with respect to the binding character of the obligations, it was clear from an early point in the NAFTA debate (and became even clearer with the election of President Clinton) that separate provisions would have to be negotiated outside the NAFTA to meet environmental concerns not addressed in the NAFTA itself. The most serious of these concerns, especially for the United States, was the question of enforcement of environmental law. It is this concern that is at the heart of the separate agreement negotiated on environmental cooperation.

---

feasibility, that achieves the appropriate level of sanitary or phytosanitary protection and is significantly less restrictive to trade"). In general, however, his comments would apply with equal force to the final text produced in 1993.

40. However, some writers have questioned whether investment flows are heavily influenced by the level of environmental standards imposed by a country. For different perspectives on this question, *see* INTERNATIONAL TRADE AND THE ENVIRONMENT, WORLD BANK DISCUSSION PAPERS NO. 159 (Patrick Low, ed., 1992).

41. NAFTA, *supra* note 1, art. 1114(2) (emphasis added).

42. *Id.*

IV. The North American Agreement on Environmental Cooperation

A. Introduction

The North American Agreement on Environmental Cooperation[43] (AEC) was, in effect, one of the prices[44] Mexico paid for admission to a North American free trade zone. Although it does not constitute a part of the NAFTA as such, it must nevertheless be viewed as part of the NAFTA package. However, the AEC differs from the NAFTA in approach in a fundamental respect. If the NAFTA can be characterized as a trade agreement with some environmental provisions, then the AEC can be characterized as an environmental agreement with some trade implications.

The examination of the AEC in this section begins with an overview of the agreement's objectives and obligations; as will be seen, many of the obligations are what at best might be called "soft law." The discussion then turns to the institutions established under the AEC, the success of which will ultimately determine the real value of the agreement. Finally, there is a discussion of the agreement's provisions on dispute resolution; while politically these were crucial to the salability of the agreement, it will be suggested that in practice they may prove less interesting than other aspects of the AEC.

B. AEC: An Overview of Objectives and Obligations

1. Objectives

The degree to which the AEC is an agreement about environment rather than trade is reflected in its first article, which sets out the objectives of the Agreement. Of the ten objectives listed, all but one are explicitly related to the promotion of environmental goals. These include references to sustainable development,[45] increased cooperation for environmental protection and conservation,[46] enhanced compliance with and enforcement of environmental requirements,[47] the promotion of transparency and public

---

43. North American Agreement on Environmental Cooperation Between The Government of the United States of America, The Government of Canada, and The Government of the United Mexican States, Sept. 13, 1993, 32 I.L.M. 1480 (*entered into force* Jan. 1, 1994) [hereinafter AEC].

44. *See also* the North American Agreement on Labor Cooperation, Sept. 9, 1993, 32 I.L.M. 1499, and the Understanding Between the Parties to the North American Free Trade Agreement Concerning Chapter Eight Emergency Action, Sept. 14, 1993, 32 I.L.M. 1519.

45. AEC, *supra* note 43, art. 1(b), and by implication art. 1(a).

46. *Id.*, art. 1 (c),(d),(f).

47. *Id.*, art. 1(g).

participation in developing environmental norms,[48] and the promotion of pollution prevention policies and practices.[49] The only explicit reference to trade obligations is in the objective to "avoid creating trade distortions or new trade barriers."[50] Some oblique reference to trade obligations may also be found in the objectives to "support the environmental goals and objectives of the NAFTA"[51] and to "promote *economically* efficient and effective environmental measures."[52]

2. *Obligations*

This environmental thrust is similarly reflected in the obligations undertaken by the Parties. The basic obligations under the AEC are of essentially two types—the first relating to domestic environmental law (which constitutes the bulk of the obligations),[53] and the second relating to international cooperation.[54] Of these, the former is by far the most important source of obligations.

The basic obligations with respect to domestic environmental law are in the main directed not at the substance of environmental laws and policy. Rather the emphasis is on secondary, albeit extremely important, issues relating primarily to procedure and enforcement. The obligations include those of a general nature, such as the broad commitments by each Party to take certain steps regarding environmental law and policy with respect to its territory,[55] to "consider implementing in its law any recommendation of

---

48. *Id.*, art. 1(h).

49. *Id.*, art. 1(j).

50. *Id.*, art. 1(e). Interestingly, the language would seem to be entirely prospective here; that is, there is no explicit goal under this agreement of eliminating or even reducing *existing* trade distortions or barriers.

51. *Id.*, art. 1(d).

52. *Id.*, art. 1(i) (emphasis added).

53. *Id.*, arts. 2–7 (Part Two, "Obligations").

54. *Id.*, arts. 20–21 (Part Four, "Cooperation and Provision of Information").

55. *Id.*, art. 2(1). These include commitments to:

> (a) periodically prepare and make publicly available reports on the state of the environment;
>
> (b) develop and review environmental emergency preparedness measures;
>
> (c) promote education in environmental matters, including environmental law;
>
> (d) further scientific research and technology development in respect of environmental matters;
>
> (e) assess, as appropriate, environmental impacts; and
>
> (f) promote the use of economic instruments for the efficient achievement of environmental goals."

the Council under Article 10(5)(b)" (discussed below),[56] and to "consider" the prohibition of toxic or pesticide exports where the substance is prohibited in that Party's own territory.[57] There are also more specific commitments directed at the issues of transparency,[58] government enforcement action,[59] effective private access to remedies,[60] and procedural guarantees.[61]

As noted, most of the obligations set out in Part Two are not directed at the level of environmental protection which a Party chooses to set, although as a practical matter it may well be the case that provisions such as those relating to improved enforcement of existing law may substantially improve the level of protection actually afforded. In general, though, the level of protection has been treated as a matter reserved to the sovereign discretion of each Party. The sole exception in this regard is the duty in Article 3, which provides: "Recognizing the right of each Party to establish its own levels of domestic environmental protection and environmental development policies and priorities . . . each Party shall ensure that its laws and regulations provide for high levels of environmental protection and shall strive to continue to improve those laws and regulations."

At first blush, this balancing of sovereign rights and environmental protection might seem to reflect the compromise that was achieved both in

56. *Id.*, art. 2(2). The Council referred to here is also established under the Agreement and is discussed *infra.*

57. *Id.*, art. 2(3). The same provision also requires that "[w]hen a Party adopts a measure prohibiting or severely restricting the use of a pesticide or toxic substance in its territory, it shall notify the other Parties of the measure, either directly or through an appropriate international organization."

58. Article 4 requires prompt publication of "laws, regulations, procedures and administrative rulings of general application" and, to the extent possible, advance publication of proposed measures and the provision of an opportunity to interested persons and Parties to comment on them. *Id.*, art. 4.

59. Article 5 requires that "each Party shall effectively enforce its environmental laws and regulations through appropriate governmental action," *id.*, art. 5(1), and then lists a number of illustrative actions that might be taken towards this end. It also addresses the issue of judicial and quasi-judicial or administrative enforcement proceedings, *id.*, art. 5(2), and speaks to the appropriateness of sanctions and remedies, *id.* art. 5(3).

60. *Id.*, art. 6.

61. Article 7 speaks to issues such as the openness and fairness of hearings, the timeliness of proceedings, the desirability of written reasons, and the availability of judicial review. In essence the procedures contemplated in Article 7 are of the sort that would typically be expected of judicial or quasi-judicial tribunals under either Canadian or US law. *Id.*, art. 7.

the Stockholm Declaration, Principle 21, and, more recently, in Principle 2 of the Rio Declaration.[62] As such, it would be disappointing to environmentalists, who have sought a stronger sense of obligation regarding environmental protection. On closer examination, however, the AEC principle goes beyond either of these declarations insofar as it strikes a balance between sovereign rights and environmental protection in the context of purely domestic environmental law. That is, the obligations in Article 3 apply even in the absence of transboundary environmental harm, whereas for both Rio and Stockholm the implicit assumption is that a duty to the international community is triggered only where there are transboundary effects.[63] As such, despite its relatively weak formulation, Article 3 represents a step forward in the articulation of binding international environmental norms.

Apart from the obligations with respect to domestic environmental protection in Part Two of the AEC, there are also obligations with respect to cooperation and provision of information in Part Four of the Agreement. These obligations include not only a general obligation to "endeavour to agree" on the application of the Agreement and to cooperate and consult in resolving matters affecting its operation,[64] but also to provide notification to "any other Party with an interest in the matter" of an environmental measure, actual or proposed, that "might materially affect the operation of [the] Agreement or otherwise substantially affect that other Party's interests under [the] Agreement."[65] There is also a requirement to provide information on such measures when requested[66] and, most interestingly, a

---

62. The Rio Declaration provides in Principle 2:

> States have, in accordance with the Charter of the United Nations and the principles of international law, the sovereign right to exploit their own resources pursuant to their own environmental and developmental policies, and the responsibility to ensure that activities within their jurisdiction or control do not cause damage to the environment of other States or of areas beyond the limits of national jurisdiction.

Rio Declaration on Environment and Development, United Nations Conference on Environment and Development, U.N. Doc. A/CONF 151/5/Rev.1 (1992), *reprinted in* 31 I.L.M.874 [hereinafter *Rio Declaration*]. This is an almost verbatim restatement of Principle 21 of the *Stockholm Declaration on the Human Environment*, U.N. Doc. A/CONF.48/14 (1972), *reprinted in* 11 I.L.M. 1416 (1972) [hereinafter *Stockholm Declaration*].

63. Admittedly, the Rio Declaration also provides for a more general obligation, not dependent on transboundary harm, in Principle 11: "States shall enact effective environmental legislation. Environmental standards, management objectives and priorities should reflect the environmental and developmental context to which they apply. Standards applied by some countries may be inappropriate and of unwarranted economic and social cost to other countries, in particular developing countries." *Rio Declaration*, *supra* note 62, princ. 11. Obviously, however, this does not speak directly to the *level* of environmental protection that should be enacted in such legislation.

64. AEC, *supra* note 43, art. 20(1).

65. *Id.*, art. 20(2).

66. *Id.*, art. 20(3).

right in any Party to bring to the attention of another Party possible violations of its environmental law.[67] There is a separate obligation to provide information to the Council and Secretariat set up under the Agreement, subject to requirements of reasonableness.[68]

The obligations under Part Four have their genesis in a number of international law documents, although in some important respects they go beyond what might be considered emerging customary norms of international environmental law. For example, there are numerous examples now in international law of the principles of cooperation,[69] consultation,[70] and notification to other states[71] concerning activities having possible environmental impacts. However, the thrust of such international obligations to date is, again, that they are predicated on extraterritorial environmental effects (usually phrased in terms of transboundary harm, although one could probably phrase a broader duty extending to effects on the global commons). Principle 19 of the Rio Declaration is typical in this respect: "States shall provide prior and timely notification and relevant information to potentially affected States on activities that may have *a significant adverse transboundary environmental effect* and shall consult with those States at an early stage and in good faith."[72]

The duties imposed on Parties under the AEC would seem to go beyond those arising merely in the context of actual or potential transboundary harm, although admittedly the language of the Agreement could be more helpful in this respect. Presumably, however, the reference to a Party with "an interest" in an environmental measure is not intended to refer only to those instances where the Party is suffering direct environmental harm, especially since the Article goes on to speak more generally of the Party's

67. *Id.*, art. 20(4).

68. *Id.*, art. 21.

69. *See, e.g.*, EXPERTS GROUP ON ENVIRONMENTAL LAW OF THE WORLD COMMISSION ON ENVIRONMENT AND DEVELOPMENT, ENVIRONMENTAL PROTECTION AND SUSTAINABLE DEVELOPMENT, LEGAL PRINCIPLES AND RECOMMENDATIONS, art. 14 (1987) [hereinafter EXPERTS GROUP]; *Rio Declaration, supra* note 62, princ. 7; *Stockholm Declaration, supra* note 62, princ. 24. Earlier examples of the duty can also be found in a number of documents relating to international water law.

70. *See* EXPERTS GROUP, *supra* note 69, art. 17; *Rio Declaration, supra* note 62, princ. 19.

71. *See* EXPERTS GROUP, *supra* note 69, arts. 16, 19; *Rio Declaration, supra* note 62, princs. 18, 19.

72. *Rio Declaration, supra* note 62, princ. 19 (emphasis added). The bulk of the articles proposed by the Experts Group are similarly phrased as "Principles Specifically Concerning Transboundary Natural Resources and Environmental Interferences." EXPERTS GROUP, *supra* note 69, arts. 9–20 (emphasis added).

interests under the Agreement.[73] Read broadly, then, this interest could extend to virtually any environmental measure, insofar as the rights under the AEC include the right to demand that the obligations with respect to "high levels of environmental protection" under Article 3 be complied with.

In summary, the obligations under the AEC have much of their genesis in international environmental law, and similarly reflect an attempt both to give effect to the principle of state sovereignty with respect to domestic environmental law and to recognize the interests of all states in environmental protection. The AEC goes beyond general international environmental law in articulating an interest by all Parties not only in environmental policies that may affect them through transboundary impacts, but also in what would normally be considered the purely domestic environmental issues of another state. While the substantive commitment to "high levels of environmental protection" is not onerous, the obligations with respect to openness, transparency, and effectiveness of environmental law may prove particularly useful when considered against the backdrop of the institutional arrangements established under the Agreement.

C. Institutional Arrangements: The Commission for Environmental Cooperation

While the obligations contained in the AEC arguably represent some modest advances in existing international environmental law, in many respects the greatest potential for innovative approaches to improving cooperative action on the environment is found in the institutional provisions of the agreement, and specifically in Part Three, which establishes the Commission for Environmental Cooperation. The Commission is to be based in Montreal and will comprise three bodies, each of which exercises distinctly different functions. These are a Council, a Secretariat, and a Joint Public Advisory Committee. The first two of these are typical of intergovernmental organizations; the last, however, is atypical and is one of the most interesting aspects of the AEC, in terms of both its role in the functioning of the Agreement and its potential as a model for other international agreements, especially those concerned with the environment.

1. The Council

The Council is the governing body of the Commission[74] and, as is typical of international organizations, comprises, in effect, the political masters ultimately responsible for the Agreement; accordingly it is com-

73. AEC, *supra* note 43, art. 20(2).
74. *Id.*, art. 10.

posed of "cabinet-level or equivalent representatives . . . or their designees."[75] The Council will meet at least once a year in regular session[76] and meet in special session at the request of any of the Parties.[77] With some important exceptions (noted below), Council decisions will normally be taken by consensus.[78] Again as is typical of international organizations, much of the work of the Council may be delegated to committees, working groups, or expert groups,[79] and it is anticipated that the Council will seek the advice of nongovernmental experts (including nongovernmental organizations).[80]

As the governing body of the Commission, the Council approves the Commission's annual program and budget;[81] oversees the operations of the Secretariat;[82] and exercises broad policy functions, including the consideration and development of recommendations on a wide range of environmental issues.[83] It is also charged with "strengthen[ing] cooperation on the development and . . . improvement of environmental laws and regulations,"[84] and "encourag[ing]" enforcement and compliance with environmental laws and regulations, and technical cooperation between Parties.[85]

The Council also serves as the link between the Commission for Environmental Cooperation and the Free Trade Commission established under the NAFTA. In this respect, it is noteworthy that the Council is charged with the duty to "cooperate with the NAFTA Free Trade Commission *to achieve the environmental goals and objectives of the NAFTA.*"[86]

---

75. *Id.*, art. 9(1).

76. *Id.*, art. 9(3)(a). The Council is required to hold public meetings in the course of regular sessions.

77. *Id.*, art. 9(3)(b).

78. *Id.*, art. 9(6).

79. *Id.*, art. 9(5)(a).

80. *Id.*, art. 9(5)(b). Nongovernmental organization (NGO) is defined broadly in Article 45 as "any scientific, professional, business, non-profit, or public interest organization or association which is neither affiliated with, nor under the direction of, a government."

81. *Id.*, art. 10(1)(e).

82. *Id.*, art. 10(1)(c).

83. *Id.*, art. 10(2). The Article lists 18 specific topics which touch on most areas of environmental law and policy, and then adds (art. 10(2)(s)) "other matters as it may decide." Additional recommendatory powers are found in Article 10(5) with respect to public access to information and decision making and to appropriate limits for specific pollutants; in Article 10(7) with respect to environmental impact assessment of projects with potential "significant adverse transboundary effects;" and in Article 10(9) with respect to reciprocal access of persons to rights and remedies in the event of harm caused by pollution originating in another Party.

84. *Id.*, art. 10(3).

85. *Id.*, art. 10(4).

86. *Id.*, art. 10(6) (emphasis added).

The essentially subordinate place of the Council vis-à-vis the Free Trade Commission is emphasized in the specification of the Council's functions. For example, the Council is to "provid[e] assistance in consultations under Article 1114 of the NAFTA."[87] Similarly, with regard to preventing or resolving "environment-related trade disputes,"[88] it is to make recommendations to the Free Trade Commission only with respect to avoiding disputes[89] and identifying appropriate experts to assist NAFTA bodies.[90] Finally, it is charged with "otherwise *assisting* the Free Trade Commission in environment-related matters."[91]

2. The Secretariat[92]

The Secretariat is, in effect, the day-to-day operating arm of the Commission.[93] It is headed by an Executive Director appointed by the Council for a three-year term.[94] Staffing of the Secretariat is then the responsibility of the Executive Director, subject to general standards established by the Council;[95] the Council has the power to reject appointments that fail to meet such standards.[96] While there is therefore room for political considerations intruding at the initial appointment stage (especially for the Executive Director, where any Party could effectively exercise a veto), the intention is that, once appointed, the Director and staff should be free of political influence.[97]

---

87. *Id.*, art. 10(6)(b). This refers to the NAFTA's provisions on environmental measures relating to investment, discussed earlier.

88. The very language is revealing; the disputes here are presented as trade-related with environmental aspects rather than environmental disputes with a trade aspect.

89. *Id.*, art. 10(6)(c)(ii).

90. *Id.*, art. 10(6)(c)(iii).

91. *Id.*, art. 10(6)(e). The Council is also charged with "considering on an ongoing basis the environmental effects of the NAFTA." *Id.*, art. 10(6)(d). However, it would appear to have no power to exercise any significant powers on the basis of its considerations.

92. The provisions dealing with the Secretariat are found in Section B of Part Three, *Id.*, arts. 11–15.

93. "The Secretariat shall provide technical, administrative and operational support to the Council . . . and such other support as the Council may direct." *Id.*, art. 11(5).

94. *Id.*, art. 11(1). The Director may be appointed for one additional term. However, the position of Executive Director is to rotate consecutively between nationals of the Parties. The Executive Director can be removed by the Council, but only for cause.

95. *Id.*, art. 11(2).

96. *Id.*, art. 11(3). Only a two-thirds majority is required for such decisions, in contrast to the consensus that is required for the appointment of the Executive Director. In making appointments to the Secretariat, the Executive Director is further required to take into account lists of possible candidates prepared not only by the Parties themselves, but also by the Joint Public Advisory Committee. *Id.*, art. 11(2)(b). Additionally, "due regard shall be paid to the importance of recruiting an equitable proportion of the professional staff from among the nationals of each Party." *Id.*, art. 11(2)(c).

97. The Executive Director and staff "shall not seek or receive instructions from any government or any other authority external to the Council. Each Party shall respect the international character of the responsibilities of the Executive Director and the staff and shall not seek to influence them in the discharge of their responsibilities." *Id.*, art. 11(4).

The Secretariat has three major functions assigned to it under the Agreement: preparation of the annual report of the Commission,[98] preparation of reports on other matters,[99] and certain duties relating to submissions on enforcement matters.[100]

The annual report is prepared under instructions from the Council.[101] The report covers not only the Commission's activities and expenses for the previous year,[102] but also the approved plan and budget for the subsequent year.[103] Additionally, it is to cover "relevant views and information" submitted by either nongovernment organizations (NGOs) or private individuals,[104] as well as other matters.[105] There is, finally, a requirement that "[t]he report shall periodically address the state of the environment in the territories of the Parties,"[106] although the timing and content of such reports would seem to rest entirely with the Council.

Of potentially more significance than its responsibility for the annual report is the Secretariat's power to undertake reports on its own initiative. Such reports are of two types. First, the Secretariat has the right to prepare a report for the Council "on any matter within the scope of the annual program."[107] Depending upon how broadly one interprets this language, this alone could amount to a substantial power of investigation. Second, the Secretariat may prepare a report on "any other environmental matter related to the cooperative functions of this Agreement" provided that it notifies the Council of its intention and provided that there is not a Council objection (based on a two-thirds majority) within thirty days of notification.[108] The Agreement is therefore tilted in favor of such reports going forward, rather than requiring permission from the Council.

It might, of course, be objected that the right to report is not a right to decide, and as such the actual powers of the Secretariat are less than impressive. However, given that this is an international forum, it would be

98. *Id.*, art. 12.
99. *Id.*, art. 13.
100. *Id.*, arts. 14–15.
101. *Id.*, art. 12(1).
102. *Id.*, art. 12(2)(a).
103. *Id.*, art. 12(2)(b).
104. *Id.*, art. 12(2)(d).
105. *Id.* The report may include recommendations falling under the Agreement and any other matter the Council wishes included. *Id.*, arts. 12(2)(e), (f).
106. *Id.*, art. 12(3).
107. *Id.*, art. 13(1).
108. *Id.* There is one significant constraint on what the Secretariat can report on under this provision, which excludes "issues related to whether a Party has failed to enforce its environmental laws and regulations." The Secretariat's role in this respect is dealt with separately in the Agreement. *Id.*, arts. 14–15.

unrealistic to expect that governments would allow final decision-making powers on significant questions of policy to pass out of the hands of political masters (and indeed, one could argue that such an approach would be questionable as a matter of democratic responsibility). As a practical matter, however, the political weight of such independent reports may be very significant, especially given that during the course of the information gathering the Secretariat may draw upon the widest array of sources, including the Joint Public Advisory Committee[109] and "public consultations, such as conferences, seminars and symposia."[110] Moreover, the report is to be made public within sixty days of its submission to the Council unless the latter decides to the contrary.[111] In summary, this power of the Secretariat to report on matters on its own initiative may well be an effective tool for raising the international visibility of environmental issues. Obviously, however, much will depend in this respect on the willingness of the Secretariat, and especially its Executive Director, to exercise a strong and independent voice. The Secretariat could also be hampered significantly in exercising a strong voice by financial constraints, given that ultimately its budget must be approved by the Council.

Apart from its reporting functions under Articles 12 and 13, the Secretariat also has separate functions with respect to the issue of effective enforcement of environmental law. In this regard, the Secretariat acts as the Commission's initial point of contact for complaints from either NGOs or private individuals that a Party is failing to effectively enforce its environmental law.[112] The Secretariat must first decide whether such a complaint meets some minimum criteria of acceptability.[113] Assuming that these criteria are met, the Secretariat then determines "whether the submission

---

109. *Id.*, art. 13(2)(c).

110. *Id.*, art. 13(2)(e).

111. *Id.*, art. 13(3). A decision *not* to publish apparently requires a consensus on the part of the Council, effectively preventing a Party from exercising a "veto" over its release.

112. This failure is defined negatively in Article 45:

> A Party has not failed to "effectively enforce its environmental law" . . . in a particular case where the action or inaction in question by agencies or officials of that Party:
>
> (a) reflects a reasonable exercise of their discretion in respect of investigatory, prosecutorial, regulatory or compliance matters; or
>
> (b) results from *bona fide* decisions to allocate resources to enforcement in respect of other environmental matters determined to have higher priorities.

Id., art. 45(1).

113. *Id.*, art. 14(1). These criteria relate primarily to clarity, certain procedural regularities, and a finding that the submission "appears to be aimed at promoting enforcement rather than at harassing industry." *Id.*, art. 14(1)(d). One can see some obvious difficulties in assessing this last requirement, especially, for example, if an NGO complainant is an industry association.

merits requesting a response from the Party."[114] Again, in making this decision, the Secretariat is to be guided by specified criteria.[115]

In the event that the Secretariat decides to request a response from a Party, the latter is given thirty days (in exceptional cases sixty days) to reply.[116] The Party may respond in two ways. First, it may advise the Secretariat that "the matter is the subject of a pending judicial or administrative proceeding," in which case the Secretariat is precluded from taking any further action.[117] Alternatively, it may submit other information as it wishes.[118]

In light of the response from the Party, the Secretariat must then make a further decision as to whether or not the submission warrants the development of a "factual record."[119] If it decides this step is appropriate, it must then approach the Council for permission, which can instruct the Secretariat to take this step by a two-thirds majority.[120] In preparing this record, the Secretariat is required to consider any information provided by any Party, and may also consider other information from a variety of sources, including that developed by itself or independent experts.[121] Following the submission of the Secretariat's draft of the factual record to the Council, further comments on the accuracy are restricted to Parties.[122]

---

114. *Id.*, art. 14(2).

115. These include whether:

> (a) the submission alleges harm to the person or organization making the submission;
>
> (b) the submission, alone or in combination with other submissions, raises matters whose further study in this process would advance the goals of this Agreement;
>
> (c) private remedies available under the Party's law have been pursued; and
>
> (d) the submission is drawn exclusively from mass media reports.

Id., art. 14(2). Unfortunately, this provision gives no indication of how these criteria should be weighted. To take only one problem, what is the significance of the reference to "harm" to the complainant as a factor guiding the Secretariat's response? Narrowly read, this could raise obstacles that have confronted plaintiffs in domestic courts with respect to standing in environmental cases (albeit the criterion here is formally directed at the remedy rather than the issue of standing).

116. *Id.*, art. 14(3).

117. *Id.*, art. 14(3)(a).

118. Examples of such information suggested in the Agreement include: "i) whether the matter was previously the subject of a judicial or administrative proceeding, and ii) whether private remedies [are available and] have been pursued." *Id.*, art. 14(3)(b).

119. *Id.*, art. 15(1).

120. *Id.*, art. 15(2).

121. *Id.*, art. 15(4). The Article also refers to information that is available publicly (art. 15(4)(a)), that is submitted by interested persons or NGOs (art. 15(4)(b)), or that is submitted by the Joint Public Advisory Committee (art. 15(4)(c)).

122. Paties have 45 days to respond. *Id.*, art. 15(5). There are, however, no time limits specified on the preparation of this draft by the Secretariat.

Following the incorporation of such comments into the draft,[123] the Council by a two-thirds majority "*may*" make the record publicly available.[124] Although there is room at this stage for the Council to withhold release permanently, this would seem highly unlikely in practice, given the voting procedure and the expectations raised by previous public input into the process.

3. The Joint Public Advisory Committee

The Joint Public Advisory Committee (JPAC) is the most innovative institution established under the AEC. However, its role is only briefly described in the Agreement[125] and its effectiveness will ultimately depend not only on the role it sees for itself, but also the financing allocated to it by the Council.

The JPAC will normally comprise fifteen members, with equal numbers appointed by each Party.[126] The JPAC would not appear to have a day-to-day operational existence. This is suggested by the lack of any supporting institutional infrastructure and by the fact that it is required to meet only once a year, coincident with the annual meeting of the Council.[127] The functions of the Advisory Committee are both generally to provide advice to the Council on virtually any matter related to the Agreement[128]

---

123. The discretion here as to which comments to include would seem to rest with the Secretariat which "shall incorporate, as appropriate" such comments. *Id.*, art. 15(6).

124. *Id.*, art. 15(7) (emphasis added). This is "normally" to be done within 60 days of submission. The Council also has the option of making the factual record available (again, by a two-thirds majority) only to the Joint Public Advisory Committee. *Id.*, art. 16(7).

125. The JPAC is established in one Article, Article 16, under Part Three, Section C (Advisory Committees). There are two other types of committees provided for in this section. The others, however—National Advisory Committees and Governmental Committees—may be set up at the discretion of each Party to advise it on the implementation and elaboration of the Agreement. Since they have no formal role at the international level, they will not be discussed here. Indeed, other than for hortatory purposes, it is not clear why they are referred to in the Agreement, since presumably a Party could establish such committees without authorization under the AEC. *Id.*, art. 16.

126. *Id.*, art. 16(1). The Council can vary this number. A Party can choose to have its members appointed by its National Advisory Committee, established pursuant to Article 17.

127. *Id.*, art. 16(3). It can also meet "at such other times as the Council, or the Committee's chair with the consent of a majority of its members, may decide."

128. Article 16 reads:

> The . . . [c]ommittee may provide advice to the Council on any matter within the scope of this Agreement, including [the Commission's proposed annual program and budget, the draft annual report, and any report prepared by the Secretariat under art. 13], and on the implementation and further elaboration of this Agreement, and may perform such other functions as the Council may direct.

Id., art. 16(4).

and to provide information to the Secretariat, including information related to the development of a factual record.[129]

The provisions on the JPAC provide cause for both disappointment and optimism. With respect to the former, of the three institutions in the Commission, the JPAC has the least defined role. While there also remain details to be fleshed out regarding the interplay of the Council and Secretariat, there is more than a mere fleshing out required for the JPAC. For example, lacking are even such basic provisions as a fixed term for members (to encourage their independence)[130] or a reference to the qualifications expected of them (to encourage appointments of a high caliber).[131] Presumably these are issues that will be worked out by the Ministers responsible for the Agreement. More problematically though—as perhaps reflected in the shortcomings noted—it is not clear that the Parties to the AEC have clearly thought out the role of a body such as the JPAC. As it stands, the JPAC would seem to be a largely reactive body, providing input to the Council and Secretariat largely on an ad hoc basis. The JPAC is not given an explicit role with respect to undertaking on its own initiative its own work agenda—a role that is given to the Secretariat. One could imagine a number of such roles for a body such as the JPAC, including actively fostering transborder ties among environmental NGOs, but there is little direction provided in this regard in the AEC.

On a positive note, it is possible of course that, with the right membership and the right chair, the JPAC could assert a strong activist presence. For example, the provision that the JPAC "may provide advice to the Council on any matter within the scope of" the AEC[132] could be read as granting a mandate to give unsolicited as well as solicited advice. Again, however, as with the Secretariat, the ability of the JPAC to pursue this course may be largely determined by the budget allocated to it by the Council.

---

129. *Id.*, art. 16(5)—although the factual record itself is not automatically provided to the JPAC, unless Council votes to make it available (by a two-thirds majority). *Id.*, art. 16(7).

130. By contrast, members of the roster of possible arbitration panelists, discussed *infra*, are given such fixed terms, *id.*, art. 25(1), as is the Executive Director of the Secretariat, *id.*, art. 11(1).

131. Again, criteria are established for members of the roster of potential arbitration panelists, *id.*, art. 25(2), and for staff of the Secretariat, *id.*, art. 11(2). There is similarly lacking any direction as to the extent to which JPAC members should represent a range of perspectives on the environment; indeed, under the wording of the Agreement it would be open to a Party to appoint nothing but government officials to the JPAC.

132. *Id.*, art. 16(4).

4. Conclusions

In summary, the institutional provisions of the AEC are a blend of features characteristic of international organizations and features that are new to this agreement. While the potential of these institutions has yet to be realized, there are at least three aspects of the AEC that hold particular promise. First, the ability of the Secretariat to exercise an independent role in the issuance of reports on a wide range of environmental issues suggests that the Commission may prove more than a captive of its political masters. Second, the procedure for the development of a factual record at the initiation of nongovernmental bodies is an interesting and innovative means of allowing citizens and NGOs a role as watchdogs on government in an international forum. Finally, while one would have hoped for more than the skeletal provisions on the JPAC, the concept is in principle encouraging and the role as defined in the agreement could allow for the development of an activist committee capable of forging and encouraging ties across borders among environmental NGOs.

It is true, of course, that the powers of the Secretariat and the JPAC are largely recommendatory, with ultimate decision-making power in the hands of the Council. However, there is much to suggest in the evolution of domestic environmental law and policy that the power to air environmental issues openly and publicly in an institutionalized forum may prove highly effective if properly utilized.

D. Dispute Resolution

A crucial aspect of the Commission in terms of its acceptability to all Parties was the regime for dispute resolution. Indeed, agreement on a regime with some teeth was critical to the larger issue of the "selling" of the NAFTA in the US Congress. By contrast, the Canadian government made it clear that if these teeth included trade sanctions, this would be a "deal breaker" for Canada.[133] The approach ultimately agreed upon reflects both these concerns. The regime is found in a separate part of the Agreement,[134] and procedurally would appear to be heavily influenced by the dispute resolution mechanisms found in the NAFTA. The approach, typical of international agreements, is a graduated series of steps, beginning with consultations, moving on to other attempts to resolve the dispute, then to

133. The Canadian insistence on the avoidance of trade sanctions as a means of inducing compliance was rooted in a long-standing distrust of the United States' willingness to use trade sanctions for protectionist ends, especially in the natural resources sector. For a discussion of the background to these fears, *see* Christian Yoder, *United States Countervailing Duty Law and Canadian Natural Resources: The Evolution of Resources Protectionism in the United States*, *in* TRADING CANADA'S NATURAL RESOURCES 81 (J. Owen Saunders ed., 1987).

134. AEC, *supra* note 43, arts. 22–36.

arbitration, implementation of the arbitral report, and, as a last resort, penalties for noncompliance. If practice under the GATT (where one finds a sequence that is in some respects similar) is instructive, it is likely that most disputes will never reach the stage of arbitration.

The most notable aspect of the AEC's dispute resolution procedures is their highly limited scope, a scope that was dictated by the most serious concern on the part of the United States which gave rise to the AEC itself. Specifically, the dispute resolution mechanism does not provide for the settlement of a broad range of environmental disputes. Rather, the mechanism is restricted only to questions concerning whether there has been a "persistent pattern of failure" by a Party "to effectively enforce its environmental law."[135] Moreover, as discussed *infra*, this ambit is restricted further in those instances where a dispute goes to arbitration. This is critical in that the mechanism does not provide a forum to address other shortcomings under the Agreement—perhaps most notably, each Party's commitment in Article 3 to "ensure that its laws and regulations provide for high levels of environmental protection."[136]

A second important restriction on the dispute resolution mechanism is that it is available only to Parties to the Agreement. While this is typical of international agreements, it does stand in contrast to the earlier discussed provisions allowing significant room for actions initiated by individuals and NGOs.

1. Consultations

One example of the influence of the NAFTA approach to dispute resolution is found in the provisions on consultation, which are very similar to those provided in Article 2006 of the NAFTA. Consultations are, of course, the first step typically provided for dispute resolution in international agreements. Under the AEC, any Party may request consultations "regarding whether there has been a persistent pattern of failure by [another] Party to effectively enforce its environmental law."[137] It is anticipated that "a third Party that considers it has a substantial interest in the matter" will also be entitled to participate in the consultations.[138]

---

135. *Id.*, art. 22(1).

136. *Id.*, art. 3.

137. *Id.*, art. 22(1). The request is to be in writing and shall be delivered by the requesting Party to the other Parties and to the Secretariat. *Id.*, art. 22(2).

138. *Id.*, art. 22(3). The Council may, however, provide otherwise in setting the rules and procedures for the Commission. This provision mirrors the third-party rights established in the NAFTA. NAFTA, *supra* note 1, art. 2006(3).

2. *Initiation of Procedures*

Failing the resolution of the matter through consultations, a consulting Party may request a special session of the Council.[139] The Council may then use its good offices, conciliation, mediation, or other procedures in an attempt to assist in the resolution of the dispute.[140] It may also make recommendations which, at the Council's option, may be made public.[141]

3. *Arbitral Panels*

If the dispute is still unresolved within sixty days of the Council convening under Article 23, a Party may request the convening of an arbitral panel to consider the matter. However, the coverage of the dispute resolution mechanism is narrowed significantly at this point, in that such panels can be convened only where the pattern of failure to enforce environmental law "relates to a situation involving workplaces, firms, companies or sectors that produce goods or provide services: (a) traded between the territories of the Parties; or (b) that compete, in the territory of the Party complained against, with goods or services produced or provided by persons of another Party."[142] This provision again emphasizes the degree to which the agreement is driven by trade considerations. Although it is certainly true that a wide range of environmental issues will be open for consideration at a number of points in the agreement, when it comes to the issue of binding arbitration, only those environmental issues with a trade nexus can trigger action.

The process for selecting the arbitral panel is similarly modeled on the process established under the NAFTA, but with some differences reflecting the need for appropriate expertise given the environmental nature of the agreement. The Council is required to establish a roster of qualified individuals[143] with expertise in environmental law or international dispute resolution or other relevant experience.[144] The professional and independent nature of the roster is emphasized, with an explicit prohibition on a member maintaining an affiliation with, or receiving instructions from, any Party, the Secretariat, or the JPAC.[145] In the event of a dispute going to

---

139. AEC, *supra* note 43, art. 23(1). This mirrors, though with some differences, a NAFTA provision. NAFTA, *supra* note 1, art. 2007.

140. AEC, *supra* note 43, art. 23(4)(b).

141. *Id.*, art. 23(4)(c).

142. *Id.*, art. 24(1). Again, a third Party may join the dispute where it considers it has a substantial interest in the matter. *Id.*, art. 24(2).

143. *Id.*, art. 25(1). The roster can comprise up to 45 individuals (no minimum is specified), who are to be appointed by consensus for three-year terms.

144. *Id.*, art. 25(2)(a).

145. *Id.*, art. 25(2)(c). Additionally, members are to "be chosen strictly on the basis of objectivity, reliability and sound judgment," and are subject to a Code of Conduct to be established by the Council. *Id.*, art. 25(2)(b), (d).

arbitration, a panel of five members is selected, with the disputing Parties jointly choosing a chair[146] and each selecting two panelists who are citizens of the other Party.[147] Panelists will normally be selected from the roster, although non-roster individuals may also be nominated, subject to a peremptory challenge from another disputing Party.[148]

After submissions and arguments by the Parties,[149] and possibly also by a third Party that wishes to be heard,[150] and after receiving any relevant expert advice,[151] the panel is then required to present an initial report to the disputing Parties. The report must contain findings of fact, a determination as required in the terms of reference, and, in the event of an affirmative finding, recommendations for resolution of the dispute.[152] After receiving any comments by disputing Parties on the initial report, the panel shall then present a final report to these Parties, who shall transmit it to the Council together with any comments a disputing Party wishes to append; five days later the report is to be published.[153]

In implementing the recommendations consequent on an affirmative finding by an arbitration panel, the disputing Parties themselves may agree

---

146. *Id.*, art. 27(1)(b). In the event of a failure to agree on a chair, the same Article provides that "the disputing Party chosen by lot shall select within five days a chair who is not a citizen of that Party."

147. *Id.*, art. 27(1)(c). Where there are more than two disputing Parties, the selection of the Panel proceeds on a similar path; for example, in choosing the four members other than the chair, the Party complained against is entitled to select two panelists: one a citizen of one complaining Party, and another a citizen of the other complaining party; and the complaining Parties shall select two citizens of the Party complained against. *Id.*, art. 27(2)(c). The provisions for selecting the chair are also similar. *Id.*, art. 27(2)(b).

148. *Id.*, art. 27(3).

149. Under rules and procedures to be established by the Council under guidelines set out in Article 28, *id.*, art. 28(1). Unless the disputing Parties agree otherwise, the panel's terms of reference shall be:

> To examine, in light of the relevant provisions of the Agreement, including those contained in Part Five, whether there has been a persistent pattern of failure by the Party complained against to effectively enforce its environmental law, and to make findings, determinations and recommendations in [an initial report pursuant to] Article 31(2).

Id., art. 28(3).

150. *Id.*, art. 29.

151. *Id.*, art. 30. The advice may be sought at the request of a disputing Party or by the panel on its own initiative, subject to agreement by the disputing Parties.

152. *Id.*, art. 31(2). Such recommendations "normally shall be that the Party complained against adopt and implement an action plan sufficient to remedy the pattern of nonenforcement." *Id.*, art. 31(2)(c).

153. *Id.*, art. 32. There does not appear to be any option of withholding the report from publication.

on a satisfactory action plan to remedy the "persistent pattern of failure."[154] Alternatively, if there is a failure to agree either to an action plan or to whether a Party is fully implementing an action plan, the Council shall reconvene the panel upon the request of a disputing Party.[155]

Once reconvened, in cases where there is nonagreement on an action plan, the panel may approve the plan proposed by the Party complained against or establish an appropriate plan,[156] and also impose a monetary penalty "where warranted."[157] This assessment is to be paid into a Commission fund "and shall be expended at the direction of the Council to improve or enhance the environment or environmental law enforcement in the Party complained against, consistent with its law."[158] In those cases where the panel is reconvened to consider whether there is indeed full implementation of an action plan, the panel, in the event of an affirmative finding, is *required* to impose a monetary penalty.[159] Continued failure to fully implement the action plan may result in a reconvening of the panel by the Council at the request of a complaining Party.[160]

As a final resort, in the event of continuing noncompliance either with respect to paying an assessed penalty or with respect to implementing an action plan, a complaining Party may suspend NAFTA benefits against the offending Party,[161] unless that Party is Canada. While enforcement through the removal of NAFTA benefits is not allowed vis-à-vis Canada,[162] in the alternative, panel determinations that could result in such trade sanctions

---

154. *Id.*, art. 33. It is contemplated that this plan "normally shall conform with the determinations and recommendations of the panel."

155. *Id.*, art. 34(1). There are time limits attached to these various stages. One practical problem that might be anticipated (but which is not addressed in the AEC), given that the option of reconvening might be exercised some considerable time after the panel's original decision, is what course should be taken if a member or members of the original panel is/are unavailable. This is a problem particularly with respect to disputes over whether or not an action plan is being fully implemented, something that might take considerable time to evaluate.

156. *Id.*, art. 34(4)(a).

157. *Id.*, art. 34(4)(b). The penalty, referred to as a "monetary enforcement assessment," is specified in greater detail in Annex 34, which both places limits on such a penalty and provides factors to consider in the determination of the assessment.

158. *Id.*, Annex 34(3).

159. *Id.*, art. 34(5). Again, this is pursuant to the guidelines set out in Annex 34.

160. *Id.*, art. 35.

161. *Id.*, art. 36. The suspension in benefits is limited, however, pursuant to Annex 36B. In the event of a request on the part of the Party complained against, the panel may be reconvened by the Council to consider whether that Party has since fully complied with the action plan or has paid the monetary assessment; given an affirmative finding, the suspension of benefits will be terminated. *Id.*, art. 36(4). The panel may be similarly reconvened to consider whether the suspension of benefits is "manifestly excessive." *Id.*, art. 36(5).

162. *Id.*, Annex 36A(3).

may be filed by the Commission in a Canadian court, where for enforcement purposes they will be treated as court orders, not subject to review or appeal.[163] The Commission may then have the order enforced by way of summary proceedings.[164]

In summary, the AEC does indeed provide the "teeth" that were promised to the environmental community. However, given the steps that must be taken to arrive at this point, it is unlikely that the teeth—at least with respect to the imposition of trade sanctions—will be often employed. This does not detract entirely from the importance of the arbitral provisions, of course; the very fact that they exist should serve as a strong inducement towards compliance. However, the scope of the disputes that can be reached by arbitration—and by the dispute resolution mechanism more generally—is such that many significant environmental issues will not fall within it. This points once again to the importance of relying on those provisions in the AEC that are geared towards cooperation.

V. CONCLUSIONS

Although the NAFTA has a number of innovative provisions dealing with the environment, it remains preeminently a trade agreement. As such, it is unlikely that any version of the NAFTA concluded by trade negotiators would meet with the full approval of the environmental community in North America. Some environmentalists, indeed, would assert that the very concept of an international trade system works against the ideal of local sustainability and is therefore bad in itself.[165] A broader range of environmentalists, while not opposed to international trade as such, would nevertheless contend that international trade institutions are inevitably biased in favor of open trade, even at the expense of legitimate environmental concerns. It is to this segment of the environmental community that the compromises in the NAFTA are directed. That the NAFTA does not go far enough in this direction is evidenced by the political demands that led to the North American Agreement on Environmental Cooperation.

---

163. *Id.*, Annex 36A(2).

164. *Id.*, Annex 36A(2)(d), (e).

165. For an argument that free trade among nations of substantially different living standards is a dubious goal, *see* HERMAN E. DALY & JOHN B. COBB, JR., FOR THE COMMON GOOD: REDIRECTING THE ECONOMY TOWARD COMMUNITY, THE ENVIRONMENT AND A SUSTAINABLE FUTURE, ch. 11 (1989). By contrast, the Brundtland Commission, although typically viewed as a commission with a strong environmental focus, spoke of the vital role of trade in advancing the economic prospects of developing countries. *See* WORLD COMMISSION ON ENVIRONMENT AND DEVELOPMENT, OUR COMMON FUTURE (1987), especially at 78-84. For a recent debate by two prominent commentators on the effects of free trade on the environment, *see* Jagdish Bhagwati, *The Case for Free Trade*, SCI. AM., Nov. 1993, at 42; Herman E. Daly, *The Perils of Free Trade*, SCI. AM., Nov. 1993, at 50.

The AEC, like the NAFTA itself, represents inevitably a series of compromises. The major compromise negotiated in the AEC is between two primary interests. On the one hand there was a demand (especially on the part of the United States) for an environmental agreement with teeth which would address concerns regarding the use of lower environmental standards to gain trade advantages and attract investment. On the other hand there was a concern (especially on the part of Mexico) that trade indeed be free and that environmental standards not be used as a justification either for protectionism or for interference with state sovereignty in purely domestic affairs. Canadian interests, somewhat quixotically, lay in both camps: while there was popular concern in Canada regarding the loss of jobs due to lower environmental standards elsewhere, there was also concern, on the basis of experience with natural resources protectionism in the United States, that an agreement which allowed for trade sanctions as a means of enforcing environmental obligations would result in unfair attacks (especially by US interests) on Canadian industry.

The compromise achieved in the AEC speaks to both these concerns. There are indeed teeth in this agreement, with the ultimate possibility of significant penalties, whether in the loss of trade sanctions or in a court-enforced monetary penalty. However, the teeth are those of an international arbitral body, not those of a domestic trade tribunal which may be suspected of playing to more parochial concerns. Moreover, the ultimate penalty most probably will never or rarely be imposed, given the likelihood of agreement or compliance with panel findings before this stage is reached. Finally, and most importantly, the very scope of the dispute resolution mechanism is highly limited, especially for those disputes that go to arbitration.

While the heavy focus on binding dispute resolution is understandable given the nature of the political concerns that gave rise to the agreement, it is nevertheless unfortunate. In this regard, resort to arbitration, or even more drastically the removal of trade sanctions to enforce a finding by an arbitral panel, should not be regarded as evidence of the strength of the AEC, but rather as evidence that it has failed. One would hope that as the AEC is implemented,[166] the focus will shift increasingly to the cooperative aspects of the agreement, which, if the AEC is to prove successful, will be its true strength. This potential for cooperation is important in at least two respects.

166. As of this writing, the responsible Ministers had met in Vancouver in March 1994 and undertaken to move towards implementation, including the early appointment of an Executive Director.

First, the institutional framework for increased intergovernmental cooperation not only holds the potential for better individual and joint action on environmental problems within North America (and, in the event of the extension of the NAFTA, within the Americas more generally), but it also provides a possible model for the resolution of other North-South environmental differences. For many developing states, the AEC may serve as a welcome departure from the threat of unilateralism that has sometimes characterized intergovernmental environmental diplomacy in recent years, and which has also raised the spectre of eco-protectionism or eco-imperialism.[167] However, to serve as such a model, the AEC must first demonstrate its effectiveness as a forum for cooperation, rather than as a body focused primarily on disciplining its members.

Second, the AEC holds the potential for encouraging much greater transborder cooperation between environmental groups in North America, both because of the transnational focus that the Commission will bring to bear on environmental problems, and because of institutional structures such as the JPAC, which will involve the cooperation at a personal level of representatives from different national environmental constituencies. This is, however, the optimistic view; it follows, of course, that without sufficient funding and high-quality appointments, the Commission could be reduced to little more than a shell. Again, this would be a missed opportunity not just for the Parties to the agreement, but also for the development of North-South environmental relations more generally.

167. The concerns of developing countries in this respect were reflected in Principle 12 of the Rio Declaration which provides:

> States should cooperate to promote a supportive and open international economic system that would lead to economic growth and sustainable development in all countries, to better address the problems of environmental degradation. *Trade policy measures for environmental purposes should not constitute a means of arbitrary or unjustifiable discrimination or a disguised restriction on international trade. Unilateral actions to deal with environmental challenges outside the jurisdiction of the importing country should be avoided.* Environmental measures addressing transboundary or global environmental problems should, as far as possible, be based on an international consensus.

Rio Declaration, *supra* note 62, princ. 12 (emphasis added).

[11]

TRADE AND ENVIRONMENT: SOME LESSONS FROM *CASTLEMAINE TOOHEYS* (AUSTRALIA) AND *DANISH BOTTLES* (EUROPEAN COMMUNITY)

DAMIEN GERADIN and RAOUL STEWARDSON*

I. INTRODUCTION

IT is frequently argued that more liberalised trade between States[1] leads to general benefits. Free trade is thought to have a series of positive economic effects on domestic economies, such as increasing the range of consumer choice, reducing the costs of inputs such as raw materials and manufactured components, and also increasing economies of scale on return on investment. More liberalised trade is also thought to stimulate social progress as contacts among societies lead to the diffusion of new ideas and technological advances. In creating links between people and a harmony of interests among societies, trade may also be a force for peace.[2] Finally, and perhaps more concretely, the economy of the State of export benefits materially from access to broader markets. In the light of these considerations, States are increasingly working to reduce barriers to trade between States and in some cases to achieve a degree of economic integration with other States.

On the other hand, and in conflict with this movement towards trade liberalisation, States are rarely prepared to allow trade, whether domestic

* Damien Geradin: "Paul-Henri Spaak" Research Fellow in European Community Law, Belgian National Fund for Scientific Research and University of Liège, Belgium; Junior Research Fellow, Wolfson College, Cambridge University, England. Raoul Stewardson: Research Fellow, Institute for European Legal Studies, University of Liège, Belgium. The authors are grateful to Professors David Caron and James Crawford for their comments on earlier drafts. The authors would like to acknowledge the material support provided by the Belgian State, Prime Minister's Office, Science Policy Programming to the University of Liège and the University of Ghent as part of the "Pôles d'attraction interuniversitaires" (PAI) programme.

1. By "State", we mean any political entity that operates within a larger trading bloc. This entity may be a province, State, or nation State, depending on the circumstances. Examples of organisations that join separate States in some form of economic integration are the US, Australia and the EC, and this article will deal with the last two. Looser forms of integration also exist; e.g. NAFTA, Mercosur, Asean and, of course, GATT or the WTO.

2. R. Gilpin, *The Political Economy of International Relations* (1986), pp.171 *et seq.* It should be noted, however, that not everyone benefits. Some places may lose industries and communities, and various other adverse impacts (social, economic or environmental) may be felt. For a more theoretical critique of the theory of comparative advantage, see Cobb and Daly, "Free Trade versus Community: Social and Environmental Consequences of Free Trade in a World with Capital Mobility and Overpopulated Regions" (1990) 11 Population and the Environment: J. of Interdisciplinary Studies 175.

or international, to be governed only by market forces. States frequently intervene in such trade, for a variety of reasons. A State may, for example, be concerned about local public health, safety or morality, its balance of payments or the protection of domestic production from foreign competition. Another purpose, which will be central to this article, is the desire to protect the environment, including air, water and soil quality and to "manage properly" natural resources (minerals, vegetation and wildlife).

To achieve all or any of these purposes, States impose taxes, subsidies, regulatory requirements or outright bans on trade, whether domestic or inter-State. Such a measure may be directed openly and explicitly at inter-State trade; or it may on its face be directed at all trade, but in effect apply to disadvantage only inter-State trade; or it may apply on its face and in effect equally to domestic and inter-State trade. Nevertheless, even in the latter case the implementation of such regulations often, either incidentally or as its main function, presents a hurdle of some form to inter-State trade, making such trade more costly, hence reducing it, and in some cases making it impossible.[3] A central question is, therefore, how to balance the purely domestic interests of a State against the interest which that State and other States have in inter-State trade. Which local regulations affecting inter-State trade should be allowed, and which should not?

In this article we will explore some of these issues in the context of environmental protection, and specifically with regard to *Castlemaine Tooheys Ltd* v. *State of South Australia*[4] and *Commission* v. *Denmark*[5] (the *Danish Bottles* case), decided by the Australian High Court and the European Court of Justice respectively. In both cases the respective Court examined the validity of State legislation attempting on its face to establish or promote schemes for the return and recycling of used bottles. Such schemes are intended to reduce litter and waste disposal problems within the State. However, return and recycling schemes are classically seen as restricting trade and disadvantaging importers as against domestic producers because of the extra costs involved for importers in setting up such schemes (far from the importer's production base) and transporting the returned bottles back to that base.

In Part II we survey the Australian law on restrictions of inter-State trade as it stood before *Castlemaine Tooheys*, and then discuss *Castlemaine Tooheys* itself. In Part III we summarise the EC law in the area, and

3. See generally Geradin, "Free Trade and Environmental Protection in an Integrated Market: A Survey of the Case Law of the United States Supreme Court and the European Court of Justice" (1993) 2 Fla. St. U.J. of Trans. L. & Pol. 141.

4. *Castlemaine Tooheys Ltd* v. *State of South Australia* (1990) 64 A.L.J.R. 145.

5. Case 302/86, *Commission of the European Communities* v. *Kingdom of Denmark* [1988] E.C.R. 4607.

then discuss *Danish Bottles*. In Part IV we compare the case law of the two jurisdictions, with particular reference to the *Castlemaine Tooheys* and *Danish Bottles* cases.

In Part IV, two main comparisons between the methodology of the two systems are made. First, we compare the relevance in each system of the question whether a trade-restrictive measure *discriminates* against inter-State trade, or treats both inter-State and domestic trade alike. Australian law presently prohibits only trade-restrictive regulations which discriminate against inter-State trade in favour of domestic trade, while EC law prohibits certain trade-restrictive measures, whether or not they are discriminatory.[6] We suggest that this difference in approach relates to the different historical and political contexts in which the two respective legal systems have evolved. The Australian approach appears to be centrally concerned about protectionism (which is discriminatory). Protectionism is the most obvious restriction of inter-State trade and is generally discriminatory. Both Australian and EC courts have moved to address this type of trade barrier. However, trade barriers are also caused by the mere presence of differing but non-discriminatory State standards. The Australian High Court did not need to take the difficult step of addressing such barriers to trade, as political union was achieved rapidly in Australia, leading to uniform laws on many matters affecting trade. In Europe, however, political union has been much harder to achieve, with the result that disparate laws in many areas affecting trade still exist in the member States. The European Court of Justice has thus felt obliged to take on a much wider role in reducing these barriers, so that EC law deals with both types of trade barrier, and concentrates more on reducing any barriers to trade, whether or not they are protectionist or discriminatory.

The second point of comparison is the way in which the tests of "necessity" and "proportionality" are used in assessing trade-restrictive measures adopted to achieve a certain goal. Although the Australian High Court and the European Court of Justice have traditionally applied a limited test of necessity, merely examining the measure adopted to achieve a goal, it is arguable that there is a trend in both jurisdictions, in practice if not explicitly, to extend this test to enable the courts to balance the importance of the goal itself against trade effects. The trend would lead to an increased degree of control over State legislation by the central court, and we discuss certain issues which could arise.

6. Although in EC law the grounds recognised as justifying trade-restrictive measures may differ depending on whether or not the measure is discriminatory, nevertheless the basic prohibition applies alike to both situations. This will be discussed in more detail *infra*.

II. THE AUSTRALIAN LAW

A. *The Legal Framework*

1. *The principle of free trade*

A central provision of the Australian Constitution[7] regarding trade between the Australian States is section 92, which reads: "On the imposition of uniform duties of customs, trade, commerce and intercourse among the states, whether by means of internal carriage or ocean navigation, shall be absolutely free."[8] It has been established that section 92 covers all types of interaction, whether trade in goods or services, or simply movement of people or capital,[9] and applies to both State and federal governments.[10] However, beyond that, the section has proved difficult to interpret. In particular, the meaning and scope of "absolutely free" have proved difficult to define.

It is clear that section 92 prohibits the imposition of tariffs on inter-State trade. However, in *Cole* v. *Whitfield*,[11] which made significant changes to the law on section 92, the High Court recognised that "section [92] cannot be easily confined to [fiscal charges and burdens] because protection against interstate trade and commerce can be secured by non-fiscal measures".[12] According to the Court: "The purpose of the section is ... to create a free trade area throughout the Commonwealth and to deny to Commonwealth and States alike a power to prevent or obstruct the free movement of people, goods and communications across State boundaries."[13]

Section 92 has thus been interpreted as extending two steps further than merely prohibiting restrictive fiscal charges. First, it also covers quantitative restrictions on trade, that is, the "restriction or partial or complete prohibition of passing into or out of the State".[14] This means that quotas and bans are prohibited by section 92. Second, and more broadly, section

7. Most of the colonies existing in what is now Australia joined together to form a new nation under the Australian Constitution on 1 Jan. 1901. The Australian Constitution was passed by the British Parliament at the request of the colonies in 1900 (63 and 64 Victoria, Ch.12). The Constitution has subsequently been amended by the Statute of Westminster 1931, the Australia Act 1986 and several referendums.

8. The introduction of uniform customs duties, over a number of years, was provided for in s.90.

9. In contrast, these matters are treated separately in the EC Treaty.

10. *James* v. *Commonwealth of Australia* (1936) 55 C.L.R. 1, 61; [1936] A.C. 578, 633.

11. *Cole* v. *Whitfield* (1988) 62 A.L.J.R. 303; 78 A.L.R. 42; 165 C.L.R. 360. For an excellent, recent and brief history of interpretation of s.92, see Christopher Staker, "Free Movement of Goods in the EEC and Australia: A Comparative Study" (1990) 10 Y.E.L. 209.

12. *Idem*, C.L.R., p.395; A.L.R., p.57.

13. *Idem*, A.L.R., p.54.

14. *Idem*, p.58.

92 also acts to prohibit a regulation that in effect places inter-State trade at a disadvantage in any other way. In *Cole* the High Court held that:[15]

> A law will discriminate against interstate trade or commerce if the law on its face subjects that trade or commerce to a disability or disadvantage or if the factual operation of the law produces such a result . . . The court looks to the practical operation of the law in order to determine its validity.

This would include regulations which, for example, required a permit for the import of certain goods, or a special licence to drive a truck across the border. Although such licences or permits may be readily granted, they impose an extra administrative burden on the inter-State trader, and leave that trader somewhat subject to the policy whims of the administration. However, as will be discussed *infra*, section 92 does not prohibit *all* legislation imposing an extra burden on inter-State trade, only that which is discriminatory and protectionist.

2. *Restrictions on the principle of free trade*

Section 92 says that trade shall be not just free but *absolutely* free. In 1936, in *James* v. *Commonwealth of Australia*, the High Court took a very literal approach to this section, holding that inter-State trade should be free of any control at all, and indicating that even where a regulation imposed an identical burden on both intra- and inter-State trade, it might contravene section 92.[16] Such an interpretation would allow inter-State trade to remain free of any regulation, including environmental regulation. This would have two consequences. First, the environment and other local interests would be completely unprotected as against inter-State trade. Second, inter-State trade would gain such a competitive advantage over intra-State trade that the latter would collapse.[17]

Such an outcome is unacceptable in the long term. From its early days the Court has recognised that some limits to the principle of free trade must exist, based on the need to regulate certain aspects of economic behaviour. In 1920 Gavan Duffy J said that:[18]

> freedom of trade and commerce never means freedom from regulation or control, or complete immunity from municipal law with respect to acts which constitute such trade or commerce . . . All that could be demanded . . .

15. *Idem*, p.60, referring also to *North Eastern Dairy Co. Ltd* v. *Dairy Industry Authority of New South Wales* (1975) 134 C.L.R. 559; 7 A.L.R. 433.

16. *James* v. *Commonwealth of Australia* (1936) 55 C.L.R. 1, 56.

17. This represents the rise of what Detmold calls the "anti-states": M. J. Detmold, "Australian Law: Federal Movement" (1991) 13 Sydney L.Rev. 31, 48–50. An anti-State is a relation between two States. The High Court in *Cole* recognises the same problem at (1988) 78 A.L.R. 42, 62–63.

18. *W. & A. McArthur Ltd* v. *Queensland* (1920) 28 C.L.R. 530, 567–568. See also *Bank of New South Wales* v. *Commonwealth* (1948) 76 C.L.R. 1 (HC); (1949) 79 C.L.R. 497 (PC). This passage was quoted with approval by the High Court in *Cole, idem*, p.57.

would be equality of trading rights for the subjects of each nation in the territory of the other.

In 1988 the High Court in *Cole* supported this interpretation, saying: "The history of the movement for abolition of colonial protection and for the achievement of intercolonial free trade does not indicate that it was intended to prohibit genuine non-protective regulation of intercolonial or interstate trade."[19] Inter-State trade is, therefore, not to be wholly free from regulation, and trade-restrictive legislation enacted to protect certain interests does not necessarily contravene section 92. It has proved harder, however, to define exactly where the limits to free trade should lie.

The principal legal test used to distinguish between permissible and prohibited trade-restrictive legislation is whether the legislation in question is protectionist or not. This approach was derived from the historical context in which the Constitution was drafted. In *Cole* the Court discussed the historical background to the drafting of the Constitution, and concluded that the section was intended primarily to prevent protectionist policies from undermining the economic integration of the new nation:[20]

> The history of s.92 points to the elimination of protection as the object of s.92 in its application to trade and commerce. The means by which that object is achieved is the prohibition of measures which burden interstate trade and commerce and which also have the effect of conferring protection on interstate trade and commerce of the same kind.

The High Court held, therefore, that use of the word "free" in section 92 means that inter-State trade is not to be hindered by legislation that is protective of a local market: "In relation to both fiscal and non-fiscal measures, history and context alike favour the approach that the freedom guaranteed to interstate trade and commerce under s.92 is freedom from discriminatory burdens in the protectionist sense already mentioned."[21] Section 92 does not, on the other hand, prohibit legislation that is a "genuine non-protective regulation of ... interstate trade".[22]

How then does a court decide what is "genuine non-protective regulation" (which does not contravene section 92) and what is protectionist regulation (which does)? Initially, courts developed an idea of a "permissible burden ... which was associated with a somewhat ill-defined notion of what is legitimate regulation in an ordered society".[23] The High Court in *Cole* dismissed this approach, and formulated its own test.[24] It set out two,

19. *Cole, supra* n.11, at C.L.R. p.403, A.L.R. p.63.

20. *Idem*, pp.394–395 and 56–57 respectively. It is widely felt that this emphasis on preventing protectionism reflects the central concern of the original drafters of s.92: see e.g. P. H. Lane, *Lane's Commentary on the Australian Constitution* (1986), pp.502–503; Staker, *op. cit. supra* n.11, at p.224.

21. *Cole, ibid.*

22. *Idem*, pp.403 and 63 respectively.

23. *Idem*, A.L.R., p.63.

24. *Idem*, p.66; C.L.R., p.408.

stepped, qualifications to the principle of free trade, based on the concepts of discrimination and protectionism.

(a) Discrimination. The first step of the test set out in *Cole* is that a State regulation restricting inter-State trade will breach section 92 only if it discriminates between inter-State trade and intra-State trade.[25] Discrimination against inter-State trade occurs "if the law on its face subjects that trade ... to a disability or disadvantage or if the factual operation of the law produces such a result".[26] A regulation which does not discriminate between inter- and intra-State trade on its face or in effect would be less likely to offend section 92.[27] However, a measure which does not discriminate between identical domestic and imported products may still breach section 92 if it regulates those products in order to protect another domestic product.[28] One example would be legislation designed to restrict the import of wine into a beer-producing country. It may be noted that, even where there is no discrimination, a measure may nevertheless impose a burden on inter-State trade (as well as on intra-State trade). However, it appears that, in the absence of some discrimination, such a measure would not be considered to be inconsistent with section 92.

(b) Protectionism. A law which in effect or form "discriminates in favour of intrastate trade" offends section 92 "if the discrimination is of a protectionist character".[29] In distinguishing between a law that discriminates in favour of intra-State trade but is non-protectionist, and a discriminatory law that is protectionist, one must look at the "real object" of that law; a regulation which "has as its real object the prescription of a standard for a product or service or a norm of commercial conduct will not ordinarily be grounded in protectionism and will not be prohibited by s.92".[30]

The courts retain a wide degree of discretion in determining what the real object of a law is. They are to deduce the object of the law from the manner or degree of the discrimination:[31]

> if a law, which may be otherwise justified by reference to an object which is not protectionist, discriminates against interstate trade or commerce in pursuit of that object in a way or to an extent which warrants characterisation of

25. The Court repeatedly said that discrimination is the first part of the test. E.g. at A.L.R., *ibid*, the Court said that a law which in effect or form "discriminates in favour of intrastate trade" offends s.92 if the second step (see *infra*) is satisfied. And at *idem*, p.59, it refers to "discriminatory burdens of a protectionist kind".
26. *Idem*, p.60.
27. Although cf. *idem*, p.66, where the Court says: "If [a regulation] applies to all trade ... interstate and intrastate alike, it is *less likely* to be protectionist" (emphasis added). The implication is that it is still possible for it to be protectionist.
28. Another example would be where a State discriminates against local and imported margarine in order to protect the domestic butter market.
29. *Cole, supra* n.11, at A.L.R. p.66.
30. *Ibid.*
31. *Ibid.*

the law as protectionist, a court will be justified in concluding that it none the less offends s.92.

In *Cole* the Court also set out a more specific test to use in determining whether or not legislation is protectionist. According to this test, legislation will not be characterised as protectionist if it is "a necessary means" of achieving a non-protectionist State objective.[32] Thus, a court will consider whether the discrimination is necessary for the achievement of a legitimate goal. If it was not necessary, the legislation is likely to be characterised as protectionist. Conversely, if the legislation is necessary to the achievement of a legitimate goal, it will be likely to be valid.

The test in *Cole* is therefore a two-step test involving the notions of discrimination and necessity. If a statute is not discriminatory, or is discriminatory but can be seen as necessary to achieve a non-protectionist goal, it will not offend section 92 and will be valid even though it burdens inter-State trade. If it is discriminatory and is not necessary to achieve a non-protectionist goal, it will probably be held to be invalid.

What would be the result in the situation where there is no domestic market in the product in question? It has been argued that, in these circumstances, it would not be possible for legislation to be protectionist as the term is used in this context by the Court, and that there would thus be no way to strike down very restrictive legislation.[33] However, it should be borne in mind that even where there is no domestic production of the same goods, the State may be protecting other goods which stand in a loose competitive relationship with the imported goods.

The application of a necessity requirement poses certain problems which were not explored in the judgment in *Cole*. On the basis of parts of the various cases to be discussed *infra* it is suggested that there are at least three components to a necessity test: is the measure likely to achieve the goal? Does it go further than is necessary? Is there a less trade-restrictive measure? The answer to the last question depends on what other options are actually available. An alternative which may appear desirable in the abstract may in practice face insuperable economic, organisational or political obstacles. For example, in *Cole*, the Tasmanian Government had banned the sale of any crayfish under a certain size in order to protect the Tasmanian cray fishery. It would be less trade-restrictive were the State simply to ban the catching of such cray in Tasmanian waters and inspect all boats fishing in Tasmanian waters. However, such inspections would require resources which the State could not readily provide, as the Court in that case noted.[34] It is generally difficult for a court properly to assess the

32. *Idem*, p.67.
33. Staker, *op. cit. supra* n.11, at pp.236–237.
34. *Cole*, *supra* n.11, at C.L.R. pp.409–410.

relevant economic, organisational and political factors and to include these in a coherent calculus of necessity as applied to each possible regulatory or fiscal regime. Furthermore, a court's view of what is equally effective may vary.[35] As will be seen *infra*, the Court tries to move away from this assessment in *Castlemaine Tooheys*.

B. Castlemaine Tooheys *v.* State of South Australia

The *Castlemaine Tooheys* case concerns a deposit-and-return scheme for beer bottles introduced in South Australia to reduce litter and encourage recycling.[36] For some time four producers brewed all the packaged beer (beer in small bottles or cans) sold in South Australia: the South Australian Brewery Company ("SAB"), Cooper and Sons Ltd ("Cooper"), Carlton and United Brewery ("CUB") and various Bond brewing companies ("Bond"). The first two brewers brew their beer in South Australia, the latter two are located outside the State. In 1975 the South Australian legislature passed the Beverage Container Act 1975 (SA) (the "1975 Act"). This Act imposed a mandatory deposit of five cents on non-refillable beer bottles and cans, refundable on return of the beverage containers.[37] CUB, SAB and Cooper sold beer in South Australia predominantly in refillable bottles, and were thus not subject to the deposit. Bond sold beer only in non-refillable bottles, and was thus subject to the five cents deposit. Production and transport costs of non-refillable bottles are generally lower than for refillable bottles, so that the deposit raised the price of Bond's beer to approximate equality with the price of the other beers on the market.

Prior to 1986 SAB held 77.4 per cent of the market, and Bond 0.1 per cent. In 1986 Bond launched an advertising campaign and in a few months increased its market share to 4 per cent, at the expense of SAB. Bond planned to continue its campaign and obtain 10 per cent of the market over the next year. The South Australian legislature then passed the Beverage Container Act Amendment Act 1986 (SA) (the "1986 Act"). This imposed a deposit of four cents on refillable bottles and increased the deposit on non-refillable beer bottles (i.e. mainly on Bond bottles) from five to 15 cents.[38] Furthermore, while consumers were entitled to return non-refillable glass containers (i.e. mainly Bond beer bottles) to any retailer stocking the same type of bottle, and receive a refund of the

35. E.g. some may consider that labelling is as effective as product regulation.

36. One of the earliest bottle-deposit schemes was introduced in Oregon in 1971. It is discussed in William J. Baumol and Wallace E. Oates, *Economics, Environmental Policy and the Quality of Life* (1979), pp.269–272.

37. Reg.5(1). Presumably there was some other collection or return system for refillable bottles; a refillable bottle on the street is as much litter as a non-refillable bottle!

38. S.4 and Reg.7(c) and (d).

deposit from that retailer,[39] retailers were not obliged to accept the return of, and pay back the deposit for, refillable beer bottles.[40] Instead, such bottles could be returned to a collection depot for refund.[41] Thus, while retailers who sold any Bond beer were, as before, liable to accept return of Bond's non-refillable bottles and pay the deposit, retailers which sold only other beers escaped this burden.

Bond challenged the constitutionality of the legislation. Both parties agreed that the object of the legislation was to "make the sale of beer in non-refillable beer bottles commercially disadvantageous".[42] Bond, however, alleged that the effect of the law was "to discriminate against sale in South Australia of packaged beer brewed interstate and to protect the beer brewed in South Australia from interstate competition",[43] thus breaching section 92 of the Constitution. South Australia argued that the objects of the law were "(1) to promote litter control by forcing non-glass containers and non-refillable bottles into a return system", and by discouraging use by imposing a deposit, and "(2) to promote energy and resource conservation by discouraging the use of non-refillable containers by imposing a higher deposit and by requiring acceptance of returns at the point of sale (thus discouraging retailers from handling them)".[44] South Australia also claimed incidentally that reuse of bottles reduces the release of carbon dioxide into the atmosphere.[45]

The Court discussed *Cole* at length, and followed its statement of the general law (although distinguishing it on the grounds that in that case the regulation did not have a discriminatory effect, whereas in the present case the law in question clearly did).[46] In *Cole* the Court had said that if a law were discriminatory, it would offend section 92 if it was also protectionist, and it would be protectionist if the measures in question were not necessary to achieve a non-protectionist goal. In *Castlemaine Tooheys* the Court subtly changed the approach to determining whether or not a law is protectionist. Recognising the problems involved in applying a necessity requirement, the Court stated that answering the question of what is necessary in a particular social and political situation was outside its competence.[47] Instead, the Court said, once it has been determined that the

39. S.7 of the 1975 Act. In the case of non-glass containers, it was refundable at a collection depot: s.12. However, very few cans were sold in South Australia.

40. S.5b(2) and notice issued by the Minister.

41. S.10; it seems that non-refillable bottles cannot be returned to a depot, though this is never stated in the judgment. The sale of refillable bottles was permitted only in a "collection area delineated in relation to a collection depot": s.10.

42. *Castlemaine Tooheys*, *supra* n.4, at p.377.

43. *Ibid.*

44. *Ibid.*

45. *Ibid.*

46. Although the Court in *Cole* did not recognise it, the regulation there did in fact impose an additional sorting burden on importers of crayfish from other States.

47. *Castlemaine Tooheys*, *supra* n.4, at pp.383–384.

law serves a legitimate purpose but has a discriminatory effect, the test should be whether the law adopts measures which are "appropriate and adapted to the resolution of those problems" and whether "any burden imposed on interstate trade was incidental and not disproportionate to the [...] achievement [of the legislation's legitimate goals]".[48]

It is not immediately clear on the basis of this language how the Court intended to modify the test to be applied. However, the requirement that a measure be "appropriate and adapted" appears to be substantially the same as the first two limbs of the necessity approach set out above, that is, is the measure suitable or likely to attain a legitimate goal and does it go too far? This interpretation seems confirmed by the holdings of the Court, discussed *infra*.

What is meant by the requirement that any burden on trade be "incidental and proportionate" to the goal? The Court mentions this requirement elsewhere, stating:[49]

> There is also some room for a comparison, if not a balancing, of means and objects in the context of s.92. The fact that a law imposes a burden upon interstate trade and commerce that is not incidental or is disproportionate to the attainment of the legitimate object of the law may show that the true purpose of the law is not to attain that object but to impose the impermissible burden.

How should this requirement be understood? At first sight, it might seem to be the same as asking, does the measure go too far? However, the Court does not ask whether the *measure* is proportionate, but whether the *burden* is proportionate, which suggests that a measure may go just the right distance, but still impose a disproportionate burden on trade. Alternatively, the incidental and disproportionality test could be the same as the third limb of the former necessity test, that is, that there must not be a less trade-restrictive measure available. However, this is not possible because, as noted *supra*, the Court had already stated that determining what is necessary in a particular context is outside its competence. Does the use of the word "disproportionate" then suggest that the goal itself and the restriction on trade may be balanced against each other so that the Court would examine whether the benefits brought by the particular goal outweigh the burdens imposed on inter-State trade? This would be a new development, but the Court also expressly rejects such an approach, stating that it cannot assess the relative weight of, or need for, a legislature's goals.[50] What is left seems to be a fairly subjective, open-ended test which will allow the Court to use its judgment as to whether the real purpose of the measure is to achieve a legitimate goal or to protect local industry.

48. *Idem*, p.384.
49. *Idem*, p.383.
50. *Idem*, pp.383–384.

The Court has thus deleted that part of the necessity requirement which it found most difficult, the assessment of whether an equally effective, but less trade-restrictive, measure is available. However, if the Court no longer considers this issue, but may still strike down a measure on grounds that it has a disproportionate impact on trade, then it could theoretically find a measure to have a disproportionate effect on trade, and hence strike it down, even if there is actually *no* less restrictive measure available. In such a case, the Court would be effectively condemning the State to lower its goal, as there would be no other way in which the State could attain that goal consistently with section 92. Conversely, the Court could find the trade effect was proportionate and uphold a measure, even where there *was* a less trade-restrictive measure available, thus supporting environmental programmes. Either way, the Court is coming very close in effect to balancing the State's goal against the restriction on trade, despite its statement that it cannot do so.

In determining whether the 1986 Act was in fact protectionist or not, the Court, somewhat confusingly, did not apply the language of its reformulated test but spoke instead in terms of necessity. In holding that the larger deposit imposed on non-refillable bottles breached section 92, the Court said that "the discrepancy between the 15 cents refund amount ... for non-refillable bottles and the 4 cents refund amount ... for refillable bottles goes beyond what is *necessary* to ensure the return of non-refillable bottles at the same rate as refillable bottles".[51] The Court then inferred that the aim of the provision was to protect local producers.[52] In relation to the retailer return requirement, imposed only on non-refillable bottles, the Court found that "no justification for this difference appears", and concluded that it must therefore be intended to achieve a goal other than litter control.[53]

The first holding, if not perhaps the second, seems relatively uncontroversial as to the result, particularly given that South Australia had admitted that a lower amount of deposit would have been as effective in ensuring return. However, in using the language of necessity, the Court seems to contradict its own statement that it is not competent to assess necessity, and to ignore its new tests. But as suggested above, the substance of the holding is consistent with an "appropriate and adapted" test even though that language is not used. This seems to indicate, therefore, that the Court meant to retain the first two limbs of the necessity requirement, concerning the likelihood of the measure to attain the goal and whether the measure goes further than necessary. Only the third limb of

51. *Ibid* (emphasis added).
52. *Ibid.*
53. *Ibid.*

the necessity requirement, concerning less trade-restrictive measures, is in fact excluded.

As the measures failed to satisfy the "appropriate and adapted" requirement, the Court did not go on to expressly consider the second requirement, concerning whether or not the impact on trade was "incidental and proportionate" to the achievement of the goal. This question therefore remains in the wings. However, although the Court has withdrawn itself from the problem of assessing the practicality of alternative methods, its "incidental and proportionate" requirement may have raised a new set of questions, and will be discussed further in Part IV.

III. THE EUROPEAN COMMUNITY LAW

A. *The Legal Framework*

1. *The principle of free trade*

The EC Treaty contains a variety of provisions designed to prohibit impediments to intra-Community trade.[54] The central provision with regard to import restrictions is Article 30, which prohibits all measures imposing a quantitative restriction on imports or having equivalent effect.[55] The concept of a measure having an equivalent effect has been interpreted by the Court of Justice in its leading judgment, *Procureur du Roi* v. *Dassonville et al.*, as covering "all trading rules enacted by Member States which are capable of hindering, actually or potentially, directly or indirectly, intra-Community trade".[56] It is clear from this statement that one must look to the effects of a measure and not to its aim in deciding whether it falls under Article 30. Consequently, in theory, any environmental measure making the import of goods from other member States more difficult or costly than the sale of domestic production falls under the Court's definition.[57] However, the prohibition is not absolute. The member States can use two categories of exceptions, one derived from Article 36 of the Treaty and the other derived from the *Cassis de Dijon* case law (the "rule of reason").[58] In the first place we have to ask to what extent

54. Measures capable of restricting inter-State trade are covered as to customs duties and charges having equivalent effect by Arts.9 and 12–17 EC; as to quantitative restrictions and measures having equivalent effect by Arts.30–36 EC; as to the free movement for natural and legal persons by Arts.48–58 EC; as to the freedom to provide services by Arts.59–66 EC; as to State aids by Arts.92–94 EC and as to discriminatory taxation by Arts.95–98 EC.

55. Art.30 reads: "Quantitative restrictions on imports and all measures having an equivalent effect shall, without prejudice to the following provisions, be prohibited between Member States." For some general literature on Art.30 see P. Oliver, *Free Movement of Goods in the EEC* (2nd edn, 1988); L. Gormley, *Prohibiting Restrictions on Trade Within the EEC* (1985).

56. Case 8/74 [1974] E.C.R. 837, 852. See, however, *infra* n.101.

57. See e.g. *Danish Bottles*, *supra* n.5.

58. P. Kapteyn and P. Verloren Van Themaat, *Introduction to the Law of the European Communities* (2nd edn, Gormley (Ed.), 1990), p.387.

unilateral environmental measures can be based on these exceptions. Then we will focus on the requirement of necessity which has to be satisfied for the use of either of them.

2. Restrictions on the principle of free trade

(a) Article 36. Assuming that certain conditions are met, Article 36 allows member States to adopt measures hindering the free movement of goods for the purpose of protecting a series of non-economic values such as public policy or public security and the protection of human health, animals and plants. The Court has made clear that Article 36 must be strictly interpreted and that it does not extend to justifications not mentioned in the Article.[59]

Environmental protection does not figure in Article 36. However, environmental protection measures are frequently designed to protect some of the values listed in Article 36. For example, it is clear that a member State can justify under Article 36 an environmental protection measure which aims at protecting the life of humans.[60] Article 36 could thus be used as a basis to justify measures aiming at controlling or limiting trade in substances that are dangerous for human beings. Moreover, environmental objectives can sometimes be related to the protection of the life of animals or plants. Article 36 could thus justify regulations prohibiting trade in endangered animals or vegetable species. For example, in *Van den Burg*[61] the Dutch government tried to use Article 36 as a justification for a measure prohibiting the importation and keeping of red grouse in the Netherlands. Although the Court of Justice did not make reference to Article 36 in its decision, for Advocate-General Van Gerven, as for the Commission, there was no doubt that the aim of improving bird stocks may be regarded as falling within the legal interests referred to in Article 36, namely the protection of human health and animals. Despite their general character, it seems to be more difficult to use the concepts of "public policy" or "public security" to justify environmental protection measures.

(b) The rule of reason. The rule of reason is a "creation of case law".[62] In the *Cassis de Dijon* case the Court phrased the rule of reason in the following way:[63]

59. Case 95/81 *Commission of the European Communities* v. *Italian Republic* [1982] E.C.R. 2187.

60. See Krämer, "Environmental Protection and Article 30" (1993) 30 C.M.L.Rev. 111, 118.

61. Case C-169/89 *Criminal Proceedings against Gourmetterie Van Den Burg* [1990] E.C.R. 2143.

62. Kapteyn and Van Themaat, *loc. cit. supra* n.58.

63. Case 120/78 *Rewe-Zentral AG* v. *Bundesmonopolverwaltung für Branntwein* [1979] E.C.R. 649, 662.

> Obstacles to movement within the Community resulting in disparities between the national laws relating to the marketing of the products in question must be accepted in so far as those provisions may be recognized as being necessary in order to satisfy mandatory requirements relating in particular to the effectiveness of fiscal supervision, the protection of health, the fairness of commercial transactions and the defence of the consumer.

Thus, it appears that the *Cassis de Dijon* judgment recognises that member States may, when applying measures which apply equally to domestic and imported products, restrict imports for motives other than those specifically mentioned by Article 36. It appears that environmental protection measures fall within the principle enunciated by the European Court of Justice in *Cassis de Dijon*. In 1980 the European Commission underlined the importance of environmental protection as a potential limitation on the rule contained in Article 30 of the Treaty.[64] This was accepted by the European Court of Justice in the *Waste Oils* case,[65] the first case to tackle the problem of the tension between the free movement of goods and environmental protection measures in the Community.

In *Waste Oils* the Court was not asked to evaluate the validity of a member State environmental measure but to determine if Council Directive 75/439/EEC of 16 June 1975 on the disposal of waste oils was in conformity with the principles of freedom of trade, the free movement of goods and free competition. Particularly at issue were the provisions of the Directive which envisaged the possibility of exclusive zones being assigned to waste-oil collectors, the prior approval of undertakings responsible for disposal and the possibility of indemnities being granted to undertakings. The Court began by recalling: "The principles of free movement of goods and freedom of competition, together with freedom of trade as a fundamental right, are general principles of Community law."[66] However, the Court insisted that:[67]

> The principle of freedom of trade is not to be viewed in absolute terms but is subject to certain limits justified by the objectives of general interest pursued by the Community provided that the rights in question are not substantially impaired ... There is no reason to conclude that the Directive has exceeded these limits. The Directive must be seen in the perspective of

64. Communication from the Commission concerning the consequences of the judgment given by the Court of Justice on 20 Feb. 1979 in Case 120/78 ("*Cassis de Dijon*") (1980) O.J. C256/2.

65. Case 240/83 *Procureur de la République* v. *Association de Défense des Brûleurs d'Huiles Usagées* [1984] E.C.R. 531.

66. *Idem*, p.548.

67. *Idem*, p.549.

environmental protection, which is one of the Community's essential objectives.

The *Waste Oils* decision may be considered a landmark, for it may be inferred from it that national measures taken for environmental protection reasons are capable of constituting "mandatory requirements" recognised in *Cassis de Dijon* as limiting the application of Article 30 of the Treaty in the absence of Community rules. As we will see, this has since been confirmed in the *Danish Bottles* case.

(c) The test of "necessity". Measures justifiable under Article 36 or the rule of reason must satisfy at least one common condition: they must fulfil a test of "necessity" (referred to, confusingly, as the principle of proportionality). According to the case law of the European Court of Justice, measures justifiable under the rule of reason or under Article 36 of the Treaty must be pertinent, i.e. there must be a causal relationship between the measure adopted and the attainment of the objective pursued, and the measure must be the least restrictive method of attaining that purpose.

The *Gilli* case[68] offers a good illustration of the first of these requirements. In that case, the Court found that the prohibitions enacted by Italy on the sale of vinegar other than wine vinegar were not justified, since the other kinds of vinegar were not damaging to human health, nor did their mere existence mislead the consumer. The Court held that "there is no factor justifying any restriction on the importation of the product in question from the point of view either of the protection of public health and the fairness of commercial transactions or of the defence of the consumer".[69] The Italian measure was struck down because it was not possible to find a causal connection between the unilateral national measures (ban on vinegar other than wine vinegar) and the objectives pursued (protection of public health and the fairness of commercial transactions).

The *De Peiper* case[70] provides a good illustration of the criterion of the least restrictive alternative. A Dutch legal provision required parallel importers of pharmaceutical products to submit to the national health authorities certain documents which could be obtained only from the manufacturers of the products or their appointed distributor. The effect of this provision was to make all parallel imports of pharmaceutical products dependent on the goodwill of the manufacturer or of the official distributor. The Court considered that such a regulation did not fall within the exception provided in Article 36, since public health could be protected as effectively by a less restrictive measure, such as a collaboration between

68. Case 788/79 *Criminal Proceedings against Herbert Gilli and Paul Andres* [1980] E.C.R. 2071.

69. *Idem*, p.2078.

70. Case 104/75 *Adriaan de Peijper, Managing director of Centrafarm BV* [1976] E.C.R. 613.

the Dutch authorities and those of the member States in which the pharmaceutical products in question were produced.

B. *The* Danish Bottles *Case*

In *Commission* v. *Denmark*[71] (*Danish Bottles*) the Commission challenged a Danish law of 2 July 1981 whose main feature was that manufacturers had to market beer and soft drinks in "returnable containers". According to the definition given in the implementing order, this meant that there had to be a system for collection and refill under which a large proportion of the containers sold would be refilled. In addition, the containers had to be approved by the National Agency for the Protection of the Environment ("NAPE"), which was entitled to refuse approval to a new container if it considered that the planned system of collection did not ensure that a sufficient proportion of the containers would be reused or if a container of equal capacity, already approved and suitable for the same use, was available.[72]

Following protests from producers of beverages and containers in other member States, the Commission urged the Danish government to change the law. As a consequence of the Commission intervention, in 1984 the Danish government amended the 1981 law so that each producer could sell up to 3,000 hl a year in non-approved containers (excluding metal containers), and could also use non-approved containers for drinks sold by foreign producers to test the market, provided in both cases that a deposit-and-return system was established for the non-approved containers.[73] The Commission was not satisfied with the 1984 amendment and in 1986 brought Article 169 proceedings to have both the compulsory deposit-and-return system and the NAPE approval system declared incompatible with Article 30 of the EC Treaty.

For the Commission, the collection system in force in Denmark clearly constituted a measure having an equivalent effect to a quantitative restriction contrary to Article 30 of the Treaty.[74] The Commission argued that the Danish government could not rely on the "rule of reason" to exclude the application of Article 30 as the contested rules had a discriminatory effect. While formally applying to both domestic and imported products, the Danish collection system placed imported products at a disadvantage in relation to domestic products.[75] Moreover, even assuming that the Danish system was not discriminatory, the Commission estimated that it could

71. *Supra* n.5.

72. It appears that a return-and-refill scheme can operate effectively only if the variety of bottle types is limited.

73. *Danish Bottles*, *supra* n.5, at p.4629.

74. *Idem*, p.4610.

75. *Ibid*.

not be justified as the restrictive effects on trade that it created were disproportionate. In particular, the Commission was of the opinion that Council Directive 85/339 of 27 June 1985[76] illustrated that it was possible to achieve the objective of environmental protection by less restrictive means, such as systems for the recycling of containers or systems designed to encourage the selective collection of containers that are not reusable.[77] The Commission finally contended that it "follows from the principle of proportionality that the level of [environmental] protection should not be fixed exaggeratedly high and that other solutions should be accepted even if they are a little less effective in assuring the aim pursued".[78]

In its reply to the Commission arguments, the Danish government contended that its bottles legislation was justified by the legitimate concern to protect the environment in general and to conserve resources, as well as to reduce the amount of waste.[79] The objective of its legislation was in no way a disguised attempt to wall off the Danish market from imports of beer and soft drinks from other member States. With regard to the question of proportionality, the Danish government agreed that an environmental measure must not be excessive if it is to comply with Community law. However, it was of the opinion that such measure would be excessive only if there were other measures just as effective and less restrictive of intra-Community trade. The Danish bottle system, according to the Danish government, should not therefore be seen as disproportionate as no alternative solutions as effective as that system were available.

In his opinion Advocate-General Slynn supported the Commission's case and argued to the Court that both the compulsory return-and-deposit system and the NAPE approval system were in breach of the EC Treaty.[80] In the first place, Advocate-General Slynn found that the Danish measures were contrary to Article 30 of the Treaty and did not fall within any of the exceptions listed in Article 36.[81] Moreover, he agreed with the Commission that the Danish measures had a discriminatory effect in that, even though on the surface indiscriminately applicable to Danish and non-Danish manufacturers, the rules bore more heavily on the latter. As a result, it was not possible for Denmark to rely on the rule of reason, even if environmental protection could be considered as a mandatory requirement.[82]

In addition, even if the Danish measures could be considered as indiscriminately applicable, they were not proportionate to achieve the legit-

76. (1985) O.J. L176/18.
77. *Danish Bottles*, *supra* n.5, at p.4611.
78. *Idem*, p.4613.
79. *Idem*, p.4615.
80. *Idem*, p.4626.
81. *Idem*, p.4621.
82. *Idem*, p.4622.

imate environmental aim. Although the Advocate-General admitted that the Danish legislation achieved the highest standard of environmental protection and that it might be difficult by other methods to achieve the same high standards, he did not consider that "Denmark must succeed in this application unless the Commission can show that the same standard can be achieved by other specified means".[83] For him it was indeed clear that:[84]

> There has to be a balancing of interests between the free movement of goods and environmental protection, even if in achieving the balance the high standard of the protection sought had to be reduced. The level of protection sought must be a reasonable level: I am not satisfied that the various methods outlined in the Council directive and referred to at the hearing—selective collection by governmental authorities or private industry, a voluntary deposit system, penalties for litter, education of the public as to waste disposal—are incapable of achieving a *reasonable* standard which impinges less on the provisions of Article 30.

The Court did not agree with the Advocate-General in respect of the deposit-and-return system. Applying the *Cassis de Dijon* case law, it found that the system was "an indispensable element of a system intended to ensure the reuse of containers and therefore . . . *necessary* to achieve the aims pursued by the contested rules. That being so, the restrictions which it imposes on the free movement of goods cannot be regarded as disproportionate."[85]

As regards the NAPE approval system, however, the Court found that by restricting the quantity of beer and soft drinks which could be marketed by a single producer in non-approved containers to 3,000 hectolitres a year Denmark had failed to fulfil its obligations under Article 30 of the Treaty. According to the Court, even though the existing system of approved containers offered a better degree of environmental protection than a system of non-approved containers:[86]

> The system for returning non-approved containers is capable of protecting the environment and, as far as imports are concerned, affects only limited quantities of beverages compared with the quantity of beverages consumed in Denmark owing to the restrictive effect which the requirement has on

83. *Idem*, p.4626.
84. *Ibid* (emphasis added).
85. *Idem*, p.4630 (emphasis added).
86. *Idem*, p.4632 (emphasis added). Empty approved containers can be returned to any retailer of beverages whereas non-approved containers can be returned only to the retailer who sold the beverage.

imports. In these circumstances, a restriction of quantity of products which may be marketed by importers is *disproportionate* to the objective pursued.

The Court's reasoning contains some troubling elements. First, it is noteworthy that although the Court held the deposit-and-return system to be justified under the rule of reason, the Court did not raise in its decision the issue of discrimination. This is surprising especially when we consider that the rule of reason may be relied on only where the national rules in question do not on their face or in effect discriminate against domestic and imported products.[87] In *Danish Bottles* it was clear that even though the Danish measures were, on the surface, indiscriminately applicable to Danish and non-Danish manufacturers, they placed a heavier burden on the latter. The Court should thus have seriously questioned the applicability of the *Cassis de Dijon* formula.

Second, the Court became involved in an ambiguous balancing process. When the Court analysed the deposit-and-return system it did so against the background of Denmark's very high rate of reutilisation of empty bottles.[88] This implies that the Court will take for granted the level of protection chosen by a member State (even if that level is very high) and thus will assess only whether the restrictions resulting from the measures are effective to achieve the aims adopted by the State (traditional test of "necessity").

In contrast, when the Court examined the approval system and the 3,000-hectolitre limit, it considered them in the context of the more general objective of environmental protection. The Court considered that this general objective could be satisfied by the deposit-and-return system, which would be less trade-restrictive than the limit.[89] However, as non-approved containers cannot be returned to all retailers (unlike approved bottles), a smaller proportion of them are returned than is the case with approved containers. Although the Court states that the requirement to set up a separate return scheme will still limit the number of non-approved bottles imported, this is not quantified, and it seems that there is likely to be at least *some* increase in imports. Thus, with an increase in the import of non-approved bottles, there will be more litter, and the Court does not suggest any other way by which Denmark might ensure an equally high level of environmental protection.

This suggests that the Court in practice followed the opinion of Advocate-General Slynn that the level of protection must be a reasonable one.[90]

87. *Gilli, supra* n.68; Case 177/83 *Theodore Kohl KG* v. *Ringelhan & Rennet SA and Ringelhan Einrichtungs GmbH* [1984] E.C.R. 3651; Case 207/83 *Commission of the European Communities* v. *United Kingdom of Great Britain and Northern Ireland* [1985] E.C.R. 1201; Case 16/83 *Criminal Proceedings against Karl Prantl* [1984] E.C.R. 1299.

88. *Danish Bottles, supra* n.5, at p.4630.

89. *Idem*, p.4632.

90. Ludwig Krämer, *op. cit. supra* n.60, at pp.123–127, appears to be of the same opinion.

In so doing, the Court in effect balanced the goal of the State against the harm done to inter-State trade, and reduced the level of protection that the State could choose.[91] Some implications of such an approach will be discussed *infra*.

IV. A COMPARATIVE ANALYSIS

DESPITE the different language of the provisions concerning inter-State trade in the EC Treaty and the Australian Constitution, respectively,[92] the tests used in the *Danish Bottles* and *Castlemaine Tooheys* cases are remarkably similar in many respects.

The Australian High Court in the earlier case of *Cole* had asked three questions: does the regulation in question discriminate against inter-State trade (this must implicitly also involve an assessment of whether a burden is placed on inter-State trade)? Does the legislation imposing the burden pursue a "legitimate" purpose? Is the measure adopted necessary to attain the objective? In *Castlemaine Tooheys* it asked the same first two questions, but for the third it asked: is the measure taken appropriate and the burden imposed not incidental or disproportionate?

When asked to assess the validity of a trade-restrictive measure hindering trade, the European Court of Justice also asks three questions: does the measure in question impose a burden on inter-State trade? Does the measure imposing the burden seek to achieve a legitimate purpose? Is the measure adopted necessary to attain the objective? In *Danish Bottles* Advocate-General Slynn suggested that the Court should also ask whether the particular objective was proportional to the burden on trade. This approach seems confirmed by the Court in its assessment of the Danish approval system.

The Courts differ in their use (or not) of a discrimination test, and both seem slightly ambiguous as to the content of their necessity/proportionality requirements. We will next examine these two issues in more detail.

91. The ambiguity may be seen in this statement by the Court: "obstacles to movement within the Community ... must be accepted in so far as such rules ... may be recognized as being *necessary* in order to satisfy mandatory requirements of Community law. It is *also* necessary for such rules to be *proportionate* to the aim in view" (emphasis added): *Danish Bottles*, *supra* n.5, at p.4630. In fact, according to the Court, there was hardly any impact on trade, as the Court claimed the deposit-and-return system would still limit imports. Thus, the Court seems more concerned with harm to the principle of free movement than actual restrictions on trade in this case.

92. Art.30 of the EC Treaty and s.92 of the Australian Constitution appear, *prima facie*, very different. The scope of s.92 is much broader in that it speaks of absolute freedom of trade, whereas Art.30 is couched in terms of the elimination of a particular type of barriers to trade.

A. Discrimination

The Australian test requires a showing of discrimination before legislation can be struck down (although evidence of discrimination is of itself not fatal). In the European Community, although discriminatory legislation is treated somewhat more severely than non-discriminatory legislation, the latter can still be struck down.[93] To satisfy the test of the European Court of Justice, legislation has to impose the least burden possible on inter-State trade, and offer legitimate benefits that outweigh harm to trade. The inclusion of discrimination in the Australian test makes it harder for a court to invalidate legislation that goes too far without discriminating, and not to invalidate legislation which does discriminate.

In practice, it may be that the language is sufficiently loose that similar results are reached under both systems. Nevertheless, the formulation is different and will thus affect the way the facts are analysed. What is the reason for this difference between the way in which discrimination is used in the two jurisdictions? The answer is to be found in the historical and political context. But it is first necessary to make some distinctions between different types of restrictive measures.

It is perhaps not new to point out that State measures restricting trade may be divided into two broad categories: protectionist and legitimately protective. Courts may react differently to each. The first type of measure may be adopted where, because of superior international competitiveness, inter-State trade threatens to drive local companies out of business with resultant economic and social dislocation (protectionism). There will always be an incentive for a State to enjoy the benefits that come from its companies trading in a larger market, while preventing foreign companies from threatening its domestic producers. A court's reaction to such a measure will generally be negative.

The second type of measure inhibiting inter-State trade is adopted to address externalities imposed on the State by trade in a particular product or service, whether that trade is domestic or inter-State.[94] For example, the

93. In the EC context, the concept of discrimination still plays an important role as only even-handed measures can be justified under the rule of reason. This has a practical impact as, due to the strict interpretation of its narrow language, Art.36 appears as a rather limited legal basis for legitimising trade-restrictive State environmental measures. Contrary to Australian law, discrimination is therefore not necessary for finding a measure unlawful.

94. We assume here that individuals are perfectly informed in choosing the imported product. Of course, this is not always the case. Labelling regulation is designed to improve consumer information about both domestic and imported products. In so far as language or labelling requirements differ from State to State, they may impose another burden on inter-State trade.

sale in the State of improperly prepared meat or an otherwise unsafe product imposes health costs on the local community; and the sale of unbiodegradable and difficult to dispose of packaging waste harms the environment and reduces the aesthetic pleasure of inhabitants and tourists alike. Consequences such as these are part of the costs of the use of the product, but are not all included in the price.[95] Instead, part of the cost is borne by other individuals (those who pay taxes to provide health care, or are harmed by dangerous products, or whose view is spoilt) or by the environment. Thus, more of the product or service will be demanded than would be if the consumers of the product or service bore its true cost.[96]

State regulation may in these circumstances internalise more of the costs to the parties, such as by taxing them or requiring special precautions to be taken. Nevertheless, even though such legislation is not protectionist in intent and may not discriminate between inter-State and domestic trade, it will significantly restrict the former by imposing extra burdens on inter-State manufacturers or service providers.[97] A manufacturer in another State will have to meet both the standards of its own State and those of the State of sale, or perhaps those of several States of sale. This will increase the costs of its product or service to the point where it may become uncompetitive. This outcome is particularly serious where the local aim is relatively insignificant or even capricious.

From the perspective of the larger trading bloc, the optimal solution to the second type of problem would in fact be for an omniscient and omnipresent legislature to pass legislation perfectly internalising all the costs of activities to the parties to those activities uniformly across all States.[98] Then there would be no need for individual States to adopt measures in respect of those activities. This would also remove the opportunity for camouflage which States may seek to use in passing essentially protection-

95. Re externalities, see William J. Baumol and Wallace E. Oates, *The Theory of Environmental Policy: Externalities, Public Outlays, and the Quality of Life* (1975), pp.14–32. The concept of externalities was identified in A. C. Pigou, *The Economics of Welfare* (4th edn, 1932), Part II.

96. Robert S. Pindyck and Daniel L. Rubinfeld, *Microeconomics* (1992), pp.639–644.

97. See e.g. A. Mattera, "De l'arrêt 'Dassonville' à l'arrêt 'Keck': l'obscure clarté d'une jurisprudence riche en principes novateurs et en contradictions" (1994) I Rev. Marché Unique Européen 117, 127.

98. In the Australian context, the central legislature has limited power, on paper, to do this. Under s.109 of the Australian Constitution, the States retain all powers not exclusively given to the federal government, or withdrawn from the States, by the Constitution. This is similar to the US Constitution; see the 10th Amendment. As power over the environment is not given (exclusively or otherwise) to the federal government, it is retained by the States. However, as James Crawford, "The Constitution and the Environment" (1991) 13 Sydney L.Rev. 11, points out, the federal government can effectively regulate most environmental matters with the powers it does have. In the EC, the EC Treaty does give the Council power to act with respect to environmental matters (see Arts.100A and 130S).

ist legislation. However, as preferences tend to vary from one State to another, agreement is not always easy to attain at the central level. Indeed, in many cases competence in particular matters is never given to the central government. This means that States are frequently left to follow their own course of action. Moreover, even if agreement is found at the central level, some "progressive" States may be tempted to adopt stricter measures than the centrally harmonised ones, therefore potentially reintroducing distortions of competition.[99]

Section 92 of the Australian Constitution was enacted at the end of the nineteenth century, at a time when free trade was understood mainly as the absence of protectionism and collusion, and in the context of an effort to unify colonies with strong trade-protectionist barriers. The essence of protectionism is discrimination against inter-State trade, and so there was initially an emphasis on differential treatment in Australian law. At the same time, however, the federated former colonies achieved political union very quickly. With such unity, the federal government was able to adopt uniform laws in many areas where different State laws, though non-discriminatory, would have severely hampered the flow of goods. Thus, a substratum of uniform laws was able to be created. In this context the Court did not have to develop its doctrine in order to address the problem that would have been posed by the presence of a substantial number of varying (non-discriminatory) laws in different States.

It appears that originally Article 30 of the EC Treaty was also considered (by the European Commission at least) to apply only to restrictive measures that were discriminatory.[100] Political union has, however, been more elusive in Europe than in Australia. This means that in many areas it has not been possible to adopt uniform legislation, and that even where uniform legislation is adopted it may be relatively flexible and leave room for member States to adopt a range of measures within certain limits (as is typically the case with Directives), or to adopt stricter measures (under Article 100A(4) of the Treaty, where applicable). Perhaps as a result of this, together with the desire of the Court to promote European inte-

99. In the EC context, this is permitted by Arts.130T and 100A(4) of the Treaty. There is no similar clause in the Australian Constitution. However, covering clause 5 and s.109 of the Australian Constitution provide that in the event of conflicting federal and State laws in the same field, the federal law prevails. Thus, where a federal law regulates a subject, a State law on that topic imposing stricter measures will be valid only if it is either consistent with the federal law (and a stricter measure would arguably not be consistent), or if the federal law provides that State laws may impose stricter measures.

100. E.g. in reply to a question from the European Parliament in 1967, the Commission said that "provisions which apply indiscriminately to imports and home products do not as a rule constitute measures having equivalent effect to quantitative restrictions": W.Q.64 (Deringer) (1967) J.O. 169/12, trans. and quoted in Kapteyn and Van Themaat, *op. cit. supra* n.58, at p.377.

gration, from the 1970s the Court dropped the discrimination criterion in order to be able also to strike down or limit the application of a broad range of non-discriminatory trade-restrictive measures which the EC legislature was unable effectively to harmonise.[101]

A parallel phenomenon may be observed in the context of the General Agreement on Tariffs and Trade. Under the GATT, signed in 1947, only discriminatory measures are prohibited. Although any measures restricting or prohibiting imports are *prima facie* prohibited by Article XI, where such measures apply in a non-discriminatory manner to both imports and domestic products they are generally considered to be permitted under Article III (the national treatment provision).[102] However, GATT law has developed to address non-discriminatory measures as well. Over the years, the contracting parties have taken steps to limit their use of non-tariff barriers to trade whether discriminatory or not. For example, Article 2.2 of the Technical Barriers to Trade Agreement[103] and paragraph 6 of the Agreement on Sanitary and Phytosanitary measures,[104] adopted at the conclusion of the Uruguay Round, do not require the showing of discrimination in order to prohibit measures which are seen as unjustifiably hindering trade.

Like EC law, GATT law thus originally focused on the most obvious form of trade barrier, or that on which there was most consensus: protectionist measures. It then began to address non-discriminatory measures. We have argued that one reason that the Australian law does not prohibit non-discriminatory trade restrictions is that Australia achieved political union quickly and thus many laws potentially affecting trade were made uniform. In the case of GATT, with over a hundred contracting parties from around the world, such uniformity is not at present feasible. Given this lack of political unity, it is difficult to address the trade barriers caused

101. E.g. *Dassonville*, *supra* n.56; *Cassis de Dijon*, *supra* n.63. It should, however, be noted that the ECJ has recently retreated somewhat from this position. See its decision in Joined Cases C-267 and C-268/91 *Keck & Mithouard* (decision of 24 Nov. 1993, not yet reported), where it was held that non-discriminatory measures relating to marketing arrangements for products (such as a prohibition on resale at a loss) would not fall within the scope of Art.30. This decision does not appear to exclude from Art.30 regulations applying to products (as opposed to regulations applying to marketing arrangements). See e.g. Mattera, *op. cit. supra* n.97; Reich, "The 'November Revolution' of the European Court of Justice: *Keck*, *Meng* and *Audi* Revisited" (1994) 31 C.M.L.Rev. 459.

102. See generally McGovern, *International Trade Regulation* (1986), p.245.

103. Art.2.2 of the Technical Barriers to Trade Agreement requires members to "ensure that technical regulations are not prepared, adopted or applied with a view or with the effect of creating unnecessary obstacles to international trade".

104. Para.6 of the Agreement on Sanitary and Phytosanitary Measures requires members to ensure that "any sanitary measure or phytosanitary measure is applied only to the extent necessary to protect human or animal health, is based on scientific principles and is not maintained against scientific evidence".

by disparate, but non-discriminatory, national laws by means of uniform measures; these problems can be more readily addressed by means of negative rules.

B. Necessity and Proportionality

1. Necessity

Once the question of discrimination has, where relevant, been addressed, the requirement of necessity arises. Even discriminatory measures may be upheld provided they are necessary for the achievement of a legitimate goal. Despite some statements to the contrary by the High Court in *Castlemaine Tooheys*,[105] both Courts have in general asked whether the measure is likely to attain the goal and whether it goes too far (the first two parts of the necessity requirement). In *Castlemaine Tooheys* the Court applied these requirements to the 1986 Act,[106] and in *Danish Bottles* the European Court did so in respect of the Danish deposit-and-return obligation.[107]

While the European Court will also consider whether other measures might be equally effective and impose less of a burden on inter-State trade, it appears that, since *Castlemaine Tooheys*, the Australian High Court is reluctant to do so.[108] This may reflect the difficulties faced by the EC legislature and the European Court's more proactive role in establishing a common market. The High Court can rely on a stronger federal legislature to address such issues if they become pressing enough.

However, it seems that in *Castlemaine Tooheys* and *Danish Bottles* the Australian High Court and the European Court of Justice have attempted either to move away from the concept of necessity or to introduce an additional, more operative requirement of proportionality.

2. Possible emergence of a "proportionality of goal" test

It seems that in the *Danish Bottles* case, and possibly also in *Castlemaine Tooheys*, there is evidence of an emerging trend to assess not just the measure but the goal itself; and not just whether the goal falls within the list of legitimate subjects of State action, but whether the goal is justified in relation to the burden it imposes on inter-State trade. As already noted, in *Danish Bottles* the European Court appears in effect to reduce slightly the level of protection which Denmark is able to pursue, on the ground that

105. See e.g. *Castlemaine Tooheys, supra* n.4, at p.383.
106. In *Cole, supra* n.11, in contrast, the Court had said that legislation will not be characterised as protectionist if it is a necessary means of achieving a non-protectionist objective, and had then gone on to discuss the viability of other methods for protecting smaller crayfish in Tasmania. See *supra* text accompanying n.50.
107. *Danish Bottles, supra* n.5, at p.4630, para.13.
108. *Cole, supra* n.11, at A.L.R. pp.67–68.

the effective pursuit of such a goal has too great an impact on trade, or on the principle of free movement.

In *Castlemaine Tooheys* the Australian High Court did not weigh the effect on trade against the level of environmental protection desired. As discussed *supra*, however, the reformulation which it adopts, by removing the "least trade-restrictive" requirement and including a requirement that the burden imposed not be "incidental and proportionate" is sufficiently ambiguous to leave such an approach open for the future. Whether the Court chooses to take advantage of this possibility remains to be seen.

We note in passing that GATT law concerning quantitative restrictions is less ambiguous and applies only the necessity (or least restrictive) test, rather than the more intrusive proportionality of goal test.[109] This is perhaps due to the low degree of political integration achieved between the contracting parties to GATT. Uruguay Round negotiators had included a proportionality test in a footnote to Article 2.2 of the 1994 Technical Barriers to Trade Agreement, but this was removed before adoption of the Agreement.

It is not clear whether a "proportionality of goal" test is in fact emerging. Below we will discuss whether such a test would be desirable and how it could be applied.

(a) Issues arising from the use of a proportionality of goal test. One implication of the development of a proportionality of goal test is that the extent of State control over certain subject areas would be reduced in favour of the central courts. With a true proportionality of goal test, courts would be able to examine, not just whether the goal pursued fell within the scope of sovereignty, or whether the measure used to achieve it was acceptable, but whether the goal itself was "reasonable". This may have positive consequences in that a court would be able to strike down legislation which brings a small environmental benefit at a significant cost (often imposed largely on other, exporting States), or legislation which is perhaps not strictly necessary (in the sense that a less restrictive measure is conceivable) but which appears a desirable policy choice, but it also entails the risk that central courts may undermine local values (from the perspective of the State adopting the measure),[110] or over-privilege them

109. See Ernst-Ulrich Petersmann, "The Settlement of International Environmental Disputes in GATT and the EEC" Conference paper London 23/24 Apr. 1993, published in Cameron, Demaret and Geradin (Eds), *Trade and the Environment—the Search for Balance* (1994). One finds such a test in e.g. Art.XX(b) and (g) of GATT; the GATT panel report in "US—Measures Affecting Alcoholic and Malt Beverages" (GATT Doc.DS 23/R, 7 Feb. 1992, para.5.52); Arts.2.2 and 2.3 of the 1994 Agreement on Technical Barriers to Trade; and para.21 of the 1994 Agreement on Sanitary and Phytosanitary measures.

110. In the GATT context, see Petersmann, *idem*; Charnowitz, "GATT and the Environment—Examining the Issues" (1992) Int. Env. Affairs 203, 215. For an opposite view, see Dunoff, "Reconciling International Trade with Preservation of the Global Commons: Can We Proposer and Protect?" (1992) 49 Wash. & Lee L.Rev. 1407, 1447.

(from the point of view of another, exporting State). Such an exercise of judicial discretion risks being controversial, and it may be suspected that the courts have been obscure in their language in this area precisely in order to avoid such controversy.

If the courts are in fact tending to assess the proportionality of the goal being pursued, two issues need to be considered. First, it seems that an accurate understanding of the facts is important. Unless the court is clear about the factual implications of measures, balancing may be unsatisfactory. However, the factual and policy issues which need to be understood in order to assess an environmental measure can be complex and novel, and one may note that in both the EC and Australian cases there appear to have been some errors or omissions in the treatment of the facts by the respective courts. For example, in *Castlemaine Tooheys*, in comparing the respective bottle cost of the Bond and other beers after the 1986 legislation the High Court appears to overlook the four cents deposit on refillable bottles, and hence to miscalculate the difference between the bottle cost of refillable and non-refillable bottles. Neither did the Court analyse fully whether the retail return requirements in the new legislation would in fact further limit Bond's ability to sell in South Australia. Retailers who sold any Bond bottles had already been obliged to accept the return and refund of Bond bottles but not of other bottles. Nevertheless, the High Court stated that this was one respect in which the "1986 Act and the new regulations disadvantaged the Bond brewing companies".[111] For its part, the European Court of Justice did not analyse what the additional cost to outside beer producers of having to use approved containers would be, nor compare that with the increased costs to Denmark of having more litter or establishing a more expensive waste collection and disposal system to remove non-approved containers; nor did it develop the reasoning behind its conclusion that there would not be a significant increase in litter if the 3,000-hectolitre limit on non-approved bottles were lifted.[112]

The second issue which arises is that such a balancing process also involves assessing the importance of vague and unspecified interests such as those of trade and environmental protection. In theory, a court could balance the benefit against the detriment and calculate whether there was a net benefit (Kaldor–Hicks criterion of efficiency).[113] However, while

111. *Castlemaine Tooheys*, *supra* n.4, at p.376.

112. Non-approved bottles may remain competitive as they do not have to be returned to the producer as approved containers do (they can instead be broken down *in situ*), nor do they have to be made to be refillable (which, as *Castlemaine Tooheys* illustrates, can increase production costs significantly). Kenneth Culp Davis criticises the US Supreme Court for its inability to deal with factual matters, and proposes that it request a research service: "Judicial, Legislative, and Administrative Lawmaking: A Proposed Research Service for the Supreme Court" (1986) 71 Minn.L.Rev. 1.

113. See generally R. Posner, *Economic Analysis of Law* (3rd edn, 1986).

inter-State trade has a large, recognised and readily quantifiable economic component, typically many of the interests protected by States, such as health, morals, culture, education and environment, are more subjective and hence less easily quantified and calculated. In weighing State benefit against harm to inter-State trade, how is a court actually to assess the benefit a particular measure brings to a particular State? Courts are not necessarily well equipped to assess the degree to which the population of a State values something. One way in which a court may approximate the value of a certain goal to citizens is to compare the standard in question with parallel standards in other States. It can be asked to what extent this was done implicitly in *Danish Bottles*, where the Advocate-General hinted that the Danish system ensured a higher level of protection than was present in other member States.[114] However, even where a court is fully informed about other systems this is not a very satisfactory solution, given that the very reason for leaving States with sovereignty in certain areas is to allow local diversity.

Another approach is for the court to use its own values in assessing the benefit of the State legislation. It can be asked whether this was not what the High Court did in *Castlemaine Tooheys*. Although the Court did not, in the end, specifically challenge the recycling goal, neither did it seriously address the values of South Australians. The majority also largely ignored the State's argument that its measure was designed in part to reduce the emission of greenhouse gases. The minority dismissed it on the grounds that such legislation would have an insignificant impact on the problem.[115] But why should an individual State not be able to take steps to contribute to the protection of a global commons, even if in a small way, particularly when action by *any* individual State is insufficient and action by all States is necessary?[116] The Court may not have dealt with these issues fully because the differential in the deposit made it a relatively clear case.

(b) Proposed necessity/proportionality test. The requirements of necessity and proportionality should be clearly distinguished and could then be used in a distinct but complementary manner by the courts.[117] The requirement of necessity concerns the relationship between the measure and the goal, whereas the justification of the goal itself, particularly in relation to

114. *Danish Bottles*, *supra* n.5, at p.4625.

115. *Idem*, p.388.

116. See Professor Crawford's discussion of this in *op. cit. supra* n.98, at pp.13–14. As Krämer, *op. cit. supra* n.60, at pp.135–136, points out, such a measure may not, however, satisfy a literal application of the necessity test, which requires that the measure be likely to achieve its goal. It is suggested that such measures should be seen as part of *globally* necessary measures.

117. In the EC context, this position was put forward by Advocate-General Van Gerven in his opinion in *Van den Burg*, *supra* n.61, at p.2156, and in Case C-159/90 *Society for the Protection of Unborn Children Ireland Ltd* v. *Stephen Grogan and Others* [1991] E.C.R. 4685, 4720.

the trade effects, is a separate issue, which may be referred to as proportionality (while noting that this does not seem to be the usual use of the term, at least in the European Community).

As noted above, the necessity requirement has at least three components: is the measure likely to achieve the goal? Does it go further than is necessary? Is there a less trade-restrictive measure? The Australian Court in *Castlemaine Tooheys* does apply the first and second questions, but has understandable reservations about the third, as discussed *supra*. The European Court seems prepared to apply all three questions, taking a more proactive role in this matter. The necessity requirement could thus be used to strike down measures, or parts of measures, which are not likely to achieve their goal or which go further than is needed, and possibly also measures to which there is a clearly practicable and less restrictive alternative.

Once it has been ascertained that a measure is necessary, it may then be asked whether the obstacle introduced is proportional to the objective pursued. This would allow the courts to invalidate local regulation that is capricious or which imposes a very much greater burden on inter-State trade. One should recall, however, that this requirement of proportionality is particularly intrusive and tends to limit State sovereignty in certain fields. Particular attention should therefore be paid to the factual and economic aspects of each case and to the legitimate local interests in protection. As a general rule, it may be useful to presume that a large degree of disproportionality should be found before legitimate and necessary local regulation is struck down.

V. CONCLUSION

As we have seen, the Australian High Court and the European Court of Justice have used rather similar tests when addressing the validity of State environmental measures hindering inter-State trade. We have also seen, however, that the concept of discrimination is given much more importance in Australia than in the European Community. Its use by the Australian High Court seems based on a concept of protectionism, whereas the European Court goes beyond the question of discrimination and addresses more directly the balancing of the interests that are involved. This may be because a greater degree of uniformity of national non-discriminatory rules affecting trade has been possible in Australia than in the Community, so that the High Court has not been called on to address the trade-restrictive effects which may flow from the existence of such measures.

In assessing trade-restrictive State measures, both Courts allow only what is necessary to achieve legitimate goals. However, the language used by the Courts in the *Castlemaine Tooheys* and *Danish Bottles* cases, as well as in earlier cases, leaves some room for confusion. Under the cover of this confusion, courts may in fact implicitly assess not only the necessity of the measure chosen by a member State to attain its legitimate goal of environmental protection (necessity of the means) but also the value of the goal itself (proportionality of the goal).

An assessment by the courts of the proportionality of the goal pursued may serve some useful purposes, but for the sake of clarity, and in order to protect legitimate State interests, courts should adopt a more open and structured approach. This would involve applying first the necessity (or least restrictive measure) test, and then the proportionality test, bearing in mind the importance of respecting State sovereignty and not intervening in the absence of a large disparity between the benefit to the State and the harm to inter-State trade.[118]

From the foregoing discussion, it will be seen that it is very difficult to design a workable, practicable test that perfectly resolves the conflicting interests involved where local legislation protects local environment at the expense of inter-State trade. This illustrates how difficult it is for the High Court of Australia and European Court of Justice to reconcile free trade and environmental protection in their respective jurisdictions. Adjudication of this type of case should therefore be reduced to a minimum. As local environmental initiatives often result from the absence, or the inadequacy, of harmonised environmental standards, one way of reducing section 92 or Article 30 conflicts is for the central legislature to adopt adequate harmonised legislation in all relevant fields.[119] Such legislation would contribute in a significant way to the balancing of trade and the environment in Australia and the European Community.

118. Some may argue that the wording of legal requirements is irrelevant, in that they are not determinative of any outcome. Yet, although not always determinative, words do matter; they can shape perceptions, define the questions and set levels of credibility. For this reason we do believe it is worthwhile to attempt to clarify legal tests.

119. See generally Geradin, "Trade and Environmental Protection: Community Harmonization and National Environmental Standards" (1993) 13 Y.E.L. 151.

[12]

The Fair Trade-Free Trade Debate: Trade, Labor, and the Environment

ROBERT HOWSE and MICHAEL J. TREBILCOCK

University of Toronto

I. Introduction

Many trade scholars—both lawyers and economists—view the increasing preoccupation with "fair trade" as the most fundamental challenge or threat to the liberal trading order that has arisen in recent decades.[1] The fair trade claims that currently generate the most heated debates in the trade community are those related to environmental and labor standards. The *Economist* magazine recently noted that ". . . . labour standards and environmental issues are playing an increasing role in international trade disputes" and are likely to be the central area of conflict between developed and developing countries in the next decade.[2]

Most free traders see recent demands that trade be linked to compliance with environmental and labor standards as motivated by the desire to protect jobs at home against increased competition from the Third World and view many fair traders as charlatans (protectionists masquerading as moralists). Where the demands of fair traders cannot so easily be reduced to protectionist pretexts, free traders are inclined to portray the advocates of linkage as irrational moral fanatics, prepared to sacrifice global economic welfare and the pressing needs of the developing countries for trivial, elusive, or purely sentimental goals.

The attitude of the free traders is reflected in two recent General Agreement on Tariffs and Trade (GATT) dispute panel rulings,[3] both concerning the legality under GATT of U.S. embargoes of tuna imports. The embargoes were targeted, either directly

We are grateful for research assistance by Ari Blicker and Peter Miller and for helpful comments from Lucian Bebchuck, Jagdish Bhagwati, Richard Craswell, Alan Deardorff, Steven Elliot, David Friedman, Douglas Ginsberg, Robert Hudec, Brian Langille, Helen Maroudas, Richard Posner, Alan Sykes, and Darlene Varaleau.

[1]See, for example, J. Bhagwati, "*The World Trading System at Risk, Aggressive Unilateralism,*" and "Fair Trade, Reciprocity and Harmonization", in *Analytical and Negotiating Issues in the Global Trading System* eds. A. Deardorff and R. Stern (Ann Arbor: University of Michigan Press, 1993); R. Hudec, "Mirror, Mirror on the Wall: The Concept of Fairness in the United States Foreign Trade Policy" *Proceedings of the Canadian Council on International Law* 88 (1990).

[2]"War of the Worlds," *The Economist,* October 1, 1994, p. 32.

[3]*United States—Restrictions on Imports of Tuna,* 30 I.L.M. 1594 (1991) (hereinafter, *Tuna/Dolphin I*); *United States—Restrictions on Imports of Tuna,* DS29/R, June 1994 (hereinafter, *Tuna/Dolphin II*). Tuna/Dolphin I is discussed at length in M.J. Trebilcock and R. Howse, *The Regulation of International Trade* (London and New York, Routledge, 1995) pp. 344–350.

International Review of Law and Economics 16:61–79, 1996

655 Avenue of the Americas, New York, NY 10010

0144-8188/96/$15.00
SSDI 0144-8188(95)00057-7

or indirectly,[4] at tuna-fishing practices in the Eastern Pacific, particularly those of Mexico, which resulted in the deaths of large numbers of dolphins. Despite some differences in interpretive approach, both panels held that the environmental exemptions in Article XX of the GATT (which refer to protection of animal life and health and to conservation of natural resources) do not extend to trade sanctions targeted at other countries' policies. While neither panel ruling has been formally adopted by the GATT Council, and while there is currently no exemption in Article XX of the GATT that applies to labor rights-based measures (except with respect to restrictions on imports of products of prison labor), the principle that trade sanctions should never be a legally permissible response to the environmental and labor policies of other countries has become an article of faith among most free traders, or at least the beginning point[5] for any discussion of the relationship between GATT rules and global environmental and labour rights concerns.

The notion that there is, or should be, no room whatever within the GATT World Trade Organization (WTO) legal framework for trade measures in response to labor and environmental policies of other countries, has arguably heightened the intuitive discomfort many citizens feel about transferring domestic sovereignty to an international institution like the WTO. It is significant that of all the GATT panel rulings in recent years, only *Tuna/Dolphin I* has attracted widespread attention and scrutiny beyond the trade law and policy community, particularly in the United States. If international trade law simply rules out of court any trade response to the policies of other countries, however abhorrent, then there will be an understandable, and dangerous, temptation to declare that international trade law is an ass. The lesson of the recent heroic exercise to gain congressional approval of the Uruguay Round Agreement, including the provisions establishing the WTO, is that any rules-based approach to international trade is unlikely to be durable unless, in the end, it is able to command significant public legitimacy.

This article suggests the idea of a blanket prohibition of trade sanctions to affect other countries' policies and advocates a more subtle legal and institutional approach to the relationship between trade, environment, and labor rights. We propose a normative framework for disaggregating and evaluating "fair trade" claims relating to labor and environmental standards. In particular, we draw a critical distinction between claims that trade measures should be used to attain a specific non-trade goal or vindicate a specific non-trade value, and arguments for a "level" competitive playing field, evening the odds, or establishing "fair" rules of the game that are internal to the trading system.

Sanctions as a Means of Inducing Other States to Alter their Environmental or Labor Practices

Environmentalists and labor rights activists may advocate trade sanctions as a means of inducing recalcitrant governments and/or firms to meet a given set of labor or envi-

---

[4] *Tuna/Dolphin II* concerned a secondary embargo of tuna from the European Union World Trade Organization (EU), aimed at pressuring the EU to itself impose a primary embargo on tuna from the Eastern Pacific caught in a dolphin-unfriendly way (i.e., with purse-seine nets).

[5] Free traders may often eventually concede some exceptional cases where sanctions ought to be permissible—for instance where both the sanctioning state and the targeted state are signatories to an international environmental agreement that contemplates sanctions.

ronmental standards.[6] This may involve trade restrictions being imposed in the case of a country violating international environmental or labor agreements that it has already signed, or to induce a country to adopt a standard or norm that it has not yet accepted as binding, even in principle. Where the conduct of another state is repugnant to the values and sensibilities of its citizens, a government has a range of responses available to it, escalating from the minimalist response of doing nothing or making diplomatic protests to a maximalist response of declaring and waging war. Economic sanctions, including trade sanctions, can be viewed as falling somewhere in the middle of this spectrum, and have characterized in recent years the main response of a wide variety of states to such practices as apartheid in South Africa and genocide in the former Yugoslavia. The embargo of Iraq is a further recent example of the use of economic sanctions in support of non-trade policy goals. To what extent does the use of trade sanctions to punish, protest, or influence behavior of other states in the name of values external to the trading system itself constitute a challenge or threat to the normative theory of the gains from trade?

The non-trade-related rationales for environment and labor sanctions. An initial issue is whether the ultimate goals of such sanctions can be justified. Here it is useful to identify the main reasons why concerns about environmental and labor laws and practices may legitimately extend beyond national borders.

EXTERNALITIES. In certain circumstances, a country may be able to externalize some of the environmental costs of economic activity within its borders to the nationals of other countries. The classic example is pollution which flows from country A into the territory of country B through common air or water bodies. These spillovers can be of major significance—for example, a significant portion of the acid rain that affects Canada can be attributed to emissions in the United States.

THE GLOBAL ENVIRONMENTAL COMMONS. The commons may be defined as "physical or biological systems that lie wholly or largely outside the jurisdiction of any of the individual members of society but that are valued resources for many members of society. International commons of current interest include Antarctica, the high seas, deep seabed minerals, the electromagnetic spectrum, the geostationary orbit, the stratospheric ozone layer, the global climate system, and outer space.[7] Protection of endangered species might be added to this list. Where unconstrained and uncoordinated, exploitation of these physical and biological systems by nationals of each individual jurisdiction may produce what is widely referred to as the "tragedy of the commons."[8]

SHARED NATURAL RESOURCES. "Shared natural resources are physical or biological systems that extend into or across the jurisdictions of two or more members of international society. They may involve nonrenewable resources (for example, pools of oil that

---

[6]See H.F. Chang, "An Economic Analysis of Trade Measures to Protect the Global Environment", *Georgetown Law Journal* 83 (1995): 4.

[7]O. Young, *International Governance: Protecting the Environment in a Stateless Society* (Ithaca, NY: Cornell University Press, 1994), p.20.

[8]G. Hardin, "The Tragedy of the Commons", in *Managing the Commons* eds. G. Hardin and J. Baden (San Francisco: W.H. Freeman, 1977).

underlie areas subject to the jurisdiction of adjacent or opposite states), renewable resources (for example, straddling stocks of fish or migratory stocks of wild animals), or complex ecosystems that transcend the boundries of national jurisdiction."[9] Property rights to these shared resources cannot easily be assigned on a purely territorial basis, and therefore each sharing state has an interest in the practices and policies of each other sharing state with respect to these resources.

Human Rights. Human rights are frequently and increasingly regarded as inalienable rights that belong to individuals regardless of their national affiliation, simply by virtue of being human. Such an understanding of rights is implicit in the Kantian understanding of human autonomy that has profoundly influenced contemporary liberal theory. Certain labor rights or standards have come to be widely regarded as basic human rights with a universal character. These include: the right to collective bargaining and freedom of association; the right not to be enslaved; the abolition of child labor; and equality of opportunity in employment for men and women.[10] These rights are reflected in the Conventions of the International Labor Organization (ILO). Some of the Conventions have been ratified by a large number of countries; others by far fewer countries.

Although labor rights are conceived of as universal in the ILO Conventions, they are not viewed as absolute. Thus, for example, in the case of the prohibition on child labor, the minimum age of 15 years applies in most circumstances, but in many developing country contexts, the applicable age may be 12 years; as well, child labor in agricultural contexts is generally permitted.[11] Respect for the universal normative content of international labor rights need not entail *identical* labor policies or standards.

International Political and Economic Spillovers. Some human rights abuses and some labor practices, particularly violent suppression of workers' rights to organize or associate, may lead to the kind of acute social conflict that gives rise to general political and economic instability. Such instability may spill over national boundaries and affect global security. Increasingly (as the cases of the former Yugoslavia, Rwanda, and Somalia illustrate), "internal" conflicts are capable of raising regional or global security, economic, or social (e.g., immigration and refugee) issues.

Altruistic or Paternalistic Concerns. Even if they are not directly affected in any of the ways described above, citizens of one country may find the purely domestic environmental practices or policies of another country to be misguided or morally wrong. Similarly, citizens of one country may believe that workers in another country would be better off if protected by higher labor standards. Such a belief may or may not be warranted. For instance, higher minimum wages or other improvements in standards that raise labor costs, may in some circumstances do more harm than good, if the result is a significant increase in unemployment. Proponents of external intervention make the strong assumption that citizens in one country are better able to make these welfare judgments than governments in another country, which seems unlikely to be systematically true, even where the government in the latter country is not democratically

---

[9] Young, *op. cit.*, p. 21.

[10] See, generally, B. Hepple, "Equality: A Global Labour Standard" in *International Labour Standards and Economic Interdependence*, eds. W. Sengenberger and D. Campbell (Geneva: International Institute for Labour Studies, 1994).

[11] *ILO Convention No. 138* (Minimum Age Convention) (1973).

elected or accountable. However, the provision of foreign aid, often with major conditions attached as to recipients' domestic policies, by international agencies such as the World Bank and the International Monetary Fund (IMF) suggests that a welfare presumption against paternalism is not irrebuttable.

The nature of the above concerns differs in important respects. In the case of externalities, the global environmental commons, and shared natural resources, the main normative basis may sound in an argument about economic welfare, primarily the welfare of citizens in the state seeking to invoke trade sanctions but perhaps indirectly also global welfare. In other cases, the most obvious and compelling normative basis for insisting on compliance with minimum standards may have little relation to economic welfare; this is particularly true in the case of universal human rights, including labor rights, where the case for universal recognition of such rights is often premised on a deontological conception of human freedom and equality. Alternatively, in welfare terms, one can conceptualize such rights as involving interdependent utility functions between citizens of different states (unlike externalities and related claims). However, it is important to stress the universal character of such rights in order to distinguish these claims from more *ad hoc* claims of paternalism or altruism, which although also ostensibly grounded in the interdependence of utility functions cannot as readily be justified on a purely deontological basis, rendering these claims contestable in both welfare (or utilitarian) terms and in deonotological terms.

In the following discussion we attempt to identify the kinds of potential welfare effects, both positive and negative, that would need to be considered in any analysis of environmental or labor rights-based trade sanctions.

Scenario 1: trade sanctions or the threat of sanctions succeed in inducing higher environmental or labor standards.

The first scenario is that the country or countries targeted by sanctions, or at least some firms within those countries, change their domestic practices and adhere to or accept the minimum standards.

Welfare Effects in Targeted Country. With respect to the *domestic welfare of the country or countries that change policies,* if the status quo prior to the alteration of the policies is welfare maximizing (either in the Pareto or Kaldor-Hicks sense), then conforming to higher standards will reduce domestic welfare. Alternatively, the policy change may be welfare enhancing. For instance, in the case of environmental standards, it may lead to a more complete internalization of environmental costs and therefore a more efficient allocation of resources within the domestic economy. Critics of "fair trade" claims from an economic perspective often assume that low environmental or labor standards do in fact reflect a welfare-maximizing outcome for poor countries, but there is no empirical work that appears to provide unambiguous support for such a conclusion. Therefore, the *assumption* that domestic polices' *ex ante* trade sanctions were welfare maximizing has to be based on the view that, absent foreign influence, the domestic political and regulatory processes within these states would maximize welfare based on revealed preferences.

With respect to labor rights abuses, some of the practices that have been singled out as justifying trade sanctions—slave labor camps in China, for instance—would be difficult to characterize as the product of political or regulatory processes likely to maximize welfare based on the revealed preferences of individuals. Since the countries concerned are not genuine democracies, the domestic political process is simply not designed to take into account the preferences of all citizens. Indeed, in a Marxist totalitarian state like China, individual preferences—except for those of the ruling elites—may well count for very little. With respect to low environmental standards, it is true that some countries singled out for attack are liberal democracies where the assumption that domestic political and regulatory processes maximize individual preferences is more plausible (e.g., the call for trade sanctions against the British Colombia forest products industry). However, in these instances it may sometimes be possible to attribute lax environmental standards to the disproportionate influence of powerful industrial interests on the political and regulatory process, or to misguided efforts to protect jobs in a particular firm, sector or region.[12] In the end, knowing whether higher environmental or labor standards is likely to result in an improvement in domestic welfare, defined either in Pareto or Kaldor-Hicks terms, would entail judgments and analysis that go far beyond the disciplinary expertise of trade economists and trade policy experts.[13]

In general, the domestic welfare gains from improved labor standards are most likely to exist where, in the first place, there is a strong case for regulation to correct specific instances of market failure[14] (e.g., information asymmetries in the case of occupational health and safety[15], or where markets fail more radically due, for instance, to the presence of coercion (slave labor, child labor, the use of violence to intimidate workers, etc).

Global Welfare Effects. Improvements in environmental standards may increase global welfare where these improvements reduce or eliminate transboundary spillovers and externalities or address the problem of the "tragedy of the commons" or correct other market failures. In the case of the environment, examples of transboundary externalities abound, whether these are conceived of in the traditional sense as spillovers or whether they concern effects on the global environmental commons.

In the environmental area, where they are effective in inducing countries to remove or reduce externalities, and therefore in more fully internalizing the costs of economic activity, trade sanctions may actually lead to an increase in global allocative efficiency.[16] With respect to labor rights or standards, international minimum standards may address in some measure a fundamental distortion in the global labor market, i.e., restrictive

[12]For an explanation along these lines of some Canadian environmental policies, see Michael E. Porter and The Monitor Company, *Canada at the Crossroads: The Reality of a New Competitive Environment* (Ottawa: Business Council on National Issues, Supply and Services Canada, 1991), pp. 92–94.

[13]See G. Hansson, *Social Clauses and International Trade: An Economic Analysis of Labour Standards in Trade Policy* (New York: St. Martin's Press, 1983), pp. 168–171.

[14]Some economists have a generally skeptical view of the possibility that minimum standards, for instance in the case of occupational health and safety, can adequately correct for market failure. However, once this skepticism is put to the test through economic modeling, the results are ambiguous. Under some assumptions, minimum standards may be effective in correcting for market failure; under others (e.g., considerable heterogeneity in workers' risk preferences) minimum standards may actually result in greater market distortion. See D.K. Brown, A.V. Deardorff, and R.M. Stern, "International Labour Standards and Trade: A Theoretical Analysis", Fairness-Harmonization Project, University of Michigan, July 1994.

[15]See, generally, C. Sunstein, *After the Rights Revolution: Reconceiving the Regulatory State* (Cambridge, MA: Harvard University Press, 1990).

[16]It is this perspective, reflected in the "polluter pays" principle, that has informed most of the work of the OECD on international environmental standards (although the OECD does not endorse trade sanctions *per se* as a means of achieving internalization of environmental costs). See OECD, *Guiding Principles Concerning International Economic Aspects of Environmental Policies* (26 May 1972) 11 I.L.M. 1172 (1972); OECD, *Council Recommendation on the Implementation of the Polluter Pays Principle* (14 Nov. 14 1974) 14 I.L.M. 234 (1975). See also, G. Feketekuty, "The Link Between Trade and Environmental Policy" Minnesota Journal of Global Trade 2 (1993): 171–178.

immigration policies that prevent people from moving to locations where their labor is more highly valued. Without the threat of exit and often without effective voice in their home countries, they may be vulnerable to oppressive domestic labor policies or practices.[17] There may be possible longer-term impacts of the reduction in oppressive labor practices that would have positive impacts on global welfare—such as accelerated political liberalization as workers become less intimidated, better organized, and generally more capable of asserting their rights.[18] Increasing liberalization of domestic political regimes was linked early on by the philosopher Immanuel Kant[19] and much more recently in empirical work by Michael Doyle,[20] to a reduced threat of global conflict, including a reduced likelihood of war. Resort to practices such as forced labor, child labor (which often amounts to the same thing since, generally, children in these regimes have little say in whether they work or not), and violent suppression of independent trade unions (e.g., the Solidarity movement in Poland) provides a means of resistance to pressures for political and economic reforms—reforms which, it has been suggested, may well in the medium or longer run produce regimes that are significantly less likely to threaten international peace and security.[21]

Welfare Effects in Sanction-Imposing Country. Depending on elasticities of supply and demand, where foreign producers are faced with higher costs due to higher environmental or labor standards, they may be able to pass on some of these costs to consumers in the country that imposed the trade sanctions. However, it may be the case that compliance with minimum environmental or labor standards will not result in significantly higher prices to consumers, where *some* producers in the targeted country are *already* meeting minimum standards. In the case of the environment, for example, producers who have more modern plants or use new technologies that are relatively speaking more environmentally friendly, may not need to incur significant additional costs in order to comply with minimum standards. Similarly, in the case of labor standards, some producers may be meeting minimum standards within existing cost structures. Where, for instance, a producer is located in a part of the country where political and social conditions have allowed trade unions to survive, it may already have had to measure up to basic levels of protection with respect to occupational health and safety. Such a producer may have been able to remain competitive with other producers who have not been meeting minimum standards, through increasing the productivity of

[17]See Albert Hirschman, *Exit, Voice and Loyalty: Responses to Decline in Firms, Organizations, and States* (Cambridge, MA: Harvard University Press, 1970).

[18]In the case of Poland, for instance, the beginnings of liberal revolution are to found in the gradual recognition of an independent trade union movement, which was able to mobilize broader social forces against the Soviet-bloc regime. See A. Pravaj, "The Workers," in *Poland: Genesis of a Revolution,* ed. A. Brumberg (New York: Vintage, 1983), pp. 68–91.

[19]I. Kant, "Perpetual Peace," in *Kant's Political Writings,* ed. Hans Reiss, trans. H.B. Nisbet (London: Cambridge University Press, 1970).

[20]See Michael W. Doyle, "Kant, Liberal Legacies and Foreign Affairs" *Philosophy and Public Affairs* 12 (1983): 205; and "Liberalism and World Politics" *American Political Science Review* 80 (1986): 1151.

[21]In recent work, Bhagwati has suggested that labor rights-related trade measures might be understood as most justifiable where the labor standards in question can be most clearly assimilated to classical human rights—for instance, prohibition of forced labor, or suppression of collective bargaining, sanctioning of violence to intimidate workers from making demands for a better workplace, etc. From a global welfare perspective, it is these kinds of labor rights that we suggest may lead to welfare gains from the resultant liberalization that occurs where a regime can no longer resist popular demands for a better life through coercive measures (or sanctioning private sector use of coercion).

labor, better employment of technology, etc.[22] However, it must be acknowledged that, making the conventional economic assumption that supply curves are never infinitely elastic, some adverse price effects on consumers in the sanction-imposing country seem likely, although in many cases these seem likely to be small.

In some circumstances the additional costs that compliance with labor or environmental standards impose on firms in the targeted country may create gains for the domestic producers of like products in the country that imposed or threatened sanctions. This would occur where producers in the sanction-imposing country have the lowest costs of *any* country whose producers comply with the labour or environmental standards in question. In this instance, producers in the sanctions-imposing country will gain both domestic and foreign market share. Consumers, however, will pay more. Nevertheless, in very many instances, the next-lowest-cost producer complying with minimum standards is likely not to be a domestic firm, but a firm in another country. For this reason, compliance with minimum labor or environmental standards will often not confer substantial benefits on producer interests in the country that has imposed sanctions, although there are always likely to be some protective price effects (depending on elasticities of supply).

Scenario 2: the case where trade sanctions fail to induce higher standards.

Welfare Effects in the Targeted Country. Here, the welfare effects will depend on how widely or narrowly cast the sanctions are. Perhaps the sanctions with the least negative welfare effects would be those that target the products of only those *firms* that do not meet minimum labor or environmental standards.[23] These sanctions, first of all, may be effective in actually securing some environmental or labor rights benefits even in the absence of a change in *government* policy, if they induce changes in firm behavior. Second, if there exist some producers who are already meeting the standards (e.g., due to deployment of more recent technologies, etc.) or who could meet them without variable costs significantly exceeding those of the most efficient firm not meeting the standards, then the sanctions may have only a small negative welfare effect, mostly shifting export market share to the more efficient producers.

Monitoring and enforcement of firm-specific sanctions may, however, entail much higher administrative costs than an outright ban of a given product from a particular country or countries. An attractive variant on firm-specific sanctions may therefore be a general ban subject to specific exemptions for firms able to satisfy the authorities of the sanctioning state that they are, in fact, in compliance with the environmental or labor standards at issue.

Global Welfare Effects. Even where sanctions fail to induce any policy change in the

[22]In the case of Mexico, for example, it is often suggested that gross violations of basic international labor rights norms are concentrated in the *maquiladora* region, whereas basic labor rights are respected throughout much of the country, particularly in unionized workplaces. See P. Morici, "Implications of a Social Charter for the North American Free Trade Agreement, in *Ties Beyond Trade: Labour and Environmental Issues under the NAFTA* eds. J. Lemco and W.B.P. Robson (Toronto and Washington D.C.: C.D. Howe Institute and National Planning Association, 1993), pp. 137–138. Morici notes that, even within the *maquiladoras*, "many employers . . . provide workers with a wide range of benefits and a safe working environment, and they adhere closely to strict environmental standards." (p. 138). See also USITC, "Review of Trade and Investment Measures by Mexico," *USITC Report No. 2326* (October 1990).

[23]In practice, however, such targeting will not always be easy. For instance, it is rumored that China falsifies the factories of origin for exported products that are manufactured with forced labor, so that these cannot be traced to the labor camps.

targeted country, there may be some positive effect on global welfare where sanctions result in a decline in the global sales of products that are manufactured in a fashion that creates significant externalities or entail labor rights abuses. If the country imposing the sanctions, or the group of countries imposing them, constitute a major market for the products in question, then global demand will now be met through production that complies with the standards in question. But for this to happen, sanctions must be imposed *consistently*—i.e., against all producers or countries worldwide that do not comply with the standards in question. Otherwise, production may simply be shifted from one firm that is responsible for the negative externalities or abuses in question to another.

Just as with domestic welfare, trade sanctions that are not carefully targeted against only those industries, sectors, or (ideally) firms that actually do not meet higher environmental or labor standards could, in theory, result in significant global welfare losses, shifting production away from least-cost producers in the targeted country to higher-cost producers elsewhere. However, many product areas are characterized by the existence of a variety of rival producers in different countries, often with closely comparable cost structures. In such a case, and assuming that some of these companies will be in compliance with the environmental and labor standards in question, global welfare losses may not in the end be significant. Rivals in compliance with international minimum standards will simply expand their market share. However, there are likely to be some price increases, assuming supply is not infinitely elastic.

With respect to the welfare effects of sanctions that fail to change government policy on those with pro-environmental or pro-labor rights preferences, these will still likely to be positive for three reasons. Two of the reasons will be evident from the above analysis. First, if the sanctions are properly targeted at *firms* they may induce higher levels of labor and environmental protection even in the absence of a change in government policy. Second, sanctions, because they reduce world demand for products made in ways that harm the environment or abuse workers' rights, will reduce the levels of these harmful activities. Third, sanctions will provide the moral satisfaction of resisting government policies or practices that violate environmental or human rights norms, even if the government does not change its policies. However, even those with pro-environmental and pro-labor rights preferences may have some of these utility gains offset from utility losses due to the knowledge that sanctions may well cause harm to "innocent" victims of the government's intransigence in the face of sanctions, i.e., workers who lose their jobs, persons who suffer from a country's reduced ability to purchase essential supplies given a reduction in its convertible currency earnings, etc.

WELFARE EFFECTS IN THE SANCTIONS-IMPOSING COUNTRY. Welfare effects on consumers and producers in the sanctions-imposing country are likely to be similar to those in Scenario 1.

SUMMARY. The above analysis has taken into account only the static effects of sanctions. A dynamic perspective could alter the analysis significantly. For instance, higher environmental standards may induce investment in environmentally friendly processes or technologies, ultimately leading to a reduction in environmental compliance costs, or even production costs generally (inasmuch as the new technology is simply more efficient). Similarly, restrictions on the use of child labor may, as with the *Factory Acts* enacted in Britain in the first half of the nineteenth century, lead to political demands for enhanced access to public education.

The very general analysis, above, of the welfare effects of environmentally or labor rights-based trade sanctions outlined above suggests that little can be said, in the abstract, about the likely effects of such sanctions on aggregate domestic welfare in either the targeting or sanction-imposing country, or on global welfare. This clearly distinguishes trade measures of this kind from conventional protectionist trade restrictions, where formal analysis suggests overall net welfare losses, both domestic and global, when one considers the welfare effects of trade restrictions on consumers as well as workers and firms.[24]

Predicting the Effectiveness of Sanctions. Clearly, as the above analysis suggests, the welfare effects of sanctions will differ considerably depending on whether or not sanctions are actually able to change policies or practices in the targeted country. This underscores the importance of examining whether and when sanctions are likely to be effective in achieving such policy changes.

While there is not much evidence on the effectiveness of environmental or labor rights trade sanctions in particular, significant empirical work has been undertaken with a view to measuring the impact of economic sanctions more generally on state behavior. To our knowledge, the most comprehensive work on this question remains the study by Hufbauer, Schott, and Elliott,[25] which examines 115 instances of the use of economic sanctions over a period of about 40 years. The authors conclude that these sanctions had an overall success rate of about 34% in achieving an alteration of the conduct of the targeting country in the desired direction.[26] Not surprisingly, they found sanctions were more likely to succeed in changing behavior where the policy changes in question were relatively modest, and where the sanctions-imposing country was larger and more powerful than the targeted country.[27] Another important observation in this study is that sanctions are least likely to succeed against intrasigent, hostile regimes as opposed to countries that are relatively friendly to the sanctions-imposing state.

Relative to many of the sanctions studied by Hufbauer, Schott, and Elliott, most environmental or labor rights trade sanctions would certainly count as aimed at only modest policy changes,[28] in comparison with sanctions that seek to topple an entire regime, or the removal of a pervasive form of social ordering (e.g., apartheid in South Africa). Moreover, Hufbauer, Schott, and Elliott's general observations on the importance of the relative size of the sanction-imposing and the targeted country, and about friends and enemies, seems consonant with recent evidence about the effectiveness of some environmental and labor rights sanctions. The threat of trade sanctions by the United States has, for instance, been credited with altering fishing practices that harmed endangered species in countries such as Japan, South Korea, Chile, Taiwan, and Peru—all of which could be described as relatively "friendly" states from the U.S.

[24] Trebilcock, Chandler, and Howse, *op. cit.* p. 45. See also R.E. Baldwin, "The Ineffectiveness of Trade Policy in Promoting Social Goals," *The World Economy* 8: 109.

[25] G.C. Hufbauer, Schott, and Elliott, *Economic Sanctions Reconsidered: History and Current Policy*, 2d ed. (Washington D.C.: Institute for International Economics, 1990). See also M. Miyagawa, *Do Economic Sanctions Work?* (New York: St. Martin's Press, 1992), and D. Baldwin, *Economic Statecraft* (Ithaca, NY: Cornell, University Press, 1985).

[26] *Ibid.* p. 93.

[27] This is consistent with more recent work by Nossal, which found that sanctions by "middle powers" such as Canada and Australia have been largely ineffective. See K.R. Nossal, *Rain Dancing: Sanctions in Canadian and Australian Foreign Policy* (Toronto: University of Toronto Press, 1994).

[28] In some cases such sanctions might, however, be aimed at goals that imply very significant regime change, for instance, in the case of China, sanctions aimed at inducing respect for the right of labor to organize and bargain freely.

point of view, and all (with the possible exception of Japan) significantly smaller and less powerful than the United States.[29] By contrast, U.S. threats to deny most favored nation (MFN) status to China, a totalitarian quasi-superpower with a hostile ideological system, has made little impact in terms of human rights, including labor rights compliance.

Overall, the evidence suggests that trade sanctions are of limited but real effectiveness, and in this respect they are no different from other, more extreme forms of coercive action such as military force where the record of effectiveness is also extremely mixed (e.g., Lebanon, Bosnia, Somalia, Rwanda, Haiti, and Vietnam). On the other hand, a systematic strategy of isolationism, appeasement, or acquiescence would largely resign us to accept grotesque human rights abuses or indeed attempted genocide without external opposition.

An issue closely related to the effectiveness of economic sanctions is the relative desirability of sanctions as opposed to other instruments for influencing the behavior of other countries and their producers. For instance, the GATT Secretariat has advocated the use of financial inducements as an alternative means to sanctions for influencing countries to adopt higher environmental standards.[30] This proposal has the virtue of attaching a price to the invocation of such sanctions and thus providing some assurance that these higher standards are truly valued for their own sake in the country desiring the changes, especially in cases of ostensible *ad hoc* paternalism or altruism, whereas trade sanctions, lacking such an explicit price (beyond price effects on consumers), may be easily subverted by protectionists. Chang argues, however, that subsidies, as opposed to sanctions, create a perverse incentive for foreign countries to engage in, or intensify, the offensive behavior (or make credible threats to this effect) in order to maximize the payments being offered.[31]

A recent study of the effects of both carrots and sticks on political change in South Africa supports Chang's skepticism about carrots; it concludes that ". . . political strategies that rely on inducements rather than commands are limited in what they can accomplish."[32] Moreover, in cases of transboundary externalities, the global environmental commons, shared natural resources, or universal human rights abuses (in contrast to exchanges of tariff concessions), a principle that victims (or their supporters) should always pay ("bribe") violators to achieve compliance would seem impossible to defend either ethically or politically. However, in some cases financial assistance to enable poor Third World countries to meet higher environmental or labor standards may be warranted or distributive justice grounds.

Another alternative[33] to trade restrictions is environmental and labor rights labeling,

---

[29]S. Charnovitz, "Encouraging Environmental Cooperation Through Trade Measures Through The Pelly Amendment and the GATT", *Journal of Environment and Development* 3 (1994): 3, 2202–2203.

[30]GATT Secretariat, *Trade and the Environment*, GATT Doc. 1529 (Feb. 3, 1992).

[31]Chang, *op. cit.*, pp. 2154–2156.

[32]K.A. Rodman, "Public and Private Sanctions against South Africa," *Political Science Quarterly* 109 (1994): 313,334.

[33]There may also be a further alternative, akin to labeling, through which individual consumers by their investment choices can attempt to discipline socially irresponsible corporate behavior. The phenomenon of socially responsible investing (SRI) refers to the "making of investment choices according to both financial and ethical criteria." For instance, individuals can choose to put their investments in firms that act in a manner consistent with their ethical values or they may choose to refrain from investing in those firms believed to be behaving in a socially unacceptable fashion. The two primary claims advanced by SRI adherents, which distinguish it from other strategies of investment, are: (i) that social screening does not entail a financial sacrifice (i.e., that advancing one's social agenda can be as profitable as investment for purely financial gain) and (ii) that SRI can alter corporate behavior insofar as it seeks to

which allows individuals as consumers to express their moral preferences for environmental or labor rights protection.[34] Products that are produced in a manner that meets a given set of labor or environmental standards would be entitled to bear a distinctive logo or statement that informs consumers of this fact. Although labeling may enable individual consumers to avoid the moral "taint" of consuming the product in question themselves, if most consumers have a preference for terminating production altogether (rather than merely reducing consumption and production) by changing a foreign country's domestic policies, then a collective action problem arises as in any approach to influencing behavior that depends upon coordinating action among large numbers of agents. Unless she can be sure that most other consumers will do likewise, the individual consumer may well not consider it rational to avoid buying the product in question.[35]

In sum, neither financial inducements nor labeling programs are self-evidently superior policy instruments to sanctions for influencing other countries' environmental and labor practices. Each has its own drawbacks. However, it must be admitted that little concrete empirical evidence exists that would allow a rigorous comparison of these alternative instruments with sanctions. In addition, the greatest effectiveness might actually be achieved by a combination of more than one of these instruments. Again, in the absence of empirical work, it is difficult to make out a clear-cut case for excluding the use of trade sanctions as an instrument for influencing the behavior of other countries' governments or firms.

The "Systemic" Threat to a Liberal Trading Order

Even in the presence of indeterminate welfare effects many free traders may still reject environmental or labor rights-based trade measures on the basis that such measures, if widely permitted or entertained, would significantly erode the coherence and sustainability of rule-based liberal trade. We ourselves, in earlier work, have argued that competitiveness-based or level playing field "fair trade" measures, such as countervailing and antidumping duties, already pose such a threat. This is based on the notion that the legal order of international trade is best understood as a set of rules and norms aimed at sustaining a long-term cooperative equilibrium, in the face of ongoing pressures to cheat on this equilibrium, given that the short-term political payoffs from cheating may be quite high (depending, of course, on the character and influence of protectionist interests within a particular country, the availability of alternative policies to deal with

---

channel funds away from firms acting in a socially unacceptable way. While this phenomenon has become quite popular, there is good reason to be skeptical about its ability to deliver on its claims. Specifically, Knoll has suggested that, at best, only one of the claims can be true because each implies the negation of the other. As he explains, "[i]f markets are efficient, the first might be true but the second is false. If markets are inefficient, the second might be true but the first is false." With respect to the second claim, Knoll found that "regardless of the efficiency or inefficiency of the market, the impact of an investor's decision not to invest in a company will have little or no impact on the firm's ability to raise capital and therefore on its activities." For a more thorough discussion, see Michael S. Knoll, "Socially Responsible Investment and Modern Financial Markets" (March 18, 1994, unpublished manuscript).

[34]On environmental labeling, see R. Howse, "Reform, Retrenchment or Revolution? The Shift to Incentives and the Future of the Regulatory State", *Alberta Law Review* 31 (1993): 486–487; D. Cohen, "Procedural Fairness and Incentive Programs: Reflections on the Environmental Choice Program", *Alberta Law Review* 31 (1993): 554–574.

[35]J. Bhagwati and T.N. Srinivasan suggest that environmental values, if sound, "will spread because of their intrinsic appeal." "Trade and the Environment: Does Environmental Diversity Detract From the Case for Free Trade?," unpublished manuscript, July 1994. The fact that moral principles such as those prohibiting murder and theft are inherently sound does not, however, obviate the need to sanction non-compliance with them.

adjustment costs etc.).[36] In the presence of a lack of fundamental normative consensus as to what constitutes "cheating" on the one hand, and the punishment of others' cheating on the other, confidence in the rules themselves could be fundamentally undermined, and the system destabilized.

In considering the systemic threat from environmental and labor rights-related trade measures, it is important to distinguish between purely unilateral measures and those that have a multilateral dimension. The former measures are based upon an environmental or labor rights concern or norm that is specific to the sanctioning country or countries. Here, there is a real risk of dissolving a clear distinction between protectionist "cheating" and genuine sanctions to further non-trade values—the sanctioning country may well be able to define or redefine its environmental or labor rights causes so as to serve protectionist interests. Measures with a multilateral dimension, by contrast, will be based upon the targeted country's violation of some multilateral or internationally recognized norm, principle, or agreement—for instance, a provision in an accord to protect endangered species or one of the ILO Labor Conventions. These norms, principles, or agreements are typically not the product of protectionist forces in particular countries, nor are they easily captured by such forces (although the example of the Multi-Fibre Arrangement suggests that this is not invariably the case).

In *Tuna/Dolphin I,* the judgment that the strictures of Article XX of the GATT would not be adequate to "screen" global as opposed to domestic environmental measures and thereby prevent abuse, is undermined by the fact that the Panel itself had little difficulty in applying (*arguendo*) a least restrictive means test (as developed in the *Thai Cigarette*[37] case) to the facts of *Tuna/Dolphin.* Thus, the Panel noted that even if Article XX were to include measures with non-domestic policy goals, the U.S. ban on dolphin-unfriendly tuna imports could not be considered "necessary" to achieve these goals, since the United States had not exhausted the avenues for a negotiated co-operative solution that would have avoided trade disruption.

It should be possible to build into Article XX of the GATT a series of limits or criteria that are likely to minimize the protectionist abuse of environmental or labor rights[38] trade sanctions, and the corresponding risk of a loss of coherence and integrity in the GATT legal framework. In developing such criteria, we believe it is important to distinguish four different contexts in which environmental or labor rights trade sanctions may be employed: (1) where trade measures are explicitly contemplated in an interna-

[36] *Trade and Transitions, op. cit.*, pp. 211–215. This view of the legal order of liberal trade has been greatly influenced by the liberal internationalist perspective of Robert Axelrod and Robert Keohane. According to Axelrod and Keohane, "The principles and rules of international regimes make governments concerned about precedents, increasing the likelihood that they will attempt to punish defectors. In this way international regimes help to link the future with the present. This is as true of arms control agreements, in which willingness to make future agreements depends on others' compliance with previous arrangements, as it is in the GATT, which embodies norms and rules against which the behavior of members can be judged. By sanctioning retaliation for those who violate rules, regimes create expectations that a given violation will be treated not as an isolated case but as one in a series of interrelated actions." R. Axelrod and R.O. Keohane, "Achieving Cooperation Under Anarchy: Strategies and Institutions", in *Neorealism and Neoliberalism* ed. D.A. Baldwin (New York: Columbia University Press, 1993), p. 94.

[37] *Thailand: Restrictions on Importation of and Internal Taxes of Cigarettes* (Report of the Panel) BISD, 37th. Supp. (1989–1990) 200. In this case, the Panel ruled that an import ban could only be found "necessary" within the meaning of Article XX (b), where alternative measures, less restrictive of trade, were not available to achieve the objectives in question.

[38] In the case of labor rights, amending the actual text of Article XX would seem to be necessary, because (apart from products manufactured with prison labor) Article XX does not contain any explicit labor rights justifications for trade restrictions.

tional treaty that establishes labor or environmental standards; (2) where trade measures are not contemplated in the treaty or agreement, but where an independent body, such as a supra-national dispute settlement panel, commission, or monitoring authority, has found the targeted country in violation of international labor or environmental standards; (3) where the sanctions-imposing country or countries themselves have determined that the targeted country is in violation of an international norm or standard, in the absence of an independent ruling by a neutral third party (e.g., international institution); and (4) where the sanctions-imposing country merely asserts a norm or standard of environmental or labor protection as appropriate, in the absence of an internationally recognized norm or standard. Trade sanctions involved to promote environmental or labor protection should be easier to justify in categories (1) and (2) than categories (3) and (4).

Competitiveness-based Arguments for Environmental or Labor-Rights-Based Trade Measures

Unlike the arguments for trade restrictions on environmental and labor rights grounds that we have been discussing up to this point, which have a normative reference point external to the trading system itself, competitiveness-based "fair-trade" claims focus largely on the effects on domestic producers and workers of other countries' environmental and labor policies, and not *per se* on the effects of those policies on the environment and on workers elsewhere. Competitiveness claims are, in principle, indifferent to the improvement of environmental or labor practices in other countries. Hence, in the case of competitiveness claims, trade measures that protect the domestic market or "equalize" comparative advantage related to environmental or labor standards are a completely acceptable *substitute* for other countries raising their standards.

Competitiveness claims usually refer to one of two kinds of supposed unfairness (and, it is often argued as well, welfare losses) that stem from trade competition with countries that have lower environmental or labor standards:

1. It is unfair (and/or inefficient) that our own firms and workers should bear the "costs" of higher environmental or labor standards through loss of market share to foreign producers who have lower costs due to laxer environmental or labor standards in their own country.
2. It is unfair that downward pressure should be placed on our environmental or labor standards by virtue of the impact of trade competition with countries with lower standards.

Competitive Fairness Claim 1

The first kind of claim is, in our view, largely incoherent and in fact in tension with the basic theory of comparative advantage in trade. Assuming there is nothing wrongful with another country's environmental or labor policies along the lines discussed in the first part of this paper, then why should a cost advantage attributable to these divergent policies not be treated like any other cost advantage, i.e., as part and parcel of comparative advantage? In fact, even if all countries had the same level of environmental consciousness, or even the same general environmental standards, approaches to instrument choice as well as the choice of risks on which to concentrate would still differ widely, due to differing climatic and other geographical or demographic conditions. For these reasons, even in a world where all citizens shared the same environmental preferences, environmental laws and regulations would still be likely to differ substantially between countries, and even where they were the same, the costs to industry of complying with those laws and regulations would still likely differ substantially from country to country.

Precisely because the implicit benchmark of fairness is so illusory—i.e., a world where governmentally imposed labor and environmental protection costs are completely equalized among producers of like products in all countries—trade measures based upon this kind of fairness claim are likely to be highly manipulable by protectionist interests. Since, of course, protectionists are really interested in obtaining trade protection, not in promoting environmental standards or labor rights, the fact that the competitive fairness claim in question does not generate a viable and principled benchmark for alteration of other countries' policies is a strength not a weakness—for it virtually guarantees that justifications for protection will always be available, even if the targeted country improves its environmental or labor standards.

Welfare Effects of Trade Restrictions Aimed at Equalizing Comparative Advantage

Trade restrictions will lead to reduced exports, with consequent welfare losses to firms and workers in the targeted country. Since *every* foreign producer whose environmental or labor rights compliance costs are less than those of domestic producers will be vulnerable to trade action, trade restrictions based on equalization of comparative advantage are likely to affect imports, potentially quite dramatically, from a wide range of countries. Firms and workers engaged in the manufacture of like products to those imports targeted by trade restrictions will benefit where the restrictions in question make imports relatively more expensive than domestic substitutes, thereby shifting demand from imports to domestic production. Consumers will pay more, probably substantially more, as domestic producers will price up to the duty imposed by the trade restriction. Here, the welfare effects essentially resemble those from the imposition of a tariff or countervailing duty. Inasmuch as production is shifted from lower to higher cost producers, there is also some loss of global allocative efficiency.

Clearly, overall, these welfare effects entail a shift in wealth to firms and workers in the trade-restricting country from firms and workers in the targeted country as well as from consumers in the trade-restricting country. In our view, it is difficult to construct a theory of distributive justice to support the fairness of these transfers.

Perhaps the transfer between workers and consumers in the trade-restricting countries might be a *prima facie* defense on the grounds that it is just that many people suffer a little to avoid a few (i.e., workers who risk dislocation) from suffering a lot. But, then, why burden consumers? Why not subsidize from general taxation revenue environmental or labor rights compliance costs for industries that, but for such subsidies, could not compete on international markets? If anything, the most coherent distributive justice argument in support of the fairness claim here points to getting rid of countervailing duty law, so that such subsidies can be provided without risk of trade retaliation (but fair traders are not known for their outspokenness in this cause!).

What seems completely unsustainable on grounds of distributive justice is the shift of the costs of higher environmental or labor standards in the trade restricting country from workers and firms in that country to workers and firms in other countries. If, as fair traders vociferously argue, it is unfair to make workers and firms in one's own country pay for the competitive consequences of higher environmental and labor standards in that country, how could it possibly be fair to make workers and firms in another country pay this price? Indeed, shifting the competitiveness costs of one's own environmental or labor standards to workers in other countries seems distributively *perverse*. No matter how high an intrinsic or instrumentalist value we may wish to put on high environmental or labor standards in our own country, there is simply an unsupportable leap of logic in the conclusion that someone else should be paying the price for them. First of all, workers in other countries do not even usually directly benefit from these higher standards, whereas workers in one's own country do. Second, most competitiveness-based fair trade claims are targeted against countries that are poorer than the trade-restricting country, often with lower *per capita* incomes, higher levels of unemployment, and weaker social welfare nets (in some instances, the revenue from trading products may be essential to obtaining foreign exchange to buy essential goods such as medicines and foods).

Competitive Fairness Claim 2

This fairness claim does appear to be based in some concern for environmental and labour rights *per se*, albeit not at the international level but within one's own country. Whereas competitiveness claim 1 presumes that governments will not respond to the competitive implications of higher labor and environmental standards, and simply let firms and workers lose out, the second competitive fairness claim assumes just the opposite—that governments will respond by lowering domestic standards below the optimal level.

We do not believe that, generally speaking, lowering environmental or labor standards is an appropriate response to competitive pressures. There is, in fact, a wide range of alternatives—such as better regulation which reduces compliance costs without lowering standards,[39] investment in training, etc. to increase the productivity of labor[40] and the investment in technologies that are likely to reduce the costs of compliance with environmental standards.

Of course, it is arguable (although there is not much hard empirical evidence on the matter) that governments and/or firms are in fact responding by lowering standards, rather than through these arguably superior activity alternatives. However, these sub-optimal policy responses surely represent a political and social problem within countries that are lowering standards in response to competitive pressures. Again, it seems hardly fair that workers (or firms for that matter) in other countries should bear the burden of avoiding choices in another country that are ultimately attributable to a flawed policy process in that country.

A variation of the claim about the effect of competitiveness pressures on domestic environmental and labor standards suggests the possibility of a form of beggar-thy-neighbor behavior that may, admittedly leave all countries worse off. This is the "race to the bottom," whereby countries competitively lower their environmental or labor standards, in an effort to capture a relatively greater share of a fixed volume of trade or investment.[41] Much like the beggar-thy-neighbor subsidies wars that characterized ag-

[39]See R. Stewart, "Environmental Regulation and International Competitiveness" *Yale Law Journal* 102 (1993): 2039.

[40]See W. Sengenberger, "Protection-Participation-Promotion: The Systemic Nature and Effects of Labour Standards," in W. Sengenberger and D. Campbell, eds., *supra* note 10.

[41]"Fair Trade is Free Trade's Destiny," forthcoming in Bhagwatti & Hudec (eds.), *Harmonization and Fair Trade: Prerequisites for Fair Trade?* (MIT, 1996).

ricultural trade among Canada, the United States, and the European Union and other countries during the 1980s, it is not difficult, using the model of a Prisoner's Dilemma game, to show that competitive reduction in environmental or labor standards will typically result in a negative sum outcome,[42] as long as one assumes that before entering the race each country's environmental or labor standards represent an optimal domestic policy outcome for that country.

The "race to the bottom" claim has a different normative basis from the other competitiveness-based claims discussed above. Those claims relate to the proper distribution of the competitiveness costs of maintaining higher environmental and labor standards than one's trading partners. The normative basis for concern over the race to the bottom, by contrast, sounds in the language of Pareto efficiency: the race ends, literally, at the bottom, with each country adopting suboptimal domestic policies, but no country in the end capturing a larger share of the gains from trade.

Frequently, beggar-thy-neighbor regulatory competition is able to flourish much more easily where it is possible to reduce on a selective basis labor or environmental standards to attract a particular investment or support a particular industry or firm. It is more difficult and more costly to engage in these activities where the formal statutory framework of labor or environmental regulation must be altered across the board. Here, some of the provisions in the NAFTA Environmental and Labor Side Agreements may create disincentives to beggar-thy-neighbor competition in as much as these agreements oblige the signatories to enforce effectively those environmental and labor rights laws that are formally on the books. At the same time, it must be acknowledged that effectively monitoring whether a country is fully enforcing its own laws is not an easy task, especially for outsiders.

Finally, it is possible simply to ban by international agreement beggar-thy-neighbor competition. This is, for instance, what Article 1114 of the NAFTA attempts to do, albeit in rather weak legal language, with respect to environmental measures, *inter alia.* Article 1114 (2) states, in part that "The Parties recognize that it is inappropriate to encourage investment by relaxing domestic health, safety, and or environmental measures. Accordingly, a Party should not waive or otherwise derogate from or offer to waive or otherwise derogate from, such measures as an encouragement for the establishment, acquisition, expansion, or retention in its territory of an investor."

Accepting, however, that cooperation is the ultimate solution to the "race to the bottom," a further difficult question remains as to the appropriateness of trade restrictions as a sanction to induce a cooperative outcome. Here, there is important further work to be done in applying the insights of game theory to beggar-thy-neighbor trade conflicts such as, for instance, the agricultural subsidies wars: Did trade retaliation facilitate or frustrate a cooperative solution, i.e., the Uruguay Round Agreement on Agriculture? Just as was suggested in the first part of this paper, the role of unilateral sanctions in inducing rules-based, cooperative solutions to conflict is a complex one. Sophisticated advocates of unilateralism or aggressive reciprocity, such as Laura Tyson[43] and Carolyn Rhodes,[44] argue for trade measures as a means of inducing a rules-based cooperative equilibrium, not as a long-term strategy of non-cooperative behavior. The

---

[42]"Competing Conceptions of Regulatory Competition in Debates on Trade Liberalization and Labour Standards," forthcoming in Bratton, McCahery, & Picciotto (eds.), *International Regulatory Competition and Co-ordination—Perspectives on Economic Regulation in Europe and the United States* (Oxford University Press, 1996).

[43]Laura Tyson, *Who's Bashing Whom?*, (Washington, D.C.: Institute for International Economics, 1992).

[44]C. Rhodes, *Reciprocity, U.S. Trade Policy and the GATT Regime* (Ithaca, NY: Cornell University Press, 1993).

problem, as has been articulated by Bhagwati and others, is that these trade restrictions usually constitute deviations from *existing cooperative outcomes* (*preexisting GATT rules*). Therefore, depending on one's standpoint such restrictions may resemble cheating on an existing cooperative equilibrium, rather than inducement to create a new one. One response of the unilateralists and reciprocitarians might be that the "race to the bottom" or "beggar-thy-neighbor" conduct of one's trading partners has, in fact, already put in danger the preexisting cooperative equilibrium, and that no return to a rules-based approach is possible unless new rules are adopted to deal with the "race to the bottom." However, free traders might well respond that an approach to inducing a new equilibrium based upon the use of technically illegal trade measures as a sanction to bring about negotiation of new rules is likely to undermine countries' overall confidence in the rule of law, and therefore actually may complicate the future prospects for rules-based solutions to trade conflict.

In the GATT WTO, there is arguably already a kind of implicit response to this dilemma, to be found in the concept of non-violation nullification and impairment in Article XXIII. In some circumstances, a GATT Panel may find that a Contracting Party's practices, even if not in technical violation of the General Agreement, nevertheless undermine reasonable expectations of another Party as to the benefit that it would receive from GATT concessions. In this situation, trade sanctions may ultimately be authorized, even if the targeted country did not engage in a technical violation of the GATT rules. Where a Contracting Party views the "beggar-thy-neighbor" but technically GATT-legal conduct of another Party as undermining the existing cooperative equilibrium of GATT rules and concessions, it may seek GATT approval of ultimate recourse to unilateral trade measures through making a case that non-violation nullification or impairment has occurred. This procedure prevents each Party being judge in its own cause, and thereby obviates the consequent potentially negative implications for overall confidence in the rule of law. Through this means, trade sanctions or the threat of sanctions, may be used as a legitimate instrument for inducing one's trading partners to bargain towards new or reformed rules to end a "race to the bottom." Thus, even where it could be shown that trade restrictions are appropriate as a means of inducing a cooperative solution, we do not see a justification for taking such measures outside the existing jurisprudential framework of the GATT WTO, or for making the framework more amenable to unilateral actions in which Contracting Parties are judges in their own cause as to whether the existing cooperative equilibrium has been undermined by purported "beggar-thy-neighbor" conduct of other Contracting Parties.

Conclusion

Once carefully disaggregated and scrutinized, "fair trade" claims related to environmental and labor standards are not necessarily groundless, nor self-serving of protectionist interests, nor as threatening to the liberal world trading order as free traders often make out. A concern to protect the rules-based liberal trading order from a loss of coherence and integrity, and a corresponding risk of a new protectionist spiral, has led free-trade oriented economists, policy experts, and lawyers to criticize and often reject wholesale trade measures related to labor and environmental standards, even where there is little persuasive evidence that such measures are welfare reducing or are motivated only by protectionist interests. However, a potentially serious threat to a liberal international trading order is posed by competitiveness-based or level playing field forms of fair trade claims, which we almost entirely dismiss as normatively incoherent and as mostly thinly disguised forms of protectionism. The institutional challenge thus posed is designing trade law regimes (both international and domestic) with the capacity to distinguish credibly between these two classes of claims. We have argued in this paper that this enterprise will entail minimizing to the greatest extent possible the scope for unilateral assertions of fair trade claims and maximizing to the greatest extent possible the role of international treaties, agreements, and norms as the basis of such claims. Free traders, by indiscriminately dismissing all fair trade claims and eliding these two classes of claims, run the risk of being discredited as moral phillistines and thus being marginalized in political debates that do indeed carry serious risks for a liberal international trading order.

[13]

Differences in National Environmental Standards: The Level-Playing-Field Dimension

Robert E. Hudec*

One of the many strands of the trade-and-environment debate is a complaint that exports from countries with weak environmental regulations are "unfair." It is argued that producers in such countries obtain an unfair cost advantage because they are excused from complying with proper environmental practices. For example, if paper producers are not required to clean up the water they discharge from their production facilities, their costs will be lower than those of producers in countries requiring clean discharges. The claim that such cost advantages are unfair rests on a general normative proposition known as the "level-playing-field" complaint: competition is unfair whenever foreign producers enjoy any advantage created by their government that is not equally available to the complaining domestic producers.

A government could satisfy the demand for a level playing field by removing the perceived cost disadvantage in one of three ways. First, the government could lower its own environmental standards. Second, the government could give domestic producers a cash subsidy to cover their environmental compliance costs. Finally, the government could tax away the foreign producers' cost advantage by imposing customs duties ("eco-duties") on imports from countries with low environmental standards.

The first two options are problematic. Environmentalists quite naturally oppose relaxing domestic environmental standards. Budget problems usually limit the extent to which subsidies can be granted. Consequently, commercial and environmental interests tend to support eco-duties. From the environmental point of view, eco-duties improve both domestic and foreign environmental policies. They mollify the competitive

---

* Melvin C. Steen Professor of Law, University of Minnesota. An earlier version of this article was delivered as a lecture on April 13, 1995, on the occasion of the author's reappointment to the Steen Professorship.

concerns of domestic producers and offer economic incentives to improve environmental standards abroad. Domestic producers prefer eco-duties because they elicit the least opposition from environmentalists and taxpayers.

Needless to say, governments of countries with low environmental standards do not concede that their lack of environmental regulations creates an unfair advantage. In most cases, they are developing countries who assert the right to formulate whatever environmental policies are best suited to their level of economic development. They therefore object to any trade measures levied on the basis of lower environmental compliance costs.

This article evaluates the claim that imports from countries with low environmental standards are unfair.[1] Part I surveys recent U.S. legislative proposals that have addressed the level-playing-field complaint. Part II examines environmental policy arguments that usually accompany unfairness claims and describes their relationship to unfairness issues. Part III explores the root concepts of fairness underlying the level-playing-field

---

1. For an earlier and somewhat differently oriented version of the analysis in this section, see Robert E. Hudec, *"Mirror, Mirror, on the Wall": The Concept of Fairness in U.S. Foreign Trade Policy*, *in* PROCEEDINGS OF THE 1990 CONFERENCE OF THE CANADIAN COUNCIL ON INTERNATIONAL LAW 88, 88-110 (1990).

For other recent works exploring the possible meanings of the fairness concept, *see* Ronald A. Cass and Richard D. Boltuck, *Antidumping and Countervailing Duty Law: The Mirage of Equitable International Competition*, *in* 2 FAIR TRADE AND HARMONIZATION: PREREQUISITES FOR FREE TRADE? (Jagdish Bhagwati and Robert E. Hudec eds., forthcoming 1996); Kenneth W. Abbott, *Defensive Unfairness: The Normative Structure of Section 301*, *in* 2 FAIR TRADE AND HARMONIZATION: PREREQUISITES FOR FREE TRADE? (Jagdish Bhagwati and Robert E. Hudec eds., forthcoming 1996); Robert T. Kudrle, *Fairness, Efficiency, and Opportunism in U.S. Trade and Investment Policy*, *in* 8 NATIONAL COMPETIVENESS IN A GLOBAL ECONOMY, 153 (1995); Robert Howse & Michael J. Trebilcock, The Fair Trade - Free Trade Debate: Trade, Labour and the Environment, (WPS - 32, University of Toronto Law and Economics Working Paper Series, 1994) (on file with author); J. Michael Finger, *The Meaning of 'Unfair' in United States Import Policy*, 1 MINN. J. GLOBAL TRADE 35 (1992); John J. Barcelo III, *An Analytical History of GATT Unfair Trade Remedy Law*, 14 WORLD ECON. 311 (1991); Susan Hutton & Michael Trebilcock, *An Empirical Study of the Application of Canadian Anti-Dumping Laws: A Search for a Normative Rationale*, 24 J. WORLD TRADE 123 (1990); Patricia I. Hansen, *Defining Unreasonableness in International Trade: Section 301 of the Trade Act of 1974*, 96 YALE L.J. 1122 (1987).

On the influence of the fairness concept in U.S. policy, see Jagdish Bhagwati, PROTECTIONISM chs. 3, 6 (1988); AGGRESSIVE UNILATERALISM: AMERICA'S 301 POLICY AND THE WORLD TRADING SYSTEM (Jagdish Bhagwati and Hugh Patrick, eds., 1990); JAGDISH BHAGWATI, THE WORLD TRADING SYSTEM AT RISK (Harry Johnson Memorial Lecture, 1990).

complaint as it appears in current U.S. trade policy debate. Part IV examines the extent to which the concepts of "subsidy" and "dumping" in both GATT law and current U.S. trade law can be applied to imports produced under low environmental standards. Part V looks beyond the level-playing-field norm and considers other, possibly more discriminating norms that might justify national differences in environmental standards. A brief conclusion examines the likely course of future developments.

I. RECENT LEGISLATIVE PROPOSALS

The legislative solution most frequently proposed to offset the price advantage of weak environmental regulations is a tax on imports from the low-standards country. The Copper Bill introduced by Senator DeConcini in 1985 provides an early example of such a "level playing field" proposal.[2] The bill, which did not pass, imposed duties on copper produced in countries that "do not employ environmental measures substantially equivalent to those imposed on [U.S.] copper producers."[3] The bill fixed the amount of the duty by comparing the import's actual cost of production to the cost if the foreign producer were required to observe U.S. environmental standards.[4]

A 1991 proposal by Senator Baucus targeted countries that refused to negotiate international environmental standards.[5] Under this proposal, if a country rejected international negotiations and its environmental standards did not meet those of the United States, the United States would be allowed to impose countervailing duties on imports from that country.[6] The United States would have imposed such duties only if three criteria were met: (1) the applicable U.S. environmental standards must have been scientifically based; (2) the same standards must have been applied to all competitive domestic production; and (3) the imported products must have been causing economic injury to competitive domestic production.[7] The duty would have set an amount to "offset any economic advantage gained by

---

2. S. 353, 99th Cong., 1st Sess. §§ 1-2 (1985).

3. *Id.* at § 2.

4. *Id.*

5. Richard Lawrence, *GATT Urged to Address Environment,* J. COM., Oct. 28, 1991, at 5A.

6. *Id.*

7. 137 Cong. Rec. S13,169 (daily ed. Sept. 17, 1991) (recommendation of Senator Baucus). *See also Baucus Calls for Environmental Code in GATT Modeled After Subsidies Code,* 8 Int'l Trade Rep. (BNA) 1568-69 (Oct. 30, 1991).

producing the product under less stringent environmental protection regulations."[8]

The International Pollution Deterrence Act of 1991, proposed by Senator Boren, would have allowed the United States to apply countervailing duties to imports produced without "effective pollution controls."[9] The duty based on the cost of complying with U.S. environmental standards. Half of the countervailing duties collected would have been placed into a "Pollution Control Export Fund" to help developing countries purchase U.S. pollution control equipment.[10] The Boren bill was not enacted or reintroduced.

A more general Congressional resolution introduced in 1993 called for creating a "fair" world economic system by ensuring that "[U.S.] laws designed to protect the environment from polluting and environmentally destructive industrial and agricultural practices not place the United States at a competitive disadvantage compared with other countries."[11] This resolution also failed.

Representative Gephardt has advanced the most recent level-playing-field measure entitled "Blue and Green 301."[12] Not yet introduced as a bill, Gephardt's proposal treats any failure to adopt effective environmental safeguards as an unfair trading practice if it yields a competitive advantage to the polluter.[13] The proposal also allows the United States to impose unilateral trade sanctions against countries failing to enforce their own environmental and labor laws.[14]

One academic commentator has suggested an antidumping approach to the problem. She recommends imposing a dumping duty equal to the cost "saved" by the exporter in a low-standards country.[15] The amount of the duty would be based on the difference between the cost of complying with the importing country's

---

8. 137 Cong. Rec. at S13,169.

9. S. 984, 102d Cong., 1st Sess. § 3 (1991). *See also Trade Incentives and Environmental Reform: The Search for a Suitable Incentive,* 4 GEO. INT'L ENVTL. L. REV. 421, 427 (1992).

10. S. 984, 102d Cong., 1st Sess. § 4 (1991).

11. H.R. Con. Res. 86 (1993).

12. The colors represent the interests protected by the bill — labor (blue collar) and the environment (green).

13. *Gephardt Bill to Allow Sanctions For Not Enforcing Environmental Laws*, 11 Int'l Trade Rep. (BNA) 500 (Mar. 30, 1994).

14. *Id.*

15. Ursula Kettlewell, *GATT — Will Liberalized Trade Aid Global Environmental Protection?* 21 DENV. J. INT'L L. & POL'Y 55, 74-76 (1992).

environmental regulations and the cost of complying with the exporting country's regulations.[16]

Another proposed solution to the perceived competitive problem would remove otherwise available preferential tariff treatment for products from countries that fail to meet some acceptable standard of environmental regulation. For example, the Baucus proposal contained a provision making adequate environmental regulation a condition for extending U.S. duty-free benefits to developing countries.[17] Similarly, the Global Environmental Protection and Trade Equity Act, introduced by Senators Lautenberg, Kasten and Dixon, would have required that countries institute and enforce "effective" pollution control programs in order to be eligible for trade preferences under the U.S. Generalized System of Preferences (GSP) and the Caribbean Basin Initiative (CBI).[18] Representative Brown introduced the GSP Renewal and Reform Act of 1993 that would have required countries to comply with internationally recognized environmental protection standards in order to qualify for GSP status.[19] Congress has yet to enact any of these GSP proposals.[20]

II. THE ENVIRONMENTAL CASE FOR A LEVEL PLAYING FIELD

Although the main focus of the level-playing-field complaint is commercial, environmental concerns add a new policy dimension. Some environmental writers argue that satisfying the unfairness claims of domestic producers promotes better environmental policies. If such producers are protected from foreign competition they may be less likely to oppose higher domestic environmental standards. Environmental advocates also assert that the threat of eco-duties creates pressure for higher environmental standards in other countries.

Environmental writers have developed a vocabulary connecting these level-playing-field concerns to other environmen-

16. *Id.* at 75.

17. 137 Cong. Rec. S13,170 (daily ed. Sept. 17, 1991). *See also* Lawrence, *supra* note 5, at 5A.

18. S. 2887, 101st Cong., 2d Sess. (1990).

19. H.R. 3625, 103d Cong., 1st Sess. (1993).

20. Section 601 of the Uruguay Round Agreements Act, 108 Stat. 4809, 4990 (1994), extended the existing GSP law, 19 U.S.C. §§ 2461-65 (1994) through July 31, 1995 to give Congress additional time to consider the long-term fate of the GSP program. The proposed renewal legislation, H.R. 1654, 104th Cong., 1st Sess. (1995), contained no environmental conditions. This renewal legislation had not been enacted as of October, 1995.

tal issues. Environmentalists once drew attention to the pollution "spillover" that weak environmental policies caused in neighboring countries. They argued that pollution that crossed national frontiers should be treated like any other tortious harm and that affected countries had a right to take action against the polluting countries. The term "spillover" acquired so much normative resonance in this context that environmental writers began to use it to describe many other kinds of environmental concerns. For example, the term "psychological spillover" is used to support a claim that mistreatment of animals has an emotional impact on citizens of other countries, an impact that harms them as much as pollution spillover and thus justifies similar retaliatory action.[21] This same "spillover" vocabulary is now used to describe the adverse political effects caused by imports from countries with low environmental standards. Such imports cause "political spillover" when they induce local producers to oppose stronger environmental policies at home.

It is true that domestic producers often cite competitive disadvantage as one reason to object to higher environmental standards at home. Moreover, if domestic producers can feasibly relocate to a "polluter haven" country, they will usually threaten to do so. One can never know, however, the extent to which lower environmental standards abroad actually do contribute to the substance or intensity of such political positions. Common sense tells us that there are usually many other factors involved in perceptions of competitive disadvantage *vis-à-vis* imports. Recent studies indicate that the cost of complying with environmental regulations to date has not been very large.[22] Some skepticism is warranted.

Assuming that discrepancies in environmental policies cause at least some cost differences and that manufacturers will call attention to them, the ultimate question is whether these cost differences deserve to be treated as more important than the dozens of other cost advantages a foreign producer may

21. *See, e.g.*, Richard Blackhurst & Arvind Sabramanian, *Promoting Multilateral Cooperation on the Environment, in* THE GREENING OF WORLD TRADE ISSUES 247 (Kym Anderson & Richard Blackhurst eds., 1992).

22. *See* Arik Levinson, *Environmental Regulations and Industry Location: International and Domestic Evidence, in* 1 FAIR TRADE AND HARMONIZATION: PREREQUISITES TO FREE TRADE? (Jagdish Bhagwati & Robert E. Hudec eds., forthcoming 1996).

Daniel Esty, while acknowledging the generally low level of current environmental compliance costs, reports a number of estimates showing that average compliance costs will rise significantly. DANIEL C. ESTY, GREENING THE GATT: TRADE, ENVIRONMENT, AND THE FUTURE 160-61 (1994).

have. International trade is based on differences of cost factors. Local producers will complain about any of them if given a chance. Unless something is thought to be wrong with a particular cost factor, however, governments do not usually feel obliged to address such complaints, nor, indeed, do such complaints tend to be pressed very far in the first place.

In sum, "political spillover" arguments are significant only to the extent they are supported by some kind of normative complaint. It is the level-playing-field complaint that gives them what vigor they have today. While environmental writers do not necessarily endorse the level-playing-field complaint on its merits (although to be fair most don't exactly oppose it, either), the strength of their political spillover arguments depends on it. It would be difficult to complain about the political spillover of low environmental standards if such standards were generally perceived to be a normal and legitimate variation between national domestic policies.

III. THE CONCEPT OF FAIRNESS IN INTERNATIONAL TRADE

The concept of fairness in international trade policy is almost entirely a U.S. contribution. No government uses unfair trade laws as vigorously as does the United States, and the U.S. Congress bows to no one in its attachment to concepts of fair and unfair trade. To understand these distinctive U.S. ideas, we must start by looking into their origins in U.S. economic life.

A. FAIR COMPETITION IN U.S. ECONOMIC POLICY

In the United States, the core substantive content of unfairness claims derives from a concept known as "fair competition." The normative assertion behind the idea of fair competition is that merit should determine business outcomes. In other words, businesses should succeed or fail according to their merit as competitors. Competition will be "fair" if none of the competitors has any advantages that are not based on merit. Competition will be fair if the playing field is level.

The concept of fair competition originated in U.S. internal economic policy. Throughout most of its history, the United States has maintained a commitment to an open internal economy. U.S. businesses are expected to compete with each other. The policy is reflected in the U.S. Constitution's Commerce

Clause,[23] and in the many components of the U.S. antitrust laws. The primary justification for this policy, of course, is its beneficial effect on national economic welfare. Over the years, however, public debate has added the concept of fair competition as a normative justification for this policy.

The idea of merit-based outcomes has broad popular appeal, at least in United States politics. The business community itself has come to welcome the idea, because a fair competition policy requires that government not intrude in business. The role of government is merely to make certain that the playing field is level, by ensuring both that local governments do not tilt the playing surface and that private parties do not impede competition through cartels or other anti-competitive behavior.

To be sure, the rhetorical image of a level playing field is somewhat fanciful to the extent that it portrays competitors grappling for commercial success in some pristine environment free from external influences. The modern world has never known such a government-free state of nature. Government is everywhere. Government presence in the market begins by providing certain very important basic conditions such as law and order, infrastructure, stable financial markets, and so forth. The modern state goes much further with economic program upon economic program, each of which influences the direction and content of business activity. The concept of fair competition, therefore, simply cannot exclude government assistance from the picture. It can make sense, however, in terms of a policy which excludes all forms of one-sided government assistance. If everyone receives essentially the same kind and amount of government assistance, as well as the same measure of government-imposed handicaps, no competitor will be advantaged by government in the end, and so competitive skills will continue to be the determining factor of commercial success.

"Fair competition" can be achieved in a general way in the internal U.S. market. Business conditions between domestic competitors are, for the most part, the same. All businesses are subject to the same federal government, providing them with the same type of government benefits and burdens. State governments do differ to some extent, and sometimes differences between states generate business complaints, as in the case of taxes or labor policy. But the disadvantages of such inter-state

23. The U.S. Constitution states that "Congress shall have Power . . . to regulate Commerce with foreign Nations, and among the several States." U.S. CONST. art. I, § 8, cl. 3.

differences tend to be muted by an underlying acceptance of business mobility as a relevant option — if you don't like it you can move. Another leveling element is the fact that businesses really can compete anywhere within the internal market. No one has an officially protected market, and antitrust laws limit the competitive barriers that can be erected privately.

In the rough-and-tumble of business competition, losers will always want to complain about the unfairness of the process and there will always be some difference in business conditions to complain about. Governments cannot run a sensible economic policy unless they are capable of considerable skepticism toward such complaints. The internal U.S. market comes equipped with a considerable supply of such skepticism. Almost all the players in the competitive contest are represented in the relevant governments, so that every claim of unfair advantage will be tested by opposing interests. Domestic economic policy is not in fact swamped with unfairness claims.

On the whole, then, the concept of fair competition works well enough in the internal U.S. market that most U.S. business and political leaders make a public commitment to these values. This is a central part of the normative education they bring to international trade affairs.

B. "Fair Competition" Applied to Foreign Trade

The concept of fair competition found an important role in United States foreign trade policy after World War II. During the U.S. economic domination of the 1950s and early 1960s, the U.S. government and the U.S. business sector utilized the rhetoric of fair competition when demanding entry into protected foreign markets. "Open your doors," they said, "and let the better competitor win." When the pressure of foreign competition started to rise in the late 1960s and early 1970s, U.S. business interests began to speak more softly, but the U.S. government kept up the rhetoric in an effort to justify an increasingly liberal trade policy.

The invocation of "fair competition" values justified two important elements of U.S. foreign trade policy. First, and most obviously, it avoided trade protection. A commitment to fair competition policy found its way into the U.S. "escape clause" legislation.[24] The escape clause law declares that, while local

24. The current version of the escape clause, which was substantially rewritten in the Omnibus Trade and Competitiveness Act of 1988, is found at 19 U.S.C. § 2251-53 (1994).

business may deserve some breathing space when import competition becomes very intense, trade remedies must be temporary. If domestic industry cannot compete in the long run without extra protection, it should get out of the business.

A second policy consequence of the commitment to fair competition was the practice of not compensating the losers in foreign trade competition. The economic theory of international trade demonstrates that trade creates welfare gains for society as a whole, but admits that there will be dislocation costs for losers. The standard academic answer to the problem of dislocation costs is to use the gains from trade to compensate the losers. The fair competition approach says "no" to the idea of compensation. It posits that losers deserved to lose because they were just not good enough competitors. Losers must accept their losses and move on. That has generally been the U.S. policy.

In order to make "fair competition" a politically credible justification for liberal trade policy, the U.S. government had to acknowledge the existence of "unfair competition" as well and promise to protect U.S. producers against it. During the early 1970s, the U.S. government almost welcomed increased attention to claims of "unfair" foreign competition because it signaled acceptance in the business community of the basic policy of openness toward "fair" foreign competition. By the time of the Trade Agreements Act of 1979, it could be said that government and business had struck a deal: business would accept the policy of unprotected and uncompensated adjustment to "fair" foreign competition in exchange for effective protection against "unfair" competition.[25]

Unfortunately, the ideas of fair and unfair competition that make sense to competition within a domestic market do not make the same kind of sense when applied to international competition. The question of whether international competition is fair or unfair depends on the net advantage produced by the differing conditions in each country. There is, however, no reliable way of ascertaining and comparing the net advantage from one country to another. Foreign and domestic competitors do not share the same governmental regulatory structures. The burdens and benefits of each government's policy are never identical

25. Trade Agreements Act, Pub. L. No. 96-39, 93 Stat. 144 (1979). This act, which ratified the results of the GATT Tokyo Round negotiations, contained a complete rewriting of the antidumping and countervailing duty (AD/CVD) laws, making them tighter in a number of respects. The AD/CVD laws continue to have a large industry support group, which periodically calls upon Congress to keep its 1979 pledge to make the AD/CVD laws effective.

to those in other countries. Moreover, government policies are so complex that one could never compile a complete list of the relevant policy measures influencing competitive outcomes in any one country, much less measure them. Nor can the effects of these differences be equalized by the mobility of producer investments or by access into the competitor's market, for neither of these alternatives can be taken for granted in the markets of other countries.

In short, there is no way to know whether the playing field is level to begin with. That being so, there is no way to know whether any particular government measure produces an unfair advantage. A single advantage, like a subsidy, is unfair only if one assumes that all other factors are equal. Eliminating a subsidy will produce a level playing field only when the playing field is otherwise level.

Critics of unfair trade laws welcome this demonstration of the normative incoherence of such laws, but advocates for liberal trade policy take no comfort in its unpleasant corollary — the impossibility of proving that any instance of foreign competition is fair. Our inability to measure and compare competitive conditions between nations means that the possibility that a foreign competitor has received greater assistance than the assistance given by one's own government can never be excluded. This is a most disturbing truth, for it means that foreign trade can never be proved to be in compliance with the seemingly all-powerful normative standard that governs U.S. business and political attitudes toward trade.

A logical response at this point may be for trade policy experts to educate the U.S. business and political community that (1) the concepts of "fair" and "unfair" cannot be applied to foreign trade, and (2) foreign trade is nonetheless clearly beneficial to the national welfare even though it is based on different business conditions. But that response has thus far not been made.

Instead, the U.S. trade laws continue to treat foreign trade as though fairness and unfairness were administrable concepts. In all probability, the decision to do so was largely unconscious. Ideas of fairness and unfairness were part of everyone's attitudes toward competition, and the simple momentum of traditional thinking could account for the importation of those ideas into the relatively unfamiliar domain of international competition. The fact that traditional ideas of fair competition were quite useful in securing broad political acceptance of trade liberalization no doubt also encouraged this tendency.

Oddly enough, U.S. trade laws have been reasonably successful in creating the illusion that the law can distinguish between fair and unfair foreign trade. The trade laws simply identify certain acts such as subsidies and dumping as unfair and further provide a tariff remedy that "cures" the unfair effects of these practices. By claiming the ability to police unfair trade, the law implicitly assures the business public that the rest of foreign trade is fair — something like the way a hanging assures the public that the streets are safe.

Business attitudes aid this illusion of legal efficacy, because most business participants are genuinely convinced of the unfairness of certain advantages enjoyed by foreign business. Fairness is very much a matter of perception, and perceptions vary considerably according to the eye of the beholder. For the average business leader, "unfair is what your government does for you that mine does not do for me." As for the nice things one's own government does, well, those are just the well-deserved fruits of having a competent government. These intuitive, perhaps even subconscious, sorting operations produce what feels like genuine convictions of unfairness. Most domestic producers become genuinely livid about the unfairness of a foreign government subsidy, their minds intuitively closed to the possibility, for example, that the subsidy does no more than correct for an overvalued exchange rate. It helps, of course, that the foreign producers to whom these attitudes are directed are not represented in the political process.

Before rejecting this entire legal edifice as make-believe, we must give make-believe its due. The U.S. laws on fair and unfair trade attempt to develop a politically acceptable rationale for a liberal trade policy. Politics is the art of working with the values and perceptions that people have, to the extent one cannot change them. If public discourse reveals a fairness-unfairness line along which the business community will accept a healthy degree of free trade, governments can be forgiven for trying to use, and even enhance, those business perceptions as a way of promoting sound policy.

The results have been quite satisfying on the whole. The world is currently experiencing the greatest degree of trade liberalization it has known since the rise of the nation state. We will never know what would have happened if a more intellectually honest approach had been taken because the success of the present policy has all but carved these wrong ideas in stone. For the foreseeable future, U.S. trade policy is condemned to follow a public religion based on the worship of fairness and unfairness. Trade policy officials will have to make the best policy they can within the confines of that theology.

C. LIMITING THE REACH OF FAIRNESS CONCEPTS

The greatest danger posed by the current attachment to fairness concepts in international trade policy is the possibility that those concepts will be used to attack almost all foreign trade. There are many differences between business conditions from one country to another. We know that there is no way to measure the net balance of advantage produced by such differences. U.S. trade law tries to circumvent this problem by focusing on one particular advantage at a time, such as a subsidy, and treating that advantage in isolation. If every advantageous difference in business conditions between countries were similarly treated in isolation, most if not all foreign trade could be branded as unfair.

The question is whether a line can be drawn between the sort of competitive advantage created by things like subsidies, which have already been declared to be unfair, and the competitive advantage created by other differences in regulatory policy such as differences in environmental standards. Logically, the fairness concept underlying these characterizations does not offer a plausible distinction between one source of advantage and another. Anything that affects competition is potentially unfair. Happily, however, logic has not been the controlling variable so far. Governments seem to recognize a practical need to limit the fairness concept at some point.

The pragmatic concern is simply that a limitless concept of fairness will destroy a country's exports as well as its imports. Most countries have a substantial investment in international trade and are not prepared to suffer the major economic dislocation that would occur if all that trade were cut off. The U.S. government's commitment to preventing unfair trade was never intended to threaten this larger interest. To the contrary, the attention to unfairness emerged primarily as a quid pro quo support for liberal trade policy. Indeed, if the unfairness concept is viewed from its political origins, it must be seen as necessarily assuming that the bulk of foreign trade as we know it is fair.

Thus far, it would appear that governments have applied the unfairness concept with the sort of restraint just suggested. As will be discussed in the following section, broader ideas of subsidy and dumping are rejected whenever they threaten to produce too many trade restrictions.

To be sure, there is always the possibility that, in the long run, the idea of unfairness will overpower its creators. Normative concepts like this one do have a capacity to generate their own growth. It would not be the first time a legal fiction had grown out of control and destroyed the values it was created to implement.[26] The main safeguard against this outcome is simply the size of the world's investment in international trade. It is probably a safe bet that these large money interests will prevail, but it is difficult to be complacent about a political issue involving anything as potentially volatile as perceptions of unfairness.

IV. FAIRNESS CONCEPTS IN ACTION: CAN LOW ENVIRONMENTAL STANDARDS BE TREATED AS "SUBSIDIES" OR "DUMPING"?

The primary legal concepts employed to root out unfair trade are those of subsidy and dumping. This section considers how present laws dealing with subsidies and dumping address low environmental standards. The analysis considers both GATT and U.S. law.

A. LOW ENVIRONMENTAL STANDARDS AS SUBSIDIES

The most common legal framework for level-playing-field claims against low environmental standards is the assertion that such low standards should be treated as a form of subsidy to producers. The subsidy is the cost saved due to the low environmental standard — the difference between the producer's actual costs and the higher costs it would have incurred if required to comply with more rigorous environmental standards. GATT law permits governments to impose "countervailing duties" (CVDs) on subsidized imports that cause material injury to a domestic industry. The amount of the countervailing duty is equal to the amount of the subsidy.

Current countervailing duty laws do not seem to provide a remedy against goods produced in countries with low environ-

26. The editors have asked for an example. One that comes to mind is the concept of "benefit" in the law of restitution, originally stretched out of shape to do justice in cases where the law of contracts failed to do so, and now routinely employed to give plaintiffs an unjustly excessive measure of damages.

mental standards. Such a legal claim would fail on several counts. First, the current definition of "subsidy" does not appear to include the cost advantage obtained from lower environmental standards. Second, in most cases the benefits of such a subsidy do not meet the requirement that they be "specific" to certain industries. Finally, it is very difficult to demonstrate, much less measure, the financial benefit conferred by low environmental standards. Most proposals calling for CVDs against environmental subsidies concede that new legislation would be required to impose such a remedy.

New legislation, of course, could remove all these legal shortcomings in a single stroke. Such legislation could declare the cost advantage of low environmental standards to be a subsidy, it could waive the specificity requirement, and establish an arbitrary formula for calculating the size of the subsidy. Such a law would probably run afoul of GATT obligations, but that has not always prevented such laws from being enacted.

The core concept of "subsidy" is extremely pliable. The term normally means the transfer by the government of something of value to a producer which increases the producer's profitability. The most common kinds of subsidies involve transfers of money, goods or services, either for free or at below market prices. But from an economic viewpoint anything the government does which alters the producer's costs or revenues in a favorable direction could just as easily be called a subsidy. The political perception is primarily a matter of visibility. Once the helping hand of government becomes conspicuous, it tends to elicit "subsidy" objections no matter what form the help takes.

Until recently, the concept of subsidy was not defined either in national law or in GATT. The lack of definition caused no major problems before the 1970's. The countervailing duty law was little used, and complaints tended to focus on the ordinary export subsidies involving financial transfers from government to business.

Pressure to expand the concept began in the 1970's when the United States decided to apply CVD law to domestic subsidies. In response, domestic producers complained about more and more kinds of government assistance. U.S. countervailing duty law resisted this pressure to expand and began to impose some limits on the subsidy concept.

The first major limitation on the subsidy concept was the so-called "specificity" requirement.[27] Countervailing duty law was held inapplicable to any governmental benefits "generally available" to all or most producers. This limitation effectively excluded most government contributions to infrastructure, as well as most economy-wide social or economic programs. The GATT subsequently adopted the specificity requirement when it issued the first formal definition of "subsidy" in the 1994 Uruguay Round revision of the GATT Subsidies Code.[28]

A second major definitional exercise is still in motion. Until about 1992, the U.S. administrative authorities limited the definition of "subsidy" in U.S. CVD law to transfers of things of value by the government. The concept included the grant of less tangible benefits like loan guarantees, but stopped short of recognizing indirect financial benefits that sometimes result from regulatory measures, such as lower input prices that certain producers obtain from an export restriction on the raw materials they use. In 1992, the U.S. Department of Commerce explicitly rejected its previous definition of subsidy in the *Softwood Lumber III* case.[29] The Department determined that a Canadian export restriction on raw logs, which effectively reduced the price of raw logs to Canadian lumber mills, was an actionable subsidy to those mills.[30] Although the Commerce ruling was ultimately reversed on other grounds, a U.S.-Canada binational panel upheld the expansion of the subsidy definition.[31]

---

27. For an account of the origins of the U.S. doctrine, see James D. Southwick, *The Lingering Problem with the Specificity Test in United States Countervailing Duty Law*, 72 MINN. L. REV. 1159 (1988).

28. Agreement on Subsidies and Countervailing Measures, *opened for signature* Apr. 15, 1994, art. 2, *in* GATT SECRETARIAT, THE RESULTS OF THE URUGUAY ROUND OF MULTILATERAL TRADE NEGOTIATIONS 264, GATT Sales No. 1994-4 (1994) [hereinafter 1994 Subsidies Code].

29. Certain Softwood Lumber Products from Canada, 14 I.T.R.D. (BNA) 2166, 2224-2237 (May 28, 1992) (the third CVD action involving a long-standing complaint about imports of softwood lumber from Canada).

30. The change had been adumbrated in a somewhat earlier decision by the Commerce Department, Leather from Argentina, 13 I.T.R.D. (BNA) 1095, 1096 (Oct. 2, 1990).

31. Certain Softwood Lumber Products from Canada, 16 I.T.R.D. 1168 (BNA) (May 6, 1993). The decision of the Commerce Department was appealed to a binational panel constituted under Chapter 19 of the U.S.-Canada Free Trade Agreement. *Id.* The binational panel accepted the "subsidy" classification of the export ban by a 3-2 decision, but remanded asking for further elaboration on the issues of "specificity" and "direct and discernable effect." *Id.* The Commerce Department elaborated on and affirmed its original findings. 1993 FTAPD LEXIS 10 (Sept. 17, 1993). On a second appeal, the binational panel found the elaborated "specificity" finding still insufficient and remanded with

Shortly after it was announced, the broad new subsidy concept articulated in *Softwood Lumber III* appeared to have been rejected by the new GATT definition of "subsidy" in the Uruguay Round Subsidies Code.[32] The new GATT definition limited the subsidy concept to measures involving a "financial contribution by a government."[33] Indeed, even the Commerce Department opinion in *Softwood Lumber III* seemed to concede that the broader definition of subsidy it adopted in that case was in conflict with the new GATT definition, then in draft.[34]

In ratifying the Uruguay Round Subsidy Code, however, the U.S. Congress made clear that it wanted the new GATT definition of "subsidy" to be interpreted as including and affirming the broader concept of regulatory subsidy employed in *Softwood Lumber III*. The consistency of Congress's position with the new GATT definition cannot be determined authoritatively without a comprehensive review of the negotiating history of the new definition, the documentation for which is still restricted,[35] but the U.S. law itself is now quite clear.

---

orders to dismiss the proceeding. 1993 FTAPD LEXIS 15 (Dec. 17, 1993). That remand order was affirmed by an Extraordinary Challenge Committee, Panel No. ECC-94-1904-01 USA, 1994 FTAPD LEXIS 11 (Aug. 3, 1994), and the Commerce Department's countervailing duty order was dismissed, 59 Fed. Reg. 42,029 (Aug. 16, 1994).

32. 1994 Subsidies Code, *supra* note 28, at art. 1.

33. *Id.*

34. The Commerce decision took note of the unadopted text of the new GATT definition, conceded that it was in conflict with the new definition of subsidy being adopted in that case, and actually sought to use the changes made by the draft GATT text as proof that the definition of "subsidy" in the older version of the Subsidies Code then in force (the Tokyo Round version) must not have been similarly limited. Certain Softwood Lumber Products from Canada, *supra* note 29, at 2235.

35. The full text of the new GATT definition reads as follows:

For the purpose of this Agreement, a subsidy shall be deemed to exist if:

(a)(1) there is a financial contribution by a government or any public body within the territory of a Member (referred to in this Agreement as "government"), i.e. where:

(i) a government practice involves a direct transfer of funds (e.g. grants, loans, and equity infusion), potential direct transfers of funds or liabilities (e.g. loan guarantees);

(ii) government revenue that is otherwise due is foregone or not collected (e.g. fiscal incentives such as tax credits);

(iii) a government provides goods or services other than general infrastructure, or purchases goods;

(iv) a government makes payments to a funding mechanism, or entrusts or directs a private body to carry out one or more of the type of functions illustrated in (i) to (iii) above which would normally be vested

Is this evolving U.S. definition of "subsidy" broad enough to include the cost advantage created by low environmental standards? Probably not. The current definition in U.S. law includes financial benefits businesses receive from private sources, but only those benefits arising from government action that "entrusts or directs a private entity to make a financial contribu-

---

> in the government and the practice, in no real sense, differs from practices normally followed by governments; or
>
> (a)(2) there is any form of income or price support in the sense of Article XVI of GATT 1994; and
>
> (b) a benefit is thereby conferred.

1994 Subsidies Code, *supra* note 28, at art. 1.1 (footnote omitted).

Congress enacted a considerably modified version of the GATT definition into U.S. countervailing duty law. The text of Article 1.1 (a)(1)(iv) of the 1994 Subsidies Code came out as:

> [an authority] makes a payment to a funding mechanism to provide a financial contribution, or entrusts or directs a private entity to make a financial contribution, if providing the contribution would normally be vested in the government and the practice does not differ in substance from practices normally followed by governments.

Uruguay Round Agreements Act, Pub. L. No. 103-465, § 251, 108 Stat. 4809, 4902 (1994) (codified at 19 U.S.C. § 1677(5)(B)(iii)).

According to the House conference report for the Act, Congress interpreted subsection 5(B)(iii) to cover any situation where "government took or imposed (through statutory, regulatory or administrative action) a formal, enforceable measure which directly led to a discernible benefit being provided to the industry under investigation." H.R. REP. No. 826, 103d Cong., 2d Sess., pt. 1, 108-09 (1994). According to the Senate Finance Committee report, "the Committee intends that the term entrusts or directs shall be interpreted broadly to prevent the 'indirect' provision of a subsidy from becoming a harmful loophole to effective enforcement of the countervailing duty law." S. REP. No. 412, 103d Cong., 2d Sess., 91 (1994). Both reports explicitly affirm the definition of "subsidy" in *Softwood Lumber III*. *Id.*; H.R. Rep. No. 826, *supra*, at 108-09.

The GATT text itself appears to limit "private" subsidies to cases where private bodies are dispensing benefits in the same manner as would a government agency. To be sure, governments have often given subsidies by selling raw material inputs below fair market value. An export restriction will usually force private sellers to reduce their price below what it would otherwise be. Whether the resulting reduced-price sale "in no real sense differs from practices normally followed by governments" is debatable. Interestingly, the U.S. implementing legislation struck "in no real sense differs" and substituted "does not differ in substance."

As well as can be determined from available negotiating records, the negotiators appear to have agreed to disagree about the meaning of the term "financial contribution," adopting that text without resolving their differences. Several months after the term "financial contribution" had been established in a July 1990 chairman's draft, the EEC and others were insisting the term should require an actual charge on the public account, while the United States was still holding to an earlier position that the definition had to include "any government action or combination of government actions which confers a benefit on the recipient firm(s)." 1 THE GATT URUGUAY ROUND: A NEGOTIATING HISTORY (1986-1992) 861, 873, 898-899, 967 (Terrence P. Stewart ed., 1993).

tion."[36] Additionally, according to the House conference report, private subsidies require "a formal, enforceable [government] measure which directly [leads] to a discernable benefit."[37] An export restriction fits within this definition because it is a concrete government measure usually intended to lower the domestic market price of the product being exported. Weak environmental laws, however, involve no government action as such. The financial benefit to producers, if any, arises from government inaction rather than action. Moreover, the financial benefit has no identifiable transferor, public or private. In sum, a definition that treated the *absence* of regulation as a subsidy — a benefit measured by the cost of what some other government decides the regulation should have been — would carry the concept of "subsidy" to a new and different level.

Nonetheless, the recent action of the U.S. Congress indicates that the legal definition of subsidy is still unsettled. Both in GATT and in U.S. law, the present legal definition of subsidy consists of arbitrary lines drawn around a rather loose concept of a government-generated benefit. The underlying concept of subsidy can always be extended to cover any additional unfair benefits that political leaders want to countervail. Only a widespread awareness that broader definitions will at some point become self-destructive holds the more limited definitions in place.

B. Low Environmental Standards as Dumping

Current antidumping laws define dumping to include sustained sales at prices below the average cost of production. When dumped imports materially injure a domestic industry, governments may levy an antidumping duty equal to the "margin of dumping" — the amount by which the import price falls below the true cost of production plus profit. If goods produced under low environmental standards can be viewed as goods being sold for less than their true cost of production, antidumping laws may provide a mechanism to impose eco-duties.

Environmental policy literature endorses the idea that goods produced under inadequate environmental standards should be viewed as goods manufactured at prices below the true costs of production.[38] The cost of the environmental resources appropriated by the pollution-causing production pro-

36. 19 U.S.C. 1677 (5)(B)(iii) (1994).

37. H.R. Rep. No. 826, *supra* note 35, at 108-09.

38. Michael Jacobs, The Green Economy: Environment, Sustainable Development and the Politics of the Future xv-xvii (1991); David W.

cess is not reflected in the price of such goods. Indeed, one of the most widely advocated reforms in this area is the proposal to create a legal framework requiring that such goods reflect their true cost.[39]

To the author's knowledge, no national antidumping law currently allows an action for environmental dumping. For the most part, current laws determine costs of production based on the producer's own data. "Cost" has meant the actual costs of the kind that businesses and tax collectors record.

As is true of the subsidy concept, however, the history of legal definition in this area suggests possibilities for growth. Some precedent exists for imposing fictitious costs where legislators believe they ought to be recognized. Until recently, U.S. antidumping law imposed an eight percent profit charge and a ten percent overheads charge when calculating the cost of imports, regardless of whether the producer actually incurred these costs.[40] Moreover, the antidumping law of most countries allows administrators to calculate hypothetical costs and prices for imports from non-market economies.[41] It would hardly be unprecedented, therefore, if a country amended its antidumping law to include a statutory environmental compliance cost, calculated from the same sort of arbitrary general average data as the eight percent profits and ten percent overhead items.

At the moment, however, the policy trend appears to be moving against imposing such fictitious costs. The 1994 Uruguay Round revision of the GATT Antidumping Code seeks to preclude governments from using the sort of arbitrary profit and overhead figures just described. The 1994 Antidumping Code provides that "costs shall normally be calculated on the basis of records kept by producers," and that cost and overhead expenses "shall be based on actual data pertaining to production and sales . . . by the exporter or producer under investigation."[42] In re-

---

PEARCE AND R. KERRY TURNER, ECONOMICS OF NATURAL RESOURCES AND THE ENVIRONMENT 3-28 (1990).

39. Jacobs, *supra* note 38, at 62-70; PEARCE AND TURNER, *supra* note 38, at 120-90.

40. In the pre-1994 version of U.S. antidumping law, these provisions were found at 19 U.S.C. 1677b (e)(1)(B)(i)-(ii) (1980).

41. For the current U.S. provision governing products from nonmarket economies *see* 19 U.S.C. 1677b(c) (1994). *See also* William P. Alford, *When is China Paraguay? An Examination of the Application of the Antidumping and Countervailing Duty Laws of the United States to China and other "Nonmarket Economy" Nations*, 61 S. CAL. L. REV. 79 (1987).

42. Agreement on Implementation of Article VI of the General Agreements on Tariffs and Trade, *opened for signature* April 15, 1994, arts. 2.2.1.1, 2.2.2,

sponse, the United States removed the statutory rates for profit and overhead from its antidumping law.[43]

At the present time, therefore, both national antidumping laws and the law of GATT seem to preclude using antidumping laws to remedy the level-playing-field complaint against low environmental standards. The idea of treating environmental degradation as a cost of production has by no means lost its appeal, however. As in the case of anti-subsidies law, the final answer to these questions has yet to be written.

V. FAIRNESS REVISITED: CAN DIFFERENCES IN ENVIRONMENTAL STANDARDS BE JUSTIFIED ON OTHER NORMATIVE GROUNDS?

The level playing field metaphor reflects a rather simple-minded concept of fairness. As usually applied, its standard is the equality of competitive conditions: competition is only fair when all conditions are equal.

In most discourse about international trade, however, experts agree that some differences in competitive conditions between countries are both natural and proper, and that trade outcomes determined by these differences are consequently "legitimate." Those who accept the legitimacy of such differences in competitive conditions include free trade economists at one end of the spectrum and dedicated disciples of unfair trade laws at the other. The willingness to accept differences suggests that there are more sophisticated concepts of fairness that may eventually displace simple level-playing-field norms — concepts that may produce a normative framework for trade that allows for at least some national differences in environmental regulatory standards.

A. LEGITIMATE DIFFERENCES IN GENERAL

Both in free trade economic theory and in the "fairness" rhetoric of modern U.S. trade law, competitive advantages arising from certain physical differences between countries are universally considered as a fair and proper basis of international trade. Economists call them factor endowments. Natural ad-

reprinted in UNITED STATES TRADE REPRESENTATIVE, FINAL TEXTS OF THE GATT URUGUAY ROUND AGREEMENTS INCLUDING THE AGREEMENT ESTABLISHING THE WORLD TRADE ORGANIZATION 168 (1994).

43. Uruguay Round Agreements Act, § 224 (e)(2)(B)(iii), Pub. L. No. 103-465, 108 Stat. 4809, 4884 (1994).

vantages such as the fertility of soil, climate, rainfall, available raw materials, and transportation facilities such as deep harbors and navigable rivers fall into this category. Economists assert that nations increase their economic welfare when they trade according to the comparative advantages stemming from such differences. The priests of fairness doctrine also bless the competitive results of these natural differences — a position not entirely consistent with their usual emphasis on awarding victory to the better competitor, but one seemingly hammered into them by 150 years of indoctrination by David Ricardo.

At the next level, both free trade economists and fair trade advocates bless the competitive advantages arising from certain societal differences between nations, such as work habits, savings rate, education, and efficient government. For economists, these qualities also determine a nation's comparative advantages, and therefore basing trade upon these qualities increases welfare. Fair traders also seem to accept the competitive advantages created by these social differences because they are part of the package of virtues that distinguish good competitors from poor competitors.

This attitude toward natural advantages seems to legitimize at least one kind of difference in national environmental policies. If a country's natural physical advantages allow it to achieve the same level of environmental quality with less rigorous regulation, the cost advantage from less rigorous standards is fair. For example, a country with fast-running, self-cleaning rivers that retains good quality water despite less stringent controls deserves the resultant cost advantage. Similarly, economists and fair traders would likely endorse cost savings gained from less rigorous air pollution standards in a country with fewer smokestacks and more trees. Additionally, lower environmental standards made possible by superior social behavior, such as recycling, auto speed limits, or turning down thermostats, would probably be accepted as well.

The national differences that cause the greatest disagreement are lower environmental standards that produce lower levels of environmental quality. At this point, the normative claims of free trade economists and fair-traders diverge. Each, however, offers an analytical framework in which some difference in environmental regulatory standards can be viewed as legitimate.

B. A FAIR-TRADER'S APPROACH TO LEGITIMATE DIFFERENCES

Fair trade advocates appear willing to accept lower levels of environmental regulation to the extent they can somehow be characterized as "natural" (like the self-cleaning river example) rather than "artificial" (like cash subsidies from the government). Consider the following policy statement by the Clinton Administration on trade-and-environment:

> The Administration is not seeking guidelines on the level of minimum wages, nor health and safety standards that are not appropriate to a country's level of development . . . . But at the same time, no country should seek to gain or maintain a comparative advantage or otherwise distort competitive conditions by maintaining artificially low labor or environmental standards.[44]

The distinction between "low" and "artificially low" is not immediately clear. The idea that lower environmental standards are legitimate because they are "appropriate to a country's level of development" is equally elusive. The word "artificial" suggests that environmental standards are acceptable if they result from pure-minded choices based only on environmental factors, as opposed to standards chosen for impure competitive business reasons. The reference to "development" suggests a similar distinction; low standards due to a lack of development are legitimate, whereas low standards based on competitive aggression are invalid.[45]

The thought that poor countries in particular can adopt environmental policies absent any competitive motivation seems particularly fanciful. To be sure, some kinds of pollution result from a lack of public funds for things like sanitation, but this is

---

44. *Proposed SAA Language on Labor, Environment and Fast Track,* INSIDE U.S. TRADE, Aug. 12, 1994, at S-7.

45. Few writers escape unscathed after wrestling with this concept of legitimacy. For example:

> Where differences in environmental policy choices reflect variations in climate, weather patterns, existing pollution levels, population density, economic needs, and risk preferences *and where* any environmental impacts are confined to local harm, the divergent standards may be considered legitimate — and therefore an inappropriate target for unilateral ecoduties or other efforts to adjust for policy differences.
>
> Where, however, the *strategic* environmental behavior results in pollution that spills over onto others, the difference in standards should be considered illegitimate, thereby making resort to ecoduties potentially appropriate.

ESTY, *supra* note 22, at 157 (emphasis added).

The distinction between local and transborder harm is clear enough, but those are distinctions of environmental policy. The intriguing distinction is the one between the first category of "legitimate" variations and the second category of "strategic environmental behavior."

not the type of low environmental standard that countries like the United States complain about. The primary complaint against developing countries involves lower environmental standards that reduce manufacturing costs. When a manufacturer is spared the cost of higher environmental standards *because* of its country's stage of development or level of poverty, the reason is a commercial one; it is simply that the lower costs created by lower standards will preserve the manufacturer's competitive position, thus preserving and expanding that manufacturer's useful economic activity. Development reasons *are* commercial reasons.

On reflection, this rather ill-defined acceptance of differences in developing-country environmental standards appears to be nothing more than an effort to accord some margin of tolerance to poor countries. This is the same normative presumption that underlies government economic assistance to poor countries. Existing assistance programs, such as those that offer tax benefits for investors, often create competitive advantages for producers in beneficiary countries. A willingness to overlook less rigorous pollution controls suggests the same normative response to poverty.

As such, the fair trader's tolerance for weaker environmental regulation in developing countries is probably not based on any principled distinction between "legitimate" and "illegitimate" differences in environmental policy. Rather, this tolerance works like most forms of charity where donors try to balance between recognizing a moral obligation to help and limiting the donation to the amount they can afford. The balance in this case will probably depend primarily on two factors.

The first factor involves the amount of commercial injury resulting from the environmental policy difference. Given that costs of environmental compliance are usually rather small, the amount of commercial injury will rarely be significant. The second factor is the amount of environmental damage caused by the lower standards in question. The more the harm exceeds what the observer thinks is reasonable, the greater the tendency to ascribe unworthy commercial motives to the underlying environmental policy.

Unclear though it may be, this fair-trader's view of legitimate differences is potentially very important. The idea has some staying power in the rough and ready debate of everyday politics in much the same way as the rather crude idea of "fairness" itself. If this idea of legitimacy can arm politicians in battle, it deserves further attention.

C. AN ECONOMIST'S APPROACH TO LEGITIMATE DIFFERENCES

Economic analysis contributes a number of distinctive ideas to the normative debate over differences in national environmental policy. First, it underlines the fact that environmental amenities do have opportunity costs. The economist stresses that local environmental amenities are purchased at the cost of other government expenditures, increased production costs, or foregone economic opportunities. By stressing cost, the economic perspective reinforces the intuitive judgment that poor nations are not able to afford the same level of environmental amenities. The economist's emphasis on opportunity cost does not rebut the fairness complaint that the commercial advantage created by weak environmental policies is somehow "artificial." Rather, like the fair trader's poverty defense, it suggests the competing value of the need to give poor countries greater leeway in using such cost advantages.[46]

Economic analysis sometimes suggests another set of normative justifications for differences in national environmental policies, based on certain perceptions of legitimacy that attach to market outcomes. One part of this legitimacy claim might be called the relativity of market outcomes. The "right" outcome for every market is the mix of products and prices that yields the greatest satisfaction to the market participants. Since it is given that the wants and needs of individual participants always differ, it follows that the optimal outcome for any market varies according to the wants and needs of its individual participants. "Right" is merely the sum of what the market participants want.

A related legitimacy claim attached to market outcomes rests on the perception that market outcomes are determined without overall human guidance. Individuals express their preferences, but the overall result of those preferences is defined through the invisible hand of the price mechanism. In this sense, the market functions "naturally." Market outcomes are not "artificial" in the sense of having been created by government policy.

46. The idea that a developing country cannot "afford" certain environmental standards is a nice way of describing the choice in a way that makes it seem like there is no choice at all. It is a way of approving the choice by denying the freedom not to make it.

Both the relativity of consumer preferences and the perceived neutrality of market processes are used to justify painful economic outcomes in international trade. Assume, for example, that consumers in Canada develop an insane attachment to skim milk. This surge of demand causes an increase in Canadian skim milk production and, with it, a sharp decline in the price of all the excess Canadian butter manufactured as a by-product of skim milk production. The low-priced Canadian butter finds its way to export markets where it displaces local U.S. production. Is this unfair trade? Economists generally decline to express an opinion about fairness, but few would hesitate to point out that the result, painful as it may be for U.S. producers, was merely the product of neutral market forces — just innocent consumer preferences acting in an unguided manner.

Economists looking at national differences in environmental policy sometimes suggest that such policy differences are another kind of market outcome. The individuals in each country have preferences regarding the choice between environmental amenities and the other things that must be given up for them. The sum of these preferences constitutes the nation's environmental policy. The analogy to market processes seeks to legitimize resulting policy differences as a result of innocent personal preferences, collated by a neutral, invisible hand. No government is trying to steal jobs from anyone.

Even if one overcomes the many other objections to viewing environmental policy differences as the product of neutral market forces,[47] the market analogy cannot answer the unfairness complaint. Assuming for the sake of argument that a nation's environmental policy is the sum of the unguided preferences of its individual citizens, the individual preferences in question are still essentially commercial in character. If people in poor countries choose fewer environmental amenities because the cost is too high, they are doing so because they want to maintain the competitive conditions that will preserve their jobs. Individuals in developing countries quite naturally prefer economic benefits

47. The traditional demonstration of optimal market outcomes assumes a market for private goods in which the participants directly bear the full cost or receive the full benefit of the goods in question. In the case of a public good like pollution control, these assumptions cannot be made. The consumer cannot restrict the benefit of the good to him or herself, nor can others who benefit from it be made to pay for it. As a consequence, environmental economists argue that the free market alone usually does not call for the correct amount of public goods, either under-producing because of free riders or over-producing when externalities are shifted to nonconsumers.

over environmental benefits, but that does not answer the question of whether they won those economic benefits fairly.

In the end, the economist's attention to cost and market choice undoubtedly sharpens the perception that the economic cost of environmental policies is relatively higher for poor countries. The ultimate normative thrust of this analysis comes down to an assertion of the same value that supports the other claims for legitimacy in this area — the notion that poor countries are to some degree entitled to spend less on environmental amenities.

D. Whither Legitimacy?

The fairness debate goes on. As long as trade policy continues to worship at the shrine of fairness, trade policy advocates will find it necessary to try to satisfy the relentless demands for proof that trade is fair. The fact that fairness concepts make no sense in international trade matters will not excuse the need to employ them.

In this second-best sort of policy debate, it is somewhat comforting to know that there are a few standards of legitimacy that can go beyond the ruthless equality of the level playing field. There seems to be some mileage in the distinction between "natural" and "artificial" differences in competitive conditions. Although the distinction does not provide a wholly convincing justification for different environmental standards, the ideas are fluid enough to provide a normative cover to other competing values. Things that are perceived as fair also tend to be perceived as natural. The perception that poor countries are entitled to employ lower standards slides easily into the idea that lower standards are natural, normal, unguided, and unaggressive. Both fair traders and economists are able to wrap their altruistic values in such normative dress. The fact that such claims do not withstand analysis may be less interesting than the fact that they seem to work anyway.

A story is told that during the early days of World War II, German camouflage experts tried to lure British bombers away from German airfields by constructing fake airfields, using wood-and-canvass mock-ups of aircraft and buildings. One day the Royal Air Force discovered the deception. The next day RAF bombers flew over and dropped wooden bombs on the canvass airplanes.

VI. CONCLUSION

If politics were completely rational, there would be little reason to be concerned about level-playing-field claims against imports from countries with weak environmental standards. The size of the commercial advantage in such cases is usually too small to generate serious business concerns. Because of the importance attached to fairness complaints in today's trade policy environment, however, there is always temptation for industries to throw in level-playing-field complaints when they seek protection from imports or oppose new environmental standards. And while legislators themselves may be skeptical about these complaints, no one ever lost an election by coming down on the side of fairness. As a result, level-playing-field complaints about weak environmental policies remain on the trade agenda.

Policy debate cannot completely answer these fairness complaints because the normative concepts that underlie the notions of fairness in this debate are simply not coherent when applied to international trade relations. No one knows whether any playing field is truly level, nor does anyone know how to make it level. Instead, the present system of unfair trade laws seems to be held in check by nothing more than a rather vague sense of restraint. We have suggested an implicit policy settlement here — a settlement under which we remedy certain highly visible fairness claims in exchange for accepting a generally liberal trade policy, with the reservation that fairness claims will not threaten the main contours of that liberal policy. The sense of restraint sometimes bends before important political needs, but it remains effective and is likely to endure so long as countries have major investments in open world markets.

The debate over level-playing-field claims is likely to continue as long as fairness claims exert some political leverage. As long as they do, those who defend trade with developing countries will have to reply. In the current debate, there does seem to be an effort in many quarters to find a normative justification for at least some differences in national environmental policies. Granted that the underlying normative concepts in this area are not wholly coherent, it still seems worthwhile to encourage further investment in analysis — or perhaps, better, artistry — to bring these different strands together into some kind of politically effective policy response.

Part III
Policy Perspectives

[14]

The demand for international regimes

Robert O. Keohane

We study international regimes because we are interested in understanding order in world politics. Conflict may be the rule; if so, institutionalized patterns of cooperation are particularly in need of explanation. The theoretical analysis of international regimes begins with what is at least an apparent anomaly from the standpoint of Realist theory: the existence of many "sets of implicit or explicit principles, norms, rules, and decision-making procedures around which actor expectations converge," in a variety of areas of international relations.

This article constitutes an attempt to improve our understanding of international order, and international cooperation, through an interpretation of international regime-formation that relies heavily on rational-choice analysis in the utilitarian social contract tradition. I explore why self-interested actors in world politics should seek, under certain circumstances, to establish international regimes through mutual agreement; and how we can account

The original idea for this paper germinated in discussions at a National Science Foundation-sponsored conference on International Politics and International Economics held in Minneapolis, Minnesota, in June 1978.

I am indebted to Robert Holt and Anne Krueger for organizing and to the NSF for funding that meeting. Several knowledgeable friends, particularly Charles Kindleberger, Timothy J. McKeown, James N. Rosse, and Laura Tyson, provided bibliographical suggestions that helped me think about the issues discussed here. For written comments on earlier versions of this article I am especially grateful to Robert Bates, John Chubb, John Conybeare, Colin Day, Alex Field, Albert Fishlow, Alexander George, Ernst B. Haas, Gerald Helleiner, Harold K. Jacobson, Robert Jervis, Stephen D. Krasner, Helen Milner, Timothy J. McKeown, Robert C. North, John Ruggie, Ken Shepsle, Arthur Stein, Susan Strange, Harrison Wagner, and David Yoffie. I also benefited from discussions of earlier drafts at meetings held at Los Angeles in October 1980 and at Palm Springs in February 1981, and from colloquia in Berkeley, California, and Cambridge, Massachusetts.

International Organization 36, 2, Spring 1982
0020-8183/82/020325-31 $1.50

for fluctuations over time in the number, extent, and strength of international regimes, on the basis of rational calculation under varying circumstances.

Previous work on this subject in the rational-choice tradition has emphasized the "theory of hegemonic stability": that is, the view that concentration of power in one dominant state facilitates the development of strong regimes, and that fragmentation of power is associated with regime collapse.[1] This theory, however, fails to explain lags between changes in power structures and changes in international regimes; does not account well for the differential durability of different institutions within a given issue-area; and avoids addressing the question of why international regimes seem so much more extensive now in world politics than during earlier periods (such as the late 19th century) of supposed hegemonic leadership.[2]

The argument of this article seeks to correct some of these faults of the hegemonic stability theory by incorporating it within a supply-demand approach that borrows extensively from microeconomic theory. The theory of hegemonic stability can be viewed as focusing only on the supply of international regimes: according to the theory, the more concentrated power is in an international system, the greater the supply of international regimes at any level of demand.[3] But fluctuations in demand for international regimes are not taken into account by the theory; thus it is necessarily incomplete. This article focuses principally on the demand for international regimes in order to provide the basis for a more comprehensive and balanced interpretation.

Emphasizing the demand for international regimes focuses our attention on why we should want them in the first place, rather than taking their desirability as a given. I do not assume that "demand" and "supply" can be specified independently and operationalized as in microeconomics. The same actors are likely to be the "demanders" and the "suppliers." Furthermore, factors affecting the demand for international regimes are likely simultaneously to affect their supply as well. Yet supply and demand language allows us to make a distinction that is useful in distinguishing phenomena that, in the first instance, affect the desire for regimes, on the one hand, or the ease of supplying them, on the other. "Supply and de-

[1] See especially Robert O. Keohane, "The Theory of Hegemonic Stability and Changes in International Economic Regimes, 1967–1977," in Ole R. Holsti, Randolph Siverson, and Alexander George, eds., *Changes in the International System* (Boulder: Westview, 1980); and Linda Cahn, "National Power and International Regimes: The United States and International Commodity Markets," Ph.D. diss., Stanford University, 1980.

[2] Current research on the nineteenth century is beginning to question the assumption that Britain was hegemonic in a meaningful sense. See Timothy J. McKeown, "Hegemony Theory and Trade in the Nineteenth Century," paper presented to the International Studies Association convention, Philadelphia, 18–21 March 1981; and Arthur A. Stein, "The Hegemon's Dilemma: Great Britain, the United States, and the International Economic Order," paper presented to the American Political Science Association annual meeting, New York, 3–6 September 1981.

[3] The essential reason for this (discussed below) is that actors that are large relative to the whole set of actors have greater incentives both to provide collective goods themselves and to organize their provision, than do actors that are small relative to the whole set. The classic discussion of this phenomenon appears in Mancur Olson Jr., *The Logic of Collective Action: Political Goods and the Theory of Groups* (Cambridge: Harvard University Press, 1965).

mand" should be seen in this analysis as a metaphor, rather than an attempt artificially to separate, or to reify, different aspects of an interrelated process.[4]

Before proceeding to the argument, two caveats are in order. First, the focus of this article is principally on the *strength* and *extent* of international regimes, rather than on their *content* or *effects*. I hope to contribute to understanding why international regimes wax and wane, leaving to others (in this volume and elsewhere) the analysis of what ideologies they encompass or how much they affect ultimate, value-laden outcomes. The only significant exception to this avoidance of questions of content comes in Section 5, which distinguishes between control-oriented and insurance-oriented regimes. Second, no claim is made here that rational-choice analysis is the only valid way to understand international regimes, or even that it is preferable to others. On the contrary, I view rational-choice analysis as one way to generate an insightful interpretation of international regimes that complements interpretations derived from analyses of conventions and of learning (illustrated in the articles in this volume by Young and Haas). My analysis is designed to be neither comprehensive nor exclusive: I suggest hypotheses and try to make what we know more intelligible, rather than seeking to put forward a definitive theory of international regimes.

The major arguments of this article are grouped in five sections. First, I outline the analytical approach by discussing the virtues and limitations of "systemic constraint-choice analysis." Section 2 lays the basis for the development of a constraint-choice theory of international regimes by specifying the context within which international regimes operate and the functions they perform. In Section 3 elements of a theory of the demand for international regimes are presented, emphasizing the role of regimes in reducing transactions costs and coping with uncertainty. In Section 4, I use insights from theories of information and uncertainty to discuss issues of closure and communication. Section 5 suggests that control-oriented regimes are likely to be increasingly supplemented in the 1980s by insurance regimes as the dominance of the advanced industrial countries in the world political economy declines.

1. Systemic constraint-choice analysis: virtues and limitations

The argument developed here is deliberately limited to the *systemic* level of analysis. In a systemic theory, the actors' characteristics are given by assumption, rather than treated as variables; changes in outcomes are explained not on the basis of variations in these actor characteristics, but on the basis of changes in the attributes of the system itself. Microeconomic theory, for instance, posits the existence of business firms, with given utility

[4] I am indebted to Albert Fishlow for clarifying this point for me.

functions, and attempts to explain their behavior on the basis of environmental factors such as the competitiveness of markets. It is therefore a systemic theory, unlike the so-called "behavioral theory of the firm," which examines the actors for internal variations that could account for behavior not predicted by microeconomic theory.

A systemic focus permits a limitation of the number of variables that need to be considered. In the initial steps of theory-building, this is a great advantage: attempting to take into account at the outset factors at the foreign policy as well as the systemic level would lead quickly to descriptive complexity and theoretical anarchy. Beginning the analysis at the systemic level establishes a baseline for future work. By seeing how well a simple model accounts for behavior, we understand better the value of introducing more variables and greater complexity into the analysis. Without the systemic microeconomic theory of the firm, for instance, it would not have been clear what puzzles needed to be solved by an actor-oriented behavioral theory.

A systems-level examination of changes in the strength and extent of international regimes over time could proceed through historical description. We could examine a large number of cases, attempting to extract generalizations about patterns from the data. Our analysis could be explicitly comparative, analyzing different regimes within a common analytical framework, employing a methodology such as George's "focused comparison."[5] Such a systematic comparative description could be quite useful, but it would not provide a theoretical framework for posing questions of why, and under what conditions, regimes should be expected to develop or become stronger. Posing such fundamental issues is greatly facilitated by *a priori* reasoning that makes specific predictions to be compared with empirical findings. Such reasoning helps us to reinterpret previously observed patterns of behavior as well as suggesting new questions about behavior or distinctions that have been ignored: it has the potential of "discovering new facts."[6] This can be useful even in a subject such as international politics, where the variety of relevant variables is likely to confound any comprehensive effort to build deductive theory. Deductive analysis can thus be used in interpretation as well as in a traditional strategy of theory-building and hypothesis-testing.

This analysis follows the tradition of microeconomic theory by focusing on constraints and incentives that affect the choices made by actors.[7] We

[5] Alexander L. George, "Case Studies and Theory Development: The Method of Structured, Focused Comparison," in Paul Lauren, ed., *Diplomacy: New Approaches in History, Theory, and Policy* (New York: Free Press, 1979).

[6] Imre Lakatos, "Falsification and the Methodology of Scientific Research Programmes," in Lakatos and Alan Musgrave, eds., *Criticism and the Growth of Scientific Knowledge* (Cambridge: Cambridge University Press, 1970).

[7] Stimulating discussions of microeconomic theory can be found in Martin Shubik, "A Curmudgeon's Guide to Microeconomics," *Journal of Economic Literature* 8 (1970): 405–434; and Spiro J. Latsis, "A Research Programme in Economics," in Latsis, ed., *Method and Appraisal in Economics* (Cambridge: Cambridge University Press, 1976).

assume that, in general, actors in world politics tend to respond rationally to constraints and incentives. Changes in the characteristics of the international system will alter the opportunity costs to actors of various courses of action, and will therefore lead to changes in behavior. In particular, decisions about creating or joining international regimes will be affected by system-level changes in this way; in this model the demand for international regimes is a function of system characteristics.

This article therefore employs a form of rational-choice analysis, which I prefer to term "constraint-choice" analysis to indicate that I do not make some of the extreme assumptions often found in the relevant literature. I assume a prior context of power, expectations, values, and conventions; I do not argue that rational-choice analysis can derive international regimes from a "state of nature" through logic alone.[8] This paper also eschews deterministic claims, or the *hubris* of believing that a complete explanation can be developed through resort to deductive models. To believe this would commit one to a narrowly rationalistic form of analysis in which expectations of gain provide both necessary and sufficient explanations of behavior.[9] Such beliefs in the power of Benthamite calculation have been undermined by the insufficiency of microeconomic theories of the firm—despite their great value as initial approximations—as shown by the work of organization theorists such as Simon, Cyert, and March.[10]

Rational-choice theory is not advanced here as a magic key to unlock the secrets of international regime change, much less as a comprehensive way of interpreting reality. Nor do I employ it as a means of explaining particular actions of specific actors. Rather, I use rational-choice theory to develop models that help to explain trends or tendencies toward which patterns of behavior tend to converge. That is, I seek to account for typical, or modal, behavior. This analysis will not accurately predict the decisions of all actors, or what will happen to all regimes; but it should help to account for overall trends in the formation, growth, decay, and dissolution of regimes. The deductive logic of this approach makes it possible to generate hypotheses about international regime change on an *a priori* basis. In this article several such hypotheses will be suggested, although their testing will have to await further specification. We shall therefore be drawing on microeconomic theories and rational-choice approaches heuristically, to help us con-

[8] I am indebted to Alexander J. Field for making the importance of this point clear to me. See his paper, "The Problem with Neoclassical Institutional Economics: A Critique with Special Reference to the North/Thomas Model of Pre-1500 Europe," *Explorations in Economic History* 18 (April 1981).

[9] Lance E. Davis and Douglass C. North adopt this strong form of rationalistic explanation when they argue that "an institutional arrangement will be innovated if the expected net gains exceed the expected costs." See their volume, *Institutional Change and American Economic Growth* (Cambridge: Cambridge University Press, 1971).

[10] Two of the classic works are James March and Herbert Simon, *Organizations* (New York: Wiley, 1958); and Richard Cyert and James March, *The Behavioral Theory of the Firm* (Englewood Cliffs, N.J.: Prentice-Hall, 1963).

struct nontrivial hypotheses about international regime change that can guide future research.

The use of rational-choice theory implies that we must view decisions involving international regimes as in some meaningful sense voluntary. Yet we know that world politics is a realm in which power is exercised regularly and in which inequalities are great. How, then, can we analyze international regimes with a voluntaristic mode of analysis?

My answer is to distinguish two aspects of the process by which international regimes come into being: the imposition of constraints, and decision making. Constraints are dictated not only by environmental factors but also by powerful actors. Thus when we speak of an "imposed regime," we are speaking (in my terminology) of a regime agreed upon within constraints that are mandated by powerful actors.[11] Any agreement that results from bargaining will be affected by the opportunity costs of alternatives faced by the various actors: that is, by which party has the greater need for agreement with the other.[12] Relationships of power and dependence in world politics will therefore be important determinants of the characteristics of international regimes. Actor choices will be constrained in such a way that the preferences of more powerful actors will be accorded greater weight. Thus in applying rational-choice theory to the formation and maintenance of international regimes, we have to be continually sensitive to the structural context within which agreements are made. Voluntary choice does not imply equality of situation or outcome.

We do not necessarily sacrifice realism when we analyze international regimes as the products of voluntary agreements among independent actors within the context of prior constraints. Constraint-choice analysis effectively captures the nonhierarchical nature of world politics without ignoring the role played by power and inequality. Within this analytical framework, a systemic analysis that emphasizes constraints on choice and effects of system characteristics on collective outcomes provides an appropriate way to address the question of regime formation.

Constraint-choice analysis emphasizes that international regimes should not be seen as quasi-governments—imperfect attempts to institutionalize centralized authority relationships in world politics. Regimes are more like contracts, when these involve actors with long-term objectives who seek to structure their relationships in stable and mutually beneficial ways.[13] In

[11] For a discussion of "spontaneous," "negotiated," and "imposed" regimes, see Oran Young's contribution to this volume.

[12] For a lucid and original discussion based on this obvious but important point, see John Harsanyi, "Measurement of Social Power, Opportunity Costs and the Theory of Two-Person Bargaining Games," *Behavioral Science* 7, 1 (1962): 67–80. See also Albert O. Hirschman, *National Power and the Structure of Foreign Trade* (1945; Berkeley: University of California Press, 1980), especially pp. 45–48.

[13] S. Todd Lowry, "Bargain and Contract Theory in Law and Economics," in Warren J. Samuels, ed., *The Economy as a System of Power* (New Brunswick, N.J.: Transaction Books, 1979), p. 276.

some respects, regimes resemble the "quasi-agreements" that Fellner discusses when analyzing the behavior of oligopolistic firms.[14] In both contracts and quasi-agreements, there may be specific rules having to do with prices, quantities, delivery dates, and the like; for contracts, some of these rules may be legally enforceable. The most important functions of these arrangements, however, are not to preclude further negotiations, but to establish stable mutual expectations about others' patterns of behavior and to develop working relationships that will allow the parties to adapt their practices to new situations. Rules of international regimes are frequently changed, bent, or broken to meet the exigencies of the moment. They are rarely enforced automatically, and they are not self-executing. Indeed, they are often matters for negotiation and renegotiation; as Puchala has argued, "attempts to enforce EEC regulations open political cleavages up and down the supranational-to-local continuum and spark intense politicking along the cleavage lines."[15]

This lack of binding authority associated with international regimes has important implications for our selection of analytical approaches within a constraint-choice framework: it leads us to rely more heavily on microeconomic, market-oriented theory than on theories of public choice. Most public-choice theory is not applicable to international regime change because it focuses on the processes by which authoritative, binding decisions are made within states.[16] Yet in international politics, binding decisions, arrived at through highly institutionalized, rule-oriented processes, are relatively rare and unimportant, and such decisions do not constitute the essence of international regimes. Traditional microeconomic supply and demand analysis, by contrast, assumes a situation in which choices are made continuously over a period of time by actors for whom "exit"—refusal to purchase goods or services that are offered—is an ever-present option. This conforms more closely to the situation faced by states contemplating whether to create, join, remain members of, or leave international regimes. Since no binding decisions can be made, it is possible to imagine a market for international regimes as one thinks of an economic market: on the basis of an analysis of relative prices and cost-benefit calculations, actors decide which regimes to "buy." In general, we expect states to join those regimes in which they expect the benefits of membership to outweigh the costs. In such an analysis, observed changes in the extent and strength of international

[14] William Fellner, *Competition among the Few* (New York: Knopf, 1949).

[15] Donald J. Puchala, "Domestic Politics and Regional Harmonization in the European Communities," *World Politics* 27,4 (July 1975), p. 509.

[16] There are exceptions to this generalization, such as Tiebout's "voting with the feet" models of population movements among communities. Yet only one chapter of fourteen in a recent survey of the public-choice literature is devoted to such models, which do not focus on authoritative decision-making processes. See Dennis C. Mueller, *Public Choice* (Cambridge: Cambridge University Press, 1980). For a brilliantly innovative work on "exit" versus "voice" processes, see Albert O. Hirschman, *Exit, Voice, and Loyalty* (Cambridge: Harvard University Press, 1970).

regimes may be explained by reference to changes either in the characteristics of the international system (the context within which actors make choices) or of the international regimes themselves (about which the choices are made).

This constraint-choice approach draws attention to the question of why disadvantaged actors join international regimes even when they receive fewer benefits than other members—an issue ignored by arguments that regard certain regimes as simply imposed. Weak actors as well as more powerful actors make choices, even if they make them within more severe constraints. (Whether such choices, made under severe constraint, imply obligations for the future is another question, one not addressed here.)[17]

2. The context and functions of international regimes

Analysis of international regime-formation within a constraint-choice framework requires that one specify the nature of the context within which actors make choices and the functions of the institutions whose patterns of growth and decay are being explained. Two features of the international context are particularly important: world politics lacks authoritative governmental institutions, and is characterized by pervasive uncertainty. Within this setting, a major function of international regimes is to facilitate the making of mutually beneficial agreements among governments, so that the structural condition of anarchy does not lead to a complete "war of all against all."

The actors in our model operate within what Waltz has called a "self-help system," in which they cannot call on higher authority to resolve difficulties or provide protection.[18] Negative externalities are common: states are forever impinging on one another's interests.[19] In the absence of authoritative global institutions, these conflicts of interest produce uncertainty and risk: possible future evils are often even more terrifying than present ones. All too obvious with respect to matters of war and peace, this is also characteristic of the international economic environment.

Actors in world politics may seek to reduce conflicts of interest and risk

[17] Anyone who has thought about Hobbes's tendentious discussion of "voluntary" agreements in *Leviathan* realizes the dangers of casuistry entailed in applying voluntaristic analysis to politics, especially when obligations are inferred from choices. This article follows Hobbes's distinction between the structure of constraints in a situation, on the one hand, and actor choices, on the other; but it does not adopt his view that even severely constrained choices ("your freedom or your life") create moral or political obligations.

[18] Kenneth N. Waltz, *Theory of International Politics* (Reading, Mass.: Addison-Wesley, 1979).

[19] Externalities exist whenever an acting unit does not bear all of the costs, or fails to reap all of the benefits, that result from its behavior. See Davis and North, *Institutional Change and American Economic Growth*, p. 16.

by coordinating their behavior. Yet coordination has many of the characteristics of a public good, which leads us to expect that its production will be too low.[20] That is, increased production of these goods, which would yield net benefits, is not undertaken. This insight is the basis of the major "supply-side" argument about international regimes, epitomized by the theory of hegemonic stability. According to this line of argument, hegemonic international systems should be characterized by levels of public goods production higher than in fragmented systems; and, if international regimes provide public goods, by stronger and more extensive international regimes.[21]

This argument, important though it is, ignores what I have called the "demand" side of the problem of international regimes: why should governments desire to institute international regimes in the first place, and how much will they be willing to contribute to maintain them? Addressing these issues will help to correct some of the deficiencies of the theory of hegemonic stability, which derive from its one-sidedness, and will contribute to a more comprehensive interpretation of international regime change. The familiar context of world politics—its competitiveness, uncertainty, and conflicts of interest—not only sets limits on the supply of international regimes, but provides a basis for understanding why they are demanded.

Before we can understand why regimes are demanded, however, it is necessary to establish what the functions of international regimes, from the perspective of states, might be.[22]

At the most specific level, students of international cooperation are interested in myriads of particular agreements made by governments: to

[20] Olson, *The Logic of Collection Action;* Bruce M. Russett and John D. Sullivan, "Collective Goods and International Organization," with a comment by Mancur Olson Jr., *International Organization* 25,4 (Autumn 1971); John Gerard Ruggie, "Collective Goods and Future International Collaboration," *American Political Science Review* 66,3 (September 1972); Duncan Snidal, "Public Goods, Property Rights, and Political Organization," *International Studies Quarterly* 23,4 (December 1979), p. 544.

[21] Keohane, "The Theory of Hegemonic Stability"; Charles P. Kindleberger, *The World in Depression, 1929–1939* (Berkeley: University of California Press, 1974); Mancur Olson and Richard Zeckhauser, "An Economic Theory of Alliances," *Review of Economics and Statistics* 48,3 (August 1966), reprinted in Bruce M. Russett, ed., *Economic Theories of International Politics* (Chicago: Markham, 1968). For a critical appraisal of work placing emphasis on public goods as a rationale for forming international organizations, see John A. C. Conybeare, "International Organizations and the Theory of Property Rights," *International Organization* 34,3 (Summer 1980), especially pp. 329–32.

[22] My use of the word "functions" here is meant to designate consequences of a certain pattern of activity, particularly in terms of the utility of the activity; it is not to be interpreted as an explanation of the behavior in question, since there is no teleological premise, or assumption that necessity is involved. Understanding the function of international regimes helps, however, to explain why actors have an incentive to create them, and may therefore help to make behavior intelligible within a rational-choice mode of analysis that emphasizes the role of incentives and constraints. For useful distinctions on functionalism, see Ernest Nagel, *The Structure of Scientific Explanation* (New York: Harcourt, Brace, 1961), especially "Functionalism and Social Science," pp. 520–35. I am grateful to Robert Packenham for this reference and discussions of this point.

maintain their exchange rates within certain limits, to refrain from trade discrimination, to reduce their imports of petroleum, or progressively to reduce tariffs. These agreements are made despite the fact that, compared to domestic political institutions, the institutions of world politics are extremely weak: an authoritative legal framework is lacking and regularized institutions for conducting transactions (such as markets backed by state authority or binding procedures for making and enforcing contracts) are often poorly developed.

Investigation of the sources of specific agreements reveals that they are not, in general, made on an *ad hoc* basis, nor do they follow a random pattern. Instead, they are "nested" within more comprehensive agreements, covering more issues. An agreement among the United States, Japan, and the European Community in the Multilateral Trade Negotiations to reduce a particular tariff is affected by the rules, norms, principles, and procedures of the General Agreement on Tariffs and Trade (GATT)—that is, by the trade regime. The trade regime, in turn, is nested within a set of other arrangements—including those for monetary relations, energy, foreign investment, aid to developing countries, and other issues—that together constitute a complex and interlinked pattern of relations among the advanced market-economy countries. These, in turn, are related to military-security relations among the major states.[23]

Within this multilayered system, a major function of international regimes is to facilitate the making of specific agreements on matters of substantive significance within the issue-area covered by the regime. International regimes help to make governments' expectations consistent with one another. Regimes are developed in part because actors in world politics believe that with such arrangements they will be able to make mutually beneficial agreements that would otherwise be difficult or impossible to attain. In other words, regimes are valuable to governments where, in their absence, certain mutually beneficial agreements would be impossible to consummate. In such situations, *ad hoc* joint action would be inferior to results of negotiation within a regime context.

Yet this characterization of regimes immediately suggests an explanatory puzzle. Why should it be worthwhile to construct regimes (themselves requiring agreement) in order to make specific agreements within the regime frameworks? Why is it not more efficient simply to avoid the regime stage and make the agreements on an *ad hoc* basis? In short, why is there any demand for international regimes apart from a demand for international agreements on particular questions?

An answer to this question is suggested by theories of "market failure" in economics. Market failure refers to situations in which the outcomes of

[23] Vinod Aggarwal has developed the concept of "nesting" in his work on international regimes in textiles since World War II. I am indebted to him for this idea, which has been elaborated in his "Hanging by a Thread: International Regime Change in the Textile/Apparel System, 1950–1979," Ph.D. diss., Stanford University, 1981.

market-mediated interaction are suboptimal (given the utility functions of actors and the resources at their disposal). Agreements that would be beneficial to all parties are not made. In situations of market failure, economic activities uncoordinated by hierarchical authority lead to *in*efficient results, rather than to the efficient outcomes expected under conditions of perfect competition. In the theory of market failure, the problems are attributed not to inadequacies of the actors themselves (who are presumed to be rational utility-maximizers) but rather to the structure of the system and the institutions, or lack thereof, that characterize it.[24] Specific attributes of the system impose transactions costs (including information costs) that create barriers to effective cooperation among the actors. Thus institutional defects are responsible for failures of coordination. To correct these defects, conscious institutional innovation may be necessary, although a good economist will always compare the costs of institutional innovation with the costs of market failure before recommending tampering with the market.

Like imperfect markets, world politics is characterized by institutional deficiencies that inhibit mutually advantageous coordination. Some of the deficiencies revolve around problems of transactions costs and uncertainty that have been cogently analyzed by students of market failure. Theories of market failure specify types of institutional imperfections that may inhibit agreement; international regimes may be interpreted as helping to correct similar institutional defects in world politics. Insofar as regimes are established through voluntary agreement among a number of states, we can interpret them, at least in part, as devices to overcome the barriers to more efficient coordination identified by theories of market failure.[25]

The analysis that follows is based on two theoretical assumptions. First, the actors whose behavior we analyze act, in general, as rational utility-maximizers in that they display consistent tendencies to adjust to external changes in ways that are calculated to increase the expected value of outcomes to them. Second, the international regimes with which we are concerned are devices to facilitate the making of agreements among these actors. From these assumptions it follows that the demand for international regimes

[24] Of particular value for understanding market failure is Kenneth J. Arrow, *Essays in the Theory of Risk-Bearing* (New York: North Holland/American Elsevier, 1974).

[25] Helen Milner suggested to me that international regimes were in this respect like credit markets, and that the history of the development of credit markets could be informative for students of international regimes. The analogy seems to hold. Richard Ehrenberg reports that the development of credit arrangements in medieval European Bourses reduced transaction costs (since money did not need to be transported in the form of specie) and provided high-quality information in the form of merchants' newsletters and exchanges of information at fairs: "during the Middle Ages the best information as to the course of events in the world was regularly to be obtained in the fairs and the Bourses" (p. 317). The Bourses also provided credit ratings, which provided information but also served as a crude substitute for effective systems of legal liability. Although the descriptions of credit market development in works such as that by Ehrenberg are fascinating, I have not been able to find a historically-grounded theory of these events. See Richard Ehrenberg, *Capital and Finance in the Age of the Renaissance: A Study of the Fuggers and Their Connections*, translated from the German by H. M. Lucas (New York: Harcourt, Brace, no date), especially chap. 3 (pp. 307–333).

at any given price will vary directly with the desirability of agreements to states and with the ability of international regimes actually to facilitate the making of such agreements. The condition for the theory's operation (that is, for regimes to be formed) is that sufficient complementary or common interests exist so that agreements benefiting all essential regime members can be made.

The value of theories of market failure for this analysis rests on the fact that they allow us to identify more precisely barriers to agreements. They therefore suggest insights into how international regimes help to reduce those barriers, and they provide richer interpretations of previously observed, but unexplained, phenomena associated with international regimes and international policy coordination. In addition, concepts of market failure help to explain the strength and extent of international regimes by identifying characteristics of international systems, or of international regimes themselves, that affect the demand for such regimes and therefore, given a supply schedule, their quantity. Insights from the market-failure literature therefore take us beyond the trivial cost-benefit or supply-demand propositions with which we began, to hypotheses about relationships that are less familiar.

The emphasis on efficiency in the market-failure literature is consistent with our constraint-choice analysis of the decision-making processes leading to the formation and maintenance of international regimes. Each actor must be as well or better off with the regime than without it—given the prior structure of constraints. This does not imply, of course, that the whole process leading to the formation of a new international regime will yield overall welfare benefits. Outsiders may suffer; indeed, some international regimes (such as alliances or cartel-type regimes) are specifically designed to impose costs on them. These costs to outsiders may well outweigh the benefits to members. In addition, powerful actors may manipulate constraints prior to the formation of a new regime. In that case, although the regime *per se* may achieve overall welfare improvements compared to the immediately preceding situation, the results of the joint process may be inferior to those that existed before the constraints were imposed.

3. Elements of a theory of the demand for international regimes

We are now in a position to address our central puzzle—why is there any demand for international regimes?—and to outline a theory to explain why this demand exists. First, it is necessary to use our distinction between "agreements" and "regimes" to pose the issue precisely: given a certain level of demand for international agreements, what will affect the demand for international regimes? The Coase theorem, from the market-failure literature, will then be used to develop a list of conditions under which international regimes are of potential value for facilitating agreements in world politics. This typological analysis turns our attention toward two central problems, *transactions cost* and *informational imperfections.* Questions of information, involving uncertainty and risk, will receive particular attention, since their exploration has rich implications for interpretation and future research.

The demand for agreements and the demand for regimes

It is crucial to distinguish clearly between international regimes, on the one hand, and mere *ad hoc* substantive agreements, on the other. Regimes, as argued above, facilitate the making of substantive agreements by providing a framework of rules, norms, principles, and procedures for negotiation. A theory of international regimes must explain why these intermediate arrangements are necessary.

In our analysis, the demand for agreements will be regarded as exogenous. It may be influenced by many factors, particularly by the perceptions that leaders of governments have about their interests in agreement or nonagreement. These perceptions will, in turn, be influenced by domestic politics, ideology, and other factors not encompassed by a systemic, constraint-choice approach. In the United States, "internationalists" have been attracted to international agreements and international organizations as useful devices for implementing American foreign policy; "isolationists" and "nationalists" have not. Clearly, such differences cannot be accounted for by our theory. We therefore assume a given desire for agreements and ask: under these conditions, what will be the demand for international regimes?

Under certain circumstances defining the demand and supply of agreements, there will be no need for regimes and we should expect none to form. This will be the situation in two extreme cases, where demand for agreements is nil and where the supply of agreements is infinitely elastic and free (so that all conceivable agreements can be made costlessly). But where the demand for agreements is positive at some level of feasible cost, and the supply of agreements is not infinitely elastic and free, there may be a demand for international regimes *if* they actually make possible agreements yielding net benefits that would not be possible on an *ad hoc* basis. In such a situation regimes can be regarded as "efficient." We can now ask: under what specific conditions will international regimes be efficient?

One way to address this question is to pose its converse. To ask about the conditions under which international regimes will be *worthless* enables us to draw on work in social choice, particularly by Ronald Coase. Coase was able to show that the presence of externalities alone does not necessarily prevent Pareto-optimal coordination among independent actors: under certain conditions, bargaining among these actors could lead to Pareto-optimal solutions. The key conditions isolated by Coase were (a) a legal framework establishing liability for actions, presumably supported by governmental authority; (b) perfect information; and (c) zero transactions costs (including organization costs and costs of making side-payments).[26] If all these conditions were met in world politics, *ad hoc* agreements would be costless and regimes unnecessary. *At least one of them must not be fulfilled if international regimes are to be of value, as facilitators of agreement, to independent utility-maximizing actors in world politics.* Inverting the Coase theorem provides us, therefore, with a list of conditions, at least one of which must apply if regimes are to be of value in facilitating agreements among governments:[27]

(a) lack of a clear legal framework establishing liability for actions;
(b) information imperfections (information is costly);
(c) positive transactions costs.[28]

In world politics, of course, *all* of these conditions are met all of the time: world government does not exist; information is extremely costly and often impossible to obtain; transactions costs, including costs of organization and side-payments, are often very high. Yet the Coase theorem is useful not merely as a way of categorizing these familiar problems, but because it suggests how international regimes can improve actors' abilities to make mutually beneficial agreements. Regimes can make agreement easier if they provide frameworks for establishing legal liability (even if these are not perfect); improve the quantity and quality of information available to actors; or reduce other transactions costs, such as costs of organization or of making side-payments. This typology allows us to specify regime functions—as devices to make agreements possible—more precisely, and therefore to understand demand for international regimes. Insofar as international regimes can correct institutional defects in world politics along any of these three dimensions (liability, information, transactions costs), they may become efficient devices for the achievement of state purposes.

Regimes do not establish binding and enforceable legal liabilities in any strict or ultimately reliable sense, although the lack of a hierarchical struc-

[26] Ronald Coase, "The Problem of Social Cost," *Journal of Law and Economics* 3 (October 1960). For a discussion, see James Buchanan and Gordon Tullock, *The Calculus of Consent: Logical Foundations of Constitutional Democracy* (Ann Arbor: University of Michigan Press, 1962), p. 186.

[27] If we were to drop the assumption that actors are strictly self-interested utility-maximizers, regimes could be important in another way: they would help to develop norms that are internalized by actors as part of their own utility functions. This is important in real-world political-economic systems, as works by Schumpeter, Polanyi, and Hirsch on the moral underpinnings of a market system indicate. It is likely to be important in many international systems as well. But it is outside the scope of the analytical approach taken in this article—which is designed to illuminate some issues, but not to provide a comprehensive account of international regime change. See Joseph Schumpeter, *Capitalism, Socialism, and Democracy* (New York: Harper & Row, 1942), especially Part II, "Can Capitalism Survive?"; Karl Polanyi, *The Great Transformation: The Political and Economic Origins of Our Time* (1944; Boston: Beacon Press, 1957); and Fred Hirsch, *Social Limits to Growth* (Cambridge: Harvard University Press, 1976).

[28] Information costs could be considered under the category of transaction costs, but they are so important that I categorize them separately in order to give them special attention.

ture does not prevent the development of bits and pieces of law.[29] Regimes are much more important in providing established negotiating frameworks (reducing transactions costs) and in helping to coordinate actor expectations (improving the quality and quantity of information available to states). An explanation of these two functions of international regimes, with the help of microeconomic analysis, will lead to hypotheses about how the demand for international regimes should be expected to vary with changes in the nature of the international system (in the case of transactions costs) and about effects of characteristics of the international regime itself (in the case of information).

International regimes and transactions costs

Neither international agreements nor international regimes are created spontaneously. Political entrepreneurs must exist who see a potential profit in organizing collaboration. For entrepreneurship to develop, not only must there be a potential social gain to be derived from the formation of an international arrangement, but the entrepreneur (usually, in world politics, a government) must expect to be able to gain more itself from the regime than it invests in organizing the activity. Thus organizational costs to the entrepreneur must be lower than the net discounted value of the benefits that the entrepreneur expects to capture for itself.[30] As a result, international cooperation that would have a positive social payoff may not be initiated unless a potential entrepreneur would profit sufficiently. This leads us back into questions of supply and the theory of hegemonic stability, since such a situation is most likely to exist where no potential entrepreneur is large relative to the whole set of potential beneficiaries, and where "free riders" cannot be prevented from benefiting from cooperation without paying proportionately.

Our attention here, however, is on the demand side: we focus on the efficiency of constructing international regimes, as opposed simply to making *ad hoc* agreements. We only expect regimes to develop where the costs of making *ad hoc* agreements on particular substantive matters are higher than the sum of the costs of making such agreements within a regime framework and the costs of establishing that framework.

With respect to transactions costs, where do we expect these conditions to be met? To answer this question, it is useful to introduce the concept of *issue density* to refer to the number and importance of issues arising within a given policy space. The denser the policy space, the more highly interdependent are the different issues, and therefore the agreements made about

[29] For a discussion of "the varieties of international law," see Louis Henkin, *How Nations Behave: Law and Foreign Policy*, 2d ed. (New York: Columbia University Press for the Council on Foreign Relations, 1979), pp. 13–22.

[30] Davis and North, *Institutional Change and American Economic Growth*, especially pp. 51–57.

them. Where issue density is low, *ad hoc* agreements are quite likely to be adequate: different agreements will not impinge on one another significantly, and there will be few economies of scale associated with establishing international regimes (each of which would encompass only one or a few agreements). Where issue density is high, on the other hand, one substantive objective may well impinge on another and regimes will achieve economies of scale, for instance in establishing negotiating procedures that are applicable to a variety of potential agreements within similar substantive areas of activity.[31]

Furthermore, in dense policy spaces, complex linkages will develop among substantive issues. Reducing industrial tariffs without damaging one's own economy may depend on agricultural tariff reductions from others; obtaining passage through straits for one's own warships may depend on wider decisions taken about territorial waters; the sale of food to one country may be more or less advantageous depending on other food-supply contracts being made at the same time. As linkages such as these develop, the organizational costs involved in reconciling distinct objectives will rise and demands for overall frameworks of rules, norms, principles, and procedures to cover certain clusters of issues—that is, for international regimes—will increase.

International regimes therefore seem often to facilitate side-payments among actors within issue-areas covered by comprehensive regimes, since they bring together negotiators to consider a whole complex of issues. Side-payments in general are difficult in world politics and raise serious issues of transaction costs: in the absence of a price system for the exchange of favors, these institutional imperfections will hinder cooperation.[32] International regimes may provide a partial corrective.[33] The well-known literature on "spillover" in bargaining, relating to the European Community and other integration schemes, can also be interpreted as being concerned with side-

[31] The concept of issue density bears some relationship to Herbert Simon's notion of "decomposability," in *The Sciences of the Artificial* (Cambridge: MIT Press, 1969). In both cases, problems that can be conceived of as separate are closely linked to one another functionally, so that it is difficult to affect one without also affecting others. Issue density is difficult to operationalize, since the universe (the "issue-area" or "policy space") whose area forms the denominator of the term cannot easily be specified precisely. But given a certain definition of the issue-area, it is possible to trace the increasing density of issues within it over time. See, for example, Robert O. Keohane and Joseph S. Nye, *Power and Interdependence: World Politics in Transition* (Boston: Little, Brown, 1977), chap. 4.

[32] On questions of linkage, see Arthur A. Stein, "The Politics of Linkage," *World Politics* 33,1 (October 1980): 62–81; Kenneth Oye, "The Domain of Choice," in Oye et al., *Eagle Entangled: U.S. Foreign Policy in a Complex World* (New York: Longmans, 1979), pp. 3–33; and Robert D. Tollison and Thomas D. Willett, "An Economic Theory of Mutually Advantageous Issue Linkage in International Negotiations," *International Organization* 33,4 (Autumn 1979).

[33] GATT negotiations and deliberations on the international monetary system have been characterized by extensive bargaining over side-payments and complex politics of issue-linkage. For a discussion see Nicholas Hutton, "The Salience of Linkage in International Economic Negotiations," *Journal of Common Market Studies* 13, 1–2 (1975): 136–60.

payments. In this literature, expectations that an integration arrangement can be expanded to new issue-areas permit the broadening of potential side-payments, thus facilitating agreement.[34]

It should be noted, however, that regimes may make it more difficult to link issues that are clustered separately. Governments tend to organize themselves consistently with how issues are treated internationally, as well as vice versa; issues considered by different regimes are often dealt with by different bureaucracies at home. Linkages and side-payments become difficult under these conditions, since they always involve losses as well as gains. Organizational subunits that would lose, on issues that matter to them, from a proposed side-payment are unlikely to support it on the basis of another agency's claim that it is in the national interest. Insofar as the dividing lines between international regimes place related issues in different jurisdictions, they may well make side-payments and linkages between these issues less feasible.

The crucial point about regimes to be derived from this discussion of transactions costs can be stated succinctly: the optimal size of a regime will increase if there are increasing rather than diminishing returns to regime-scale (reflecting the high costs of making separate agreements in a dense policy space), or if the marginal costs of organization decline as regime size grows. The point about increasing returns suggests an analogy with the theory of imperfect competition among firms. As Samuelson notes, "increasing returns is the prime case of deviations from perfect competition."[35] In world politics, increasing returns to scale lead to more extensive international regimes.

The research hypothesis to be derived from this analysis is that increased issue density will lead to greater demand for international regimes and to more extensive regimes. Since greater issue density is likely to be a feature of situations of high interdependence, this forges a link between interdependence and international regimes: increases in the former can be expected to lead to increases in demand for the latter.[36]

The demand for principles and norms

The definition of international regimes provided in the introduction to this volume stipulates that regimes must embody principles ("beliefs of fact, causation, and rectitude") and norms ("standards of behavior defined in

[34] Ernst B. Haas, *The Uniting of Europe* (Stanford: Stanford University Press, 1958).

[35] Paul A. Samuelson, "The Monopolistic Competition Revolution," in R. E. Kuenne, ed., *Monopolistic Competition Theory* (New York: Wiley, 1967), p. 117.

[36] Increases in issue density could make it more difficult to supply regimes; the costs of providing regimes could grow, for instance, as a result of multiple linkages across issues. The 1970s Law of the Sea negotiations illustrate this problem. As a result, it will not necessarily be the case that increases in interdependence will lead to increases in the number, extensiveness, and strength of international regimes.

terms of rights and obligations") as well as rules and decision-making procedures.[37] Otherwise, international regimes would be difficult to distinguish from any regular patterns of action in world politics that create common expectations about behavior: even hostile patterns of interactions could be seen as embodying regimes if the observer could infer implied rules and decision-making procedures from behavior.

Arguments about definitions are often tedious. What is important is not whether this definition is "correct," but that principles and norms are integral parts of many, if not all, of the arrangements that we regard as international regimes. This raises the question of why, in interactions (such as those of world politics) characterized by conflict arising from self-interest, norms and principles should play any role at all.

The constraint-choice framework used in this article is not the best approach for describing how principles and norms of state behavior evolve over time. The legal and sociological approaches discussed in this volume by Young are better adapted to the task of historical interpretation of norm-development. Nevertheless, a brief analysis of the function of principles and norms in an uncertain environment will suggest why they are important for fulfilling the overall function of international regimes: to facilitate mutually advantageous international agreements.

An important principle that is shared by most, if not all, international regimes is what Jervis calls "reciprocation": the belief that if one helps others or fails to hurt them, even at some opportunity cost to oneself, they will reciprocate when the tables are turned. In the Concert of Europe, this became a norm specific to the regime, a standard of behavior providing that statesmen should avoid maximizing their interests in the short term for the sake of expected long-run gains.[38]

This norm requires action that does not reflect specific calculations of self-interest: the actor making a short-run sacrifice does not know that future benefits will flow from comparable restraint by others, and can hardly be regarded as making precise calculations of expected utility. What Jervis calls the norm of reciprocation—or (to avoid confusion with the concept of reciprocity in international law) what I shall call a norm of generalized commitment—precisely forbids specific interest calculations. It rests on the premise that a veil of ignorance stands between us and the future, but that we should nevertheless assume that regime-supporting behavior will be beneficial to us even though we have no convincing evidence to that effect.

At first glance, it may seem puzzling that governments ever subscribe either to the principle of generalized commitment (that regime-supporting behavior will yield better results than self-help in the long run) or to the corresponding norm in a given regime (that they should act in a regime-supporting fashion). But if we think about international regimes as devices to

[37] Stephen D. Krasner, article in this volume, p. 186.
[38] Robert Jervis, article in this volume, p. 364.

facilitate mutually beneficial agreements the puzzle can be readily resolved. Without such a norm, each agreement would have to provide net gains for every essential actor, or side-payments would have to be arranged so that the net gains of the package were positive for all. Yet as we have seen, side-payments are difficult to organize. Thus, packages of agreements will usually be difficult if not impossible to construct, particularly when time is short, as in a balance of payments crisis or a sudden military threat. The principle of generalized commitment, however, removes the necessity for specific clusters of agreements, each of which is mutually beneficial. Within the context of a regime, help can be extended by those in a position to do so, on the assumption that such regime-supporting behavior will be reciprocated in the future. States may demand that others follow the norm of generalized commitment even if they are thereby required to supply it themselves, because the result will facilitate agreements that in the long run can be expected to be beneficial for all concerned.

The demand for specific information

The problems of organization costs discussed earlier arise even in situations where actors have entirely consistent interests (pure coordination games with stable equilibria). In such situations, however, severe information problems are not embedded in the structure of relationships, since actors have incentives to reveal information and their own preferences fully to one another. In these games the problem is to reach some agreement point; but it may not matter much which of several is chosen.[39] Conventions are important and ingenuity may be required, but serious systemic impediments to the acquisition and exchange of information are lacking.[40]

The norm of generalized commitment can be seen as a device for coping with the conflictual implications of uncertainty by imposing favorable assumptions about others' future behavior. The norm of generalized commitment requires that one accept the veil of ignorance but act *as if* one will benefit from others' behavior in the future if one behaves now in a regime-supporting way. Thus it creates a coordination game by ruling out potentially antagonistic calculations.

Yet in many situations in world politics, specific and calculable conflicts of interest exist among the actors. In such situations, they all have an interest in agreement (the situation is not zero-sum), but they prefer different types of agreement or different patterns of behavior (e.g., one may prefer to

[39] The classic discussion is in Thomas C. Schelling, *The Strategy of Conflict* (1960; Cambridge: Harvard University Press, 1980), chap. 4, "Toward a Theory of Interdependent Decision." See also Schelling, *Micromotives and Macrobehavior* (New York: Norton, 1978).

[40] For an interesting discussion of regimes in these terms, see the paper in this volume by Oran R. Young. On conventions, see David K. Lewis, *Convention: A Philosophical Study* (Cambridge: Cambridge University Press, 1969).

cheat without the other being allowed to do so). As Stein points out in this volume, these situations are characterized typically by unstable equilibria. Without enforcement, actors have incentives to deviate from the agreement point:

> [Each] actor requires assurances that the other will also eschew its rational choice [and will not cheat, and] such collaboration requires a degree of formalization. The regime must specify what constitutes cooperation and what constitutes cheating.[41]

In such situations of strategic interaction, as in oligopolistic competition and world politics, systemic constraint-choice theory yields no determinate results or stable equilibria. Indeed, discussions of "blackmailing" or games such as "prisoners' dilemma" indicate that, under certain conditions, suboptimal equilibria are quite likely to appear. Game theory, as Simon has commented, only illustrates the severity of the problem; it does not solve it.[42]

Under these circumstances, power factors are important. They are particularly relevant to the supply of international regimes: regimes involving enforcement can only be supplied if there is authority backed by coercive resources. As we have seen, regimes themselves do not possess such resources. For the means necessary to uphold sanctions, one has to look to the states belonging to the regime.

Yet even under conditions of strategic interaction and unstable equilibria, regimes may be of value to actors by providing information. Since high-quality information reduces uncertainty, we can expect that there will be a demand for international regimes that provide such information.

Firms that consider relying on the behavior of other firms within a context of strategic interaction—for instance, in oligopolistic competition—face similar information problems. They also do not understand reality fully. Students of market failure have pointed out that risk-averse firms will make fewer and less far-reaching agreements than they would under conditions of perfect information. Indeed, they will eschew agreements that would produce mutual benefits. Three specific problems facing firms in such a context are also serious for governments in world politics and give rise to demands for international regimes to ameliorate them.

(1) Asymmetric information. Some actors may have more information about a situation than others. Expecting that the resulting bargains would be unfair, "outsiders" may therefore be reluctant to make agreements with "insiders."[43] One aspect of this in the microeconomic literature is "quality uncertainty," in which a buyer is uncertain about the real value of goods

[41] Arthur A. Stein, article in this volume, p. 312.

[42] Herbert Simon, "From Substantive to Procedural Rationality," in Latsis, ed., *Method and Appraisal in Economics;* Spiro J. Latsis, "A Research Programme in Economics," in ibid.; and on blackmailing, Oye, "The Domain of Choice."

[43] Oliver E. Williamson, *Markets and Hierarchies: Analysis and Anti-Trust Implications* (New York: Free Press, 1975).

being offered. In such a situation (typified by the market for used cars when sellers are seen as unscrupulous), no exchange may take place despite the fact that with perfect information, there would be extensive trading.[44]

(2) Moral hazard. Agreements may alter incentives in such a way as to encourage less cooperative behavior. Insurance companies face this problem of "moral hazard." Property insurance, for instance, may make people less careful with their property and therefore increase the risk of loss.[45]

(3) Deception and irresponsibility. Some actors may be dishonest, and enter into agreements that they have no intention of fulfilling. Others may be "irresponsible," and make commitments that they are unlikely to be able to carry out. Governments or firms may enter into agreements that they intend to keep, assuming that the environment will continue to be benign; if adversity sets in, they may be unable to keep their commitments. Banks regularly face this problem, leading them to devise standards of "creditworthiness." Large governments trying to gain adherents to international agreements may face similar difficulties: countries that are enthusiastic about cooperation are likely to be those that expect to gain more, proportionately, than they contribute. This is analogous to problems of self-selection in the market-failure literature. For instance, if rates are not properly adjusted, people with high risks of heart attack will seek life insurance more avidly than those with longer life expectancies; people who purchased "lemons" will tend to sell them earlier on the used-car market than people with "creampuffs."[46] In international politics, self-selection means that for certain types of activities—for example, sharing research and development information—weak states (with much to gain but little to give) may have greater incentives to participate than strong ones. But without the strong states, the enterprise as a whole will fail. From the perspective of the outside observer, irresponsibility is an aspect of the problem of public goods and free-riding;[47] but from the standpoint of the actor trying to determine whether to rely on a potentially irresponsible partner, it is a problem of uncertainty and risk. Either way, information costs may prevent mutually beneficial agreement, and the presence of these costs will provide incentives to states to demand international regimes (either new regimes or the maintenance of existing ones) that will ameliorate problems of uncertainty and risk.

4. Information, openness, and communication in international regimes

International regimes, and the institutions and procedures that develop in conjunction with them, perform the function of reducing uncertainty and

[44] George A. Ackerlof, "The Market for 'Lemons': Qualitative Uncertainty and the Market Mechanism," *Quarterly Journal of Economics* 84,3 (August 1970).

[45] Arrow, *Essays in the Theory of Risk-Bearing*.

[46] Ackerlof, "The Market for 'Lemons' "; Arrow, *Essays in the Theory of Risk-Bearing*.

[47] For an analysis along these lines, see Davis B. Bobrow and Robert T. Kudrle, "Energy R&D: In Tepid Pursuit of Collective Goods," *International Organization* 33,2 (Spring 1979): 149–76.

risk by linking discrete issues to one another and by improving the quantity and quality of information available to participants. Linking issues is important as a way to deal with potential deception. Deception is less profitable in a continuing "game," involving many issues, in which the cheater's behavior is closely monitored by others and in which those actors retaliate for deception with actions in other areas, than in a "single-shot" game. The larger the number of issues in a regime, or linked to it, and the less important each issue is in proportion to the whole, the less serious is the problem of deception likely to be.

Another means of reducing problems of uncertainty is to increase the quantity and quality of communication, thus alleviating the information problems that create risk and uncertainty in the first place. Williamson argues on the basis of the organization theory literature that communication tends to increase adherence to group goals: "Although the precise statement of the relation varies slightly, the general proposition that intragroup communication promotes shared goals appears to be a well-established empirical finding."[48] Yet not all communication is of equal value: after all, communication may lead to asymmetrical or unfair bargaining outcomes, deception, or agreements entered into irresponsibly. And in world politics, governmental officials and diplomats are carefully trained to communicate precisely what they wish to convey rather than fully to reveal their preferences and evaluations. Effective communication is not measured well by the amount of talking that used-car salespersons do to customers or that governmental officials do to one another in negotiating international regimes. Strange has commented, perhaps with some exaggeration:

> One of the paradoxes of international economic relations in the 1970s has been that the soft words exchanged in trade organizations have coexisted with hard deeds perpetuated by national governments. The reversion to economic nationalism has been accompanied by constant reiterations of continued commitment to international cooperation and consultation. The international bureaucracies of Geneva, New York, Paris and Brussels have been kept busier than ever exchanging papers and proposals and patiently concocting endless draft documents to which, it is hoped, even deeply divided states might subscribe. But the reality has increasingly been one of unilateral action, even where policy is supposedly subject to multilateral agreement.[49]

The information that is required in entering into an international regime is not merely information about other governments' resources and formal negotiating positions, but rather knowledge of their internal evaluations of the situation, their intentions, the intensity of their preferences, and their

[48] Oliver E. Williamson, "A Dynamic Theory of Interfirm Behavior," *Quarterly Journal of Economics* 79 (1965), p. 584.

[49] Susan Strange, "The Management of Surplus Capacity: or How Does Theory Stand Up to Protectionism 1970s Style?", *International Organization* 33,3 (Summer 1979): 303–334.

willingness to adhere to an agreement even in adverse future circumstances. As Hirsch points out with respect to the "Bagehot Problem" in banking, lenders need to know the moral as well as the financial character of borrowers.[50] Likewise, governments contemplating international cooperation need to *know* their partners, not merely know *about* them.

This line of argument suggests that governments that successfully maintain "closure," protecting the autonomy of their decision-making processes from outside penetration, will have more difficulty participating in international regimes than more open, apparently disorganized governments. "Closed" governments will be viewed with more skepticism by potential partners, who will anticipate more serious problems of bounded rationality in relations with these closed governments than toward their more open counterparts. Similarly, among given governments, politicization of issues and increases in the power of political appointees are likely to reduce the quality of information and will therefore tend to reduce cooperation. Thus as an issue gains salience in domestic politics, other governments will begin to anticipate more problems of bounded rationality and will therefore perceive greater risks in cooperation. International cooperation may therefore decline quite apart from the real intentions or objectives of the policy makers involved.

This conclusion is important: international policy coordination and the development of international regimes depend not merely on interests and power, or on the negotiating skills of diplomats, but also on expectations and information, which themselves are in part functions of the political structures of governments and their openness to one another. Intergovernmental relationships that are characterized by ongoing communication among working-level officials, "unauthorized" as well as authorized, are inherently more conducive to information-exchange and agreements than are traditional relationships between internally coherent bureaucracies that effectively control their communications with the external world.[51]

Focusing on information and risk can help us to understand the performance of international regimes over time, and therefore to comprehend better the sources of demands for such regimes. Again, reference to theories of oligopoly, as in Williamson's work, is helpful. Williamson assumes that cooperation—which he refers to as "adherence to group goals"—will be a function both of communication and of the past performance of the oligopoly; reciprocally, communication levels will be a function of cooperation. In addition, performance will be affected by the condition of the environment. Using these assumptions, Williamson derives a model that has two points of equilibrium, one at high levels and one at low levels of cooperation.

[50] Fred Hirsch, "The Bagehot Problem," *The Manchester School* 45,3 (1977): 241–57.

[51] Notice that here, through a functional logic, a systemic analysis has implications for the performance of different governmental structures at the level of the actor. The value of high-quality information in making agreements does not force governments to become more open, but it gives advantages to those that do.

His oligopolies are characterized by substantial inertia. Once a given equilibrium has been reached, substantial environmental changes are necessary to alter it:

> If the system is operating at a low level of adherence and communication (i.e., the competitive solution), a substantial improvement in the environment will be necessary before the system will shift to a high level of adherence and communication. *Indeed, the condition of the environment required to drive the system to the collusive solution is much higher than the level required to maintain it once it has achieved this position. Similarly, a much more unfavorable condition of the environment is required to move the system from a high to a low level equilibrium than is required to maintain it there.*[52]

It seems reasonable to suppose that Williamson's assumptions about relationships among communication, cooperation or adherence, and performance have considerable validity for international regimes as well as for cartels. If so, his emphasis on the role of information, for explaining persistent behavior (competitive or oligopolistic) by groups of firms, helps us to understand the lags between structural change and regime change that are so puzzling to students of international regimes. In our earlier work, Nye and I observed discrepancies between the predictions of structural models (such as what I later called the "theory of hegemonic stability") and actual patterns of change; in particular, changes in international regimes tend to lag behind changes in structure.[53] But our explanation for this phenomenon was essentially *ad hoc:* we simply posited the existence of inertia, assuming that "a set of networks, norms, and institutions, once established, will be difficult either to eradicate or drastically to rearrange."[54] Understanding the role of communication and information in the formation and maintenance of international regimes helps locate this observation in a theoretical context. The institutions and procedures that develop around international regimes acquire value as arrangements permitting communication, and therefore facilitating the exchange of information. As they prove themselves in this way, demand for them increases. Thus, even if the structure of a system becomes more fragmented—presumably increasing the costs of providing regime-related collective goods (as suggested by public goods theory)—increased demand for a particular, well-established, information-providing international regime may, at least for a time, outweigh the effects of increasing costs on supply.

These arguments about information suggest two novel interpretations of puzzling contemporary phenomena in world politics, as well as providing the

[52] Williamson, "A Dynamic Theory of Interfirm Behavior," p. 592, original italics.

[53] *Power and Interdependence*, especially pp. 54–58 and 146–53. Linda Cahn also found lags, particularly in the wheat regime; see "National Power and International Regimes."

[54] *Power and Interdependence*, p. 55.

basis for hypotheses that could guide research on fluctuations in the strength and extent of international regimes.

Understanding the value of governmental openness for making mutually beneficial agreements helps to account for the often-observed fact that effective international regimes—such as the GATT in its heyday, or the Bretton Woods international monetary regime[55]—are often associated with a great deal of informal contact and communication among officials. Governments no longer act within such regimes as unitary, self-contained actors. "Transgovernmental" networks of acquaintance and friendship develop, with the consequences that supposedly confidential internal documents of one government may be seen by officials of another; informal coalitions of like-minded officials develop to achieve common purposes; and critical discussions by professionals probe the assumptions and assertions of state policies.[56] These transgovernmental relationships increase opportunities for cooperation in world politics by providing policy makers with high-quality information about what their counterparts are likely to do. Insofar as they are valued by policy makers, they help to generate demand for international regimes.

The information-producing "technology" that becomes embedded in a particular international regime also helps us to understand why the erosion of American hegemony during the 1970s has not been accompanied by an immediate collapse of international regimes, as a theory based entirely on supply-side public goods analysis would have predicted. Since the level of institutionalization of postwar regimes was exceptionally high, with intricate and extensive networks of communication among working-level officials, we should expect the lag between the decline of American hegemony and the disruption of international regimes to be quite long and the "inertia" of the existing regimes relatively great.

The major hypothesis to be derived from this discussion of information is that demand for international regimes should be in part a function of the effectiveness of the regimes themselves in providing high-quality information to policy makers. The success of the institutions associated with a regime in providing such information will itself be a source of regime persistence.

Three inferences can be made from this hypothesis. First, regimes accompanied by highly regularized procedures and rules will provide more information to participants than less regularized regimes and will therefore, on

[55] On the GATT, see Gardner Patterson, *Discrimination in International Trade: The Policy Issues* (Princeton: Princeton University Press, 1966); on the international monetary regime, see Robert W. Russell, "Transgovernmental Interaction in the International Monetary System, 1960–1972," *International Organization* 27,4 (Autumn 1973) and Fred Hirsch, *Money International*, rev. ed. (Harmondsworth, England: Pelican Books, 1969), especially chap. 11, "Central Bankers International."

[56] Robert O. Keohane and Joseph S. Nye, "Transgovernmental Relations and International Organizations," *World Politics* 27,1 (October 1974): 39–62.

information grounds, be in greater demand. Thus, considerations of high-quality information will help to counteract the normal tendencies of states to create vague rules and poorly specified procedures as a way of preventing conflict or maintaining freedom of action where interests differ.

Second, regimes that develop norms internalized by participants—in particular, norms of honesty and straightforwardness—will be in greater demand and will be valued more than regimes that fail to develop such norms.

Third, regimes that are accompanied by open governmental arrangements and are characterized by extensive transgovernmental relations will be in greater demand and will be valued more than regimes whose relationships are limited to traditional state-to-state ties.[57]

Perhaps other nontrivial inferences can also be drawn from the basic hypothesis linking a regime's information-provision with actors' demands for it. In any event, this emphasis on information turns our attention back toward the regime, and the process of institutionalization that accompanies regime formation, and away from an exclusive concern with the power structure of world politics. The extent to which institutionalized cooperation has been developed will be an important determinant, along with power-structural conditions and issue density, of the extent and strength of international regimes.

From a future-oriented or policy perspective, this argument introduces the question of whether governments (particularly those of the advanced industrial countries) could compensate for the increasing fragmentation of power among them by building communication-facilitating institutions that are rich in information. The answer depends in part on whether hegemony is really a necessary condition for effective international cooperation or only a facilitative one. Kindleberger claims the former, but the evidence is inconclusive.[58] Analysis of the demand for international regimes, focusing on questions of information and transactions costs, suggests the possibility that international institutions could help to compensate for eroding hegemony. International regimes could not only reduce the organization costs and other transactions costs associated with international negotiations; they could also provide information that would make bargains easier to strike.

How effectively international regimes could compensate for the erosion of hegemony is unknown. Neither the development of a theory of international regimes nor the testing of hypotheses derived from such a theory is likely to resolve the question in definitive terms. But from a contemporary policy standpoint, both theory development and theory testing would at least

[57] These first three inferences focus only on the *demand* side. To understand the degree to which norms, for example, will develop, one needs also to look at supply considerations. Problems of organization, such as those discussed in the public goods literature and the theory of hegemonic stability, may prevent even strongly desired regimes from materializing.

[58] Kindleberger has asserted that "for the world economy to be stabilized, there has to be a stabilizer, one stabilizer." *The World in Depression*, p. 305.

help to define the dimensions of the problem and provide some guidance for thinking about the future consequences of present actions.

5. Coping with uncertainties: insurance regimes

Creating international regimes hardly disposes of risks or uncertainty. Indeed, participating in schemes for international cooperation entails risk for the cooperating state. If others fail to carry out their commitments, it may suffer. If (as part of an international growth scheme) it reflates its economy and others do not, it may run a larger-than-desired current-account deficit; if it liberalizes trade in particular sectors and its partners fail to reciprocate, import-competing industries may become less competitive without compensation being received elsewhere; if it curbs bribery by its multinational corporations without comparable action by others, its firms may lose markets abroad. In world politics, therefore, governments frequently find themselves comparing the risks they would run from lack of regulation of particular issue-areas (i.e., the absence of international regimes) with the risks of entering into such regimes. International regimes are designed to mitigate the effects on individual states of uncertainty deriving from rapid and often unpredictable changes in world politics. Yet they create another kind of uncertainty, uncertainty about whether other governments will keep their commitments.

In one sense, this is simply the old question of dependence: dependence on an international regime may expose one to risks, just as dependence on any given state may. Governments always need to compare the risks they run by being outside a regime with the risks they run by being within one. If the price of achieving short-term stability by constructing a regime is increasing one's dependence on the future decisions of others, that price may be too high.

Yet the question of coping with risk also suggests the possibility of different types of international regimes. Most international regimes are *control-oriented.* Through a set of more or less institutionalized arrangements, members maintain some degree of control over each other's behavior, thus decreasing harmful externalities arising from independent action as well as reducing uncertainty stemming from uncoordinated activity. A necessary condition for this type of regime is that the benefits of the regularity achieved thereby must exceed the organizational and autonomy costs of submitting to the rules, both for the membership as a whole and for each necessary member.

Control-oriented regimes typically seek to ensure two kinds of regularity, internal and environmental. Internal regularity refers to orderly patterns of behavior among members of the regime. The Bretton Woods international monetary regime and the GATT trade regime have focused, first of all, on members' obligations, assuming that, if members behaved according to the rules, the international monetary and trade systems would be orderly. Where all significant actors within an issue-area are members of the regime, this assumption is warranted and mutual-control regimes tend to be effective.

Yet there are probably few, if any, pure cases of mutual-control regimes. Typically, an international regime is established to regularize behavior not only among the members but also between them and outsiders. This is a side-benefit of stable international monetary regimes involving convertible currencies.[59] It was an explicit purpose of the nonproliferation regime of the 1970s, in particular the "suppliers' club," designed to keep nuclear material and knowledge from diffusing rapidly to potential nuclear powers. Military alliances can be viewed as an extreme case of attempts at environmental control, in which the crucial benefits of collaboration stem not from the direct results of cooperation but from their effects on the behavior of outsiders. Alliances seek to induce particular states of minds in nonmembers, to deter or to intimidate.

Observers of world politics have often assumed implicitly that all significant international regimes are control-oriented. The economic literature, however, suggests another approach to the problem of risk. Instead of expanding to control the market, firms or individuals may diversify to reduce risk or may attempt to purchase insurance against unlikely but costly contingencies. Portfolio diversification and insurance thus compensate for deficiencies in markets that lack these institutions. Insurance and diversification are appropriate strategies where actors cannot exercise control over their environment at reasonable cost, but where, in the absence of such strategies, economic activity would be suboptimal.[60]

In world politics, such strategies are appropriate under similar conditions. The group of states forming the insurance or diversification "pool" is only likely to resort to this course of action if it cannot control its environment effectively. Second, for insurance regimes to make sense, the risks insured against must be specific to individual members of the group. If the catastrophic events against which one wishes to insure are likely (should they occur at all) to affect all members simultaneously and with equal severity, risk sharing will make little sense.[61]

[59] Charles P. Kindleberger, "Systems of International Economic Organization," in David P. Calleo, ed., *Money and the Coming World Order* (New York: New York University Press for the Lehrman Institute, 1978); Ronald McKinnon, *Money in International Exchange: The Convertible Currency System* (New York: Oxford University Press, 1979).

[60] Arrow, *Essays in the Theory of Risk-Bearing*, pp. 134–43.

[61] In personal correspondence, Robert Jervis has suggested an interesting qualification to this argument. He writes: "If we look at relations that involve at least the potential for high conflict, then schemes that tie the fates of all the actors together may have utility even if the actors are concerned about catastrophic events which will affect them all. They can worry that if some states are not affected, the latter will be much stronger than the ones who have been injured. So it would make sense for them to work out a scheme which would insure that a disaster would not affect their relative positions, even though this would not mean that they would all not be worse off in absolute terms." The point is certainly well taken, although one may wonder whether such an agreement would in fact be implemented by the states that would make large relative gains in the absence of insurance payments.

International regimes designed to share risks are less common than those designed to control events, but three examples from the 1970s can be cited that contain elements of this sort of regime:

(1) The STABEX scheme of the Lomé Convention, concluded between the European Community and forty-six African, Caribbean, and Pacific states in 1975. "Under the STABEX scheme, any of the 46 ACP countries dependent for more than 7.5 percent (2.5 percent for the poorest members of the ACP) of their export earnings on one of a list of commodities, such as tea, cocoa, coffee, bananas, cotton, and iron ore, will be eligible for financial help if these earnings fall below a certain level."[62] STABEX, of course, is not a genuine mutual-insurance regime because the guarantee is made by one set of actors to another set.

(2) The emergency sharing arrangements of the International Energy Agency, which provide for the mandatory sharing of oil supplies in emergencies, under allocation rules devised and administered by the IEA.[63]

(3) The Financial Support Fund of the OECD, agreed on in April 1975 but never put into effect, which would have provided a "lender of last resort" at the international level, so that risks on loans to particular countries in difficulty would have been "shared among all members, in proportion to their quotas and subject to the limits of their quotas, however the loans are financed."[64]

Control-oriented and insurance strategies for coping with risk and uncertainty have different advantages and liabilities. Control-oriented approaches are more ambitious; when effective, they may eliminate adversity rather than simply spread risks around. After all, it is more satisfactory to prevent floods than merely to insure against them; likewise, it would be preferable for consumers to be able to forestall commodity embargoes rather than simply to share their meager supplies fairly if such an embargo should take place.

Yet the conditions for an effective control-oriented regime are more stringent than those for insurance arrangements. An effective control-oriented regime must be supported by a coalition that has effective power in the issue-area being regulated, and whose members have sufficient incentives to exercise such power.[65] Where these conditions are not met, insurance regimes may be "second-best" strategies, but they are better than no strategies at all. Under conditions of eroding hegemony, one can expect the increasing emergence of insurance regimes, in some cases as a result of the

[62] Isebill V. Gruhn, "The Lomé Convention: Inching toward Interdependence," *International Organization* 30,2 (Spring 1976), pp. 255–56.

[63] Robert O. Keohane, "The International Energy Agency: State Influence and Transgovernmental Politics," *International Organization* 32,4 (Autumn 1978): 929–52.

[64] OECD *Observer*, no. 74 (March–April 1975), pp. 9–13.

[65] The optimal condition under which such a coalition may emerge could be called the "paper tiger condition": a potential external threat to the coalition exists but is too weak to frighten or persuade coalition members to defect or to desist from effective action. OPEC has been viewed by western policy makers since 1973 as a real rather than paper tiger, although some observers keep insisting that there is less to the organization than meets the eye.

unwillingness of powerful states to adopt control-oriented strategies (as in the case of STABEX), in other cases as replacements for control-oriented regimes that have collapsed (as in the cases of the IEA emergency sharing arrangements and the OECD Financial Support Fund or "safety net"). Economic theories of risk and uncertainty suggest that as power conditions shift, so will strategies to manage risk, and therefore the nature of international regimes.

6. Conclusions

The argument of this paper can be summarized under six headings. First, international regimes can be interpreted, in part, as devices to facilitate the making of substantive agreements in world politics, particularly among states. Regimes facilitate agreements by providing rules, norms, principles, and procedures that help actors to overcome barriers to agreement identified by economic theories of market failure. That is, regimes make it easier for actors to realize their interests collectively.

Second, public goods problems affect the supply of international regimes, as the "theory of hegemonic stability" suggests. But they also give rise to demand for international regimes, which can ameliorate problems of transactions costs and information imperfections that hinder effective decentralized responses to problems of providing public goods.

Third, two major research hypotheses are suggested by the demand-side analysis of this article.

(a) Increased issue density will lead to increased demand for international regimes.
(b) The demand for international regimes will be in part a function of the effectiveness of the regimes themselves in developing norms of generalized commitment and in providing high-quality information to policymakers.

Fourth, our analysis helps us to interpret certain otherwise puzzling phenomena, since our constraint-choice approach allows us to see how demands for such behavior would be generated. We can better understand transgovernmental relations, as well as the lags observed between structural change and regime change in general, and between the decline of the United States' hegemony and regime disruption in particular.

Fifth, in the light of our analysis, several assertions of structural theories appear problematic. In particular, it is less clear that hegemony is a necessary condition for stable international regimes under all circumstances. Past patterns of institutionalized cooperation may be able to compensate, to some extent, for increasing fragmentation of power.

Sixth, distinguishing between conventional control-oriented international regimes, on the one hand, and insurance regimes, on the other, may help us to understand emerging adaptations of advanced industrialized countries to a global situation in which their capacity for control over events is much less than it was during the postwar quarter-century.

None of these observations implies an underlying harmony of interests in world politics. Regimes can be used to pursue particularistic and parochial interests, as well as more widely shared objectives. They do not necessarily increase overall levels of welfare. Even when they do, conflicts among units will continue. States will attempt to force the burdens of adapting to change onto one another. Nevertheless, as long as the situations involved are not constant-sum, actors will have incentives to coordinate their behavior, implicitly or explicitly, in order to achieve greater collective benefits without reducing the utility of any unit. When such incentives exist, and when sufficient interdependence exists that *ad hoc* agreements are insufficient, opportunities will arise for the development of international regimes. If international regimes did not exist, they would surely have to be invented.

[15]

Trade Measures and the Design of International Regimes

STEVE CHARNOVITZ

This article examines the use of trade measures in international regimes. The catalyst for this research is the high-level international debate on trade and the environment, which is now focusing on the appropriateness of using trade measures in multilateral environmental agreements.[1] *The World Trade Organization is expected to consider recommendations on this issue at its first ministerial meeting in December 1996.*

Overview

The goal of this article is to present a framework for thinking about the use of trade measures in multilateral agreements. Although there is analytical literature on the role of trade measures in particular regimes (e.g., the United Nations Security Council), very little work has been done to compare the use of trade measures across regimes. Therefore, although this article emphasizes environmental regimes, it also considers the utilization of trade measures in other regimes, such as the trade regime.

The first part presents a conceptual framework for analyzing how trade measures are used. The second part examines 30 cases in which trade measures were incorporated into international regimes. The third part extracts some lessons from these cases and suggests policy implications. The article concludes that trade measures are employed in similar ways in different regimes. Such measures can prevent physical harm from/to a product, physical harm engendered by the market, and economic harm engendered by the market.

The issue of the use of trade measures in environmental treaties has become more salient during the past few years as the General Agreement on Tariffs and Trade (GATT) and its successor, the World Trade Organization (WTO), have questioned such use. The WTO, the Organization for Economic Cooperation and Development (OECD), and the United

1. For example, see World Trade Organization (1995).

AUTHOR'S NOTE: An earlier version of this article was delivered at the Aspen Global Change Institute in August 1995.

Journal of Environment & Development, Vol. 5, No. 2, June 1996 168-196

Nations Environment Programme (UNEP) are currently examining environmental treaties that employ trade measures.[2] The outcome of these discussions may have important implications for the workability of environmental treaties. For example, trade measures may be needed for future agreements on global warming, persistent organic substances, fisheries, or timber.[3] If negotiators are instructed not to use trade instruments, achieving effective environmental protection may become more difficult (Barrett, 1994, p. 31).[4]

Framework for Trade Measures

This section considers several fundamental questions about the use of trade measures. First, why would a government want to interfere with private trade? Second, what harms spring directly or indirectly from trade? Third, what exactly is a trade measure, and how does it differ from a domestic measure? Fourth, should trade measures be reserved for trade purposes? Finally, how do trade measures operate within international regimes?

THE SIDE EFFECTS OF INTERNATIONAL TRADE

Being a voluntary transaction, trade in goods (or services) across national borders can be expected to improve the welfare of both the buyer and the seller (Abbott, 1992). But trade can have side effects on others that undermine their welfare. Thus governments may find it appropriate to use trade measures to limit certain cross-border exchanges.[5]

Harm from commerce can be divided into three categories:

1. The traded product causes physical harm.
2. Trade engenders physical harm through the market.
3. Trade engenders economic harm through the market.

By *physical*, I mean a direct, tangible effect. By *harm*, I mean negative impact on people, communities, animals, markets, or an ecosystem anywhere in the world. Each of these three categories will be discussed in turn.

2. For example, see United Nations Environment Programme (1995).

3. On timber, see Sonner (1995).

4. See also Cameron and Arden-Clarke (1996).

5. If there was one worldwide polity, there would be no international trade across borders. There would still be commerce, however, and that commerce would require regulation. For example, phytosanitary measures would be needed, just as they are currently used to monitor goods moving from the mainland to Hawaii.

Physical harm from a traded product may occur in several ways. First, harm can spring from relocation. For example, an innocuous insect in one country can create havoc in another when it arrives as part of cargo. An animal taken from the wild and put in a zoo may die quickly. Second, consumption can have negative side effects. For example, smuggled Freon for automobile air conditioners may reduce the ozone layer (McGrory, 1995; Tyson, 1995). Heroin use may lead to violent crime. Third, disposal can have negative side effects. For example, imported toxic waste may leak after it is buried. Fourth, transportation can have negative side effects. For example, oil may spill from tankers. Fifth, the commodity itself can be harmed in transit. For example, tropical birds may die in transit to receiving nations.

Physical harm engendered by the market may occur in several ways. First, domestic demand for an import can increase production, harvesting, or extraction in other countries. For example, feather fashions in the early 20th century caused the destruction of many birds (Kastner, 1994). Second, trade can strengthen potential adversaries by enabling them to buy weapons of aggression. For example, oil trade can finance terrorism. Physical harm from a traded product differs from physical harm engendered by the market in that with the former, the introduction of the product through trade can directly transmit ill effects. In the latter, the physical harm typically occurs before the trade and can occur again as a result of trade-induced demand.

Economic harm engendered by the market may occur in several ways. First, imports can displace internal production, leading to unemployment and loss of profits.[6] Second, excessive importing can lead to currency depreciation and excessive exporting can lead to currency appreciation. Third, defective or injurious exports can damage the reputation of producers. Fourth, trade in counterfeit goods can undermine the innovation process in the country of invention. Physical harm differs from economic harm in that the former involves life and health and the latter involves pecuniary concerns. Whereas economic harm is fully remediable by money, physical harm may not be.

It should be noted that for all three categories, these harms are not caused solely by imports. Similar harms can occur from domestic-origin products. In a few cases, however, there is so little demand in the country of origin that certain harms would be sharply lessened without trade. For example, as Harland (1994) has noted, "there is little doubt that the international trade in ivory was largely responsible for the crash in elephant populations between 1979 and 1989" (p. 167).[7]

6. This is not to suggest that trade in both directions causes net unemployment or loss of profits. But imports alone can have that effect on particular individuals or businesses.

7. Harland (1994) notes that habitat loss is also a critical problem.

WHAT ARE TRADE MEASURES?

Before discussing the use of trade measures in international regimes, I should first clarify what trade measures are. A trade measure (or instrument) is the application of a tax or regulation exclusively to a traded good—typically an import but sometimes also an export. This contrasts with a domestic measure, which is the application of a tax or a regulation to an internally produced good or to the like imported good. Some applications of domestic measures to imported goods may resemble trade measures. For example, a domestic product ban (e.g., no unpasteurized cheese) may prevent the entry of a tasty import. To the disappointed exporter, that may look like a trade measure, even though the same rule is applied to internal production.

Following this definition, it is apparent that the WTO has rules not only about trade measures but also about domestic measures.[8] Domestic measures must meet the test of "national treatment" under the rule of the GATT (GATT, 1947).[9] National treatment requires that imported goods be treated no less favorably than internally produced goods. Until the Uruguay Round, this was the only substantive requirement for domestic measures. Now the multilateral trade regime has additional requirements for domestic measures, such as the new Agreement on the Application of Sanitary and Phytosanitary Measures.

When used as a trade measure, taxes can be nondiscriminatory (e.g., tariffs) or discriminatory (e.g., antidumping duties). Discrimination means that like products are treated differently. Regulations can be standards or bans. Bans can be absolute, or they can be contingent—that is, contingent on actions by governments or practices of producers.[10]

For domestic measures, taxes and regulations can be aimed at production, consumption, or disposal. Although this article will generally focus on trade measures, it is important to remember that international regimes can also utilize domestic measures. For example, an agreement to remove lead from gasoline would not involve trade measures per se, although imported fuel would be held to the same standard as domestically produced fuel.

USE OF TRADE MEASURES IN GENERAL

Because a trade measure, by definition, can only act upon trade, the efficacy of a trade measure depends on the nexus between trade and the harmful behavior being addressed. Although trade measures could be used for purposes wholly unconnected to trade, this is unlikely to occur

8. See WTO (1994).

9. The GATT is now part of the WTO.

10. For further discussion of these categories, see Charnovitz (1994). See also GATT Secretariat (1993).

in a multilateral agreement (as opposed to a unilateral action). Thus, in the prototypical situation, a trade measure in an environmental treaty is used to control trade as part of a program for preventing future environmental harm.

Do trade measures work? It is often said that trade instruments are not likely to be an effective way to deal with environmental problems. Agenda 21 counsels governments to "deal with the root causes of environment and developmental problems" in a manner that avoids unjustified restrictions on trade (United Nations, 1992). Lloyd (1992) points out that in very few, if any, instances is the actual cause of an environmental failure international trade in commodities itself. Petersmann (1995) finds six different approaches for addressing cross-border pollution that would likely be more effective than trade instruments.[11] Kirchgässner and Mohr (1996) report that "in most cases trade restrictions are—at best—third-best solutions"[12] because trade restrictions usually attack a problem only indirectly and are much too far away from the source of the problem to be fully effective.

In considering when trade measures should be used, it may be helpful to start by dismissing the simplistic notion (prevalent in the "trade and the environment" literature[13]) that trade instruments should be used to address trade problems, whereas environmental instruments should be used to address environmental problems.[14] There are two difficulties with this matchup. First, as noted above, many environmental problems are trade related. Of course, one can define some problems as "environmental" by pointing to the root cause. For instance, we might say that endangered species trade is not a trade problem because the root cause is harvesting, not trade. But if we do that for the environment, we should also do so for other issues. Thus the root cause of import-induced unemployment is not trade, but, rather, uncompetitive domestic industry (or perhaps overvalued currency). The root cause of injurious dumping is not trade but, rather, unharmonized competition policies. Viewed in this manner, all trade problems melt away. There are no pure trade problems unrelated to nontrade goals.

The second difficulty with the simplistic notion is that the distinction between trade and environment instruments is ambiguous. Is a tax a

11. The six approaches are (a) avoidance of intergovernmental disputes through decentralized international private law solutions, (b) international "coast negotiations" between the private parties affected or their respective home countries, (c) intergovernmental environmental agreements, (d) dispute settlement proceedings on damage prevention or compensation, (e) supranational primary law rules like the Treaty on European Union, and (f) supranational secondary law rules, like European Commission regulations and directives.

12. This chapter considers many of the issues discussed in this article.

13. For example, see Feketekuty (1993). See also Esty (1994).

14. A further difficulty with this notion can be seen if one tries to apply it to the health regime. Should biological weapons be used as an instrument in getting other countries to eradicate disease?

trade instrument or an environmental instrument? How about regulations or quotas?[15] These are instruments of both trade and environmental policy makers. They do not "belong" more to one regime than the other. Of course, a tariff might be viewed as principally a trade instrument. But so far, none of the trade and environment conflicts have involved tariffs.

A related misconception is that trade instruments are used to solve trade problems. Actually, trade instruments are commonly directed at nontrade problems (e.g., unemployment, industry uncompetitiveness, aggressive foreign pricing, etc.) and typically "solve" them only by helping favored groups while hurting consumers, exporters, or unprotected industries.[16] Trade itself is only rarely a real problem. Thus, while the use of a trade instrument for an environmental purpose might indeed be third best, it is important to keep in mind that the use of a trade instrument for a trade purpose may be fourth best (or even first worst).

TRADE MEASURES IN TREATIES

Although many applications of trade measures are unilateral, treaties also utilize trade measures, meaning the treaty requires or authorizes the use of trade measures. An example of a treaty requiring a trade measure is the Convention on International Trade in Endangered Species of Wild Fauna and Flora (CITES; 1973), which imposes import bans contingent on foreign and domestic government certification. An example of a treaty authorizing a trade measure is the Wellington Convention, which states that parties "may also take measures, consistent with international law, to . . . prohibit the importation of any fish . . . which was caught using a driftnet" (Convention for the Prohibition of Fishing With Long Driftnets in the South Pacific, 1989, Article 3[2][c]). Another example is the GATT (1947), which states that parties "shall be free" to use trade measures in cases of serious economic injury from imports (Article XIX[1]). In some instances, treaty-based institutions, such as a conference of the parties, will call for the use of trade measures.

Trade measures in treaties can be nondiscriminatory or discriminatory. For example, the phosphorus match convention (Convention Respecting the Prohibition of the Use of White (Yellow) Phosphorus in the Manufacture of Matches, 1906) is nondiscriminatory in banning the importation of phosphorus matches regardless of the source. The Bamako Convention on hazardous wastes (1989) is discriminatory in prohibiting the importation of waste from nonparties.[17] Provisions that discriminate against nonparties are not uncommon. One factor to consider in determining the appropriateness of such provisions is whether

15. For a good discussion of the use of quotas for environmental purposes, see Wilder (1995).

16. See Bovard (1991) and Hufbauer and Elliott (1994).

17. For a discussion, see Ovink (1995).

the treaty has open entry. The Bamako Convention (1989, Article 22:1) is not open to countries outside of Africa. The Montreal Protocol (1987)—which also requires import bans against nonparties—is open to universal membership.[18]

An in-between case is the WTO, which permits, but does not explicitly authorize, discrimination against nonparties. The new WTO is technically open to universal membership, but some countries have been denied entry (WTO, 1994).[19] For example, China has sought membership for 10 years. This antimultilateral feature of the WTO has been subject to criticism (Walker, 1995).[20]

Trade measures are included in environmental treaties in order to facilitate multilateral cooperation.[21] The aim of trade measures is variously to deflect, halt, reduce, or increase international trade. Some trade measures are aimed at affecting private producer behavior (e.g., the phosphorus match treaty). The rest are aimed at affecting the policies of governments.

Trade measures can be divided into several different categories, some based on purpose and some based on type of harm. These categories are shown below:

Purpose

A. *To encourage governments to join a treaty.* Trade benefits can be used as incentives for membership; penalties can be used as disincentives against nonmembership.

B. *To encourage conformity to the harmonization prescribed by the treaty.* Trade controls can be used to change production practices or government policies.

C. *To encourage parties to comply with a treaty.* Trade sanctions or countervailing duties can be used to police compliance with a treaty. (This category includes only active rather than passive measures.)

D. *To make a treaty more effective by preventing diversion of trade or leakage of traffic.* Trade controls can be used to attain a closed system or to maintain the equilibrium of a regime.

E. *To prevent free riders from gaining economic benefits from nonmembership.* Trade controls can be used to raise the cost of noncooperation (Caldwell, 1994, pp. 173, 178).

F. *To assist other countries in enforcing their laws.* Trade controls can be used by one government to help another government. These are purely consensual arrangements.

18. See also Vienna Convention (1985).

19. Article XII provides that approval of new members shall require a two-thirds vote.

20. China is eager to rejoin to prevent WTO members from discriminating against it in trade. It is interesting to note that China is a signatory to the WTO Agreement.

21. For a good analysis and critique of the use of trade measures in environmental agreements, see Blackhurst and Subramanian (1992).

G. *To prevent relocation through trade.* Trade controls can be used to stop certain transfers.

Type of Harm

X. *Physical harm from/to a product.*
Y. *Physical harm engendered by the market.*
Z. *Economic harm engendered by the market.*

Each specific utilization of a trade measure in a treaty can be described by its purpose and the type of harm it addresses. In many instances, trade provisions involve a mix of purposes. Because treaties are the result of a negotiation, it is sometimes difficult to specify after the fact why the parties wrote a particular provision. Negotiating history tends to be vague or ambiguous. It should be noted that no distinction is made here regarding whether the term *trade* appears in the title of the treaty.

SUMMARY

Trade measures are governmental tools to influence trade. When used in international regimes, they are intended to make the regime more effective. The simplistic argument that trade measures should be reserved for trade treaties must be rejected. Whether trade measures are appropriate for any particular treaty depends on their role in that treaty. This section concludes by proposing 10 ways of categorizing trade measures. The first 7 relate to purpose, that is, why the trade measure is used.[22] The last 3 relate to the type of harm that the trade measure seeks to prevent.

Case Studies

This second section examines 30 cases in which trade measures were drawn on in the design of a treaty.[23] All of these cases involve bilateral, plurilateral, or multilateral treaties; no cases of unilateral trade measures are presented. To maintain the clarity of the presentation, this section does not discuss every trade measure included in these 30 treaties. Instead, specific provisions are selected to illustrate how trade instruments can be used. Thus, for example, although the Basel Convention contains multiple trade measures, only one is discussed here. The case write-ups provide some background information, but not a full explanation of the political circumstances surrounding each treaty.

22. Purposes A-E involve the use of trade measures to make a treaty more effective. Purpose G is to prevent trade itself.

23. Although trade measures are not explicitly mentioned in the Whaling Convention (International Convention for the Regulation of Whaling, 1946), it authorizes the IWC to make recommendations to parties on any matters that relate to whales.

The cases presented are neither exhaustive nor random. They were selected to illustrate the broad range of possible uses of trade measures. Thus the reader should not infer that the inclusion of trade measures is typical of multilateral treaties in general or of multilateral environmental treaties.[24] Although the final section makes some observations about the frequency of certain types of trade measures, no guarantee is implied about statistical validity.

In explaining the purpose of each trade measure (i.e., categories A-G) and what harms the trade measure aims to address (i.e., categories X-Z), I have tried to select the best category or categories that fit each case. Readers may find other plausible categories, but I hope not more accurate ones.

Phylloxera. The earliest treaty to use trade measures for a health/environment purpose was the Convention on Measures to Be Taken Against *Phylloxera Vastatrix* (1878), an agreement to protect against a plant louse that damages wine vineyards. The treaty called for common internal measures (e.g., delimitation of areas affected by the disease) as well as trade bans.[25] Torn vines and dried shoots were excluded from international commerce. All plants and nursery products were to be imported through designated customs offices and had to be accompanied by a certificate stating that they were not infected and had not recently been imported. There were also rules requiring that packaging be sealed yet easily accessible for inspection. Improperly packaged goods were to be returned to their point of origin. The purpose of the trade ban on torn vines was to prevent relocation of *Phylloxera* through trade. The harm addressed was physical harm to the vineyards of other countries.

Sugar bounties. The International Convention Relative to Bounties on Sugar (1902) sought to limit the use of governmental subsidies. As enforcement, the Convention had a provision requiring parties to impose countervailing duties on sugar imports from parties and nonparties that continued to use proscribed bounties on production or export. The purpose of these trade penalties was to encourage parties to comply with the antisubsidy regime and to encourage nonmembers to conform. The harm addressed was economic harm to domestic producers engendered by foreign government action that affects the market.

Birds useful to agriculture. The Convention for the Protection of Birds Useful to Agriculture (1902) provided for common action to protect

24. In the author's view, these cases are representative of treaties that do use trade measures.

25. For a summary of the treaty, see Rüster and Simma (1975, pp. 1565-1566).

certain birds that eat insects.[26] This included a prohibition on killing such birds and a ban on the importation and sale of the nests, eggs, and broods of such birds (Rüster & Simma, 1975).[27] The main purpose of the import ban was to prevent relocation of birds through trade. The harm addressed was physical harm to bird populations engendered by the market.

Phosphorus matches. The Convention Respecting the Prohibition of the Use of White (Yellow) Phosphorus in the Manufacture of Matches (1906) was established to deal with the problem of "phossy jaw" among match workers, a dread occupational disease (U.S. Bureau of Labor Statistics, 1919).[28] The treaty provided for the prohibition of the manufacture, importation, and sale of matches made with phosphorus. Although the dangers of phosphorus were well recognized, many governments were reluctant to forbid the use of that chemical because the substitute production methods were more expensive. The solution found was for governments to act jointly to outlaw the use of phosphorus. The purpose of the import ban was to encourage other governments to forbid phosphorus match production and to prevent any country from increasing its market share by retaining the noxious production method. The harm addressed was physical harm to match workers engendered by the market.

Fur seals. The Convention Respecting Measures for the Preservation and Protection of Fur Seals in the North Pacific Ocean (1911) established the first international environmental regime to protect an endangered species. The four parties agreed to prohibit their nationals from engaging in pelagic sealing. They also agreed to ban the import of sealskins taken from a protected area in the ocean and the import of other sealskins except those marked as taken from approved breeding grounds. In addition, the parties agreed to share the sealskins lawfully taken in order to reduce the incentive to defect (Peterson, 1993). Furthermore, the United States agreed to make advance monetary payments to Canada and Japan to be reimbursed in sealskins. The purpose of the import ban on skins taken from the ocean was to encourage conformity to the pelagic sealing ban. The purpose of the contingent import ban on skins taken on land was to assist parties in enforcing their own laws. The harm addressed was physical harm to seals engendered by the market for sealskin.

Migratory birds. The Convention for the Protection of Migratory Birds (1916) established a close season for game birds and prohibited all

26. For a summary of the treaty, see Rüster and Simma (1975, p. 1615).

27. See Lyster (1985).

28. A few countries had acted in advance of the treaty.

hunting of insectivorous and nongame birds. The treaty prohibits the export of birds or bird eggs during the close season and prohibits international traffic of birds taken or shipped contrary to municipal law. This treaty was a landmark in North American environmental law in the recognition that joint action was needed to protect shared natural resources (Lyster, 1985). The purpose of the export ban may have been to prevent Canada and the United States from diverting bird trade to other countries. The purpose of the contingent trade ban was to assist both countries in enforcing their laws. The harm addressed was physical harm to birds engendered by the market.

African liquor. The Convention Relating to Liquor Traffic in Africa (1919) was a treaty of colonial powers who agreed to cooperate in keeping distilled beverages out of Africa because they were "especially dangerous to the native populations" (Article 3).[29] The treaty forbade the import, sale, or possession of certain "injurious" beverages, such as absinthe. The purpose of the import ban was to prevent relocation of liquor through trade. The harm addressed was physical harm to African natives from the consumption of liquor.

Livestock. The Convention to Safeguard Livestock Interests by Prevention of Infectious and Contagious Diseases (1928) between Mexico and the United States provided for joint measures to prevent the spread of livestock disease. The measures included the maintenance of livestock "sanitary police" at ports of importation, disinfection of vessels, and an import ban on ruminants from countries with a recent outbreak of disease. The purpose of the import ban was to prevent relocation of infectious ruminants through trade. The harm addressed was physical harm to domestic livestock from imported livestock.

Plaice and flounder. The Agreement Regarding the Regulation of Plaice and Flounder in the Baltic Sea (1929) provided for a close season and set minimum size requirements. Fish smaller than the prescribed size were not to be landed in port. The purpose of the import ban was to promote conformity in following the minimum size rule. The harm addressed was physical harm to fisheries engendered by the market.

Ivory. The Agreement for the Control of Illicit Traffic in Ivory and Rhinoceros Horn (1932) between Great Britain and Italy on ivory and rhino horn trade across the frontiers of Kenya and Somalia provided that cross-border trade be contingent on certificates of legal possession from the country of origin. The purpose of the trade ban was to assist countries

29. The United States was a party to this treaty; it had just enacted the constitutional amendment on prohibition.

in enforcing their own conservation laws. The harm addressed was physical harm to species engendered by the market for ivory and horn.

Transit of animals. The International Convention Concerning the Transit of Animals, Meat and Other Products of Animal Origin (1935) provided for international rules relating to sanitary problems and to "unnecessary suffering" of animals. One of the rules was that animals could only be transported in wagons constructed to prevent the dissemination of excreta. The purpose of this rule was to encourage harmonization to salutary sanitary practices. The harm addressed was physical harm to domestic humans and animals from foreign animal waste.

Animal products. The International Convention Concerning the Export and Import of Animal Products (Other Than Meat, Meat Preparations, Fresh Animal Products, Milk, and Milk Products) (1935) provided disciplines on the use of trade measures for sanitary purposes. The Convention also required that listed animal products be imported duty-free from countries that had ratified the International Convention for the Campaign Against Contagious Diseases of Animals.[30] This was one of the earliest linkages of trade to social policy—in this case, making tariff benefits contingent on whether other countries had ratified a health treaty. The purpose of the trade preference (which increased trade) was to encourage other governments to join the campaign against contagious diseases. The harm addressed was physical harm to agriculture and human health from disease-laden products. It was not limited to harm in the country granting duty-free treatment.

Property of historic value. The Pan-American Treaty on the Protection of Movable Property of Historic Value (Hudson, 1941, p. 59) restricted the export of monuments unless specimens of similar value remained in the country. In the definition of "natural movable wealth," the treaty included rare species threatened with extermination. The purpose of the contingent export ban was to stop relocation of rare birds. The harm addressed was physical harm to rare species engendered by the market.

Protection of birds. The International Convention for the Protection of Birds (1950) provided for close seasons and for the elimination of certain hunting practices such as the use of automatic guns and stupefying agents. The Convention bans taking or trade in young, wild birds during breeding season and bans trade in birds captured in violation of the Convention. The purpose of these trade bans is to encourage conformity to the rules in the treaty. The harm addressed is physical harm to birds engendered by the market.

30. See also International Convention for the Campaign Against Contagious Diseases of Animals (1935).

Opium. The Protocol for Limiting and Regulating the Cultivation of the Poppy Plant, the Production of, International and Wholesale Trade in, and Use of Opium (1953) promulgated international rules for opium manufacture and traffic. It provided that if a party failed to carry out its obligations, or a nonparty seriously impeded the administration of the convention, the Opium Board could order parties to embargo the import or export of opium to that country. The purpose of the embargo was to encourage parties to comply with the treaty and to encourage nonparties to conform. The harm addressed was physical harm from products of opium.

Narcotic drugs. The Single Convention on Narcotic Drugs (1961) consolidated international rules on narcotics traffic. The Convention provides that parties shall not knowingly permit the export of drugs to any country except in accordance with the laws of that country. The purpose of this contingent export ban is to assist countries in enforcing their laws. The harm addressed is physical harm from narcotics to the people of another country.

Convention on International Trade in Endangered Species of Wild Fauna and Flora. CITES (1973) provides comprehensive regulation of trade in endangered species (Burgess, 1994). Trade with nonparties is permitted, but only when competent authorities in that government issue "comparable documentation to that required of the parties (CITES, 1973, Article X). This provision removes some incentive for nonmembership but does not provide a disincentive to nonmembership (Favre, 1989, pp. 251-256). The purpose of applying the same trade rules to nonparties was to encourage their conformity with the certification requirements in CITES.[31] This provision also prevents trade diversion, that is, parties using nonparties as intermediaries. The harm addressed by CITES is physical harm to species engendered by the market.

Polar bears. The Agreement on the Conservation of Polar Bears (1973) commits parties to take action to protect polar bears and their ecosystems. For example, the use of aircraft for hunting polar bears is generally prohibited. The Agreement forbids imports of polar bears (or bear parts) taken in violation of the Agreement (e.g., using aircraft). The purpose of the contingent ban on imports is to encourage governments to conform to the treaty. The harm addressed is physical harm to polar bears engendered by the market.

31. The UN Charter also applies some of its rules to nonmembers. Article 2(6) states that the UN shall ensure that nonmember states "act in accordance" with UN principles so far as may be necessary for the maintenance of international peace and security (Charter of the United Nations, 1945).

Textiles. The Agreement Regarding International Trade in Textiles (ARITT; GATT, 1973) or the Multi-Fiber Arrangement provides a special procedure to deal with countries whose textile exports are causing market disruption. Importing countries begin by consulting formally with exporting countries to seek export restraints or another settlement. If the exporting country prefers to maintain a free-market approach, the importing country "may decline to accept imports" above a certain level (GATT, 1973, Article 3). By permitting such import quotas, the Arrangement gives importing governments leverage to force changes in the domestic policies of exporting governments. The purpose of these quotas is to encourage other governments to conform to the protectionist goals of the Multi-Fiber Arrangement and to prevent diversion of trade. The harm addressed is economic harm to importing-nation producers engendered by the textile market.

Whaling. The International Whaling Commission (IWC; 1978) has directed member nations to take all practicable steps to prevent the transfer of factory ships or gear used in whaling operations to any nation that is not a member of the IWC. The purpose of this export ban is to encourage governments to join the treaty and to prevent nonparties (who would not be adhering to IWC quotas) from free-riding on the conservation efforts of other countries. The harm addressed is physical harm to whales engendered by the market.

Ozone layer. The Montreal Protocol on Substances That Deplete the Ozone Layer (1987) provides a comprehensive regime regarding the production, consumption, and trade of certain controlled substances.[32] The treaty requires parties to ban the importation of controlled substances, or products containing them, from nonparties unless those nonparties are determined (by a meeting of the parties) "to be in full compliance" with the production and consumption regime of the Protocol.[33] The main purpose of the import ban on nonparties is to prevent leakage of trade in chlorofluorocarbons (CFCs) and other controlled substances (Lang, 1993).[34] The import bans also serve the purpose of encouraging countries to join or, if they remain nonparties, to comply with the regime (Benedick, 1991, p. 91).[35] Although the harm addressed

32. For amendments to the Protocol, see 30 ILM 537 and 32 ILM 874.

33. For background on the trade provisions, see Lammers (1988). See also Enders and Porges (1992), Runge (1994), and Brack (1996).

34. Lang (1993, pp. 364-368) notes that the aim was to establish a watertight system and to block evasion. Lang was chairman of the Montreal conference.

35. See Benedick (1991, p. 91). Benedick notes that the United States proposed the trade restrictions to encourage membership, to prevent nonparticipating countries from enjoying competitive advantages, and to discourage the movement of CFC production to those countries.

by the Protocol is a physical harm from CFCs and similar substances, the trade provisions address the physical harm engendered by the market. A CFC is no more harmful in one country than another. Thus the trade bans aim to suppress demand that could stimulate future production of CFCs.

Hazardous waste. The Basel Convention on the Control of Transboundary Movements of Hazardous Wastes and Their Disposal (1989) provides a comprehensive regime concerning the disposal of waste and its trade.[36] Among its numerous trade provisions, the Convention bans the export of wastes (including recyclables) to a nonparty (Article 4:5).[37] One purpose of the export ban to nonparties is to encourage nonparties to become members, especially those that desire to engage in reprocessing. Another purpose of this ban is to render the treaty more effective by preventing diversion and, therefore, to reinforce the need for countries to develop better waste control practices. The harm addressed is physical harm from waste to the receiving country. It should be noted that hazardous waste differs from CFCs in that waste can be more harmful in one country than in another. This can occur if the quality of waste treatment differs or if absorptive capacity differs.

Iraq. Following the invasion of Kuwait by Iraq, the UN Security Council imposed a trade embargo on Iraq ("The Iraqi Invasion," 1990).[38] The Resolution for Sanctions on Iraq directed UN members to prevent imports of all commodities originating in Iraq. The purpose of the embargo was to encourage Iraq to comply with its UN treaty obligations and a previous Security Council resolution. The harm addressed by the embargo was the potential physical harm to other countries from an economically strong Iraq. The embargo also had nontrade goals, namely, to force Iraq to withdraw from Kuwait.

CITES. According to CITES (1973), when the Secretariat determines that CITES provisions "are not being effectively implemented," it shall communicate that information to the party concerned. Information provided by the party is reviewed at the next CITES Conference, which "may take whatever recommendations it deems appropriate" (Article XIII). Perhaps relying on this authority, in 1991 the CITES Standing Committee recommended that parties prohibit all trade with Thailand

36. For a comprehensive discussion, see, Kummer (1994).

37. But exportation may occur pursuant to an agreement with that country that includes provisions "not less environmentally sound than those in the Basel Convention. See Kummer (1994), Article 11.

38. This case was included because it is well known. Multilaterally agreed economic sanctions have a long history going back at least as early as 1921. See Hufbauer, Schott, & Elliott (1990, pp. 17-19). See also, Martin (1992).

in fauna and flora species covered by the Convention.[39] The purpose of this recommendation was to encourage Thailand to comply with the treaty (Petersmann, 1995). The harm addressed was physical harm to monkeys, birds, and reptiles engendered by the market.

Antarctica. The Protocol on Environmental Protection to the Antarctica Treaty (1991) establishes a protective regime for the Antarctic environment. Among its provisions is a ban on the importation of live poultry into Antarctica. The purpose of this trade ban is to prevent relocation of certain microorganisms through trade. The harm addressed is physical harm to the Antarctic ecology.

The North American Free Trade Agreement. NAFTA (1992) directs a phaseout of tariffs and provides for a harmonization of certain policies. Parties are required to "give effect" to the provisions of four treaties relating to phonograms, literary and artistic works, industrial property, and plant varieties. Parties also agreed to make every effort to accede to these treaties. Failure to comply could subject a party to NAFTA enforcement provisions, which could ultimately lead to trade sanctions. Parties are also required to detain goods at the border at the request of holders of property rights. The purpose of such trade enforcement is to encourage parties either to join the four property-rights treaties or to conform to them. The harm addressed is economic harm engendered by the market.

World Trade Organization. The WTO (1994) established a comprehensive regime of rights and duties related to trade policy. To gain the benefits of the various agreements, including market access, nations must become members of the WTO. To do so, nations undertake accession procedures whereby they offer to change their domestic legislation as a "price" for entry. The underlying idea is that a new WTO member receives tariff benefits immediately, under the most-favored-nation rule, and therefore must reciprocate in advance. The purpose of requiring prospective members to undertake trade measures (i.e., liberalization) is to prevent free-riding. The harm addressed is economic harm engendered by the market.

Bananas. The Framework Agreement on Banana Imports (1994) is a trade agreement between the European Union (EU) and developing countries to limit the importation of bananas into the EU and to allocate trade by national quota. In return for large quotas, four nations agreed not to seek adoption of a GATT panel report criticizing the EU's banana

39. 56 C.F.R. 32260 (1991). For a discussion of enforcement provisions in CITES, see Crawford (1995).

regime. One purpose of the quotas is to encourage governments to join the Framework, thus neutralizing opposition to a continuation of the EU's banana restrictions. The harm addressed is economic harm to EU farmers and former colonies engendered by the banana market.

Shipbuilding. The OECD Agreement Respecting Normal Competitive Conditions in the Commercial Shipbuilding and Repair Industry (1994) seeks to eliminate most governmental subsidies granted directly to shipbuilders or indirectly to ship operators. The Agreement contains tough dispute settlement mechanisms to respond to export subsidies and certain kinds of domestic support. Under these mechanisms, a complaining party receiving a favorable judgment by a dispute panel may suspend trade benefits to the defendant government if that government does not take the remedial steps dictated by the panel. Parties forgo their right to complain about this trade sanction under the rules of any other agreement (e.g., the WTO). The purpose of such trade enforcement is to encourage parties to comply with the treaty. The harm addressed is economic harm engendered by foreign governmental action affecting the market.

Fish stocks. The UN Agreement Relating to the Conservation and Management of Straddling Fish Stocks and Highly Migratory Fish Stocks (1995) provides for new methods of international cooperation to respond to dwindling fish stocks. According to the treaty, parties "may" adopt regulations to prohibit the landing or transshipment of fish where it has been established "that the catch has been taken in a manner which undermines the effectiveness of subregional, regional or global conservation and management measures on the high seas" (Article 23). The purpose of this import ban is to encourage conformity to the prescribed conservation and to prevent free riders from undermining the treaty. The harm addressed was physical harm to fisheries engendered by the market.

Table 1 summarizes the trade measures in these 30 cases and lists the most pertinent categories for each. Purpose is shown on the top part of each row in Column 3; type of harm is shown on the bottom of that row.

Lessons and Policy Implications

SUMMARY OF FINDINGS

For more than a century, drafters of treaties have made use of trade measures in the design of international regimes. Trade measures continue to be used (see cases concerning bananas, shipbuilding, and fish stocks above). As the previous part shows, trade measures have been

Table 1
Summary of Case Studies

Year	*Case*	*Categories*	*Summary*
1878	*Phylloxera*	G X	Bans trade in vines and shoots.
1902	Sugar bounties	B, C Z	Requires countervailing duties against member and nonmember countries using sugar bounties.
1902	Birds useful to agriculture	G Y	Bans import of certain bird eggs.
1906	Phosphorus matches	B, E Y	Bans import of phosphorus matches.
1911	Fur seals	B Y	Bans import of sealskins taken from ocean.
		F Y	Bans import of sealskins when unlawfully taken from land.
1916	Migratory birds	D Y	Bans export of birds during close season.
		F Y	Bans trade in birds caught contrary to local law.
1919	African liquor	G X	Bans import of liquor into Africa.
1928	Livestock	G X	Bans import from countries with a recent outbreak of disease.
1929	Plaice and founder	B Y	Bans import of fish below a minimum length.
1932	Ivory	F Y	Bans trade in ivory without certificate of legal possession.
1935	Transit of animals	B X	Requires that animals be transported in wagons designed to prevent the dissemination of excreta.
1935	Animal products	A X	Requires duty-free treatment of animal products from countries ratifying the Contagious Diseases Convention.
1935	Property of historic value	G Y	Forbids export of irreplaceable objects, including rare species.
1950	Birds	B Y	Bans import of birds caught in prohibited ways.
1953	Opium	B, C X	Authorizes Opium Board to impose embargo on the export or import of opium to a country.

(continued)

Table 1 Continued

Year	Case	Categories	Summary
1961	Narcotic drugs	F X	Bans export of opium except in accordance with law of importing country.
1973	CITES	B, D Y	Applies the same trade controls on endangered species to nonparties.
1973	Polar bears	B Y	Bans trade in polar bears taken in violation of agreement.
1973	Textiles	B, D Z	Authorizes import bans to force countries to adopt export restraints.
1978	Whaling	A, E Y	Directs countries to ban export of whale hunting equipment to nonmembers.
1987	Ozone layer	A, B, D Y	Bans import of controlled substances from nonparties.
1989	Hazardous waste	A, D X	Bans export of waste to nonparties.
1990	Iraq	C Y	UN embargo on Iraq following invasion of Kuwait.
1991	CITES	C Y	Recommends trade ban applying to Thailand on CITES-covered species.
1991	Antarctica	G X	Bans import of live poultry into Antarctica.
1992	NAFTA	A, B Z	Requires parties to give effect to private property treaties and to make every effort to ratify them. Enforces with potential trade sanctions.
1993	WTO	E Z	Requires prospective members to undertake trade measures.
1994	Bananas	A Z	Establishes managed trade in bananas.
1994	Shipbuilding	C Z	Provides for trade sanction against governments found to subsidize shipbuilding.
1995	Fish stocks	B, E Y	Permits import bans on fish catch that undermines treaty.

employed in a wide range of regimes. Of the 30 cases presented, 3 relate to sanitary and phytosanitary matters, 6 relate to commerce, 14 relate to the environment, 6 relate to human health, and 1 relates to security.[40]

The first section of this article outlines seven purposes for which trade measures might be used. I presented at least three examples of each purpose. Environmental treaties employed trade measures for all seven of these purposes. Commercial/trade treaties employed trade measures for five of these purposes.

The first section also outlines three harms from trade to which trade measures could be addressed. I presented several examples of each. Environmental treaties used trade measures to address two harms (X and Y). Commercial treaties used trade measures to address only one harm (Z). There is no overlap here.

There were 21 possible combinations (7 × 3) of purpose and type of harm. I found examples of 18 of them. There are no cases of EX, FZ, and GZ. Because the cases presented are neither exhaustive nor random, one cannot make any judgments about the distribution of the combinations. One should also not infer that most environmental, commerce, health, or sanitary treaties use trade instruments; most do not.

ARE TRADE MEASURES NECESSARY?

In assessing whether an international regime needs to use a trade measure, one should logically start by asking whether a real problem exists that requires governmental attention. For example, is the ozone layer truly threatened by CFCs? That level of inquiry is beyond the scope of this article. Our focus here is on how treaty designers address problems that they perceive as real.

Assuming that a problem does exist, the next logical question is whether an international regime is needed to address it. For purely local environmental problems (such as noise pollution) or purely local trade problems (such as high domestic tariffs), effective solutions may be accomplishable through national policy alone. For transborder environmental problems (such as air pollution) or transborder economic problems (such as recession), effective solutions may require intergovernmental cooperation. In the 30 cases above, it was assumed by governments that a regional or international regime was either essential or highly desirable. It is beyond the scope of this article to evaluate whether those judgments were in fact correct. Some analysts have suggested that international regimes do not really need to use trade measures. That may often be right. Certainly, many effective international regimes do not draw on trade measures.

40. The Basel Convention (1989) is counted as human health; it is also environment.

In general, it will always be possible to address physical and economic harms by agreement on actions that governments can take as an exercise of their own sovereign jurisdiction. If an appropriate agreement can be reached and if all parties can be relied on to honor it, there is no need for trade measures. For example, in the *Phylloxera* convention, the parties could have agreed to stamp out the plant louse and to prevent any movement on vines and shoots. In the Ivory treaty, the parties could have agreed to upgrade their internal enforcement of ivory commerce.

Yet, although there is always a hypothetical compact that may have been obtainable, trade measures have been used as epoxy where parties were unable to dovetail their positions. The case of CITES is particularly instructive because the parties would never have agreed to harmonize their domestic wildlife conservation policies. CITES is about commerce only because deeper harmonization was unachievable. Because CITES, as designed, does concern trade, it seems appropriate that trade measures are used as a tool.[41]

Because perfect treaties are elusive, negotiators use available instruments to cobble together regimes that might work. Trade measures can be helpful in dealing with complications of intentional noncompliance (e.g., shipbuilding subsidies), inadvertent inspection failure (e.g., *Phylloxera*), or transitional periods (e.g., CFC phaseouts). Without trade measures, many of the treaties discussed above may never have been consummated, because the remaining regime might have looked ineffectual or one-sided. International cooperation often stumbles over free riders. Trade measures provide one way of responding to that problem (cases concerning phosphorus matches, whaling, WTO, and fish stocks).

International agreements are typically about transborder issues involving either physical or economic harms.[42] Because of the transborder nature of the problem, a transborder tool (like a trade measure) may enable a workable remedy. In all of the environmental cases discussed above, the trade tool used was directly related to the perceived harm. For example, the Polar Bear treaty applies only to trade in polar bears. It does not ban trade in widgets as a means of enforcing better conservation behavior. By contrast, some of the commerce treaties do use trade tools unrelated to the perceived harm. For example, NAFTA threatens trade sanctions against parties that do not conform to international treaties on property. The shipbuilding agreement also threatens trade sanctions on unrelated products. This points to a significant difference between the environment and trade regimes.[43] The environment regime has never followed the lead of the trade regime in using trade measures merely to punish or to provide restitution.

41. See Lang (1991, pp. 183-185).

42. Some treaties are about physical harms to humans in other countries. For example, see cases 1906 and 1919.

43. See Dam (1970, p. 81). Controlled retaliation is made the heart of the GATT system.

ARE TRADE MEASURES EFFECTIVE?

The short answer to the question of whether trade measures are effective is, *Compared to what?* There is an infinite variety of carrots and sticks that might be substituted for trade measures and that might be more effective. For example, in the Fur Seals treaty, the United States could have agreed not merely to make advance payments but to compensate Canada and Japan for forgoing seal hunting entirely. In the shipbuilding agreement, each country could have posted a $50 million bond with the OECD to be surrendered if they were caught breaking the antisubsidy rules. But there is little use in comparing politically feasible trade measures to unfeasible carrots and sticks.[44]

It is beyond the scope of this article to present a detailed evaluation of the 30 cases to determine whether the regimes worked and, if so, whether trade measures were critical to the success. Such an evaluation might find many successes, however. For example, the phosphorus match treaty solved the problem of phossy jaw. That import ban proved effective in forcing several countries, such as Great Britain, to join the agreement (Reinsch, 1911). Although it remains a bit leaky, the Montreal Protocol has been an overall success. The trade bans were important in promoting new membership.[45]

Of course, trade measures work in bad treaties as well as good ones. The Multi-Fiber Arrangement continues to prevent "market disruption" 23 years after its inception. Perhaps the WTO will be successful in emancipating textile trade.

Although many of the 30 treaties were unsuccessful, there is no obvious evidence that the use of trade measures was responsible for that lack of success. If anything, it was the failure to follow through with trade measures that undermined some of these treaties. But trade measures can only go so far. They cannot create a meeting of the minds between countries when that does not exist. Moreover, border measures have diminished effectiveness in dealing with smuggling. This was a problem in several of the cases discussed such as ivory, opium, narcotic drugs, CITES, and, most recently, with the Montreal Protocol.

DO TRADE MEASURES NEED TO BE DISCRIMINATORY?

Some commentators have suggested that if environmental treaties use any trade measures, such measures should only be nondiscriminatory.[46]

44. It is interesting to note that the Maastricht Treaty permits the European Court of Justice to levy penalty payments against EU member nations that do not comply with a judgment of the Court. See Treaty on European Union (1992, Article 171).

45. See Twum-Barima and Campbell (1994, pp. 52, 53, 100), and Brack (1995, p. 504).

46. For example, see Eglin (1993, pp. 304, 311). (Nondiscrimination is the principal GATT requirement in every case, and it is hard to accept that environmental policy making needs trade discrimination to be effective.) Eglin is the director of the WTO division responsible for environmental issues.

Any trade measure that distinguishes between countries is discriminatory. This includes cases concerning sugar bounties, livestock, animal products, opium, textiles, whaling, ozone, hazardous waste, Iraq, CITES, bananas, and shipbuilding. In addition, any trade measure that treats like products differently depending on their production method would also be viewed as discriminatory by most GATT experts. This includes cases concerning fur seals, birds, polar bears, and fish stocks. Trade measures aimed at helping another country enforce its law are also technical discrimination. This includes cases concerning migratory birds, ivory, and narcotic drugs. But those trade measures would probably never be adjudged discriminatory because the other country is unlikely to lodge a complaint.

There is no reason why the environmental regime should eschew trade discrimination when the trade regime utilizes it. Several of the clearest examples of trade discrimination occur in commodity agreements (see cases concerning sugar bounties, textiles, and bananas). The GATT permits discrimination in Article VI (countervailing duties) and Article XXIII (dispute settlement) to force changes in the domestic policies of other countries.

But even if the trade regime did not violate its own norm of nondiscrimination, there would still be a justification for the environment regime to do so. Although "equal treatment" may be very useful in deregulating trade, it is not so useful in regulating production to safeguard the environment. Environmental regulation needs to be targeted. This illustrates one of the basic clashes between the trade and environment regimes. The environment regime cannot operate on the norm that it does not matter how an item is produced or where it is produced.

One useful distinction is between trade measures used to control the flow of trade (see cases concerning birds useful to agriculture, African liquor, property of historic value, CITES, ozone layer, Antarctica, and bananas) and trade measures used as punishment (see cases concerning sugar bounties, opium, Iraq, and shipbuilding; Chayes & Chayes, 1995, pp. 29-32). The latter might be viewed as a less essential use of a trade measure.[47] For example, in the sugar bounties convention, any punishment could have been used to thwart subsidies. But in the 1902 birds convention, trade controls on eggs were part of the strategy to preserve bird populations.

Although there have been several environmental treaties that ban trade in items whose production (using the term loosely) violates the treaty (see cases concerning fur seals, birds, polar bears, and CITES), the fish stocks agreement goes one step further in linking the trade ban to actions that undermine a treaty.[48] This is expanded enforcement. It will be interesting to see whether it proves effective.

47. Insights from game theory might be useful here. See McMillan (1990).

48. For a discussion of the earlier technique, see Mander (1941).

A few of the treaties discussed in the previous section recommend or require trade discrimination against nonparties (see cases concerning whaling, ozone layer, and hazardous waste). One treaty, the WTO, can require countries to change their trade laws as the price for membership.[49] The issue of trade relations with nonmembers is a difficult issue that will continue to arise in new treaties. We will probably see more Category A and E cases in the future if new environmental agreements are negotiated that are costly to implement.

LINKAGE TO OTHER REGIMES

In two cases, trade measures were used in one treaty to promote the goals of another treaty. The animal products treaty provided trade preferences to countries that ratified the International Convention for the Campaign Against Contagious Diseases of Animals. NAFTA required parties to give effect to property-rights treaties. In another case, not included in the previous section, the GATT required members to join the International Monetary Fund (IMF) or enter into a special exchange rate agreement with the GATT (1947, Article XV:6).

These cases differ from the more common circumstance where a trade measure was used to promote a noneconomic objective of the treaty itself.[50] For example, the Multi-Fiber Arrangement sought to preserve textile production in certain countries. The fur seals treaty sought to preserve seals. But these goals were inherent to the textile and fur seal regimes.

We will likely see more interregime linkage in the future.[51] For example, as of 1998, the European Commission may give additional trade preferences to developing countries that "have adopted and actually apply domestic legal provisions incorporating the substance of the standards laid down by the ITTO [International Tropical Timber Organization] relating to the sustainable management of forests."[52] Interregime linkage will be driven by new paradigms, such as sustainable development, that attempt to balance and meld fundamental goals.[53]

49. It is interesting to note that the OECD also negotiates accession with new member nations (e.g., Mexico) that involve discussions about previous OECD recommendations including environmental policy.

50. For a discussion of the efficiency of trade and subsidy measures used for noneconomic objectives, see Bhagwati and Srinivasan (1983).

51. One case, not included here, is the original GATT, which permitted quantitative trade restrictions having the equivalent effect of exchange restrictions authorized under Article VII(3)(b) of the Agreement of the International Monetary Fund. See GATT (1947, Article XIV[5][a]).

52. Council Regulation No. 3281/94, *OJ* L348/1.

53. See Moltke (1996).

FUTURE OF TRADE MEASURES IN INTERNATIONAL REGIMES

For more than a century, multilaterally approved trade measures have been used in the design of international regimes. This article has tried to explain the logic of such use. I have also tried to point out that the use of trade measures in treaties about commerce bears similarity to such use in treaties about the environment.

Although trade measures have shown their utility, their use in the 21st century may be less than in the 20th. There are several reasons for this. First, the channels of trade have greatly expanded. Trade stopped at one border can easily flow to another. Second, trade in services is expanding faster than trade in goods, and services are less likely to cause health, sanitary, or environmental problems. Third, the increasingly globalized economy, and the ensuing interdependence, makes it more costly to restrict trade.[54] For all three reasons, economic borders are likely to be less important in the future. Borders that are permeable to information and money find it harder to be impermeable to goods.

On top of market-driven economic integration, there will be more politically driven governmental integration. Nations will venture into deeper harmonization of their domestic policies. These trends can be seen in the European Union, where the Maastricht Treaty contains strong provisions on economic and monetary policy (and considerably weaker ones on environmental policy).[55] Integration will forestall the need for trade measures if new commitments are legally enforceable in supranational or national courts. A step in that direction was taken by Canada in the NAFTA environmental and labor side agreements when it agreed that dispute panel decisions would be enforceable in Canadian courts.[56]

The final reason why trade measures will be used less is that they are too blunt.[57] Trade measures fit into "command-and-control" environmental regulation but are less suited to market-based economic instruments. It is one thing to prevent relocation through trade (i.e., Category G). It is quite another to achieve ecoefficiency through trade restrictions.

If trade measures are to retain their usefulness for treaties, there will need to be a new generation of trade measures. One possibility is an international tariff (or tax) approved by a multilateral authority and applied to goods based on their production process. For example, there could be a tax on fossil fuel use. There could be a tariff on fish caught in excess of an internationally set quota. Such a system could rely on

54. However, a reduction in self-sufficiency may also make countries more vulnerable to trade restrictions.

55. Treaty on European Union (1992, Title VI). The limitations on government deficits may increase unemployment, which can lower public support for environmental quality.

56. North American Agreement on Environmental Cooperation (1993, Annex 36A); North American Agreement on Labor Cooperation (1993, Annex 41A). For a discussion, see Johnson and Beaulieu (1996).

57. See Barbier (1995).

certifications, or ecolabels, granted by a neutral authority. We have already seen a greater use of product documentation in recent treaties, such as the Basel Convention, which operates by officializing waste flows.

Perhaps the most fruitful feature of the trade-and-environment debate is that both regimes are reflecting on their own goals and mechanisms in light of the practices in the other regime. Until recently, the contribution of trade measures to regime effectiveness has been given insufficient attention. This article has sought to shed new light on this little-explored topic.

Manuscript submitted December 30, 1995; revised manuscript accepted for publication February 9, 1996.

Acknowledgments

Support for this research was provided by the Rockefeller Brothers Fund and The Pew Charitable Trusts. The author wishes to thank two anonymous reviewers for helpful critiques.

References

Abbott, F. M. (1992, Fall). Trade and democratic values. *Minnesota Journal of Global Trade*, 15-20.

Agreement for the Control of Illicit Traffic in Ivory and Rhinoceros Horn, 136 LNTS 386, ¶2 (1932).

Agreement on the Conservation of Polar Bears, 27 UST 3918 (1973).

Agreement Regarding the Regulation of Plaice and Flounder in the Baltic Sea, 115 LNTS 107 (1929).

Agreement Relating to the Conservation and Management of Straddling Fish Stocks and Highly Migratory Fish Stocks, 34 ILM 1542 (1995).

Agreement Respecting Normal Competitive Conditions in the Commercial Shipbuilding and Repair Industry (OECD 1994).

Bamako Convention on the Ban of the Import into Africa and the Control of Transboundary Movement and Management of Hazardous Wastes Within Africa, 30 ILM 773 (1989).

Barbier, E. B. (1995). Elephant ivory and tropical timber: The role of trade interventions in sustainable management. *Journal of Environment and Development*, 4(2), 1-32.

Barrett, S. (1994). *Trade restrictions in international environmental agreements*. Center for Social and Economic Work on the Global Environment Working Paper, GEC 94-13.

Basel Convention on the Control of Transboundary Movements of Hazardous Wastes and their Disposal, 28 ILM 649 (1989).

Benedick, R. E. (1991). *Ozone diplomacy*. Cambridge, MA: Harvard University Press.

Bhagwati, J. N., & Srinivasan, T. N. (1983). *Lectures on International Trade*. Cambridge, MA: MIT Press.

Blackhurst, R., & Subramanian, A. (1992). Promoting multilateral cooperation on the environment. In K. Anderson & R. Blackhurst (Eds.), *The Greening of World Trade Issues* (pp. 247-268). London: Harvester Wheatsheaf.

Bovard, J. (1991). *The fair trade fraud: How Congress pillages the consumer and decimates American competitiveness.* New York: St. Martin's.

Brack, D. (1995). Balancing trade and the environment. *International Affairs, 71,* 504.

Brack, D. (1996). *International trade and the Montreal Protocol.* London: Earthscan.

Burgess, J. (1994). The environmental effects of trade in endangered species. In OECD, *The Environmental Effects of Trade* (pp. 123-150). Paris: OECD.

Caldwell, D. J. (1994, Fall). International environmental agreements and the GATT: An analysis of the potential conflict and the role of a GATT "waiver" resolution. *Maryland Journal of International Law and Trade,* 173, 178.

Cameron, J., & Arden-Clarke, C. (1996). *The relationship between the provisions of the multilateral trading system and trade measures for environmental purposes, including those pursuant to multilateral environment agreements* (WWF Legal Briefing #2).

Charnovitz, S. (1994, Summer). Green roots, bad pruning: GATT rules and their application to environmental trade measures. *Tulane Environmental Journal,* 299.

Charter of the United Nations, 1 UNTS xvi (1945).

Chayes, A., & Handler Chayes, A. (1995). *The new sovereignty: Compliance with international regulatory agreements.* Cambridge, MA: Harvard University Press.

Convention for the Prohibition of Fishing With Long Driftnets in the South Pacific, 29 ILM 1454, Article 3(2)(c) (1989).

Convention for the Protection of Birds Useful to Agriculture, 191 CTS 91 (1902).

Convention for the Protection of Migratory Birds, 39 Stat. 1702 (1916).

Convention on International Trade in Endangered Species of Wild Fauna and Flora, 993 UNTS 243 (1973).

Convention on Measures to be Taken Against *Phylloxera Vastarix,* 153 CTS 247 (1878).

Convention Relating to Liquor Traffic in Africa, 7 LNTS 332 (1919).

Convention Respecting Measures for the Preservation and Protection of Fur Seals in the North Pacific Ocean, 214 CTS 80 (1911).

Convention Respecting the Prohibition of the Use of White (Yellow) Phosphorus in the Manufacture of Matches, 203 CTS 12, Article 1 (1906).

Convention to Safeguard Livestock Interests by Prevention of Infectious and Contagious Diseases, 46 Stat. 2451 (1928).

Crawford, C. (1995, Spring). An examination of conflicts between the convention on international trade in endangered species and the GATT in light of actions to halt the rhinoceros and tiger trade. *Georgetown International Environmental Law Review,* 555-585.

Dam, K. W. (1970). *The GATT: Law and the International Economic Organization.* Chicago, IL: University of Chicago Press.

Eglin, R. (1993). International economics, international trade, and international environmental protection. *Wirtschaftspolitische Blätter,* 3(4), 304, 314.

Enders, A., & Porges, A. (1992). Successful conventions and conventional success: Saving the ozone layer. In K. Anderson & R. Blackhurst (Eds.), *The greening of world trade issues* (pp. 130-144). London: Harvester Wheatsheaf.

Esty, D. C. (1994). *Greening the GATT.* Washington, DC: Institute for International Economics.

Favre, D. S. (1989). *International trade in endangered species: A guide to CITES.* Dordrecht, Netherlands: Martinus Nijhoff.

Feketekuty, G. (1993, Summer). The link between trade and environment policy. *Minnesota Journal of Global Trade,* 171, 182-185.

Framework Agreement on Banana Imports, 34 ILM 1 (1994).

GATT Secretariat (1993). *Trade provisions contained in Multilateral Environmental Agreements* (GATT Doc. TRE/Wq Rev. 1). Geneva, Switzerland: Author.

General Agreement on Tariffs and Trade, 55 UNTS 188 (1947). (The WTO has renamed this agreement *GATT 1994.*)

General Agreement on Tariffs and Trade. (1973). Agreement regarding international trade in textiles. In *Basic instruments and selected documents, 21,* 3.

Harland, D. (1994). *Killing game: International law and the African elephant*. Westport, CT: Praeger.

Hudson, M. O. (1941). *International Legislation, Vol. VII*. Washington, DC: Carnegie Endowment.

Hufbauer, G. C., & Elliott, K. A. (1994). *Measuring the costs of protection in the United States*. Washington, DC: Institute for International Economics.

Hufbauer, G. C., Schott, J. J., & Elliott, K. A. (1990). *Economic sanctions reconsidered: Supplemental case histories*, 2. Washington, DC: Institute for International Economics.

International Convention Concerning the Export and Import of Animal Products (Other than Meat, Meat Preparations, Fresh Animal Products, Milk, and Milk Products), 193 LNTS 61 (1935).

International Convention Concerning the Transit of Animals, Meat and Other Products of Animal Origin, 193 LNTS 39, Article 5 (1935).

International Convention for the Campaign Against Contagious Diseases of Animals, 186 LNTS 175 (1935).

International Convention for the Protection of Birds, 638 UNTS 187 (1950).

International Convention for the Regulation of Whaling, 161 UNTS 72, Article VI (1946).

International Convention Relative to Bounties on Sugar, 95 B.F.S.P. 6, Articles IV & VII (1902).

International Whaling Commission (1978). 29th Annual Meeting, Appendix 8.

The Iraqi invasion: Text of the Resolution for Sanctions on Iraq. (1990, August 7). *The New York Times*, p. A9.

Johnson, P. M., & Beaulieu, A. (1996). *The environment and NAFTA*. Washington, DC: Island.

Kastner, J. (1994). Long before furs, it was feathers that stirred reformist ire. *Smithsonian, 25*(4), 96.

Kirchgässner, R., & Mohr, E. (1996). Trade restrictions as viable means of enforcing compliance with international environmental law: An economic assessment. In J. A. Frowein et al. (Eds.), *Beiträge zum ausländischen öffentlichen Recht und Völkerrecht*. Heidelberg, Germany: Springer Verlag.

Kummer, K. (1994). The use of trade measures in selected multilateral environmental agreements. In *Environment and trade, 7*. Geneva, Switzerland: United Nations Environment Programme.

Lammers, J. G. (1988). Effort to develop a protocol on chlorofluorocarbons to the Vienna Convention for the Protection of the Ozone Layer. *Hague Yearbook of International Law, 1*, 225.

Lang, J. T. (1991). Some implications of the Montreal Protocol to the Ozone Convention. In W. Lang et al. (Eds.), *Environmental protection and international law* (pp. 183-185). London: Graham & Trotman.

Lang, W. (1993). International environmental agreements and the GATT. *Wirtschaftspolitische Blätter, 3*(4), 364-368.

Lloyd, P. J. (1992). The problem of optimal environmental policy choice. In K. Anderson & R. Blackhurst (Eds.), *The greening of world trade issues*. London: Harvester Wheatsheaf.

Lyster, S. (1985). *International wildlife law*. Cambridge, UK: Grotius.

McGrory, B. (1995, November 2). Freon hot in Miami: Smugglers find big profits in soon-to-be-banned gas. *The Boston Globe*, p. F6.

Mander, L. A. (1941). *Foundations of modern world society*. Stanford, CA: Stanford University Press.

Martin, L. L. (1992). *Coercive cooperation: Explaining multilateral economic sanctions*. Princeton, NJ: Princeton University Press.

McMillan, J. (1990). Strategic bargaining and Section 301. In J. Bhagwati & H. T. Patrick (Eds.), *Aggressive unilateralism: America's 301 trade policy and the world trading system*. Ann Arbor: University of Michigan Press. (Reprinted from *Economics and Politics*, (1990, Spring), 45-58.

Moltke, K. von. (1996). *International environmental management, trade regimes and sustainability*. Winnipeg, Manitoba: International Institute for Sustainable Development.

Montreal Protocol on Substances that Deplete the Ozone Layer, 26 ILM 1541, Articles 4 & 17 (1987).

North American Agreement on Environmental Cooperation, 32 ILM 1480, Annex 36A (1993).

North American Agreement on Labor Cooperation, 32 ILM 1499, Annex 41A (1993).

North American Free Trade Agreement, 32 ILM 605 (1992).

Ovink, B. J. (1995, Winter). Transboundary shipments of toxic waste: The Basel and Bamako Conventions: Do Third World countries have a choice? *Dickinson Journal of International Law*, 281.

Petersmann, E.-U. (1995). *International and European trade and environmental law after the Uruguay Round*, London: Kluwer Law International.

Peterson, M. J. (1993). International fisheries management. In P. Haas et al. (Eds.), *Institutions for the Earth* (pp. 261-262). Cambridge, MA: MIT Press.

Protocol for Limiting and Regulating the Cultivation of the Poppy Plant, the Production of, International and Wholesale Trade in, and Use of Opium, 14 UST 10 (1953).

Protocol on Environmental Protection to the Antarctica Treaty, 30 ILM 1460 (1991).

Reinsch, P. (1911). *Public international unions*. Boston: Ginn.

Runge, F. (1994). *Freer trade: Protected environment* (chapter 5). New York: Council on Foreign Relations.

Rüster, B., & Simma, B. (1975). *International protection of the environment* (Vol. IV). Dobbs Ferry, NY: Oceana.

Single Convention on Narcotic Drugs, 520 UNTS 204 (1961).

Sonner, S. (1995). "Group Blames Timber Trade for Deforestation," *Journal of Commerce*, December 29, p. 5A.

Treaty on European Union. (1992). Brussels, Belgium: European Commission.

Twum-Barima, R., & Campbell, L. B. (1994). Protecting the ozone layer through trade measures: Reconciling the trade provisions of the Montreal Protocol and the rules of GATT. In *Environment and Trade, 6*. Geneva, Switzerland: United Nations Environment Programme, 52, 53, 100.

Tyson, R. (1995, December 21). Nearly banned coolants are hot illegal imports. *USA Today*, p. 5A.

United Nations. (1992). *Earth Summit Agenda 21*. Geneva, Switzerland: Author.

United Nations Environment Programme. (1995). The Use of Trade Measures in Selected Multilateral Environmental Agreements. In *Environment and Trade, 10* Geneva, Switzerland: Author.

U.S. Bureau of Labor Statistics. (1919). *International Labor Legislation and the Society of Nations* (Bulletin No. 254). Washington, DC: Author.

Vienna Convention for the Protection of the Ozone Layer, 26 ILM 1516, Article 14 (1985).

Walker, T. (1995, October 18). China accuses US over WTO. *Financial Times*, p. 4.

Wilder, M. (1995, Summer). Quota systems in international wildlife and fisheries regimes. *Journal of Environment and Development*, 55.

World Trade Organization. (1994). Agreement Establishing the World Trade Organization (WTO). Reprinted in *Uruguay Round*. Washington: Government Printing Office.

World Trade Organization (1995, December). WTO Trade and Environment Committee agrees on work programme in preparation for the Singapore Ministerial Meeting. *Trade and the Environment*.

Steve Charnovitz is the director of Global Environment and Trade Study (GETS), New Haven, CT.

[16]

Trade Protectionism and Environmental Regulations: The New Nontariff Barriers*

*C. Ford Runge***

I. Introduction

This article reviews some economic and legal aspects of the growing role of environmental, health, and safety regulations operating as disguised barriers to trade. While this has always been a recognized problem in trade policy, the issue has gained new force as environmental policies move to the forefront of many national agendas. Because environmental standards have a growing national constituency, they are especially attractive candidates for disguised protectionism. International distinctions in the tolerable level of environmental risks are created because the weight attached to environmental standards tends to vary with the income levels of different countries. Incentives are created to move restricted product and processes into areas of lax regulation, notably developing countries, while denying import access to countries that may not subscribe to the regulatory policies of the developed countries. Without multilateral action, environmental standards become sources of trade tension.

The article is organized as follows. First, the issue of environmental

* This article is based in part on a chapter appearing in AGRICULTURE AND WATER QUALITY: INTERNATIONAL PERSPECTIVES (John B. Braden and Stephen B. Lovejoy, eds.), Lynn Rienner, Boulder, Colorado, 1990, and in revised form in *Environmental Risks and International Trade Policy*, THE AMERICAN PROSPECT, March 1990 and with Richard Nolan in Trade in *Disservices: Environmental Regulation and Agricultural Trade*, FOOD POLICY, February, 1990. Financial support provided by Northwest Area Foundation, St. Paul, Minnesota.

** Director, Center for International Food and Agricultural Policy; Associate Professor, Department of Agricultural and Applied Economics, Hubert H. Humphrey Institute of Public Affairs, and Department of Forest Resources, University of Minnesota

Northwestern Journal of International Law & Business 11:47(1990)

regulation is discussed in an international context, with special emphasis on food, health, and safety. Second, the problems created by national income disparities and the different priorities of national governments are noted. Third, a case study based on a recent United States - Canada dispute over salmon and herring exports is analyzed. The article closes by suggesting an agenda for both domestic and international policy reforms, focusing on a multi-tiered set of international standards that will help distinguish legitimate health and environmental regulations from disguised non-tariff barriers.

II. The Internationalization of Environmental Risks

On January 1, 1989, the European Community (EC) announced a ban on all beef imports from the United States containing hormones used to help increase cattle growth. Citing health risks, the EC action touched off a cycle of retaliation worth hundreds of millions of dollars that has affected the world trading system. This apparently isolated example of health regulations acting as trade barriers is part of an emerging pattern of environmental and health issues with major consequences for the world economy. These consequences are especially important to trade between developed and developing nations.

Other developments include discussions by the European Commission in September, 1989 of rules to further restrict imports of cattle or dairy products produced with the aid of bovine somatotropin (BST), a bovine growth hormone. In February of 1989, the Natural Resources Defense Council released a report citing significant health risk from the use of Alar, a chemical used to prevent blemishes on apples. United States regulatory agencies may ultimately ban its use, and the EPA announced that it would increase its capacity to ban certain agricultural chemicals. Senator Pete Wilson (R, Ca), the governor elect for California, introduced federal legislation in December, 1989 that would ban companies from exporting pesticides that are illegal in the United States. Responding to the political influence of the Western Growers Association, Wilson stated that "export of dangerous pesticides creates a competitive inequity between foreign and American farmers and growers." In October, 1989, a dispute settlement panel formed under the United States/Canada free trade agreement determined that Canadian restrictions on foreign salmon and herring fishing were an effective barrier to trade.

These examples are part of an emerging pattern in which environmental and health risks are increasingly traded among nations along with goods and services. These risks arise directly from the transfer of technology, and will increasingly affect international investment, trade, and development.[1]

This pattern of trade underscores the problem of formulating government policies in an interdependent world economy. While the United States and other signatories to the General Agreement on Tariffs and Trade (hereinafter "GATT") pursue more open borders in the ongoing Uruguay Round, safety and environmental regulation grows in importance for domestic electorates — especially in wealthy countries of the North. Increasingly, different national regulatory priorities will pose problems for trade harmonization, blurring the distinction between domestic and foreign economic policy. Without additional attempts to come to terms with environmental issues through multilateral institutions such as the United Nations, OECD, World Bank, and GATT, differences in national regulatory approaches will bedevil both the environment and the trade system in the next decade and beyond.

The examples cited above demonstrate that environmental regulations are not purely domestic policy issues. As economist Ingo Walter of New York University has written, "the fact of national sovereignty in environmental policy, when coupled with its economic consequences, leads directly to repercussions on international economic relations."[2]

Indeed, there has been longstanding recognition of the possibility of conflicts between national environmental policy and more liberal international trade. The GATT articles, adopted in 1947, explicitly recognize the possibility that domestic health, safety, and environmental policies might override general attempts to lower trade barriers.[3] GATT Article XI headed "General Elimination of Quantitative Restrictions", states in paragraph (1)

> No prohibitions or restrictions other than duties, taxes, or other charges, whether made effective through quotas, import or export licenses or other measures, shall be instituted or maintained by any contracting party on the importation of any product of the territory of any contracting party or on the exportation or sale for export of any product destined for the territory of any other contracting party.

---

[1] Nolan, Hon. Richard and C. Ford Runge, *Trade in Disservices: Environmental and Health Damages in International Trade*, Staff Paper P89-8, February 1989. Department of Agricultural and Applied Economics, University of Minnesota.

[2] Walter, Ingo, *International Economic Repercussions of Environmental Policy: An Economist's Perspective*, in Rubin and Graham, ENVIRONMENT AND TRADE (Rubin & Graham ed.) (Allanheld, Osmun 1982).

[3] JACKSON, J.H., WORLD TRADE AND THE LAW OF GATT (Bobbs-Merrill NY 1969).

Northwestern Journal of International Law & Business 11:47(1990)

Yet Article XX, headed "General Exceptions", provides

> . . .nothing in this Agreement shall be construed to prevent the adoption or enforcement by any contracting part of measures:
>
> . . .(g) relating to the conservation of exhaustible natural resources if such measures are made effective in conjunction with restrictions on domestic production or consumption; provided that such measures:
>
> . . .are not applied in a manner which would constitute a means of arbitrary or unjustifiable discrimination between countries where the same conditions prevail, or a disguised restriction on international trade. . .

A similar set of exceptions is applied to health-related measures under Article XX(b). GATT law emphasizes that any restrictions posed on foreign practices for environmental or health reasons must also reflect a domestic commitment, so that the exceptions cannot be misused as a disguised form of protection.

These attempts in the GATT articles to balance the objectives of more open trade with national sovereignty over environmental and health measures have not successfully defused the problem. Indeed, although tariff barriers, especially in the manufacturing sector, have fallen several-fold since 1947, nontariff barriers have become an increasingly seductive means of protection.[4] Recognizing this problem, in 1971 a special commission (the Williams Commission) sought to identify key areas of potential trade conflict, and to recommend policies to prevent the spread of nontariff protectionism. In that year the Williams Commission recommended that "serious efforts be made to harmonize environmental quality standards to the greatest possible extent". But that goal has been far easier to state than to achieve. Writing in the early 1980's, Rubin and Graham noted that developed countries were moving along a far faster track of environmental regulations than other parts of the world. As they emphasized, a strong political constituency had emerged in the developed countries for environmental standards. Less obvious was the fact that this constituency could also be turned to the purpose of protectionism. "In the United States, and perhaps elsewhere hard political battles to establish environmental standards have recently been fought and won. Proponents of these standards will fight equally hard to prevent their modification to accommodate an international consensus."[5]

At roughly the same time, the Tokyo Round of Multilateral Trade

[4] RUBIN AND GRAHAM, ENVIRONMENT AND TRADE (Allanheld Osmun NJ 1982).

[5] *Id.*

Trade Protectionism
11:47(1990)

Negotiations promulgated a "Standards Code" that has tried (also largely without success) to grapple with the balance between health, safety, and environmental standards and trade liberalization.[6] This 1979 code supplemented the GATT rules that require "national treatment" (no less favorable to importers than to domestic parties) and prohibit the "nullification or impairment" of trade concessions through the back door device of nontariff barriers.[7] The purpose of the Code was to prevent any product, technical, health, safety, or environmental standard from creating "unnecessary obstacles to international trade."[8]

The main principles of the Code are reiterated in United States domestic trade legislation. However, this legislation clearly indicates congressional reluctance to surrender sovereignty over such wide-ranging standards to the GATT or other multilateral bodies. In addition to the usual caveats concerning why international standards may be inappropriate to the United States (e.g. national security), The Trade Agreements Act of 1979[9] explicitly notes in section 402 that the United States may elect nonconformance with international standards in order to assure "the protection of human health or safety, animal or plant life, or health, or the environment."[10]

Despite an additional decade of discussions including substantial attention to both technical standards and nontariff barriers in the Uruguay Round, scheduled to end in 1990, it is still unclear when and where such standards constitute an unnecessary obstacle to international trade. If anything, the temptation to use environmental and health standards to deny access to home markets is stronger now than in the 1980's. As the European Community moves toward its goal of market integration in 1992, it will have strong incentives to create common regulations for internal purposes, but to impose restrictions vis-a-vis the rest of the world. A similar propensity may occur as a result of harmonization under the United States/Canada free trade agreement. However, even if national standards can be harmonized there is every reason to expect subnational jurisdictions to utilize various health and environmental standards to protect certain markets.

6 Code of Conduct for Preventing Technical Barriers to Trade, GATT, Multilateral Trade Negotiations, Doc. MTN/NTM/W1192/Rev. 5; *See Supra* note 4, at 162.

7 *Supra* note 3.

8 *Supra* note 5, at 8.

9 19 U.S.C.S. §§ 2501-2581 (West 1990).

10 *Supra* note 5, at 9.

A. The North/South Gap in Regulation

Underlying the development of these trade tensions are fundamental differences in the views of developed and developing countries (the "North" and "South") concerning the appropriate level and extent of environmental regulation. Differences in the domestic policy response to these problems are well represented in the food systems of the North and South. Since so much recent attention has focused on food and agricultural chemical use in the North, and because the agricultural sector is of key importance in almost all developing economies of the South, it provides a useful case in point.

In the developed countries of North America and Western Europe, the "food problem" arises not from too little food and land in production, but generally too much. As predicted by Engels' Law, the incomes of developed countries have increased, and the share of this income spent on food has fallen in proportion to other goods and services. This characteristic makes food an "inferior good" in economics jargon. In contrast, environmental quality and health concerns have grown in importance with increasing income levels. They are what economists call "superior goods," in the sense that they play a larger role in the national budget as national incomes increase.[11]

In low-income developing countries, while the share of national resources devoted to food and agriculture remains large (creating substantial markets for yield-increasing products), environmental quality and occupational health risks are widely perceived as concerns of the rich. Even if these risks are acknowledged, the income levels of most developing countries do not permit a structure of environmental regulation comparable to that in the North. This two-tiered structure of international environmental regulation, with stricter regulatory regimes in developed countries paired with lax or non-existent regulations in developing countries, increases the North-South flow of environmental risks. A kind of "environmental arbitrage" results, in which profits are gained by exploiting the differential in regulations. This environmental arbitrage results from conscious policy choices that reveal differences in the value attached to environmental quality by rich and poor countries. As these paths of institutional innovation increasingly diverge, so will the differential impact of environmental constraints on producers in the North and competitors in the South such as Argentina and Brazil.[12]

---

[11] Runge, *Induced Agricultural Innovation and Environmental Quality: The Case of Groundwater Regulation*, LAND ECONOMICS at 249-58 (1987).

[12] Runge, Houck, and Halback, *Implications of Environmental Regulations for Competitiveness*

The competitiveness implications of these trends are not lost on Northern producers. They have been quick to see the trade relevance of environmental and health standards. Growing consumer concerns with the health and environmental impacts of agriculture create a natural (and much larger) constituency for nontariff barriers to trade, justified in the name of health and safety. As between countries in the North, obvious differences in values also exist, although the regulatory gap is less yawning.

An example of the problem created by this regulatory gap arises in the agricultural fertilizer and chemical industry. Since World War II, food systems in both the North and South have become increasingly dependent on chemicals and fertilizers in order to raise agricultural productivity. Chemical "inputs" have been responsible for dramatic increases in yields, and have made food an important meeting point for environmental, health, and trade issues. Yet many of the chemical and fertilizer inputs on which agriculture now depends have been found to have health and environmental impacts, especially if poorly managed or inappropriately used. In response, the food systems of developed countries have been constrained by regulations designed to protect environmental quality and human health.

In most developing countries, however, food production and agricultural development remain the primary focus of concern. Because agriculture is a major trade sector, incentives are created to export restricted agricultural and industrial production methods from North to South. In addition, when products produced by methods regulated in the North are imported from the South where such regulation is lax or nonexistent (e.g., Mexican or Chilean fruits and vegetables), competing producers may demand protection. As a specific example, consider the evolution of U.S. policies toward pesticides, herbicides and fungicides. How does the regulatory climate, affecting sales of these chemicals, interact with trade flows in this sector?

U.S. sales of these products grew at an average of 6 percent per year between 1965 and 1974, fluctuated throughout the 1970s, and fell along with farm financial conditions and acreage cut-backs in the 1980s.[13] From the perspective of U.S. industry, softening domestic demand in the 1980s had stimulated a search for foreign marketing opportunities. By 1986, the U. S. pesticide industry exported 34 percent of its total sales

in Agricultural Trade, Chapter 4 in AGRICULTURAL TRADE AND NATURAL RESOURCES: DISCOVERING THE CRITICAL LINKAGES (Boulder and London) (Sutton and Reinner ed. 1988).

13 *See* International Trade Commission, *Synthetic Organic Chemicals*, 1978-86; 1965-78 (USDA 1978); *The Pesticide Review* (U.S. Bureau of the Census Report No.s FT210, FT410, FT610).

Northwestern Journal of
International Law & Business 11:47(1990)

value ($1.4 billion) compared with 26 percent in 1965. Part of the incentive to increase foreign sales arose from the substantial fixed costs of bringing new products to market in the face of internal research and development expenses and U.S. Environmental Protection Agency (EPA) registration requirements. Research and development in the industry is a major expenditure due to specialized personnel, manufacturing specifications, and tight government controls. Large quantities of chemicals must now be screened to find those that target specific markets and conform to environmental regulations.[14]

In 1986, for example, pesticide researchers screened 13,500 compounds for every one registered by the EPA, compared with 5,500 compounds screened per registration in 1967. The time lag between product discovery and marketing likewise rose from an estimated 5 years in 1967 to 10 years in 1986. Anticipated amendments to the Federal Insecticide, Fungicide, and Rodenticide Act (FIFRA), the Safe Drinking Water Act (SDWA) and the 1990 Farm Bill are all likely to effectively constrain agricultural chemical uses.[15]

These are but several examples which may raise the fixed costs of doing business domestically, creating incentives for firms producing fertilizers and chemicals to expand markets where regulatory oversight is less constraining. These fixed costs create powerful motivation, once a chemical is registered and in use, to build long-term markets. If domestic markets tighten due to market or regulatory factors, foreign markets are all the more crucial in spreading these fixed costs over sufficient sales volume. Finally, this process is likely to make entry into the pesticide industry by smaller firms more difficult, concentrating industry activity in larger firms with international marketing strategies.

Studies examining the general impact of environmental regulations on the location decisions of major industries have been relatively inconclusive, although there is a growing evidence that the regulatory gap between North and South will have long-term implications for both environmental and trade policy. As Walter noted, ". . . environmental factors may gradually take on greater importance in the decisions and planning of multinational firms, so that the international locational effects on industry of differential environmental policies throughout the

[14] Swanson and Dahl, *The U.S. Pesticide Industry: Usage Trends and Market Development*, Staff Paper P89—5, January 1989, Department of Agricultural and Applied Economics, University of Minnesota.

[15] Batie, *Agriculture as the Problem: The Case of Groundwater Contamination*, CHOICES (3rd Quarter, 1988); Benbrook, *The Environment and the 1990 Farm Bill*, J. SOIL AND WATER CONSERV. (November-December 1988).

decision system of international firms may take on somewhat greater significance in the years ahead."[16] Of perhaps even more importance will be the response of farmers and others in both developed and developing countries for whom relocation is *not* an option. In the North, these producers will have an incentive to raise protectionist nontariff barriers in the name of health, safety and the environment, while in the South, they may be compelled to suffer higher risks in order to maintain competitive advantage.

Increasing production and consumption of chemicals in the food industry over the last forty years have thus created a flow of trade that is both beneficial and fraught with risks. Despite current criticism of their use in agriculture, these products have been responsible for much of the global increase in agricultural output, without which billions of people would be both poorer and more hungry than they are today. In the postwar period, gains in food production throughout the developed and developing world have been powered by significantly increased applications of these products. But this trend has been accompanied by growing concern over environmental impacts. The point is not to end the use of these chemicals, but to use them responsibly and knowledgeably.[17]

To do so immediately raises the question of regulatory standards affecting their use. Modern chemical inputs require substantially more information to use safely and effectively, and such standards are complicated both to develop and to apply. Especially in the South, the inputs themselves are aggressively marketed and subsidized, yet farm-level education (including the basic literacy necessary to read package instructions) is seldom given comparable attention. Yet the absence of such standards exacts a high toll. Human poisoning in developing countries due to overapplication of pesticides is common. For example, per capita pesticide poisonings in the seven countries of Central America are 1,800 times higher than in the United States, according to Jeffrey Leonard of the Conservation Foundation.[18] How are standards to be developed that reflect the North's concerns with environmental quality, while attending to the different needs and priorities of the South?

Given the tension separating North and South, and the lesser differences between countries in the North, it would appear that a single set of

---

16 Walter, *International Economic Repercussions of Environmental Policy: An Economist's Perspective*, in Seymour and Rubin, ENVIRONMENT AND TRADE (Allaneld, Osmun, N.J. 1982).

17 Baanante, Bumb, & Thompson, *The Benefits of Fertilizer Use in Developing Countries*, International Fertilizer Development Center, Muscle Shoals, Alabama (1989).

18 Leonard, *Remedies are Available for Latin America's Environmental Ills*, CONSERVATION FOUNDATION LETTER, No. 2 (1989).

Northwestern Journal of
International Law & Business 11:47(1990)

standards is unlikely to be successful. The Subsidies Code adopted during the Tokyo Round is at least a necessary staring point, but some mechanism must be found to accommodate differences in national priorities linked to levels of economic development and cultural factors.

B. Determining When a Standard Is an "Unnecessary Obstacle to Trade"

How might such standards be developed? Consider a 1989 case heard by a panel convened under the U.S./Canada Free Trade Agreement.[19] The case involved a panel established to hear testimony over Canadian restrictions on exports of Pacific Coast unprocessed salmon and herring. Such restrictions date to 1908, but were found illegal under GATT in 1987 after the United States complained that they were unjustifiable restrictions on trade. In 1988, Canada accepted the GATT finding, but stated that it would continue a "landing" requirement for foreign boats which would allow inspection of their catch. The ostensible reason for the requirement was an environmental one: to allow the fish harvest to be counted and monitored so as to preserve the fishery from overexploitation.

According to the United States, the requirement that its boats must land in Canada constituted an export restriction, because of the extra time and expense U.S. buyers must incur in landing and unloading, as well as due to dockage fees and product deterioration. The Canadians held that they were pursuing "conservation and management goals" for five varieties of salmon (some of which had previously not been covered by the landing requirement) as well as herring. Essentially, the Canadians sought to justify under Article XX of the GATT (the "General Exceptions" section noted above) what had otherwise been found GATT-illegal, by appealing to an environmental claim under Article XX(g): conservation of exhaustible natural resources.

The U.S. argued that although the new herring and salmon regulations "are carefully worded to avoid the appearance of creating direct export prohibitions or restrictions, their clear effect is to restrict exports".[20] Moreover, the Canadian landing requirement was argued not to be "primarily aimed" at the conservation of herring and salmon stocks, which had been the interpretation given to Article XX(g) by the 1987 GATT ruling. Thus, the United States held that the Canadian landing requirement was an environmental policy acting as a disguised

19 McRae, *Canada's Landing Requirements for Pacific Coast Salmon and Herring*, (1989).
20 *Id.* at 13.

restriction on international trade. Canada argued that the landing requirement was "primarily aimed" at the conservation of the salmon and herring fisheries.

In a significant decision, the Panel found that if the effect of such a measure is to impose a "materially greater commercial burden on exports than on domestic sales," it amounted to a restriction on trade, whether or not its trade effects could be quantitatively demonstrated. The Panel "was satisfied that the cost of complying with the landing requirement would be more than an insignificant expense for those buyers who would have otherwise shipped directly from the fishing ground to a landing site in the United States."[21] With regard to the Article XX(g) exception, the Panel was conscious "of the need to allow governments appropriate latitude in implementing their conservation policies," and that the trade interests of one state should not be allowed to override the "legitimate environmental concerns of another."[22] "If the measure would have been adopted for conservation reasons alone," the Panel found, "Article XX(g) permits a government the freedom to employ it." However, balancing this is the "primarily aimed at" test, which determines whether the measure is part of a genuine conservation or environmental policy, or is in fact a disguised barrier to trade.

This line of reasoning led the Panel to two conclusions. First, "since governments do not adopt conservation measures unless the benefits to conservation are worth the costs," the magnitude of costs to the parties— foreign and domestic—who actually bear them must be examined." Second, "how genuine the conservation purpose of a measure is, must be determined by whether the government would have been prepared to adopt that measure *if its own nationals had to bear the actual costs of the measure*."[23] In this case, the Panel was unconvinced that the measure would have been imposed on all Canadian boats primarily for conservation reasons. Specifically, the Panel found that Canada would not have adopted such a measure "if it had required an equivalent number of Canadian buyers to land and unload elsewhere than at their intended destination."[24] Alternative methods of monitoring catch rates were available which posed far fewer restrictions on trade.

Generalizing from this case, it seems possible to envision the development of criteria based on (a) estimated costs of health, safety and environmental regulations; (b) evidence on who bears these costs; and (c)

21 *Id.* at 25.
22 *Id.* at 29.
23 *Id.* at 31 (emphasis added).
24 *Id.* at 32.

judgments of whether such measures would be imposed *in the absence of any trade effects*. Such criteria can serve as a basis for the development of standards determining which environmental and health measures constitute unnecessary obstacles to trade.

Consider a specific example arising from the 1989 United States decision to embargo Chilean fruit and vegetable imports after traces of cyanide were found in two grapes. Would the costs imposed on Chile by a complete embargo have been imposed on domestic U.S. interests if two California grapes had been adulterated? In estimating these costs, and their trade effects, differences in national levels of living must also come into play. Since Canadian and U.S. fishing interests are in the main a homogeneous group, the problem does not arise. Where the measures promulgated in one country loom much larger in relation to incomes in another (e.g., Chile and the United States), an *a priori* argument for a differentiated approach exists.

In view of differences in levels of economic development and national priorities, it is clear that standards cannot be wholly uniform. Jeffrey James, in *The Economics of New Technology in Developing Countries*,[25] suggests that despite valid arguments for improved health and environmental regulations in the South, "it does not follow from this that countries of the Third World should adopt either the same *number* or the same *level* of standards as developed countries." James suggests what may be called *intermediate* standards, "in the same sense and for the same basic reasons as that which underlies the widespread advocacy of inter-mediate technology in the Third World." This does not imply a "downgrading" of U.S. regulations, but an "upgrading" of developing countries' norms, together with the recognition that the social costs of regulation are relative to national income.

Under GATT law, these distinctions are recognized as "Special and Differential Treatment" of lower income countries. While "S&D" often creates serious long run distortions, the terms under which it is granted, as James emphasizes, may actually reduce current regulatory differentials by raising norms in the South, thus improving developing countries' environmental policies. While this may not satisfy all competing producers in the North, it can contribute to reductions in overall trade tension while improving environmental quality in the South.

---

[25] James, The Economics of New Technology in Developing Countries (Stewart and James eds. 1982).

Trade Protectionism
11:47(1990)

III. Conclusion: Toward Activist Multilateral Environmental Policies

The global consequences of failure to confront these complex problems are increasingly clear, in both environmental and trade terms. The Brundtland Commission Report, undertaken by the United Nations and the World Commission on Environment and Development, has underscored the need for international action on a wide range of environmental issues.[26] Despite such calls to action, little has yet been done to move effectively to reduce environmental and health hazards at the international level, and to coordinate environmental and trade policy through GATT, the World Bank, and other multilateral institutions.

Environmental risks traded across national borders require international policy responses. The World Bank has recently raised the profile of environmental issues in project planning and appraisal. But many, both inside and outside the Bank, are skeptical of the commitment. It is vital that the United States government, as a principal financial supporter, emphasize the seriousness of the issues to Bank staff. Similarly, United States activities in U.N. agencies such as the Food and Agriculture Organization (FAO) and U.N. Environmental Program (UNEP) need to place environmental needs in developing countries far higher on the agenda than in the past. By raising the level of environmental standards in the South, the gap in regulations with the North will be reduced, easing trade tensions.

Unfortunately, despite recent attempts to deal with these issues in forums such as GATT, the linkages from environmental regulation to international trade have not been clearly recognized. The Food and Agriculture Organization of the United Nations has worked to develop comprehensive rules affecting food and agricultural health and safety, called the "Codex Alimentarius."[27] A special technical working group at the GATT Secretariat in Geneva is attempting to use this code as the basis for harmonizing member countries' regulations. Unfortunately, there are no agreed-upon standards except for a few items, and none are regarded as binding in law. With the exception of the beleaguered GATT working group, the issue has not been given priority by international institutions.

Beyond environmental considerations are shorter term problems of trade distortion and market access. These distortions threaten more lib-

[26] World Commission on Environment and Development, Our Common Future (Oxford University Press 1987).

[27] Food and Agriculture Organization, *Introducing Codex Alimentarius*, FAO/WHO Food Standards Program (Rome 1987).

eral international trade in ways that are damaging to both developed and developing country interests. In spite of the vital importance of environmental quality, as well as more open trade, to developed country interests, those industries most clearly victimized by the changing structure of environmental regulations in the North are likely either to resist environmental regulatory reform, or to demand import protection from countries that do not face similar constraints. In periods when rapid growth in trade is one of the only avenues out of debt and deficits (for both the North and the South), these distortions cannot be dismissed as unimportant.

Given the complexity of formulating international approaches to environmental and trade policies, it is understandable that some have argued for loosening the environmental regulatory constraints affecting industry in order to allow it to compete more effectively in global markets. However, this appears to be inconsistent with the growing importance attached to the environment and health in the political processes of all countries. Yet tight regulatory constraints in developed economies *do* have cost and competitiveness implications. The perception that foreign competition does not face similar constraints breeds animosity and protectionism. Both at home and internationally, environmental standards must therefore be strengthened.

The key is to recognize the inherently international character of environmental quality and health—issues which are similar in nature to human rights. Only the force of international standards defining the duties of nations, corporations and individuals, can hope to resolve these difficult issues. This does not, as I have emphasized, suggest that these standards cannot be sensitive to levels of development.

To begin this process, the United States must take the lead in urging existing multilateral institutions to coordinate their efforts. Some of this coordination is underway. The GATT, IMF and World Bank, for example, have agreed to work more closely on issues of trade, aid and development. The use of environmental and health regulations as trade barriers would provide an especially appropriate focal point for these efforts.

In addition to the development of carefully reasoned legal arguments determining when environmental and health standards are in fact trade barriers, an international accord on environmental and health regulations would be appropriate. Similar in nature to the 1988 Montreal Protocol agreed to by 40 nations to reduce emissions shown harmful to the ozone layer, its purpose would be primarily invocational—to call for the rights, duties and liabilities that define national regulations on environment and health—which can then be brought more nearly into ac-

Trade Protectionism
11:47(1990)

cord. In absence of such an agreement, groups within nations will continue to advocate the use of regulations as disguised protectionism, or loosening standards of environmental quality in the name of greater competitiveness.

[17]

DAVID VOGEL

Environmental Protection and the Creation of a Single European Market

Introduction

This article examines the efforts of the European Community (EC) to balance two objectives: the creation of a single European market, and the improvement of environmental quality in its member states. The first section presents an overview of the development of EC environmental policy from the 1960s to the present; the second explores the development of a number of Community environment regulations which directly affect intra-Community trade. Specifically, we examine product regulations for automobile emissions.

The issue of auto emissions illustrates the uneasy relationship between economic integration and the improvement of environmental quality. Through the mid-1980s, the Community generally favored the former goal over the latter; national governments were frequently forbidden from enacting stricter environmental regulations than those of other member states in order to prevent the emergence of non-tariff barriers. The passage of the Single European Act brought a more equal balance between the two: the EC's commitment to create a single European market has, on balance, significantly strengthened European environmental standards. More recently, the balance appears to be shifting even further: the EC now appears willing, or at least reconciled, to sacrifice some degree of integration in the interests of environmental protection.

Environmental Regulation under the Treaty of Rome

While the word "environment" does not appear in the 1957 Treaty of Rome which established the European Community, the Community began, during the mid-1960s, to recognize that establishing a common market required the enactment of common environmental regulations. The EC adopted its first environmental directive in 1967, establishing standards for classifying, packaging, and labelling dangerous substances. Three years later the Council approved a directive on automotive emissions. In October 1972, at the Paris Summit, the EC Heads of State issued a communique stating that economic

---

This article is part of a forthcoming book-length study of the relationship between government regulation and international trade.

David Vogel is professor in the Graduate School of Business Administration at the University of California and editor of the California Management Review.

expansion was "not an end in itself," and that economic growth should be linked to the "improvement in living and working conditions of life of the citizens of the EC,"—a phrase taken from the Preamble to the Rome Treaty.[1] The summit called upon the Commission to draw up a Community environmental policy and authorized the European Commission to establish a separate administrative body or directorate whose responsibilities included environmental protection.

The following year, the Council of Ministers adopted the EC's first official environmental program. Based on Article 2 of the Treaty of Rome, which defined one of the Community's objectives as the promotion of "a harmonious development of economic activities," the EC's "action plan" stated that "major aspects of environmental policy in individual countries must no longer be planned or implemented in isolation ... and national policies should be harmonized within the community."[2]

The EC's environmental policy, according to the plan, would be guided by three objectives or principles.[3] The first was to reduce and prevent pollution by "developing protective measures" and by requiring that the "polluter pay." The second principle stated that both national and Community regulations should seek to protect the environment as well as improve the quality of life. Third, the Community pledged its support for "international initiatives" to address environmental problems that could not be adequately addressed on either a regional or national basis.

The Community's Second Environmental Action Program, adopted in 1977, restated and extended these aims, stressing the need for additional research and data collection, and expressing the EC's intention of developing a system of environmental-impact assessment. The Community's Third Program, approved in 1983, reflected growing concern about unemployment and resource depletion: it emphasized the role of environmental regulation in both preserving scarce resources for future use and "creating employment by developing environmentally compatible industries and technologies."[4] It also shifted the Community's priorities from pollution reduction to pollution prevention.

Each of these three action plans was accompanied by a steady expansion in the scope of Community environmental regulations. Between the early 1970s and the mid-1980s, the Community issued 120 regulations and directives. (A regulation is directly applicable to all member states and thus automatically becomes part of national law. A directive establishes a framework for national policies; it only becomes effective after member states have enacted legislation implementing it. Directives generally specify the result to be achieved, relying upon national authorities to determine the means and mechanisms of implementation. Most EC environmental rules are directives.)

The EC's environmental policies enacted during this fifteen-year period covered a wide range of areas: the regulation of air, water, noise pollution, and waste disposal; the prevention of accidents; safety requirements for chemicals; environmental impact assessment; and wildlife and habitat protection. By the mid-1980s, virtually all aspects of national environmental policy had been addressed, in one form or other, at the Community level.[5] In many critical areas of environmental policymaking Brussels had come to play as important a role as any nation-state.

The growth of EC environmental regulation during the 1970s was due to various factors. EC environmental policy was in part a response to the increase in public concern throughout the industrialized world, during the late 1960s and early 1970s, about environmental issues. A 1973 survey taken in the then nine EC member states reported that "pollution was cited as the most important problem, ahead of inflation, poverty, and unemployment."[6] Political developments in Europe also played an important role. Environmental organizations became more active politically in a number of European countries, and most national governments significantly expanded and strengthened the scope of their own regulatory controls over industry.

In order to preserve their legitimacy, EC institutions attempted to respond to these new political forces and public pressures by enacting environmental regulations as well. EC environmental policy represented a way for Community officials to address the "democratic deficit": the gap between the Community's power and its lack of accountability to the electorate of its member states. At the same time, environmental policymaking provided a way for officials in Brussels to preserve the momentum of European integration, which in other respects had stagnated during the 1970s. Indeed, the steady pace of environmental regulations, directives, and decisions enacted during this period stands in sharp contrast to the "political vicissitudes, budgetary crises, and recurrent waves of Europepessimisn of the 1970s and early 1980s."[7]

Economic considerations also contributed to the expansion of EC environmental regulation. The expansion of *national* environmental regulation posed a serious economic threat to both the creation and maintenance of a common market. If nations were allowed to adopt their own product standards, such as ones regarding the safety of chemicals or emissions from vehicles, nations with stricter environmental standards would then likely to attempt "protect" both their citizens and their industries by excluding goods produced in member states with weaker regulatory requirements. Consequently, the free flow of goods within the EC would be impaired.

In the case of production standards, nations that had adopted more stringent pollution controls than other member states would find the goods produced by their industries placed at a competitive disadvantage. They would therefore find themselves forced to chose between excluding goods produced by member states with weaker regulatory requirements or lowering their own standards to those of other EC member states. The former course would threaten economic integration; the latter would make national regulatory policies hostage to those of the least strict member state.

A third motivation for EC environmental policy was geographic. The twelve nations of the EC comprise a large land-area—roughly 1.6 million square kilometers—and encompass a considerable diversity of climate and topography. The environmental problems of nations on the periphery of the Community, such as Greece and the Netherlands, have little in common with each other, and neither nation's environmental policies affect the citizens of the other.

However, a number of member states are physically close to one another and the quality of their physical environment, as well as the health of their population, is significantly affected by the environmental policies of their neighbors. For example, the Rhine flows west through three EC member states—Germany, France, and the Netherlands; accordingly the quality of Dutch water is largely determined by the severity of German and French pollution controls. On the other hand, because winds in Europe travel from west to east, the air quality in northern Europe is affected by industrial emissions from Britain. As one journalist observed, "Environmental regulations are among the world's toughest in ... West Germany and the Netherlands. But that does little good when winds waft Britain's loosely regulated power-plant fumes and their product, acid rain, eastward."[8] Equally importantly, industrial accidents do not respect national boundaries.

A number of important EC environmental initiatives reflect the high degree of physical interdependence among the Community's members. For example, the "Seveso Directive" was adopted in 1982 following a major industrial accident in Italy that unleashed large quantities of the chemical dioxin into the atmosphere. The directive addressed the issue of accident prevention and required industries to prepare safety reports and emergency response plans. The EC's Directive on the Conservation of Wild Birds, adopted in 1979, required member states "to preserve, maintain or reestablish a sufficient diversity and area of habitats for birds," many of which migrated across national boundaries.[9] And following the disclosure that forty-one drums of waste from Seveso which had been lost in transit had been found in the French countryside, a directive was approved that established a system for controlling and regulating the collection and disposal of hazardous wastes moving across frontiers.

For all these reasons—political, economic,

and geographic—the Community attempted to harmonize a wide range of national environmental regulations. Not surprisingly, this effort led to considerable conflict between those nations that favored stricter environmental standards and those that did not. The former, most notably Germany, Denmark, and the Netherlands, were relatively affluent and had strong domestic environmental movements. Other nations, such as Great Britain, France, and Italy, had weaker environmental pressure groups and their industries were less willing or able to absorb the costs of stricter environmental controls. Still others, such as Greece and Spain, were even less interested in Community air and water-quality standards. Not only were they relatively poor, but they were physically distant from the "core" of the EC and thus unaffected by acid-rain emissions or the quality of the EC's major rivers. Further complicating agreement was the requirement of the Treaty of Rome that all directives be approved unanimously.

Thus it took the Community five years before it could reach agreement on a directive reducing emissions of sulphur dioxide.[10] The positions of the member states fell into four groups. West Germany, the Netherlands, and Denmark were prepared to spend substantial sums on retrofitting their existing plants. However, less affluent Britain and Italy, whose power plants burned considerable quantities of coal, were not. France and Belgium were relatively indifferent to sulphur-emission standards since they relied heavily on nuclear power. Most of the remaining nations were not interested in the directive since they were not affected by acid rain in the first place.

The Large Combustion Directive, which was finally approved in June 1988, advanced a rather complex formula to reconcile these differences. Emissions of sulphur dioxide would be reduced in three stages—1993, 1998, and 2003—while nitrogen oxide emissions would be reduced in two stages. In addition, the percentage reductions of each pollutant for each stage varied by country. Thus Belgium, Germany, France, the Netherlands, and Luxembourg were required to reduce their sulphur-dioxide emissions by 40 percent by 1993. On the other hand, Spain was not required to reduce its emissions at all while Portugal was permitted to increase its emissions.

The form of pollution control also led to disputes among the member states. For example, most nations favored uniform emission standards for water pollutants, since that would impose roughly similar costs on firms throughout the EC. The British, however, argued that since their rapidly flowing rivers could absorb relatively large amounts of pollution without impairing water quality, uniform emission standards were inappropriate; they instead favored water-quality standards. "As one British official put it, 'Italy economically benefits from the amount of sunshine it receives each year. Why should not our industry be able to take similar advantage of our long coastline ... and rapidly flowing waters?' "[11] Once again the result was a complex compromise: the emissions of highly hazardous substances would be controlled by uniform emission standards, while less dangerous substances would be regulated by water-quality standards.

Notwithstanding the steady growth of EC environmental regulation, the legal basis of EC environmental policy remained somewhat tenuous. Most Community environmental policy could be justified under Article 100 of the Treaty, which authorized the harmonization of all national regulations that directly affected the functioning or establishment of a common market. However in a number of cases, the link between EC environmental regulations and the common market was less clear.

What, for example, did establishing EC standards for drinking or bathing-water quality have to do with economic integration? Why should the Community require the member states to protect wild birds? To justify its environmental regulations in these areas, the EC was forced to rely upon Article 235 of the Treaty, which authorized legislation not envisaged elsewhere if it was "necessary to attain ... one of the objectives of the Community."[12] Since the Preamble to the Treaty of Rome had declared that improving the "living and working conditions of life of the citizens of the EC" was a legitimate Community objective, it presumably followed that the EC could legislate on any aspect of the environment that it chose. Not surprisingly, this somewhat strained legal defense was not entirely persuasive.[13]

Moreover, the Treaty of Rome, by not explicitly mentioning environmental protection, provided no framework for EC policymakers to balance environmental protection with other EC goals, the most important of which was obviously the creation of the common market itself. Virtually any level of environmental regulation was compatible with increased economic integration, providing that it was decided at the Community level. Accordingly, several observers argued that many EC directives tended to reflect the "least common denominator" and that therefore the Community had, in effect, subordinated environmental goals to the creation of a common market.

The Single European Act

On July 1, 1987, the Treaty of Rome was revised by the Single European Act (SEA). While the most important purpose of this amendment to the Community's constitution was to facilitate the creation of a single European market, it also introduced important changes into Community environmental policy and policymaking.

Most importantly, Article 100A of the SEA explicitly recognized the improvement of environmental quality as a legitimate Community objective in its own right. This meant that EC environmental policies need no longer be justified in terms of their contribution to economic integration. The EC now had a firm constitutional basis for regulating any aspect of the environment. Even more importantly, the SEA stated that in harmonizing national regulations, "the Commission ... will take as a base a high level of [environmental] protection." Thus harmonization was associated with the improvement of environmental quality, rather than with, as under the Treaty of Rome, only economic integration.

Article 130R further declared that "environmental protection requirements shall be a component of the Community's other policies."[14] This provision accorded environmental protection an unusually high priority among the Community's objectives, since no other EC goal was granted a commensurate provision. In practical terms, it strengthened the hands of the Commission's Environmental Directorate (DG XI) in its conflicts with those Directorates whose focus was essentially economic.

To reassure those member states who feared that harmonization would require them to relax existing national regulations, both Article 100A and 130T explicitly granted member states the right to maintain or introduce national environmental standards stricter than those approved by Brussels, provided they did not constitute a form of "hidden protectionism" and were otherwise compatible with the Treaty of Rome.[15] The determination as to whether a national regulation that affected the completion of the internal market created an open or disguised barrier to trade was left up to the European Court of Justice.[16]

The Single European Act also facilitated the adoption of environmental regulations by the Council. Prior to 1987, all Community legislation had to be approved unanimously. Also, legislation approved under Article 130, the SEA's environmental article, still required unanimity. However, under Article 100A—which provides for the approximation of laws concerned with the functioning of the common market—the SEA permitted the approval of directives by a "qualified majority," defined as fifty-four of seventy-six votes. This provided an alternative means for enacting environmental legislation, one which deprived any single member state of the power to block approval. (In fact, virtually all environmental directives enacted since the passage of the SEA have been based on 100A.)

The Single European Act also expanded the role of the European Parliament (EP), which has generally been more supportive of stricter environmental standards than the Council, in shaping Community legislation. For ten articles of the EC Treaty, the SEA established a "cooperation procedure" under which Parliament has the right to propose amendments to legislation approved by the Council of Ministers. If the Commission chooses to retain these amendments, then the Council must then either reject them unanimously or adopt them by a qualified majority.

The SEA also contributed to the strengthening of EC environmental policy in another, more indirect, way. A primary purpose of the new Community treaty was to accelerate the move toward the creation of a single internal market—a goal which had been formally outlined in a Commission White Paper issued a few years earlier. However, Community officials recognized that the removal of all barriers to intra-Community trade by the end of 1992 was also likely to exacerbate Europe's environmental problems. A report entitled, *"1992" the Environmental Dimension*, released in 1989, examined some of the adverse environmental consequences of the completion of the internal market. The most important of these was a dramatic increase in transportation, which would significantly increase emissions of both sulphur dioxide and nitrogen oxides. In addition, economic integration, by accelerating intracommunity trade, increased the exposure of member states to the import of environmental "bads" such as toxic and hazardous wastes from other member states. Thus the Community's renewed commitment to economic integration made the strengthening of EC environmental standards even more urgent.

The strengthening of environmental protection within the Community's constitution both reflected and reinforced a major heightening of public concern with environmental issues occurring throughout Europe during the latter part of the 1980s. Stimulated in part by the Soviets' Chernobyl disaster and a massive chemical spill of toxins into the Rhine River that destroyed a half million fish in four countries—events that took place in 1986—environmental issues moved rapidly to a prominent position on the political agenda in a number of EC member states. The *Washington Post* observed:

> Dead seals in the North Sea, a chemical fire on the Loire, killer algae off the coast of Sweden, contaminated drinking water in Cornwall (England). A drumbeat of emergencies has intensified the environmental debate this year in Europe, where public concern about pollution has never been higher.[17]

A poll taken in December 1986 reported that 52 percent of the Germany electorate regarded environment quality as the most important issue facing their nation.[18] In 1987, the German Green Party received 8.3 percent of the votes cast for the Bundestag and increased their number of seats in the legislative body of the Federal Republic to forty-two. More significantly, in European Parliament elections held in June 1989, Europe's Green parties captured an additional seventeen seats, bringing their total representation to thirty-seven and placing them among the biggest "winners" of the first "European" election held after the enactment of the SEA. An EC official publication observed in 1990 that,

> Major disasters (and) global problems like ozone depletion and the greenhouse effect, and quality of life issues such as drinking water and air pollution have all contributed in recent years to a 'greening' of European public opinion, to a widening consensus in flavor of 'cleaner' and more sustainable economic growth.[19]

A survey published by the EC in 1989, reported "strong support for a common EC-wide approach to environmental protection."[20]

Since the passage of SEA, the "momentum for environmental protection [has] accelerated dramatically."[21] Between 1989 and 1991, the EC enacted more environmental legislation than in the previous twenty years combined. "It now has over 450 regulations in effect and is adding new ones at a rate of about 100 a year."[22] Not only have many EC standards been significantly strengthened—in some cases approaching American ones—but the EC has also come to play a leadership role in the making of global environmental policy. One example concerns the protection of the ozone layer. In 1987, thirty-one nations, including the EC, signed the Montreal Protocols in which they pledged to reduce the production of chlorofluorocarbons by 50 percent by the end of the century. In March 1989, the EC went a step further: it announced that its member states had agred to cut production of this chemical by 85 percent as soon as possible and to eliminate production entirely by the year 2000.

That same year, the European Council voted to create a European Environmental Agency, though to date it has not been established due to disagreement over where it will be located. The agency is not to make or enforce EC environmental policy; rather it is to seive as a central information clearinghouse and a coordinator for national centers of environmental monitoring and evaluation.

Environmental Regulation and Economic Integration

Environmental regulations primarily affect EC economic integration in one of two ways: indirectly through production standards which alter the relative costs of production among EC member states, or directly though product standards, which may make intra-Community trade more difficult. A detailed study of EC environmental policy concerning automobile emissions falls into the latter category, and illustrates the complex dynamics of the relationship between free trade, or economic integration, and environmental regulation.

Automobile Emissions

One of the most important and contentious EC environmental policy disputes has been over automotive emission standards. The Community's nearly twenty-year effort to develop common standards for both car emissions and fuel content illustrates some of the difficulties of reconciling environmental protection and economic integration. The design and performance of automobiles, which are among the EC's most widely traded goods, have historically been heavily influenced by national regulations for approval of new motor vehicles in order to create a single market for automobiles.

While motor vehicles are sold throughout the EC, significant automobile manufacturing takes place in only seven of the Community's twelve member states. Germany, France, Italy, and Great Britain have their own national car industries, and a number of both European and U.S. multinationals have production facilities in the Netherlands, Spain, and Belgium. The former nations tend to identify closely with the economic interests of their domestic firms, which in turn has made agreement on Community-wide standards both time-consuming and difficult. In the case of emissions control, there is a further complication: the political strength of environmental movements varies considerably. Support for strict emissions controls has been strongest in Denmark, the Netherlands, and Germany, while green movements have enjoyed much less influence in Great Britain, Italy, and France.

In 1970, the European Community, like the United States, established emission levels for carbon monoxide and unburnt hydrocarbons. Four years later, the EC also imposed restrictions on emissions of nitrogen oxides. All three standards were tightened in 1977, 1978, and 1983. However, unlike the United States, which had imposed uniform national standards (with the exception of California, which was permitted to exceed them by an amount specified by Congress), the EC opted for "optional harmonization by setting maximum requirements and leaving member states the power to allow operation of vehicles on their territory that do not meet the EEC emission standards."[23] Thus, while member states were not required to impose the EC's standards on cars sold within their borders, they were permitted to do so. At the same time, they were obligated to permit the sale of any cars that did meet the EC's minimum standards. The EC's standards thus functioned more as a ceiling than a floor: no member nation was permitted to unilaterally impose stricter standards than that specified in the directives.

Nevertheless, because of the export-oriented nature of Europe's car industry, auto producers had a strong incentive to comply with Community standards. Thus, in fact, the agreement approximated "a system of total harmonization."[24] Moreover, as the standards became progressively stricter, nations which wished to place stronger controls of vehicular emissions were gradually permitted to do so.

Through 1983, the establishment of EC emission standards had a relatively low political profile within the Community. Indeed, the Community itself did not initially develop its own emission standards. Rather, the EC essentially adopted the standards established by the U.N. Economic Commission for Europe, a European-wide standards body headquartered in Geneva. These standards applied equally to EC member states as well as to members of the European Free Trade Association (EFTA).

By contrast, the EC's initial efforts to regulate the content of motor fuel were a source of considerable conflict. By the late 1960s, there was growing evidence that airborne lead—a significant proportion of which came from motor vehicles—threatened childrens' mental development. As a result, two member states began to restrict the lead content of gasoline sold within their borders. In 1972, the German government announced a two-stage reduction: it set the maximum lead content for gasoline at .4 grams per liter for 1972 and .15 for 1976; the latter level was chosen because it represented the lowest amount of lead content that did not require changes in engine design. The British established less severe limits on the lead content of petrol: in 1972 Parliament limited lead to .84 grams per liter. Other EC member nations imposed no restrictions.

The resulting disparity in national rules and regulations presented an "obstacle to the free movement of both fuel and motor vehicles within the Community."[25] Not only did these divergent national product regulations limit intra-EC trade in gasoline, but, even more importantly, since different car engines were designed to run on fuels containing different amounts of lead, they created potential non-tariff barriers to trade in motor vehicles.

In December 1973, the Commission forwarded to the Council a directive that sought to establish a uniform standard for the lead content of gasoline sold anywhere in the Community. The Commission was motivated not only by the need to prevent technical barriers to trade, but also by an internal committee report that had concluded: "although there was no immediate danger for public health, it was desirable to prevent an increase in air pollution by lead and hence to limit lead because of the increase in car use."[26]

The debate over the lead directive was dominated by Germany, which was reluctant to weaken its standard in the interests of economic integration. As the debate proceeded, other nations tightened their standards; for example, in 1978 the British adopted a phased reduction to .45. However agreement on a single, uniform standard proved impossible. Eventually, after prolonged negotiations, the Community agreed to, "accommodate the decisions the Germans had already made."[27] Accordingly, in 1978, a directive was approved establishing both maximum and minimum standards. The former was set at .4; the latter at .15 grams per liter—"in view of the situation in Germany where lead content had already been reduced to 0.15 grams per litre."[28]

The inclusion of a lower limit for the lead content of gasoline was added at the initiative of the British government, which wanted to insure that "no barriers to trade in motor cars would be created by any one Member State insisting on lead free petrol."[29] Thus the final form of this directive had as much, if not more, to do with preventing trade barriers as with reducing lead emissions. At the time of its adoption, the Commission stated that its long-term goal was to impose further restrictions on lead emissions from motor vehicles, but to do so in such a way as to not create additional trade barriers within the EC.

As the visibility of environmental issues increased in Europe during the first half of the 1980s, the EC found itself under increased pressure to enact new restrictions on automobile emissions. In 1984, the Commission presented to the Council two new, related directives on automobile emissions.

One dealt with lead, the other with motor vehicle pollutants. The former proposed the total elimination of lead from gasoline; the latter required a further 70 percent reduction in CO, HC, and NOX emissions. The two were linked, since the EC's proposed emissions standards required that all new cars be equipped with catalytic converters. Vehicles equipped with converters in turn required unleaded gasoline, while unleaded gasoline could only be used in engines equipped with converters.

The Council's proposal on emissions marked a significant departure in EC environmental policy-making. For the first time the EC was attempting to formulate its own distinctive body of regulation for automobile emissions, rather than, as in the past, adopting European-wide standards. Equally importantly, the EC's proposed new emission standards were as strict as those of the United States. (Significantly, several EFTA countries had recently broken from the EEC and adopted standards modeled on those of the United States.) Subsequently the American standards of 1983—widely referred to as "US '83"—became an important reference point for the debate over automobile emissions in Europe.

The adoption of a new directive on the lead content of gasoline proved relatively straightforward; only six months elapsed between the Commission proposal and the adoption of a directive by the Council. The Council's 1985 directive on lead in gasoline maintained the maximum and minimum standards enacted seven years earlier. However, it contained two additional provisions. First, it urged each member state to achieve the .15 level as soon as possible. Second, the directive required all member states to offer at least some unleaded gasoline for sale beginning in October 1989. The delay was intended to give the petroleum and automobile industries sufficient time to make the necessary design changes, although the voluntary introduction of lead-free gasoline was permitted prior to the October 1 deadline.

The EC's endorsement of the goal of unleaded gasoline represented a major change in Community policy. It was due primarily to three factors. First, European environmentalists had become increasingly critical of the EC's prohibition of national legislation requiring lead content below 0.15 grams per liter. In June, 1983, the European Parliament had approved a resolution urging that this restriction be ended and this in turn put considerable pressure on the Commission.

Second, following the recommendation of the Royal Commission on Environmental Pollution in June 1983, the British government reversed its previous opposition to lead-free petrol. Persuaded by the arguments of CLEAR, the "Campaign for Lead-Free Air," a coalition of environmental, public-health and social-welfare organizations which had been campaigning for the abolition of lead in gasoline since 1981, it now urged the Council to permit member states to require the removal of lead from gasoline. Third, the British position coincided with that of Germany, which favored lead-free gasoline, though for a rather different reason: the new emission requirements that Germany wanted the Community to adopt required the use of catalytic converters, which in turn required that unleaded gasoline be made widely available throughout the EC. Otherwise how would German tourists be able to drive to (and from) Greece for their summer vacations?

The Luxembourg Compromise

Agreement on new automotive emission standards proved much more difficult. The Council's proposed emissions guidelines were designed "so that the[ir] effect on the European environment [would] be equivalent to that produced by U.S. standards."[30] But meeting the strict U.S. guidelines required the installation of three-way catalysts and electronic fuel-injection control systems on all vehicles. This in turn became the focus of considerable controversy.

Nations with strong environmental movements, led by the Netherlands, Denmark, and Germany, supported full conformity with U.S. regulations. Dutch environmentalist Lucas Reijnders went so far as to argue that EC standards should be "replaced" by U.S. standards.[31] German environmentalists, increasingly alarmed about the death of Germany's forests ("Waldsterben"), also supported the adoption of American standards by the EC—a position endorsed by their government. On the other hand, nations with weaker environmental movements, namely France, Italy, and Great Britain, strongly opposed the adoption of the U.S. requirements.

Underlying, and for the most part, reinforcing, the differing strengths of environmentalism within Europe were the conflicting interests of European automotive producers. The dispute over EC pollution controls essentially pitted countries whose motor-vehicle manufacturers produced larger, more expensive cars against those nations whose automotive firms specialized in smaller, less expensive vehicles. In practice, this primarily amounted to a battle between Germany—home to Mercedes, BMW, and Audi—and France and Italy, whose major producers were Fiat, Peugeot and Renault. Britain, which primarily produced medium-size cars, had interests similar to those of the manufacturers of smaller cars.

There was virtually no dispute over whether convertors should be required on all new, large cars. Both the German and non-German manufacturers of larger vehicles supported this requirement. Rather, the dispute centered on whether they should be mandatory for all new small-and medium-size vehicles as well. For a number of reasons German producers favored—and French and Italian producers opposed—standards requiring the mandatory use of catalytic convertors in all vehicles.[32]

First, the installation of expensive, technically complex, abatement technologies raised the price of large cars proportionately less than that of smaller vehicles. Moreover, many large vehicles were already equipped with fuel-injection systems in order to improve their engine performance. Since the major cost of the technology required to meet "US '83" standards was the fuel-injection system rather than the converter itself, the installation of this abatement technology was absolutely, as well as relatively, more expensive for the manufactures of small cars. Moreover, since consumers who purchase smaller vehicles tend to be more sensitive to costs, the mandatory installation of converters on all vehicles threatened to disproportionately depress the sales of smaller ones.

Second, in contrast to most French and Italian car producers, whose markets were primarily domestic, most German car manufacturers were already producing large numbers of cars for sale in the United States and Japan, where catalytic converters had long been mandatory. (This was also true of the relatively small British and French producers of luxury vehicles.) Thus, unlike their French and Italian competitors, they already had considerable experience in manufacturing and marketing vehicles equipped with this abatement technology. Indeed, the adoption of U.S. regulations by the EC would reduce their production costs by allowing them to make roughly similar vehicles for sale both within and outside Europe.

Third, as has already been noted, vehicles equipped with catalytic convertors required the use of unleaded gasoline. But the availability of unleaded gasoline varied widely within the European Community: the portion of stations carrying unleaded gasoline ranged from 98 percent in Germany and nearly 100 percent in the Netherlands, to 3.5 percent in Britain and less than 2 percent in France, Italy, and Spain.[33] These differences largely reflected "the severity of the stance taken by the national authority towards the tighter control of vehicle emissions."[34] They also meant that it would be much more difficult for British, French, and Italian gasoline firms to supply fuel for converter-equipped vehicles.

Finally, the market demand for vehicles equipped with advanced pollution-control technology varied considerably within Europe. In July 1985, Germany began to provide tax incentives to increase the sale of less polluting cars. In 1985, both BMW and Daimler-Benz reported increased demand for cars equipped with catalytic convertors; thanks to the government's tax incentives, even 20 percent of all Volkswagens sold in Germany were being ordered with some form of emission controls. By contrast, the national markets in France, Britain, and Italy, were considerably less "green"; there was much less consumer demand, and no tax incentives, for the purchase of "clean" vehicles.

Britain was also opposed to catalytic converters, but for different reasons. The U.K. government favored the use of the "lean-burn engines," which were designed to decrease engine pollutants by changing the engine design. Ford UK had invested substantial sums in this technology, which the catalytic converter threatened to make obsolete. Indeed, the British argued that the catalytic converter was an outdated, 1960s technology. One British official stated: "We are not supporters of the outdated idea of bolting bits on the back of autos. There is no way that the British government is going to change its mind on this point."[35] Underlying the British position was Ford Britain's inexperience in converter production and design. In addition, reflecting the then relatively limited political influence of Britain's environmental movement, British Prime Minister Thatcher, told German Chancellor Kohl that she thought U.S. standards were too high.[36]

Not surprisingly, Germany was the leader in the drive for emissions standards that made the catalytic converter mandatory for all cars; the interests of their powerful automobile industry and their influential environmental movement complimented one another. For the French and the Italians, the interests of their domestic automobile producers and relatively weak domestic environmental movements, also reinforced one another. The French Trade Association of Automakers argued that "catalytic converters on automobiles would be costly and unnecessary" and that "the usefulness of catalytic converters remains to be demonstrated."[37] In a move directed against Germany, which had no speed limits on its highways, French Prime Minister Laurent Fabius suggested that "governments should consider lowering speed limits rather than introducing catalytic converters as an immediate means of reducing pollution from automobile exhausts."[38] Pierre Perrin-Pelletier of the French Auto Makers Commission added that the United States is a "good example" of how strict regulations "do not necessarily lead to correspondingly low levels of air pollution."[39]

The German government first threatened to impose its own emission standards, requiring that all cars sold in Germany be equipped with converters. This would have make it very difficult for most French or Italian-made vehicles to be exported to Germany, wreaking havoc on intra-Community trade. While this initiative pleased Germany's green constituencies, who had become increasingly impatient with the slow pace of Community environmental policy, the possibility of an intra-EC trade war terrified Germany's export-oriented car makers. The latter persuaded Bonn to back off on its threat to unilaterally establish its own automobile emission standards. Although the FRG did enact legislation requiring that all new cars be fitted with catalytic converters, it subsequently agreed to delay the law's implementation from 1986 until 1988 for cars above 2.0 liters and to 1989 for all other cars, in order to give the Community more time to act. In return the German automobile industry agreed to conform to the US'83 standards as soon as possible and to offer vehicles with catalytic converters for sale immediately.

To accommodate the interests of France, Italy, and Great Britain, the Council altered its guidelines on pollutants so that medium cars could meet them by employing "lean-burn" engines or comparable cost-effective measures, while still looser standards were set for smaller cars. In addition to laxer standards for smaller vehicles, the manufacturers of both medium and small cars were given additional time to comply with them. In effect, the German government had traded off lower standards for vehicles made outside of Germany in exchange for the ability to impose stricter standards on its domestic manufacturers.

In July 1985, nine members of the Council finally reached a compromise agreement. The basis of the "Luxembourg Compromise" was the classification of motor vehicles into three categories, based on their cylinder capacity: large (more than 2 liters), medium (from 1.4 to 2 liters), and small (less than 1.4 liters). Different emission limits, along with different deadlines for meeting them, were established for cars in each category. In addition, different deadlines were set for new-model and new-vehicle standards, based on the recognition that the latter imposed substantially greater burdens on car manufacturers since it was more difficult to change the specifications of a vehicle already in production than to change the design of a new model.

The standards for new, large cars were scheduled to come into effect on October 1, 1989 and for mid-size cars on either October 1, 1991 or October 1, 1993 (depending on whether they were new models). The much looser standards for small cars would be phased in by 1990 and 1991. Like previous EC emissions directives, the 1987 legislation set a ceiling rather than a floor: member states were still allowed to set lower emission levels than those specified in the directive, but they could not exclude cars that complied with the directive's emission standards.

The Luxembourg compromise also addressed another important source of tension between national environmental regulation and European economic integration. During the mid-1980s, the German and Dutch governments had announced that they would introduce tax incentives to encourage the purchase of low-emission cars. These initiatives were strongly criticized by other EC member states and the Commission began proceedings to determine their legality. Some Commission officials concluded these measures were "'compatible' with Community regulations because they provide for tax derogations to the final consumer on a 'non-discriminatory basis.'"[40] Others maintained that the incentives would lead to the distortion of free trade, arguing that they worked "in favor of German automobile and catalytic converter manufacturers."[41] In particular, the manufacturers of small vehicles feared that the incentives would hurt their sales in favor of German and Japanese producers. The Luxembourg compromise addressed these concerns by allowing nations to offer fiscal incentives for the purchase of cleaner vehicles, but restricted the terms under which they were allowed to do so.

The Luxembourg agreement represented a considerable departure from the EC's original objective of matching U.S. emission standards. Acknowledging that its emission limits remained weaker than those of the United States, the Community now argued that their "ultimate effect on the environment" was comparable to those of the United States. Accordingly, the EC would be matching U.S. standards in the sense that the overall amount of pollution generated by European autos would be the same as in the United States. Individual cars in Europe would, however, continue to emit more pollutants than their U.S. counterparts.

Thus, on balance, the Luxembourg compromise favored the interests of the manufacturers of smaller vehicles over those of the European environmental movement: economic integration took precedence over more radical emissions reductions. Not surprisingly, European environmentalists were very disappointed with the Luxembourg Compromise: once again the Community appeared to have sacrificed pollution control in order to prevent the emergence of new non-tariff barriers. However environmentalists did secure one concession: the Luxembourg agreement included a provision requiring the EC to adopt new, stricter emissions requirements for small-and medium-size vehicles. These would go into effect in 1992 and 1993.

Although France, Italy, and the United Kingdom remained unenthusiastic with the proposed compromise, all three countries were prepared to go along with the proposed directive, largely to head off the possibility of unilateral action by Germany. However, the Commission's proposal was vetoed by Denmark, on the grounds that it was too lenient. It was not until after the passage of the Single European Act, when Denmark lost its veto power over the enactment of EC legislation, that the "Luxembourg Compromise" was finally adopted by the Council. Approved in July 1987, it was the first directive to be adopted under the EC's new qualified-majority voting procedures.

The directive still had one more hurdle to pass, namely the European Parliament, which, under the provisions of the SEA, had the right to review Council directives. In view of the political strength of environmentalists within the EP, debate was heated. Many members strongly criticized the Council for ignoring a (non-binding) resolution the

Parliament had adopted in 1984 calling for much stricter emission standards for all vehicles. One member of Parliament accused the Council and the Commission of "deliberately spurning" the Parliament, adding that "it is high time the strictest limits should be defined, and they must be mandatory. It seems that even in this Year of the Environment, the interests of industry are placed higher than those of the environment. One can only speak of scandal."[42] Another stated, "This situation is intolerable...If we maintain the dates in this compromise, we will wait nine years. A child will have walked nine years ingesting all the dirt that escapes from our cars, with our complicity and connivance."[43]

A defender of the Council agreement countered that, "all that is excessive is derisory ... 1992 requires the Europeans preserve the unity of their market...This objective is as important for the German and French automakers."[44] The EC's Environment Commissioner, Clinton Davis, spoke at the end of the debate. He pleaded with the Parliament not to undermine a hard fought, and fragile, compromise and warned it that the Commission would reject any amendments approved by the Parliament. Davis concluded; "Some progress is better than none at all."[45] On November 18, 1987, with many MEPs abstaining, an amendment that would have tightened the proposed emission standards was defeated and the following month the Luxembourg Compromise became law.

The Small Car Directive

Within a few months, the Commission began work on a directive to establish stricter emission standards for smaller vehicles. However, the context for the making of emission standards had changed considerably since the mid-1980s. First, the European environmental movement had gained considerable strength in a number of European countries, including Britain. Its influence in the European Parliament had also grown, and, with the passage of the SEA, Parliament now was in a position to affect Community regulations. This in turn created considerable pressure on both the Council and the Commission to put forward stricter standards that they might otherwise have supported.

Equally importantly, with the approach of "1992," the EC's self-imposed deadline for creating a single European market, the EC was under growing pressure to harmonize its environmental regulations—particularly those that directly affected free trade. The device of "optimal harmonization," which the Council had used in the past to reconcile different national environmental and economic interests with respect to automotive emissions, was no longer a viable option. In short, the Community was under pressure both to enact strict automobile emission standards and to make them mandatory.

At the outset, nonetheless, the by-now familiar divisions reappeared. The British, French, and Italian governments, attempting to maintain the spirit of the Luxembourg Compromise, urged that smaller vehicles continue to be allowed to meet laxer standards. The Dutch, Germans, and Danes countered by proposing standards for smaller vehicles that were stricter than the 1987 standards for medium-sized ones, thus, effectively abandoning the basis of the Luxembourg Compromise. In February 1988, the Commission struck a compromise between the two positions; it proposed to subject small vehicles to the same standards as medium-size ones, but to maintain lower standards for both.

In June 1988, the Council tentatively approved the Commission's compromise, with Denmark, the Netherlands, and Greece dissenting. It also agreed to propose a further emissions reduction by the end of 1991. Furthermore, the Council agreed to forbid member states from offering financial incentives for the purchase of "cleaner" vehicles. However, the following month, after the Dutch announced that they planned to offer fiscal incentives for consumers to purchase "cleaner" small cars, the French government abruptly withdrew its support for the small-car plan. German auto leaders immediately criticized the French for putting "financial interests before environmental aspects."[46] But the

French government's opposition to the mandatory use of converters for small vehicles no longer reflected the position of its domestic industry. The opposition of a number of Europe's small-and medium-car producers to catalytic converters had diminished since 1987. Not only had they acquired more experience with this technology, but the demand for cleaner vehicles on the part of European consumers had grown considerably; in a number of European markets, the "cleanliness" of a car had become a quality symbol. In addition both Renault and Fiat had begun to manufacturer vehicles equipped with three-way catalysts, the former for the U.S. market and the latter for the Dutch.

Faced with Renault's change of position, and concerned that their opposition to the Small Car Directive had created the impression, in the words of France's Environment Minister, that "cleanliness was a German vice and dirtiness a French virtue," the French government now decided to support the Council's resolution.[47] The United Kingdom also initially expressed reservations about the Small Car Directive, hoping to buy time for its industry to perfect a cheaper lean-burn engine technology. However, by 1989, Britain had given up on such hopes, and was "totally in agreement about using catalytic converters."[48] It too supported the directive.

The focus of debate now switched to the European Parliament. The European Environmental Bureau, a lobbying group representing one hundred European environmental organizations, criticized the Council's position as a "revealing example of the inadequate character of the European strategy for environmental protection."[49] It demanded that the EC require emission standards as strict as those of the United States, beginning in January 1993. One MEP argued, "It is not with limits like these that we can end the defoliation of our forests." Another stated: "Trees are dying, walls are cracking, and people are falling ill. We in Denmark don't want to wear oxygen masks, like they do in Tokyo."[50]

Recognizing that the Parliament, faced with coming European elections, was likely to insist on standards which might prevent the enactment of any directive at all, the Commission and the Council were forced to compromise. They also were spurred to modify their position by the decision of the Netherlands to require catalytic converters on all vehicles sold in that country. While the EC could have successfully challenged the Dutch requirement in the European Court, such a move would have proven politically unpopular and clearly undermined the Commission's "green" credentials.[51] Accordingly, one week before the EP was to vote, the Commission announced that it would shortly propose much stricter emission standards for small cars.

The adoption of a new proposal by the Council was delayed by two disagreements. One concerned timing. The Dutch, Germans, the Danes wanted new standards for small automobiles to be implemented as quickly as possible. However the British, French, and Italians, anxious to give their domestic manufacturers as much time as possible to adjust, pressed for a later date. The Council compromised by setting a deadline of July 1, 1992 for all new models and January 1, 1993 for new vehicles.

A second issue concerned whether or not governments could offer financial incentives for the purchase of cleaner vehicles—an issue which the EC had addressed a few years earlier. The Dutch had already done so and the Germans and Danes indicated that they planned to follow suit. "The question of fiscal incentives was seen as particularly important because without a coordinated system, competition among car sellers in different countries could become distorted."[52] Once again, the Council compromised: member states were allowed to offer fiscal incentives to new-car purchasers until July 1992, providing the amount did not exceed 85 percent of the cost of the catalytic converter.

In July 1989, a second, revised version of the Small Car Directive was approved by the Council of Ministers by a qualified majority; Denmark and Greece voted against it. Its passage marked a significant step forward in both the tightening and harmonization of pollution-control standards within the Community. Strict new limits on emissions were established for *all* small cars sold in the European Community. To meet these standards, small cars would be required to be fitted with catalytic converters—and thus run on unleaded gasoline. In fact, the new limits, which aimed to cut existing emissions levels by 73 percent, were even lower than the 1987 standards for medium and large cars, effectively standing the Luxembourg Compromise on its head.

Thus, after nearly two decades of wrangling, the EC had finally managed to harmonize emission standards for the majority of vehicles sold in Europe. Moreover, it had done so by setting them at an extremely high level. Integration and environmental protection had finally managed to reinforce one another.

The directive was hailed by environmentalists as a major victory. EP Environment Committee Chair Ken Collins boasted: "We forced the catalytic converter on a reluctant Britain and France."[53] EC Environment Commissioner Carlo Ripa di Meana described the agreement on the Small Car Directive as, "a milestone for Europe," and announced that the Commission planed to put forward new proposals to impose stricter emission standards on medium and large cars that would bring them into line with U.S.norms.[54]

Nonetheless, despite this substantial progress toward both the harmonization and strengthening of European auto-emission standards, serious tensions among the member states persisted. For example, in September 1990, the issue of German speed control, or to be more precise, the lack thereof, was again raised by the French government. In a newspaper interview, French Environment Minister Brice Lalonde threatened that "Paris [would] ban imports of West German BMWs, Mercedes, and other fast cars if Bonn did not introduce speed limits to help the environment.[55] Lalonde added, "I want talks on speed limits and carbon monoxide gas emissions. A West German commitment on this point is indispensable."[56]

A somewhat more substantive disagreement emerged in 1990, when Denmark enacted legislation establishing anti-pollution standards for cars considerably stricter than those mandated by the Community. It based its action on Article 100A, paragraph 4 of the SEA, which permits member states to exceed Community standards if necessary to improve environmental quality. The Commission, in turn, expressed the fear that the excessive use of this provision would create "islands" within the single market and argued that this "escape clause" applied only to national laws enacted prior to the SEA.[57] The Commission, however, decided not to take Denmark to court since the Council was about to approve the first draft of a new directive on car emissions that set standards comparable to those enacted by Denmark. In July 1991, the EC gave its final approval to a directive which significantly tightened emission standards for all vehicles, thus obviating the Danish challenge.

Conclusion

Two sets of conclusions emerge. The first concerns the difficulty that the Community has faced in harmonizing environmental product regulations. The second has to do with the dynamics of creating the single European market.

It is clear that the EC's effort to develop common product standards with respect to the environmental impact of tradable goods has proven extremely difficult, complicated, and time-consuming. Why?

The first, and most significant reason, is that environmental product regulation and the creation of a single European market are so closely connected. The regulation of environmental quality at the product level invariably has important implications for intra-Community trade; virtually every environmental issue and regulation represents a potential threat to creation of a single European market. But the Community is not supposed to chose between economic integration and environmental protection: the Single European Act charged the Community with simultaneously achieving *both*. Indeed, both goals emerged about the same time: the enactment of the SEA coincided with an upsurge of public support for environment protection in Europe.[58]

No other political system faces such a difficult and complex challenge.

Second, the economic costs and benefits of environmental regulation at both the national and Community level are not randomly distributed among the member states; virtually every regulation at either the national or Community level makes some country's producers relatively better off and those of another nation less competitive. Since the nation-state remains the primary lobbying force and decision-making unit in Brussels, conflicts over environmental regulation invariably produce divisions among the EC's member states. Moreover, the central role played by the nation-state in the Community's structure and deliberations not only encourages members of the Council of Minsters to seek to safeguard the interests of their national firms or industries, but also encourages them to propose Community regulations that will create advantages for domestic producers.

Their task has been relatively easy—and the formulation of EC policy correspondingly more difficult—because support for strong environmental regulation is distributed unevenly among the electorates of the twelve member states, and because national producers and national environmental groups frequently shared similar interests. At least in the case described here, there have been relatively few cross-cutting loyalties, and therefore maximum opportunities for Baptist-bootlegger coalitions. Consider for example, how different the politics of automobile emissions would have been had the division between large-and small-car producers not fallen along national lines and/or the producers who had the most to gain from strict emission standards were of a different nationality than Europe's most "green" electorate.

These patterns of differences are exacerbated by another one. The individual member states or coalitions of states favoring stricter and less strict environmental regulations have tended to be remarkably similar from issue to issue. Thus Germany and Denmark have consistently been the strongest proponents of tougher regulations at both the national and Community levels in areas ranging from automobile emissions to waste disposal. With equal consistency, Britain, frequently joined by France and Italy, have been on the other side. This has tended to make compromise more difficult since the resentments and suspicions engendered by one dispute spill over onto the next.

This analysis also has important implications for our understanding of the dynamics of European integration. First, the ongoing debate over the Maastricht treaty aside, the Community, at least in the area of environmental regulation, is clearly already a federal structure. There are no longer any significant regulatory policies, certainly with respect to traded goods, which are exclusively decided at either the national or Community level. Even the decision as to what areas of environmental policymaking should be left up to the member states is now decided in Brussels. Nonetheless, as in any federal system, the degree of autonomy granted to or reserved to political subunits can vary over time. The principle of subsidiarity embedded in the Maastricht treaty may well result in national governments being allowed to maintain more control over environmental policies that do not directly affect economic integration.

Second, the creation of the single European market is an ongoing process. Not only will it not be concluded at the end of 1992; it will *never* be concluded. The reason is simple: the regulatory agenda is constantly changing. As new issues, such as packaging and eco-labeling, emerge, they present additional potential obstacles for intra-Community trade that could not have been anticipated at the time the White Paper was written. As long as both the priority placed on environmental protection and the competitive impact of regulation varies across the EC, member states will attempt to initiate regulations that will in turn be perceived by other member states as non-tariff barriers. The opportunities are endless: as soon as one kind of regulation is harmonized, another source of contention among the member states or between the member states and Brussels emerges. The year 1992 is not so much a date as a moving target.

Consider for example, the long-standing, and continuing controversy over the ability of the member states to provide financial incentives for the purchase of cleaner products, or alternatively to tax the production or use of harmful substances.[59] On one hand, the use of market incentives to encourage "greener" behavior represents a viable, and in many respects, more efficient alternative to command-and-control-style regulation. Yet at the same time, green taxes, incentives, and subsidies can easily be designed to favor the products produced in some nations over those of others. Moreover, their growing use enormously complicates the efforts of the EC's finance ministers to harmonize fiscal policies. The harmonization of green taxes, subsidies, is likely to prove no less difficult or time-consuming than the harmonization of environmental product standards, or the EC's ongoing efforts to harmonize national tax policies.

Finally, the case described in this article suggests the importance of placing the creation of a single European market within a global context. Many scholars have noted the important role played by European fears of Japanese economic power in the decision to place priority on the creation of a single European market in the mid-1980s. Yet relatively little attention has been played to the international dimension of EC regulatory policies. However in the case we have examined, American regulations played a critical role in strengthening those eventually enacted by the Community. The U.S. standard created a benchmark against which the EC measured its progress, or lack thereof, in enacting strict emissions controls. In addition, the success of European producers in marketing their vehicles in America made them more willing to support a tightening of EC requirements.

More generally, the EC's efforts to harmonize the environmental policies of its member states can be understood as part of a much broader effort on the part of the industrialized nations to harmonize regulatory policy and standards and reduce the role of regulation as a non-tariff barrier. For example, the OECD has played an important role in attempting to coordinate both chemical safety standards and policies regarding the export of hazardous wastes among its members. In addition, in order to address global environmental policies a growing number of national environmental policies that affect trade are now subject to international negotiations. The interdependency of trade and regulatory policies is no longer confined to the EC; it is now a global phenomenon.

Notes

1. David Freestone, "European Community Environmental Policy and Law," *Journal of Law and Society* 18, 1 (Spring 1991): 135.
2. Timothy O'Riordan, "Role of Environmental Quality Objectives: The Politics of Pollution Control," O'Riordan and D'Arge, eds., *Progress in Resources Management and Environmental Planning*, vol. 1 (New York: Wiley, 1979), 249.
3. David Briggs, "Environmental Problems and Policies in the European Community," Chris Park, ed., *Environmental Policies: An International Review* (London: Croom Helm, 1986), 110-11.
4. Ibid.
5. Nigel Haigh, *EEC Environmental Policy and Britain*, 2nd ed. (Harlow: Longman, 1989).
6. Angela Liberatore, "Problems of Transnational Policymaking: Environmental Policy in the European Community," *European Journal of Political Research* 19 (1991): 289.
7. Giandomenico Majone, "Cross-National Sources of Regulatory Policymaking in Europe and the United States," *Journal of Public Policy* 11, 95.
8. Jackson Diehl, "Choking on Their Own Development," *Washington Post National Weekly Edition*, 29 May-4 June 1988, 9.
9. Haigh, *EEC Environmental Policy and Britain*, 288.

10. Nigel Haigh, "New Tools for European Pollution Control," *International Environmental Affairs* (Winter 1989): 32-35.
11. Quoted in David Vogel's, *National Styles of Regulation* (Ithaca, NY: Cornell University Press, 1986), 103.
12. Freestone, 136.
13. See, for example, George Close, "Harmonization of Laws: Use or Abuse of the Powers Under the EEC Treaty," *European Law Review* (December 1978): 461-81.
14. Ludwig Kramer, "The Single European Act and Environmental Protection: Reflections on Several New Provisions in Community Law," Common Market Law Review 24 (1987): 651.
15. Ibid., 681.
16. Dirk Vandermeersch, "The Single European Act and the Environmental Policy of the European Community," *European Law Review* 12 (December 1987): 407-29, 559-88.
17. Robin Herman, "An Ecological Epiphany," *Washington Post National Weekly Review*, 5-11 December 1988, 19.
18. Richard Kirkland, "Environmental Anxiety Goes Global," *Fortune*, 21 November 1988, 118.
19. *Environmental Policy in the European Community*, 4th ed. (Luxembourg, Office of Official Publications on the European Communities, 1990), 5.
20. Ibid., 15.
21. Alberta Sbragia, "Environmental Policy in the Political Economy of the European Community," prepared for the Workshop of "The Consortium for 1992," Stanford, California, May 1992, 4.
22. Elizabeth Bomberg, "European Community Environmental Policy: The Role of the European Parliament," presented at the Eighth Annual Conference of Europeanists, March 1992.
23. Eckard Rehbinder and Richard Stewart, "Legal Integration in Federal Systems: European Community Environmental Law," *American Journal of Comparative Law* 33 (1985): 77.
24. Ibid.
25. Stanley P. Johnson and Guy Corcelle, *The Environmental Policy of the European Communities* (London: Graham and Trotman, 1989), 124.
26. Haigh, *EEC Environmental Policy and Britain*, 203.
27. Turner T. Smith, Jr. and Pascale Kromarek, *Understanding US and European Environmental Law; A Practitioner's Guide* (London: Graham and Trotman, 1989), 71.
28. Johnson and Corcelle, 124.
29. Haigh, *EEC Environmental Policy and Britain*, 204.
30. "Agreement on New Auto Emission Standards Starting in 1988 Called Major Breakthrough," *International Environmental Reporter*, 4 April 1985, 109.
31. "Auto Industry Environmentalists Disagree over Need for U.S. Auto Emission Standards," *International Environmental Reporter*, 13 November 1985, 368.
32. This section draws extensively from Henning Arp, "Interest Groups in EC Legislation: The Case of Car Emission Standards," presented in the workshop, "European Lobbying Towards the Year 2000" at the ECPR Joint Session of Workshops, University of Essex, March 22-28, 1991.
33. Kevin Done, "A two-speed Europe on Exhaust Fumes," *Financial Times*, 18 July 1988, 11.
34. Ibid.
35. "Government Says It Stands Firm on Refusal to Require Catalytic Converters on New Cars," *International Environmental Reporter*, 9 April 1986, 114.
36. "France, Britain Oppose German Attempt to Win Agreement in Emission Standards," *International Environmental Reporter*, 13 February 1985, 40.
37. "Trade Association of Automakers Opposes Use of Catalytic Converters to Meet Limits," *International Environmental Reporter*, 13 November 1985, 39.
38. "France, Britain Oppose German Attempt to Win Agreement in Emission Standards," 40-41.
39. "Auto Industry Environmentalists Disagree over Need for U.S. Auto Emission Standards," 368.
40. "Commission to Consider Legal Proceedings on West German Incentives for Cleaner Cars," *International Environmental Reporter*, 13 February 1985, 39.
41. Ibid.
42. Jonathan Story and Ethan Schwartz, "Auto Emissions and the European Parliament: A Test of the Single European Act," INSEAD-CEDEP, 1990, 23, 24.
43. Ibid., 24.
44. Ibid.
45. "Franco-German Row Looms over Car Emission Rules," *Reuters*, 25 July 1988.

46. "European Community Environment Ministers Agree on New Emission Level for Small Cars," *International Environment Reporter*, June 1989, 283.
47. *Le Monde*, 4 August 1988.
48. "European Community Environment Ministers Agree on New Emission Level for Small Cars," 283.
49. Quoted in Elizabeth Bomberg, "EC Environmental Policy: The Role of the European Parliament," prepared for delivery at the Eighth International Conference of Europeanists, Chicago, March 27-29, 1992, 23.
50. Story and Schwartz, 27.
51. "Green greener greenest?" *Economist*, 6 May 1989, 67.
52. "European Community Environment Ministers Agree on New Emission Levels for Small Cars," 283.
53. Quoted in Bomberg, "EC Environmental Policy: The Role of the European Parliament," 25.
54. Ibid.
55. "France Ready to Ban Big West German Cars, Minister Says," *Reuters*, 12 September 1990.
56. Ibid.
57. "Danish Car Emission Law in the EEC Spotlight," *Europe Information Service*, November 6, 1990.
58. This point has been insightfully made by Sbragia.
59. See, Eberhard Grabitz and Christian Zacker, "Scope for Action by the EC Member States for the Improvement of Environmental Protection Under EEC Law: The Example of Environmental Taxes and Subsidies," *Common Market Law Review* 26 (1989): 423-47.

[18]

The North American Free Trade Agreement's Lessons for Reconciling Trade and the Environment

ROBERT HOUSMAN*

I. Introduction

The North American Free Trade Agreement[1] (NAFTA) creates a free trade zone that stretches from the Yukon to the Yucatan, encompassing Mexico, Canada and the United States. The NAFTA has been touted as creating a US$6 trillion market made up of some 360 million consumers—the world's largest.[2]

* Staff Attorney, Center for International Environmental Law (CIEL), Adjunct Professor of Law, the American University. Prepared for the United Nations Environment Programme with the assistance of Durwood Zaelke, CIEL. The author wishes to thank Gary Horlick, Dan Esty, Ambassador Ambler Moss, Ambassador Mike Smith, Professor John Jackson, Mark Ritchie, David Hunter, Konrad Von Moltke, Justin Ward, Mary Kelly, Gustavo Alanis and the Mexican Center for Environmental Law, Scott Vaughan, Art Farrance, and the staff of the *Stanford Journal of International Law* for their assistance. CIEL also wishes to thank the Pew Charitable Trusts, the C.S. Mott Foundation, the Jesse Smith Noyes Foundation and the U.S. Environmental Protection Agency for additional financial support for research on trade and the environment. This paper does not represent the views of the United Nations Environment Programme or any other individual or organization named above. Any errors are the author's.

1 North American Free Trade Agreement Between the Government of the United States, the Government of Canada and the Government of the United Mexican States, Dec. 17, 1992, 32 I.L.M. 289 (1993) (preamble to chapter 10); 32 I.L.M. 605 (1993) (chapter 10 to Errata table) [hereinafter NAFTA].

2 Actually, the Canada-U.S. market alone reached the six trillion dollar mark in 1990 operating under the 1988 Canada-United States Free Trade Agreement. *See* William A. Orme, Jr., *Myths Versus Facts; The Whole Truths About the Half Truths*, 72 For. Affs. 2, 3-4 (1993). The NAFTA both brings Mexico into the fold and expands the range of areas (such as financial services) covered by the hemispheric trade rules. In fact, however, claims as to the NAFTA's market are often misleading. *Id.* For example, the NAFTA does not create the world's largest market. *Id.* When fully implemented, the European Union, which entered into effect November 1, 1993, will be more integrated and larger in dollar terms than the NAFTA zone. *See generally* Peter Ludlow, *The Maastricht Treaty and the Future of Europe*, Wash. Q. No. 4, Autumn, 1992, at 119. Although the accords setting up the

While these numbers were the primary driving force behind the agreement, the NAFTA's importance is not limited solely to the size of its market or the number of its consumers. As the first major free trade agreement adopted after the recent attention to the integration of trade and environmental policies, the NAFTA, and the process by which it was negotiated, provide many valuable lessons for future trade agreements and other efforts that will address trade and environment.[3] This paper summarizes these lessons. Part II discusses the process of the NAFTA's creation. Part III discusses the substantive environmental issues related to the NAFTA.

II. PROCESS ISSUES

A. *The Role of Regional Trade Agreements in the Integration of Trade and Environmental Policies*

Although some may fear the negative impact of regional trade agreements on the international trading system,[4] the confluence of regional interests clearly played a major role in allowing the parties to achieve the environmental gains provided by the NAFTA package. This dynamic is of particular note when one considers the disparate political, social, and economic situations of the three NAFTA parties.

The importance of the NAFTA and other regional trade agreements as testing grounds for addressing environmental concerns is illustrated by the NAFTA-inspired advances in the final Uruguay Round text[5] of the General Agreement on Tariffs and Trade (GATT).[6] The NAFTA parties were able to bring to the GATT ta-

Union do include certain environmental provisions, they are less comprehensive and require less integration of trade and environment than occurred in the NAFTA.

[3] *See* Ambler H. Moss, Jr., *Free Trade and Environmental Enhancement: Are They Compatible in the Americas?*, *in* TRADE AND THE ENVIRONMENT: LAW, ECONOMICS AND POLICY 109, 116 (Durwood Zaelke et al. eds., 1993) [hereinafter TRADE AND THE ENVIRONMENT] ("It necessarily follows that environmental concerns should be integrated into the actual text of future free trade agreements. The model to follow is NAFTA . . . .").

[4] *See* C. Michael Aho, *More Bilateral Trade Agreements Would Be a Blunder: What the New President Should Do*, 22 CORNELL INT'L L.J. 25, 25 (1989) (arguing that bilateral agreements harm international trade system). *But see* C. Michael Hathaway & Sandra Masur, *The Right Emphasis for US Trade Policy for the 1990s: Positive Bilateralism*, 8 B.U. INT'L L.J. 207, 211-16 (1990) (arguing that bilateral agreements can help extend and develop the international trade system).

[5] *See infra* notes 138-140 (discussing NAFTA-like changes in Uruguay Round final text); *see also* Trade Negotiations Committee, Final Act Embodying the Results of the Uruguay Round of Multilateral Trade Negotiations, Dec. 15, 1993, MTN/FA-UR-93-0246 [hereinafter Uruguay Round Final Act].

[6] General Agreement on Tariffs and Trade, *opened for signature* Oct. 30, 1947, 61 Stat. A3, 55 U.N.T.S. 187.

ble environmental provisions that were demonstrably workable. This, coupled with U.S. political pressure and environmental pressure from within Europe, allowed the NAFTA gains to be accepted at the wider international level.[7]

B. *Integration of Environmental Issues Within the NAFTA Process*

Selecting a method for integrating environmental and trade issues into a coordinated and cohesive policy-making framework is central to the trade and environment debate. Closely related is the question of when such integration between trade and environmental issues should occur. The NAFTA experience speaks to both questions.

Environmental issues related to the NAFTA first rose to prominence during the U.S. Congressional debate over the granting of "fast track"[8] authority to the President to commence formal negotiations over a free trade agreement with Mexico and Canada.[9] In order to secure the votes necessary to obtain fast track authority, then-President Bush was compelled to provide Congress with a plan to address the environmental ramifications of the NAFTA.[10]

During the early stages of the NAFTA negotiations, and following the Bush environmental response, the three parties agreed that environmental discussions related to the NAFTA would occur on a parallel track separate from the actual trade negotiations.[11] The parties argued the parallel track approach was necessary to keep the trade negotiations as streamlined and straightforward as possible.[12] During this early stage, environmental issues were raised directly in the trade agreement negotiations only in the discussions

7 *See infra* notes 138-140 and accompanying text (discussing NAFTA-inspired changes in Uruguay Round of GATT).

8 Trade Act of 1974, §§ 101-102, 151, Pub. L. No. 93-618, 88 Stat. 1978, 1982, 2001 (1975) (codified at 19 U.S.C. §§ 2101, 2111-2112, 2191 (1988)); Omnibus Trade and Competitiveness Act of 1988, Pub. L. No. 100-418, 102 Stat. 1107, 1102-03 (codified at 19 U.S.C. §§ 2902-2903). Fast track procedures limit Congressional input into the negotiation of trade agreements to ease the President's ability to enter into such agreements. *See* Alan F. Homer & Judith H. Bello, *The Fast Track Debate: A Prescription for Pragmatism*, 26 INT'L LAW. 183, 184 (1992).

9 *See* Robert F. Housman & Paul M. Orbuch, *Integrating Labor and Environmental Concerns Into the North American Free Trade Agreement: A Look Back and a Look Ahead*, 8 AM. U. J. INT'L L. & POL'Y 719, 724-25 (1993) (discussing role of environmental issues in the fast track debate).

10 Executive Office of the President, Response of the Administration to Issues Raised in Connection with the Negotiation of the North American Free Trade Agreement, May 1, 1991.

11 *See Unions, Employers, and Federal Government Debate Effect of NAFTA on U.S. Safety Rules*, Daily Labor Rep. (BNA) A8 (1992) (discussing parallel tracks).

12 *Id.*

over the NAFTA's standards provisions—an area where the parties acknowledged such linkage was inherently unavoidable. The decision to separate environmental issues from trade issues was widely criticized by the environmental communities of all three nations.[13] Environmental groups argued that placing environmental issues on a parallel track would seriously limit the parties' ability to make the cross-track trade-offs necessary to "green" the NAFTA.[14]

As pressure continued to grow from environmental groups and members of the U.S. Congress, environmental issues began to take on greater significance for the agreement's chances of obtaining Congressional approval in the United States. Environmental efforts gained further momentum through alliances among environmental groups, labor, and consumer organizations.[15] Groups outside the United States began extensive efforts to influence their governments as well.[16] These trilateral efforts ultimately caused the distinctions between the environmental and trade tracks to implode. A number of environmental issues then made their way onto the trade track and some of these, in turn, ultimately found a place in the trade agreement's text.[17]

While environmental changes to the agreement occurred, in principle, during the tenures of Bush, Salinas and Mulroney, some of the most important NAFTA-related trade and environment integration efforts came after the change of presidential administrations in the United States. During the 1992 U.S. presidential campaign, the NAFTA's impacts on both labor and the environment were important issues.[18] Recognizing the difficulties the agreement faced, particularly in Congress, U.S. presidential candidate Bill Clinton called for supplemental agreements to address at least some of the outstanding labor and environmental concerns.[19]

13 *See* David Marchick & Amit K. Misra, *Trade Wars*, ATLANTA CONST., Apr. 11, 1991, at A19.

14 Housman & Orbuch, *supra* note 9, at 768.

15 *See* Bruce Stokes, *Greens Talk Trade*, NAT'L J., Apr. 13, 1991, at 864; Nancy Dunne, *Fast-track train runs off the rails*, FIN. TIMES, Apr. 26, 1991, at 6.

16 *See, e.g.*, Regina Barba, *NAFTA and NACE: A Mexican Perspective*, *in* SHAPING CONSENSUS: THE NORTH AMERICAN COMMISSION ON THE ENVIRONMENT AND NAFTA 10, 10-12 (Sarah Richardson ed., 1993) (discussing Mexican efforts); Steven Shrybman, *Trading Away the Environment*, 9 WORLD POL'Y J. 93, 93-110 (Winter 1991-1992) (Mr. Shrybman served as Counsel to the Canadian Environmental Law Association).

17 *See* Housman & Orbuch, *supra* note 9, at 768.

18 *See* James Risen, *Dynamite Deal; Trade Pact Could Backfire on Bush in the Rust Belt*, L.A. TIMES, Aug. 7, 1992, at B5-B6.

19 *See* Expanding Trade and Creating American Jobs, Remarks of Governor Bill Clinton at North Carolina State University (Oct. 4, 1992). While certain aspects of the supplemental environmental agreement were discussed on the parallel track, the election

Candidate Clinton's NAFTA position was straightforward: there would be no NAFTA without these supplemental agreements.[20]

Shortly after the U.S. election, representatives of the Clinton Administration and their counterparts from Mexico and Canada began working in earnest on developing the labor and environmental supplemental agreements. Completed on September 14, 1993, these supplemental agreements,[21] coupled with other NAFTA-related environmental efforts, became the NAFTA parallel environmental package.

Although the parallel track approach was intended to ease the NAFTA process, ultimately it had the opposite effect. The failure to integrate trade and environmental issues from the outset created obstacles to a final agreement both during negotiation and Congressional consideration. During the negotiations it became clear that environmental issues would have to be dealt with to some degree in the agreement itself, and new and unanticipated issues had to be added to an already extensive negotiating docket.

Had these emerging issues been on the negotiation docket from the outset they could have been handled more effectively and deliberately. Instead, their late addition caused difficult eleventh-hour negotiations that delayed and threatened passage of the agreement as a whole.[22] At the Congressional stage, the fact that the environmental supplemental agreement was not part of the NAFTA proper raised serious concerns as to the side agreement's effectiveness.[23] Congressional members questioned the binding qualities of the supplemental agreement and the commitment of each party to the agreement's mandates.[24] These concerns made

fundamentally changed the direction of these negotiations. For example, prior to the U.S. election, a North American Commission on the Environment had been agreed to in principle. *See NRDC Warns Administration Not to Rush Creation of NAFTA Environmental Body*, INSIDE U.S. TRADE, Oct. 30, 1992, at 14. However, the Commission as envisioned during the Bush administration bears little resemblance to the one ultimately created.

20 *See* Expanding Trade and Creating American Jobs, *supra* note 19.

21 *See* North American Agreement on Environmental Cooperation Between the Government of the United States of America, the Government of Canada and the Government of the United Mexican States, Sept. 14, 1993, 32 I.L.M. 1480 (1993) [hereinafter NAAEC]; North American Agreement on Labor Cooperation Between the Government of the United States of America, the Government of Canada, and the Government of the United Mexican States, Sept. 13, 1993.

22 *Cf. Administration to Release NAFTA Text Next Week as Officials Scramble to Finish*, INSIDE U.S. TRADE, Sept. 4, 1992, at 1, 11.

23 *Cf. Gephardt Criticizes NAFTA Side Accord as 'Not Supportable'*, INSIDE U.S. TRADE, Aug. 16, 1993, at S-5, S-6 [hereinafter *Gephardt Criticizes*].

24 *Id.* For example, the failure of the supplemental agreement's withdrawal clause to include a penalty to inhibit parties from dropping out from their environmental responsibilities but continuing to participate in the NAFTA's trade benefits was a subject of much

the process of building early Congressional support for the NAFTA package more difficult.[25] In the end, however, the relative weaknesses of the supplemental agreements may have allowed more Republicans in the U.S. House of Representatives to support the agreement.[26]

The NAFTA's lessons here are twofold. On one level, the NAFTA process shows that a trade agreement can integrate trade and environmental issues, however late in the process. On a second level, the difficulties caused by the NAFTA parallel track approach suggest that both from a trade perspective and an environmental perspective, it would have been far better to integrate trade and environmental concerns from the outset.

Finally, despite its positive lessons for integrating trade and environment, the NAFTA process also suggests the difficulties that accompany broad-based integration of trade and environment. While the NAFTA was successful at addressing relatively discrete environmental issues (for example, the effect on certain environmental laws of certain provisions on standards),[27] the process was less successful at dealing with larger issues that were raised during the debate (for example, the environmental effects of NAFTA-driven agriculture).[28] This aversion to complex macro-issues seems to plague the trade and environment debate generally. The NAFTA, however, suggests the value of parcelling the trade and environment debate into issues or issue groups that are easier to handle. Parcelling may even assist the debate to deal more easily with the macro-issues that must be addressed at the outset of any meaningful integration effort.

C. *Participation by Environmental Agencies in the Formal NAFTA Process*

One of the most important examples of the NAFTA success in integrating environmental and trade issues was the high degree of participation by the federal environmental agencies of each of the

concern. *See* Janet Perez, *Opponents Voice Fears on NAFTA*, PHOENIX GAZETTE, Nov. 6, 1993, at E1; Peter Behr, *U.S. Tells Canada, Mexico Side Agreements are Vital*, WASH. POST, Oct. 30, 1993, at A4.

25 *See Gephardt Criticizes*, *supra* note 23.

26 *Cf.* Letter from Ambassador Kantor, U.S. Trade Representative, to the Honorable Bill Archer, *reprinted in* INSIDE U.S. TRADE, Oct. 22, 1993, at 16-17.

27 *See, e.g.*, *infra* notes 100-140 and accompanying text (discussing the NAFTA's advances in the standards area).

28 *See, e.g.*, Mark Ritchie, *Free Trade versus Sustainable Agriculture: The Implications of NAFTA*, 22 ECOLOGIST 221 (1992).

parties. This sharply contrasts with prior efforts on trade and environmental issues, where the trade (or, at times, environmental) agency with primary jurisdiction over a matter traditionally operated without the degree of consultation found during the NAFTA process.[29] Not only did the environmental agencies of all three parties lead efforts on the parallel track, but, in addition, they all played substantial roles in developing the NAFTA's sections on environmental issues.[30] For example, in the United States, the Environmental Protection Agency and the Food and Drug Administration served as co-chairs of the U.S. delegation to two of the three standards-negotiating subgroups.[31]

Without the involvement of both the trade and environment agencies, the NAFTA could not possibly have addressed the complex interactions of trade and environment as successfully as it did. Thus, the NAFTA's lesson here is the value of blending regulatory expertise in coming to grips with trade and environment issues. The NAFTA experience argues strongly for involving from the outset both trade and environment agencies as co-equals in efforts to address the linkages between trade and the environment.

D. *Participation by Environmental Groups in the Formal NAFTA Process*

In addition to the significant role played by the environmental agencies, non-governmental environmental groups also played an expanded role in the U.S. and Canadian formal NAFTA trade advisory processes. In Canada, environmental representatives were appointed to the International Trade Advisory Committee and to eight of the Sectoral Advisory Groups on International Trade.[32] Similarly, as part of his NAFTA environmental package, U.S. President Bush placed five representatives of national environmental groups on committees within the Private Sector Advisory Committee System. As private advisors with government clearance, both

29 *See generally* Jan C. McAlpine & Pat LeDonne, *The United States Government, Public Participation, and Trade and Environment*, *in* TRADE AND THE ENVIRONMENT, *supra* note 3, at 203. This criticism is more commonly directed at trade agencies, which tend to hold greater sway in many government decision-making fora related to trade and the environment. *Id.*

30 Peter L. Lallas, *NAFTA and Evolving Approaches to Identify and Address "Indirect" Environmental Impacts of International Trade*, 5 GEO. INT'L ENVTL. L. REV. 519, 543 (1993) (Mr. Lallas is an Attorney Advisor with the U.S. Environmental Protection Agency's Office of the General Counsel; he also served as a member of the EPA's NAFTA delegation).

31 *Id.*

32 Government of Canada, North American Free Trade Agreement: Canadian Environmental Review, Oct. 1992, at 1.

the Canadian and U.S. environmental representatives enjoyed access to confidential negotiating texts and were able to provide direct input into the NAFTA environmental process. While serious concerns were voiced, particularly in the United States, about the small number of environmental advisors and the narrow scope of constituencies and views they represented, these advisors arguably played a significant role in the NAFTA's environmental efforts.[33]

The NAFTA lesson here is that non-governmental environmental groups can play an important role in shaping trade agreements without compromising the ability of the parties to negotiate effectively. This experience provides the foundation for incorporating additional non-governmental environmental consultation into future trade negotiations.

E. *Participation by Sub-Federal Entities in the NAFTA Process*

Because all of the NAFTA parties have federal systems of government, and many of their environmental protection responsibilities are delegated to the sub-federal level,[34] the role of sub-federal governmental entities in the NAFTA process is also important. Concerns over the NAFTA's effects on the ability of sub-federal governments to enact and implement environmental protections were heightened because of two recent challenges by Canada to the practices of certain U.S. entities: (1) a challenge to Puerto Rico's milk safety laws[35] and (2) a GATT panel decision finding that U.S. state practices related to beer violated the United States'

[33] *See* Daniel C. Esty, *Integrating Trade and Environment Policy Making: First Steps in the North American Free Trade Agreement*, *in* TRADE AND THE ENVIRONMENT, *supra* note 3, at 45, 48.

[34] *See* Anne L. Alonzo, *Mexico*, 15 LOY. L.A. INT'L & COMP. L.J. 87, 89 (1992) (discussing Mexico's environmental regulatory system) (Ms. Alonzo is an attorney with the U.S. Environmental Protection Agency at the American Embassy in Mexico City, Mexico); M. Paul Brown, *Environment Canada and the Pursuit of Administrative Decentralization*, 29 CAN. PUB. ADMIN. 218 (1986); *see generally* Daniel P. Selmi & Kenneth A. Manaster, STATE ENVIRONMENTAL LAW ch. 7 (1989).

[35] *See* In re Ultra-High Temperature Milk from Quebec, No.USA-92-1807-02 (1992) (appearing before a panel convened pursuant to Chapter 18 of the CFTA) (Puerto Rico is a commonwealth of the United States and for the purposes of both setting standards and trade challenges to these standards, it functions much like a state). The milk case involved a Canadian challenge to the testing and certification standards imposed on facilities manufacturing ultra-high temperature processed milk for sale in Puerto Rico. *Id.* The standards in question required the use of certified inspectors and laboratories to test the milk's safety, and periodic (as opposed to one time) certification of all manufacturing facilities. *Id.* All manufacturers of ultra-high temperature milk are required to meet these standards. *Id.* Canada argued that the standards were an unnecessary and discriminatory trade barrier.

GATT obligations.[36] Environmentalists, analogizing developments within the NAFTA process to the GATT case and the milk challenge, expressed serious concerns over the NAFTA's effects on state, provincial, and local environmental protections.[37]

In response to these concerns, all three parties attempted to coordinate developments in the NAFTA process with affected sub-federal authorities to ensure that their views and needs were considered. For example, Canada formed a Federal-Provincial Committee on the NAFTA at both the ministerial and staff levels.[38] This committee met regularly during the course of the NAFTA process to ensure that provincial officials had a voice in the NAFTA developments.[39]

Also of interest is the degree to which sub-federal environmental efforts related to the NAFTA were coordinated internationally. For example, the California Environmental Protection Agency worked with the environmental protection authorities from the neighboring Mexican State of Baja California Norte to, among other things: (1) increase enforcement capacity in the two states; (2) adopt protocols and procedures for information sharing; and (3) address the problem of air pollution from Tijuana.[40] These sub-federal efforts designed to address the localized impacts of the NAFTA provide an important model for ensuring greater local input into future trade agreements.[41]

The NAFTA's lesson here is that sub-federal entities can and must play a role in addressing any potential impacts of trade agreements. First, sub-federal entities must play a role because they often have legally mandated responsibilities that must be integrated into the framework of any trade agreement. Second, sub-

36 *See* GATT, *United States — Measures Affecting Alcoholic and Malt Beverages, Report of the Panel* (Feb. 7, 1992). Prior cases have raised similar problems that federal systems face with regard to the actions of their sub-federal entities. *See Canada Import, Distribution and Sale of Alcoholic Drinks by Canadian Provincial Marketing Agencies,* (adopted Mar. 22, 1988), 35 BISD 37 (1988); Springfield Rare Coin Galleries, Inc. v. Johnson, 115 Ill. 2d 221, 503 N.W.2d 300 (1986). The proximity in time of the beer and milk cases to the NAFTA, however, caused them to play special roles in the NAFTA process.

37 *See, e.g.*, Kate Tambour, *NAFTA's Cloud Over the States*, 9 POLICY ALTERNATIVES ON THE ENVIRONMENT — A STATE REPORT 1, 5 (1992).

38 Canadian Environmental Review, *supra* note 32, at 6.

39 *Id.*

40 Gail Severns, *NAFTA Prompts Environmental Cooperation on California Border with Mexico*, 2 ENVIROMEXICO, Dec. 1993, at 4.

41 *See generally* Scott McCallum, *Trade and the Environment: Local Action in a New World Order*, 23 ENVTL. L. 621 (1992) (discussing the important role cross-border state-to-state coordination must play with the increasing internationalization of commerce) (Mr. McCallum is the Lieutenant Governor of the U.S. State of Wisconsin).

federal entities have a unique ability to ameliorate the localized impacts of such agreements.[42]

F. *Participation by the Public in the NAFTA Process*

The NAFTA also proved notable because of the general and widespread interest the agreement generated throughout the North American citizenry.[43] Although subsectors of private industry typically are involved in developing specific provisions of trade agreements that could affect their pecuniary interests (for example, French agriculture or the American film industry), the public interest in the NAFTA process was decidedly different in several respects.

First, public interest in the NAFTA extended to the grassroots level.[44] Local groups throughout all three nations significantly affected the course of the NAFTA.[45] Local efforts on the NAFTA were uniquely strong in the U.S.-Mexico border region where special trade rules have already caused serious local environmental threats.[46] Second, public interest in the NAFTA process involved significant coordination of non-governmental activities across national borders. Here again, the efforts were particularly strong in the U.S.-Mexico border region but also existed among the nationals of all the parties.[47] Third, while public interest in the NAFTA at times stressed the specific impacts of select NAFTA provisions, in general this interest focused on larger trade policy issues, such as

[42] *See id.*

[43] *See* George E. Brown, Jr. et al., *Making Trade Fair*, 9 WORLD POL'Y J. 309, 315 (1992) (discussing development of public participation in the United States, Canada, and Mexico on trade issues).

[44] *See* Lori Wallach, *Panel Discussion: Environmental Standards, Enforcement and NAFTA*, 5 GEO. INT'L ENVTL. L. REV. 568, 569 (1993) (noting that the U.S. "Congress received a monumental 20 million postcards" in the wake of the Tuna/Dolphin case).

[45] *Id.* at 573 (discussing role of a citizens trade network made up of 40 million citizens in all 50 of the United States).

[46] *See, e.g.*, Texas Center for Policy Studies, NAFTA and the U.S./Mexico Border Environment: Options for Congressional Action, Sept. 1992; Letter to Ambassador Kantor, U.S. Trade Representative, from Texas Center for Policy Studies, Southwest Voter Research Institute, Mexican American Legal Defense and Education Fund, Border Ecology Project, Udall Center for Public Policy, Arizona Toxics Information, International Transboundary Research Center, and Domingo Gonzales, May 18, 1993 (regarding U.S.-Mexico border issues).

[47] *See, e.g.*, Coalition for Justice in the Maquiladoras, Annual Report 1990-1991, at 19 (listing diverse membership including groups from all of the NAFTA countries); North American Institute, The North American Environment: Opportunities for Trinational Cooperation by Canada, the United States, and Mexico — Report and Recommendations, Feb. 12-14, 1993 (trilateral colloquium report). These cross-border efforts build upon similar efforts between U.S. and Canadian groups aimed at the environmental effects of the Canada-U.S. Free Trade Agreement. *See, e.g.*, Shrybman, *supra* note 16.

the NAFTA's potential effects on sustainable development and environmental protection, democracy, sub-federal environmental protections, industrial relocation and investment flight, and employment.

Fourth, public participation in the NAFTA process was unique because it was actively facilitated by the parties. Nothing demonstrated this more than the nationally-televised debate held in the United States between Vice President Gore and Texas billionaire and NAFTA naysayer Ross Perot.[48] In addition to this highly publicized debate, the parties conducted a range of activities designed to build public support for the NAFTA. For example, the United States conducted a series of hearings—both within the border region and beyond—concerning the Border Plan, where oral and written testimony was submitted by more than 650 witnesses.[49]

Governmental responses to public attention to the NAFTA, however, were not uniform.[50] For example, the Mexican government has been criticized for its failure to engage the general public in a debate over the NAFTA.[51] Although the Mexican approach may have enabled the government to streamline negotiations of the NAFTA, this approach is already raising questions as to how the agreement will be received by the Mexican people when implemented.[52]

The nature of public interest in the NAFTA highlights an important trend for trade policy-making. As economic development increasingly emphasizes expanded international trade, international and domestic public interest in these new policies is likely to continue expanding. Increasing public attention to trade matters is also likely to continue to place heavy emphasis on how these

48 *See, e.g.*, Nancy Dunne, *Gore Up Front and Deals in the Backrooms — What Turned the Tide in the Fight for NAFTA*, FIN. TIMES, Nov. 19, 1993, at 6.

49 Lallas, *supra* note 30, at 543. The Border Plan is discussed more fully at notes 158-162 and accompanying text.

50 *Cf.* Barba, *supra* note 16, at 10-12; Adolfo Aguilar Zinser, *Authoritarianism and North American Free Trade*, *in* THE POLITICAL ECONOMY OF NORTH AMERICAN FREE TRADE 205, 205-11 (Ricardo Grinspun & Maxwell A. Cameron eds., 1993).

51 *See* Zinser, *supra* note 50, at 207. One critic summarized the Mexican government's approach to the NAFTA as giving the "negotiations equivalent status of a national security affair, keeping information almost a state secret, preventing any meaningful public debate, maintaining a close vigilance on its opponents, and transmitting only general propaganda messages to the public." *Id.* The lack of public debate in Mexico produced startling results. For example, one survey of Mexican citizens found that 45.8% of those interviewed supported the NAFTA because it would make it easier for Mexicans to get jobs in the United States. Jorge G. Castañeda, *Can NAFTA Change Mexico?*, 72 FOR. AFFS. No. 4, Sept.-Oct. 1993, at 66, 74.

52 *See, e.g.*, Tod Robberson, *How Mexico Brewed a Rebellion*, WASH. POST, Jan. 9, 1994, at A31 (discussing the NAFTA as a root cause of the Chiapas uprising).

newly emerging trade policies will affect non-economic interests. Faced with growing public pressure from the grassroots level, it will be difficult for trade negotiations to continue shading themselves from the spotlight of public attention.

The NAFTA experience here has two central lessons for public participation in trade and environment. First, with rising public interest in trade agreements, the public will increasingly demand to participate in crafting these agreements.[53] The failure to provide for such participation will only serve, in the long term, as an impediment to the acceptance of any trade agreement.[54] Thus, it is in the best interests of the involved parties to ensure that this participation is informed and considered in the decisionmaking process. Second, the NAFTA holds an important lesson for environmental proponents: international alliances among environmental groups are vital to advancing an environmental agenda in trade fora.

G. *Environmental Assessments of the NAFTA*

Although public interest in the NAFTA was intense, effective public participation in the NAFTA debate required information about the potential environmental impacts of the NAFTA. This raised the issue of whether environmental assessments must be prepared for the agreement.

In general, environmental assessments are designed to provide information to government decisionmakers (both negotiators and parliamentarians) and the public in order to assist in understanding the environmental effects of proposed policies and projects, thereby allowing adverse impacts to be eliminated or minimized or the action in question to be rejected.[55] From a trade perspective, some argue that the public disclosure required in an environmental assessment process conflicts with the need of each party in trade

[53] Wallach, *supra* note 44, at 571-72; *see also* David B. Hunter, *Toward Global Citizenship in International Environmental Law*, 28 WILLAMETTE L. REV. 547, 552 (1992) (discussing need to democratize international institutions). This trend toward public involvement in trade decision-making reflects a general trend in international law toward the recognition of non-governmental organizations and persons. *See* John H. Barton & Barry E. Carter, *International Law and Institutions for a New Age*, 81 GEO. L.J. 535, 538 (1993).

[54] *Cf.* Nancy Dunne, *Clinton Woes Environmentalists: Washington Seeks Support in Congress for GATT Accord*, FIN. TIMES, Dec. 22, 1993, at 4 (discussing public opposition in the United States to the Uruguay Round).

[55] *See* 1 WORLD BANK, ENVIRONMENTAL ASSESSMENT SOURCE BOOK 1 (1991); UNEP, CONCEPTS AND PRINCIPLES IN INTERNATIONAL ENVIRONMENTAL LAW: AN INTRODUCTION 17-18 (1994).

negotiations to keep its own negotiating positions secret.[56] The NAFTA process not only displays this tension, but also shows how it can be reduced.

The NAFTA parties took different approaches to environmental assessments. At the beginning of the NAFTA process in the United States, a number of environmental groups petitioned the Bush administration to prepare an Environmental Impact Statement (EIS) for the NAFTA in accordance with the U.S. National Environmental Policy Act of 1969 (NEPA).[57] The Bush administration refused this request, but did prepare a very limited "Environmental Review" of the agreement.[58] Despite its limitations, the Review did identify environmental problems with the NAFTA, which in some instances, enabled the three parties to alter the agreement to address these concerns.[59] The Bush administration's Review admittedly did not satisfy the legal requirements of NEPA, causing three environmental groups (Public Citizen, Sierra Club, and Friends of the Earth) to use judicial means to try to require the United States to comply with NEPA as it applied to the NAFTA.[60]

With the change of administrations in the United States, further attention was focused on the application of NEPA to the NAFTA. Although the Clinton administration continued fighting the application of NEPA in the courts, the new administration did recognize that the environmental information remained incomplete and inadequate. Even though a U.S. Court of Appeals held that the administration could not be required to comply with NEPA for the NAFTA,[61] in an effort to address the need for more complete environmental information, the Clinton administration

56 *See* Brief of Amici Curiae American Automobile Manufacturers Association et al., Public Citizen v. United States Trade Representative, No. 92-2102 (CRR), at 27-29.

57 42 U.S.C. § 4341.

58 Interagency Task Force Coordinated by the Office of the United States Trade Representative, Review of U.S.-Mexico Environmental Issues (Feb. 1992).

59 For example, the Review recommended that the NAFTA "respect existing international agreements to which the U.S. is a party." *See id.* at 217. This recommendation provided a framework for the agreements' protections provided to certain international environmental agreements. *See infra* notes 91-99 and accompanying text (discussing NAFTA article 104).

60 *See* Public Citizen v. United States Trade Representative, 782 F. Supp. 139 (D.D.C.), *aff'd*, 970 F.2d 916 (D.C. Cir. 1992) (finding that plaintiffs' claims were not yet ripe for review because no agreement existed at that time).

61 *See* Public Citizen v. United States Trade Representative, 5 F.3d 549 (D.C. Cir. 1993) (holding that because the President submitted the NAFTA to Congress there was no "final agency action" upon which plaintiffs could seek review of the decision not to prepare an EIS). No U.S. federal court has held that NEPA does not apply to trade agreements. The cases involving the NAFTA merely discuss the procedural impediments to judicial review of the decision not to apply NEPA to the NAFTA. *Id.*

prepared and submitted to Congress along with the NAFTA a "Report on Environmental Issues."[62] While the Report came late in the NAFTA process, it proved to be one of the most detailed and balanced environmental overviews of the agreement. Most notably, the Report dealt with both the macro-effects of the NAFTA on the hemispheric environment and the environmental impacts on the entire U.S.-Mexico border region, although it did not focus on discrete domestic environmental impacts of the NAFTA.[63]

Each of the other two NAFTA parties also took its own distinct approach to the NAFTA environmental review process. On the one hand, the Canadian government also refused to prepare a formal Environmental Impact Assessment (EIA) for the NAFTA, sparking debate within the Canadian House of Commons.[64] However, the Canadian government moved more quickly to address the root cause of the debate—the need for environmental information pertaining to the agreement. Acting on its own initiative, the Canadian government prepared an "Environmental Review" for the NAFTA.[65] By initiating this review, the Canadian government avoided the somewhat bitter battle that occurred in the United States over whether to prepare an environmental assessment. Instead, the major issue in Canada focused on the limited public consultation process provided in formulating the environmental review.[66]

On the other hand, although Mexico prepared environmental studies for the NAFTA, the government never released a public environmental review for the agreement.[67] Mexican environmental groups sought to use the administrative means provided by Mexican law to force the government to prepare an environmental statement on the NAFTA.[68] However, the limited access citizens enjoy to the Mexican courts allowed Mexico largely to avoid the

62 OFFICE OF THE U.S. TRADE REPRESENTATIVE, THE NAFTA: REPORT ON ENVIRONMENTAL ISSUES, Nov. 1993 [hereinafter REPORT ON ENVIRONMENTAL ISSUES].

63 *See generally id.*

64 *Cf.* Constance D. Hunt, *A Note on Environmental Impact Assessment in Canada*, 20 ENVTL. L. 789 (1990).

65 *See* Canadian Environmental Review, *supra* note 32; *see also* Robert Page, *Negotiating the Environmental Provisions of NAFTA: What Gains Were Made?*, *in* THE NORTH AMERICAN FREE TRADE AGREEMENT AND THE NORTH AMERICAN COMMISSION ON THE ENVIRONMENT 10, 10-13 (Sarah Richardson ed., 1993) (prepared for the National Roundtable on the Environment and the Economy, Canada).

66 Page, *supra* note 65 at 10-11.

67 *See* Mark Ritchie, *The Green Lobby Raises a Red Flag on Agreement*, INT'L BUS., Nov. 1991, at 82, 82; Mark Ritchie, *Mexican Environmental Groups File Suit Challenging NAFTA, Outlook Considered Dim*, Sept. 1, 1993 DAILY EXEC. REP. (BNA), at A168.

68 *See Mexican Environmental Groups File Suit*, *supra* note 67.

public scrutiny that accompanied the U.S. decision not to apply NEPA to the NAFTA.

Although the Mexican and Canadian processes both avoided the tension over an environmental assessment that marked the U.S. process, the results of each of these alternative processes were markedly different. Because Canada chose to prepare and release an environmental assessment for the NAFTA, Canadian citizens had access to environmental information specific to their interests that allowed for a more informed debate. In contrast, Mexican citizens had more limited access to such information.[69] Much of the NAFTA environmental information available in Mexico was "imported" from Canada and the United States.[70] The limited access of Mexican citizens to such information hindered their effective participation.[71]

There are several lessons suggested by the different approaches to an environmental assessment taken by each of the parties. At the most basic level these assessments show that it is possible to successfully craft basic environmental assessments of trade agreements.[72] More importantly, they illustrate that environmental assessments can be useful policy tools, which can actually lead to environmental improvements of a given trade agreement—without fundamentally altering the process of trade negotiation or compromising the agreement or the benefits sought from the agreement. Moreover, the NAFTA experience demonstrates that the failure to comply with procedural laws such as NEPA can needlessly endanger the underlying trade treaty.[73] The NAFTA's environmental assessment efforts, however, represent only the first steps in the process of determining *how* such assessments for trade agreements may best be conducted. The NAFTA environmental assessment ef-

69 *Cf.* Zinser, *supra* note 50, at 207-11 (discussing lack of NAFTA information in Mexico).

70 *Id.* at 207 (noting that Mexicans learned that their government was negotiating a NAFTA from a leaked *Wall Street Journal* article).

71 *Id.* at 207-11.

72 In contrast, the NAFTA process shows the difficulties faced with the preparation of more in-depth environmental analyses, or EISs, for trade agreements. No party prepared either an EIS or an EIA for the NAFTA process. *See supra* note 61 (discussing *Public Citizen* case).

73 *See* Susan Dentzer, *Hasta la Vista, In Court, Baby*, U.S. NEWS & WORLD REP., July 12, 1993, at 47 ("What [NEPA's application to the NAFTA] means is that the proposed free-trade zone . . . could be in more limbo than ever."); *Constitutional Issue Main Focus of NAFTA EIS Hearing*, WORLD ENVT. REP., July 23, 1993, *available in* NEXIS, NEWS Library, CURNWS File ("An EIS, in fact, would put some members of Congress at ease, helping to dismiss doomsayers who say the environment will suffer tremendously as a result of [the NAFTA].").

forts leave unanswered a range of questions concerning the scope, timing, and justiciability of such assessments. For example, in the United States, despite two separate lawsuits and appeals, the courts left unanswered questions as to whether and how NEPA's EIS requirements apply to trade agreements.[74]

Despite these uncertainties, the NAFTA's overall lesson on environmental assessments is that it is not only possible to prepare such assessments for trade treaties, but it is preferable to prepare them early and on the government's own initiative.

III. SUBSTANTIVE ISSUES

The heightened attention to the environmental aspects of the NAFTA resulted in an agreement that breaks new environmental ground both within the agreement's provisions and through the developments on the parallel track. While many of the NAFTA's environmental efforts are modest, others are truly ambitious. Each offers insights into the path that future trade agreements are likely to follow on environmental issues.

A. *Provisions of the NAFTA Text*

1. *Preamble*

The central and self-proclaimed goals of most modern trade agreements are directed at trade liberalization. Coming in the wake of the United Nations Conference on Environment and Development, the NAFTA differs somewhat from previous trade agreements in that it places the goal of trade liberalization in the context of the overarching goal of sustainable development. To this end, the NAFTA's preamble specifically provides that the agreement is intended to:

> Contribute to the harmonious development and expansion of world trade . . . in a manner consistent with environmental protection and conservation; . . . promote sustainable development . . . ; [and] strengthen the development and enforcement of environmental laws and regulations.[75]

Although this preambulatory language is without binding effect, the basic premise—that trade should advance sustainable development—remains important.[76]

74 *See supra* notes 60-61 (discussing *Public Citizen* suits).

75 NAFTA, *supra* note 1, at Preamble, 32 I.L.M. at 297.

76 *See* Lallas, *supra* note 30, at 544. *But see* John Audley, *Why Environmentalists Are Angry about the North American Free Trade Agreement, in* TRADE AND THE ENVIRONMENT, *supra* note 3,

2. *Investment*

The NAFTA's approach to environment-driven industrial relocation and investment flight is one example of how the agreement seeks to implement its commitment to sustainable development. Throughout the NAFTA process various interests feared that Mexico's nascent environmental protection and enforcement system, relative to the systems of its NAFTA partners, provided businesses operating in Mexico a competitive advantage *vis-à-vis* their American and Canadian competitors.[77] This in turn fueled concerns that lower environmental costs of operation in Mexico could contribute to both industrial relocation and investment flight to Mexico by northern industries.[78] Although the actual impact of differences in the environmental costs of doing business on industrial relocation and investment flight remains a hotly debated topic, the NAFTA parties sought to address this issue within the agreement.

To this end, Canada proposed that a party's lowering or waiver of an environmental protection standard to encourage investment should be an actionable violation of the NAFTA.[79] Although this proposal would have provided a significant incentive to the parties to avoid officially lowering or waiving standards to encourage investment, it suffered from a number of significant shortcomings. First, the proposal would have applied only where a party officially waived or lowered an existing standard. Thus, the proposal did not cover the far more common instances where the waiver or lowering was not provided through the "official" regulatory or legislative process. For example, the provision would not have applied where the regulatory body provided tacit approval of an action or inaction that violated an environmental law.[80] Second, it was feared

at 191, 198 (arguing the NAFTA's preambulatory language on sustainable development "is difficult to take seriously" given the environmental questions the agreement leaves unanswered).

77 *See* Senator Max Baucus, *NAFTA Needs Environmental Side Agreement*, 10 ENVTL. F. 30, 30 (1993); Jane Bussey, *Trade Pact Doomed if It Ignores Labor, Environment, Critics Warn*, MIAMI HERALD, Apr. 4, 1993, at A28.

78 *See, e.g.*, U.S. General Accounting Office, U.S.-Mexico Trade: Some U.S. Wood Furniture Firms Relocated From Los Angeles Area to Mexico, Report to the Chairman, Comm. on Energy, House of Representatives, 1-4, GAO/NSIAD-91-191 (Apr. 1991) (furniture firms relocated to Mexico to avoid environmental compliance costs). *But see* MYTHS & REALITIES: THE NORTH AMERICAN FREE TRADE AGREEMENT 2 (1992) (arguing that no pollution haven problem exists).

79 Steve Charnovitz, *NAFTA: An Analysis of its Environmental Provisions*, 23 ENVTL. L. REP. 10,067, 10,072 (1993).

80 The only scenarios where the Canadian proposal would have definitely applied were: (1) a legislature changed or eliminated a law specifically to induce investment; or (2) a regulatory agency altered a rule specifically to induce investment.

that the proposal's emphasis on tightly binding the parties to existing laws and rules, without addressing a party's failure to regulate, could inhibit the enactment of new environmental protections. Without an incentive to act a party might refrain from regulating in fear of binding itself into a rigid legal requirement.

While the NAFTA did not adopt the Canadian proposal, it did adopt a provision designed to address the issue of investment flight. Article 1114.2 of the NAFTA provides that:

> The Parties recognize that it is inappropriate to encourage investment by relaxing domestic health, safety or environmental measures. Accordingly, a Party should not waive or otherwise derogate from, or offer to waive or otherwise derogate from, such measures as an encouragement for the establishment, acquisition, expansion or retention in its territory of an investment of an investment of an investor.[81]

If a party believes that another party has violated this prohibition, the party may request official consultations with the party whose actions are in question.[82] These consultations are to be conducted with a view towards avoiding the waiver or derogation from the environmental protection at issue.[83]

Article 1114.2 differs from the Canadian proposal in that it applies to a far greater range of activities aimed at encouraging investment at the expense of environmental protection. In exchange for its expanded scope, article 1114.2, however, limits an aggrieved party's recourse to consultations and publicity.[84] Article 1114.2's lack of enforcement measures has raised serious questions regarding the provision's ultimate ability to discourage investment flight.[85] In addition, even if article 1114.2 proves effective in dealing with future problems, it fails to address pre-existing differences in regulatory programs that may encourage industrial relocation or investment flight. In effect, article 1114.2 simply preserves the legal status quo.

81 NAFTA, *supra* note 1, art. 1114.2, 32 I.L.M. at 642.

82 *Id.*

83 *Id.*

84 *Id.*; *see also* Michelle Swenarchuk, *The Environmental Implications of NAFTA: A Legal Analysis*, *in* CANADIAN ENVIRONMENTAL LAW ASSOCIATION, THE ENVIRONMENTAL IMPLICATIONS OF TRADE AGREEMENTS 101, 125 (1993) (prepared for the Ontario Ministry of Environment and Energy).

85 *See* Esty, *supra* note 33, at 53 ("There has been considerable debate over this 'pollution haven' provision because the remedy provided to a party that believes another has induced investment through a reduction in the rigor of its environmental regime is consultations and not binding dispute resolution.").

Despite its limitations, the NAFTA investment provision may have a significant impact internationally. As more nations require their domestic industries to adopt increasingly stringent environmental measures, it is likely that the investment flight and environmental competitiveness concerns that drove the NAFTA's investment provision will spread.[86] The NAFTA investment provision is one of the first instances where a group of nations has determined that the failure of environmental protection is an unacceptable means of encouraging investment and development, and has addressed this objectionable behavior in a trade agreement. Clearly, there are more effective ways to thwart investment flight and industrial relocation than those provided in the NAFTA; however, the NAFTA provisions are a first step in this direction.[87]

Ironically, while environmental attention to the NAFTA's investment provisions has focused on the relative merits or flaws of article 1114.2, the more traditional investment provisions of the chapter may be equally important for environmental protection. The vast majority of the NAFTA investment chapter sets forth protections that the NAFTA parties agree to extend to foreign investors to provide them with the confidence necessary to invest throughout the NAFTA trade block.

Although these more traditional investment provisions are not generally thought of as having a positive environmental impact, these provisions are important for providing the environmental goods and services industry and other environmentally sound investors with the security needed to invest abroad and bring their technologies and expertise with them. Coupled with the NAFTA's basic trade obligations (such as national treatment),[88] these investment security provisions may speed the diffusion of environmental technologies and expertise.[89] In addition, the investment provisions can be expected to promote a stronger role, especially in

86 John Zarocostas, *GATT Chief Blasts West's Call for Sanctions against Poor Nations*, J. COM., Mar. 22, 1994, at A3.

87 *See generally*, Robert Housman et al., *Enforcement of Environmental Laws Under a Supplemental Agreement to the North American Free Trade Agreement*, 5 GEO. INT'L ENVTL. L. REV. 593, 593-622 (1993).

88 *See* U.S. General Accounting Office, Report to Congress: North American Free Trade Agreement — Assessment of Major Issues, Sept. 1993, Doc. No. GAO/GGD-93-137B, Vol. 2, 21 (discussing basic obligations under the NAFTA).

89 *See* Interagency Environmental Technologies Exports Working Group, Environmental Technologies Exports: Strategic Framework for U.S. Leadership, Nov. 1993, Appendix A: Mexico, NAFTA, and Environmental Export Opportunities, at 33 (noting that the NAFTA will stimulate environmental technology exports through the removal of non-tariff barriers).

Mexico, for law in general and the judiciary in particular—essential conditions for further environmental protection.

3. *International Environmental Agreements*

The NAFTA's approach to the interrelationship between international environmental agreements ("IEAs") and trade rules is one of the agreement's most aggressive attempts to advance the trade and environment debate. Throughout the trade and environment debate a great deal of emphasis has been placed on the preference for multilateral solutions to multilateral environmental problems. Thus, it follows that there has been considerable support for protecting the trade provisions of certain widely accepted IEAs from trade challenges.[90]

Article 104 and its annexes attempt to realize this protection.[91] These provisions of the NAFTA list three multilateral agreements[92] and two bilateral agreements[93] for protection. (The parties have subsequently agreed to list two other bilateral treaties once the NAFTA takes effect.)[94] Article 104 then provides that in the event of an inconsistency between the NAFTA and the trade provisions of these listed IEAs, the obligations of a party under the IEA "shall prevail to the extent of the inconsistency, provided that where a Party has a choice among equally effective and reasonably available means of complying with such obligations, the Party chooses the

90 *See, e.g.*, Michael Smith, *Afterword*, *in* TRADE AND THE ENVIRONMENT, *supra* note 3, at 287, 292 ("While a recognition of environmental trade measures contained in multilateral agreements is not a panacea, it is a major and necessary first step.").

91 NAFTA, *supra* note 1, art. 104, Annex 104.1, 32 I.L.M. at 297-98.

92 *See id.* art. 104, 32 I.L.M. at 297-98. The multilateral agreements are: (1) The Montreal Protocol on Substances that Deplete the Ozone Layer, *adopted and opened for signature* Sept. 16, 1987, *entered into force* Jan. 1, 1989, S. Treaty Doc. No 100-10, 26 I.L.M. at 1541 (the Montreal Protocol); (2) the Basel Convention on Transboundary Movements of Hazardous Wastes and Their Disposal, *opened for signature* Mar. 22, 1989, U.N. Doc. EP/16.80/3, 28 I.L.M. at 649 (the Basel Convention); and (3) the Convention on International Trade in Endangered Species of Wild Fauna and Flora, *opened for signature* Mar. 3, 1973, 27 U.S.T. 1087, 993 U.N.T.S. 243.

93 *See* NAFTA, *supra* note 1, art. 104, Annex 104, 32 I.L.M. at 297-98. The listed bilateral agreements are: Agreement on Cooperation for the Protection and Improvement of the Environment in the Border Area, Aug. 14, 1983, T.I.A.S. No. 10,827; Agreement Between the Government of Canada and the Government of the United States of America Concerning the Transboundary Movement of Hazardous Waste, signed Oct. 26, 1986, T.I.A.S. No. 1109.

94 *See infra* note 99; Report on Environmental Issues, *supra* note 62, at 11. The United States has obtained commitments from Canada and Mexico to list: The Convention on the Protection of Migratory Birds, Aug. 16, 1916, U.S.-Great Britain (on behalf of Canada) 39 Stat. 1702, T.I.A.S. No. 628 ; and The Convention Between the United States of America and the United Mexican States for the Protection of Migratory Birds and Game Mammals, Feb. 7, 1936, 50 Stat. 1311, T.I.A.S. No. 912.

alternative that is least inconsistent with the other provisions of [the NAFTA]."[95] Although the parties fully believe that article 104 preserves their ability to take actions that would otherwise be inconsistent under the NAFTA, environmentalists fear that article 104's "least inconsistent" language can be used to challenge such actions.[96]

The NAFTA also provides that the parties may add other existing and future IEAs to the protected list through the unanimous consent of the NAFTA parties.[97] Environmental groups have expressed concern that the requirement of unanimity to add additional IEAs[98] may unnecessarily hinder the ability of the parties to list other IEAs. Although the requirement of unanimous consent raises serious concerns, the parties have succeeded in adding at least two bilateral treaties to this list.[99] In the future, however, if the parties prove less successful in adding additional IEAs to the protected list, the flaws of this listing approach will become apparent. In the meantime, there is the danger that listing certain treaties leaves all unlisted treaties open to challenge without any additional protection.

Despite the limitations of article 104's protection for IEAs, the ramifications of the provision cannot be easily discounted. The NAFTA parties' ability to agree on article 104 serves as important notice that the provisions of certain IEAs must and can be pro-

95 NAFTA, *supra* note 1, art. 104.1, 32 I.L.M. at 298.

96 *Id.*; *see also* Housman & Orbuch, *supra* note 9, at 754-55. Environmentalists argue that article 104 only protects the IEAs proper and not the domestic laws of the NAFTA parties implementing those IEAs; the implementing laws of the parties are required to be "least inconsistent with the other provisions of [the NAFTA]." Housman & Orbuch, *supra* note 9, at 754. Thus, while the terms of a listed IEA may prevail, the law implementing the IEA may not.

97 NAFTA, *supra* note 1, art. 104.2, 32 I.L.M. at 298.

98 Environmentalists fear that the unanimity requirement will allow one foot-dragging NAFTA party to undermine the ability of the other NAFTA parties to implement non-listed IEAs effectively. This fear is compounded by NAFTA's accession clause, which does not require acceding parties to also accede to the IEAs listed under article 104. Thus, if the list of NAFTA parties grows, the requirement of unanimity could prove increasingly troublesome.

99 The original NAFTA text failed to list for protection the Convention on the Protection of Migratory Birds and the Convention Between the United States of America and the United Mexican States for the Protection of Migratory Birds and Game Mammals. *See Key Officials Address House Committee on Environmental Benefits of Agreement*, Int'l Trade Daily (BNA), Nov. 15, 1993. In an effort to secure the support of the U.S.-based National Audubon Society, the Clinton administration was able to obtain the consent of Canada and Mexico to place these bilateral treaties on the list of protected IEAs. This process, however, occurred at a time when the leverage for environmental gains was at its highest. Whether the parties will be able to agree on future IEAs absent that leverage remains to be seen.

tected from challenge. More broadly, the provision also affirms the belief of three important nations within the world trade system that there are instances where trade restrictions are both necessary and proper to advance environmental goals.

Moreover, the fact that the NAFTA parties were able to reach agreement on this provision may also provide much needed stimulus to move similar protection for IEAs forward at the international level, where widespread agreement has yet to translate into any concrete protection. The NAFTA's lesson here is that it is possible to provide added protections from trade challenges for IEAs without undercutting the goals of a trade agreement.

4. *Standards Provisions*

Within the trade and environment debate, many of the most difficult issues revolve around the requirements a party imposes on its domestic products and also on products in international commerce when they enter its market. The difficulty here lies in the tension that exists between the trade community's desire to eliminate unnecessary trade barriers[100] and the environmental community's desire to preserve the rights of each nation to enact and implement needed environmental protections.[101]

The frictions that exist in the area of standards can be divided into three general categories: (1) frictions over the role of the harmonization of standards; (2) frictions over the trade rules that will be used to determine when an environmental standard violates a trade obligation; and (3) frictions over the right or ability of a party to use standards that discriminate between products because of differences in their production process methods. The NAFTA standards provisions are arguably the first systematic attempt to develop, within a trade agreement, a comprehensive set of standards rules that address environmental concerns.[102] Thus, the

100 *See, e.g.*, GATT, International Trade 20 (Vol. I, ch. III) (1990-1991), at 24, 31 (Report on Trade and Environment).

101 *See, e.g.*, Audley, *supra* note 76, at 195-96; Patti A. Goldman, *Resolving the Trade and Environment Debate: In Search of a Neutral Forum and Neutral Principles*, 49 WASH. & LEE L. REV. 1278, 1292-96 (1992).

102 The NAFTA's attempt to craft "environmentally friendly" standards provisions can be traced, in large measure, to the "Waxman/Gephardt" resolution. H.R. Cong. Res. 246 § 2, 102d Sess., 138 Cong. Rec. H7699 (Aug. 6, 1992). This resolution provided that the U.S. House of Representatives "[would] not approve legislation to implement any trade agreement including [the GATT and the NAFTA] if such agreement jeopardizes United States health, safety, labor, or environmental laws (including the Federal Food, Drug, and Cosmetic Act and the Clean Air Act)." *Id.* Thus, the fate of the NAFTA was intimately tied to the agreement's standards provision.

NAFTA's standards provisions provide valuable lessons for balancing trade and environmental concerns.

The NAFTA's standards provisions are set forth in chapters 7 and 9 of the agreement. Chapter 7, section B,[103] establishes sanitary and phytosanitary (SPS) measures. Chapter 9[104] sets forth rules on all other standards-related measures (SRM), except those covered under the SPS and government procurement rules. The standards rules set forth in both chapters 7B and 9 are unique in a number of respects important to environmental protection.

a. *Right to Set Appropriate Levels of Protection*

First, both the SPS and SRM rules begin with the basic premise that all the NAFTA parties have the right to establish their own "appropriate levels of protection."[105] If a party determines that the risks from a given product or service are too great, the party can choose to ban that product or service outright—set a zero risk standard—and so long as that ban is implemented in a non-discriminatory fashion, the ban cannot violate the NAFTA.[106]

Thus, while the NAFTA generally requires that scientific evidence support the finding of a potential risk to the environment, health or safety, the social value judgement as to what level of risk is acceptable is left solely to each party without any requirement of scientific justification.[107] In insulating the risk management decisions of the parties from trade challenges the NAFTA differs sharply from what has been, prior to the close of the Uruguay Round, the emerging practice under GATT.[108]

b. *Right to Apply Standards*

Despite the NAFTA's gains in recognizing the right of a party to set its own appropriate levels of protection, the NAFTA still leaves

103 NAFTA, *supra* note 1, ch. 7, section B, 32 I.L.M. at 377-78.

104 *Id.* ch. 9, 32 I.L.M. at 386-92.

105 *Id.* arts. 712.2, 904.2, 32 I.L.M. at 378, 387; *see also* Report on Environmental Issues, *supra* note 62, at 6, 7, 9; Lallas, *supra* note 30, at 545.

106 *See* Page, *supra* note 65, at 12.

107 *See* NAFTA, *supra* note 1, art. 712.3, 32 I.L.M. at 378; *see also* Report on Environmental Issues, *supra* note 62, at 5-6.

108 *See United States — Restrictions on Imports of Tuna*, adopted Sept. 3, 1991 (Panel Report No. DS21/R), at 46. The panel decision found that the U.S. restrictions were not "necessary" within the meaning of GATT article XX because the restriction's means-ends fit was insufficiently close. *See id.*; *see also* Robert F. Housman & Durwood J. Zaelke, *The Collision of Environment and Trade: The GATT Tuna/Dolphin Decision*, 22 Envtl. L. Rep. 10,268, 10,273 (1992); *infra* note 133 (discussing limits of extrapolating from the Tuna/Dolphin decision).

environmentalists concerned over restrictions on the manner in which a party may apply its standards once a level of protection has been selected. The NAFTA SPS text requires a party to apply its standards "only to the extent necessary to achieve its appropriate level of protection, taking into account technical and economic feasibility."[109] The SRM text similarly requires parties not to create "unnecessary obstacles" to trade in applying their standards.[110]

Environmentalists believe that this "necessary" language is subject to interpretation under GATT jurisprudence, which could require environmental standards to be "least trade restrictive" as applied.[111] Such a reading could seriously hinder the abilities of the parties to enact and implement environmental protections. The NAFTA parties, however, do not believe that this test lends itself to the development of a least trade restrictive jurisprudence under the NAFTA.[112]

The NAFTA standards provisions are also notable because they avoid the concept of proportionality where the environmental gains of a measure must be proportional to the trade burdens the measure imposes.[113] While the NAFTA requires disciplines on a party's application of its standard, it does not require that the burdens of application be proportional to the ends; so long as the standard satisfies all other tests, its burdens are irrelevant.

c. *Role of Science*

The NAFTA also differs in the requirement imposed on a party to advance a scientific justification for its standard. Under NAFTA's SPS rules a party does not need to prove a scientific justification for its measures. It must only show that its standards are "based on scientific principles"[114] and the product of an acceptable risk assessment process.[115] Similarly, under chapter 9's SRM rules,

109 NAFTA, *supra* note 1, art. 712.5, 32 I.L.M. at 378.

110 *Id.* art. 904.4, 32 I.L.M. at 387.

111 *See Thailand — Restrictions on Importation of and Internal Taxes on Cigarettes*, (adopted Nov. 7, 1990), 37 BISD 223, para. 74 (1990).

112 *Cf.* Lallas, *supra* note 30, at 545.

113 Jeffrey L. Dunoff, *Reconciling International Trade with Preservation of the Global Commons: Can We Prosper and Protect?*, 49 WASH. & LEE L. REV. 1407, 1447-48 (1992) (discussing proportionality). *See also* Lallas, *supra* note 30, at 545.

114 NAFTA, *supra* note 1, art. 712.3, 32 I.L.M. at 378. The NAFTA further provides that a "scientific basis" is "a reason based on data or information derived using scientific methods." *Id.* art. 724, 32 I.L.M. at 382-83.

115 *See id.* art. 712.3, 32 I.L.M. at 378. While this standard seeks to prevent "duelling science," it does provide discipline against protectionism by requiring that some science must support a measure (except in the case of precautionary standards, *see infra* notes 128-131 and accompanying text). If a party can show that no scientific basis exists for a stan-

a party need not conduct a risk assessment before setting a standard.[116] Nor does the SRM text require a party to advance a scientific rationale for its standard. All a party must do is ensure that the "demonstrable purpose" of its standard is to advance the legitimate goals of, among other things: "safety," "protection of human, animal or plant life or health, the environment, or consumers," or "sustainable development."[117] While the NAFTA requires that environmental, health and safety decisions be informed by scientific evidence,[118] the NAFTA leaves the value-laden process of risk management up to the domestic experts.[119] Once a risk has been identified (not proven) by a NAFTA party, that party is free to decide how much of that risk is acceptable (for example, a 1 in 100 risk of cancer versus a 1 in 10 risk).

Thus, the NAFTA SRM and SPS provisions attempt to prevent "duelling science" from serving as a justification to find an environmental, health or safety measure inconsistent with the NAFTA's standards obligations. These provisions are among the NAFTA's most important accomplishments in dealing with environmental protections. They provide a valuable lesson about the important role science can play in trade and environmental decisionmaking without unduly burdening the ability to preserve and protect a country's standards.

Although the NAFTA makes progress in eliminating the problem of "dueling science," the somewhat rigid risk assessment requirements of the NAFTA SPS text could inadvertently serve as an obstacle to enhanced environmental, health, and safety protec-

dard, the standard would violate the NAFTA. This balance was vital to the United States in that it preserved the United States' long-standing position, as seen in the U.S.-E.C. beef hormone dispute, that standards must have some scientific basis to be proper. *See* Holly Hammonds, *A U.S. Perspective on the EC Hormones Directive*, 11 MICH. J. INT'L L. 840, 843-44 (1990).

116 *See* NAFTA, *supra* note 1, art. 907.1, 32 I.L.M. at 387-88 (a party "may" conduct a risk assessment).

117 *See id.* art. 904.4 and 915.1, 32 I.L.M. at 387, 391-92. The "demonstrable purpose" requirement does provide discipline to prevent unbridled protectionism. Under this test, if a party can show that the purpose of a provision was to erect a discriminatory barrier to trade, for example where science shows that the harm the standard is predicated on is nonexistent, then the standard would violate the NAFTA. *Id.* art. 904.3, 32 I.L.M. at 387.

118 *See id.* arts. 712.3, 907.1, 32 I.L.M. at 378, 387-88.

119 *See* Ellen J. Case, Note, *The Public's Role in Risk Assessment*, 5 GEO. INT'L ENVTL. L. REV. 479, 494-95 (1993). While risk assessment focuses on the science of identifying risks, risk management is the process of determining how to address such risk. *Id.* Risk management decisions must weigh not only science, but also ethical, social, political and economic considerations. *Id.*

tion.[120] A technical reading of the SPS text would require that a risk assessment be available to the actual decision-makers prior to the enactment of a standard. Such a reading raises four concerns. First, it is unclear how such a requirement would apply where a standard is adopted as a political decision, without a prior risk assessment, but a subsequent risk assessment confirms the risk addressed by the standard.

Second, it is unclear how such a requirement would apply to environmental standards adopted by referendum or popular vote. These unanswered questions place at potential risk a wide range of environmental, health, and safety protections especially at the subnational (state, provincial and local) level in the United States. Third, the human and fiscal costs associated with requiring a risk assessment before any SPS measure is taken may have a chilling effect on future environmental, health and safety measures, especially at the sub-federal level. Fourth, the NAFTA's risk assessment requirement may also place at risk environmental standards that are based on consumer preference[121] and not on scientific data.

d. *Harmonization*

The NAFTA also attempts to chart a new path for the harmonization of standards. First, the NAFTA seeks to ensure that the harmonization of standards will not occur in a downward fashion towards a lowest common denominator. To this end, the NAFTA's SPS rules explicitly provide that any harmonization is to occur "without reducing the level of protection of human, animal or plant life or health."[122]

In addition, although the NAFTA maintains clear preference for the increased harmonization of environmental, health, and safety standards,[123] the NAFTA seeks to address the threat of downward harmonization by concentrating on alternative means of en-

120 *See The Role of Science in Adjudicating Trade Disputes Under the North American Free Trade Agreement: 1992 Hearing Before the House of Representatives Committee on Science, Space, and Technology*, 102d Cong., 2d Sess. 38, 50-51 (statement of David Wirth). Interestingly, the NAFTA's risk assessment requirement substantially buoys the discipline of risk assessment, which has faced considerable criticism within the United States. *See* Case, *supra* note 119, at 479, 480 ("The science of risk assessment has suffered from its inability to deliver a foundation and credibility for regulatory decisions and policies.").

121 *See, e.g.*, 7 U.S.C. §§ 1901-04, 2142-43 (1991). Humane transport, slaughter and sale laws require that certain humane or ethical standards be applied to commerce in livestock, pets, and show animals. Humane slaughter laws, in particular, have no bearing on the quality of the product, which will meet its demise anyway.

122 *See* NAFTA, *supra* note 1, art. 713.1, 32 I.L.M. at 378.

123 *See, e.g.*, *id.* art. 906, 32 I.L.M. at 387.

couraging voluntary harmonization. Internationally, the drive to harmonize standards has focused largely on either mandatory rules aimed at requiring the use of international standards or rules that provide significant incentives to adopt international standards at the cost of domestic standards.[124]

The NAFTA's harmonization efforts rely principally on technical cooperation and increased transparency to facilitate: (1) the actual harmonization of standards; and (2) where technical standards may be different but provide similar protections, equivalency determinations.[125] Thus, while the NAFTA encourages harmonization and the use of international standards,[126] it does so with the explicit recognition of each party's right to exceed the protections of such international standards.[127]

e. *Precautionary Principle*

The standards provisions of the NAFTA also break new ground for the formation of trade policy by explicitly recognizing the precautionary principle of environmental law.[128] Articles 715.4 of the SPS text and 907.3 of the SRM text each allow the NAFTA parties leeway to adopt environmental, health and safety measures where the scientific evidence is insufficient to determine the actual risk posed by a given product or service.[129] Whereas the other NAFTA standards provisions, discussed above, provide leeway for environmental protections where the science is conflicting,[130] these precautionary provisions provide leeway where the science in incomplete. A party must, however, revisit a precautionary stan-

124 *See, e.g.*, Uruguay Round Final Act, *supra* note 5, art. 2.4.

125 *See* NAFTA, *supra* note 1, art. 714.1, 32 I.L.M. at 378.

126 *Id.* arts. 713, 905, 32 I.L.M. at 378, 387.

127 *Id.* arts. 713.3, 905.3, 32 I.L.M. at 378, 387. For example, article 905 provides, in pertinent part:

> 1. Each Party shall use, as a basis for its standards-related measures, relevant international standards . . . except where such standards would be an ineffective or inappropriate means to fulfill its legitimate objectives, for example because of . . . the level of protection that Party considers appropriate.
>
> 2. A Party's standards-related measure that conforms to an international standard shall be presumed consistent with [the Party's Basic Rights and Obligations].
>
> 3. Nothing in paragraph 1 shall be construed to prevent a Party, in pursuing its legitimate objectives, from adopting, maintaining or applying any standards-related measure that results in a higher level of protection than would be achieved if the measure were based on the relevant international standard.

Id. art. 905, 32 I.L.M. at 387.

128 *See* UNEP, *supra* note 55, at 25-26.

129 *See* NAFTA, *supra* note 1, arts. 715.4, 907.3, 32 I.L.M. at 378-79, 387-88.

130 *See generally supra* text accompanying notes 100-140 (discussing the NAFTA standards rules).

dard once adequate information becomes available and eliminate the standard if no scientific basis can be found for it.[131]

These provisions allow the domestic authorities of each party to adopt measures aimed at avoiding environmental, health, and safety risks before real, and often times irreversible, harms actually occur. Thus, for example, although some may still question the environmental risks associated with global climate change, even in the absence of perfect science the NAFTA parties remain free to take measures aimed at addressing the threats from climate change.

f. *Production Process Methods*

Negotiations over restrictions based on production process methods ("PPMs") proved more difficult than in other standards areas. The essential issue in the NAFTA and other PPM negotiations is determining when a party may restrict trade in products based upon the PPMs of the products in question.[132] Given the United States and Mexico's history on PPM issues,[133] the difficulties encountered during the PPM negotiations should come as no surprise.

Going into the NAFTA negotiations a number of U.S. environmental groups sought to have the NAFTA provide disciplines on PPM-based SRMs that would differentiate between allowable and unallowable restrictions (as opposed to the current GATT framework, which generally disallows all PPM-based restrictions). Although PPM-based restrictions were the topic of much discussion, in the end, the NAFTA text did not adopt this approach.

The NAFTA's SRM text provides that a standard may include rules that apply to "goods or related processes and production methods."[134] Although article 915.1 of the SRM text recognizes

131 *Id.* arts. 712, 715.4, 907, 32 I.L.M. at 377-79, 387-88.

132 For an excellent discussion of the PPM issues, see John H. Jackson, *World Trade Rules and Environmental Policies: Congruence or Conflict?*, *in* TRADE AND THE ENVIRONMENT, *supra* note 3, at 219, 226-29.

133 *See United States — Restrictions on Imports of Tuna* (adopted Sept. 3, 1991) (Panel Report No. DS21/R) (panel decision finding U.S. Marine Mammal Protection Act failed to comply with GATT because, among other things, it applied to the production process methods of tuna harvesting outside the territory of the United States and not to tuna as a product). While the Tuna/Dolphin decision is generally informative, its further application may be limited. Generally speaking, the facts of the Tuna/Dolphin decision presented a bad test case. The case involved standards that applied to PPMs outside U.S. territory. In addition, these standards were arguably somewhat discriminatory. The decision has never been adopted by the GATT Contracting Parties.

134 NAFTA, *supra* note 1, art. 915, 32 I.L.M. at 391-92.

PPM restrictions as standards, neither article 907 nor article 915 explicitly includes PPM-based restrictions as "legitimate objectives" that are protected from challenge.[135] Thus, it appears that while an environmental PPM-based restriction may be considered a standard, it may not be able to receive the additional protections the SRM text typically provides for other environmental SRMs. The effect of this duality may be to leave PPMs essentially in the same posture as they are under the GATT: at risk in all instances.[136]

The NAFTA's inability to resolve the PPM issue reflects the issue's inherent difficulty. From an environmental perspective, the manner in which a product is produced is an essential element of the product that cannot be parceled off in determining how a given product is to be treated at market. This perspective finds support in the fact that the greatest environmental impacts of most products often occur not at the consumer or post-consumer stages, but at the production stage.

The trade perspective, however, views PPMs as the proverbial slippery slope—allowances for regulating environmental PPMs will open the door for restrictions on a vast array of issues related to production (such as labor standards) that will completely disrupt international trade.[137] The NAFTA's inability to resolve the PPM issue simply reflects the incredible difficulties this issue will pose for future trade negotiations.

g. *The Impact of the NAFTA's Standards Provisions*

The NAFTA's standards provisions have already begun to affect international trade decisionmaking. In the final days of the Uruguay Round, many of the premises underlying the NAFTA SPS provisions were incorporated into the Final Uruguay Round SPS

135 *Id.* art. 904, 907, 32 I.L.M at 387-88.

136 *See* Richard B. Stewart, *The NAFTA: Trade, Competition, Environmental Protection*, 27 Int'l Law. 751, 761 (1993); Housman & Orbuch, *supra* note 9, at 738-39. The only exception to this statement is with regard to the PPM-based restrictions provided for in the IEAs listed under article 104 of the NAFTA. *See supra* notes 91-99 and accompanying text (discussing article 104). By protecting the PPM provisions of these IEAs, the NAFTA has essentially recognized certain internationally agreed-to PPMs.

137 Ambassador Smith eloquently summarizes this fear:

> Today we will use trade to dictate to the rest of the world how many parts per million of benzene is permissible, tomorrow it will be how many hours in the day a worker can work, next it will be the per capita number of schools a country must have. Surely, these seemingly innocent and laudable social goals will sooner or later be hijacked by protectionist interests .... We will have opened a Pandora's box of protectionism.

Smith, *supra* note 90, at 287-88.

text.[138] For example, the Final Uruguay Round SPS text incorporates the basic premise behind the NAFTA's affirmation of the right of the parties to adopt their own appropriate levels of protection, even where such levels exceed international standards.[139] Similarly, the Uruguay Round SPS text on harmonization acknowledges the NAFTA's premise that any harmonization should not compromise the protections afforded by a party's chosen level of protection.[140] Although the final Uruguay Round text adopted many of the NAFTA SPS changes, the parties refused to adopt a similar set of changes proposed by the United States for the Technical Barriers to Trade text (the GATT equivalent to the NAFTA SRM text).[141]

While the NAFTA standards rules are likely to play a substantial role in future standards rule-setting efforts, it is likely that the NAFTA's standards rules are only an intermediary step. The failure of the Uruguay Round to incorporate the SRM rules suggests that the NAFTA provisions are not the last word and future negotiations will be needed to address the unresolved environmental issues. The remaining shortcomings of the NAFTA text also show that additional refinements to the NAFTA framework will be needed before the proper trade and environment balance can be found.

That the NAFTA's standards rules may serve an interim function is, however, not to downplay the effect these rules will have on future trade negotiations. The NAFTA's rules are already playing a major role in setting the terms of the debate for future efforts in this area and this will probably continue at least for the foreseeable future.[142] Moreover, assuming that the NAFTA rules are applied fairly and rationally, they will be refined and the weight accorded these rules in international circles is likely to increase. Thus, while the NAFTA standards rules do not solve all the standards issues in the trade and environment debate, they are a substantial step forward.

138 *See GATT TBT Agreement Reveals Failure of U.S. to Secure Changes*, INSIDE U.S. TRADE, Dec. 24, 1993, at 11.

139 *See* Uruguay Round Final Act, *supra* note 5, Agreement on the Application of Sanitary and Phytosanitary Measures, preamble, art. 11 n.2.

140 *See id.*

141 *See GATT TBT Agreement Reveals Failure of U.S. to Secure Changes, supra* note 138, at 11.

142 *See supra* text accompanying notes 138-140 (discussing NAFTA's effect on the GATT Uruguay Round).

5. *Dispute Resolution*

The NAFTA's dispute resolution provisions also attempt to move the trade and environment debate forward. First, the NAFTA provides that in disputes among the NAFTA parties concerning IEAs or an environmental, health, or safety measure, the challenged party has the right to have the case heard exclusively under the substantive and procedural provisions of the NAFTA.[143] This provision secures the added protections the NAFTA provides to environmental measures by preventing the challenging party from undercutting these protections by bringing the dispute under GATT where no such protections exist.[144]

The NAFTA also explicitly provides that a NAFTA party challenging another NAFTA party's environmental, health, or safety standards bears the burden of proof in the dispute.[145] The Canadian government has summarized the effect of this provision: "[I]n the event of a dispute, the environment would be given the benefit of the doubt."[146] The degree of protection actually provided by these burden-shifting provisions is, however, unclear because the NAFTA text is silent as to the level of burden imposed on the challenging party (*prima facie* or reasonable doubt).[147]

In addition, the NAFTA clarifies the role of experts in trade disputes and seeks to provide dispute panels with greater access to such experts. Trade panels are typically made up solely of international trade experts. Thus, the panel members' access to environmental expertise in disputes concerning environmental issues is of great importance to environmentalists. The NAFTA provides two different mechanisms for panels to receive environmental expertise. First, subject to the terms and conditions set by the parties to a dispute, dispute panels can request formation of an independent scientific review board to prepare a "written report . . . on any factual issue concerning environmental, health, safety or other scientific matters raised" in a dispute.[148] Only if both parties disapprove this request can the panel be denied access to such a review board.[149] The review board's membership is selected by the panel

143 NAFTA, *supra* note 1, arts. 2005.3, 2005.4, 32 I.L.M. at 684.

144 *See* Esty, *supra* note 33, at 54.

145 NAFTA, *supra* note 1, arts. 723.6, 914.4, 32 I.L.M. at 382, 391.

146 Canadian Environmental Review, *supra* note 32, at 70.

147 *See* Housman & Orbuch, *supra* note 9, at 744; James E. Bailey, *Free Trade and the Environment — Can NAFTA Reconcile the Irreconcilable*, 8 AM. UNIV. J. INT'L L. & POL'Y 839, 853 (1993).

148 *See* NAFTA, *supra* note 1, art. 2015.1, 32 I.L.M. at 696-97.

149 *Id.* art. 2015.1, 32 I.L.M. at 696.

in consultation with the parties.[150] Second, on request of a party, or at its own initiative, a NAFTA panel "may seek information and technical advice from any person or body that it deems appropriate, provided that the disputing Parties so agree and subject to such terms and conditions as such Parties may agree."[151] Following the NAFTA model, the Final Uruguay Round text also provides for access for panels to outside expertise. This movement in the Uruguay Round suggests that the NAFTA's increased access for panels to outside expertise has already influenced other international trade fora.[152]

Despite the advances made in the NAFTA dispute resolution provisions, these provisions have come under strong criticism for their failure to provide greater public participation and transparency in trade disputes. Under the NAFTA's dispute resolution provisions, interested members of the general public and non-governmental organizations cannot participate in, or have access to, the hearings or consultations conducted during a dispute.[153] Nor can these individuals and groups obtain the filings of the parties in a dispute.[154] Similarly, in certain instances the public can even be denied access to the panel's final decision.[155]

The NAFTA's failure to reflect greater transparency and participatory rights in trade disputes will diminish the long-term viability of the NAFTA procedural rules as a framework for future trade agreements.[156] For example, although the Final Uruguay Round text is itself weak on transparency and public participation, the text does surpass the NAFTA by providing that, at the request of one of the parties to a dispute, the parties must make their briefs, or summaries of their briefs, available to the general public. The NAFTA's lesson for transparency then seems to be that while increased transparency and access to trade decisionmaking seems inevitable, it is likely to be an incremental process.[157]

150 *Id.* art. 2015.1, 32 I.L.M. at 697.

151 *Id.* art. 2014, 32 I.L.M. at 696.

152 A panel's access to outside expertise is not without precedent. In the *Thai Cigarettes* case, the GATT dispute panel consulted with and received a submission from the World Health Organization. *See Thailand — Restrictions on Importation of and Internal Taxes on Cigarettes, supra* note 111, at 201, 216-20. Thus, the NAFTA-related movements in the Uruguay Round may be seen as a clarification or enunciation of the existing status of expert information under the GATT.

153 *See* NAFTA, *supra* note 1, art. 2012.1(b), 32 I.L.M. at 696.

154 *Id.*

155 *See id.* art. 2017.4, 32 I.L.M. at 697.

156 *Cf.* Jackson, *supra* note 132, at 232 (discussing need for greater transparency in international trade decision-making).

157 Note: Author's opinion.

B. *Elements of the Parallel Track*

Although the NAFTA text breaks new ground in the trade and environment debate, many of the most interesting NAFTA trade and environment developments occurred on the parallel environmental track.

1. *The Mexican-U.S. Border Plan*

From the outset of the NAFTA process, the deplorable environmental situation on the U.S.-Mexico border was one of the most pressing issues confronting further hemispheric economic integration. "Driven by the commencement of the Maquiladora Program, a program of U.S. trade incentives . . . , and the liberalization of Mexican trade rules in 1987, industrial development in the Border Region has turned the area into a 'virtual cesspool and a breeding ground for infectious disease.' "[158]

In an effort to deal with the border's problems, in February of 1992, the environmental ministers of the United States and Mexico released the Integrated Environmental Plan for the Mexican-U.S. Border Area ("Border Plan").[159] The Border Plan focuses on four major objectives: (1) cooperative efforts to strengthen the enforcement of environmental laws relating to polluting activities; (2) increases in investments for pollution control efforts; (3) cooperative efforts to increase the understanding of pollution problems confronting citizens in the border region; and (4) cooperative efforts in environmental education and training.[160]

Although the Border Plan makes an effort to deal with the region's environmental problems, the plan was criticized for failing to provide: (1) sufficient financing to conduct the actions called for;[161] (2) adequate enforcement strategies to deal with polluters who use the border as a shield from prosecution; and (3) effective

[158] *See* Housman & Orbuch, *supra* note 9, at 777 (quoting American Medical Association report) (citations omitted).

[159] EPA-SEDUE, Integrated Environmental Plan for the Mexican-U.S. Border Area (First Stage, 1992-1994).

[160] *See* Timothy Atkeson, *The Mexican-U.S. Border Environmental Plan*, 1 J. ENVT. & DEV. 143, 147 (1992).

[161] Ironically, the U.S. Congress cut the already small amounts of funding that were to be made available for these efforts. *See* Report of the Administration on the North American Free Trade Agreement and Actions Taken in Fulfillment of the May 1, 1991 Commitments, Sept 18, 1992, at 126.

means to deal with the region's tremendous water quality and supply problems.[162]

The Border Plan provides at least two important lessons. First, despite its shortcomings, the plan provides a model for future economic integration among parties that share common borders. While the severity of the environmental problems on the U.S.-Mexico border may be somewhat unique, where economic integration occurs over a shared border, the environmental effects of such integration tend to concentrate at border crossings. The Border Plan provides one strategy for dealing with the concentrated environmental effects of economic expansion. Future efforts at addressing similar concentrated impacts would do well, however, to learn from the NAFTA experience and avoid the sometimes substantial flaws in the plan.

Second, and more importantly, the plan's shortcomings stand as a vivid example of why environmental protection must occur contemporaneously with economic development. Despite the added growth obtained through the largely unregulated economic expansion in the region, the resources now available appear insufficient to correct the current environmental situation. Thus, the border region is an apt reminder that, when it comes to environmental issues, truly "an ounce of prevention is worth a pound of cure."

2. *The North American Agreement on Environmental Cooperation*

The North American Agreement on Environmental Cooperation (NAAEC) supplements the NAFTA and commits the NAFTA parties to a series of obligations and institutions intended to advance both environmental protection and the environmental sustainability of NAFTA-related trade. Specifically, the NAAEC's stated goals include the promotion of sustainable development, support for the environmental objectives of the NAFTA, and the promotion of transparency and public participation in the development and enhancement of environmental protections.[163]

a. *General Obligations*

Under the NAAEC, the parties' obligations include: (1) ensuring high levels of environmental protection and striving to improve

162 *See* Jan Gilbreath Rich, *Planning the Border's Future: The Mexican-U.S. Integrated Border Environmental Plan*, U.S.-Mexican Occasional Paper No. 1, Mar. 1992, at 1, 4.; Housman & Orbuch, *supra*, note 9, at 778-79, 782.

163 NAAEC, *supra* note 21, art. 1, 32 I.L.M. at 1483.

these levels;[164] (2) effectively enforcing their environmental laws;[165] and (3) ensuring that the procedures for developing and implementing their environmental laws are impartial, transparent, and equitable.[166]

One of the most important commitments secured by the NAAEC is the agreement of the parties to provide citizens access to judicial and administrative procedures for the enforcement of environmental laws.[167] While this provision does not guarantee that citizens will have actual standing in domestic courts to secure the enforcement of environmental laws, it does ensure that, consistent with a party's laws, citizens will have the right to petition their governments to enforce these laws. This provision also requires the parties to provide citizens who have suffered real damages because of an environmental harm the right to sue the person or legal entity that caused the harm.[168]

b. *The Commission for Environmental Cooperation*

The NAAEC also establishes a new trilateral Commission for Environmental Cooperation (CEC).[169] The CEC is a continent-wide institution that is intended to complement existing bilateral environmental institutions in North America. The CEC is headed by the environmental ministers of the three parties who sit as the governing Council of Ministers.[170] The day-to-day affairs of the CEC will be directed by an independent Secretariat serving an Executive Director selected by the Council of Ministers.[171] The Secretariat and the Council of Ministers will also have input from a Joint Public Advisory Committee made up of five non-governmental individuals from each of the member states.[172]

Although the CEC has a wide range of responsibilities related to environmental protection, for the purposes of this paper its

164 *Id.* art. 3, 32 I.L.M. at 1483.

165 *Id.* art. 5, 32 I.L.M. at 1483-84. This obligation includes the responsibility to: appoint and train inspectors; monitor compliance with environmental laws; investigate suspected violations of environmental laws; seek voluntary compliance agreements to avoid or end violations of environmental laws; and use legal proceedings and sanctions, or otherwise seek appropriate remedies for violations of environmental laws. *Id.* A party's failure to fulfill its article 5 obligations can serve as grounds for dispute settlement and sanctions under the other provisions of the NAAEC.

166 *Cf. id.* art. 4, 32 I.L.M. at 1483.

167 *Id.* arts. 5-6, 32 I.L.M. at 1483-84.

168 *Id.* art. 6, 32 I.L.M. at 1484.

169 *Id.* art. 8, 32 I.L.M. at 1485.

170 *Id.* art. 9, 32 I.L.M. at 1485.

171 *Id.* art. 11, 32 I.L.M. at 1487.

172 *Id.* art. 16, 32 I.L.M. at 1489.

most important responsibilities are those that relate directly to the NAFTA. These NAFTA-related responsibilities fall into two general categories: (1) the CEC's responsibilities towards the NAFTA institutions; and (2) the CEC's responsibilities directed at ensuring effective enforcement of environmental laws.

i. *NAFTA Activities*

The CEC is charged with a number of responsibilities that relate directly to the NAFTA. The CEC is responsible for serving as a point of public inquiry and comment concerning the fulfillment of the NAFTA's environmental goals.[173] Additionally, the CEC may be called upon to provide information when, under article 114.2 of the NAFTA, a party seeks consultations with another party concerning the alleged derogation from environmental laws for the purposes of attracting or securing investment.[174]

The CEC is also charged with helping to avoid environmental trade disputes under the NAFTA. To this end the CEC shall provide recommendations to the NAFTA Free Trade Commission—the trilateral NAFTA oversight body—as to how such disputes may be avoided.[175] The CEC is responsible for identifying experts to assist NAFTA panels hearing trade disputes that involve environmental matters.[176]

ii. *Enforcement Activities*

The CEC will play a role in encouraging the enforcement of national laws. One of the principal motivations for the creation of the CEC was the need to address the potential that the NAFTA would encourage industrial flight as companies seek to avoid environmental laws and regulations. Although for the most part all three NAFTA countries have similar environmental regulatory requirements, serious concerns were raised concerning the failure to enforce those requirements.[177] Absent effective environmental enforcement in all the NAFTA parties, some feared the NAFTA could encourage industrial flight and investment displacement as companies relocate to avoid the costs of environmental compliance.[178]

[173] *Id.* art. 10.6(a), 32 I.L.M. at 1486.

[174] *Id.* art. 10.6(b), 32 I.L.M. at 1486.

[175] *Id.* art. 10.6(c), 32 I.L.M. at 1486.

[176] *Id.* art. 10.6(c)(iii), 32 I.L.M. at 1486.

[177] *See supra* text accompanying notes 77-78 (discussing concerns over enforcement of environmental laws).

[178] The actual effect of environmental regulations on investment and industrial siting decisions is heavily disputed. *Compare* Friends of the Earth, Standards Down Profits Up!,

The fear that the NAFTA might become an instrument for environmental degradation led the NAFTA parties to provide the CEC with ground-breaking responsibilities and powers to oversee environmental enforcement.

The NAAEC establishes, under the auspices of the CEC, a dispute resolution procedure to help ensure that the parties effectively enforce their environmental laws.[179] Through this procedure, a party may request an arbitral panel be formed:

> where the alleged persistent pattern of failure by the Party complained against to effectively enforce its environmental law relates to a situation involving workplaces, firms, companies or sectors that produce goods or provide services: (a) traded between the territories of the Parties; or (b) that compete, in the territory of the Party complained against, with goods or services produced or provided by persons of another Party.[180]

This request for a panel requires a two-thirds vote of the CEC.[181]

Article 45.1 of the NAAEC provides guidance regarding what constitutes effective enforcement for the purposes of the NAAEC:

> [a] Party has not failed to "effectively enforce its environmental law" . . . where the action or inaction in question by agencies or officials of that Party:
> (a) reflects a reasonable exercise of their discretion in respect of investigatory, prosecutorial, regulatory or compliance matters; or
> (b) results from *bona fide* decisions to allocate resources to enforcement in respect of other environmental matters determined to have higher priorities[.][182]

Panels will be made up of five members[183] selected from a previously-agreed-upon roster of independent and objective experts ex-

Jan. 1993 (finding that the failure to comply with environmental laws can increase some industries' profits by upwards of 200%) *with* Patrick Low & Alexander Yeats, *Do Dirty Industries Migrate? in* WORLD BANK DISCUSSION PAPERS, INTERNATIONAL TRADE AND THE ENVIRONMENT, 89, 103 (1992) (finding that environmental costs of compliance are too low to affect investment and siting decisions). Most economic studies tend to find that, in most instances, current environmental regulations do not alone play a major role in such decisions. *See* Norman A. Bailey, *Foreign Direct Investment and Environmental Protection in the Third World, in* TRADE AND THE ENVIRONMENT, *supra* note 3, at 133, 135-36.

179 NAAEC, *supra* note 21, at arts. 22-36, 32 I.L.M. at 1490-94.

180 *Id.* art. 24.1, 32 I.L.M. at 1490. Disputes concerning laws primarily aimed at managing natural resources are, however, excepted from these procedures. *Id.* art. 45.2(b), 32 I.L.M. at 1495.

181 *Id.* art. 24.1, 32 I.L.M. at 1490.

182 *Id.* art. 45.1, 32 I.L.M. at 1494-95.

183 *Id.* art 27.1(a), 32 I.L.M. at 1491.

perienced in environmental law and its enforcement, or in the resolution of international disputes.[184] Once a panel is formed, it will review the information provided to it by the parties to the dispute and any other interested NAAEC party. Additionally, on the approval of the parties to the dispute, an arbitral panel "may seek information and technical advice from any person or body that it deems appropriate."[185]

After hearing all the evidence in a dispute, the panel will furnish an initial report to the parties.[186] If, after receiving and consulting on the initial report, the parties are still unable to resolve the dispute, then the panel shall prepare a final report to the parties and the CEC.[187] This final report shall be made public five days after its submission to the CEC.

If the final panel report finds that the challenged party has persistently failed to enforce its environmental laws effectively, then the parties may agree upon a corrective "action plan."[188] If the parties cannot agree on a plan, then the panel may impose one.[189]

Panels are also empowered under article 34.4 of the NAAEC to impose a "monetary enforcement assessment" against the party found to have failed to enforce its laws.[190] For the first year after the entry into force of the NAAEC these assessments are limited to US$20 million.[191] Thereafter, no single assessments can exceed .007% of the total trade in goods between the parties in the most recent year for which data is available.[192] Monies obtained through an assessment are paid into a fund established under the CEC, and the CEC is directed to expend these monies to improve or enhance enforcement of environmental law in the country against which the claim is filed.[193]

If a party fails to pay a monetary assessment or continues in its failure to enforce its environmental laws, the complaining party or parties may suspend annually the application of the NAFTA benefits (such as tariff reductions) in an amount no greater than the

184 *Id.* art. 25, 32 I.L.M. at 1491.
185 *Id.* art. 30, 32 I.L.M. at 1492.
186 *Id.* art. 31, 32 I.L.M. at 1492.
187 *Id.* art. 32, 32 I.L.M. at 1492.
188 *Id.* arts. 33, 34, 32 I.L.M. at 1492.
189 *Id.* art. 34.4, 32 I.L.M. at 1493.
190 *Id.* art. 34.5, 32 I.L.M. at 1493.
191 *Id.* Annex 34.1, 32 I.L.M. at 1496.
192 *Id.*
193 *Id.* Annex 34.3, 32 I.L.M. at 1496.

monetary assessment imposed by the panel.[194] The suspension of benefits provisions of the NAAEC is not applicable to Canada. Instead, if the Canadian government fails to pay an assessment, the CEC, on the request of the complaining party, will collect the assessment through a summary proceeding before a Canadian court of competent jurisdiction.[195] The different direct collection approach for Canada was necessitated because of provisions within the Canadian constitution. Because this approach uses the power of the domestic judiciary, it may prove more effective in securing compliance over the long-term.

While the dispute resolution provisions of the NAAEC are ground-breaking, they suffer from important limitations. First and foremost, the dispute proceedings are government-to-government; the public is not accorded any role in these proceedings nor is the public entitled to obtain information from these proceedings. Second, the range of disputes that may be brought to an arbitral panel is limited. For example, the definition of effective enforcement eliminates entire classes of potential disputes from these proceedings. Third, the standard for what disputes may be heard is high in that it requires a "persistent pattern" of non-enforcement. Fourth, the definition of what constitutes enforcement also allows the parties tremendous leeway to avoid having a dispute brought to a panel. Fifth, the entire dispute process is unnecessarily time-consuming and convoluted, raising serious concerns as to whether the process will ever result in environmental gains.

In addition to the dispute resolution procedures set up under the NAAEC, the Secretariat of the CEC is also charged with a special role in ensuring enforcement. Under article 14 of the NAAEC, the Secretariat "may consider a submission from any non-governmental organization or person asserting that a Party is failing to effectively enforce its environmental law."[196] The Secretariat then will determine, on the basis of a number of explicitly delineated criteria, whether the submission warrants a request for a response from the party complained against.[197] If the Secretariat finds that a

194 *Id.* art. 36, 32 I.L.M. at 1493-94. A party cannot, without violating the NAFTA, unilaterally suspend benefits; it may only do so at the direction of the CEC.

195 *Id.* Annex 36A, 32 I.L.M. at 1496-97.

196 *Id.* art. 14.1, 32 I.L.M. at 1488.

197 *Id.* art. 14.2, 32 I.L.M. at 1488. For a submission to be considered it must: (1) be in the party's designated notification language; (2) clearly identify the individual or group making the submission; (3) provide sufficient information to allow review; (4) appear to be aimed at promoting enforcement and not harassment; (5) indicate that the matter has been raised with the party in question; and (6) be filed by an individual or group residing in a NAFTA territory. *Id.* art. 14.1(a)-(f), 32 I.L.M. at 1488. If a submission meets the

response is warranted, then the Secretariat shall ask for such a response and provide the party with the submission and any supporting materials. The party must then provide a reply to the Secretariat.

If, after the party's reply, the Secretariat believes that the submission deserves further consideration, then the Secretariat may request authorization from the CEC to prepare a "factual record."[198] Such authorization requires a two-thirds vote of the CEC in favor of the Secretariat's request. Once approval is granted by the CEC, the Secretariat then prepares a factual record from publicly available information, information submitted by the public, information developed by or for the Secretariat, and information provided by the party or parties.[199] Upon completion of its efforts, the Secretariat submits a draft and then a final factual record to the CEC.[200] This final factual record may be made public by a two-thirds vote of the CEC. These factual reports, however, do not necessarily trigger any process to correct any problems identified. This is a significant shortcoming in the CEC structure.

While these factual records do not necessarily lead to anything more than a report, they do offer two advantages for NAFTA-related environmental protection. First, they allow the public to focus attention on the behavior of the NAFTA parties. Second, these factual records can be used to identify "persistent patterns" of nonenforcement that can lead to formal dispute resolution proceedings as described above.

The Secretariat inquiry process is not without limitations, or in the eyes of others, checks. For example, the Secretariat can be prevented from developing a factual record if two-thirds of the Commission vote against allowing the Secretariat to proceed.[201] Similarly, the party complained against can preclude further inquiry by the Secretariat if the party asserts that the "matter is the subject of a pending judicial or administrative proceeding."[202] Whether or not these limits will detract from the value of the Secre-

above criteria, then the Secretariat is to look at the following criteria to determine if a response is appropriate: (1) does the submission allege a harm to the submitting individual or group?; (2) does the submission, alone or in conjunction with other submissions, raise issues for which further study would advance the goals of the NAAEC?; (3) have the private remedies available under law been pursued?; and (4) is the submission drawn exclusively from mass media reports? *Id.* art. 14.2(a)-(d), 32 I.L.M. at 1488.

198 *Id.* art. 15, 32 I.L.M. at 1488-89.

199 *Id.* arts. 15.2, 15.4, 32 I.L.M. at 1488-89.

200 *Id.* arts. 15.5, 15.6, 32 I.L.M. at 1488-89.

201 *Id.* art 15.2, 32 I.L.M. at 1488.

202 *Id.* art. 14.3(a), 32 I.L.M. at 1488.

tariat's role in ensuring enforcement of environmental laws remains to be seen.

3. *The U.S.-Mexico Border Environment Cooperation Agreement: The Funding Package*

Throughout the NAFTA process a great deal of attention was focused on the serious environmental problems present in the U.S.-Mexico border region. Although a number of bilateral agreements exist that are aimed at addressing elements of these border problems, these agreements have been unable to stem the tide of environmental degradation that plagues the region.

Building upon the U.S.-Mexico Border Plan, and in an effort to address the environmental plight of the border region, the United States and Mexico agreed to the U.S.-Mexico Border Environment Cooperation Agreement (BECA).[203] The BECA establishes two new institutions dedicated to rectifying the environmental problems of the border: The Border Environment Cooperation Commission (BECC) and the North American Development Bank (NADBank).[204]

a. *The BECC*

The BECC is intended to work with local communities and state governments to coordinate and facilitate environmental infrastructure (such as sewage treatment plants) development in the region. The BECC will be headed by a binational Board of Directors drawn from both government and non-governmental sectors.[205] On major issues the Board is required to consult with an advisory council drawn predominantly from the border area and representing community, business and environmental interests. The advisory council will consult on issues regarding the project certification process, general guidelines, and environmental criteria. The BECA also provides that the BECC must give the public notice and an opportunity to comment on important decisions.[206]

The BECC will not develop projects itself, but instead it will work with interested governmental and non-governmental groups

203 Agreement Between the Government of the United States of America and the Government of the United Mexican States Concerning the Establishment of a Border Environment Cooperation Commission and a North American Development Bank, Nov. 16, 18, 1993, 32 I.L.M. 1545 [hereinafter BECA].

204 *Id.*

205 *Id.* ch. I, art. III, section 3, 32 I.L.M. at 1551.

206 *Id.* ch. I, art. II, section 4, 32 I.L.M. at 1550.

and entities on implementing the projects they determine are necessary. One important element of the BECC is its coordination function. The BECC will assist in coordinating border efforts to help ensure that the most effective solutions are brought to bear on environmental problems. This is of particular importance because many of the problems present in the region straddle the border, thus necessitating internationally coordinated efforts to address them effectively.

The BECC will also play an important role in developing the financing necessary to implement these infrastructure projects. The BECC will help in the financial planning of projects and will assist project sponsors to obtain public and private funding. To this end, the BECC is authorized to certify projects for NADBank funding.[207] For a project to obtain NADBank certification, the project must meet all environmental requirements of the applicable jurisdictions. In certifying a project the BECC must also determine, in consultation with affected states and localities, whether the project will provide a significant level of environmental protection.[208]

b. *The NADBank*

The NADBank is designed to address the environmental impacts of prior unregulated and concentrated economic activity in the border region.[209] The NADBank is intended to supplement other sources of financing for the border, in particular national government assistance and World Bank and Inter-American Development Bank funding. All told, the two countries estimate that approximately US$7-8 billion will be made available for environmental projects in the border region.

The NADBank will be capitalized and governed equally by the United States and Mexico.[210] The NADBank's principal purpose is to provide the financial resources needed to carry out projects certified to it from the BECC.[211] The total initial paid-in capital of the

207 *Id.* ch. I, art. II, section 3, 32 I.L.M. at 1549-50.

208 *Id.* ch. I. art. II, section 3(c)(2), 32 I.L.M. at 1550.

209 *But see NADBank to Start Soon—How Long Will it Last?*, BANK LETTER, Dec. 20, 1993, at 4 (discussing U.S. Congressional critics attempts to limit NADBank to one year duration).

210 BECA, *supra* note 203, at ch. II, art. II sections 2, art. VI, section 2, 32 I.L.M. at 1557, 1564.

211 In addition to its environmental component, each country can elect to have the NADBank use up to 10% of its capital payments for community adjustment and investment.

NADBank is US$450 million, and its callable capital amounts to US$4.55 billion. Based on these capital contributions, Mexico and the United States believe that the NADBank will be able to provide roughly US$2 billion for loans and guarantees to infrastructure projects, with an upper limit of US$3 billion.

While the funding package for the border includes a substantial sum of money and provides perhaps the most publicly accountable institutions in the entire NAFTA package, the funding package is not without its limitations. First, the package only really attempts to deal with infrastructure projects, such as sewage treatment plants, most of which are over the long-term revenue generating. The package does not seriously address the costs of environmental cleanup of existing problems, such as toxic hot spots, which do not generate revenue.

Second, the overall cost of rectifying the border's environmental problems is estimated by some experts as up to US$20 billion. Assuming that the financing package is capable of generating US$8 billion, if these cost estimates prove accurate, that leaves a shortfall of US$12 billion in needed additional funding. Thus, while the NADBank will play a major role in funding environmental activities related to the NAFTA, it cannot be looked at as the sole environmental funding source for the environmental needs of the border region.

4. *Impact of Efforts on the Parallel Environmental Track*

One of the most interesting features of the entire NAFTA process is the relative success of the efforts on the parallel track. Although each of the institutions and processes created on the parallel track has its flaws, these institutions without question break new ground. The success of the parties in developing these institutions may be a result of the mix of institutions that were created. The ability of the parties to agree on a CEC with both monetary assessment and trade sanction powers seems to have been aided by the offer of a substantial funding package aimed at solving some of the worst environmental problems shared by at least two of the parties. This combination of carrots and sticks provided each party with incentives necessary for accepting the least appealing elements of the package. Now, as the NAFTA is implemented, it will be interesting to see what effect any shift in the balance between carrots and sticks will have on the efficacy of the parallel track efforts.

In addition to the process-based lessons of the parallel track as a whole, the efforts on the parallel track are also each important in their own respect. For example, the linkages in the CEC between the failure to provide adequate environmental protection, the competitiveness impacts of this failure, and the ability of a country to use a trade measure to address these impacts are important steps in the trade and environment debate. If the CEC's dispute resolution processes, as implemented, can function in a nondiscriminatory, non-protectionist fashion that results in increased environmental protection, then these processes will serve as an important model for future trade and environment efforts.

Similarly, the NAFTA funding package provides an important lesson in how developed nations can provide assistance to developing nations to enable them to conduct trade more sustainably. These incentives for environmentally sound trade may, in the long run, prove equally or more important to environmental protection than the coercive elements of the package. Moreover, the NAFTA's approach of linking the funding incentives to binding responsibilities backed by sanctions is also informative. While this approach is less coercive than the pure sanctions approach, it avoids the perception that plagues the pure positive incentive approach that every environmental gain must be purchased. This carrot and stick model may hold the solution to many of the most difficult issues at play in the trade and environment debate.

Although the specific structures and functions of the NAFTA parallel track institutions are perhaps best suited to the particular circumstances of the NAFTA, the basic premises behind each of these institutions are important for charting the course of future trade and environment efforts.

IV. CONCLUSION

The environmental provisions of the NAFTA all hold important lessons for future trade and environment efforts. As these provisions are implemented, their successes and shortcomings will serve as an important laboratory for cultivating solutions to many issues in the trade and environment field.

[19]

North American Environmental Cooperation: Bilateral, Trilateral, Multilateral

by Don Munton and John Kirton

An ever increasing level of trade in goods and services is not all that flows across what Canada and the United States are fond of calling the world's longest undefended border. There is also, as a former Canadian environment minister has put it, "a massive international exchange of pollutants."[1] Environmentally, the effort of recent years has been not to open borders and reduce barriers but rather to reduce these transboundary flows. Given the impossibility of closing the borders to water- and air-borne pollutants, the governments have attempted to reduce their production and to control their emission at the source. In conjunction with these domestic measures, they have negotiated and signed various bilateral agreements. Most recently, Canada and the United States have broadened this area of cooperation by signing with Mexico an important trilateral environmental side agreement in the creation of the North American Free Trade Agreement (NAFTA). This article will review these arrangements, both bilateral and trilateral, and it will speculate about their implications for the three countries, the continent, and beyond.[2]

Environmental cooperation is becoming an inherent and inescapable part of living not only in the global village but also next door. The international boundary lines of North America have never been particularly effective fences against pollutants. Now, when those barriers are becoming ever more permeable to economic exchanges, the need to deal cooperatively with transboundary environmental phenomena is readily evident.

Without doubt, the two major Canada-U.S. transboundary environmental issues in recent decades have been the serious water pollution problems long affecting the Great Lakes and the more recently addressed problem of acid rain. Without doubt, one of the central concerns of the coming decades will be the relationship among the environment, economic activity, and trade, as the United States, Mexico, and Canada proceed to implement the North American Free Trade Agreement. The bilateral issues of water quality in the Great Lakes and of transboundary air pollution and the looming, trilateral trade-environment questions seem destined to be long on the agenda. These will be the focus here. To understand the current state of affairs of these issues, some history is essential. To deal with these issues in an innovative and effective manner will require new thinking and new approaches.

In addition to transboundary water and air pollution and trade-environment links, there are other problems and solutions to be sought, including the bilateral long-range transport of airborne toxins, the treatment and disposal of hazardous waste, the protection of migratory species, and the preservation of wildlife habitats. The way in which these may be handled can only be the subject of speculation here and cannot be discussed in detail.

A MIXED HISTORY OF TRANSBOUNDARY POLLUTION CONTROLS

Basic Principles

Canadian, American, and Mexican efforts to deal with environmental issues are creating a new environmental regime for North America. The basis of that regime for Canada and the United States dates from the early years of the century. The 1909 Canada-U.S. Boundary Waters Treaty dealt mainly with the "levels and flows" of the boundary waters,[3] but it also included an extraordinary principle—nothing less than a general prohibition on the pollution of the boundary waters.[4] The second paragraph of Article IV states that "the waters herein defined as boundary waters and waters flowing across the boundary shall not be polluted on either side to the injury of health or property on the other." Ironically, the absolute nature of this injunction was its weakness; it was virtually impossible to prevent all injurious pollution from crossing the border given the common environment, water currents, and wind patterns. Article IV was so sweeping a prohibition that it became more empty rhetoric than enforced rule.

The earliest case of Canada-U.S. transboundary air pollution, the well-cited Trail Smelter Case of the 1930s and 1940s, broadened the principle enshrined in Article IV to include the idea that it was the responsibility of good neighbors not to pollute each other's territory via the winds as well as the waters. The joint Canada-U.S. International Joint Commission (IJC), created by the 1909 treaty,[5] ultimately awarded damages to American farmers affected by "fumes" from the large Cominco smelter located only a few miles north of the 49th parallel. The IJC declared that "no state has the right to use or permit the use of its territory in such a manner as to cause damages to another state or to the properties or persons therein, when the case is of serious consequence and the injury is established by clear and convincing evidence."[6]

The Great Lakes Water Quality Agreements

The principles that the Boundary Waters Treaty and the Trail Smelter Case incorporated had little effect on the more established practices of governments and industries. Only a few years after the Boundary Waters Treaty was signed, serious typhoid epidemics occurred in the cities on the Great Lakes due to water-borne bacteria from human sewage. Governments on both sides responded, not by eliminating raw sewage outflows or treating the sewage (which would have been consistent with Article IV), but by continuing to pollute and adopting the less expensive measure of chlorinating drinking water supplies. Industries along the Great Lakes also used the waters to dispose of an ever widening array of wastes. By the mid 1960s, it was clear that pollution in the Great Lakes had become steadily and dangerously worse.

The response was the 1972 Canada-U.S. Great Lakes Water Quality Agreement.[7] It emerged in part out of considerable scientific work pointing to new and alarming pollution threats, the principal of which was the problem of eutrophication, or the accelerated aging, of the lower Lakes due to excessive nutrients. The agreement also stemmed from mounting public concern over water pollution in the late 1960s-early 1970s, which in the United States was partly focused on the "death" of Lake Erie.

The essence of the 1972 accord (which was maintained when it was renegotiated and broadened in 1978 and when it was modestly revised in 1987) was agreement on general water quality objectives and specific regulatory standards and on the collaborative monitoring of subsequent progress, along with mutual commitments to implement national programs to achieve these objectives.[8] The accord specified water quality objectives and standards in terms of maximum levels of particular pollutants allowed in open waters.

In one sense, then, the 1972 agreement represented an elaboration and definition of the key clause (Article IV) of the Boundary Waters Treaty. As an attempt to translate this article into practical goals, the 1972 agreement was an essential refinement of the bilateral environmental regime.

A major point, often misunderstood, is that while the objectives and standards are joint and the monitoring of progress is a collaborative effort under the IJC, the pollution control programs are national. Although intended to be complementary, the regulatory programs of the various jurisdictions—federal, state, provincial, and municipal—are designed to meet their own differing needs and are implemented more or less autonomously within each country and jurisdiction. The Great Lakes agreements, therefore, effected no significant diminution of sovereign authority for pollution control actions.

The 1972 agreement gave the International Joint Commission new responsibilities—for the collection and analysis of information on water quality objectives and pollution control programs, for the independent verification of data, and for the publication of reports, on at least a biennial basis, assessing progress toward these objectives. In addition, the IJC gained broad responsibility for providing "assistance in the coordination of the joint activities." However, this broad and unclear mandate has largely been stripped from the commission in recent years.

When originally negotiated, the 1972 Great Lakes agreement focused primarily on the problem of eutrophication caused by excessive nutrients, especially phosphates, in the Lakes. As a result of improved detection (making possible the identification of trace pollutants) and more research into the consequences of other substances through the 1970s, industrial effluents and toxic chemicals pushed their way onto the Great Lakes agenda. The spotlight moved from municipal sources to nonmunicipal sources, particularly industries and agricultural runoff. This shift, in turn, caused the political focus to move, highlighting not only American sources but also Canadian sources. Ontario's industrial pollution control programs, which lagged far behind its own municipal ones, became a target for U.S. officials now tired of being on the defensive.

Implementation continued. The IJC reports during the 1980s tended to focus on what the Water Quality Board called "areas of concern," particularly polluted and degraded areas of the Lakes where remedial action was most needed. One perennial area of concern has been the harbor of Hamilton, Ontario; another has been the complex of chemical industrial dumps near Niagara Falls,

New York. Under a new and separate accord concluded in 1987, both federal governments, New York, and Ontario agreed to cut these emissions in half by 1996, thus reaffirming their commitments implied in the 1978 agreement. An extensive multistakeholder consultative process to develop "Remedial Action Plans," or RAPs, for local areas around the Lakes has achieved varied success, although some in the nongovernmental organization (NGO) community have concluded that such consultation has generally been a waste of time and energy. More recently, pressure has been building from environmental groups for an outright ban on the use of one of the most ubiquitous chemicals, chlorine. The binational citizen organization Great Lakes United made this ban its main issue at the 1993 IJC meeting. The chemical industry is beginning to take the challenge seriously.[9]

The United States and Canada have thus had a mixed record with respect to improving the quality of the Great Lakes. On the one hand, the nutrient reduction objectives of the original agreement have largely been met. The phosphate loadings have been reduced from both sides (particularly from the United States), and the eutrophication problem is under control. On the other hand, increasing scientific evidence points to the seriousness and complexity of the toxic waste problem in the Lakes, and government programs in this area have not yet begun to show substantial results. The most recent bilateral nongovernmental review of the state of the Great Lakes suggests that the pattern of failure to implement commitments to abstract principles remains strong. The Conservation Foundation and the Institute for Research on Public Policy concluded that "neither country is spending enough, or doing enough, to check the insidious long-term decline of the Great Lakes ecosystem. On the remedial front, it is painfully clear that only the easiest problems have been tackled and the cheapest remedies applied."[10] These issues, pushed from center stage during the long acid rain debate of the 1980s, seem to be reasserting themselves and will likely dominate the environmental agenda of the latter 1990s.

Acid Rain

The popular term "acid rain" has come to stand for a complex set of physical and chemical phenomena by which gases, especially sulfur dioxide (SO_2) and nitrogen oxides (NO_x), are emitted as a result of combustion and other processes and transformed into acidic compounds while being transported through the atmosphere. They are then deposited by rain, snow, and dry particles onto land and water surfaces.[11] A bilateral Canada-U.S. report in 1979, which offered the first compilation of existing scientific information on the origins, transport, and deleterious effects of acid precipitation in North America, warned of "irreversible" damage being caused to lakes, rivers, and fish.[12] Subsequent research and reports also examined the evidence more fully for the impact on forests, human-made structures, and human health,[13] but the evidence has remained less convincing in these areas than for aquatic systems.

There are some striking parallels between acid rain and water pollution in the Great Lakes in terms of their sources and respective transboundary flows and, as a result, in terms of their politics. The 1979 bilateral report noted above estimated that American emissions of SO_2 were five times greater than Canadian ones and that American emissions of NO_x were 10 times greater. Although both countries polluted their own and the other's territory to some extent, because of the prevailing southwesterly winds on the eastern half of the continent, the United States produced overall about 70-80 percent of transboundary air pollution. Subsequent scientific studies of the atmospheric chemistry and meteorology of acid rain have shown that most of southern Ontario and Quebec, where the most obvious acid rain damage has occurred, have been more affected by pollution from U.S. than from Canadian sources. Canadian government estimates in the late 1980s were that about 750,000 lakes in eastern Canada were vulnerable to acid rain and about 14,000 were already acidified to some degree. American estimates of aquatic damage, actual or potential, were considerably lower but still sufficient to cause alarm in New York and New England, the most severely affected areas.

A bilateral agreement to reduce acid rain had been sought by Canada for over a decade, but negotiation of such an accord and new acid rain controls in domestic legislation had been successfully resisted by the United States for years. The Canadian government set as its objective reductions of 50 percent in U.S. and Canadian emissions to control acid rain. Domestically, federal environment officials through the mid 1970s slowly patched together an agreement with the seven eastern provinces to reduce their emissions by 50 percent. This agreement was not expected to solve Canada's acid rain problem unilaterally, but was designed to fulfill the Canadian commitments in an eventual Canada-U.S. acid rain program.

U.S. action took somewhat longer due to a combination of strenuous industry opposition to SO_2 and NO_x controls, reluctance within the Reagan administration to strengthen U.S. air pollution laws, and the fierce interregional controversy the issue provoked within the United States. The Bush administration eventually proposed revisions to the Clean Air Act that contained provisions to reduce significantly the emissions from U.S. electrical generating plants that were causing much of the acid rain in the northeastern states and, incidentally, in Canada. The U.S. Congress agreed, and by late 1990 legislation was passed and signed that provided the necessary basis for Washington to deal with acid rain.

The Bilateral Air Quality Agreement

Although the 1909 Boundary Waters Treaty had provided a framework for cooperation largely on transboundary water pollution problems, no similar framework existed specifically for air quality issues. Now, however, the new act allowed the United States to negotiate the bilateral Air Quality Agreement, which the two countries signed in March 1991. This accord represented an important breakthrough not only in rendering both bilateral and cooperative the effort to reduce the specific problem of acid rain, but also in establishing a framework within which the two countries could deal with other air quality issues in the future.

In the agreement, the two countries promised to reduce emissions of sulfur dioxide by somewhat less than 50 percent by 2000. Both countries are also committed to lesser reductions in nitrogen oxide emissions. It is particularly significant that Canada, for the first time, committed itself to the establishment of a permanent national cap on SO_2 emissions (3.2 million tonnes), similar to the cap (8.95 million tons) set by the new U.S. act. As a result of the agreement, Canada has also put into effect new vehicle emissions standards (roughly equivalent to those in the Clean Air Act) and promised to initiate programs to improve visibility and ensure air quality in parks and wilderness areas similar to the U.S. "prevention of serious deterioration" programs. The latter commitments were the price Canada had to pay to get the kind of agreement it wanted on its key issue, acid rain.

In terms of process, the agreement provided for the creation of a bilateral (intergovernmental) Air Quality Committee to oversee implementation. Unlike the Great Lakes Water Quality Agreements, there is no direct role for the International Joint Commission except possibly holding public hearings and submitting a summary of them. (Note that the IJC was not empowered to prepare its own report, but only to summarize the hearings.) The Air Quality Committee has created two subgroups, one to deal with emissions and reductions and the other to handle scientific research and monitoring.

The committee produced its first "progress report" in March 1992, as required under the agreement. This report focused almost entirely on coordination of scientific and technical data, especially on developing consistent emissions inventories and reviewing ongoing scientific research such as the impact of acid rain on trees. Given that the emissions programs on the U.S. side are only now under way, the lack of attention in the report to progress in meeting reduction commitments is not unexpected. There are some key deadlines approaching, however. The Canadian emissions program targets reducing SO_2 to no more than 2.3 million tonnes in the seven easternmost provinces by the end of 1994. In Canada, the largest sources of SO_2, ore smelters, have reduced emissions through process changes and modernization. Phase I limits for SO_2 from 261 units at 110 U.S. electric utilities will become effective also at the end of 1994. Affected utilities have been developing plans for their own emissions reductions. In general, phase I reduction plans seem to be emphasizing fuel switching (mainly from higher to lower sulfur coals) rather than technological controls. Given the low cost of coal, fuel switching is a more cost-effective option than expensive emissions control equipment such as stack scrubbers. In many cases, the reductions through fuel switching will be accomplished with no increase in fuel costs. The much publicized marketable allowances program of the acid rain section of the U.S. act (Title IV) has already begun operation, although allowances cannot be used until 1995. The current going price for an individual allowance, less than $200, is much lower than many experts anticipated.

Has the battle against acid rain been won? The *Globe and Mail* newspaper, among others, seems to think so, announcing in 1990 that "Canada finally won its fight."[14] Is passage of the Air Quality Agreement reason to think that this thorny issue has been dealt with? Not entirely; such thoughts are at best premature.

To be sure, the signs are at present relatively positive. The Canadian acid rain program is "ahead of schedule"[15] in meeting emissions reduction targets. The implementation of U.S. controls appears to be proceeding smoothly, indeed with an unusual degree of government-industry cooperation and goodwill.

If the track record of implementing Canada-U.S. environmental agreements were good, there might be reason to begin to celebrate. But the track record has been far from good. In fact, most Canadian and U.S. commitments to bilateral environmental actions over the past half century have been broken, usually sooner than later. For example, within months of coming to Ottawa to sign the Great Lakes accord in 1972, Richard Nixon impounded the federal funds necessary to clean up municipal pollution on the U.S. side of the Lakes. Further, as noted above, effective steps have yet to be taken to deal with the toxic chemical threat in the Great Lakes, actions not only envisaged but required by the 1978 accord and subsequent agreements. In terms of pollution control, the experience with Great Lakes water quality has thus shown that policy implementation is at least as important to the eventual outcome as is policymaking. Moreover, it is by no means certain that the actions taken to date to reduce the emissions that cause acid rain will prove sufficient to protect sensitive ecosystems. Further reductions may be necessary after scientists have been able to assess the impact of the cuts under way.

What is important about the bilateral agreement, therefore, is not only its mutual commitments to emissions reductions but also its provisions concerning the monitoring and review of the implementation of air quality programs. In the latter sense the accord falls short in several respects. It has relatively weak provisions for monitoring the progress of national reduction programs or for what is called in the arms control area, verification. Twenty years ago, Ottawa and Washington broke new ground in the 1972 Great Lakes Water Quality Agreement by asking an independent body, the respected International Joint Commission, to monitor what the governments were doing and to report publicly on the progress achieved—or on the lack thereof. In effect, they created a watchdog to evaluate continually these efforts and ensure that the public had the necessary information to make certain that the governments' promises were being kept.

Perhaps because the governments had more than once been embarrassed politically by the IJC's scrutiny of their performance with respect to water pollution, the 1991 Air Quality Agreement created no such watchdog. Indeed, it took a further step to insulate the governments from public criticism and pressure. While the agreement provides for a public hearing process, those hearings will involve only the IJC, not the governments themselves, with invited briefs and with the commission mandated only to provide a summary of the views presented, not the commission's own expert evaluation. The governments could choose, in effect, to hide behind an emasculated, powerless commission. The only reports to be released are those of the joint Air Quality Committee, that is, of the governments themselves. These reports are most unlikely to contain information that will embarrass the governments.

Further, the Air Quality Agreement does not contain a clear statement of principle that damaging transboundary air pollution will not be allowed, similar to the principle in Article IV of the Boundary Waters Treaty of 1909 that has formed the legal basis of all subsequent joint efforts to deal with transboundary water pollution.

Finally, the focus of the commitments in the accord is on acid rain; there are no programs that address airborne toxic pollutants, transboundary ozone, or volatile organic compounds (VOCs). In short, the 1991 Air Quality Agreement seems likely to soon undergo revision and expansion to deal with a broader spectrum of pollutants, as did the first Great Lakes accord.

These bilateral commitments and institutions to deal with transboundary air and water pollution, while important mechanisms, do not represent fundamental transformations in the way that Canada and the United States deal with each other. They are essentially evolutions in long-standing arrangements. However, more fundamental changes are occurring in the way that the three nations of North America will deal in the future with common trilateral environmental problems. These changes, the result of the movement toward a North American (Canada-U.S.-Mexico) trading bloc, seem likely to have implications at the bilateral and multilateral as well as trilateral levels.

THE NAFTA REGIME

Perhaps the most potent political force shaping Canada-U.S. environmental relations during the 1990s has been the evolution of the new regime established by the North American Free Trade Agreement, its accompanying Agreement on Environmental Cooperation (AEC), and its Commission on Environmental Cooperation (CEC). Taken together, the NAFTA regime represents a potentially revolutionary development in Canadian-American environmental relations in three important ways. It takes continental environmental concerns and integrates them directly and substantially into the core economic domain of the relationship—in trade, investment, standards, and other trade-related domestic policies.[16] It extends the almost century-old bilateral cooperation of Canada and the United States into a trilateral arrangement involving Mexico—and into the expanded array of environmental issues that results from including a developing country. It marks a step toward organizational and procedural supranational governance on the broader North American continent through the establishment of an international organization with potentially important majority voting provisions, and perhaps sufficient provisions for public participation to create a new center of political activity and legitimacy on the continent.

Although attention in the United States and Canada has recently focused on the debate over the need for, and adequacy of, the environmental side accord to NAFTA (i.e., the negotiation of the AEC), the incorporation of environmental into economic concerns and the resulting trilateralization of the hitherto bilateral environmental agenda were substantially accomplished with the initial NAFTA. Its preparation began with a trilateral summit declaration on February 9, 1991, and it was concluded by the three governments' trade ministers on August 12, 1992. From an environmental perspective, NAFTA represented a sharp departure from the 1988 Canada-U.S. Free Trade Agreement (CUSFTA), the General Agreement on Tariffs and Trade (GATT), and the Uruguay Round of multilateral trade negotiations. These pillars of the Canada-U.S. and multilateral trading systems, reflecting the environmental degradation, science, and awareness of the late 1940s, have virtually ignored the relevance of the environment to international trade and the importance of ecological values in their own right. Despite the emergence of environmental concerns in the early 1970s (registered in the Great Lakes Water Quality Agreement, the United Nations Stockholm Declaration on the Human Environment, and the creation of the United Nations Environment Program), the rise of the broader philosophy of sustainable development in the late 1980s through the Brundtland Commission Report of 1987 and the 1992 United Nations Conference on Environment and Development in Rio de Janeiro, and the emergence of major multilateral environmental agreements with trade provisions, the international trade regime still dealt with environmental issues only indirectly and tangentially, under provisions for protecting health and conserving natural resources.

In contrast, NAFTA's preamble specifies that the purpose of this trade agreement is to "promote sustainable development" and to "strengthen the development of environmental laws and regulations." Indeed, the parties pledged to undertake their obligations "in a manner consistent with environmental protection and conservation." These seminal pledges were important for their normative force and also for their legal value, as recent international law has given increasing weight to preamble statements as signaling the intent of the parties and thus guiding the interpretation and application of subsequent provisions.

Furthermore, NAFTA specifies that in cases where its trade and economic provisions conflict with the obligations of the world's major multilateral environmental agreements—notably the 1973 convention on trade in endangered species, the 1987 Montreal protocol on ozone depletion, and the 1989 Basel convention on hazardous waste—the latter will prevail. Although the parties were obliged to respect these agreements in a way consistent with their NAFTA commitments, it was clear that the claims of the global environment took precedence over those of the continental economy. This deference to environmental values was reinforced by the detailed treatment of ecological considerations in many of the more important chapters of the NAFTA text, notably that for standards.[17]

Despite this environmental focus, NAFTA's critics and some environmental nongovernmental organizations (ENGOs) in Canada and the United States saw the agreement as essentially the product and property of the trade policy community. They were concerned that NAFTA gave inadequate expression to ecological values and to the broader philosophy of sustainable development. In particular, they questioned how effectively the new textual commitments could be implemented through a NAFTA dispute settlement process that was based almost entirely on trade expertise, with limited provisions for the incorporation of environmental sensitivity, science, and NGOs.

By September 17, 1992, these concerns had led the environment ministers from Canada, the United States, and Mexico, meeting in Washington, D.C., to announce the initiation of negotiations to design an environmental accord to NAFTA and an accompanying trilateral institution (then known as the North American Commission on the Environment). The importance of generating a strong environmental side agreement and institution was underscored in October when Bill Clinton, during his campaign for the presidency, declared his support for a strong North American Commission on the Environment and repeated this commitment upon his election in November. Although the President also appealed to the traditional Democratic Party constituency by demanding a parallel accord on labor, it was clear that capturing the support of American ENGOs, which could collectively claim as many committed members as the labor union movement, was critical to the eventual passage of the Republican-initiated NAFTA.

Led by the National Wildlife Federation, the only major ENGO to endorse NAFTA's environmental provisions, American environmentalists pressed for an agreement and institution that would lead to the upward harmonization of Mexican standards to U.S. levels, allow for ample public participation and transparency in advice, deliberation, and reporting, and permit the use of trade sanctions to enforce compliance by the parties with their domestic and international environmental obligations. Their core concern, shared by the U.S. labor movement and vulnerable U.S. industry, was that Mexico's systematic inability or unwillingness to enforce its generally very high national environmental standards would lead to environmental degradation that would harm Americans across the border, influence U.S. and other industries to locate in Mexico to avoid high compliance costs in the United States, and thus generate political pressure to lower environmental standards and compliance costs to save industries and jobs back home.

The demands of U.S. environmentalists provoked resistance from three quarters.[18] The first was from Americans, centered in the Republican Party and the big business community, who feared that "their" original NAFTA would now be encumbered by trade sanctions that would contradict its core trade-liberalizing purposes and lead to a large, expensive new trilateral bureaucracy with extensive powers of enforcement and regulation over the private sector. The second was from the Canadian government, opposition Liberal Party, business community, and others. This group felt that the introduction of trade sanctions (aimed at Mexico) would provide an opportunity for protectionist forces in the United States to overwhelm the CUSFTA protection that Canada currently enjoyed, and thus do major economic damage to the export-dependent Canadian economy in return for little if any environmental gain in Mexico. The third source of resistance came from sovereignty-sensitive Mexico, which felt that improvements in its environmental performance depended not on wealth-reducing trade sanctions or threats, but on the economic, technological, and fiscal resources that trade and investment liberalization would bring, supplemented by direct transfers of enlarged environmentally focused development aid.

The Agreement on Environmental Cooperation

After a full year of negotiation led by trade officials from each country, the three countries on September 13, 1993 concluded a final North American Agreement on Environmental Cooperation.[19] The preamble and objectives (Part One) of the agreement expressed a substantial commitment to the goals of sustainable development and the commitments of Stockholm and Rio and placed new emphasis on public participation and transparency. Part Two listed the general obligations of the parties (in reporting, emergency preparedness, education, science and technology, environmental assessment, and economic instruments), their commitment to high and continually improving levels of environmental protection, the prompt publication and serious enforcement of environmental laws and regulations, the rights of private persons, and the transparency of domestic legal processes. Part Three defined composition, powers, and procedures of the new Commission for Environmental Cooperation. Part Four set forth the obligations of each party for the prior notification of proposed or actual environmental measures and the prompt provision of relevant information. Part Five dealt with the consultation and resolution of disputes through the stages of consultation, initiation of procedures, request for and composition of an arbitral panel, rules of procedure and participation, preparation of initial and final reports, implementation of the reports, and suspension of benefits in the event of noncompliance. Part Six provided general definitions, and Part Seven dealt with the coming into force of, amendments and accession to, and withdrawal from, the agreement.

As a document designed to allow each of the three governments to maintain and mobilize the support necessary to secure legislative and electoral approval for NAFTA, the agreement is a remarkable success. It gives each country the freedom to set and alter its own environmental policies and procedures, but obliges each to provide high levels of protection, to strive for continual improvements, to promptly publish proposed measures, and to offer where possible advance notification and opportunity for comment. It mandates a process aimed at developing greater compatibility of environmental technical regulations, standards, and conformity assessment procedures, without reducing levels of environmental protection. Further, it obliges each country to effectively enforce its environmental laws and regulations through national government action and to ensure that its domestic legal system allows "interested persons" to pursue alleged violations.

At the core of the agreement is a well crafted compromise over the critical issue of international enforcement. In cases where one party is alleged to have a persistent pattern of failure to effectively enforce its domestic environmental laws over economic activity involved in or affecting North American trade, international action is possible. Here the CEC's council can establish an international arbitral panel to provide a remedial action plan, and, if necessary, levy monetary fines. These fines are limited to US$20 million for any single assessment in the first year, and to no more than .007 percent of the annual total trade in goods between the parties thereafter, with the fines being given to the CEC for use in environmental remediation in the violating country. If the fines are not paid, the agreement gives the United States the ultimate power to impose trade sanctions on Mexico in the event of a "persistent pattern" of domestic noncompliance and enforcement, while sparing Canada such a CUSFTA-negating threat or right. Instead, Canada will permit its international compliance obligations to be enforced through its domestic judicial process.

Together, the package promises to maintain the scope for economic gain, minimize the potential for protectionist distortions, and raise the record of actual environmental compliance and performance in Mexico, Canada, and the United States. International trade restricting action for environmental purposes is limited to cases involving a persistent pattern of environmental noncompliance; comes at the end of a long process of consultation, arbitration by an expert panel, creation of an implementation plan, and relatively modest monetary fines; and applies to only two of the three NAFTA parties. At the same time, environmentalists have a layered network of voluntary compliance, fines, and ultimately trade and domestic judicial remedies to ensure compliance, with the revenues raised devoted directly to remediating the environmental offense.

The agreement also injects significant additional environmental sensitivity and expertise into the trade dispute settlement mechanisms of NAFTA. Article 10.6 directs that the CEC's council "shall co-operate with the NAFTA Free Trade Commission" to achieve that agreement's environmental purposes by receiving comments from NGOs, by assisting in Article 1114 consultations over alleged "pollution-haven" investment encouragement, by recommending and identifying experts for all NAFTA bodies, and, most broadly, by "considering on an ongoing basis the environmental effects of the NAFTA." Although this is a formidable array of mandates, the wording suggests that the initiative for seeking such enhanced environmental activity rests with the NAFTA Free Trade Commission and the trade policy community that controls it.

Beyond environmental standards and enforcement and the settlement of trade disputes lie the tasks of environmental cooperation. The agreement (in Article 2) mandates that the parties, with respect to their own territory, report on the state of the environment; develop environmental emergency preparedness measures; promote education, scientific research, technology development, and economic instruments; and assess environmental impacts. It specifies that the CEC's council shall promote and facilitate environmental cooperation, exchange of information, and technical cooperation, and develop recommendations for public access to information, appropriate limits for specific pollutants, and environmental impact assessment of projects with transborder effects (Article 10.3-5,7). In addition, it specifies that the council may consider and develop recommendations on 19 specific subjects, including those aimed at strengthening the role of environmental considerations in national and trilateral economic activity.

With such a broad array of standard-setting, enforcement, trade dispute, and environmental enhancement functions of both mandatory and discretionary activities, the effect of the agreement will depend critically on the operation of—and the resources made available to—the new Commission on Environmental Cooperation. This entity was deliberately set up as a minimum framework or platform to be developed and shaped as environmental demands and political pressures evolved. In its essential architecture, the CEC represents a major advance on previous, all bilateral, environmentally relevant institutions on the North American continent.

Institutionally, the CEC has at its apex a CUSFTA-like "council," which, at a minimum, is an annual meeting of the cabinet-level or "equivalent representatives" of the three countries. Thus, it will not, like so many joint ministerial committees before it, wither away due to lack of interest or political changes at the top of national governments. Although it could be relegated to junior cabinet ministers or other functionaries (including political appointees along the lines of the IJC), it is also possible that it might expand to include additional ministers (from the economic as well as the environmental domains) or even be linked to meetings of leaders themselves.

More important, the CEC marks the advent of a trilateral international organization in North America (in a field outside defense). For the CEC is not an assemblage of national sections periodically coming together as a joint institution, but a single, permanent, trilateral organization. It features a single executive director, a single bureaucratic staff (the secretariat) located in a single location (in Canada), and a 15-member Joint Public Advisory Committee

(JPAC), conceived as a single trinational group rather than three national sections meeting together.

Affirming the single character of the body, and endowing it with genuine supranational characteristics regarding procedures, is the provision for two-thirds majority voting among the three-country participants on several important procedural issues. Although in general the council will operate by consensus (and thus empower each of the three countries with a veto), the agreement specifies several important exceptions. Thus, the council must mobilize only a two-thirds majority vote (rather than the full three votes) to reject appointments to the secretariat proposed by the executive director (Article 11.3); to prevent the secretariat from preparing a report "on any other environmental matter related to the co-operative functions of this Agreement" (excluding cases of alleged nonenforcement) (Article 13.1); to instruct the secretariat to prepare a factual record on allegations of noncompliance made by NGOs (Article 15.2); to make the final factual record public (Article 15.7); to make a factual record available to the JPAC (Article 16.7); to prevent the secretariat from requesting information from a party (Article 21.2); to make public the council recommendation to parties about the resolution of a dispute (Article 23.4); and to convene an arbitral panel to consider an alleged persistent pattern of enforcement failure (Article 24.1).

For the United States, which has long resisted international organizational constraints on its sovereign prerogatives, and for a U.S.-Canadian relationship that has long avoided formal international organization, these NAFTA institutions represent a significant departure. Although motivated by a desire to remove a Mexican government veto over the effective environmental enforcement and open decisionmaking cherished by U.S. NGOs, the institutions allow for the possibility that a future U.S. government deemed unsympathetic to environmental concerns could itself be outvoted by a Canadian-Mexican majority, especially if the latter were supported by ENGOs, the public, and legislators in the United States. However, it is more likely that any prospective Canadian-Mexican majority would be exercised in the direction of supporting national prerogatives and governmental discretion, given the even greater sensitivity about sovereignty and the less well developed network of ENGOs in the two smaller NAFTA countries. Further, any government that feels consistently outvoted or otherwise discriminated against retains the ability to curtail the operation of the ACE by reducing or withholding financial support, as the agreement specifies that each party shall contribute an unspecified but equal share of the annual budget of the commission "subject to the availability of appropriated funds in accordance with the Party's legal procedures" (Article 43).

Although the council is a small body that will rely overwhelmingly on consensus decisionmaking, the presence of a permanent secretariat, the Joint Public Advisory Committee, and numerous requirements for publicity will help ensure that the CEC does not easily become the captive of national governments. The secretariat is to be recruited on the basis of merit, is not to receive instructions from any external authority other than the council, and is to issue a public report on the activities under the agreement, including the state of the environment in the territories of the parties. The secretariat also has considerable investigatory powers, as it may take up complaints about noncompliance from NGOs, investigate their merits, and request permission from the council to prepare a factual record (Articles 14-15). The JPAC will meet at least once a year at the time of the regular session of the council, which is obliged (under Article 8.4) to hold a public meeting. The JPAC may advise the council on any matter within the scope of the agreement, and it is entitled to review the CEC's annual program, budget, report, and any secretariat reports on other environmental matters. These requirements and the public participation and reporting provisions elsewhere in the agreement make it possible for the CEC to become an important center of political activity, agenda setting, and legitimacy on North American environmental matters in ways that the national governments will find difficult to ignore.

The actual importance of the CEC depends in the first instance on how the immediate institutional and budgetary issues are resolved.[20] During 1994, activity will focus on recruiting the executive director and staff, establishing the size of the resources the institution can draw upon, selecting its headquarters location, and determining the openness of its procedures to public participation and media attention. A second critical institutional issue will be the composition of its bureaucracy and advisory body, as nongovernmental environmental activists, scientists, the standards community, industrialists, and other stakeholders seek to have their constituencies and concerns amply represented. Robust resources, respected staff, and a location in a major center for media, scientists, and ENGOs will be important for the new institution if it is to acquire the scientific credibility, public visibility, and citizen scrutiny required to influence the environmental activities of otherwise distracted, cost-conscious member governments.

TRILATERAL COOPERATION

Only a few years ago, the three countries of the North American continent would have seemed an unlikely trio for institutionalized cooperation on environmental issues. Although one of the three, the United States, has rather intense cooperative and conflictual relations with each of the other two in many areas, including the environment, the two distinct bilateral relationships have rarely intersected. They have been characterized less by a cooperative spirit than by irritation and neglect. Despite some efforts by the Canadian and Mexican governments over the past decade to develop a broader and deeper bilateral relationship, the main point of commonality for the two may still seem to be not so much any tangible interests they might pursue together as their need to deal—almost invariably separately—with the United States.

Most of the environmental issues on these two distinct bilateral agendas, moreover, have been almost resolutely border-fixated and therefore nontrilateral. As discussed earlier, Canada-U.S. environmental concerns and the work of the International Joint Commission have long focused on boundary river levels and flows issues, including dams and hydropower development. More recently, these efforts have focused on boundary water pollution problems, especially those of the Great Lakes, and on transboundary air pollution problems of a regional and local nature, such as acid rain and pollution in the Detroit-Windsor area.[21] The Mexico-U.S. agenda and that of the International Boundary and Water Commission (IBWC) have traditionally been similarly dominated by boundary river concerns, especially water shortage and salinity. In recent years, prominent transboundary air pollution issues have arisen. On both borders, local-regional issues have fostered a strong tradition of bilateralism. The strength of this tradition is reflected in the fact that the Canada-U.S. IJC and the Mexico-U.S. IBWC, though functionally similar, have never in their entire histories met, even informally or socially, to share perspectives.

However, it is by no means inevitable that these historical patterns will continue into the future. In addition to the institutionalized cooperation of the CEC, it is arguable that the challenge of managing the North American environment will bring changes in government-to-government relationships.

One factor for change is the growing realization of the interconnectedness of the global ecosystem, not only in theory but in practical manifestations. At the same time that gas chromatography-electron spectrometry instruments are extending the limits of detection of minute quantities of toxins in drinking water and food supplies, huge computer models are showing the extent of the global movement of pollutants. A powerful, concrete symbol of this interconnectedness, the Chernobyl nuclear accident, was not only an immense tragedy for those living near and downwind from the plant in the Ukraine but also the source of radiation effects as far away as Welsh sheep fields and Scandinavian tundra. In North America, for example, pesticides banned in Canada and the United States, but not in Mexico, continue to show up in analyses of Great Lakes water samples.

The need to think through some initial steps toward the rather grand notion of ecomanagement of the North American continent is thus greater than would be suggested by the historical pattern of handling environmental issues bilaterally.

The Need for North American-wide Ecomanagement

But what objectives might be served by a greater degree of cooperative environmental management? These might be grouped into three categories—educational, substantive, and process objectives.

For educational objectives, the argument is straightforward, although the priority of the needs and likely payoffs may seem less than compelling. Governments stand to gain by sharing their often different experiences and views, and therefore any such exchange would be of general benefit, though perhaps ill defined and long term in nature. With respect to substantive objectives, there are, in fact, environmental problems that mutually engage the interests of all three countries. These continental issues need to be examined and dealt with in appropriate trilateral forums. As for process-oriented objectives, the cooperation of the three rather disparate countries of North America could potentially facilitate management of some global environmental problems and perhaps provide some institutional models for resolution of these problems. These three objectives could be pursued in a number of ways. The nature of the diplomacy could be trilateral, multilateral, or even bilateral.

The primary substantive benefits to be derived from North American ecomanagement likely rest in improved cooperation on problems that affect the continent and the interests of the three neighbors. Contrary to what would seem to be the evidence of the historical pattern, there are some important environmental issues, now well recognized, that are continental in nature. One of these is the agricultural use of herbicides and pesticides and another is the long-range atmospheric transport of these toxins. Another issue involves migratory species that link the three countries. As North American free trade develops and continental agricultural trade becomes a reality, these issues will become even more prominent. Indeed, quite apart from the purely environmental implications of herbicide and pesticide use, the national regulation of these substances poses possible trade barrier implications. It is also very likely that, beyond currently recognized issues, new continent-wide environmental problems will come to light, requiring new policy actions.

Creating Trilateral Mechanisms for North American-wide Ecomanagement

The nature of this continental cooperation could take a variety of forms. First, the tradition of joint fact-finding on mutual environmental problems could be strengthened. This tradition is a strong one along both the U.S.-Mexico and the U.S.-Canada borders. Undertaking similar investigations into continent-wide (or perhaps continent-long) problems would seem but a natural outgrowth of this practice. The fact-finding could be carried out by the CEC or, in the case of more bilateral issues, by investigatory boards operating under the joint aegis of the IJC and the IBWC. In this sense the investigation would be similar to that conducted by the IBWC on Colorado River salinity in conjunction with "domestic" U.S. government agencies or those that the IJC alone undertook for the Great Lakes or the Garrison Diversion. Alternatively, but less desirably, the investigation could be done by scientific experts from the three governments, as was done by Canada and the United States in the case of acid rain.[22]

The work of the IJC and the IBWC has often involved not mere fact-finding but also the formulation of recommendations for changes in government policy, and the CEC seems likely to provide this in the trade area. The credibility and force of this policy advice rests very much on the acknowledged expertise of the advisor and on the scientific and technical information that is brought together and assessed. Such policy studies might, for example, propose the establishment of common water or air pollution objectives or standards, the adoption of new regulatory or other pollution control policies, or the improvement of environmental assessment procedures. Such an advisory function would be the trilateral equivalent of the now famous 1970 IJC report on Great Lakes water quality, the 1979 and 1981 Bilateral Research Consultation Group reports on acidic precipitation, or the charge to the IBWC in 1971 for technical advice on resolving the long-standing salinity problem in the Colorado River.[23]

Policy measures could take either of two forms. On the one hand, they might involve concerted joint action by the three governments about a particular problem, such as the adoption of new standards for the use of agricultural pesticides. Alternatively, and more likely, national policy measures could be taken by each government, suitable to the domestic situation of each and according to the constitutional procedures of each, to achieve some common environmental objective or desired result. With respect to the problem of acid rain, for example, both Canada and the United States are committed as a matter of national policy to reduce emissions of SO_2 by approximately 50 percent, but each has adopted its own quite distinct measures to accomplish this goal.

Consistent with developing international law, all three countries could formally accept and develop the principle of prior notice and consultation as an essential element in their mutual environmental relations. Such declarations could serve to solidify the standing of this procedure and its underlying principles, multilaterally as well as bilaterally.

The global community of states being what it is, differences of view and conflicting interests can arise on occasion, even with the best intentioned rhetoric and sincere cooperative or consultative efforts. Therefore, the growing need for a variety of dispute resolution mechanisms seems unarguable.

Critics might suggest that such North American-wide arrangements beyond what has traditionally existed and what now exists with NAFTA would be superfluous if not unnecessary, especially in the absence of any abundance of environmental disputes needing settlement. It would amount to creating trilateral mechanisms to deal with essentially bilateral problems. Even if there were few genuinely trilateral issues to be addressed—although the clear assumption here is that there are some and that there will be more—it does not follow that trilateral mechanisms would be inappropriate. There are clear precedents for such an approach in contemporary international affairs. The General Agreement on Tariffs and Trade, as a multilateral arrangement dedicated to an open world trading system, plays a key role in resolving bilateral disputes among its members. A North American environmental dispute settlement mechanism for managing bilateral conflicts—for example, between the United States and Canada—could usefully involve the third party—for example, Mexico—in a neutral or mediatory role.

The states of the global community also being as they are, agreements made are not necessarily agreements kept. Any Mexico-U.S.-Canada environmental agreement in which the parties make commitments to take future action should provide for a vigorous review by an independent body or bodies and a public reporting process. Any agreement should also explicitly provide for open and effective public participation.

MULTILATERAL COOPERATION

As discussed, bilateral environmental problems commonly arise out of downstream or downwind situations that involve transboundary pollution flows from one jurisdiction into another. These can be conceptualized as creating an asymmetrical "environmental dependence" for the affected state. The flow of pollutants across the Canada-U.S. border that leads to acidic precipitation is one example. While the transboundary flows move in both directions, the bulk of the pollutants move from the U.S. Midwest into the central and eastern Canadian provinces, thus creating a situation of environmental dependence for Canada. Similarly, the salination of the Colorado River is a problem of environmental dependence for Mexico.

Global environmental problems, on the other hand, are much more characteristically common property situations. All users of a resource, whether it is the earth's oceans or its atmosphere, contribute in some measure to the problem, the people and ecosystems of all countries are affected or potentially threatened by it, and action by all, or at least most, is necessary to deal with the problem. Given the disparities in wealth and industrial production among countries, the politics of global environmental issues thus tend quite naturally to divide rich and poor, industrialized and nonindustrialized. This characteristic of global environmental problems makes it particularly difficult to take action on issues, such as global warming, that are inextricably tied to national economic development policies, energy use policies, and others. This political divide has been more than evident at international gatherings such as the 1972 United Nations Stockholm Conference on the Human Environment, in efforts to reduce emissions that deplete the ozone layer, and, more recently, at the United Nations Conference on Environment and Development in Rio.

The Need for a Collaborative North-South Approach

One of the less certain but most intriguing aspects of North American ecomanagement is the possibility of exploring and forging, on key global issues, a tripartite "north-south" alliance of two developed and one developing state. Such an alliance would not only represent a symbolic bridging of the north-south political chasm, but it would also represent a minor substantive breakthrough and a potentially potent diplomatic front. Each of the three countries has particularly good relations with other key groupings of states involved in these issues. Canada, for example, has close ties with both the Commonwealth and la francophonie communities, and especially with Asian and African members of each. Mexico, on the other hand, has a position of influence in the Group of 77 as well as with the other Latin Americans. The United States, of course, has both global interests and unparalleled influence in world affairs generally, although its negative and even obstructionist positions on various international environmental issues during the 1980s too often squandered what influence it might have had. Even a modestly enlightened collaborative approach out of Washington, Ottawa, and Mexico City on matters such as global warming could reap important political dividends.

ASSESSMENT AND CONCLUSIONS

Despite its important innovations, the NAFTA environmental regime is the product not of any fundamental, enduring commitment to environmental values on the part of governments in North America, but of a temporary need on the part of a Republican and then a Democratic President to secure sufficient domestic support to ensure legislative passage of a historic free trade agreement. That need has now been met. As historically slow economic growth rates and persistent employment insecurity continue to affect the three countries and as their governments of necessity turn to a stronger emphasis on fiscal deficit control, the priority attached to environmental issues could well diminish from the peak it reached in the half decade from the Brundtland Commission Report to the Rio conference. In such a climate, the new CEC could follow the IJC into relative political obscurity and impotence. To avoid this fate, the CEC will require continuing injections of energy from ENGOs throughout North America and from the business community, which is offered an important place and role.

Moreover, in the spirit of sustainable development, the CEC will require high level political attention not merely from environment ministers in junior portfolios or burdened with other responsibilities and preoccupations, but also from the political leaders who alone have the ability to direct the integration of environmental and economic concerns. A trilateral North American Summit, at which environmental issues were on the agenda, could serve to mobilize the resources and set the priorities that the CEC needs as it embarks with high expectations upon its formidable tasks.

The agenda of Canada-U.S. environmental relations has become much more complex not only because of the side agreements under NAFTA and the need to reconcile trade and environmental objectives, but also because of developing science and technology, changing global priorities, and growing ecological consciousness. Trilateral and multilateral issues will never eliminate long-standing bilateral concerns from the agenda, but they will increasingly compete for attention. At the same time, bilateral concerns such as Great Lakes water quality and acid rain will continue to evolve and demand new energy. The pattern of dealing with environmental issues, in which they are proclaimed and then forgotten, in which commitments are made and then broken, must be changed.

If the three North American nations are unlikely to encourage the early emergence of a genuinely supranational environmental regulatory agency with its own powers and authority above those of the national governments, there is still a wide range of initiatives that can realistically be contemplated.

The new issues will require government responses, including joint fact-finding and policy studies by expert advisory bodies; policy collaboration on multilateral as well as trilateral issues, through either informal arrangements or formal trilateral agreements; prior notice and consultation with respect to economic development that might have a transboundary impact; dispute settlement procedures for environmental problems (as well as trade problems); verification of compliance with existing agreements; policy planning in key areas such as energy, fisheries, agriculture, and industrial development; and NGO cooperation involving linkage of environmental groups in the three countries.

The need for these measures already exists to some degree. Indeed, the need for steps toward the development of a comprehensive North American environmental regime is clear. Current trends, and especially the creation of a trilateral free trade area, underscore the desirability. Environmental cooperation is becoming an inherent and inescapable part of living not only in the global village but also next door. The international boundary lines of North America have never been particularly effective fences against pollutants. Now, when those barriers are becoming ever more permeable to economic exchanges, the need to deal cooperatively with transboundary environmental phenomena is readily evident.

Notes

1. Howard Ross, "Industrial Pollutants Time Bomb, LeBlanc Warns," *Toronto Star*, June 21, 1977, p. B2

2. Because this article primarily discusses Canada and the United States, the long history of environmental cooperation and conflict between the United States and Mexico is not covered. For recent discussions of the U.S.-Mexico agenda, see Alberto Szekely, "Emerging Boundary Environmental Challenges and Institutional Issues: Mexico and the United States," *National Resources Journal*, Vol. 33 (Winter 1993), pp. 33–46; Milton H. Jamail and Stephen P. Mumme, "The International Boundary and Water Commission as a Conflict Management Agency in the U.S-Mexico Borderlands," *The Social Science Journal*, Vol. 19, No. 1 (January 1982), pp. 45–62; and Stephen P. Mumme, "State and Local Influence in Transboundary Environmental Policy Making Along the U.S.-Mexico Border: The Case of Air Quality Management," *Journal of Borderlands Studies*, Vol. II, No. 1, pp. 1–16.

3. A short history of the Boundary Waters Treaty is provided by N.F. Dreisziger, "Dreams and Disappointments," in Robert Spencer, John Kirton, and Kim Richard Nossal, eds., *The International Joint Commission Seventy Years On* (Toronto: Centre for International Studies, University of Toronto, 1981), pp. 8–23.

4. Former IJC Commissioner Maxwell Cohen in *The Regime of Boundary Waters—The Canadian-United States Experience* (Leyden, The Netherlands: A.W. Sijthoff, 1977) discusses what he sees as a reasonably well developed regime in international law for the boundary waters covering both water quantity and water quality issues. The focus of the present article does not include the former area.

5. The International Joint Commission was to comprise six commissioners, three appointed by the United States and three by Canada, with significant quasi-judicial authority over levels and flows issues in the boundary waters and a general investigatory function. The IJC quickly became the key intergovernmental body in development of the Canada-US. environmental regime. For a discussion of the commission, see Spencer, Kirton, and Nossal, *The International Joint Commission*, especially the chapter by William Willoughby, "Expectations and Experience," pp. 24–32.

6. Decision reported on March 11, 1941 to the government of the United States of America and to the government of the Dominion of Canada by the Trail Smelter Arbitral Tribunal. The Trail Smelter Case had involved an earlier report (February 28, 1931) by the IJC on findings and then an initial tribunal decision (April 16, 1938). The Trail Smelter principle, it might be noted, qualified the broad principle of Article IV to the extent that the injury had to be "of serious consequence" and had to be "established by clear and convincing evidence."

7. For the background to the negotiations of the 1972 and 1978 agreements, see Don Munton, "Great Lakes Water Quality: A Study in Environmental Politics and Diplomacy," in O.P. Dwivedi, ed., *Resources and the Environment: Policy Perspectives for Canada* (Toronto: McClelland and Stewart, 1980), pp. 153–178.
8. For the texts of the 1972 and 1978 agreements, see Canada and the United States, *Great Lakes Water Quality Agreement of 1972*, International Joint Commission, 1974; and Canada and the United States, *Great Lakes Water Quality Agreement of 1978*, International Joint Commission, 1978.
9. Bette Hileman, "Concerns Broaden over Chlorine and Chlorinated Hydrocarbons," *Chemical and Engineering News*, April 19, 1993. *C&EN* is a publication of the American Chemical Society.
10. Theodora E. Colborn et al., *Great Lakes Great Legacy?* (Washington, D.C.: The Conservation Foundation; and Ottawa: The Institute for Research on Public Policy, 1990), p. xxxviii.
11. Given that rain, snow, and dry particles can all deposit acidic compounds, the term "acidic deposition" is more descriptive. Given that other substances, particularly toxic chemicals, are also emitted and transported long distances through the atmosphere and pose significant environmental hazards, the term "long-range transport of air pollution" (LRTAP) is also used. Acidity is conventionally measured on the pH scale, with low values being highly acidic.
12. Canada-United States Research Consultation Group (RCG) on the Long-Range Transport of Air Pollutants, *The LRTAP Problem in North America: An Overview* (Ottawa and Washington, D.C., 1979). This and a second Research Consultation Group report (see note 13) were the only bilateral vehicles for other ongoing government and nongovernment studies. President Carter had designated $10 million for acid rain research, and Congress had authorized $68 million for similar purposes. The Clark government in Ottawa and the Ontario government both increased Canadian funding of acid rain research in this period.
13. RCG, *Second Report of the Canada-United States Research Consultation Group on the Long-Range Transport of Air Pollutants* (Ottawa and Washington, D.C., 1980).
14. Colin MacKenzie, "Clean Air Act Nearing Deadline on Capitol Hill," *Globe and Mail*, October 13, 1990.
15. Confidential interview, October 1990, Environment Canada.
16. For an initial overview from a Canadian perspective of the trade-environment relationship and its application to NAFTA, see John Kirton and Sarah Richardson, eds., *Trade, Environment and Competitiveness: Sustaining Canada's Prosperity* (Ottawa: National Roundtable on the Environment and the Economy, 1992). Another assessment of the NAFTA environmental regime can be found in Stephen P. Mumme, "Environmentalists, NAFTA, and North American Environmental Management," *Journal of Environment and Development*, Vol. 2, No. 1 (Winter 1993), pp. 205–219.
17. For a comprehensive, if not critical, overview, see Canada, *North American Free Trade Agreement: Canadian Environmental Review* (Ottawa, 1992).
18. For a sense of the debate, see Sarah Richardson, ed., *The North American Free Trade Agreement and the North American Commission on the Environment* (Ottawa: National Roundtable on the Environment and the Economy, March 1993); and Sarah Richardson, ed., *Shaping Consensus: The North American Commission on the Environment and NAFTA* (Ottawa: National Roundtable on the Environment and the Economy, May 1993).
19. Canada, *North American Agreement on Environmental Co-operation Between the*

Government of Canada, the Government of the United Mexican States, and the Government of the United States of America, final draft, September 13, 1993.
20. For an ambitious conception of its role, see Richardson, *The North American Free Trade Agreement*: and Richardson, *Shaping Consensus.*
21. The evolution of the IJC agenda is traced by Cohen in *The Regime of Boundary Waters*; by William R. Willoughby, "Expectations and Experience," in Robert Spencer, John Kirton, and Kim Richard Nossal, eds., *The International Joint Commission Seventy Years On* (Toronto: Centre for International Studies, University of Toronto, 1981); and by Willoughby, *The Joint Organizations of Canada and the United States* (Toronto: University of Toronto, 1979).
22. For the IJC reports, see Don Munton, "Dependence and Interdependence in Transboundary Environmental Relations," *International Journal (1980–81)*, Vol. 36, No. 1, pp. 139–184.
23. For the Great Lakes study, see Munton, "Great Lakes Water Quality." For the acid rain process, see Munton and Geoffrey Castle, "Controlling Acid Rain," in Don Munton and John Kirton, eds., *Canadian Foreign Policy: Selected Cases* (Toronto: Prentice-Hall, 1992). For the IBWC role in the Colorado problem, see, among other references, Herbert Brownell and Samuel D. Eaton, "The Colorado River Salinity Problem with Mexico," *American Journal of International Law (1975)*, Vol. 69, pp. 255–271; and Stephen P. Mumme, "Regional Power in National Diplomacy: The Case of the U.S. Section of the International Boundary and Water Commission," *Publius*, Vol. 14 (Fall 1984), pp. 115–135.

Name Index

The International Library of Critical Writings in Economics

1. Multinational Corporations
   Mark Casson
2. The Economics of Innovation
   Christopher Freeman
3. Entrepreneurship
   Mark Casson
4. International Investment
   Peter J. Buckley
5. Game Theory in Economics
   Ariel Rubinstein
6. The History of Economic Thought
   Mark Blaug
7. Monetary Theory
   Thomas Mayer
8. Joint Production of Commodities
   Neri Salvadori and Ian Steedman
9. Industrial Organization
   Oliver E. Williamson
10. Growth Theory (Volumes I, II and III)
    R. Becker and E. Burmeister
11. Microeconomics: Theoretical and Applied (Volumes I, II and III)
    Robert E. Kuenne
12. The Economics of Health (Volumes I and II)
    A.J. Culyer
13. Recent Developments in Macroeconomics (Volumes I, II and III)
    Edmund S. Phelps
14. Urban and Regional Economics
    Paul C. Cheshire and Alan W. Evans
15. Modern Public Finance (Volumes I and II)
    A.B. Atkinson
16. Exchange Rate Economics (Volumes I and II)
    Ronald MacDonald and Mark P. Taylor

17. The Economic Value of Education: Studies in the Economics of Education
Mark Blaug

18. Development Economics (Volumes I, II, III and IV)
Deepak Lal

19. The New Classical Macroeconomics (Volumes I, II and III)
Kevin D. Hoover

20. The Economics of the Environment
Wallace E. Oates

21. Post Keynesian Theory of Growth and Distribution
Carlo Panico and Neri Salvadori

22. Dynamic Labor Demand and Adjustment Costs
Giorgio Galeazzi and Daniel S. Hamermesh

23. The Philosophy and Methodology of Economics (Volumes I, II and III)
Bruce J. Caldwell

24. Public Choice Theory (Volumes I, II and III)
Charles K. Rowley

25. Evolutionary Economics
Ulrich Witt

26. Economics and Psychology
Shlomo Maital and Sharone L. Maital

27. Social Choice Theory (Volumes I, II and III)
Charles K. Rowley

28. Non-Linear Dynamics in Economic Theory
Marc Jarsulic

29. Recent Developments in Experimental Economics (Volumes I and II)
John D. Hey and Graham Loomes

30. Monopoly and Competition Policy (Volumes I and II)
F.M. Scherer

31. The Economics of Technical Change
Edwin Mansfield and Elizabeth Mansfield

32. The Economics of Exhaustible Resources
Geoffrey Heal

33. The Economics of Institutions
Geoffrey M. Hodgson

34. The Economics of Transport (Volumes I and II)
Herbert Mohring

35. Implicit Contract Theory
Sherwin Rosen

36. Foundations of Analytical Marxism (Volumes I and II)
John E. Roemer

37. The Economics of Product Differentiation (Volumes I and II)
Jacques-François Thisse and George Norman

38. Economic Growth in Theory and Practice: A Kaldorian Perspective
John E. King

39. Markets and Socialism
Alec Nove and Ian D. Thatcher

40. Recent Developments in the Economics of Education
Elchanan Cohn and Geraint Johnes

41. The Theory of Inflation
Michael Parkin

42. The Economics of Location (Volumes I, II and III)
Melvin L. Greenhut and George Norman

43. Financial Intermediaries
Mervyn K. Lewis

44. The Political Economy of Privatization and Deregulation
Elizabeth E. Bailey and Janet Rothenberg Pack

45. Gender and Economics
Jane Humphries

46. Macroeconomics and Imperfect Competition
Jean-Pascal Bénassy

47. Labor Economics (Volumes I, II, III and IV)
Orley C. Ashenfelter and Kevin F. Hallock

48. The Economics of Altruism
Stefano Zamagni

49. The Economic Analysis of Rent Seeking
Robert D. Tollison and Roger D. Congleton

50. Economics and Biology
Geoffrey M. Hodgson

51. The Economics of Ageing
John Creedy

52. Fiscal and Monetary Policy (Volumes I and II)
Thomas Mayer and Steven M. Sheffrin

53. The Economics of Information (Volumes I and II)
David K. Levine and Steven A. Lippman

54. Transaction Cost Economics (Volumes I and II)
Oliver E. Williamson and Scott E. Masten

55. Agricultural Economics
George H. Peters

56. International Debt (Volumes I and II)
Graham Bird and P. Nicholas Snowden

57. Economics and Discrimination (Volumes I and II)
William A. Darity, Jr

58. Business Cycle Theory
Finn E. Kydland

59. International Trade (Volumes I and II)
J. Peter Neary

60. The Money Supply in the Economic Process
Marco Musella and Carlo Panico

61. Small Firms and Economic Growth (Volumes I and II)
Zoltan J. Acs

62. Producer Cooperatives and Labor-Managed Systems (Volumes I and II)
David L. Prychitko and Jaroslav Vanek

63. Ethics and Economics (Volumes I and II)
Alan P. Hamlin

64. The Economics of the Family
Nancy Folbre

65. The Economics of Training (Volumes I and II)
Orley C. Ashenfelter and Robert J. LaLonde

66. Chaos Theory in Economics: Methods, Models and Evidence
W. Davis Dechert

67. General Equilibrium Theory (Volumes I, II and III)
Gérard Debreu

68. Economic Growth: Theory and Evidence (Volumes I and II)
Gene M. Grossman

69. Long Wave Theory
Christopher Freeman

70. The Economics of Communication and Information
Donald M. Lamberton

71. The Foundations of Public Finance (Volumes I and II)
Peter Jackson

72. The Theory of the Firm
Mark Casson

73. The Economics of Uncertainty (Volumes I and II)
John D. Hey

74. The Economics of Global Warming
Tom Tietenberg

75. The Development of Ecological Economics
Robert Costanza, Charles Perrings and Cutler Cleveland

76. Economic Growth in the Long Run: A History of Empirical Evidence (Volumes I, II and III)
Bart van Ark

77. The Economics of Productivity (Volumes I and II)
Edward N. Wolff

78. The Economics of Population: Key Modern Writings (Volumes I and II)
Julian L. Simon

79. Political Business Cycles
Bruno S. Frey

80. Cultural Economics: The Arts, the Heritage and the Media Industries (Volumes I and II)
Ruth Towse

81. Law and Economics (Volumes I, II and III)
Richard A. Posner and Francesco Parisi

82. Independent Central Banks and Economic Performance
Sylvester Eijffinger

83. Culture, Social Norms and Economics (Volumes I and II)
Mark Casson

84. Industrial Policy and Competitive Advantage (Volumes I, II and III)
David B. Audretsch

85. The Economics of Housing (Volumes I and II)
John M. Quigley

86. Economic Demography (Volumes I and II)
T. Paul Schultz

87. Trade and the Environment: Economic, Legal and Policy Perspectives
Alan M. Rugman and John J. Kirton with Julie A. Soloway

88. The Economics of Fiscal Federalism and Local Finance
Wallace E. Oates

89. Price Theory and its Applications
Bernard Saffran and F.M. Scherer

90. Women in the Labor Market (Volumes I and II)
Marianne A. Ferber

91. Market Process Theories (Volumes I and II)
Peter Boettke and David Prychitko

Future titles will include:

Mathematical Economics
Graciela Chichilnisky

Input-Output Analysis
Heinz Kurz, Erik Dietzenbacher and Christian Lager

The Economics of Unemployment
P.N. Junankar

The Economics of Energy
Paul Stevens

The Economics of Science and Innovation
Paula E. Stephan and David B. Audretsch

International Finance
Robert Z. Aliber

Welfare Economics
William J. Baumol and Janusz A. Ordover

The Economics of Inequality and Poverty
A.B. Atkinson

The Economics of Crime
Isaac Ehrlich

The Economics of Integration
Willem Molle

The Rhetoric of Economics
Deirdre McCloskey

The Economics of Defence
Keith Hartley and Nicholas Hooper

Consumer Theory
Kelvin Lancaster

The Economics of Business Policy
John Kay

Microeconomic Theories of Imperfect Competition
Jacques Thisse and Jean Gabszewicz

'he Economics of Increasing Returns
;eoffrey Heal

'he Balance of Payments
lichael J. Artis

ost-Benefit Analysis
rnold Harberger and Glenn P. Jenkins

ender in Economic and Social History
.J. Humphries and J. Lewis

rivatization in Developing and Transitional Economies
olin Kirkpatrick and Paul Cook

he Economics of Intellectual Property
uth Towse

ne Economics of Tourism
lem Tisdell

ne Economics of Organization and Bureaucracy
ter Jackson

ne Economics of Commodity Markets
avid Greenaway and Wyn Morgan

alism and Economics: Studies in Ontology
ny Lawson

w Developments in Game Theory
ic S. Maskin

e International Economic Institutions of the Twentieth Century
avid Greenaway

e Economics of Structural Change
rald Hagemann, Michael Landesmann and Roberto Scazzieri

onomic Justice
rold Hochman and Georgio Brosio

e Economics of Famine
n Drèze

e Foundations of Regulatory Economics
bert B. Ekelund

e Economics of the Welfare State
holas Barr

h Dependence and Economic Dynamics
n Cantwell

Alternative Theories of the Firm
Richard Langlois, Paul Robertson and Tony F. Yu

Economic Anthropology
Stephen Gudeman

The Economics of Executive Compensation
Kevin F. Hallock and Kevin J. Murphy

The Economics of Marketing
Martin Carter, Mark Casson and Vivek Suneja

Foreign Exchange Intervention: Theory and Evidence
Sylvester C.W. Eijffinger

The Economics of the Mass Media
Glenn Withers

The Foundations of Long Wave Theory
Francisco Louçã and Jan Reijnders

The Economics of Budget Deficits
Charles Rowley

Economic Forecasting
Terence C. Mills